Eleanor Mee
5432 San Jose
Montclair, Calif.

THE FIELD OF SOCIAL WORK

HOLT, RINEHART AND WINSTON

NEW YORK — CHICAGO — SAN FRANCISCO — TORONTO — LONDON

THE
FIELD OF
SOCIAL WORK

FOURTH EDITION

ARTHUR E. FINK

School of Social Work
University of North Carolina

EVERETT E. WILSON

School of Social Work
Yeshiva University

MERRILL B. CONOVER

Health and Welfare Council, Inc.
Philadelphia

September, 1964

Copyright 1942, 1949, © 1955, 1963 by
HOLT, RINEHART AND WINSTON, INC.
All rights reserved
Library of Congress Catalogue Card Number: 63–11337

22827–0413

Printed in The United States of America

To

WILLIAM POSNER

Pioneer in Social Services for the Aged

PREFACE

THIS EDITION CARRIES THE CORE CONTENT OF THE PRECEDING EDITIONS and records the changes in thinking and practice that have strengthened social work and increased its usefulness in the lives of the people it serves. New illustrative material has been drawn from the fields of practice and has been associated with the appropriate chapter. A new first chapter places social work in its contemporary setting, measures to some extent its size and cost, and assays some of the undone tasks.

As in the previous edition Everett Wilson carries responsibility for the chapter on social casework, and Merrill Conover for the chapters on social group work and community organization, while each has been helpful in the selection of illustrative material.

Grateful acknowledgment is given of the substantial assistance of Mrs. W. Bruce Stephens and Kathleen Boles Fink with respect to the myriad details of manuscript preparation.

This volume is dedicated to William Posner. Mr. Posner was responsible for the case material illustrative of services to the aging in the previous edition and was helpful in persuading Miss Helen Lokshin to carry that assignment in the present edition. Mr. Posner's death of a heart attack in April 1961 at the early age of forty-seven has deprived us all of many years of creative administering and teaching.

Chapel Hill   A.E.F.
New York   E.E.W.
Philadelphia   M.B.C.

JANUARY 1963

CONTENTS

velopment—Fund Raising—Coordinating and Stand-
ard-setting Programs—The Social Work Component of
Community Organization—Social Intergroup Work
Process—The Educational and Promotional Process—
The Administrative Process in Community Organi-
zation—Roles of the Social Worker in Community
Organization: Direct Practice; Administration; Super-
vision; Consultation; Teaching—Local Programs—State
Programs—National Programs—International Programs
—Trends: Tendency toward Wider Planning Areas;
Wider Scope of Community Organization Efforts;
Streamlining Planning Structure; Relation of United
Funds to Other Major Fund Drives; Conceptualization
and Identification of Basic Community Organization
Principles; Community Organization as a Two-Year
Program—Bibliography

1

SOCIAL WORK
IN MODERN
SOCIETY

The core of social welfare

For centuries in Europe, with especial reference to Great Britain, there have been organized efforts to deal to some extent with human needs —welfare needs. The monies paid out or the services rendered usually came after all other measures or efforts had failed, after the exhaustion of the individual's or his family's resources. The help came *after* the breakdown or the exhaustion. The funds or the services were deemed to be temporary and usually of an emergency nature and were to be withdrawn or stopped when the individual or the family resumed its normal and accustomed role. Some of the contemporary social scientists term this a residual conception of social welfare in contrast to the institutional conception. According to the latter notion it is a reasonable, indeed an essential, expectation that social welfare programs are to be "accepted as a proper, legitimate function of modern industrial society in helping individuals achieve self-fulfillment." [1]

The residual concept characterized the approach to dealing with human need from the pre-Elizabethan I era, through our own colonial period, and up to the Depression of the 1930s. The institutional concept may be said to express more of the programs that emerged through legislation, notably the Social Security Act, as America struggled with the problems that beset it with accelerating industrialization. Clearly this is an oversimplification, for there remain many of the residual aspects in the social welfare programs of the 1940s, the 1950s, and even into the 1960s

---

[1] Harold L. Wilensky and Charles N. LeBeaux, *Industrial Society and Social Welfare* (New York: Russell Sage Foundation, 1958), p. 14.

1

during which we are presently living; but there is sufficient demarcation, pre-Depression and post-Depression, for an identifiable shift to be noted.

The reader may well ask what are these programs that are called social welfare and wherein lies their distinction from those others that may be termed educational, or health, or religious, or just plain governmental, for is not the aim of all government to provide for the general welfare? It may be well in dealing with something as broad as welfare—social welfare—to ask what is the core concern. To this the answer must be that of help in the area of relationships—relationships of individual to individual, of individual to family, of individuals to groups, of groups to groups, of individuals to communities, of groups to communities, and even of communities to communities. All of this to be directed toward the achievement of self-realization of individuals, of families, of groups, and of communities and within a framework of genuine democracy with its commitment to the rights of individuals and respect for human dignity and the human personality.

True, other services provided by workers in other professions are related to some of these concerns, but with all of them the core concern is clearly differentiated from the one just stated for social welfare. In the educational field the central concern is the inculcation of the knowledges and the skills that are deemed important for useful and satisfying living. The structure through which these services are offered, the school system, is recognized by us all. In the area of health there are services—preventive, curative, and restorative—that are related to one's physical (and mental) well-being, and that are offered in physician's offices, health departments, and hospitals, public and private. A third area of services are those related to man's spiritual needs, offered by ministers and largely through churches. Of course, these three areas of education, health, and religion are related to man's needs and to helping him attain to the maximum his satisfactions of living and working, but even upon cursory examination they are clearly distinct from social welfare. Likewise, there are other programs, largely governmental, that conduce to man's improved well-being and yet, while related to, are distinguishable from what is usually termed social welfare. Some of these measures are the abolition of child labor, regulation of hours of work for children and women, minimum wage legislation, slum clearance and low-cost housing.

It is also pertinent to ask at the outset what the dimensions of contemporary social services are and the amount of money spent in relation to them. The services may be offered under governmental or nongovernmental auspices; that is, they may be termed public or private, supported by tax or by voluntary contributions. If governmental, the auspice may be federal, state, county, township, city; if nongovernmental, the auspice may be an organization (board, staff) chartered by law. Put another way, the governmental agency may provide services through the federal Department of Health, Education, and Welfare, a state department of public welfare, or a county or city department of public welfare; or through a federal center in the District of Columbia for disturbed children, a state training school for delinquent children, or a city or county program for aged persons. On the other hand, the private agency service may be offered or facilitated by a national organization in the family or child service field, by a state-wide adoption agency or denominational children's home, or, locally, by a social settlement or a child guidance clinic. The important point at this stage of discussion is not so much whether a particular service is paid for out of tax funds or by voluntary contributions (usually united funds or community chest funds), but rather that services are available under these two auspices, and that in a democracy like ours there is a place and an opportunity for citizens to find expression for their concerns about meeting human needs by using the machinery of government or the organization of voluntary effort.

The cost of welfare

How much does this all cost? Is it possible to arrive at some figure that will record with reasonable accurateness the amount of our income that goes into what may be termed social welfare expenditures? The answer to this will depend upon what is included in the classification of social welfare and the availability of the figures, whether these figures be of governmental expenditures or of nongovernmental, or both.[2] For example, Ida Merriam places the figure at something over $36 billion for several years ago; in this she included public welfare expenditures of $28 billion, private philanthropic expenditures of over $2 billion, and expenditures under private employee benefit plans of about $6 billion. Another estimate is made by Wilensky and LeBeaux upon the basis of a percentage of the gross national product—5 percent for public expenditures and 1 percent for private welfare expenditures. When these percentages are related to the gross national product for the same year as Dr. Merriam used, the amount comes to about $25 billion. On the other hand, Wilbur Cohen comes up with a figure of $60 billion (which includes welfare, health, and education), but he also mentions the Rockefeller Report of 1958 with the figure of $20 billion (not including education) of public expenditures only. Alongside of this should be placed the Dewhurst (Twentieth Century Fund) estimate of almost $23 billion (again without education).

---

[2] See "Definition of Social Welfare" in Ida Merriam, "Social Welfare Expenditures, 1959–60," *Social Security Bulletin*, November 1961.

The reader quite understandably may become confused when confronted with such variations, and the confusion may be furthered when estimates must be made of the cost of social services in programs when such services are subsidiary to the principal function, as in mental hospitals, courts, prisons, schools, the military establishments, etc. A large item, one that almost defies calculation, is the money spent by religious denominations for welfare purposes. Nevertheless, taking into account all of the calculable as well as incalculable considerations, it is possible to say that expenditures for welfare purposes constitute an important and an essential part of our economy.

There are at least two questions that are suggested immediately by the foregoing approximations: Is this an increasing or decreasing amount and proportion, and is it enough? The evidence supports the contention that the amounts and the percentage of gross national product devoted to social welfare, as judged by governmental expenditures, have increased. Dr. Merriam cites the percentage in 1889–1890 as 2.4; in 1928–1929 the percent was 4.2; in 1934–1935 it was 9.4; in 1949–1950 it was 8.7, while in 1959–1960 it was 10.5 percent. (Incidentally, it should be noted that in 1944–1945, when the total expenditure for war purposes was so high, the percentage for social welfare stood at 4.2.) Expenditures from all private sources for social welfare purposes, while not as readily ascertainable, have undoubtedly followed this same pattern. From all of this it is possible to conclude that increased expenditures during the twentieth century reflect an increasing commitment to provide services according to our enlarging concept of social responsibility. Such enlarging responsibility may be related to meeting destitution or want; it may also betoken a conviction about the desirability of providing resources for prevention as well as as for creative self-realization on the part of individuals, families, and communities.

The second question, Is it enough, has anything but a simple answer. Human wants are seemingly illimitable. While wants and needs are not necessarily synonymous, it can also be maintained that there are many more needs—yes, social welfare needs—that people ask satisfaction of than there are resources to supply those needs. True, our needs are not static. What today we may be acutely aware of as need may hardly have been related to our consciousness a century, a half century, or even a decade ago. In many instances of this kind there may have been a more basic or elemental need or needs that seemed much more urgent. As some or most of those elemental needs are met, we become aware of other needs that call for satisfaction.

Looking at the question in historical perspective it must be clear there has never been enough money or services, or both, to meet the many needs that people express; it is as equally clear that our notion of need has been changing constantly. Consider a century ago in America: What were the needs as they were then expressed and were there sufficient resources to meet them? What of the ills besetting children, the blind, the aged, the handicapped, the offender, the unemployed, the mentally disturbed and mentally defective? Even though we may be able to say that there are many more resources and services for such persons today than a century ago, we must also admit how inadequate those provisions are in relation to the extent of the needs.

It would be well to ask ourselves specifically about some of these and other needs and the extent to which resources are available or are used. Is there adequate financial provision for all of the aged persons in this country, either by reason of their own savings or through the use of our social insurance system? What of the disabled and handicapped—has provision been made within industry or through the use of our social insurance or public assistance systems? Are they being helped in sufficient numbers to enter into productive employment and to attain satisfying living within the limits of their affliction? What of the unemployed, temporarily or permanently—do our social insurance or public assistance systems provide adequate protection? What of our children who are in need because of what has happened to their parents or because of what their parents have done? What about the offender, granted he has broken the law—are there sufficient services, as he atones for his crimes, to help him to make something different of himself, to achieve a more constructive use of himself? What of the mentally disturbed or the mentally defective—is enough money being spent to provide adequate services for them? What of migrants and their families performing essential services in harvesting crops but compelled to exist in almost intolerable living situations; of shabby housing for millions of Americans; of medical care unavailable to many families and old people because of financial considerations; of employment denied or granted on restricted terms because of minority status? What of those whose needs call for activities of various kinds, involving usually participation with other persons in groups—are we using enough of our resources for Boy Scouts, Girl Scouts, boys' clubs, social settlements, community centers, leisure-time programs for older people as well as for the young?

The list could be much longer and the questions could become tiresome, but the answers would still be the same: We are not using enough of our resources to meet these many unmet welfare needs. Rich as we are, and we are the possessors of a large share of the world's goods and services, we still do not minister adequately to the expressed social welfare needs of our people.

Perhaps a rather rudimentary analysis might not be inappropriate here. In our economic system goods and services are distributed according to the demands of the market and usually in relation to the ability of the individual to pay for those goods and services. Those goods and services are made possible by those who are producing them. All people are consumers of these goods and services, and yet not everyone is a producer, so that the nonproducers, to the extent of their capacity, compete with the producers for a share of the total product. Who shall say what the share of the nonproducers shall be, and how those shares shall be distributed to them? Who makes these kinds of decisions for children deprived of a parent or both parents, for the unemployable or even the unemployed, for the handicapped, the offender, the aged, etc.? Obviously, the answers to many of these questions lie in the area of public social policy. Usually, the persons to whom those shares are allocated are not effectively articulate, except possibly the aged, on their own behalf, and the decisions reflect the values that one places upon helping others and constitute a measure of our social responsibility. Even in those instances where the monies come from other than taxes, that is, from voluntary contributions through united funds, community chest and other drives, or from denominational sources, there is still a measure of society's commitment to the notion of social welfare and of a conviction about paying for it.

We come back to an earlier question: How much social welfare can America afford? Dr. Eveline M. Burns dealt with this question over a decade ago in a National Conference of Social Work paper by that very title. Quite appropriately she observed that "The amount of social welfare America can afford is, in the last resort, limited by the level of the national output." She also added, ". . . it is true that the amount of social welfare that America can afford is largely a matter of how much social welfare the people of America want, but want, mark you, as compared with other things." [3]

The American economy is a dynamic economy; its productive system is an expanding one; its output is increasing at the rate of 3 percent per year. It can include within its expanding productivity an increasing amount, as well as an increasing percentage, for social welfare purposes. Likewise, as our ideas change—and they have changed—as to what social welfare measures we want, we will enlarge this share of goods and services.

Another way to look at this is to regard much of the expenditure for social welfare purposes as an investment in people. This means not only an increase in the well-being of more people, but as more people have the opportunity to discover, and to express their capacities to the full, they in turn will make their contribution to a greater productivity

---

[3] Eveline M. Burns, "How Much Social Welfare Can America Afford?" *The Social Welfare Forum*, 1949, p. 71.

for the country as a whole. As more persons become healthy or stay healthy, their contribution is greater. As youngsters are helped to lead constructive lives, instead of destructive delinquent lives, their contribution is greater. As the crippled and the handicapped are helped to develop their abilities through training or retraining, their contribution is greater. Wilbur Cohen, along with others, not only is convinced of this investment aspect but warns of the price one otherwise pays when he says: "The denial of opportunities to any individual, or their restriction to the privileged few, for economic or other reasons results in the loss of sorely needed talents and abilities. Moreover, it results in long-range increases in social and economic costs and large-scale social neglect, attributable to lack of vision and investment in meeting the needs of individuals and families." [4] We have known for a long time the value of education and have esteemed it highly as an investment, but it is only recently that we have come to apply the same thinking to social welfare.

Is poverty inevitable?

Interestingly, a decade after Dr. Burns asked, "How much Social Welfare can America afford?" another speaker, Dr. Ida Merriam, before the same assembly—the National Conference on Social Welfare—asked, "Are We Spending Enough for Social Welfare?" [5] In this article Dr. Merriam remarked: "We have taken the fruits of expanding productivity partly in the form of fewer hours of work, partly in greatly increased levels of real family income, partly in a substantial growth of social services." This observation is followed by "For the first time in history we have the technical means of wiping out poverty." Dr. Merriam was expressing what a number of persons have raised in question form: Is poverty in this country inevitable? Instead of being willing to accept too easily the assumption that the poor will always be with us, these persons have asked what it would take to abolish poverty. One of the boldest of these, Wilbur Cohen, is even willing to move past the wish or hope and to make a forthright declaration: "Stated simply, and without qualifications, it is this: Want and poverty can and should be abolished in the United States in our lifetime." In a subsequent paragraph he adds, "Depending upon where the standard is set, want or poverty could be abolished in this country at a cost of about $10 billion a year." [6]

---

[4] Wilbur J. Cohen, "Needed Changes in Social Welfare Programs and Objectives," *Social Service Review*, XXXIII (March 1959), p. 41.

[5] Ida C. Merriam, "Are We Spending Enough for Social Welfare?" *The Social Welfare Forum*, 1959, pp. 49–66.

[6] *Loc. cit.*, p. 37; see also Michael Harrington, *The Other America* (New York: Macmillan, 1962).

Marion B. Folsom, while Secretary of the U.S. Department of Health, Education, and Welfare, speaking before the American Philosophical Society in 1958 could also say:

> For the first time in human history a great nation will have the material resources, the wealth in being, to eliminate hunger and scarcity and poverty, to provide a decent level of living for a *whole* people. Life may no longer *have* to be, for anyone, a grim struggle for bare existence.
>
> I say our society will have the resources and the power to do these things. But will we *use* the power—and use it wisely? Will we have the vision to assign the proper priorities for the investment of the resources available? Will we take a sufficiently long view of our goals? [7]

One cannot contemplate such hopeful declarations in the second half of the twentieth century without contrasting them with the beginning of the same century, or the previous century. One has only to recall the wealth created by the fulfilling of the industrial revolution and to realize at the same time the degradation, squalor, ill health, and poverty that followed in its train. Nor can we fail to recall the condition that necessitated the Elizabethan Poor Law of more than three centuries ago and to realize with all of our shortcomings the long way we have come.

Concern with poverty lies not entirely with social work or the social worker. The economist also has his concern and he too is aware of what poverty does to the human spirit and to communities. Such an economist is John K. Galbraith who in *The Affluent Society* calls poverty in contemporary America a disgrace. Interested as he is, as an economist, in production, he can express the same sentiments as any social worker when he observes: "The limiting factor is not our knowledge of what can be done. Overwhelmingly it is our failure to invest in people." [8] In his proposals for attacking poverty he sees the necessity for helping the individual and the community. Here again his emphasis is upon investment. The families, especially the children in those families, that need the greatest help should get it, and likewise the communities in which those families and those children live should get the greatest, not the least, help.

> If the children of poor families have first-rate schools and school attendance is properly enforced; if the children, though badly fed at home, are well nourished at school; if the community has sound health services, and the physical well-being of the children is vigilantly watched; if there is opportunity for advanced education for those who qualify regardless of means; and if, especially in the use of urban communities, law and order

---

[7] Marion B. Folsom, "Some Suggested Adjustments in the Use of Our Resources," *Proceedings of the American Philosophical Society*, CII (August 1958), p. 321.

[8] John Kenneth Galbraith, *The Affluent Society* (Boston: Houghton Mifflin Company, 1958), pp. 331–332.

are well enforced and recreation is adequate—then there is a very good chance that the children of the very poor will come to maturity without grave disadvantage. . . . Poverty is self-perpetuating because the poorest communities are poorest in the services which would eliminate it. To eliminate poverty efficiently we should invest more than proportionately in the children of the poor community.[9]

Social work's original and, for centuries, abiding concern has been with poverty, but within more recent times it has become evident that not all of our ills are caused by poverty, nor do they all disappear as poverty is diminished, nor will they end as poverty is ended. For one, poverty is relative as to time and place. What may be regarded as poverty today might not have been so regarded a century ago. What is poverty in community A may not be regarded as poverty in community B; or substitute country A and country B for these communities. Secondly, there is another aspect to this matter of our ills, namely that people of all incomes have their difficulties, and those difficulties are not all necessarily related to lack of income or sufficiency of income. We are all human beings; we begin, each of us, with different endowments, we grow up with different experiences, we each respond differently to the demands of life upon us; we make our adaptations or we fail to make them in relation to forces internal or external. Many of these situations we deal with ourselves and achieve reasonable satisfaction in our living and working; for some we must seek help from other persons or from institutional resources that society has set up for this purpose. A third reason why our troubles will not all disappear as we make considerable headway against poverty is that as we deal with one problem we find there is another, or perhaps two others, waiting for solution. Ewan Clague, an economist, puts it this way in 1960: "Individuals and families are still unable to adjust to many of the problems engendered by our industrial and commercial life. There is scarcely a problem of the 1930s which is not with us in some form. We cure one disease and encounter another. We solve one problem and discover two more." [10] These remarks are recorded here not to diminish the ugliness and degradation of poverty, but as a corrective to an unrealistic optimism as to the nature of our human troubles. Throughout the pages that follow there will be discussion and presentation of those several aspects.

----

[9] *Ibid.*, p. 330. Chapter XXIII, "The New Position of Poverty" is well worth reading—so is the entire volume.

[10] Ewan Clague, "Economic Myth and Fact in Social Work," in Weaver, W. Wallace, ed., *Frontiers in Social Work* (Philadelphia: University of Pennsylvania Press, 1960), p. 26.

Social work in an expanding economy

Granted that it is within the bounds of possibility to diminish or even to eliminate poverty, if we are so minded, it is entirely pertinent to ask why in the expanding economy of the 1960s there is still financial need among segments of the population. An examination of certain changes that are taking place will provide a basis for understanding this seeming contradiction. Basically our population is growing and it is growing older. During the Depression of the 1930s there were predictions by qualified researchers of a slowing up and a leveling off of population. However, in the 1940s, especially following the close of World War II, and during the decade of the 1950s and into the 1960s there has been a tremendous population increase, frequently referred to as the population explosion. One effect of this has been the increase in the number of children, as well as their percentage, in the population. At the very time this increase is taking place, there is a continuing trend that delays the entrance of youth into productive employment. But also continuing are the misfortunes that befall families, especially the children of those families: death, disablement, imprisonment or commitment to mental hospital of wage earner, and, increasingly, divorce and desertion. True, the provisions of the Social Security Act for survivors of insured workers is of some help, but the larger number of children affected by those other happenings are obliged to turn to other forms of help, chiefly public assistance.

Another aspect of population increase pertains to the other end of the scale, namely, the increase in the number, as well as the percentage, of older people. Some of these older persons have resources to carry them through their remaining years; some are able to turn to their families, principally their children; but by far the largest number must turn to some form of assistance, either from private or public welfare agencies. Here again, there is increasing provision through the insurance part of the Social Security Act, but reliance must as yet be placed upon public assistance for a portion of our older population.

A third segment, or age group, of the population that is affected by these changes is to be found in the age category 45 to 64 years. Of all the workers in the productive system these are most likely to be affected adversely by the swift changes in industry that are associated with technological advances, automation. For these workers, it is a far more complicated and difficult adjustment to locate other employments or to go to other locations than is true for the younger worker. Part of the price that must be paid for automation is the provision of funds and services for these dislocated workers: vocational training or retraining, counseling, and unemployment insurance.

Thus even though ours is an expanding economy, it does not automatically follow that all of our problems are solved, or that need disappears. Indeed, what we are obliged to learn—if we will—is that, as population increases and as our productive system expands, it is essential to understand what is happening, indeed to foresee what will happen, and to make sensible and humane provision for dealing with the problems that will arise and for helping the people who will be affected.[11]

What does social work stand for?

In the last two decades tremendous changes have taken place. On a world-wide scale a global war has been waged; new nations have come into being; giant nations have striven for the world-wide extension of their ideas, of their political and economic systems. In America we have emerged from an economic depression; have participated in that world-wide war; have learned that other peoples do not accept our ideas just because they are ours. We have had to ask ourselves what as a nation and a people we are for. When we undertake to state as simply as possible what we are for, we say we are for democracy. Then it is that we are obliged to examine not only our protestations or affirmations, but, more importantly, our practices, what we *do*.

In the field of welfare, to take only one aspect of government, we must ask what is the role of government in relation to people's needs. Is it to be based on a concept of human nature that any "help" provided a human being is destructive of morale and encourages dependence? Or is it to be based on a conviction that human beings seek to develop whatever potentials they have within them, and that whatever help they require from sources other than themselves should be offered in such a way and on such terms that they have the opportunity to realize their capacities to the full? This is the difference between a negative use of government in the area of social welfare and a positive use. It means the difference between the use of tax monies as a constructive investment in people and the use of tax monies in such a way as actually to be destructive of human potentials. Perhaps the most important point to emphasize in this connection is that the social welfare services should be available to all the people and as a normal and responsible function of government, local, state and federal; a concept that the reader will recognize as the institutional one discussed in the opening of this chapter.

[11] William Haber, "Why Financial Need in an Expanding Economy?" *Public Welfare*, XV (January 1957), pp. 7–10, 29, 30.

Social workers through their professional association, the National Association of Social Workers, have put themselves on record as to what they stand for. However, it must be recognized that many other persons hold to these convictions and also strive for the enactment of programs that embody them; indeed, without the participation of workers in other fields, including just plain citizens, social welfare programs would not be possible. In 1958 the association adopted a statement known as *Goals of Public Social Policy*, which while it referred to programs largely in the area of tax supported services nevertheless took as its broad base the responsibilities wherever and under whatever auspice social welfare services were offered. A section of that report is so pertinent to the material not only in this chapter but in all the chapters that follow that it is reproduced below in its entirety.

SOCIAL WORK AND A CHANGING SOCIETY   1. *Obligations of Society to Individuals.* The profession of social work is committed to the principle that democratic society exists for the benefit of its individual members. Such a society must, therefore, be so ordered that its common resources are devoted to assuring to each of those members (a) opportunity for full growth and development; (b) the means for meeting economic needs in terms of the standards its productivity makes possible; (c) provisions of mutual aid for meeting those needs in which social interdependence is a basic factor; (d) a share in advancing and benefiting from the cumulative human heritage of knowledge, culture, and social organization; and (e) full participation in democratic social relationships. To achieve these objectives each member of society has an obligation to respect the dignity and rights of other members, to maintain himself and his dependents by his own resources to the extent that his capacity and circumstances permit, and to contribute his fair share to the common welfare, both financially and otherwise.

2. *Role of Social Institutions.* A free society fulfills these obligations to its members through a wide range of social institutions, including the family, voluntary association, economic enterprise, and government. All of these are necessary to a functioning social order and each develops in terms of its own appropriate role in meeting changing needs. While this document is concerned with governmental functions and policies, it is important that these be seen in their total social context. Support for a governmental policy implies no lack of support for the corresponding functions of the family, voluntary association, or private economic enterprise. On the contrary, the very variety of our social institutions provides a basic dynamism for social progress and a safeguard for the welfare of the individual.

3. *Responsibilities of Social Work.* Social work is the profession which concerns itself with the facilitating and strengthening of basic social relationships between individuals, groups, and social institutions. It has, therefore, a social action responsibility which derives directly from its social function and professional knowledge. This responsibility lies in the following three areas: (a) the identification, analysis, and interpretation of specific unmet

needs among individuals and groups of individuals, (b) advancing the standard of recognized social obligation between society and its individual members so that those needs will be met and a more satisfying environment for all achieved, and (c) the application of specific knowledge, experience, and inventiveness to those problems which can be solved through social welfare programs. Each of these is briefly discussed in the following paragraphs.

Identifying Needs. Most social workers, whatever their specialty or setting, act as agents of society in meeting the needs or facilitating the social adjustments of individuals. They serve in this sense as a link between society, with its vast and changing array of social institutions, and the individuals for whose benefit all social organization exists. It is their job to make a very complex social machinery meet the needs of its individual members in two ways: (a) by bringing to such needs the benefits of existing programs, policies, and knowledge, and (b) by identifying and interpreting the areas where such machinery is proving deficient in terms of actual unmet needs.

This second aspect of the social work function is a major factor in all social progress, for it is obviously impossible to apply a social remedy to a problem until it is recognized to exist. This is especially important in a dynamic society like our own where rapidly shifting economic conditions, a high degree of population mobility, and accelerated social change constantly create new needs for particular groups in the population. The social worker, whatever his function or setting, is in a key position to spot these needs as they begin to emerge and to interpret their development to the society which he serves.

Advancing the Social Standard. Basic to all social work functioning is the concept of an accepted but devolping standard of mutual obligation between individuals and their social organization. Not only is there a constantly changing standard of what people "owe" to the members of their own family, their community, their employers and employees, and their nation, but there is a comparable change in what society is believed to owe its individual members in particular circumstances and what, therefore, constitutes a socially recognized "need" on the part of such individuals.

Social workers have a major responsibility to contribute their knowledge of social conditions, social institutions, social needs, and social feasibility to advancing the evolution of this social standard. They have an obligation with respect not only to such functions of society as lie within their own area of competence—discussed below—but also to those social measures and policies that will prevent the needs with which they deal. They are necessarily concerned with all social conditions which affect the welfare of individuals, groups, and communities in terms of this established and evolving social standard. It is for this reason that this policy statement ranges over a wide variety of social measures, in many of which the profession of social work plays either no functional part or an auxiliary, facilitating role.

Social Welfare Programs and Organization. In areas of social policy and program in which the profession of social work plays a central or major facilitating role, its social action function involves the additional component or professional knowledge concerning organization and operation, policy implications, financing requirements, and personnel standards without which successful social policy can be neither made nor implemented. In the growing complexity of modern social organization, both governmental and voluntary, few policymakers can be expected to have the technical knowledge implicit in all the fields of social responsibility with which they deal. Nor is it socially desirable that they should be exclusively dependent on those who administer such policies and programs for their guidance. The professional social work organization has, therefore, a positive responsibility to make the technical knowledge and experience of its membership available to those who make social welfare policies, whether in legislative, administrative, or community leadership capacities.

4. *Co-operation and Co-ordination.* It is recognized that many other groups and professions share the concern of social workers for these areas of social policy and action. Social advances will be furthered through the broadest co-operation by social workers with all such groups. Moreover, it is basic to social progress that means should exist for co-operative planning among all elements in society, so that each may effectively fulfill its own role and society may make the best use of all its institutional resources in advancing the welfare and meeting the needs of its members. Social workers can often make their most effective contribution to social progress by lending their support and knowledge to these broadly based democratic instruments for effecting social change.[12]

The profession of social work

In the forepart of this chapter the attempt was made to identify the core concern of social welfare as distinguishable from other areas. Within the present century those persons who have made the decision to devote their skills to providing social welfare services on a professional basis have committed themselves to professional training and to professional organization. Their training is carried on through sixty-three schools of social work brought together in a Council on Social Work Education, and their professional organization is known as the National Association of Social Workers. Not only do the 25,000 members (approximate) subscribe to such positions contained in the aforementioned *Goals of Public Social Policy* (and many other so-called position papers) but also to a code of ethics that enunciates principles of professional conduct relating to clients, to employing agency, to colleagues, to the community, and to the profession. Specifically, the worker's commitments are as follows:

He regards the welfare of the individual or group served as his primary obligation.

---

[12] *Goals of Public Social Policy* (New York: National Association of Social Workers, 1959), pp. 11–13; also to be found in Russell H. Kurtz, ed., *Social Work Year Book, 1960* (New York: National Association of Social Workers, 1960), pp. 72–73.

He gives precedence to his professional responsibility over his personal interests.

He holds himself responsible for the quality and extent of the service he performs.

He respects the privacy of persons served.

He uses information gained in professional relationships in a responsible manner.

He treats with respect the findings, views, and actions of colleagues, and uses appropriate channels to express judgment on these matters.

He practices social work only within the recognized knowledge and competence of the profession.

He recognizes his professional responsibility for adding his findings and ideas to the body of social work knowledge and practice.

He accepts responsibility for helping to protect the community against unethical practice on the part of individuals or organizations engaged in social welfare activities.

He gives appropriate professional service in public emergencies.

He distinguishes clearly, in public, between his statements and actions as an individual and as a representative of an organization.

He supports the principle that professional practice requires professional education.

He accepts and continues employment in an agency only when its policies and procedures enable him to conduct himself in keeping with this code.

He contributes his knowledge, skills, and support to programs of human welfare.

Most social work services are offered by workers who are staff members of agencies, whether those agencies are financed by taxes, such as a county welfare department, or are supported by voluntary contributions or endowments such as a family service society. Occasionally, a qualified social worker may establish himself in private practice. Here again the professional association, consistent with its concern for the quality of service to be offered clients, has recommended that certain minimum qualifications be possessed by persons offering social service on such a basis. In addition to graduation from an accredited school of social work and five years of acceptable full-time employment, the minimum qualifications call for membership in the National Association of Social Workers and in the Academy of Certified Social Workers, the latter membership being a recent development, 1961, toward which the association has been pointing for many years for all of its members.[13]

---

[13] There will be no extended discussion in the present volume about private practice in social work, but the interested reader is referred to Saul Hoffstein's exposition "Social Work Process in Private Practice," *Journal of Social Work Process,* 1961; and, for a divergent view, to Sherman Merle's "Some Arguments Against Private Practice," *Social Work,* January 1962.

The responsibility of schools
of social work

The beginnings of professional education for social work are to be found in the first training courses held in the summer of 1898 by the New York Charity Organization Society. In 1903 the training programs included a six months' winter session, and in the following year the New York School of Philanthropy opened (now the New York School of Social Work of Columbia University). Since then other schools have developed, many of them as integral parts of state universities, so that by 1962 there were sixty-three schools in the United States, Canada, and Puerto Rico.

Throughout these years the schools have modified their programs as the demands made upon professional workers have changed and as creativity in social work education has manifested itself. Significant changes have come about in public welfare practice since the Social Security Act of 1935; while the developments in chemotherapy in the treatment of mental illness have called for a reassessment of the role of the psychiatric social worker, to mention only two instances. There are many indications that the changes in these areas, and others, are by no means over, and that increasingly in both tax supported and voluntarily supported programs the changes in practice and education will be interrelated.

Social work education has pressed toward a strengthening and a broadening of an integrated and integrating social work curriculum of class and field instruction. Within a decade it has initiated and participated in two important self-surveys, the latest culminating in a thirteen-volume edition. This continuing movement toward a more effective training program is based upon the need not only to supply workers for the immediate lower echelon positions in the welfare departments but also to provide students with the basis and the substance for eventual progression to the higher administrative and policy-making positions.[14]

Social work and the international
scene

Social work is not the exclusive prerogative of the United States of America. True, it has developed in certain ways in this country in response to our conditions and to the thought and the feeling that has been ex-

---

[14] For a review of the development of education for social work including current emphases see Ernest F. Witte, "Education for Social Work," *Social Work Year Book, 1960* (New York: National Association of Social Workers, 1960), pp. 223–240.

pressed in relation to our needs. People in other countries also have needs; some are different from ours and many are like ours. The changes that have taken place all over the world since World War II have made all peoples more sharply aware of their needs and have accelerated their determination to do something about those needs. Kenneth Pray, speaking as president of the National Conference of Social Work in 1946, took note of the release of a new form of energy and referred to the revolutionary age that was being ushered in and the opportunity for social work in that new age:

> The goals of this revolution are our goals. The kind of world it is creating is the kind of world—the only kind of world—in which social work can feel truly at home. For only in such a world can social work achieve its one ancient, simple, all-inclusive objective of helping human beings to find the opportunity and the incentive to make the most of themselves and so to make the largest possible contributions to the progress and well-being of the whole society. Only in such a world can our profound faith in the inviolable integrity and the inherent creative capacity of the free human personality be finally tested and validated.[15]

These words are as true in the 1960s as they were in the first postwar year. They are real wherever there are people. They inhere in all the efforts expended by American social workers and American social work organizations in every part of the world. They apply as services are offered throughout the world by the American Red Cross, the American Friends Service Committee, the World Health Organization (WHO), the United Nations Children's Fund (UNICEF), the United Nations Educational, Scientific and Cultural Organization (UNESCO), the Food and Agricultural Organization (FAO), the refugee organizations, the Organization of American States (OAS), and more recently, under the leadership of President Kennedy and the dynamic energy and vision of Sargent Shriver, the Peace Corps. This is a formidable list, by no means complete, but it serves to show there is a place for social work throughout the world. It does not have to be the kind of social work that is in operation in this country, but it must be the kind that is usable by the people who are sensitive to their own needs. If, however, our services are offered and if they are accepted, they should be governed by the principle enunciated by Mr. Pray: to help people to find the opportunity and the incentive to make the most of themselves and so to make the largest contribution to the progress and well-being of the whole society. It is here that social work stands in the second half of the twentieth century.

---

[15] Kenneth L. M. Pray, "Social Work in a Revolutionary Age," *Proceedings of the National Conference of Social Work*, 1946, pp. 6–7.

Bibliography

Anderson, Joseph P., "Social Work Status and Trends," *Social Work Year Book, 1960,* New York: National Association of Social Workers, 1960, pp. 62–73.

Bremner, Robert H., *From the Depths.* New York: New York University Press, 1956.

Burns, Eveline M., "How Much Social Welfare Can America Afford?" *Social Welfare Forum,* 1949. New York: Columbia University Press, 1950, pp. 57–78.

———, "Social Welfare Is Our Commitment," *Social Welfare Forum,* 1958. New York: Columbia University Press, 1958, pp. 3–19.

Cohen, Nathan Edward, *Social Work in the American Tradition.* New York: Holt, Rinehart and Winston, Inc., 1958.

Cohen, Wilbur J., "Trends and Issues in Welfare Expenditures and Programs," *American Journal of Public Health,* XLIX (October 1959), pp. 1299–1306.

Dewhurst, J. Frederic, and Associates, *America's Needs and Resources: A New Survey.* New York: The Twentieth Century Fund, Inc., 1955, pp. 430–468.

Folsom, Marion B., "Some Suggested Adjustments in the Use of Our Resources," *Proceedings of the American Philosophical Society,* CII (August 1958), pp. 321–327.

Friedlander, Walter A., *Introduction to Social Welfare,* 2d ed. Englewood Cliffs, New Jersey: Prentice-Hall, Inc., 1961.

Harrington, Michael, *The Other America.* New York: The Macmillan Company, 1962.

Kahn, Alfred J., ed., *Issues in American Social Work.* New York: Columbia University Press, 1959.

Merriam, Ida C., "Are We Spending Enough for Social Welfare?" *Social Welfare Forum,* 1959. New York: Columbia University Press, 1959, pp. 49–66.

———, "Financing Social Welfare Services," *Social Work Year Book, 1960.* New York: National Association of Social Workers, 1960, pp. 267–276.

———, "Social Welfare Expenditures, 1959–60," *Social Security Bulletin,* XXIV (November 1961), pp. 3–11.

Morgan, James N., Martin H. David, Wilbur J. Cohen, and Harvey E. Brazer, *Income and Welfare in the United States.* New York: McGraw-Hill Book Company, Inc., 1962.

Myrdal, Alva, Arthur J. Altmeyer, and Dean Rusk, *America's Role in International Social Welfare.* New York: Columbia University Press, 1955.

Perlman, Helen Harris, *So You Want to be a Social Worker.* New York: Harper & Row, Publishers, 1962.

Rockefeller Brothers Fund, Inc., *The Challenge to America: Its Economic and Social Aspects.* New York: Doubleday & Company, Inc., 1958.

Wilensky, Harold L., and Charles N. LeBeaux, *Industrial Society and Social Welfare.* New York: Russell Sage Foundation, 1958.

2

THE
DEVELOPMENT
OF SOCIAL
SERVICES

European Background

Origins—religious and secular

There is ample historical evidence that among early civilized peoples precept and practice ministered to the poor, the unfortunate, the afflicted. This is true of the early Egyptians, the Jewish people, and Christians. Judaism, and later Christianity, enjoined benevolence and mutual aid, and for more than twenty centuries our expressions of fellow feeling have taken form within the bounds of religious teachings. In Europe monastic orders offered food, clothing, and shelter to the destitute. No state stepped in to define the relations of giver and receiver, although a feudalistic society had long since been molded in the pattern of mutual interest and mutual dependency. And in a static world, a world that looked not to this one for solace and comfort but to the world beyond, these relations of mutuality remained fixed.

The ferment of ideas that characterized the Renaissance and that enlarged man's mental horizon and eventually his physical world also affected the relation of man and his church, and serf and his master. The *status quo* had changed, and in its place stood the emerging modern political state. It is one of these states, the British, whose history of public aid shall be sketched briefly as a prelude to the experience in America and in our own day.

As is so common in dealing with unpleasant situations, the answer given to the increasing problem of distress and vagrancy was repression and still more repression—this in contrast to the benevolences of the Church and the monastic orders. Not only was the feudal system in dissolution but also England had been struck by a plague called the "Black

19

Death" in 1348 that drastically reduced its working population. The loosing of serfs, many of whom wandered about aimlessly and in bewilderment, coupled with a depleted labor supply moved the landed gentry to prevail upon King Edward III to initiate repressive measures. Whereupon the King issued in 1349 the Statute of Laborers, which required ablebodied workers who were without means of support to accept employment tendered to them, forbade them to leave their own parish, and prohibited alms to able-bodied beggars.

Not only were there recurrences of pestilences, though none so scourging as the "Black Death," but there were also crop failures and famines, and wars on the Continent. Added to all these were the Acts of Enclosure (the conversion of tilled land into pasture for more profitable sheep raising), which dislocated rural laborers. The accumulation of a century and a half of such ills finally obliged Henry VIII to seek the enactmen of a statute in 1531, which in effect was the first expression of a positive responsibility for the relief of economic distress. Mayors and justices of the peace were required to seek out the aged poor and those compelled to live by alms and to authorize such persons to restrict their begging to designated areas. In order to control unauthorized begging by the able-bodied unemployed, fines were imposed on persons who gave money or lodging to such beggars. Furthermore an able-bodied beggar was to be whipped and returned to his place of birth and there to "put himself to labour as a true man oweth to do."

This expression of positive responsibility was but a beginning and within five years was supplemented by the Statute of 1536, as a further acceptance of governmental responsibility. Local officials, including church officers, were to secure funds through church collections to be used to help the poor, impotent, lame, sick and diseased in such wise that they would not be reduced to begging. Justices and other local officers were given authority to take children between the ages of 5 and 14 who had been begging and to appoint them to masters to be trained to earn a suitable living. Sturdy vagabonds and "valiant beggars" were to be whipped and even mutilated if found guilty of continual loitering and idleness. Severe and primitive though this may have been, in the sixteenth century it signalized the transition of poor relief from an unregulated dispensing of aid by the church to the beginnings of regulations by the state.

During this same year, 1536, and again in 1539, Henry VIII expropriated the monasteries. Not a few of those whose lives had been within these monasteries, monks and nuns, and the many families that had been sheltered or employed in the monasteries and convents were turned out. Some of these joined the ranks of the other poor and wanderers.

It was not long before it was generally recognized that a system of voluntary collection under voluntary agents furnished neither the necessary funds nor the essential stability of personnel to ensure even a modicum of relief. By 1572 overseers of the poor were appointed as civil officers to direct the expenditure of tax funds levied upon the local community for the purpose of relieving the poor. Within four years the justices of each county were empowered to secure by purchase or lease the buildings to be used as houses of correction. Here materials for work were to be provided for the unemployed to the end that work habits might be instilled, and relief be administered on a *quid pro quo* basis.

Commenting on these early years, Karl de Schweinitz in the volume so aptly titled *England's Road to Social Security* wrote in 1943:

> The statutes from Henry VIII to Elizabeth established a principle and a tradition of relief locally financed and locally administered for local residents, with the overseer of the poor as the responsible official, and a system of public assistance that included direct grants of aid to the unemployable and a policy of work for the able-bodied. After two centuries of attempts to control poverty by repressive measures, government slowly and reluctantly came to accept positive obligation for the help of people who could not provide for themselves. The experience of the years between 1349 and 1601 had convinced the rulers of England of the presence of a destitution among the poor that punishment could not abolish and that could be relieved only by the application of public resources to individual need.[1]

The Elizabethan Poor Law

It was during the latter days of the reign of Queen Elizabeth that the confused jumble of vagrancy and poverty laws came to be welded into the organic unity that we have since called the Elizabethan Poor Law. It is the 1601 revision of the act passed in 1598 which brought order out of chaos and established the basis of poor relief in England, and even America, for over three hundred years. The act of 1601, often referred to as 43 Elizabeth, established three categories of relief recipients: the able-bodied poor, the impotent poor (unemployables), and dependent children. For the able-bodied poor employment was to be provided under pain of a session in jail or in the stocks for refusal to work. The almshouse was to be the sanctuary of the second group, the unemployables; while children who could not be supported by their parents or grandparents were to be apprenticed, the boys until they were 24 years old and the girls until they were 21 or married. For the execution of these legal provisions

---

[1] Karl de Schweinitz, *England's Road to Social Security*, (Philadelphia: University of Pennsylvania Press, 1943), p. 29. This volume is invaluable as a record of England's efforts over six centuries to deal with the welfare of people as a governmental responsibility. Every student who would understand developments in America as well as England should familiarize himself with it.

a tax was to be levied in the parish upon lands, houses, and tithes, which was supplemented by private charitable bequests of land or money, and by the use of fines for the violation of certain laws.

Though there were some who regarded this law as the model for all time, it soon yielded to an addition here, a repair there, an alteration in some other place. Inevitably the poor moved from one place to another, from parishes where relief was lean to parishes where, if relief was not ample, at least it was comfortable. Several hundred years before, by the Statute of Laborers of 1349, Parliament had ordered laborers to stay in their own parishes; but so acute had the condition of laborers become that no man would root himself to a spot where he was doomed to slow starvation. By the Settlement Act of 1662 each parish became responsible only for those who had legal residence within its bounds, which usually meant residence by birth. Furthermore those without legal settlement were returnable to their proper parish, while newcomers could only be accepted upon posting surety against becoming public charges.

Another extension of the Poor Law was the development of the workhouse test. Despite the supposedly deterrent or therapeutic effects of a parish list of relief recipients and their grants, there seemed no letup in the size of the list. If anything, the public list grew longer and longer until in desperation, it may be, the workhouse test was devised. Bristol's experience, after the enabling act of 1697, whereby expenses were reduced, gave impetus to this method of work relief. Parishes were permitted to join forces for the purpose of establishing workhouses in which the poor might be lodged and worked. To refuse to work, however, was to court dismissal and to be denied any relief. To make matters even worse, at least so far as the abled-bodied poor were concerned, parishes were permitted to "farm out" the poor on contract. This amounted, in essence, to an invitation to the lowest private bidder to exploit human labor to the utmost. So criminal and so degrading had such practices become through the years that finally, in 1782, Parliament was obliged to abolish "farming out."

A system of allowances was later devised which added to the miseries of the unemployed as well as those who were barely managing to eke out a living. It is not intimated here that there was any deliberate effort on any individual's part to demean the condition of English labor, but the fact, nevertheless, remains that the effect of legislation presumably designed to improve the lot of the worker actually achieved the opposite result. The able-bodied poor were to be provided with work by the overseers of the poor and to retain their own domiciles. However, when the overseer had collected the wage and found it insufficient to support the worker and his family, a supplementary grant from relief funds was to be made. Such a wage subsidy, as might have been foreseen, depressed wages throughout England and tended to pauperize the entire working population. What employer would not pay a low wage if he knew the government would supplement it? What incentive was there to pay a "living" wage when the "dying" wage was sure to be added to? Was it any consolation to the poor that the same Parliament that enacted the allowance system also rescinded the workhouse test? Surely here was first-hand material for the pen of the English cleric, Thomas Malthus, upon which to base his population theory and his dire predictions of the tendency of population to outrun the food supply.

The Poor Law Revision of 1834

For two centuries England had struggled with the problem of a changing social order: the feudal system had disintegrated, the control of the church over the lives of communicants had been slackened, a commercial and industrial economy had gained a dominant position. All the while, however, the lot of the worker and his dependents had fallen to lower and lower estate. In 1834 a Parliamentary commission presented a report that aimed to revise the Elizabethan and post-Elizabethan Poor Laws. Upon the basis of the committee's report legislation was enacted enunciating the following principles: doctrine of least eligibility, reestablishment of the workhouse test, and centralization of control.

An analysis of these principles substantiates the penetrating description of them, by the Webbs, as the "framework of repression." The doctrine of least eligibility meant "that the condition of paupers shall in no case be so eligible as the condition of persons of the lowest class subsisting on the fruits of their own industry." It mattered not how low the standard might be of the lowest paid common workman in Great Britain, no person receiving aid was to be as well off. Then, as if this were not enough, the authorities could always hold out as a threat the ever impending workhouse. Able-bodied poor could apply for assistance in the public workhouse, but refusal to accept the lodging and fare of the workhouse disbarred them from qualifying for any aid. Outdoor relief, that is, outside of an institution, was reduced to an absolute minimum. The third principle, centralized control, was the only one that could be said to look forward rather than backward. A central authority consisting of three Poor Law Commissioners had power to consolidate and coordinate poor law services throughout the land. Parishes were no longer to be the administrative units; in their stead were to be poor law districts or unions administered by an unpaid Board of Guardians. This was really the beginning of the recognition that the problem of relief was larger than any single local unit.

Between 1834 and 1909 there were numerous changes in poor law legislation, the cumulative effect of which was to veer the entire system away from the principles of 1834. The most important changes were those that began to develop specialized care for certain disadvantaged groups. For dependent children district schools and foster homes were provided; for the sick, hospitals, dispensaries and infirmaries; for the insane and feeble-minded, specialized institutions; for the blind and the deaf, special schools.

Yet even these developments did not alter the fundamental changes which were taking place in this three-quarters of a century. The effects of the industrial revolution penetrated to the depths of British life. Pauperization, bad housing, poor health and faulty sanitation—these and many more effects became progressively accumulative like a snowball rolling downhill. By 1909 Great Britain needed another revision, and, judging by the signs of the times, one far more fundamental than that of 1834.

The Poor Law Report of 1909

Great Britain was fortunate to have the dissenting voices of the Webbs (Beatrice and Sidney) on the Royal Commission on Poor Laws and the Unemployed. Through the Webbs (Mrs. Webb was an official member of the commission) was expressed much of the enlightened thought on the fundamental problems of the British social and industrial order. It was no accident that the report of 1909 and its subsequent adaptations gave strength to principles which stressed curative treatment and rehabilitation, universal provision, and what for lack of a better term may be called compulsion. Cure was to be substituted for repression, and provision for all in the place of the punishingly selective workhouse test. Furthermore it was recognized that the state on occasion would have to exercise compulsion in the best interests of both the community and the individual, specifically, in instances involving restraint of vagrants, isolation of mental cases, removal of children from unfit parents, compulsory vaccination, regulation of child labor, and compulsory schooling.

If the principles of 1834 provided a framework of repression, those of 1909 may be characterized in the Webbs' terms as the "framework of prevention." A positive approach was to be substituted for a negative, an approach that made possible the utilization of human potentialities. The philosophy of *laissez faire*, that had built and sanctioned eighteenth- and nineteenth-century industrial Britain, was giving way before a philosophy that recognized the interdependence of the individual and the state as well as their mutual obligations. As a measure of this shift we need only look at the translation into action of the majority and minority reports. The majority report advocated the widening, strengthening and humanizing of the Poor Law; the minority favored the breaking up of the Poor Law and the abolition of the poorhouse and in its place the establishment of a national minimum of services. In the generation that has followed the dissenting opinion, as so often happens, has become the majority opinion. Great Britain's present-day organization for social security, although by no means perfect, transcends the Elizabethan Poor Law as the modern airplane transcends the cart of 1601.

Developments since 1909

The legislative enactments from 1909 to date substantiate this statement. In 1911 the National Insurance Act which provided compulsory insurance against sickness and unemployment was passed.[2] In 1925 the Widows', Orphans' and Old Age Contributory Pensions Act extended the insurance principle to cover old age and death. Cash payments provided for: (1) pensions for widows of insured men, with temporary allowances for dependent children; (2) allowances during childhood for the orphans of insured persons; and (3) old-age pensions for insured persons, and for insured men between 65 and 70 years of age.

The Local Government Act of 1929 moved closer to the breakup of the old Poor Law which the minority report advocated. The Boards of Guardians were abolished and their functions turned over to the county (rural) and county borough (urban) councils which had been established in the latter part of the nineteenth century as the largest unit of local administration. Administration of relief through public assistance committees was to follow the general pattern of administration in health, education, and other activities carried on by the councils.

The Unemployment Act of June 28, 1934, created an Unemployment Assistance Board operating on a national scale throughout Great Britain. Under its provisions unemployment assistance was to be available to the unemployed who were not covered by insurance or whose term of benefits had expired. Supplementary pensions were also to be granted to any person "entitled to receive weekly payments on account of an old-age pension, or a person who has attained the age of sixty and is entitled to receive weekly payments on account of a widow's pension." Once more de Schweinitz's observation must be relayed:

---

[2] de Schweinitz remarks that this legislation "applied an innovation only to be compared in importance with the legislation that between 1536 and 1601 established the responsibility of the state for guaranteeing the individual a protection against starvation." *Op. cit.*, p. 208.

The development of National Assistance affected the unemployed, the aged and widows, and the war sufferers. Outside these categories local relief as administered by the counties continued, but with a diminishing part in the program of social security. That program at the end of the fourth decade of the twentieth century consisted of three defenses against want: social insurance, the largest; then national assistance; and for those not protected by the first two provisions, public assistance.[3]

The Beveridge Report

On November 20, 1942, Sir William Beveridge (now Lord Beveridge), chairman of the Inter-Departmental Committee on Social Insurance and Allied Services, presented the Committee's Report to His Majesty's government. During the preceding eighteen months Sir William and his associates had been executing the charge to survey "existing national schemes of social insurance and allied services, including workmen's compensation, and to make recommendations." The report emphasized four major principles: (1) every citizen to be covered, (2) the major risks of loss of earning power—sickness, unemployment, accident, old age, widowhood, maternity—to be included in a single insurance, (3) a flat rate of contribution to be paid regardless of the contributor's income, and (4) a flat rate of benefit to be paid, also without regard to income, as a right to all who qualify.

At the same time the Beveridge report was being prepared, Great Britain was engaged in a war for its very existence as a free nation. A coalition government was in power, but before World War II was over the report already was receiving consideration in Parliament. In June 1945 legislation was enacted providing for the initiation, a year later, of a system of family allowances, one of the recommendations of the Beveridge report. In July 1945 the Labor Party came into power, and then acted upon most of the other recommendations of the report. On July 5, 1948, the National Insurance program went into full operation.

Public services in contemporary
Britain

The National Insurance program took the place of the preexisting Unemployment Insurance, National Health and Contributory Pension, and the Workmen's Compensation Acts. For all practical purposes everyone in Great Britain over school-leaving age pays contributions according

---

[3] *Op. cit.*, p. 226.

into which of the three categories he falls— (1) employed persons, (2) self-employed persons, (3) nonemployed persons; and everyone is likewise entitled to benefits. The benefits are: maternity, sickness, unemployment, industrial injury, retirement, widow's, guardianship, and death grant.

The related services are (1) Family Allowances, (2) National Health Services, and (3) National Assistance. The system of Family Allowances provides a payment for each child other than the first: 8 shillings a week for the second child in a family and 10 shillings for each subsequent child. The National Health Service provides, without charge, medical, hospital, and dental service for every man, woman, and child in Great Britain—the cost of this service being provided for almost entirely out of general taxation. The National Assistance scheme provides for those who for one reason or another are not *fully* covered by National Insurance. National Assistance was intended to make provision, especially in the early days of the National Insurance program, for those who would not have paid enough contributions to be able to draw retirement benefits or other benefits, and for others with special needs that are not met by their insurance.

The simplest and clearest statement of the program, which went into full operation July 5, 1948, is to be found in a pamphlet prepared by the British Information Services entitled *Britain's Charter of Social Security*, July 1948. Its concluding statement is:

> July 5th, then, marks one more stage on the long road of British social development. No one claims that the new charter is perfect; it will certainly be added to, modified and improved upon as time goes on, and as experience shows where its shortcomings lie. But in spite of whatever shortcomings there may be, it puts Britain well in the forefront of progress toward complete social security. . . .
>
> The charter as a whole is, in effect an expression of the duty of the community to the individual. By his work and his social conduct the individual helps the community, and in return the community helps him when he is in need of help—and in the long run it is the individual who counts for most. The retention of the principle of contributions means that these social benefits are not simply a form of charity which pauperizes the individual, but the fact that the individual does not have to pay the whole cost himself means that society is not blind to its duties.
>
> In conception the scheme is a compromise between fully government-financed services and services completely paid for by contributions, just as in administration it is a compromise between centralism and devolution of responsibility. In each, the compromise can be adjusted in the light of changing needs, and the scheme retains the advantages of flexibility without losing the other advantages of uniformity.
>
> This division of responsibility between the central government, the local

authorities and the individual himself is perhaps the keynote of the whole, but it is the individual for whom the whole exists. In a democratic country such as Britain that is as it should be.[4]

To the British the provision of these services is not considered as a condescending charity of the state. They are the services which an enlightened and democratic state, through its elected and accountable representatives, deem to be the right of a responsible people. Furthermore, they are regarded as an investment in the lives of the people as their energies and wills are directed to the survival of their country in this highly competitive contemporary world. This emphasis upon constructiveness and prevention, upon a healthier, more productive, and happier people is in marked contrast to the repressive legislation of the Statute of Laborers of 1349. It is also some measure of the creative humanity of a democratically oriented people.[5]

Private and voluntary services— European background

Even before the rise of modern European states there were social services of a primitive sort provided through the agency of the Church. Individual and institutional benevolences in obedience to religious teachings were manifested through alms to the poor, shelter to the homeless, and care and comfort to the sick. Monasteries and hospitals, the latter being charitable foundations for the sick, the destitute, and the aged, were most prominently identified in the alms-giving and sheltering role. Throughout the Middle Ages the religious guilds and craft associations also undertook to provide shelter and alms.

Yet for all the good intentions of individuals or organizations, private charity persisted without order or coordination. Rather than reducing begging and vagrancy, the indiscriminate giving of alms only encouraged greater reliance thereon. The Elizabethan Poor Laws had attempted to bring order out of the chaos of public relief, but it remained for the Ger-

---

[4] See *Britain's Charter of Social Security* (British Information Services, July 1948), pp. 22, 23–24.

[5] For further information on the Beveridge Plan and subsequent developments the reader is referred to: William H. Beveridge, *Social Insurance and Allied Services* (New York: Macmillan, 1942); Geoffrey May, "Social Security in Britain," *Public Welfare*, V, January 1947, pp. 13–16, 24; February, 1947, pp. 30–35; Martha D. Ring, "Social Security for Great Britain—A Review of the Beveridge Report," *Social Security Bulletin* VI (January 1943), pp. 3–30; see also M. Penelope Hall, *The Social Services of Modern England* (London: Routledge & Kegan Paul Ltd., 1952), and A. F. Young and E. T. Ashton, *British Social Work in the Nineteenth Century* (London: Routledge & Kegan Paul Ltd., 1956).

man cities of Hamburg and Elberfeld in the eighteenth and nineteenth centuries to develop the beginnings of an organized system. In Hamburg the first steps consisted of the establishment of a central bureau followed by the apportionment of the city into districts. To each district an overseer or supervisor was assigned, and associated with him were others who served voluntarily. These visitors called upon the poor in their districts and sought to render assistance as well as to keep themselves informed of conditions producing distress and poverty. Each visitor was to maintain close and friendly relations with the poor within his district. This friendly visiting, together with the districting principle and the over-all direction and coordination of a central board for the entire city, were the unique features of the plan. The only paid and officially constituted person was the chairman of the central bureau. As the work expanded from its beginnings in Hamburg in 1788 to its elaboration in Elberfeld in 1852 greater stress was placed upon the relation of the visitor to the person in need, the enlargement of the power of the visitor actually to grant relief, and the emphasis upon removing the causes of pauperism. While the Hamburg-Elberfeld system began essentially as a private venture and while much of the leadership and support, including the use of volunteers, continued from private sources, it eventually received public funds and operated under municipal ordinances. Its significance lies in its early enunciation of principles which underlay the later charity organization movement in Great Britain and America.

The Charity Organization Society

Between the period 1788 (Hamburg) and 1852 (Elberfeld) a Scottish preacher, teacher, and writer, Thomas Chalmers, had developed a program of dealing with poverty that years later found expression in the charity organization society movement. Chalmers detested the Poor Law and its administration as he observed it, especially in Glasgow where he had been called, in 1814, as the preacher of one of its most important churches. In the parish of St. Johns, one of the poorest in Glasgow, he established some twenty-five units, each unit under the direction of a deacon of his church. The deacon's task was to know each of the fifty families of his unit and to investigate all calls for help that were made upon him. The first response was to encourage self-help, then help from family, then from others, and ultimately from the well-to-do. A Court of Deacons served as a clearinghouse or what at a later time might be termed a case committee. Even though the primary emphasis was of help directed toward moral and educational ends, nevertheless there was provision for the disbursement of funds whose service was the "Evening Collection" at Chalmers' church.

These various principles and practices as worked out in the Hamburg system, then by Chalmers, and then in Elberfeld found expression in the first charity organization society in London in 1869. In the years before numerous societies had developed, many of them espousing pet philanthropies with very little relation to one another. Each went its own way, unmindful of duplication and, not infrequently, indifferent to a responsible sharing in the totality of privately supported welfare services. This state of affairs had become so intolerable that steps were taken to deal with the situation. In 1869 the "Society for Organizing Charitable Relief and Repressing Mendicity" was organized, which within a year became the Charity Organization Society.

As the name implies, the Charity Organization Society aimed to effect a coordination among existing welfare services and agencies. The granting of relief was the function of the existing agencies as it had been heretofore. The purpose of the COS was to develop a machinery and a technique whereby relief could be expeditiously and economically administered without duplication and competition. A central committee was established to which district committees were answerable. The district committees served as clearinghouse and central registration bureau. They were also to relieve such as fell outside the Poor Law, but only after making a thorough investigation. Arrangements were worked out between the district committees and the Poor Law officials so that there would be no overlapping or duplication of services. This society, while important for what it did for organizing private initiative and philanthropy in a coordinated service for the poor of London, is equally famous as a pioneering model, which other cities, principally those in the United States, were to follow.

Contemporary voluntary services
in Great Britain

Social services under voluntary auspices (the British prefer the term "voluntary," while we in America incline toward the expression "private social services") have continued to expand since the COS days. Many charitable societies were in existence before 1869, many have developed since then, and very few have gone out of existence. There are many organizations, some of them with titled or royal patronage, that continue to provide social services to meet the needs of the British people. In some instances these organizations continue to provide services for which the need persists even beyond the existing tax-supported services. In other instances organizations will have modified their service offerings or will have developed new programs to meet emerging needs not yet within the scope of the public social services; the "meals on wheels" services to older persons, many of whom are housebound but who insist stoutly on maintaining their accustomed habitation, is an example of the latter.

Without listing organizations by titles, it is possible to mention groupings of social services as evidence of the continued vitality of the voluntary effort throughout Great Britain: prenatal services, infancy and child welfare, youth services, old people's welfare, mental health, welfare of the blind, the correctional services, religious organizations for social service, marriage counseling, family welfare, social settlements.

The British have faced directly the respective roles of the voluntary and the statutory (in America, public welfare) services, and have a place for both; indeed, in the British democratic system the two are essential. Dr. W. G. S. Adams, formerly Warden of All Souls College, Oxford, expressed it in these words:

> Great as was the nineteenth century both in the field of state development and of voluntary service, it was only a prelude to the greater developments of the twentieth century. The first quarter of this century, especially the years 1906 to 1912, saw an unparalleled advance of state functions in the field of social security and wellbeing. The first world war greatly extended the organisation and controls of the state. The movement continued in the second quarter of the century and was carried much further by the extension of state control in the second world war and the period following. But with this great expansion of the state there came also in this country a remarkable development of voluntary organisations. Here, as in the Dominions and in the United States of America—countries with much in common in their idea of constitutional and personal liberty—state action itself encouraged and used the resources of voluntary organisations. It was found in one field after another that, in order to realise the policy of national security and social wellbeing, the state had in increasing measure to call upon the resourceful co-operation of voluntary organisations. This is characteristic of our way of life. At one time it seemed to some as if the statutory bodies would do away with the need for voluntary organisations. But more and more it came to be realised that we were reaching out to a vision of community life in which the co-operation of voluntary and statutory bodies was essential. Their services were complementary, not competitive, still less antagonistic in a true view of community development. At least this was the British way of life.[6]

---

[6] W. G. S. Adams, "Voluntary Social Service in the 20th Century," *Voluntary Social Services, Handbook of Information and Directory of Organisations* (London: National Council of Social Service, 1948), pp. 11–12.

Bibliography

Beveridge, Janet, *Beveridge and His Plan*. London: Hodder & Stoughton, Ltd., 1954.

Beveridge, Lord (William), *Social Insurance and the Allied Services*. New York: The Macmillan Company, 1942.

Bosanquet, Helen, *Social Work in London*, 1869–1912. London: John Murray, 1914.

Bourdillon, A. F. C., ed., *Voluntary Social Services: Their Place in the Modern State*. London: Methuen & Co., Ltd., 1945.

Cole, Margaret, *Beatrice Webb*. New York: Harcourt, Brace & World, Inc., 1946.

de Schweinitz, Karl, *England's Road to Social Security*. Philadelphia: University of Pennsylvania Press, 1943.

Hall, M. Penelope, *The Social Services of Modern England*. London: Routledge & Kegan Paul, Ltd., 1952.

Marsh, David C., *National Insurance and Assistance in Great Britain*. London: Sir Isaac Pitman & Sons, Ltd., 1950.

Masterman, N., ed., *Voluntary Social Services since 1918*. London: Routledge & Kegan Paul, Ltd., 1948.

Mowatt, Charles Loch, *The Charity Organization Society, 1869–1913*. London: Methuen & Co., Ltd., 1961.

Queen, Stuart Alfred, *Social Work in the Light of History*. Philadelphia: J. B. Lippincott Company, 1922.

Rathbone, Eleanor, *Family Allowances*. London: George Allen & Unwin Ltd., 1949.

Titmuss, Richard M., *Problems of Social Policy*. London: H. M. Stationery Office, 1950: also New York: Longmans, Green & Co., Inc., 1950.

———, *Essays on the Welfare State*. New Haven: Yale University Press, 1959.

Webb, Beatrice, *Our Partnership*, Barbara Drake and Margaret Cole, eds. London and New York: Longmans, Green & Co., Inc. 1948.

Webb, Beatrice and Sidney Webb, *English Poor Law Policy*. London and New York: Longmans, Green & Co., Inc., 1910.

Young, A. F., and E. T. Ashton, *British Social Work in the Nineteenth Century*. Routledge & Kegan Paul Ltd., 1956.

3

THE SOCIAL
SERVICES
IN AMERICA

From the almshouse to social security

American experience with poor relief ...

The main outlines of the English Poor Law have been presented as the background for the development of American systems of relief. When colonists came to America, they were largely from England, and brought with them English ideas, English common law, English institutions, English customs. The almshouse is a case in point. Pauperism was not to be made respectable. Poverty was an individual matter, signifying some moral flaw. Relief was to be as unpalatable as possible. The catchall institution in the local community was the almshouse into which were herded the old and the young, the sick and the well, the mentally normal and the mentally diseased, the epileptic, the blind, the feeble-minded, the alcoholic, and improvident. As in England, almshouse paupers could be farmed out and children apprenticed. Those who managed to avoid the poorhouse—to call it what it really was—received outdoor relief (that is, in their own homes). We stressed repression, we centered responsibility in the local community, we permitted only a minimum of state supervision and control, and, lastly, a generation later than England we passed our first social security act.

Local public welfare

Public welfare is a relatively new term. In the Elizabethan law of 1601 and the revision of 1834 the term was unknown. Destitution was a

33

local problem and even though a governmental unit may have granted relief the service was termed neither public nor welfare. We of today who speak so glibly of public welfare need some perspective on its development in order to realize the long way we have come and, incidentally, to appreciate the long way we still have to go.

The people and the situations (but not necessarily the problem) with which public welfare has dealt have been essentially local, and the governmental unit that has usually granted assistance has been either the smallest or the one traditionally associated with the relief of distress. In our own country as far back as colonial days it was the parish, the township, the town, or the county rather than the colony which furnished aid. Even with statehood the tradition continued for almost a century in most of the Eastern seaboard states. This chapter is the story of the transition from the local, to the state-local, and finally to the federal-state-local area of welfare services.

From local to state welfare

Ever since colonial days and the early days of statehood there has been some form or other of welfare service provided by the local community. This has usually been relief granted in the home or relief granted in an institution, commonly known as the almshouse or poorhouse. However, as time went on, it became apparent that there were some services that were too costly and some that required institutional care beyond the capacity of the local community to handle. One of the earliest instances of this was the establishment of a hospital for the insane in Virginia in 1773. Every town, county or parish had its insane members, most of whom were lodged either in jail or the almshouse, but no local unit had enough of these individuals to warrant a separate institution. What was more natural than to look to the state to furnish care for this class of afflicted persons wherever they were found. An added advantage from the point of view of the town, county, or parish was that a local burden was shared, in some instances assumed, by the state. Later (in Kentucky, 1822) another group, the deaf and dumb, became special objects of state institutional care; followed in 1837 (in Ohio) by the blind, in 1848 (in Massachusetts) by the juvenile delinquent and the feeble-minded. The list is by no means complete nor is it brought down to date. It merely indicates that public services for the needy, the delinquent, and the handicapped of all kinds began in the local community and expanded outward to state areas.

So long as all welfare services were provided by the local community, there was little need for or concern with welfare organization.

The overseer of the poor dispensed personally all forms of aid whether of cash or produce and operated the poorhouse as well. The only other local service available was that of the jail or house of correction and that usually came under the direction of the sheriff's office. When, however, the state assumed responsibilities for certain classes of what used to be called the "dependent, the defective, and the delinquent," some definite form of organization was necessary. Massachusetts was the first state to establish a state-wide organization. Created in 1863, the Massachusetts Board of State Charities was charged with the investigation and supervision of the entire system of charitable and correction institutions and empowered to recommend changes directed toward the economical and efficient operation of such institutions. Furthermore, the secretary was required to oversee and conduct the "outdoor business" of the state, that is, relating to the unsettled poor who had residence in no county and hence were chargeable to the state. By the exercise of these powers the state was able to check on the reimbursements for the unsettled poor and to achieve some degree of control over pauper relief whether it was on a state or a local basis.

From supervision to administration

The limitations placed upon a state board that could only supervise, investigate, report, and recommend were corrected through the establishment of boards with powers of administration and control. The state boards of control of Rhode Island and Wisconsin may be cited as examples. Salaried and full-time members of such boards were charged with the maintenance and direction of the charitable agencies of the state. They hired and fired personnel, controlled financial operations, and established policies for the conduct of the agencies and institutions. Such direct forms of control naturally lent themselves more readily to the institutional phase of the welfare program, but services traditionally local were touched as well. Some boards of control sought by suggestions and pressures of various kinds to raise standards of local relief, to encourage additional services for those in need, and to improve already existent services, particularly in the case of the almshouse and other local institutions such as the jail and the house of correction.

A glance in retrospect reveals that by the second decade of the twentieth century a decided shift in emphasis had occurred. Originally, local communities whether in Elizabethan England or colonial America were slow to acknowledge the presence of need. The next step was no more willingly taken, namely, to meet these needs. It followed as an inevitable corollary to these two propositions that relief should be made as distasteful as possible and that the recipient or would-be recipient be discouraged from seeking public funds. State boards of charity or control represented little if any change of belief concerning the unfitness of the poor and handicapped. Their aims were to apply business methods in the realm of "charities and corrections," to increase efficiency of administration, to eliminate waste and, if not to show a profit, at least to show low operating costs.

However, by 1917 a positive approach was beginning to replace the negativism of the past three centuries. Public welfare was coming to be regarded as a service with constructive possibilities. True, there were individuals who always would need some kind of help, other individuals who would rather live on the public treasury than by their own efforts; but on the other hand there were many others, perhaps the bulk of all the disadvantaged, who required efforts directed toward their rehabilitation and self-maintenance. Once this latter conviction began to prevail it became necessary to implement it with effective organization. Although Kansas City, Missouri, had anticipated this development as early as 1910 with the creation of a Board of Public Welfare, it was not until action by Illinois and North Carolina in 1917 that the movement of state-wide organization really got under way. In that year North Carolina established a State Board of Charities and Public Welfare consisting of seven unpaid members who appointed a commissioner as the executive officer of the board. The board and the commissioner were charged with certain duties of study, investigation, reporting, licensing, and direct service. The latter pertained particularly to providing for the placement and supervision of dependent and delinquent children. An unprecedented feature was the specific instruction to encourage counties to appoint county superintendents of public welfare by joint action of the board of county commissioners and the county board of education. The Illinois setup contrasted in many ways with that of North Carolina. A Board of Welfare Commissioners had advisory functions only, while the actual power lay with the State Department of Public Welfare and the director who was appointed by the governor. The department was responsible for the administration of the state eleemosynary and penal institutions as well as for the granting of paroles and the supervision of parolees.

From 1917 to 1929 most of the states had joined in the movement toward consolidation and coordination of welfare services into a state-wide system. Each state sought to work out its own problems according to the exigencies of the situation and of the time. Thus some states established welfare departments headed by an executive appointed by the governor, with a board solely advisory to the executive. Other states have an appointed board that selects the administrator to operate the welfare department, with certain responsibilities allocated to the executive and certain to the board. A third group of states still retain a salaried board of three or five members performing all the functions of an executive board. In some states all penal, correctional, relief, health, and mental hygiene services are under the direction of one department or board, while in other states, largely for historical reasons, there are two or more boards, departments, or commissions dividing the field. Some states make an organizational division between the institutional and the noninstitutional services. However, regardless of how administrative responsibility was delegated or whether agencies were single or multiple, there was an unmistakable trend in the direction of coordinating administration and supervision in a state department or board as well as tying in the local communities with the state agency. Yet throughout all these developments pauper relief still remained in the local town, township, or county.

The federal government and public welfare

Social work usage conceives of public welfare as those tax-supported services which are directed to the alleviation of distress, the prevention and rehabilitation of disablement, and the self-maintenance of the individual and the group of which he is a part. While no two readers will accept this tentatively offered description in its entirety, they will agree that at least the source of the funds for the initiation and support of such services is from taxes. It may be disputed whether public welfare work is concerned with alleviation of distress, prevention and rehabilitation of disablement, or self-maintenance, but there is no denial of the fact that the essential core of public welfare services can be distinguished from other governmental services such as public health, public safety, public works, public education. While there is, inevitably, a certain amount of overlapping of these services, nevertheless the central focus of each is readily identifiable and establishes it as one of the commonly accepted public services.

The very nature of public welfare organization and organizations prior to 1929 reflected the limited role which public welfare played in the life of most communities throughout the United States. Of the three areas of government—national, state, local—the first named offered the least share of services. The national government, narrowly interpreting the welfare clause of the Constitution since President Pierce's precedent-making veto in 1854 of the bill to provide care for the insane, had restricted its public welfare activities to traditionally federal, noncontroversial areas. Four departments carried on services that are classifiable as welfare: Treasury, Interior, Labor, and Justice. The oldest of these services was that of the United States Public Health Service in the Treasury Department, which as far back as 1798 administered a health insurance plan for seamen. In later years the Service has administered hospitals and relief stations for seamen, Coast Guard workers, government employees, and federal prisoners, in addition to promoting public health work through supervision, research, education and publication. The Office of Indian Affairs (and its predecessors) had been providing services for Indians, as wards of the government, long before there was the Department of the Interior with which more recently it has been affiliated. In the main the objective of these services was to assist the Indian to achieve and preserve his own self-maintenance and cultural integrity. The Department of Labor, through its Women's Bureau and Children's Bureau, has done more than any single agency to make welfare an understandable function of the federal government. The contributions through study and research, supervision and consultation, interpretation, and publication, have long since justified the hopes of those who projected the Children's Bureau in the first decade of the present century. A fourth department which has carried out welfare services has been the Department of Justice, through the Bureau of Prisons and the Board of Parole. Before 1930 these services were under the direction of a Superintendent of Prisons. Five penal institutions were used, three of them penitentiaries for men: McNeil Island, Washington (1890), Leavenworth, Kansas (1895), and Atlanta, Georgia (1902), a reformatory for men at Chillicothe, Ohio (1926), and an institution for women at Alderson, West Virginia (1927). Parole supervision as an adjunct to prison administration was authorized as early as 1911, and federal probation in 1925, but both services were limited in their operation prior to the fundamental reorganization which resulted in the U.S. Bureau of Prisons in 1930.

A review of the first century and a half of our national existence reveals that welfare activities have been circumscribed by narrowly defined unquestioned federal functions. The national government has hewed to the Constitution line throughout that period. Two early deviations, a grant of land to Connecticut in 1819 and a similar grant to Kentucky in 1826 for education of the deaf and dumb, were scored by President Pierce as being beyond the province of the federal government. Indians, offenders against the laws of the United States, seamen, war veterans, government employees—these were considered legitimate charges upon the federal government.

However, the establishment of the Children's Bureau in 1912 signalized an enlarging concept of federal welfare function. Although the charge of the law creating the bureau to "investigate and report . . . upon all matters pertaining to the welfare of children and child life among all classes of our people" stressed information and research rather than the direct service aspects of child welfare, nevertheless it was a recognition for the first time that the federal government had a share in the promotion of the welfare of children of America.

Federal subsidies and grants-in-aid

One very significant factor that profoundly affected federal public welfare programs was the extension of the federal subsidy and the grants to states principle. Grants of land to states, the proceeds from the sale of which were to be used by the states for certain federally designated purposes, was a practice reaching as far back in our national history as the Northwest Ordinance of 1787. Later the Morrill Act of 1862 provided grants for specific educational purposes, that is, for the support of land-grant colleges. Other grants of land were made subsequently for allied services such as a girls' industrial school (Alabama, 1899), a school and asylum for deaf, dumb, and blind (Arizona, 1910, New Mexico, 1898), a deaf and dumb asylum (Montana, 1889), charitable penal and reformatory institutions (Arizona, 1910, Idaho, 1890), reform schools (Montana, 1889, New Mexico, 1898).

The shift from grants of land to grants of money was readily effected. As early as 1837 Congress distributed a treasury surplus to the states in the form of loans without the expectation of repayment. By 1887 money grants were made to state agricultural stations, a year later for state veterans' homes, then in 1890 to provide instruction in land-grant colleges. Succeeding these grants came others for forest services (1911), agricultural extension work (1914), highways (1916), vocational education (1917), venereal disease control (1918), vocational rehabilitation (1920), and welfare and hygiene of maternity and infancy (1921). These early developments may seem to bear little relation to present-day public welfare until it is realized that many of the current federal-state welfare programs are financed on the grant (grant-in-aid, matched grant, or subsidy) principle, and have derived from these early anticipations. During the booming 1920s few additional welfare services were taken on or supported by the federal government. Before the depression 1930s were over, the federal government had been irrevocably committed not only to the principle of contribution, but also to the necessity and desirability of assuming a partnership role with the states and local communities. This practice has continued to the present day, with grants being made available in a number of postwar programs of which one of the largest is in the area of mental health.

Noninstitutional services
before 1929

Early in the twentieth century certain noninstitutional services such as pension laws for the blind, the aged, and widowed mothers with dependent children began to make their appearance. Although restricted in their original application, these services assumed ever-increasing proportions until they were embodied in the Social Security Act of 1935 and became the predominant and characteristic form of public welfare in the century.

Aid to the Needy Blind

Before 1929 the care of the blind had been assumed in some places by private organizations, in other places by public ones. Sometimes it involved institutional care, at other times educational and vocational training or retraining. Because the blind are frequently at a disadvantage in the labor market and less likely to earn sufficient money for self-maintenance, the movement for allowances from public funds got under way, long before public aid to dependent children or the aged. As early as 1840 the state of Indiana passed a statute to provide for the support of the indigent blind. Later, in 1866, the Board of Aldermen and Board of Councilmen of New York City passed a resolution outlining a procedure for handling applications for assistance to the blind. Before the century was out, one state, Ohio, had enacted a law providing for the relief of the blind. This law of 1898 was declared unconstitutional as was that of 1904. However, in 1908 a further enactment stood the test of constitutionality. In the meantime two other states had acted affirmatively and established precedent for pensions for the blind. The Illinois legislature acted in 1903 and Wisconsin in 1907. Thus by 1910, before any state had made pension provision for its widowed mothers or aged, three states had granted public aid to the blind. In the next decade, beginning with Kansas in 1911 and ending with Nebraska in 1917, eight other states enacted assistance laws for the blind, and a like number legislated during the decade ending in 1929.

Aid to Widows and Children

A second departure from the poor law principles as well as from traditional institutional care was the provision of financial aid to widows and other mothers with dependent children. Several centuries of poor law "treatment" of dependent children had revealed the tragic waste to so

many families and children of methods of care that pauperized or institutionalized the child. The foster home movement which originated under
private auspices in 1853 was an early innovation in child care, but it
remained for the White House Conference of 1909 to advocate a form of
aid designed to keep mothers and children in their own homes. That conference went on record as declaring that children should not be deprived
of their homes except for urgent and compelling reasons. Poverty of itself
was not deemed an urgent or compelling reason. When aid was necessary
to keep the home together, the conference declared, it "should be given
by such methods and from such sources as may be determined by the
general relief policy of each community, preferably in the form of private
charity rather than of public relief." The recognition of the vital role of
the mother in the lives of her children and of the importance of the early
developmental years in the home had found expression in a new concept
of child care.

The first mothers' aid law in the United States was enacted in April
1911 for one county in Missouri, Jackson County. Allowances were made
to mothers who were in need, whose husbands were dead or prisoners,
and whose children were under fourteen years of age. In June of the same
year the first law on a state-wide basis was placed on the statute books of
Illinois, known as the "Funds to Parents Act." The Juvenile Court of each
county was empowered to determine the eligibility of parents and children
for such assistance and to decide upon the money necessary to provide
adequate care for the child. Colorado, in 1912, followed Illinois and
adopted a Mothers' Compensation Act.

Once having started, the movement spread rapidly. By the end of
1919 thirty-nine states and two territories had passed laws of various titles
—mothers' pensions, mothers' allowances, child welfare, mothers' assistance
fund, widows' compensation, aid to dependent children, "an act to promote Home Life for Dependent Children"—all aimed to meet the same
need. Within another decade, that is, by the end of 1929, five states and
the District of Columbia had followed suit so that at the time of the
depression of the 1930s there were forty-four states, the District of Columbia and the territories of Alaska and Hawaii that had made provision
for aid to children in their own homes.

Old-Age "Pensions"

Chronologically, assistance to the blind and to mothers of dependent children preceded assistance to the aged. The first state law providing
financial aid to the blind was enacted in 1840, the first (state-wide)
widows' pension law in 1911. Actually it was not until 1923 that the first
operable old-age pension was on the statute books of an American state.

Long before 1923 it had become clear that relief granted according to the methods and philosophy of the poor law was self-defeating. Not only did it demoralize the recipient, but because of the damage it did to the individual and the family of which he in most instances was a part, it actually proved to be a costly form of assistance. Even though the per capita relief grant was low, the perpetuation of pauperization swelled the grand total of relief to large figures. Almshouse conditions were being exposed to public airing and the resulting stench often reached the nostrils not only of the social worker or of the sensitive public-spirited citizen, but also the ordinary hardheaded businessman and the equally vociferous taxpayer. Private relief with its best of intentions was in no position to meet so great a need. Private institutions reached only a relatively few needy aged. Social insurance schemes had not yet taken hold in this country. In the face of such convincing reasons for some form of assistance to the needy aged the wonder is that state aid was delayed so long. Even when the movement for old-age pensions did begin to produce tangible results the effects were not as pronounced as in the case of the blind or dependent children. The first state to enact a law that withstood the constitutional test and furnished a statutory base for a program was Montana in 1923. (Arizona had passed a law in 1914 that was declared unconstitutional. However it was the territory of Alaska, now a state, that may rightly claim the first law, 1915, to stay on the statute books.) In the same year, 1923, another state, Nevada, passed laws that withstood the courts (Pennsylvania's law did not). Wisconsin in 1925, Kentucky in 1926, Maryland in 1927, and four states—California, Minnesota, Utah, Wyoming—in 1929 complete the roll by the close of the pre-Depression era. Nine states and one territory had made their break with the poor law principle of relief for the aged.

Although the poor law had not yet been scrapped, at least its preeminence as a philosophy of adequately meeting human needs had been seriously questioned. Looking back on the comparative record of assistance to the blind, to children and the aged, one is tempted to observe that there may be a connection between the feverish activity on behalf of children between 1911 and 1929 and the prior neglect of them for three centuries. It may be as much in order to observe that apparently a correlation exists between the tardiness of care of aged prior to 1929 and the extreme solicitude, not to say generosity, that has been manifested toward them in subsequent legislation. A basic trend within recent decades toward an aging population cannot have been without its effect on old-age security legislation!

Public welfare following 1929

A new way of looking at the problems of people and new ways of dealing with those problems and people began to emerge once we realized that the debacle of 1929 spelled finis to the postwar philosophy of the twenties. Prosperity, despite reassurances from high places, was not around the corner. Depression had come. Translated into human terms, depression meant that millions of workers were unable to earn a living for their families; that people, plain ordinary people, went hungry and sick; that despair and frustration seized those who became dependent; that rebellion swelled inside people who saw threats of mass starvation in a land of plenty. The efforts to find a balance in such a topsy-turvy world, to meet the immediacy of countless needs, demanded not a return to the poor law principles but an abandonment of them, as the Webb Minority Report of 1909 in England had foreseen. True we fumbled through the time-precious years of 1929 to 1932 trying to hold on to the old while fearful of the new. Yet although the dates 1933 and 1935 mark the legislative expression of a new philosophy of public welfare, the era begins not with the stamp of legislative endorsement but with the days and events that culminated in that legislation.

From private to public agency

Until 1929 the private social work agencies had dominated the field of social work. The profession had been built largely through the efforts of workers associated with privately supported agencies. These workers and these agencies have fought for and achieved standards. They had initiated and developed social work training largely under private auspices. They looked with distrust, not to say disdain, upon the caliber of the work, and often the workers, in the public field. Furthermore, the private agency, particularly the family societies, had come to carry more and more of the load of granting relief to clients. In that process certain skills and techniques of handling relief had developed and the workers had been able to see on every hand the values of such service to the profession as well as to the client.

In view of all this, and of the very real fact, in many instances, that the public welfare field was poorly manned by incompetent people who were politically subservient, it is quite understandable that the private agencies would look with misgivings upon proposals to use public funds through public agencies for relief purposes. The response was to assert the willingness and the fitness of the private agency to do the job. At first this meant the expansion of community fund drives and the allotment of the increased sums to the various private agencies to dispense wisely. But the demands of the unemployed and their dependents increased enormously and private funds were obviously insufficient for the task. Many influential persons and a large number of private agencies conceded that the funds might come from the public treasury but be distributed by private agencies. After several years of experimentation the decision was made that public funds were to be administered by public agencies.

In the spring of 1929 there were almost 3 million unemployed workers. Instead of an expected decrease during the spring, the number kept swelling until in January 1930 there were 4 million unemployed. Before the year was out the total had reached 7 million, and by the spring of 1933 there was an estimated unemployed population of 13 to 15 million. These figures should be related to a gainfully employed population that usually numbered around 48 million workers.

Private social work agencies, which had usually carried the bulk of the relief load, were alarmed at the size of the job to be done. Their philosophy committed them to a policy of continuing to carry the load. This meant whipping up unprecedented drives for private funds. Thus a community chest that formerly raised annually about $3 million found itself faced with the demand to raise $5 million in 1931, $7 million in 1932, and $10 million in 1933, only to realize that the unmet needs exceeded the help already given. Community chests that had formerly conducted separate drives, that is, the nonsectarian community fund and the Jewish Fund, were joined but still their combined drives raised only a fraction of the money needed.

Besides financial drives to raise funds to be administered by the private agencies, a movement got under way for private charity and individuals to provide work for the unemployed. "Share-the-work" and "give-a-job" plans were put forth everywhere, and finally yielded to the American genius for organization. The block-aid plan, whereby individuals living within a designated area made job provisions for all the unemployed contained therein, expressed unmistakably the emphasis upon local and private responsibility. Apple-selling on busy street corners did the same.

Private charity was finding the size of the task far too large. Public agencies already in existence seemed even more powerless to contend with the very magnitude of the situation. Not even the administration, in an already existing local department of public welfare, of funds jointly provided from public and private sources proved adequate. The problem and the approach to it was no more local than it had been private. The next step was inevitable, namely, the assumption by the state of a share of the total responsibility. Accordingly state organizations were created outside the established departments to administer the "emergency" program. Significantly enough, the first of many such state agencies was titled "temporary emergency relief administration," and was entirely separate from the department of public welfare.

The first Temporary Emergency Relief Administration

On September 23, 1931, the New York Temporary Emergency Relief Administration was established by the Legislature to provide state aid for the unemployed. Funds were appropriated to reimburse cities and counties up to 40 percent of their expenditures for unemployment relief. Furthermore the TERA, as it came to be called, was empowered to make and enforce rules for the proper and efficient administration of relief. In October Governor Franklin D. Roosevelt appointed Harry Hopkins, an experienced social worker, to be Executive Secretary of the TERA. New Jersey and Pennsylvania also set up emergency relief organizations before the end of 1931, and were followed within the next year by Wisconsin, Rhode Island, Illinois, and Ohio. The size of the appropriations was unprecedented. New York's initial $20 million proved to be only one-half the total appropriation for the year; Pennsylvania had to revise its figures upward before its first year was out, and other states did likewise. As important as the size of the appropriations was the principle that such legislation embodied—a responsibility shared by the state and the local community for the relief of distress resulting from unemployment.

Despite these early state measures, the situation throughout the country grew worse and worse. Many states were constitutionally barred from using public funds for unemployment purposes; other states, particularly the smaller and nonindustrial ones, were without resources. To darken the picture still further, many local communities were unable to raise funds from taxes to receive state reimbursement, and in some instances there were individuals and groups that refused to admit a depression had arrived and that starvation was on hand. The valiant, if misguided, efforts of high government officials as well as leading industrialists and managerial talent to deal with the problem on a private charity basis were proving more and more fruitless. Already the movement had begun toward federal participation.

Two senators, Costigan and La Follette, succeeded in presenting overwhelming evidence of the need for federal assistance to the states, but apparently the time was not yet ripe for federal assumption of the burden, or even part of the burden. Their efforts bore no immediate fruit, for the Congress that first heard their daring proposals rejected the bills, under

administration direction, in February 1932. The common arguments occurred over and over again. The government's credit would be impaired;
age-old principles of local responsibility and relief would be abandoned;
states rights would be violated; a bureaucracy would result; and federal
aid, after all, was only a dole.

The Federal Emergency
Relief Act

But the matter would not die. Within six months Congress passed
a bill entitled the Emergency Relief and Construction Act. It authorized
the Reconstruction Finance Corporation to lend to the states $300 million
of federal funds "to be used in furnishing relief and work relief to needy
and distressed people and in relieving the hardships resulting from unemployment." Time soon proved this sum inadequate. Conditions throughout the country grew worse. An election turned out the administration.
Two months later, in May 1933, a new Congress passed the Federal
Emergency Relief Act whereby $500 million was appropriated for relief
purposes. Grants were made to states either on a matching basis, if the
state was able to match federal funds, or as an outright grant if it was
unable to do so. Before a year was over $1 billion had been appropriated.

The Federal Emergency Relief Act shattered all precedent. It
closed the door on three centuries of the poor law. It signalized the acceptance of federal responsibility for the welfare of over 100 million people. It
provided for federal leadership and for federal cooperation with the states
and local communities in helping them to meet the costs of unemployment
relief.

On May 22, 1933, the first day after he assumed office, Administrator Harry Hopkins approved the first grants to seven states. By the end of
June grants had been made to forty-five states. In November of the same
year the experiment known as the Civil Works Administration was begun
for the purpose of putting a large number of workers on civil works
projects at current rates of pay. From then until its termination in March
1934, over 4 million workers, half from the unemployed not yet on relief
rolls, were placed on work projects. The admitted purpose of the CWA
was to give a "shot in the arm" to the economic system by putting men
to work and money into circulation. But the expenditure of almost $1 bil-
lion in less than half a year proved too costly even for the federal
government.

From the end of the CWA to the inauguration of the Works Progress Administration several other experiments and expedients were tried.
These consisted of programs for the relief of distress in (1) "stranded

areas" or with "stranded populations" (such as the cut-over lumber regions, or the worked-out coal areas, etc.), (2) rural areas (Resettlement Administration, subsequently Farm Security Administration), and (3) urban areas (Emergency Work Programs with federal funds supplementing local funds).

In January 1935 President Franklin D. Roosevelt declared that "the Federal Government must and shall quit this business of relief." Lest it be feared that this meant a return to the Elizabethan days of 1601, it must be explained immediately that what the President intended was that home relief should be carried on by the local community, but that two other services were to be available. The immediate service was to be a work relief program under federal direction, the contemplated service was to be the enactment of social security legislation. In theory, then, all needs were to be met: for the employable a work program, for the unemployed with adequate work records unemployment insurance and old-age insurance upon retirement, for the unemployable, that is, the young, the aged, the blind, an assistance program, and finally, for those who fall into none of these categories, local relief.

The WPA

The largest governmental work program the world has ever known began to take form under the Works Progress Administration, beginning in May 1935 with an initial appropriation of almost $5 billion. Despite reshuffling, title-changing, and retrenchments the WPA (subsequently Work Projects Administration) continued to provide a work program with the federal government paying the wage bill largely, and the state or local community serving as sponsor and supplying a share of the materials.

The CCC and the NYA

Two other developments must be mentioned, the Civilian Conservation Corps and the National Youth Administration. The titles obviously indicate the accent on youth. These services were pointed not so much at relief as an end in itself but as a means of maintaining and developing the natural resources of the nation and at the same time of maintaining and developing its human resources. In the CCC camps young workers, largely from relief families, were to carry on conservation projects such as reforestation, prevention of forest fires, soil erosion control, flood control and like work. The NYA projects were also for the younger adult group and were directed toward (a) aiding needy high school and college students, (b) assisting other young people on constructive work projects, (c) providing job training, counseling, and placement services, and (d) the development of constructive leisure-time activities.

While no one would claim perfection for any of these programs since 1933, least of all the leaders of them, nevertheless one cannot contemplate the imagination, determination, and energy that went into them without realizing the profound changes that had taken place within the span of half a decade. President Pierce's doctrine of a static welfare had given way to a dynamic concept of human welfare. The government, federal, state, local, did exist to insure the well-being of the people who constituted that government. If the "welfare" of 1854 did not meet the needs of people in 1933, what was more realistic and human than to broaden the area of welfare?

The Social Security Act

The experience during the Depression of the 1930s with emergency relief and work programs demonstrated the necessity for more stabilized programs for dealing with some of the critical problems of unemployment, aging, illness, and disability, and the welfare of mothers and children. Steps were directed toward legislation that eventuated in the Social Security Act.

The Social Security Act became law on August 14, 1935. There are three main aspects or divisions of the original act and its subsequent amendments. One pertains to the social insurance features; another to the public assistance provisions; and a third to public health and welfare services, especially services for children. The social insurance sections adhere to principles of social insurance by providing for contributions by and in behalf of workers against the contingency of unemployment and the certainty of retirement or death. The unemployment insurance (or compensation) provisions are worked out on a federal-state basis, while the old-age and survivors insurance provisions are entirely federally administered.

The public assistance provisions are based upon federal-state cooperation in the financing and administration of aid to the aged, the blind, dependent children, the permanently and totally disabled, and, since August, 1961, to the medically indigent aged. The source of the funds is federal and state, and, in many instances, from local communities (usually counties) within the state.

The third portion of the act as amended to date provides for (a) maternal and child health services, (b) services for crippled children, and (c) child welfare services. These funds are provided for by allotment according to appropriations authorized by the Congress, and with provision for matching of federal funds by the states. Administration, as with public assistance, is federal-state-local. Vocational rehabilitation and certain aspects of public health work that were included in the 1935 Social Security Act are now in the Vocational Rehabilitation Act Amendments of 1943, known as the Barden-La Follette Act, and in the Public Health Service Act of 1944.

Unemployment Insurance

Further examination of the original Social Security Act as amended to date should be helpful in understanding the principles inherent in it, and to some degree, its operation. According to the unemployment insurance provisions, the federal government levies an excise tax of 3 percent of payroll of employers whose employees come within the definition of the Act. The first $3000 of the worker's wage is subject to tax, although several states have laws that tax the first $3600 of wages. While in all jurisdictions the tax is upon the employer there are three states in which the employee is also subject to the tax. Employers pay their state taxes according to their state unemployment insurance law, and in computing their federal tax they may offset the amount of the state tax up to a total of 90 percent of the federal tax. The remaining 10 percent of the federal tax is paid directly to the federal government.[1]

In accordance with the provisions of the Social Security Act, the states have passed acceptable unemployment insurance laws so that employers could qualify for credit against the federal tax. Furthermore, in order for the Secretary of Labor to certify grants for administrative purposes to the states there must be other acceptable elements in the state law. The effect of these two sets of requirements has been for the state laws to contain a number of provisions of which the most important are:

1. Establishment and maintenance of personnel upon a merit basis
2. Opportunity for a fair hearing, before an impartial tribunal, for all individuals whose claims for unemployment compensation are denied
3. The making of reports as required
4. Payment of unemployment compensation solely through public employment offices
5. The payment of all money received in the unemployment fund of the state to the Secretary of the Treasury to the credit of the Unemployment Trust Fund

---

[1] It should be noted that under experience rating, that is, the higher the employer's employment rate the lower his tax, taxes in many states actually have been less than 3 percent; averaging under 2 percent throughout the country within recent years.

6. Moneys withdrawn by the states from the Unemployment Trust Fund to be used solely for the payment of unemployment benefits
7. Compensation shall not be denied if an otherwise eligible individual refuses work because (a) the job offered him is vacant due to a strike, lockout, or other labor dispute, or because the wage, hours, or working conditions are substantially less favorable than those prevailing for similar work in the locality, or (b) if as a condition of employment the individual is required to sign a "yellow-dog" contract, that is, to join a company union or resign from or refrain from joining any bona fide labor organization

Unemployment insurance is not available for all workers. The federal tax that governs contributions applies, generally speaking, to employers who employ four or more workers "on each of some twenty days during the taxable year, each day being in a different calendar week." [2] Other workers are not provided for because they are in certain employments excluded from the tax provisions. The most important of these excluded employments are:

1. Agricultural labor
2. Domestic service in a private home, local college club, or local chapter of a college fraternity or sorority
3. Casual labor not in the course of the employer's trade or business
4. Service performed by an individual in the employ of his son, daughter, or spouse, and service performed by a child under 21 years of age in the employ of his father or mother
5. Service performed in the employ of the United States
6. Service performed in the employ of a state or any political subdivision thereof
7. Service performed in the employ of a foreign government
8. Service performed in the employ of a nonprofit agency organized exclusively for religious, charitable, scientific, literary, or educational purposes, or for the prevention of cruelty to children
9. Certain specified miscellaneous services

When the worker's employment ceases, he is required to notify the nearest public employment office of his situation, to register there for reemployment, and to indicate his fitness and willingness to work. His waiting period (usually one or two weeks, although Maryland and Nevada have no waiting period) must end before he can receive unemployment compensation. The weekly benefit paid bears a relationship to the worker's weekly earnings, varying, according to state laws, from about 35 percent to about 50 percent. It continues for a stated number of weeks, usually up to twenty to twenty-six weeks, or until a maximum sum has been paid.

---

[2] A number of states, however, extend unemployment insurance to workers in firms employing less than four workers.

There are certain disqualifications that affect benefit payments, such as voluntarily leaving a job, refusal of a suitable job, discharge for misconduct, or unemployment due to a work stoppage existing because of a labor dispute in which the individual is participating. Because the laws of the states vary, there is no uniformity of provisions for dealing with such situations. In some states the benefit payments are postponed, in others the benefit payments may be reduced or canceled entirely.

Even though a worker may have been on the job for a number of years and then become unemployed because of illness, there is usually no unemployment benefit paid to him while he is out of work. Four states are exceptions. Three of these states have separate provisions to pay disability benefits when illness or disability prevents the worker from being on the job. However, the worker must be covered under the unemployment insurance laws of the state. A fourth state provides temporary disability benefits through its state workmen's compensation agency. Unemployment benefits and disability benefits are not intended as a substitute for a job. Such benefits aim to give workers some protection against loss of income during the interval between jobs or before restoration to a job.

Old-Age, Survivors, and Disability Insurance

Twenty-five years after the passage of the Social Security Act, the Director of the Bureau of Old-Age and Survivors Insurance observed, as have others, that "the old-age, survivors, and disability insurance program is firmly established as the basic method in the United States of assuring income to individuals and families who suffer a loss of earnings when the worker retires, becomes disabled, or dies." When the act was passed in 1935, provision was made only for the covered wage earner upon retirement; in 1939 the survivors of the wage earner were added; in 1956 provision was made for insured wage earners between ages 50 and 64 who became disabled, permanently and totally, as well as for disabled children (aged 18 or over) of retired or deceased workers, if their disability began before the age of 18 years; and in 1960, the 50-year age limit for disability benefits was eliminated.

In other respects the act has undergone improvements during its first quarter century. Beginning in 1935 there was a long list of exclusions, similar to those under the unemployment insurance part of the act, but as amendment has succeeded amendment in ensuing years more and more workers have been brought within the OASDI (as it is called) provisions. As of 1960 only about 10 percent of the labor force was still excluded by law from coverage, in marked contrast to about 40 percent exclusion in 1935. At the present time somewhat more than half of these workers are self-employed persons and domestic employees who do not meet certain minimum requirements as to the amount of their earnings or the length of time worked. The others not included within the program are largely federal employees who have a civil service retirement system, some policemen and firemen under state or local retirement systems, and self-employed physicians.

Another change is the increase in the amount of the benefit payments, which is related both to the increase in the contribution rate (tax) as well as to the raising of the wage base. In the beginning of the program the tax was 1 percent on the employee and the employer and the base to which this tax applied was the first $3000 of the worker's wage. By September 1, 1961 the tax rate was placed at 3⅛ percent for the employee and 3⅛ percent for the employer upon a wage base of $4800. The benefit payments as of 1961 are, as is to be expected, considerably above those of the late 1930s: $40 per month is the minimum benefit payment in contrast to the earlier $10 minimum.

A still further improvement relates to the amount of money a retired worker may earn without his benefit payment being decreased. Originally the retired worker could receive full benefits if his monthly earnings were less than $15 a month; on a year's computation this would be $180. Later this was raised to $50 a month, then to $75, then to $100 ($1200 a year), and in the summer of 1961 this was modified so that a retired worker could earn $1700 per year with only a $250 deduction from his annual benefits. After 72 years of age there is no limitation on his earnings and he receives his full benefit payments for the remainder of his life.

The age at which benefits may be paid has also changed since 1935. In 1956 the act was amended to permit women to retire at 62 years of age, and in 1961 the change was made to permit men to retire at 62 years of age. In both instances the benefits to be received will be less per year than if retirement were to take place at 65 years, the age originally in the 1935 Act.

These modifications signify a continuous evaluation of the experience of administering the Social Security Act, and a determination to change it for the greater usefulness of the American people. A year never passes without the annual report of the Commissioner of Social Security and the Secretary of Health, Education, and Welfare embodying operational analysis and recommendations. There are also special study groups and advisory committees working toward a greater effectuation of the act's purpose. Likewise, practically every session of Congress since 1935 has examined the workings of the act and has been attentive to suggestions for improvement. True, there have been honest differences of opinion as to how far to go, or how quickly to move, in bringing about changes—witness the controversy of the early 1960s over medical care for the aged, whether medical care for the aged should be related to social insurance or public assistance—but it is inescapable that the intention has been to use the social security program as a constructive force in our lives in the twentieth century.[3]

Bibliography

Abbott, Edith, *Public Assistance: American Principles and Policies.* Chicago: University of Chicago Press, 1940.

Abbott, Grace, *From Relief to Social Security.* Chicago: University of Chicago Press, 1941.

Basic Readings in Social Security. Washington, D.C.: Government Printing Office, 1960.

Breckinridge, Sophonisba, *Public Welfare Administration in the United States.* Chicago: University of Chicago Press, 1938.

Brown, Josephine C., *Public Relief, 1929–1939.* New York: Holt, Rinehart and Winston, Inc., 1940.

Bruno, Frank J., *Trends in Social Work, 1874–1956,* 2d ed. New York: Columbia University Press, 1957.

Burns, Eveline M., *The American Social Security System.* Boston: Houghton Mifflin Company, 1949.

———, *Social Security and Public Policy.* New York: McGraw-Hill Book Company, Inc., 1956.

de Schweinitz, Karl, *People and Process in Social Security.* Washington, D.C.: American Council on Education, 1948.

Haber, William, *Readings in Social Security.* New York: Prentice-Hall, Inc., 1948.

———, and Wilbur J. Cohen, *Programs, Problems and Policies, Related Readings.* Homewood, Illinois: R. D. Irwin, 1960.

Kelso, Robert W., *The Science of Public Welfare.* New York: Holt, Rinehart and Winston, Inc., 1928.

Lane, Marie D., and Francis Steegmuller, *America on Relief.* New York: Harcourt, Brace & World, Inc., 1938.

Leyendecker, Hilary, *Problems and Policy in Public Assistance.* New York: Harper & Brothers, 1955.

Schlesinger, Arthur M., Jr., *The Coming of the New Deal.* Boston: Houghton Mifflin Company, 1959.

[3] No attempt has been made to record the detailed features of the Social Security Act. It is suggested that the interested reader, whether teacher or student, will find the most up-to-date material in the nearest Social Security office, or in the office of the Commissioner of Social Security in Washington, or in the pages of the *Social Security Bulletin,* published each month.

Those parts of the Social Security Act that pertain to public assistance, child welfare services, crippled children services, and vocational rehabilitation are discussed in Chapter 7, "Services in Local Welfare Departments."

Shannon, David A., ed., *The Great Depression*. Englewood Cliffs, N.J.: Prentice-
    Hall, Inc., 1960.
Warner, Amos G., *American Charities*. New York: Thomas Y. Crowell Com-
    pany, 1894.
Warner, Amos G., Stuart G. Queen, and Ernest B. Harper, *American Charities
    and Social Work*. New York: Thomas Y. Crowell Company, 1930.

4

THE SOCIAL SERVICES IN AMERICA

From the church to the Charity Organization Society movement

Development of private social work in America

From the earliest immigration—meaning our English forebears—through succeeding years, there have been concerns expressed by members of various religious groups for the welfare of people. This was true of Protestants, of Catholics, of Jews, and of members of the Society of Friends from the first day they set foot on American soil. Indeed, it was true once they came to America because it was true from whence they came. In all religious teachings there is a like commitment, which finds expression in whatever place and in whatever circumstances the members find themselves.

Later as nationality groups came they too, regardless of religious affiliation, bound themselves to come to the aid of their compatriots: the St. Andrews Society of New York (1756) for the English, the German Society of New York (1784) for the Germans, the French Benevolent Society of New York (1807) for the French.

Still another early group, but one without religious or nationality affiliation, was the New York Society for the Prevention of Pauperism formed in 1817. Its purpose was to study the causes of pauperism and to promote measures for its prevention and elimination. The members of the society were convinced that the forces making for pauperism were within the individual as well as outside of him, and that prevention called for certain actions with respect to the internal as well as to the external. A number of the proposed measures anticipated programs eventually elaborated by the charity organization movement later in the century, as well as by such commercial promotions as savings banks, mutual benefit societies, and life insurance. What seemed to characterize this early society was the disparity between the excellence of many of the proposals and the execution of them through effective action.

The Association for Improving
the Condition of the Poor

The most impressive, and by far the most far-reaching in influence of the early societies concerned with the immediate problems of the city poor, was the Association for Improving the Condition of the Poor, organized in 1843 in New York City. According to its first constitution the association's aim was ". . . the elevation of the moral and physical condition of the indigent; and so far as compatible with these objects, the relief of their necessities." Relief was granted to individuals, but studies were made of the conditions under which people lived as well as causes of their poverty. Measures were initiated to improve the conditions and to prevent them in the future.

When the association began its work there were some thirty to forty societies in operation in New York City, each undertaking to provide for a particular need. The association was determined not to grant relief to those for whom the public authorities had responsibility nor to those who were known to the other relief societies. It was to select "from the mass, for our own care and relief, every individual whose condition we can morally and physically elevate and to reject all others." [1]

The city was divided into districts and then subdivided into sections. Each district had an advisory committee, and each section a visitor. The visitors, all of whom were men, were unpaid volunteers.

Besides the relief-giving function, the association aimed to do something about the conditions that beset the poor. Among its earliest efforts were those directed toward the improvement of housing and sanitation. It is said that the report made by a committee to the board of the association in 1853 was the first tenement house report made in America. In 1855 a model tenement, "The Workingmen's Home," was constructed largely through the efforts of the association. Other efforts during its early period resulted in legislation to prevent adulteration of milk, the establishment of medical dispensaries for the indigent sick, the construction of a public bath and wash house, the creation of a special institution for the ruptured and crippled, and, in 1849, the incorporation of the New York Juvenile

---

[1] Lillian Brandt, *Growth and Development of AICP and COS* (New York: Community Service Society of New York, 1942), p. 19.

Asylum, "a reformatory and disciplinary institution, for the education and elevation of vicious children and their subsequent indenture."

During the next period of its history—up to the end of the nine-teenth century—the association actively promoted many causes, among them: fresh-air outings (later homes and camps) for mothers and children, vacation schools (later taken over by the public school system), and a settlement house, Hartley House, in 1897.

From the turn of the twentieth century until its merger with the New York Charity Organization Society in 1939, the association furthered its program of improving the conditions affecting people. Many of the enterprises it encouraged, sponsored, or initiated have since become a part of the community's social services: tuberculosis hospitals, health services for school children, convalescent homes for mothers and babies, school lunches, dental clinics, work relief projects, legislation for widows' pensions, venereal disease clinics, health centers, vocational guidance bureaus, mental hygiene clinics, apartment housing for aged, homes for aged.

Other cities followed the example of the AICP with equal emphasis upon a personalized relief-giving service and the improvement prevention of conditions adversely affecting people: Brooklyn AICP, 1853; Baltimore AICP, 1849; Boston Provident Association, 1851; Philadelphia Society for the Prevention of Pauperism and the Relief of the Deserving Poor, 1855; Chicago Relief and Aid Society, 1854; St. Louis Provident Association, 1860; and the St. Paul Society for the Relief of the Poor, 1876, the last society to be established before the onset of the charity organization movement.

The Charity Organization Society
movement in America

Watson, in his volume on the charity organization movement in the United States, takes note of these early relief societies and conjectures upon their demise or their eclipse by the COS movement. The gist of his observations is that the AICPs, despite their good intentions when founded, became just one more relief society, failing to keep moving with changed conditions.

Within four years of the organization of the London COS the United States encountered the serious Depression of 1873 as an aftermath of the Civil War. Despite the hundreds of local relief societies, or perhaps because of them, it was generally recognized that the existing methods of private charity were inefficient and inadequate. Private organizations in such cities as Philadelphia and Boston had made some use of the

Hamburg-Elberfeld system of poor relief, but it was not until 1877, when Reverend S. H. Gurteen in Buffalo, New York, drew upon his prior experience with the London COS, that the first similar society took form in America. Buffalo was divided into eight districts, each with a committee and a number of family visitors. No relief funds were administered. The COS let it be known that its sole purpose was to help to organize existing local charities, and that each society was to keep its own autonomy. The new society decided it would cut across religious, political and nationality lines. The early purpose to investigate cases and refer them to the proper existing agencies demonstrated the compelling necessity of effecting some reform in the prevailing system of municipal relief and secured at the same time the interest of a number of public-spirited citizens.

Within six years twenty-five cities had adopted the central principles of the charity organization movement: (1) investigation of every applicant, (2) central registration, (3) cooperation of all relief agencies within the community, and (4) the use, in the main, of volunteer friendly visitors. By 1883 societies had been initiated throughout the East and Midwest: New Haven, Philadelphia, Brooklyn, Syracuse, Newport (Rhode Island), Boston, Indianapolis, Detroit, Cincinnati, Baltimore, District of Columbia, New York, to mention some of the earlier organizations. In some instances the societies were known as COS; in others they were called Society for Organizing Charity (Philadelphia), Bureau of Charities (Brooklyn), Associated Charities (Boston). Regardless, however, of title their function was the same, namely to organize the relief resources of the community in order to meet effectively the needs of those who were without means or those who possessed meager resources of their own.

A movement that met such widespread acceptance must have had much to recommend it. In practically every sense the time was ripe for it, and it was ripe for the time. The niggardliness of the Elizabethan Poor Law survivals in this country had reduced, or rather maintained, public outdoor relief to the beggar's level. Private charity, which had made a thousand beginnings in as many places, had incorporated the individualism of industrialists who had grown wealthy in an expanding economy. Not infrequently a prosperous donor sought to impress his particular private phinanthropy upon any relief society willing to accept his largess. As a result there was such an overlapping and waste of private charity funds that more needs were unmet than were met. Coincident with the creation of large cities and scores of factory towns, much of the neighborliness that characterized a simpler society was gone. Coupled with this was the strong conviction that pauperism indicated a character deficiency and required the maximum of personal influence of the donor or the donor's agent upon the recipient.

Yet all of these conditions might have been present and no charity organization movement would have eventuated had there not been leadership ready and able to assume an active and energizing role. That leadership was on hand both here and abroad. Indeed the whole history of humanitarianism reveals that the very forces that create the needs by an alternate reaction produce individuals to whom these needs become a concern. One must only study the reform movements in England from 1832 on, or the efforts of humanitarians in this country from the time of the early Quakers and prison reformers, to realize the compensating effects of any system that carries its own inherent excesses. In short, the COS movement in America was no fortuitous or haphazard occurrence. The effects of the industrial revolution were felt acutely. The efforts of social thinkers and even of social reformers, joined with the rising temper of humanitarianism, were substantiated by a comfortable financial surplus. To all of this came a leadership that pointed the way to a sounder use of human resources. This movement illustrated the dynamic growth principles of any movement: a perceived need, a growing body of knowledge and experience to deal with that need, the material means available or discoverable, and all these fused into a unity by a driving leadership directed toward certain socially desirable goals or ends.

Expansion of the COS movement

As one surveys the whole field of social work today, three main groupings of interest and activities centered around them are readily apparent. First, the preoccupation with the individual per se; second, concentration upon the group of individuals as the working unit; and third, concern with developing resources to meet human needs. To these three we have given the terms social casework, social group work, and community organization. The division within the charity organization movement exemplifies the first and third of these, while the social settlement expresses the second. Consideration of group work will be left for a later chapter, but the developments within the COS with respect to the trends toward individualization and community organization must necessarily be dealt with here.

An attitude that regarded the needy as victims of their own vices and failings tended to absolve the social order of any responsibility for the conditions that reduced individuals to destitution. So long as such an attitude prevailed, it was consistent to make relief as unattractive as possible. A maximum premium was placed upon gratuitous advice, the arts of persuasion and the rigors of exhortation. But an awakened social conscience, coupled with some comprehension of the economic and social order, gave pause to so easy and comfortable a proposition and compelled attention to some of the factors that lay outside the individual. This realization was based, understandably enough, upon a rather fragmentary knowledge of "causes," but it tended to shift some emphasis from an internal to an external causation. It may be more accurate to say that the approach became twofold: first, to continue to give an individualized service in the light of a growing insight into human character (the more technical term "behavior" was to appear later); and second, to seek for changes within the existing framework of society that would produce less devastating effects upon the individual.

Among the earliest of these concerns was housing. Long before the charity organization movement had taken form, proposals had been made for improving housing conditions for the poor in order to reduce the incidence of pauperism. Under the Hamburg-Elberfeld system efforts had been made to better housing for the poor. In London, Octavia Hill and Edward Denison, leaders in reform movements, had agitated for years in the same cause. Brooklyn, however, was one of the early American cities to secure the enactment of a tenement house law in 1879, and later, under the inspired leadership of Alfred T. White, to erect model tenements. Edward T. Devine, in his reminiscent volume *When Social Work Was Young*, has recounted the work of the New York Society in making available to the city of New York the services of housing authorities through the organizational channels of COS. Other cities also gave attention to housing reform, among which must be mentioned Chicago, Washington, and Youngstown and Columbus, Ohio.

The prevention of tuberculosis was another crusade in which COS workers were enlisted. As in the case of housing reform, the initial body was a committee within the New York Society (in 1902), which was still under the leadership of Edward T. Devine. This Committee on Prevention of Tuberculosis wisely utilized the services of capable physicians and lay persons in working out a program of research into the social and medical aspects of tuberculosis, education of the public, encouragement of sanataria for the care of patients, and relief of indigent consumptives. Several years later, in 1904, at a meeting of the American Medical Association, the National Association for the Study and Prevention of Tuberculosis was organized. In other cities, Washington, Minneapolis, Boston, Buffalo, Pittsburgh, and Chicago, the Charity Organization Society or its equivalent was active in tuberculosis work, laying the groundwork for an effective nationalization of a preventive program.

Shortly after the establishment of the first and second juvenile courts in Chicago and Denver, workers within the charity organization movement had become active in the field of juvenile probation. In 1900 the Buffalo Society organized a committee on probation, which was instrumental in the passage of a state law to amend Buffalo's city charter permitting the appointment of two probation officers. Later the New York Society placed a woman probation officer at the disposal of a magistrate's court to effect a closer relation between the legal aspect of the court and the social rehabilitation of the offender. Societies in other cities followed with close interest developments within the court structure, particularly within the juvenile court.

One aspect of this concern with the operation of the courts was the effort stimulated by charity organization societies to secure a fairer distribution of legal services to persons with limited means. Too often clients who came to the attention of social workers were in need of legal services but lacked resources to take advantage of or even to secure the protection of their legal rights. Both Baltimore and Buffalo established legal aid bureaus within their own societies to make legal services available to clients either without cost or at minimum cost.

Other areas in which the societies came to operate were those of desertion and nonsupport cases. Especially was this true in Boston, Philadelphia, and Chicago. Problems within the family also called for action, such as the inadequacies and lack of facilities for dealing with dependent and neglected children. The Children's Aid Society of Pennsylvania was launched in 1882 largely through the efforts of those associated with the work of the Philadelphia Society for Organizing Charity. Beggars and vagrants, whether within or outside of a family group, were touched by COS efforts. For a time in New York all beggars and vagrants were turned over by the Police Department to the COS, where aid was administered by means of wayfarer's lodges; these lodges were also provided in Chicago, Philadelphia, and Boston.

Social reform and individual service

At this stage in the development of the movement two well-defined divergent trends could be identified. First, there were those who maintained that the major effort of the charity organization movement should be to correct the external factors in the social organization responsible for poverty—lack of opportunity and individual and family demoralization. Accordingly, this group devoted its energies to such activities as proper housing, suitable health and sanitary facilities, compulsory education, control of labor exploitation by industry, provision of play facilities in congested areas, adequate relief, and varied forms of social legislation. Second, there were those who restricted their labors to the individual client with the aim of effecting a change within the individual that would enable him to utilize to the full his own potentialities. Quite naturally this latter group developed a more intensive approach to the individual client and gave form to the specialization of social casework within the larger field of social work.

A professional journal and a professional school

Two developments in the latter years of the nineteenth century and the early twentieth need to be mentioned here because of their continuing contribution to the field of social work. One of these was the establishment of a professional journal, the other the founding of a professional school for the training of social workers.

The *Survey* and *Survey Graphic* date back to the Charity Organization Society of New York. As long ago as 1891, the society had published the *Charities Review* and for the next ten years it continued to speak for the social work of that day. In 1897 *Lend-A-Hand,* published in Boston, was merged with the *Charities Review.* At this same time the COS had begun a kind of house organ called *Charities,* which aimed to promote directly the work of the organization. Before the merger of the *Charities Review* and *Charities* to be known as *Charities* in 1901, each journal had published material of outstanding merit. Mergers were not yet over, for in 1905 *Charities* was joined by Graham Taylor's *Chicago Commons,* and early in 1906 by *Jewish Charity* to become *Charities and Commons.* After four years *Charities and Commons* became the *Survey,* taking its name from the monumental study in six volumes of the city of Pittsburgh. During all these years these publications had been under the wing of the New York COS, but in 1912 the *Survey* was separately incorporated. From then until it ceased publication in 1952 it was unequaled in the field of social work publications for pithiness, timeliness, and sprightliness of style.

Just as the *Survey* sprang from the charity organization movement so also have professional schools of social work. Staff conferences and supervision for employed as well as volunteer workers soon proved inadequate to keep abreast of changing demands of the job. Then followed informal courses and lectures for workers in the various societies, of which perhaps the earliest was Brooklyn, in 1891. The first decisive step was taken when, in 1898, the New York Society offered its summer school of philanthropy with Philip W. Ayres, assistant secretary of the society, as its director and with an enrollment of 30 students. For six years this Summer School of Philanthropic Workers continued until it was reorganized upon an eight months' instruction basis. In that year, 1904, the director of the New York Society, Edward T. Devine, along with his other duties, assumed the directorship of the first school of social work in this country.[2]

Everything that has been written here of the charity organization movement is pertinent to family welfare since it is from that movement that the family societies of today have developed. The immediate relation was the creation of the Field Department within the New York COS in 1905. Four years later this led directly to the Charity Organization Department of the Russell Sage Foundation with Mary Richmond as director. In 1911 the National Association of Societies for Organizing Charity was formed with Francis H. McLean, formerly secretary of the Field Department of COS, as its first executive secretary. Name changes since then indicate the trend in thinking: American Association for Organizing Charity (to include Canadian Societies), American Association for Organizing Family Social Work, the Family Welfare Association of America, and in 1946 the Family Service Association of America. In 1919 the periodical *The Family* was established and since then has served as an organ of education and opinion of much of the best of casework practice in the family welfare field. In October 1946 it was named *The Journal of Social Casework*, and in 1950 *Social Casework*.

The origins of the social settlements

At least one other movement must be mentioned in this retrospective survey of the development of social work. It began, understandingly enough, in an area that had suffered earliest and most acutely the effects of industrialization—London, England. By the 1880s social work in England had consisted largely of the meager grants of a poor relief authority, the unorganized philanthropies (church and private) of benevolent individuals, and the organized efforts of the Charity Organization Society. It will be observed that in practically every instance relief was directed toward the individual. It remained for the social settlement to shift this focus from the individual as an individual to the individual within a group. The unit of service had become the group. What was more natural, too, than that such work should emanate from, be supported by, and engaged in by the class that had benefited most by the industrialization of England—the upper middle class. The social settlement emerged from Oxford University and centered largely in the slums of London. Toynbee Hall, the first social settlement in the world, expressed from the moment of its founding in 1884 the conviction that individuals more fortunately endowed with this world's goods could, by taking residence in poorer areas

---

[2] Elizabeth G. Meier, *A History of the New York School of Social Work* (New York: Columbia University Press, 1954).

of the city, share their culture and advantages with those to whom opportunity had never come. This sharing process was the substance of the early efforts of the "settlers," a contribution of the more fortunate out of his experience as well as a learning from the poor out of their experience.

The example of Toynbee Hall was carried to America, and in 1886 the first settlement in the United States, Neighborhood Guild, was established in New York City. Industrialization in America had not only created tremendous wealth but also the very conditions that made that wealth unattainable to all but a few. Social work, including the latest addition of the settlements, tried to understand the problems of the disadvantaged and to help them to realize opportunities for effective living in a social order that was none too tender with those who had failed to succeed.

Conclusion

It must be obvious from the foregoing account that the beginnings of social work have been inextricably bound up with the fundamental economic conditions and changes within the social order and with the concomitant philosophies expressed therein. From the breakup of the old feudal order through the successive changes of mercantilism, commercialism, and industrialism, there has persisted the basic and unavoidable fact of human need. To meet these needs society established certain services early based on the premise of individual responsibility. The individual who was in want had brought that condition upon himself through his own shiftlessness, ignorance, or incapacity. The answer was to meet that need as sparingly as possible; relief was not to be attractive enough, for instance, to tempt the lowest paid workman in England away from his job, nor was any individual to be allowed to feel that society approved of his need. This all sounds quite Elizabethan, but it must be remembered that such was the philosophy dominant throughout the two centuries that followed.

Several centuries of attempts at alleviation had clearly shown the limitations of any program that dealt only with the result instead of the cause. It was like trying to sweep back the ocean with a broom. Little insight was gained into the nature of social problems until our understanding took in more than merely the fault of the individual. Only after we began to realize that there were factors larger than and beyond any individual did we proceed to the next phase, prevention. Then the role played by the entire nation—its industry and trade, its philosophies and social institutions—became evident. An awakened understanding of these forces showed their relation to the fate of the individual. Only with such understanding could an ameliorative and preventive program that saw the connection between cause and effect take hold. Social work became a part of the economy of the nation. As the new profession developed, it became clear that social workers who were called in after the damage to the individual had been done might well be looked to for consultation, direction, and action before the fact. This early concern with social problems gradually expanded (some would say narrowed) to working with those capacities within the individual that enable him to adjust to and use effectively his environment of things and people.

Important and as far-reaching as public welfare is today, it is evident, from even this sketchy historical review, how essential a part social work under private and voluntary auspices has played in the over-all development of social work. Even though the bulk of financial assistance is now carried by the public welfare agencies, it was the private societies during the one hundred years before our social security program that developed the basis for the present individualized services in all welfare programs. It was the private individual, or incorporations of a number of individuals, that early provided institutional care for disadvantaged persons—children, the aged, the chronically ill, the mentally ill, the feeble-minded, the blind, the deaf, the juvenile offender—and then later experimented with noninstitutional services for many of these. It was the private agencies that developed the basis for much of what today passes for social action whether through private or public channels. It was the private agencies that developed the basis for current group work services, whether today as social settlements or community centers under public or private auspices. It was the private agencies whose labors furnished the groundwork for much of present-day community organization whether in the area of voluntary community chest financing or joint planning by private and public representatives through the medium of community planning councils.

With all their mistakes, inevitable in any pioneering, the private agencies have consistently and conscientiously pushed for standards that ultimately have been accepted into sound social work practice. Furthermore, the adoption through public financing of many of the services developed by the private agencies has enabled them to move into new areas of exploration. These words are added not by way of defense or justification of the private agencies—they will stand on their record—but by way of explanation of the complementary role of the private and public agencies. These words also undertake to give some measure of the as yet undefined tasks lying ahead and calling for the necessary experimentation preliminary to public adoption and tax support.

Bibliography

Abbott, Edith, *Some American Pioneers in Social Welfare*. Chicago: The University of Chicago Press, 1937.

Andrews, F. Emerson, *Attitudes towards Giving*. New York: Russell Sage Foundation, 1953.

———, *Philanthropic Foundations*. New York: Russell Sage Foundation, 1956.

———, *Philanthropic Giving*. New York: Russell Sage Foundation, 1950.

Bogen, Boris D., *Jewish Philanthropy*. New York: The Macmillan Company, 1917.

Boylan, Marguerite, *Social Welfare in the Catholic Church*. New York: Columbia University Press, 1941.

Brandt, Lillian, *Growth and Development of the AICP and COS*. New York: Community Service Society, 1942.

Bremner, Robert H., *American Philanthropy*. Chicago: The University of Chicago Press, 1960.

Bruno, Frank J., *Trends in Social Work, 1874–1956: A History Based on the Proceedings of the National Conference of Social Work*, 2d ed. New York: Columbia University Press, 1957.

Devine, Edward T., *The Principles of Relief*. New York: The Macmillan Company, 1904.

———, *When Social Work Was Young*. New York: The Macmillan Company, 1939.

Frisch, Ephraim, *An Historical Survey of Jewish Philanthropy*. New York: The Macmillan Company, 1924.

Glenn, John M. and Lillian Brandt, *Russell Sage Foundation, 1907–1946*, 2 vols. New York: Russell Sage Foundation, 1947.

Henderson, Charles R., *Introduction to the Study of the Dependent, Defective and Delinquent Classes*. Boston: D. C. Heath and Company, 1893.

Konopka, Gisela, *Eduard C. Lindeman and Social Work Philosophy*. Minneapolis: University of Minnesota Press, 1958.

Lowell, Josephine S., *Public Relief and Private Charity*. New York: G. P. Putnam's Sons, 1884.

Matthews, William H., *Adventures in Giving*. New York: Dodd, Mead & Company, Inc., 1939.

Miller, Haskell M., *Compassion and Community: An Appraisal of the Church's Changing Role in Social Welfare*. New York: Association Press, 1961.

Niebuhr, Reinhold, *The Contribution of Religion to Social Work*. New York: Columbia University Press, 1932.

O'Grady, John, *Catholic Charities in the United States*. Washington, D.C.: National Conference of Catholic Charities, 1930.

Pumphrey, Ralph E., and Muriel W. Pumphrey, eds., *The Heritage of American Social Work*. New York: Columbia University Press, 1961.

Queen, Stuart Alfred, *Social Work in the Light of History*. Philadelphia: J. B. Lippincott Company, 1922.

Rich, Margaret E., *A Belief in People*. New York: Family Service Association of America, 1956.

Richmond, Mary E., *Friendly Visiting among the Poor, A Handbook for Charity Workers*. New York: The Macmillan Company, 1899.

———, *The Long View*. New York: Russell Sage Foundation, 1930.

———, *Social Diagnosis*. New York: Russell Sage Foundation, 1917.

Stein, Herman D., "Jewish Social Work in the United States, 1654–1954," *American Jewish Year Book*, LVII (1956), pp. 3–98.

Stewart, William Rhinelander, *The Philanthropic Work of Josephine Shaw Lowell*. New York: The Macmillan Company, 1911.

Warner, Amos G., *American Charities*. New York: Thomas Y. Crowell Company, 1894.

Watson, Frank D., *The Charity Organization Movement in the United States*. New York: The Macmillan Company, 1922.

Zimand, Savel, *Public Health and Welfare: The Citizen's Responsibility, Selected Papers of Homer Folks*. New York: The Macmillan Company, 1958.

5

SOCIAL
CASEWORK

The nature of social casework

As has already been indicated, while programs were developing to meet the needs of people on a nationwide basis, those who were engaged in their operation were continually reminded of the fact that the ultimate consumers of their services were individual human beings. It is unquestionably true that common problems are to be found among large numbers of people. In a population as large as ours, for example, there will always be a sizable number of children who are deprived of adequate parental care. It is also true that common solutions can be devised to solve these problems. All children can be given care in institutions or foster homes. But it is finally true that both the problems and the solutions have peculiar meaning for each of the individuals who encounters them. For some children, institutional care may represent the epitome of comfort, while for others it is pure agony. In a society that draws strength from a respect for, and the consequent contributions of, individuality it should not be surprising that a regard for the peculiar meaning that experience has for the individual has led to the development of the unique process that has come to be known as social casework.

All of us live in association with other people and in relation to such institutions as the family, the school, the church, and the job. Many of us, at one time or another, need to call upon the services of such professional practitioners as lawyers, doctors, and psychiatrists. These associations and relationships and services bring us many satisfactions, but they may also bring vexations. Social casework is a method by which one individual, representing a social agency, offers help to another in meeting some of the problems that arise out of the fact that the world in which we live is organized as it is. While not inimical to change and, indeed, placing a premium upon human growth and development, social casework is not primarily a method of manipulating society to serve people. Its goal is to help the individual whose needs and resources are in conflict with the vicissitudes and exigencies of life. The following pages present a general description of this method in operation, together with a consideration of some of the basic elements and current issues related to it.

Social Agencies

Social agencies, within which casework practice is to be found, exist in this country in great variety. They may be large organizations, employing several hundreds of workers, or they may be so small as to have but a single caseworker. They may serve a very restricted clientele, perhaps in relation to a single highly specialized service, or they may offer services related to a great variety of problems to all the citizens of a large community, a state, or the nation. They are to be found in large cities, where they may be organized in district units serving neighborhood areas, and in rural territories, where one small office may be expected to give service to a county or to several counties covering hundreds of square miles. They may be staffed entirely by trained members of the profession of social work, or by untrained people with perhaps a small admixture of those with professional education. Casework may be offered in agencies operating primarily to make such service available, as a family service agency, or in a social service division that is but a small part of a larger organization such as a hospital, a school system, or the mammoth Veterans' Administration. Because of all these differences it is not possible to present a picture of truly typical casework practice in a truly representative agency. Nevertheless, the description that follows contains characteristics that are quite generally found in such agencies.

The physical setting itself is likely to present a variety of faces, but the odds are very great that it will not be pretentious. The agency may be housed in an ordinary office building, in an old residence that has been converted into office space, or in an otherwise unused portion of a municipal building. It is only in recent years, little more than the past decade, that a few buildings have actually been designed and constructed for the specific use of social work agencies, and it will be interesting to see what impact such conscious design may have upon the practice itself. We have seen the consequences in the medical profession of a shift from medical practice in the home to medical practice in the hospital or other medical center. For the present, however, it is more likely that the physical setting of the social agency will be on the dingy side than that it will possess such comforts as air conditioning or comfortable and attractive furnishings. It is likely that magazines and toys, bright pictures, and perhaps even drapes or an aquarium will reveal an effort to make the setting somewhat more congenial for the human beings whose cares are the objects of its concern.

The atmosphere is likely to be coolly businesslike and calmly unhurried, but also warmly responsive to the client. Based on an unsurprised and uncondemning acceptance of the peculiarities and eccentricities of human behavior, it is permeated by a feeling of consideration and permissiveness. It reveals a depth of interest in the client that is quite different from idle or morbid curiosity, and it implies a guarantee against prying into matters that the client is not presently willing to share. Also implicit is an assumption that the problem that brings him, while it might seem shameful or frivolous to others, is of importance to the client and therefore of importance to the agency. Somehow the impression will be given that the primary interest of the agency is in helping its clients rather than in judging them. This atmosphere of concern and respect for the client, which also carries with it something of expectation of him, is a product of the behavior of all the staff members with whom the client is likely to have contact. In a sound agency, even clerical workers are expected to make their contribution to the maintenance of an atmosphere of this character.

The Application

The casework process begins, in the great majority of cases, when a client makes application to an agency for service in connection with a problem that troubles him. A good bit of significance attaches to this matter of the initiation of the contact, for there is one thing of which caseworkers are quite certain and that is that their efforts can only be successful when they are directed in general conformity with the interests and purposes of their clients and that they are foredoomed to failure when they move in a direction that is in essential contradiction to the client's will. If this suggests that casework is not a method for coercing or beguiling people into doing "what is right," the inference is correctly drawn. It would not be correct to assume further, however, that the caseworker would support his client in antisocial or illegal activities simply because the client's will ran in that direction.

Because casework can be successful only when the client himself is somehow engaged in grappling with his own problems, it is now quite general practice for agencies to wait for the client to make some move toward them in the way of requesting the service they may have to offer. This represents a kind of testing of the strength of the client's interest in achieving the sort of change that effective use of the casework process is likely to entail. Exceptions are to be found when the agency is a probation or parole department, a mental or correctional institution, or one to which are brought complaints about the care that is being given to children. In these instances it is likely to be the caseworker who will make the initial step toward the client. Research in recent years has demonstrated the existence of "multiproblem families" that account for a substantial amount of social disorganization in our communities. As the means of identifying such families have been in process of refinement, some few agencies have experimented with an *aggressive* or *reaching out* type of casework, which seems to hold some promise of usefulness. Special problems appear in such agencies but these problems can be met in ways that do not disturb the essential validity of the principle that the client must be actively engaged in the casework process. Casework is not something that is done to the client; it is a joint undertaking in which he can and must actively engage.

When the applicant first presents himself he may find that he cannot be immediately seen. Inadequacies in staffing in some agencies result in waiting lists, and the applicant may find that he must wait from a few days to perhaps a number of months. He can expect some explanation for the delay and, sooner or later, an appointment for a specific hour. Ultimately he will find himself face to face with the intake worker, who will help him as he completes his application. In the best of circumstances, this interview will be held in a private office. Less desirably, it may be in a kind of interviewing booth, which provides some, but by no means complete, privacy. In special situations the interview may even be held in the client's home.

In the course of the application interview, which is likely to last for approximately an hour, the caseworker will help the applicant to express the problem as it appears to him and also to give information about the situation that forms the background for his problem. In doing this, the caseworker may make use of an application form from the beginning or he may introduce it in the course of the interview. In any event, he will make a record of pertinent information about the problem and about the surrounding situation. The applicant may be asked to sign the form.

The application worker soon learns that applicants cannot always ask immediately for help with the problem that is their major concern. Qualities of shame and guilt may make it impossible for them to reveal at once that which is really disturbing them. Applicants make their requests for help against a background of feeling, and the varieties of feelings seem almost as numerous as the number of applicants. Some, to be sure, may make their requests as casually as though they were ordering eggs from the corner grocer, but it is not really characteristic for the person seeking help with a serious problem to be in quite such complete control of his feelings. He is more likely to come obsequiously—meek, fearful, imploring—or demandingly—bitter, angry, accusing—or with some other combination of rather intense feeling. Even though these feelings are aimed directly at him, the intake worker knows from his training and experience that they are primarily an expression of the concern the applicant has for the trouble he, the client, faces. Drawing upon this understanding and the patience it makes possible, the worker attempts to help the client move, at a pace that will be possible for him, toward a formulation and recognition of the basic problem and a readiness to make use of the services that the agency can make available. This is not to suggest that application workers are people who calmly and impassively accept vituperation and abuse, but it may suggest the reason why many agencies assign to their reception service workers who are particularly well trained, experienced, and skillful.

At the same time the worker is securing from the applicant information about his problems and the attendant circumstances, he will also be offering information about the way in which the agency may be able to help. This will include some statement of the services that the agency offers, the circumstances under which these can be made available, and what effort the agency will expect the client to invest in making constructive use of those services. If the request has been for financial assistance, the applicant will be given some idea of the amount that may be available, the conditions of eligibility under which it is given, and the extent to which he well be expected to be responsible to the agency in the way of supplying necessary information. If the request has to do with assistance in regard to family or social relationships, it is very probable that he will be given to understand that this is not something that he can leave with the agency, like a broken watch, to be returned to him later fully repaired and in operating order. On the contrary, it will be explained to him that, while this is the sort of problem with which the agency can give help, such help can only be given on the basis of a joint undertaking between the agency and himself. An almost certain probability is that the agency would expect him to return, at scheduled intervals, for further consultation on this problem. Also, if the case involves marital difficulties, the agency may request or require that the marriage partner participate to at least some degree in the casework process. In any event, unless the problem is one which can be adequately dealt with in the initial interview, the caseworker and the applicant will arrive, at some point before its conclusion, at some mutually agreed upon understanding of what the next step will be. This may involve withdrawal of the request on the part of the applicant, consideration of the possibility of referral to a more appropriate agency, a visit on the part of an agency representative to the applicant's home or to some other person involved in the situation, or a plan for the applicant to have a series of interviews, probably with a different worker, for continuing exploration and treatment with regard to his problem.

Continuing Service

From this point onward the nature of the casework process can be expected to vary greatly in accordance with the nature of the problem and the particular agency to which the client has come for help. In many agencies a large portion of the balance of the contacts would be held in the home of the client. This would be particularly true in rural areas where problems of transportation are serious ones for the client. On the other hand, the trend in a great many agencies is toward office interviews at scheduled times. This practice is consistent with the principle, stated earlier, with regard to the expectation that the client come to the agency to make application. His willingness to come to the agency for further help is an indication of his continuing interest and concern in arriving at a solution. Home visits, on the other hand, may promote the feeling that it is the agency's need and urgency to arrive at a solution that is more important than the client's.

Many agencies in which the casework process is carried on through scheduled interviews of an agreed-upon length also limit the number of interviews. The agreement may be for a series of four weekly interviews of an hour each, with the understanding that at the end of the series a reassessment will be made by the worker and the client as to the progress that has been made and the prospect for further progress if the interviews are continued. The belief supporting this practice is that human beings grow in relation to the limitations they must overcome. Strength, it is held, can only be evidenced in situations in which one's strength is taxed. Continuing dependency upon the agency is not to be promoted. Many other agencies, however, do not operate on the basis of such planful use of time. Continuing interviews in such agencies may be held at quite irregular intervals, frequently depending upon the way in which the situation moves the worker or the client, and each interview may go on for as long or as short a period of time as the worker or the client see fit. Likewise, some agencies are disinclined to set a maximum period for which they will carry a given case and consequently may have cases open for quite indefinite periods of time.

Except in unusual circumstances, the same caseworker will be responsible for all of the agency's activities in regard to a particular client. The total of all cases assigned to him constitutes the worker's "caseload," and all interviews, all telephone calls, and all correspondence will be handled by him. Only in emergency situations, arising from such causes as illness or other unavoidable absences, would one worker undertake to substitute for another.

Case Records

It is characteristic of nearly all casework agencies that they keep a complete and detailed record of all their activities in relation to each case. Variations will be found in the form and extensiveness of this record from agency to agency, but maintaining some form of case record is one of the regular duties of nearly every caseworker. In many agencies the record begins with the application form or a "face sheet" which contains a summary statement of all the pertinent factual information about the client and his situation. It continues with a chronological narrative, which usually gives in detail the substance of what went on between client and worker in each interview. The record also contains all correspondence, reports of examinations, and any other pertinent material that may have come into the agency's possession. Since much of what passes between the client and the worker is of a highly personal nature, agencies commonly take precautions to protect the confidentiality of their records from idly prying eyes. They may be kept in locked files, sometimes located in a special "file room," which can be securely locked when the agency is not open for business. The records are available only to responsible members of the staff, and even clerical and maintenance workers may be given instruction on the need to protect the agency's records, in keeping with the social work principle of confidentiality.

These case records serve many useful purposes. When, in an emergency, one worker must take over for another, or when a worker leaves the staff and is replaced by another, the record provides an account of the course of treatment that has been pursued and frequently suggests the plan for future treatment. The case record is also of value to the worker as he attempts to increase his knowledge and skill in the practice of casework. As he reads the account of the interviews and studies the ways in which the client has responded to the things that have been said, he gains new insights into the workings of the client's personality and new ideas as to ways in which to be helpful. Indeed, caseworkers often find this sort of heightened awareness occurring at the very time they are organizing their thoughts and recollections in connection with the process of recording. The case record can also serve as a tool for professional education when the worker presents a problem case to his supervisor, to a case consultant or consulting psychiatrist, or to a staff meeting. It similarly serves an educational purpose when used as a basis for learning in a professional school of social work. Records can be a source of useful statistical information about an agency's operation and a source of basic data for research projects designed to increase knowledge and improve efficiency. They are frequently encountered in professional literature as illustrations of theoretical and technical points.

While recording is of demonstrable value, it is also an expensive and time-consuming procedure. Consequently, a good bit of experimentation has been undertaken in the way of substituting summarized recording for detailed recording of the complete casework process, limiting the so-called "process recording" to a few selected cases that seem to have special problems or special educational values, using forms and check lists in place of the narrative record, and utilizing such mechanical devices as disc and tape recorders. It is interesting to note that agencies and practitioners have hesitated to use mechanical devices without the knowledge and approval of their clients, although they have seldom had similar misgivings about the more usual forms of recording.

The End of the Process

As has already been suggested, the method of ending the casework process is likely to vary considerably from agency to agency and from worker to worker. In some instances the ending may be quite clear-cut and perhaps even arbitrary. This would be true when a family is no longer eligible for public assistance, or when a child's adoption has become final, or when a homemaker can be removed from a family because the mother, who has been in a hospital, has returned and is prepared to resume her housewifely duties. In some instances the process may end arbitrarily because the agency has set a limit to the amount of time it is prepared to invest in a given case. In all such cases, however, it is likely that the client would be given to understand that he would be free to return for additional service should his circumstances change in such a way as to again make him eligible for help. In many instances, however, the ending of the process is less perceptible. It may be that the client will gradually reduce his visits to the agency, or the significance of the problems he brings may diminish so that there is in effect a gradual withdrawal from service. Such cases may sometimes be kept open for long periods of time with only sporadic and relatively insignificant contact with the agency. In the best casework practice, however, the ending is likely to be quite clear-cut, for the client will have indicated some readiness to resume a life that is independent of the help of the agency, the worker will have helped him assess his capacities for such a life, and they will together have arrived at a mutually acceptable decision that it is now appropriate for the client to attempt this.

No description of the casework process can typify an activity that is so complex and varied as this. The description that has been presented may, perhaps, serve as a basis for the somewhat more theoretical discussion that follows.

Basic elements of the casework process

Problems of Definition

It may well be that the term "social casework" is as inefficient a device for the communication of meaning as any word or phrase in the English language. In themselves the component parts do not represent any very clear meanings and taken together they do not suggest anything with which most people have had direct experience. The titles of such professions as medicine, teaching, and the law, while they conceal great professional mysteries, still carry to us quite reasonably clear impressions of the kinds of activities in which their practitioners engage. Most people have a fairly accurate picture of what is likely to happen to them when they call upon their doctor. There are probably few whose preconceptions about a visit to a social caseworker would be at all realistic.

Of course efforts have been made to provide a definition. Perhaps the best known is that put forward in 1922 by Mary Richmond: "Case work consists of those processes which develop personality through adjustments consciously effected individual by individual, between men and their social environment." More recently, Father Bowers has examined no less than thirty-four definitions of social casework formulated by many leaders in the field and produced, as a sort of distillation from his studies, a definition of his own: "Social casework is an art in which knowledge of the science of human relations and skill in relationship are used to mobilize capacities in the individual and resources in the community appropriate for better adjustment between the client and all or any part of his total environment."

Probably the most up-to-date definition is that of Werner Boehm, formulated in connection with his efforts on behalf of the Curriculum Study of the Council on Social Work Education. According to Dr. Boehm:

> Social casework is a method of social work which intervenes in the psychosocial aspects of a person's life to improve, restore, maintain, or enhance his social functioning by improving his role performance. Intervention occurs when the person, or members of his group or community, realize that his role performance is hampered or threatened. The intervention takes place through a professional relationship between the worker and the person, and also between the worker and other individuals whose interaction with the person affects his role performance. Since social functioning is the

product of interaction among intrapsychic, somatic, and social forces, social casework involves assessing the internal and social factors which impair or threaten the person's role performance and helping him to find and use the somatic, psychic and social resources at his disposal, to eliminate or reduce malfunction and to enhance functioning in social roles.

Since social casework is an evolving and expanding sort of activity, it should not be surprising that no definition has yet achieved acceptance as one that is final and authoritative. As indicated at several points in this book, there have been a number of occasions when social workers have seen and seized upon opportunities of extending their services to new groups of people through casework offered in new situations. A definition based upon the practice of the beginning of the century would be quite inadequate to describe the casework of today, and any definition that fits today's practice is likely to be equally inadequate for the casework of tomorrow. Another obstacle to adequate definition arises from the great variety of people who are covered by the title of caseworker, by the great variety of activities that they perform, and the great variety of agencies in which they are employed. The activities range all the way from the distribution of food, gifts, and toys at holiday seasons, through the administration of a variety of tangible services such as financial assistance or special care for children or the aged, to a kind of interpersonal counseling that is almost indistinguishable from the therapeutic practice of a psychiatrist or psychoanalyst.

With this vast range of differences, it must be obvious that any definition broad enough to encompass all of them would of necessity be so broad as to set almost no practical limits or boundaries to the process of social casework. Still, the process *is* recognizable; it is distinguishable in general, if not in every particular, from other kinds of similar activities; and it includes certain elements about which there is quite general agreement on the part of the profession of social work as a whole.

In the first place, there would be just about universal agreement that casework has to do with individual people who have problems with which they want and need and seek help and that the goal of casework activity is to be helpful and not hurtful to these clients. Other areas of agreement might include the fact that this help is sought and given within the framework of a social agency; that the process of helping is carried on between a particular professional helping person, the caseworker, and individual clients; and that the helpfulness arises partially from the resources of the agency, partially from the unrealized resources of the client, and partially from the resources of the caseworker—from his strength and knowledge and feeling and his ability to make these available for the use of his clients. It seems unlikely that there would be much dispute over the statement that services may be offered, through case-work, to the economically disadvantaged and also to those whose diffi-culties arise from the nature of their social relationships, whether these be the result of breakdowns such as the dependency of children resulting from death of parents, or of psychological conflict as is likely to be found in situations of marital discord. It would probably be further agreed that these categories are not mutually exclusive, that they are ordinarily found to overlap, but that one or another is likely to provide a primary focus of attention.

It is unfortunate but true that these elements cannot be combined to form the perfect definition of social casework. There is just enough doubt about each of them to give us pause before we can with confidence include it in a general statement.

A Goal of Helpfulness

Perhaps the greatest difficulty arises with regard to the proposition that the purpose of casework is to be helpful rather than hurtful. This is without doubt a simple and universally accepted idea. However, its very simplicity and ready acceptance constitute a problem, for it relates to matters that are really quite complex. Difficult questions need to be acknowledged. What is the nature of helpfulness, and what determines whether an act is helpful or harmful? Where does—or should—helpfulness begin and end? An examination of such questions will reveal, perhaps, that the proposition is not so much erroneous as it is inadequate.

The question as to what constitutes helpfulness may seem, at first glance and in most situations, to be a simple matter. Helpfulness would seem to consist of those acts and services that are responsive to the felt needs and stated requests of the client. Complications arise, however, when, as is often the case, the client is uncertain about the nature of his needs or is vague in the way he presents them. No worker who has ever faced the distraught wife who wonders whether or not to leave her hus-band, or the confused mother who wonders whether or not to place her baby for adoption, or the fearful patient who wonders whether or not to submit to the serious operation, will have illusions that this question is a simple one. Additional complications arise when the needs and requests of the client are at variance with the objectives of the agency which the worker must represent. For example, the worker in a parole department has as his purpose helping men released from prison make the sort of ad-justment to the world outside that will be acceptable to society. If a par-ticular parolee sees his need to be the procurement of a gun with which to commit new crimes, the caseworker can scarcely be expected to be helpful to him in this matter. In the same way, the worker in a public assistance agency must adhere to the standards of eligibility and the methods of determining the amount of assistance that have been developed by his agency even though these may be quite inconsistent with an individual client's assessment of his own need.

The implication in all of this is that while helpfulness may come from the outside—from the resources of the agency and its tangible goods and from the resources of the caseworker in the intangible attributes of his personality—it must also come from within the client and express itself in some reorganization of his own resources. There is a good bit of agreement that caseworkers cannot know what will be "the right answer" or what will constitute helpfulness for their clients. This is a judgment they can never properly make. The client alone can decide this, on the basis of his own needs and desires. The caseworker can only help the client to arrive at that answer which will be right for him. There is a good bit of agreement that even if they knew the right answer, caseworkers would not know how to incorporate that right answer into the lives of their clients and that they would not have a right to impose it upon them either by force or by guile.

The question that has to do with the extent and limits of helpfulness suggests the need for some means of determining when caseworkers have helped enough and when too much and when too little. This implies that the purpose is not helping alone, but helping toward some goal. There is a timeworn phrase that is subscribed to by many social workers as well as by many other professional and lay people—"helping people to help themselves." This suggests that the caseworker's helpfulness should begin when the client cannot help himself and should end when he can live independently of help. Unfortunately for simplicity, no human being can live independently. All of us are dependent upon others, to some degree, both for tangible things and for feeling responses; strangely and conversely, no human being can ever encounter a problem in life for which there is not an ultimate solution, which can be arrived at without help, in death. Somewhere within these broad extremes exists an area within which casework can operate.

With the reservations implicit in the foregoing considerations, perhaps the simple purpose, for casework, of being helpful rather than hurtful, can now be accepted with more reality and conviction. In any event, it should be more acceptable than would be its opposite—that the goal of the caseworker is to be hurtful rather than helpful.

The Role of the Client

The other generally accepted elements of the casework process do not present quite such formidable difficulties as does this matter of helpfulness. That a client stands at the center of the casework process seems obvious. There may be question whether the process exists for him or because of him, whether it represents society's effort to serve him or to control him, but there can be no doubt that his is a central role. This is a plain but not entirely simple fact. There is one major and one minor consideration, each of which needs to be weighed before this element can be comfortably accepted for purposes of definition or description. The major consideration has to do with the nature of the role the client plays in the casework process. It is one with regard to which there is a good bit of agreement in theory but perhaps a bit less consistency in practice.

It is only as the client has some recognition of a need to change and some readiness to engage in a process of change that significant change is likely to occur. Most of us have had the experience of being placed under pressure from someone else to acquire new knowledge or attain new skill. (The experiences of children with music lessons imposed by demanding parents may come to mind.) Under such conditions our efforts are seldom successful to any remarkable degree. The situation is different when our own concern to learn has become involved. It is true that many individuals present an apparent pliability of character that seems to respond easily to attempts to mold it, so much so that they sometimes seem to be asking others to assume virtually full responsibility for their choices and decisions; it is equally true that even the sturdiest characters do at times yield to external pressures. Still, caseworkers are quite generally convinced that there is little substance or stability, and therefore little virtue, in change that is induced from the outside, whether by the force of authority or the subtlety of persuasion. They are inclined to a belief that even the weakest individual has a capacity to bear, and indeed an inability to evade, responsibility for the consequences of his own choices. While recognizing that the demands of society represent different things to different people and while believing firmly that society's demands should not be exorbitant for any individual, still they believe that every individual must and can face these demands in his own person, that he can often do this more effectively, or less disastrously, with help from another person, and finally that it has been possible to develop a professional sort of helping that is cognizant of the interest both of the individual and of society. Casework in the administration of financial assistance and other tangible services, in counseling, and in authoritarian settings, despite technical variations, is quite consistent in its recognition of this fundamental idea.

The minor consideration with regard to the central role of the client in the casework process has to do with the fact that occasionally the caseworker will work with more than one person at a time. There is a persistently recurrent tendency to regard *the family unit* as the central client in some situations, and in such instances the worker may see both parties to a marriage, or a parent and child, or brothers and sisters, or some other combination of people, either in separate individual interviews or all together in a joint interview. In other circumstances, the worker may be seeing a small group of people who are unrelated but who share a common problem or a common interest. Examples might be a group of men about to be released from prison who meet together to consider how they might plan to meet the pressures they may expect to encounter in the world outside, or a group of prospective adoptive parents who meet together to consider what special implications there may be for them in taking into their homes babies who come under the aegis of a social agency. It must be conceded that in these cases the line of demarcation between casework and group work is blurred; still, the caseworker will always have a basic regard for the centrality and uniqueness of the individual.

The Role of the Agency

That a social agency provides the framework within which the casework process takes place is perhaps as obvious as the fact that a client plays a central role. But here, again, we must take into account a major consideration as to the nature of the agency's role and a minor consideration as to whether casework can ever take place outside such an institutional framework.

To deal with the minor consideration first, it must be recognized as a fact that nearly all of the activity carried on in the name of social casework does occur within an agency setting. The only bar to the automatic and unequivocal inclusion of agency as an essential element in the casework process is the fact that some few people who are trained in casework do maintain private practices quite apart from any agency structure. Without challenging the quality and effectiveness of what they do, an unanswered question stands as to whether the activities they carry on fall within the range of social casework or whether they represent a kind of helping activity that is sufficiently distinctive as to require a new and different title.

Although most caseworkers do carry on their work within the framework of a social agency, there is difference of opinion on their part as to the significance of this fact. Most would agree that the agency does establish the general area within which they will operate. It tells them the kinds of needs they will be expected to serve, the kinds of services they will be able to offer, and in at least a general manner the ways in which they will be expected to go about their duties. Similarly, the agency tells the community, and particularly prospective clients, something about the kinds of services they can expect to receive from it and from its workers.

However, agencies differ in the importance they attach to the matter of defining their services and establishing the rules or policies under which those services shall be given. Some agencies restrict their services to certain groups of people or to those whose problem arises from a certain type of situation. An example of the former would be a sectarian agency set up to offer services to the members of a particular religious group; examples of the latter would be agencies that offer only financial assistance, or services to men in conflict with the law, or services related to the adoption of children, or to unmarried mothers. Even within those agencies that have established a relatively restricted and clear-cut area of service, difficulties will be encountered, for there are some caseworkers who take the position that once a client has come to them for help in connection with the particular need their agency has been established to meet, they then become responsible for any other problems that may emerge as they continue to work with the client. In support of this position they would say that the casework skill with which they offer their specific service is based upon generic principles that can and must be applied in the offering of any help through the casework process. They would say, in further support of their position, that it is senselessly uneconomical, if not absurd, to ask or expect a client to go to a variety of agencies for help simply because he has more than one problem.

On the other hand there are a good many other workers in this same sort of rather highly specialized agency who would be inclined to maintain that the area of their responsibility is rather narrowly restricted to the specific service their agency has been established to offer or to the particular need it has been established to meet. They would readily agree that they have a responsibility to be sensitively alert to the presence of other problems, which may relate to the one that brings the client to their attention or which might be quite separate from it, and they would further agree that they have a responsibility not only to provide him with information about available resources for meeting such problems but also to help him in whatever ways they can to make effective use of such resources. They, too, would say that the skill with which they offer their particular service is based on sound generic principles that are applicable to casework activities in any area, but they would further say that it is not possible for them to develop the highest standard of performance in a specialized area such as, let us say, child adoption, and at the same time maintain adequate standards in such disparate areas as child guidance, probation, marital counseling, and the administration of financial assistance. They would also be inclined to say that it is no more senseless for a client to go to several agencies, or to several workers within the same agency if it is departmentalized, for help with a variety of problems than it is for him to go to his doctor when his head hurts but to his dentist when a tooth aches, or to go to one lawyer when he is a party to a civil suit but to a different one when he is involved in a criminal action. In general, workers of this persuasion feel that if the caseworker's service is of genuine value and meaning to the client, he will be entirely satisfied to go to some trouble to attain it; workers of the opposite persuasion are inclined to the view that it is part of the caseworker's responsibility to do everything reasonably possible to make the agency's services available in the most convenient and least demanding form.

In addition to the agencies that serve a rather restricted clientele or that operate in a highly specialized problem area, there are other agencies, sometimes called "multiple-function agencies," which offer service to quite large groups of people and which cover quite a variety of problem areas. In these agencies the same considerations with regard to specialization are to be found. Should one worker carry all the cases coming from a given geographical area or should he carry cases of a particular kind? Should the agency be organized on the basis of functional departments, or will this in effect make of it only a conglomerate of substantially independent agencies? Such questions become particularly acute in localities where there are few agencies and few workers who nevertheless must face the full variety of problems which human beings normally encounter.

This question of specialization is, of course, an important one not only for social work but for many other areas of modern life. An apparently increasing number of caseworkers are expressing the view that only through specialization can they hope that their capacities and skills, and consequently their professional effectiveness, will achieve their highest development. Many others, looking to the experience of other fields and particularly of medicine, are fearful that with specialization will come a decrease in that sensitivity to the individual client which has long been characteristic of social casework. Perhaps it may be urged that insensitivity need not be a concomitant of specialization and that it may occasionally be found among those who make no claim to specialized skill.

In addition to setting these broad limits, the agency also enunciates a basic philosophy and establishes certain more specific rules and regulations under which it, and its caseworkers, will carry on their operations. This philosophy and the attendant policies and procedures are, in most cases, a product of the combined thought of the governing board, the executive staff, and the operating personnel. Some agencies place considerable emphasis upon having this material reduced to the clearest possible writing in a manual or set of administrative bulletins, and they devote staff and committee meetings to the task of ensuring that the material is up to date with reference to the kinds of needs the workers are currently encountering. In other agencies, similar material may be stated in only the most general terms, with refinements and amendments promulgated and communicated only by word of mouth.

Although agencies vary in the extent to which they enjoy the whole-hearted support of the community, their laws or charters and policies and procedures do constitute a sort of contract by which the community gives its sanction to the agency's method of operation. While policies and procedures sometimes seem to restrict the caseworker's freedom of operation, for they set limits for him as well as for the clients, they also serve him as a source of strength when they make it unnecessary for him to exercise personal judgment at times and in situations in which this might be unsound. In public assistance agencies, for example, it is essential that all applicants and recipients be accorded equal treatment. Uniform rules of eligibility, including a standard budget, are one means by which the agency can attempt to attain this equality of treatment. Without such rules the worker would need to decide every aspect of each case on the basis of his personal judgment and the client would thus be subject to the predilections and prejudices of his particular worker. Of course, no matter how meticulously the rules may be drawn, there will be times when it will be necessary for the worker to exercise his judgment, for human individuality seldom fits neatly and comfortably into the categories that are devised for it. The hope remains that when such judgment is necessary it will be based upon professional discipline and not upon personal whim.

Despite the many variations in agency structure and the different ways in which this is used in different agencies, perhaps it is reasonable now to conclude that in a great majority of instances the agency is an essential and significant element of the casework process.

The Role of the Caseworker

Just as the client and the agency are obvious, but far from uncomplicated, elements of the casework process, so too is the presence of a caseworker obvious while the nature of his role is complex. Just as, in order to understand the meaning of the client and the agency, we must attempt to understand their individual peculiarities and differences, so too will we need to recognize that the caseworker also brings something of his own unique personality to the process. When we remember that the title of caseworker is accorded both to people who have received professional education in social work and to people who are quite without such education, we shall have little reason to be surprised to find that different caseworkers do different things in what seem to be similar circumstances. It may be a matter of some surprise to learn that differences of quite considerable magnitude, however, exist even within the group of professionally educated caseworkers. This fact will perhaps be a bit less disconcerting if we remember that even in the much older and more firmly established profession of medicine, with its more secure base of rigorous scientific knowledge, there nevertheless exist quite marked differences in the methods and procedures of individual practitioners. Medical diagnosis is by no means infallibly and precisely uniform, and different methods of treatment for what seem to be similar ailments are preferred by individual doctors. Beyond this, there is reason to believe that the physician's success in a given case is dependent not alone on the objective methods of treatment but also upon the quality of the relationship that exists between himself and his patient. This is without any doubt whatever a similarly important consideration in the casework process.

While it is not reasonable to expect that all caseworkers will fit into a neatly simple pattern, it may nevertheless be possible to find certain attributes that would be generally characteristic of caseworkers as a group or that would at least be the characteristics one would hope to find in that group. As has already been suggested, caseworkers are quite likely to be warmly interested in, concerned about, and respectful of other people. These attributes will find expression in a friendliness that is also characterized by restraint. In their professional relationships caseworkers will be under an unobtrusive but nonetheless real professional discipline. They may be inclined to talk too much or too little, but the chances are good that they will have a rather keen awareness of their natural projective and receptive tendencies, and that they will be inclined to exercise control over those tendencies in keeping with the needs and interests of their clients and associates. The chances are also good that they will be relatively, but certainly not completely, free from prejudice. There will be some tendency for them to be aware of the prejudices they do have and, again, some tendency for them to exercise a discipline in their responses which will, as best it may, counteract those prejudices. In general, however, caseworkers will be inclined to be interested and intrigued, rather than repelled by, difference. They are likely to understand that different values are attached to human behavior in different cultures, and when a client presents some vagary to them, they will likely regard it as an expression of difference in background. They will understand that the same words can mean different things to different people and that the same idea can be expressed in a variety of ways. Consequently, they will make a special effort to be sure they grasp the import, and not just the superficial meaning, of what their clients say to them. Similarly, they will make special efforts to ensure that what they say is expressed in a way that will be comprehensible to the particular client. While one of their goals is to help their clients adjust to and live comfortably within the demands of society, they will have little tendency to try to induce their clients to adopt the coloration of gray conformity. Finally, caseworkers are likely to combine humility and an awareness of human limitations with faith in the capacity of all people to be both creators as well as the creatures of their circumstances.

If all of this sounds as though caseworkers represent a paragon of all the virtues, nothing could be further from the truth. While they strive to achieve a knowledge and understanding of human behavior, drawing upon the findings of psychology and the social sciences, and while they attempt to increase their sensitivity and freedom from prejudice and ability to be useful, they never attain perfection in these efforts. For the very reason that caseworkers fall short of their ideals of performance, social work has provided a rather unique process in the form of professional supervision, which is designed to protect the interest of the agency in its clients and at the same time to help the caseworker improve and develop his own skill in serving the client.

In this process of supervision the supervisor and the worker regularly confer together and the supervisor regularly reads a portion of the records in the worker's caseload. To the conferences, usually held at weekly intervals, both worker and supervisor bring for discussion problems that have become apparent in the worker's performance, and the worker frequently arrives at new insights and new ideas as to possible ways of proceeding. A customary accompaniment to supervision is the preparation at regular intervals by worker and supervisor together of an evaluatory statement of the worker's performance in practice. Throughout the process of supervision a principle obtains that is similar to one which underlies casework practice: Growth can come, for the worker as well as the client, only from the capacity of the individual for change and from his interest in changing; help can be offered, but it is only as it is taken and used that it is meaningful.

This process of supervision has not been without its critics, who maintain that caseworkers should achieve a level of competence at which they do not need this sort of support. They feel the process prevents workers from reaching a desirable degree of professional independence and that they will always stand in inferior status to the relatively more independent practitioners of medicine and psychology. Agencies have experimented with various means of altering the pattern for their more experienced workers. In some, weekly conferences are replaced by consultative sessions held at less frequent intervals; others make use of group supervision, in which a small group of experienced workers meet together to study problems that they are commonly experiencing in their practice.

From all of this it may be seen that the caseworker is an essential but highly complicated element in the casework process.

In the case illustrations that accompany various chapters of this book it will be possible to see in operation the elements of the casework process: the goal of helpfulness, the individuality of the client, the structure of the agency, and the professional discipline of the caseworker.

Current issues in casework practice

Casework, Counseling, and Psychotherapy

Because casework is, as already noted, an evolving and expanding activity which has not reached the limits of its development, it is beset by many questions for which answers are today only imperfectly known. One of these has to do with the relationship between that form of casework which is concerned with the administration of concrete services and that which deals with the adjustment of interpersonal relationships. Related to this is the question of the relationship between both of these kinds of casework activity and the somewhat similar activities of the psychotherapist, be he psychiatrist, psychoanalyst, or clinical psychologist. There is a discernible tendency on the part of some caseworkers to limit the meaning of the word "casework" to the area of tangible services and to refer to work in interpersonal adjustment as counseling. However, the title customarily given to practitioners in both these areas remains that of caseworker, possibly because the title of counselor has already been claimed by practitioners in psychology, education, the ministry, and the law. Distinguishing between casework, and particularly the kind of activity that has just been referred to as counseling, and the various psychotherapies is a difficult matter. All of these disciplines draw heavily upon knowledge provided by modern behavioral science, and all of them operate very largely on the basis of the individualized relationship between the worker and the client (or the therapist and the patient). Distinguishing features are evident when the caseworker is concerned with tangible services or is utilizing the structural framework of the agency, since psychotherapists do not ordinarily concern themselves with considerations of this character. Some caseworkers, however, particularly those working in psychiatric settings such as mental hospitals and mental hygiene clinics, have some inclination to view their practice as being substantially the same as that of the therapist, and some psychiatrists assert the view that all casework is, in fact, a kind of psychotherapy. Despite the confusion suggested by this state of affairs, and the indubitable desirability of achieving more clarity on all these points, experience has demonstrated that representatives of the various helping professions can practice cooperatively, and the team approach that has been developed in some settings may hold promise of increasingly effective service.

Service on a Fee Basis

Early casework activities were almost exclusively associated with matters of financial need. Indeed it might not be too much to say that a point of departure for its developing philosophy was the now discarded view that financial need was a reflection of personal inadequacy. At our present stage of development it is recognized that financial needs can exist and can be met with relatively little additional preoccupation with the individual's life. Our programs of social insurance are designed on this premise. But it is similarly recognized that other kinds of problems—social, psychological, or medical, for example—can arise without regard for the individual's financial status. The affluent individual, like the affluent society, is not immune to problematical developments. Since it is a cultural fact in our society that social agencies are looked upon as resources only for the economically disadvantaged, social workers have been interested in trying to find ways of making their services available to those who have been more inclined to see themselves as contributors to such agencies than as beneficiaries. It is an interesting fact that in hospitals and clinics that have social service departments it is most likely to be the ward or nonpaying patients who receive these services, while private or fee-paying patients receive few such services, and social service in relation to the private practice of medicine or psychiatry is virtually nonexistent. In the belief that individuals should not be deprived of service either because of financial or cultural bars, caseworkers have initiated two developments designed to alter the situation. The older of these has been the development of services on a fee basis in existing social agencies, while the more recent has been the development of private practice, also on a fee basis. All of the consequences and implications of these developments are not yet clear, but it is apparent that at least some economically secure individuals are finding it possible to secure the benefits that can be provided by social caseworkers.

Casework in Authoritative Settings

Another issue not completely resolved at this time is the matter of the applicability of casework in such nonvoluntary settings as correctional institutions, courts, and parole departments. It is sometimes maintained that, because successful casework is dependent upon a voluntary association of the client with the casework agency and the caseworker, these agencies with their underlying authority do not provide an appropriate setting for casework practice. The fact of the matter is that, while the client can usually be compelled to make his physical appearance before the caseworker (and even this is not always possible, as in the case of the parolee who refuses to report to the parole office), there is no power on earth that can force him to bring to the process his own vital participation. For this reason, even in these agencies the caseworker offers service on the basis of understanding and respect for the client as a human being, and the client is free to accept or reject the service as he wishes. If he rejects the service, it is then his own responsibility to work out his own destiny on the basis of his own resources, and one of the factors he will need to consider is the authority and the power that the agency may have to impose restrictions upon him. This is an authority that is delegated by society and properly exercised by the agency. It is not inherent in the role of the caseworker, and neither is it a proper part of his role to attempt to exert a kind of extralegal sanction upon his client.

There are some who believe that the mere suggestion of this authority in the background destroys the opportunity for successful casework. Steadily increasing, however, is the number of caseworkers who have come to the conclusion that it is entirely possible to offer the casework relationship on such terms that it can be actively entered into by the client and not merely endured by him. The facts of law are frequently as hard for the criminal to bear as are the facts of medicine for the dangerously ill patient. In neither case can it be the responsibility of the caseworker to mitigate the hardship, but it is his responsibility to help the client come to some terms with those hard facts that will be right for him. In a surprising number of instances the terms that are reached are also right for society.

Research in Social Casework

One of the greatest needs in social casework today is for a strengthening of the scientific base upon which it rests. Caseworkers have seemed reluctant to engage in the sort of research that might bring progress in this direction. This is not to suggest that modern casework is based on nothing more rigorous than good will and fine intuition. An outstanding characteristic of casework through the years has been the critical self-examination to which its practitioners have exposed themselves. Evidence of this is to be found in their use of case records, the supervisory process, periodic evaluations of the quality of their work, and the growing literature of the field. Nevertheless, there is some reason to believe that caseworkers have been fearful lest the pursuit of knowledge become an end in itself which might deflect them from their primary goal, which remains steadfastly to render helpful service to fellow human beings. Slowly in recent years, there has been growing recognition of the fact that competent research may bring them new tools and new skills to make their services more helpful, and there is now increasing evidence of attempts to subject their practice to more carefully controlled examination.

A number of other obstacles have stood in the way of more thorough research. One has been the fear lest clients lose their identity as human beings when submitted to scientific analysis. Interestingly enough, this fear has not always been substantiated in experience. Another obstacle arose from the fact that in recent years the field was split by the emergence of two quite articulate, if not indeed vehement, schools of thought with regard to casework practice. This development, not unlike those in other fields such as medicine, psychology, and even architecture and anthropology, provided rich stimulation, but the proponents of the two schools seemed sometimes inclined to belabor their opponents more with assertions of their convictions than with evidence supporting their views. There was some tendency to examine practice more on the basis of its orthodoxy with regard to the tenets of one school or the other than on the basis of its effectiveness in terms of the results that could be demonstrably attributed to the efforts of the caseworker. At present, the field appears to be moving on to a new synthesis of theory and a new effort, in new ways, to validate the results of casework practice. This is not an easy task. Since other disciplines concerned with the helping process have been able to provide little reliable information on this subject, it is not to be expected that the field of casework will be able to make substantially greater contribution. It does seem significant that, increasingly, an effort is being made in this direction.

Conclusion

The elements of the casework process, while they may be stated with relative simplicity, are in reality matters of considerable complexity. Combined, they constitute a process designed to be helpful rather than hurtful, which is carried on within the structure of a social agency between a caseworker, who is concerned for the welfare of his clients but who is also ready to represent the will of the community as expressed in the agency's policies, and an individual client who has come to the agency for assistance in connection with a problem, which can be expressed in finite terms, that arises in the course of his efforts to achieve his own well-being in relation to his financial affairs, his feelings about himself, or his relationships with others. It is not a process designed to bring about broad social change but, when it is successful, it is likely to result in renewed strength for the client, which may make it possible for him to participate

more vigorously and more effectively in creative and meaningful life with
his fellow men.

―――――――

Bibliography

Aptekar, Herbert H., *Basic Concepts in Social Case Work*. Chapel Hill: Univer-
      sity of North Carolina Press, 1941.
―――, "Casework, Counseling, and Psychotherapy—Their Likeness and Differ-
      ence," *Jewish Social Service Quarterly*, XXVII (December 1950), pp.
      163–171.
―――, *The Dynamics of Casework and Counseling*. Boston: Houghton Mifflin
      Company, 1955.
―――, "Evolving Concepts in Casework and Counseling," *The Social Service
      Review*, XXVIII (March 1954), pp. 74–82.
Behrens, Marjorie L., and Nathan W. Ackerman, M.D., "The Home Visit as an
      Aid in Family Diagnosis and Therapy," *Social Casework*, XXXVII
      (January 1956), pp. 11–19.
Bernstein, Saul, "Self-Determination: King or Citizen in the Realm of Values?"
      Social Work, vol. 5 (January 1960), pp. 3–8.
Biestek, Felix P., S.J., *The Casework Relationship*. Chicago: Loyola University
      Press, 1957.
Boehm, Werner W., *The Social Casework Method in Social Work Education*.
      New York: Council on Social Work Education, 1959.
Bowers, Swithun, O. M. I. "The Nature and Definition of Social Casework,"
      Part I, *Journal of Social Casework*, XXX (October 1949), pp. 311–317;
      Part II, XXX (November 1949), pp. 369–375; Part III, XXX (Decem-
      ber 1949), pp. 412–417.
Faatz, Anita J., *The Nature of Choice in Casework Process*. Chapel Hill: Uni-
      versity of North Carolina Press, 1953.
Fizdale, Ruth, "The Challenge of the Middle Class—Casework off the Beaten
      Path," *Journal of Jewish Communal Service*, XXXVII (September 1960),
      pp. 103–111.
Garrett, Annette, *Interviewing—Its Principles and Method*. New York: Family
      Service Association of America, 1942.
Gomberg, M. Robert and Frances T. Levinson, *Diagnosis and Process in Family
      Counseling: Evolving Concepts through Practice*. New York: Family
      Service Association of America, 1951.
Goodman, Nathaniel, "Are There Differences between Fee and Non-Fee Cases?"
      Social Work, vol. 5 (October 1960), pp. 46–52.
Hamilton, Gordon, *Theory and Practice of Social Casework*, rev. ed. New York:
      Columbia University Press, 1951.
Kasius, Cora, ed., *Principles and Techniques in Social Casework, Selected Arti-
      cles 1940–1950*. New York: Family Service Association of America, 1950.
Mencher, Samuel, "Evaluating Productivity in Social Casework," *Social Work*,
      vol. 5 (April 1960), pp. 79–83.
Nicholds, Elizabeth, *A Primer of Social Casework*. New York: Columbia Uni-
      versity Press, 1960.

Perlman, Helen Harris, "Are We Creating Dependency?" *The Social Service Review*, XXXIV (September 1960), pp. 323–333.
———, *Social Casework: A Problem Solving Process*. Chicago: The University of Chicago Press, 1957.
Rawley, Callman, "A Sampling of Expert Opinion on Some Principles of Casework," *Social Casework*, XXXV (April 1954), pp. 154–161.
Reynolds, Bertha C., *Learning and Teaching in the Practice of Social Work*. New York: Holt, Rinehart and Winston, Inc., 1942.
Richmond, Mary E., *Social Diagnosis*. New York: Russell Sage Foundation, 1917.
———, *What Is Social Case Work?* New York: Russell Sage Foundation, 1922.
Robinson, Virginia P., *A Changing Psychology in Social Case Work*. Chapel Hill: University of North Carolina Press, 1930.
Shafer, Carl M., "The Family Agency and the Private Casework Practitioner," *Social Casework*, XL (December 1959), pp. 531–538.
Sherman, Sanford H., "Joint Interviews in Casework Practice," *Social Work*, vol. 4 (April 1959), pp. 20–28.
Taft, Jessie, ed., *The Relation of Function to Process in Social Case Work*. Philadelphia: Pennsylvania School of Social Work, 1937.
Towle, Charlotte, *Common Human Needs*. Washington, D.C.: Government Printing Office, 1945; New York: American Association of Social Workers, 1952.

6

SOCIAL SERVICES IN A FAMILY FOCUSED AGENCY

Early emphases

The early agencies ministering to the manifold needs of family members naturally reflected the prevailing thought currents of the times. Throughout the nineteenth century, and particularly in the last half, a preoccupation with the social conditions external to the individual bounded the scope and determined very largely the methods of working with individuals applying for help. Manipulation of situations and people was the accepted mode. If a family was in distress because the principal wage earner had lost his job, what was more natural than to expend efforts toward securing work for him? If children were not in school, the obvious thing to do was to get them into school and keep them there. If a husband and father deserted, there was always the force of the law to be invoked. If children were neglected or mistreated, it seemed a simple matter to remove them from their homes and place them in an institution. If they were delinquent, recourse could always be had to the court or, better perhaps, to some recreation center or settlement house, or even to the church. Everything had its "cause," and the "cause" so often lay in the environment. The ready answer was to change the environment or remove the individual from the environment. A part of this service consisted of a plan brought by the worker to which the applicant was expected to subscribe. It might or might not be the client's plan, but what was important was that it was a plan.

Several decades of environmental emphasis were followed by an era during which psychology and biology reigned supreme. Toward the

close of the first decade of the present century, Dr. H. H. Goddard, director of research at the Vineland Training School for the feeble-minded, introduced into America the work of two French schoolmen, Binet and
Simon. Under the stimulus of the many studies undertaken throughout
the country, it became more or less a part of the scientific folkways of the
day to apply mental tests to every individual who in any way became a
charge upon the community. Family caseworkers succumbed to this
mental-testing mania and emerged from it little wiser. Biologists, too, had
propounded their theories of the inheritance of defects, mental and physical, and for a while welfare workers found an easy explanation for all
destitution, whether of the Jukes, the Kallikaks, the Tribe of Ishmael, the
Pineys, or others in the community not so visibly affected.

Looking back upon those years of groping one can readily understand the stability that Mary Richmond's *Social Diagnosis* must have introduced in 1917. Here for the first time was a philosophy and a definite
technique of casework which afforded caseworkers, to use a technical expression, "a framework of reference." Investigation was for the purpose
of establishing facts of personality and the situation upon which a diagnosis was to be made. The end of diagnosis was treatment, which consisted of a plan that took into consideration the entire family, for to Miss
Richmond the family in its social setting was the basic social unit of our
society.

Influences from psychiatry

Nor were influences from psychiatry and the early efforts of psychoanalysis lacking. From an examination of the mental capacity and heredi-
tary structure of the individual, workers began to inquire into the
functioning of the emotional life. The shift from an economic and sociological determinism to a psychological determinism was evidenced by the
social worker's appreciation of the emotional factors as they affected the
development of the individual from the time of birth. For family workers
emotional elements took on new significance in the recognition of the basic
importance of the family and of family relationships in molding the life
of individuals, especially during the early formative years.

World War I and the years that followed brought new impressions
into the field of social work. Insight into the nature of war neuroses, the
deepening knowledge gained from the mental hygiene movement spear-
headed by the work of Clifford Beers, the unfolding of many of the earlier
theories from psychoanalysis, and the contributions from medical social
service departments of hospitals all served to give direction to a newer
emphasis in social casework.

This orientation was definitely around the personality of the individual in contrast to the emphasis upon environmental factors. The dynamic psychology that was energized by contributions from psychiatry and psychoanalysis—whether of Freud, Adler, Jung, or Rank—turned attention to the inner life of the client. What assumed significant importance were feelings, emotions, attitudes, as these reflected the repressions, the conflicts, and the struggles within the unconscious life of the individual. The influence of the detailed and searching case history persisted. Instead of the social history, however, bearing accounts of grandparents, parents, births, deaths, operations, schooling, work experience, delinquencies, etc., there developed the technique of permitting the client to reveal at length his feelings and attitudes toward these events—the case history carrying in full this recital. The worker helped the client to express his feelings, and to work with these as they were expressed. Much of the worker's effectiveness depended upon his capacity to introduce those elements into the relationship that enabled the client to assume responsibility for his feelings and for his way of life. Many of these feelings were expressions of conflicts deep within the client's personality which required help in bringing them to the surface, facing them, and then going on to alter their basis or to go on living with them more comfortably than before. It was realized very soon that no worker could take over the client's feelings or his way of life. What the worker did was to help the client—when in need and asking for help—to utilize his own resources in managing his life on a self-sustaining basis.

The Depression of the 1930s

The year 1929 is generally agreed upon as marking the inception of the Depression, yet for social workers, particularly family welfare and settlement workers, the anticipations of a collapse were discernible and already tangible a year or more before. The community as a whole, however, did not become actively aroused until 1931–1932. Until it did become aroused, the burden of relief fell most heavily upon the family welfare societies. Case loads which normally had been forty or fifty per month rose to sixty, then eighty, then 100. By this time private philanthropy had reached the end of its resources, and government aid was inescapable. Public agency case loads began at 100 and quickly climbed to 200, 250, and then to 300 and higher. What became now of all this specialized psychiatric knowledge and skill when fathers were unemployed, mothers overworked, youth despondent, and the whole family starving?

The immediate task was to meet material needs. Food, shelter and clothing had to be supplied. Efforts had to be made to help wage earners

find work, to keep children in school, to provide recreational and leisure-
time facilities to individuals dangerously near deterioration. In the public
relief office with its staggering caseloads workers soon found need for all
the skills developed during the preceding decade. People in need were of
all classes: many could hardly bring themselves to ask for public help;
some fought, in devious ways, against taking relief in any form; others had
no hesitation in demanding their "due." Each of these "cases" was an individual, each with his own needs requiring more than merely material
gratification. Caseworkers had to be sensitive to these individual needs
and to discriminate between those instances in which material assistance
was the chief factor and those others in which destitution accentuated existing difficulties and called for a specialized service beyond relief.

The family welfare societies naturally were not unaffected by the
events of these turbulent days. Workers literally were swamped with the
volume of cases. As the governmental agencies took over more and more
of the financial load, family societies were faced with definite decisions
about their own functions. Somewhat against their wills they were cata-
pulted into being out-and-out relief agencies in the early years of the
depression. Once, however, government had assumed the bulk of relief
cases, the family agency was enabled to consolidate its previous casework
gains with the experience of mass relief and was better prepared to work
out a surer philosophy of family casework than ever before.

The role of culture

Note must be made of one more development, which affected the
whole field of social work. Anthropologists, and particularly the social
anthropologists who had studied the life of contemporary primitive peoples, had been producing an enormous literature of the influence of custom, habit, and forms of social organization upon the behavior of human
beings. Sociologists who studied modern society were equally impressed
with the role of custom, habit and forms of social organization. Culture,
which consists of ways of doing things, ideas, attitudes, habits, behavior,
and the material objects attached to these, came to be regarded as the all
important aspect of human existence and a determinant of all human behavior. Social workers in turn were affected by the discussion of these
culture phenomena and incorporated much anthropological thinking into
their own philosophy and practice of casework. Particularly was this true
in the family field because the family was regarded as the most fundamental of social groupings and the one which affected the development of the
human personality more than any other. The insights that had been
gained into the structure and functioning of the personality were fused

with the knowledge derived from cultural anthropology. From this came a greater appreciation of the reciprocal interaction of the personality and the culture.

It is not without significance that one of the widely read books in this period (written by a psychiatrist) was called *Personality and the Culture Pattern*, a title that came from Ruth Benedict's *Patterns of Culture*. Caseworkers were constantly called upon to distinguish between difficulties that derived from the seemingly external cultural factors and those imbedded within the emotional make-up of the individual. Caseworkers needed to know and understand that even though man is born into a culture, grows to accept it, fills his status and plays his role within it, he nevertheless also becomes a dynamic agent within it, changing it to meet his own needs more satisfyingly. The skill of the worker very often consisted of an ability to select, out of the many difficulties with which a client was concerned, those for which the client was willing and able to assume some responsibility. This obviously was a shift in emphasis from that day when all problems were to be solved within the self and without relation to the reality factors in the social situations. A further complication lay in the fact that very often individuals were caught between conflicting cultures, of nationality groups, of age groups, and even of behavior norms. What was needed here was an outside person who could understand such conflicting situations and introduce a casework skill by working with the client on the problems of his own confusion and his capacity for mobilizing his own resources toward self-help.

Family social work today

Although public welfare services go back to Elizabethan days in Great Britain and to colonial days in America, it was not until the time of the Charity Organization Societies that the rudiments of a professionalized helping skill were developed. From those Charity Organization Societies have come the modern family service agencies, offering increasingly, an effective helping service to persons with a variety of difficulties affecting them as family members. The aim of these services is to preserve and strengthen family life. The focus is upon the family as a whole; the help is offered to family members for them to use in relation to their own difficulties as these difficulties affect their own lives and the lives of family members around them. A relatively recent statement from the national organization of family service agencies, the Family Service Association of America, makes clear that "the central purpose of the family service agency is to contribute to harmonious family interrelationships, to strengthen the positive values in family life, and to promote healthy

personality development and satisfactory social functioning of various
family members." This central purpose is consistent with, indeed follows
from, a basic conviction about the critical importance of family life:

> The quality of family relationships has profound effects, both positive
> and negative, on the emotional development and the social adjustment of
> all members of the family. Positive experiences within a family provide the
> foundation for satisfactory personality growth as the individual passes
> through the various phases of development from birth to maturity. The
> family, as the basic unit of society, has the major responsibility for child
> rearing and for preparing its members to fulfill their social roles at the pro-
> gressive stages of their development.[1]

What are the troubles that beset families and who are the persons
who ask for help? Again, it is the Family Service Association of America,
FSAA, drawing upon the experience of the workers in family service
agencies throughout the country, that offers the following instances as
reasonably representative:

> Marital discord, ranging from deep-rooted incompatibility to more
> transient and superficial conflicts
> Disturbed parent-child relationships, ranging from severe reactions in
> both parent and child, to the less complicated ones
> Fatherless families in which the mother seeks help with employment
> and child care services for the children
> Adolescents, both at home and separated from their families, who are
> having difficulties in their work and social adjustments or who may be pre-
> senting antisocial behavior
> Unmarried mothers who seek help with practical problems associated
> with illegitimate parenthood
> Individuals with physical incapacity who are having difficulty in carry-
> ing their normal responsibilities
> Adults who are separated from their families and are having difficulty in
> their social relations or in their work adjustment
> Aging persons who are encountering difficulties in their employment, in
> their living arrangements, or in their social adjustments
> Persons or families who seek help in money management, housing, or
> with problems of unemployment, work adjustment, and so forth [2]

These generalized categories could be itemized in a thousand or
ten thousand separate "cases," each unique, and yet all having a certain
common denominator. The common denominator is the reaching out be-

---

[1] *Scope and Methods of the Family Service Agency,* Report of the Committee
on Methods and Scope (New York: Family Service Association of America, 1953),
p. 3.

[2] "The Content of Family Social Work," *Social Casework,* XXXVII (July 1956),
p. 322.

yond the immediate family grouping for help. Not a family exists that does not have its troubles. Perhaps the great majority of families manage to handle their difficulties themselves. Others may reach out for help to relatives and friends. It is when help from those sources is not available or is not effective (and nearness to a person often militates against the effectiveness of help) that the approach may be made to something as impersonal as a social service agency. It may be that this very impersonalness, coupled with experience and skill as offered by a professional worker, is what renders the family service agency a useful resource.

Family service agencies are supported by voluntary contributions usually through local community chests. Since the funds are limited and since the public welfare department is responsible for meeting the inadequacies of basic maintenance, the family agency cannot, and should not try to, make any long-time indefinite financial commitments to applicants or clients. The public welfare department grants financial aid according to rules of eligibility that have been defined in the law or developed through administrative regulations consistent with the meaning and purpose of the law: old-age assistance, aid to the blind, aid to dependent children, aid to the permanently and totally disabled, and general assistance. Most family service agencies have a modicum of financial assistance available which is used as an emergency and short-term resource. It may be used to help the client to use the service of the agency, but in no wise should it be used as a bait or a trap. The problems that bring persons to family agencies and with which such agencies are qualified to help usually involve emotional and behavioral complications that go far beyond the matter of financial asistance. The role of the worker is to focus on the basic problem that brings the client and to deal with it as such rather than to tease or coerce the client by a proffer of financial assistance. When, however, funds are granted on an emergency and facilitating basis, the accountability for their constructive use is just as great, even though voluntarily contributed, as is true of the accountability of public funds according to law and administrative interpretation. In the responsible family agency funds used with the client are not an end in themselves, they are a means to a constructive end, designed to contribute toward the integrity—the wholeness—of the family group.

The foregoing reference requires a word further about the use of funds in a public welfare department. The worker in such an agency is offering, essentially, a family casework service. The same quality of casework service may be expected of the worker as in other caseworking agencies. It is not one bit less professional service because financial assistance is requested or granted. Nor is it a matter of granting assistance on a coin-slot basis and then assuming that casework service will follow. The entire service should be casework in essence. This point will be elaborated in the succeeding chapter, which discusses public assistance as casework.

In the search for a focus for family casework, there seems to be fairly general agreement upon the necessity of dealing with the problems which concern the family as a whole. In discussing this M. Robert Gomberg observes:

> It is accepted generally that the essential purpose of the family agency is to help preserve and enhance family life and coherence, wherever this represents a solution for the family and is within the facilities of the agency. It follows, then, that in carrying out the agency's purpose, the worker's perspective must necessarily embrace the relation of the client's application to the family as a whole, and the effect that the agency's service may have on it. True, the client must be individualized, but certainly he need not be isolated from his role as a family member.[3]

In addition to all of the skills discussed in the previous pages that apply in all casework settings, the family caseworker must be aware, eternally, of the roles of the respective members within the family group. In our culture the roles of father, mother, and children are fairly well defined and service to the family as a whole must be related to this. On this point Gomberg, with insight, remarks:

> No worker must be concerned as to whether meeting a particular request in the way it is presented, while serving a specific physical need of the family, may, on the other hand, only widen the breach in family unity. Neither the worker nor the agency can decide for the client what he is ready or willing or able to do in meeting his individual family problem. But the agency does have a responsibility for the role it assumes in the client's life in offering or withholding service. It has a responsibility for the way in which it offers services and the condition under which it offers them.[4]

In the chapters that follow it will be evident that the focus of the service differentiates the various areas of social casework practice. The boundaries cannot be defined clearly in all instances; in fact there may appear to be overlapping, but a recognition of the focus of the service makes possible a clarity that leads to increasingly useful service.[5]

---

[3] M. Robert Gomberg, "The Specific Nature of Family Case Work," in Jessie Taft, ed., *A Functional Approach to Family Case Work* (Philadelphia: University of Pennsylvania Press, 1944), p. 114.

[4] *Op. cit.*, pp. 117–118.

[5] As in every field of human endeavor, so in family casework, there are differences of approaches, points of view, emphases, procedures, and techniques. The earlier review of developments from the early Charity Organization movement, through the period heavily influenced by the diagnostic approach of Mary Richmond, then the varying emphases from psychiatry and psychoanalysis did not give, perhaps, enough sense of differences up to the depression period of the 1920s and 1930s. The differences were there, but it is not necessary here to be detained too long with their

In all likelihood the most fundamental conviction expressed in family casework is that of a belief in people. Hardly has this been stated an it becomes clear that this same belief in people underlies all social work, indeed all social work. Nor is it limited to social work; it is d in many other services. However, social work has been explicit its conviction and has embodied the substance of Francis McLean's terization of the Family Service Association of America when he n Margaret Rich's volume *A Belief in People* as follows: "A belief le, a belief in the complexity of each person no matter how simple seem outwardly, a belief that each human being is different from s and has a different contribution to make to this common living . . ."

How a family service agency works

The agencies in the United States that commit themselves to certain commonly agreed upon standards of casework services to families group themselves in the Family Service Association of America, which in 1962 had some 304, including premember, affiliates. These agencies are located almost without exception in cities, although their services are available to residents in adjacent areas, county-wide as well as across county lines. Although by far the greatest number of the agencies are what are known as private or voluntary family societies there are a few instances in which local public welfare departments, city or county, are members of the association.

Where the size of the community and funds permit it, a staff will consist of an executive secretary, a supervisor or supervisors, and a number of caseworkers. A laymen's board of men and women usually serves in an advisory capacity to the executive and acts in a liaison capacity between the agency and the community. In the larger cities much of the executive's time and skill is spent in working with the board, with the

exposition. What is important for our present purpose is to recognize the existence of two fairly well-defined points of view within the family casework field—or the larger casework field as well. Recent usage has placed the label *diagnostic* on one and *functional* on the other. Each has drawn upon different psychological orientations—the diagnostic largely from Freudian (Sigmund Freud) phychoanalysis, the functional from the Rankian (Otto Rank) therapy. Each stoutly defends its particular approach, emphasis, and technique as fundamentally sound and effective—that is, helpful to clients. A provocative, but hardly productive, effort to deal with these two conceptualizations is found in Cora Kasius, *A Comparison of Diagnostic and Functional Casework Concepts* (New York, Family Service Association of America, 1950). For a recent statement of the functional approach see Anita J. Faatz, *The Natur*: *of Choice in Casework Process* (Chapel Hill, University of North Carolina Press, 1953).

supervisory personnel, and with various agencies in the community. Where the size of the agency does not warrant such specialization the executive may often serve as a supervisor and in addition carry a caseload. Funds are usually allocated on an annual basis and may be derived from individual contribution, or the local chest or financial federation, or income from endowments that have been placed with the society.

The agency offers to provide a service to the entire community, and unless there are sectarian or racial restrictions, all classes of applicants are eligible. Individual members of the family group may apply of their own initiative, having known about the agency or having been told by a friend or a past or present client. Others may come by referral from another social agency, such as a children's aid society, a probation department, a medical social service department, or a public welfare office. In still other instances various groups in the community, such as the school, a church, or a service club, may suggest to a possible applicant the nature of the family society services.

In the course of the application interview the applicant has the opportunity to tell his story, the reason for coming, how he sees the difficulty that brings him to the agency, and where and how he wants the agency to help. Some of the worker's activity may consist of listening as well as in helping the applicant to express himself. From time to time the worker may enter a question or make a simple remark that will do much to bring out the real situation that troubles the person asking for help. The worker needs to know enough of the applicant's difficulty to be convinced that it is of such a nature that the family agency can help. The intake worker, or application secretary, realizes that most frequently the presenting symptom—what the applicant sees as the trouble—may not be the real difficulty, but the worker accepts the situation as the applicant brings it, simply because it concerns such apparent external factors as unemployment, dependency, desertion, legal action, etc. If the worker has helped the applicant to express his situation as he sees it and to ask for the services of the agency and if the worker feels the agency can be of assistance, the applicant becomes a client, and another worker or sometimes the same worker, called a caseworker, becomes active. Social work usage now calls the client's situation a case, the record of the client's relation to the agency a case history, and the worker who continues the service with the client a caseworker.

The caseworker begins by meeting the client's difficulties where the client places them. It may very well be that the distress which brings the client is that of unemployment, desertion, legal action or the hundred and one other situations that convince the client of the need for help; and if this proves to be true, it is in that area that the caseworker exercises his skill in endeavoring to help the client mobilize his own resources and also to make available those of the agency and the community.

Interviews may continue over a period of time depending upon the needs of the case. They may be held at regular intervals, say once a week or month, or irregularly according to the client's needs or the worker's understanding of the situation. The visits may be made by the client to the worker's office, or by the worker to the client's home. All of these details of client-worker-agency relationship are mutually agreed upon.

Service will continue until such time as the client feels he has received sufficient help not to need the worker any more, or until the worker raises the question about ending the visits. Occasionally visits will stop because the client cannot take help and sometimes because the worker cannot give help. In some instances the trouble may be so deep-seated as to require an intensive service beyond the bounds of a family agency. Frequently the worker will mention the possibility of getting further help in another agency or with a psychiatrist, provided the client is ready to use such help.

Family casework and agency settings

Family casework is practiced in family service agencies. That seems like a fairly obvious and complete statement. However, an analysis shows that it is neither obvious nor complete. The latest Directory of Member Agencies of the Family Service Association of America shows that, while every agency member provides family casework services and while the bulk of the agencies provide only that, nevertheless, a number of them also provide child placement and travelers aid services. The fact that a family service agency houses the travelers aid service or provides the travelers aid service through staff members may be a sign that it is more economical to accomplish all that within one agency setting, or that quite properly the travelers aid function is essentially a family casework function. For the time being a family member, as a lone person, may be in transit and in distress, but the service needed is generally related to his family situation. These remarks are not to be interpreted as intending that the family service agency is taking over the travelers aid function. Travelers aid agencies still carry the bulk of their services in the familiar settings of railroad stations, bus terminals, and even airport terminals in cities where there is considerable in and out traffic. In many smaller communities where the volume of traffic does not warrant a service at the terminals, it may be provided through existing agencies—such as family service. The important point here is that wherever it is offered, it demands essentially a family casework skill and service.

Another service, provided under different auspices but essentially a family casework service, is that offered by the Home Service offices of the American Red Cross. This service developed out of World War I and had been strengthened in the intervening years up to World War II. During and after World War II these services were accelerated, not only because of the size of our army but also because of the rush by which we sought to demobilize our armed forces. With Selective Service now apparently a permanent part of our national life, there is every indication that the services performed by Red Cross Home Service offices will continue as a characteristic part of the community's service linking the soldier away from home with his home and vice versa.

The Home Service program provides a casework service in personal and family problems to members of the armed forces and their dependents. It offers assistance in applying for government benefits. It renders temporary financial assistance to wives and children during the period pending the first receipt of family allowance or allotment and during periods when such payments are delayed or interrupted. It assists veterans and their dependents in the development and preparation of applications for veterans' benefits. It also makes appropriate referral to other community agencies for whose services the applicants may appear to be eligible. Throughout all of the foregoing there is emphasis upon the essential family casework care of Home Service.[6]

Family casework services are being offered under religious auspice —Catholic, Jewish, Protestant. In some instances these services may be set up within a family agency supported entirely by a denomination within a particular city or by the central or national administrative body of the organization. In other instances the family service may be set up by a number of churches or denominations within a given area, that is, Family Service of the Main Line Federation of Churches, Inc. In some communities, while there may not be a denominationally supported family service agency, there may be well-defined policies worked out between churches and the agency—particularly concerning referrals, etc. There are many signs of an increased awareness by both churches and social agencies of the relatedness of their services. Instead of, as formerly, a strict delineation between the two areas, there is increasingly a disposition to deal with the respective forms of interest and to appreciate their essential mutuality. As social workers become more comfortable and less defensive in dealing

---

[6] Home Service is one of the many services provided by the American Red Cross and is mentioned in this chapter because its focus is family social work. Other services are within the area of psychiatric social work, medical social work, hospital recreation work and will be considered in the appropriate chapters.

with the clergy, and as ministers receive more knowledge of social welfare during seminary training and later by service on social agency boards, a more workable relationship is established between the two helping professions.[7]

A number of the accredited member agencies of the Family Service Association of America are public welfare departments whose services are made possible through the appropriation of tax funds. The source of these funds may be local, state, or federal. The workers in these departments are offering, basically, a social casework service that is essentially family-oriented. True, there may be some instances in which a cash grant or a service may be provided to a lone person who has qualified for an old-age assistance grant. In other instances the cash grant and the service may be provided to a mother and her dependent children who are without, temporarily or permanently, a father. Nevertheless, the intent, by the use of tax funds for either a grant or service or both, is to serve the person or persons in relation to a family constellation. Indeed, so aware was the Congress of the desirability to be explicit on this point, after twenty years of a public assistance and child welfare program, that in 1956 it amended the Social Security Act to enjoin state and local efforts to help assistance recipients toward independent living, the achievement of self-care or self-support, and the strengthening of family life. This was followed, five years later, by the action of the Secretary of the Department of Health, Education, and Welfare in changing significantly the name of the Bureau of Public Assistance to the Bureau of Family Service. This does not convert a county public welfare department into a family service agency, but it does underscore the fundamental place of the family in our culture and the necessity to focus our thinking and our casework services upon all family members.

It must be clear from the foregoing pages how all pervasive the family is in our culture, and how anything that affects one member of it must affect all others. This certainly is borne out by experience, whether the family consists only of two young married people without children or

---

[7] This reference to family casework services under denominational auspices is not intended to imply that religious groups restrict themselves to this area, broad and basic as it is, only. Rather, ever since there have been Catholics, Jews, and Protestants in America, they have provided a wide range of social services not only to their own members but frequently to the entire community. In addition to family casework services there have been services to children in institutions and out of institutions, to older people, to persons in court or in prison. Religious organizations have been active in social group work as well as in community organization—and of course in social action. Many of social work's leaders, formerly and presently, have carried deep conviction about the spiritual aspects of social work and have insisted that many of the values that social work holds dear—the worth and dignity of the human being, the respect for human personality, the opportunity for self-development—are essentially spiritual values at the same time that they are fundamental to all helping. For particular references see bibliography at end of this chapter.

of these same two persons, years later, who have added children to themselves. It is not unlikely that, before their union took form, after they were
united, and during the years their numbers were being added, they encountered difficulties that obliged them to seek help. The family service,
over the years, has been one of the agencies that has held out to the community a specialized skill on the part of its workers designed to help
people with difficulties in marital adjustment.[8] The family service agency,
basing its philosophy of usefulness upon the wholeness of the family, has
offered husbands and wives an opportunity to discuss difficulties with a
person skilled in social casework. Not only may the discussion of attitudes,
ideas, and feelings be helpful to the marriage partners who are in conflict
but also the response of the partners to the participation of the worker
may make for movement toward unity rather than separation. However,
even though the abiding interest of the family agency is directed toward
the unity of the family, there are times when neither the disposition of the
partner (or partners) nor the skill of the worker can bring this about; no
more in this area than in any other can success be guaranteed. Family
agency workers must, and do, employ the essential knowledge and casework skills that are called for in the provision of those other services for
which clients come for help.[9]

The use of homemaker service has increased considerably within
recent years as family welfare and other agencies, including public welfare departments, have sought to preserve the integrity of the family and
the household. Begun in the early 1920s by some casework agencies in
Baltimore, Chicago, and Philadelphia, the program has moved from a
"visiting housekeeper" person to one who is especially recruited, trained,
and paid by the family agency and who works closely with a caseworker
on the agency staff. While much of the homemaker service throughout
the country is related to those families in which there are children, usually young children, nevertheless its use has spread to the provision of
care for the chronically ill, the handicapped, and the aging, the intention
being to make it possible for such persons to remain in their own homes
rather than to be placed in institutions or boarding homes during periods

---

[8] The family service agency does not have, nor ever did have, a monopoly in
this area. Ministers, physicians, psychiatrists, psychologists, and sociologists—to mention the principal persons—have offered a counseling service. Within recent years the
American Association of Marriage Counselors, organized in 1943, has sought to bring
together practitioners in this area and to work toward the development and improvement of standards, including professional training of practitioners.

[9] For an emphasis on casework and the family service agency role in marital
counseling see: Jeannette Hanford, "The Place of the Family Agency in Marital
Counseling," Social Casework XXXIV (June 1953), pp. 247–253; Eleanor A. Moore,
"Casework Skills in Marital Counseling," Social Casewor':, XXXIX (June 1953),
pp. 253–258; for a broad view of the diverse field of marriage counseling, see Emily H.
Mudd, The Practice of Marriage Counseling (New York: Association Press, 1951).

of illness, incapacity, or family stress. While family service agencies have pioneered in the development of the homemaker program, its usefulness has been recognized by other agencies such as public welfare departments, children's agencies, as well as health agencies, public and private. Indeed, it is significant to note that tax funds through the Social Security Act are now available to public agencies for homemaker services. As so frequently has happened, the private and voluntary agency has experimented, demonstrated, and proven the usefulness and workability of an idea, and then, as the service is made available to a larger segment of the population, there follows tax support for programs on a state-wide and nationwide basis. This development in nowise precludes the continuance of the service by the voluntary agency; rather it insures its availability and usefulness to larger numbers throughout the nation.

The inclusion of services to children and the joining of family and children's services within one agency has progressed further in late years. While family service agencies and child welfare agencies have existed separately over the past century, each undertaking to focus appropriately its service, there has been an underlying conviction about the essential unity of the family and its members. Not infrequently caseworkers in family agencies have served all members of the family while caseworkers in child welfare agencies have specialized in adoption and foster care placement, principally. More recently there has been some disposition, especially when mergers have been considered, to offer services within a single agency to all family members. This is reflected in the number of agencies whose titles include the words "family" and "children," or if only the word "family" is in the title there are nevertheless foster family placement or adoption services, or both, available. Indeed, of the 262 member agencies listed in the 1960 directory of the Family Service Asociation of America, 112 offered foster family placement and eighty-four offered adoption services.

The calling, in January 1961, of the first White House Conference on Aging by the President of the United States dramatized the increasing attention accorded to the fact of our aging population—distribution-wise, percentage-wise, and number-wise. For years these population changes had been reflected in the services made available to older persons by family welfare agencies. Recently, this increasing awareness of aging has found expression in the family agencies in a specialized section or division that concentrates on the characteristic needs and demands of older clients. The conviction has strengthened that these needs and demands are basically those to which workers with their family casework skills can respond helpfully. In recognition of this, a succeeding chapter will deal with many aspects of aging but will emphasize throughout the essential nature of the family casework service.

There has never been a time when the community has not been aware that certain of its families seem to have more than the usual amount of difficulties. Within the last decade this concern has come to be expressed, increasingly, in an insistence upon a reaching out to such families, and in response to this certain agencies, public as well as private, have developed concentrated programs to minister to them. These families, whether described as hard-core, hard-to-reach, or as multiproblem families, have been characterized by an excess of problems, a chronic inability to restore themselves to self-sufficient, socially approved living, a resistance to taking help, and a holding on to attitudes that continue to handicap both adults and children in their ordinary relationships to other individuals or to the community's agencies such as the school, the police, and the court. Sometimes the public welfare department will try to do an intensive job with these families, assigning highly skilled workers to a relatively small number of clients. In other instances, the private family agency may concentrate on a relatively restricted number of families or in those areas within the city where the index of social pathology may be quite high. The programs under way in St. Paul, Minnesota, Hagerstown, Maryland, San Matao County, California, New York City, and up-state New York, as well as in other parts of the country, will be watched with unusual interest as social agencies stress what are being termed family-centered projects or programs.[10]

Social welfare agencies have been alert to population changes, with respect not only to aging but also to the movement of the population out of the city—especially the larger cities. Earlier, many agency clients were in the lower income brackets and lived in lower cost sections of cities. Perceptively, however, agencies have seen a change in the economic status of some of their clients and an improvement in their housing location. The latest discernible movement has been out to suburbia, but despite a further improvement in family income and quality of housing the many problems of adjustment that people—because they are people—experience continue to be with them. Furthermore, many families that have not utilized family casework services find, when they have moved to suburbia, they can and do use such services—especially when agency policies and practices relate to problem rather than to income. In these suburban

---

[10] The pioneering effort of Community Research Associates, which produced *Community Planning for Human Services* (Columbia Press, 1952), has stimulated other projects that have been reported analytically in such monographs as *Patterns of Change in Problem Families* (Family Centered Project, St. Paul, 1959) and *Multi-Problem Families* (New York State Charities Aid Association, 1960). The most recent (1962) of these vitally important studies is that reported by Alice Voiland in *Family Casework Diagnosis*, which records some major findings about disordered family types—the perfectionistic, the inadequate, the egocentric, the unsocial—that will bear testing and retesting by family caseworkers everywhere.

areas agencies have developed to help people with their difficulties. Either the urban-located agency may establish a branch or a district office in suburbia, or, as is now not infrequently happening, the suburban area may choose to establish its own social agency—usually one that is family problem oriented.[11]

The payment for service on a fee basis has been adopted increasingly since its introduction by family agencies in 1943. Several years ago it was reported that 75 percent of member agencies of the Family Service Association of America utilized the fee principle, either with a fixed fee per interview or on a graduated ability-to-pay basis. While the sums are not a negligible item in agency budgets, the values inherent in the fee payment are what commend it to caseworkers. In some instances, fee may serve as a focal point around which the client expresses his resistance to the service and affords the client and the worker an opportunity to engage themselves in the casework process. Some clients may try to use fee as a means of avoiding real involvement in taking help. Others may use fee constructively throughout the experience and finally come to the ending phase with genuine appreciation for the reality of the fee payment in relation to the completion of casework help. The actual fact that no two clients use fee in the same way places upon the caseworker the necessity to be sure of his own conviction about fees and of his flexibility in meeting each client on an individualized basis.

Conclusion

Perhaps no more fitting conclusion for this chapter can be found than the words of Linton Swift, the General Director of the Family Welfare Association of America for the last twenty-one years of his life. Before his death in 1946 Mr. Swift had enunciated his philosophy in what he termed a creed for social workers. This creed stands not only for the principles of social casework but for all of social work under whatever auspices and in whatever agencies it is practiced. Mr. Swift saw these principles as an ideal toward which all social workers might well strive.

I respect the dignity of the individual human personality as the basis for all social relationships.

I have faith in the ultimate capacity of the common man to advance toward higher goals.

---

[11] Not only families living in suburbia but also other families in the middle and upper income groups have turned, increasingly, to outside service agencies for help with family and personal problems. For a fascinating study of a one-day cross section of applicants from coast to coast see "Patterns of Use in Family Service Agencies" by Dr. Dorothy Fahs Beck.

I shall base my relations with others on their qualities as individual human beings, without distinction as to race or creed or color or economic or social status.

I stand ready to sacrifice my own immediate interests when they conflict with the ultimate good of all.

I recognize that my greatest gift to another person may be an opportunity for him to develop and exercise his own capacities.

I shall not invade the personal affairs of another individual without his consent, except when in an emergency I must act to prevent injury to him or to others.

I believe that an individual's greatest pride, as well as his greatest contribution to society, may lie in the ways in which he is different from me and from others, rather than in the ways in which he conforms to the crowd. I shall therefore accept these differences and endeavor to build a useful relationship upon them.

I shall always base my opinion of another person on a genuine attempt to understand him—to understand not merely his words, but the man himself and his whole situation and what it means to him.

As a first essential to the understanding of others, I shall constantly seek a deeper understanding and control of myself and of my own attitudes and prejudices which may affect my relationships.[12]

Bibliography

Ackerman, Nathan W., *The Psychodynamics of Family Life*. New York: Basic Books, Inc., 1958.
———, Frances L. Beatman, and Sanford N. Sherman, eds., *Exploring the Base for Family Therapy*. New York: Family Service Association of America, 1961.
Aptekar, Herbert H., "Casework, Counseling, and Psychotherapy—Their Likeness and Difference," *Jewish Social Service Quarterly*, XXVII (December 1950), pp. 163–171.
———, *The Dynamics of Casework and Counseling*. Boston: Houghton Mifflin Company, 1955.
Brangwin, Lorna C., "Marriage Counseling—The Viewpoint of the Caseworker," *Social Casework*, XXXVI (April 1955), pp. 155–162.
Chakerian, Charles G., ed., *The Churches and Social Welfare*. Hartford: Hartford Seminary Foundation, 1955.
Faatz, Anita J., *The Nature of Choice in Casework Process*. Chapel Hill: University of North Carolina Press, 1953.
"Family Casework in the Interest of Children," entire issue of *Social Casework*, XXXIX (February-March 1958).
Gomberg, M. Robert, and Frances T. Levinson, *Diagnosis and Process in Family Counseling*. New York: Family Service Association of America, 1951.

---

[12] Linton B. Swift, *The Family*, XXVII (May 1946), pp. 117–118.

Hanford, Jeanette, "The Place of the Family Agency in Marital Counseling," *Social Casework*, XXXIV (June 1953), pp. 247–258.

Hoffstein, Saul, "Fee Payment in Social Work Counseling," *Social Casework*, XXXVI (July 1955), pp. 313–318.

Hollis, Florence, *Women in Marital Conflict: A Casework Study*. New York: Family Service Association of America, 1949.

Hush, Howard, *Eastwick, U. S. A.* New York: E. P. Dutton & Co., Inc., 1948.

Keith-Lucas, Alan, "The Nature of the Helping Process," *The Christian Scholar*, XLIII (Summer 1960), pp. 119–127.

———, "Some Notes on Theology and Social Work," *Social Casework*, XLI (February 1960), pp. 87–91.

Mudd, Emily H., *Marriage Counseling: A Casebook*. New York: Association Press, 1958.

Parad, Howard J., ed., *Ego Psychology and Dynamic Casework*. New York: Family Service Association of America, 1958.

Perlman, Helen Harris, *Social Casework: A Problem Solving Process*. Chicago: University of Chicago Press, 1957.

Posner, William, "The Family Agency's Responsibility to the Families of Aged Clients," *Social Casework*, XXXIX (November 1958), pp. 512–516.

Rich, Margaret, *A Belief in People*. New York: Family Service Association of America, 1956.

Richmond, Mary E., *The Long View*. New York: Russell Sage Foundation, 1930.

———, *Social Diagnosis*. New York: Russell Sage Foundation, 1917.

Robinson, Virginia P., *A Changing Psychology in Social Case Work*. Chapel Hill: University of North Carolina Press, 1930.

Scherz, Frances H., "What's Family-Centered Casework?" *Social Casework*, XXXIV (October 1953), pp. 343–349.

Smalley, Ruth E., "The Significance of the Family for the Development of Personality," *Social Service Review*, XXIV (March 1950), pp. 59–66.

Spencer, Sue W., "Religious and Spiritual Values in Social Casework Practice," *Social Casework*, XXXVIII (December 1957), pp. 519–526.

Taft, Jessie, *Family Casework and Counseling: A Functional Approach*. Philadelphia: University of Pennsylvania Press, 1948.

———, *A Functional Approach to Family Case Work*. Philadelphia: University of Pennsylvania Press, 1944.

Towle, Charlotte, *Common Human Needs*. Washington, D. C.: U. S. Government Printing Office, 1945; New York: American Association of Social Workers, 1952.

Voiland, Alice L., and Associates, *Family Casework Diagnosis*. New York: Columbia University Press, 1962.

THE CUTTER FAMILY

EDITH MITROCSAK, SUPERVISOR
Family Service of Northern Delaware
Wilmington, Delaware

Family Service of Northern Delaware is one of the many private family agencies throughout the United States and Canada, set up by communities "to contribute to harmonious family interrelationships, to strengthen the positive values in family life and to promote healthy personality development and satisfactory social functioning of various family members." [1] The history of this family agency, established 1884, corresponds with that of most older agencies, and as such, periodic reexamination of its services is an essential part of its responsibility if the agency is to continue an alive, useful program available for use by families with present day problems.

In its early days, Family Service championed the cause of the underprivileged. As the agency was released from the responsibility of meeting the concrete needs of the "economically deprived" cititzen, development of casework skills appropriate to the successful discharge of the stated agency purpose, as interpreted in terms of present day problems, became an area of concentration. This area has become familiarly known as family counseling. We live in a decade when families are beset by socioeconomic expectations and pressures that often confuse fundamental values. Thus Family Service has had to prepare for and meet the challenge of the increased numbers of people with problems who are seeking new meaning to family life.

The Cutter case, which follows, is an example of the current use being made by the families in this community who are seeking help with their perplexing interpersonal relationships.

Mrs. Cutter, aged 37, was referred to Family Service by her clergyman to whom she had turned for help with a marital problem. While this discord had existed in her marriage for many years, she now described it as untenable for her. The Reverend Stone telephoned the Family Service office and, after a brief discussion of the situation with the counselor, he agreed Mrs. Cutter should be encouraged to consider casework counseling. Mrs. Cutter telephoned the same day, and an appointment was arranged with the same family counselor for 5/21/59.

---

[1] *Scope and Methods of Family Service Agency* (New York: Family Service Association of America, 1953), p. 3.

The application interview had a twofold purpose. First, it provided an opportunity for the client "to tell her story," more specifically to define her problem; and secondly, an opportunity to decide whether she wanted to use the agency's counseling service as a means of finding a solution to the problem that was threatening her marriage. The "story" generally consisted of releasing to the counselor all the unhappiness she was feeling, the lack of satisfaction in the marriage, and her own ideas as to the solution to all this. The counselor listened sympathetically but also began to test out the client's motivation for help as well as the way in which she proposed to use the service. The excerpts that follow are parts taken from the first interview with Mrs. Cutter.

[5/21/59]   Mrs. Cutter was prompt for her appointment. She was an attractive woman, meticulously dressed in a smart black summer cotton with a large white collar. She was tastefully made-up, and her graying hair, which was beautifully arranged in a short cut, made her appear a youthful 37. Though she was trying to control herself, she could barely contain her anxiety and the pressure to "do something quickly." After acknowledging my introduction and the fact that I had talked briefly with her clergyman, she plunged into her story, which she described as beginning to "sound like a broken record" as she had told it so often. I expressed understanding of this and said how very true this often was, when trouble was of long duration. With a deep sigh she said it seemed as though it had been "forever." Mrs. Cutter began in an agitated, emotional voice to explain that the differences between her husband and herself existed almost from the very inception of their marriage fifteen years ago. Their courtship lasted two years, and, while she could not admit to "loving" her husband in the romantic sense, she was strongly attracted to him because of what she described as his "masculineness." In a pensive tone she spoke of how happy she had been in her job as a secretary and how she tried to delay the marriage date, but, when Mr. Cutter gave her an ultimatum, they were married late in 1943. Three children were born to them, all girls, currently age 13, 11, and 9. Though she described their oldest daughter Marian as "unplanned," she was "welcome." Judy and Barbara were born under more anxious circumstances, and Mrs. Cutter expressed great fear about becoming pregnant again, saying she would just as soon die as have another child. While she did not say too much about their sex relations, it was apparent that this had been a difficult area for her as she accepted this part of the marriage relationship primarily as a duty. Some of this was related to their struggle economically, as her husband was not considered "successful." After a number of unskilled jobs, Mr. Cutter purchased a one man sandwich-grocery shop in a depressed section of the city. This was their source of income—approximately $75–$80 a week. Mrs. Cutter spends a part of every day in the store—helping Mr. Cutter and almost all of Friday and Saturday. She saw this as necessary but was obviously resentful.

The main areas of difficulty seemed to Mrs. C. to be a lack of appreciation from her husband for all her efforts and his frequent verbal abuse in which he made fun of her in a sarcastic manner, all of which created considerable anxiety for her and had her in a continual state of turmoil. As Mrs. Cutter related this she was tearful and frustrated. With considerable crying, she pictured herself as the "sufferer" and said she was always the one to attempt to make up to him after a quarrel and then was often rebuffed by him. On the other hand, she described him as jealous and suspicious without cause and related an incident where he even objected to her dancing with her own brother. With rising feeling Mrs. Cutter told of his sarcastic manner in public, presenting him as crude and boorish, and felt he deliberately set out to do things he "knew embarrassed her."

Mrs. Cutter's misery and unhappiness was most genuine, and I gave recognition to her suffering. At that same time, when I considered with her what precipitated her coming for help at this time in light of the long history of incompatability, I learned that the one area they were together on was their love and concern for the children. A recent argument, which started over Mr. Cutter wearing "sneakers" to church in a "deliberate" attempt to embarrass her, reached such proportions that she became physically sick. Conversation between them ceased, and the atmosphere became so charged that Marian came to her mother in tears saying she was so unhappy at home. This apparently shocked Mrs. Cutter who felt that until this incident they had successfully shielded the children from their trouble. For the most part Mrs. Cutter saw her husband as the one at fault, but as I focused on what was happening she could accept some personal responsibility for the fact that the children were being affected by their conflict. While she could see that this was her motivation in seeking help, she indicated she had played around with thoughts of whether or not she could survive in this marriage. As I verbalized this to her she could admit to this but, having said it, she felt less ready to face separation. She made quite a point of being critical of women who left their husbands.

I expressed considerable understanding for the burden she was carrying and was glad she had decided not to continue to do this, so all alone. She had tears in her eyes as she decided her relatives' sympathy hadn't helped much and she was ready to try "outside help." As the agency's way of helping was outlined (frequency of interviews, payment of fee based on income, and need to see her husband) Mrs. C. moved quickly on a decision to come in each week but then seemed blocked by the fact that she had not told her husband of coming here today. She was sure he wouldn't be interested; he would say this was "all foolishness," and besides she couldn't see herself telling him. I agreed this was a problem but wondered if she was going to feel very satisfied to return next week having said nothing about all of this. Mrs. C. looked pained as she thought this over and after a moment asked if I would call him. I assured her of my willingness to do this, but she would have to understand that I would need to tell him why I was calling. She finally decided she would try to mention being here, though she seemed very tentative as she left. I agreed to call him tomorrow, and the time of our next appointment would be held open.

The next day Mrs. C. telephoned, just as the office opened, to tell me how she "broke the news" to her husband. She was extremely nervous because he didn't respond to anything she said. I thought it was good she could tell him, and I would let her know if Mr. C. accepted an appointment.

The telephone call to Mr. C. brought a reserved response, but there was no doubt that Mr. C. wanted a chance to talk this over, and an appointment was arranged for that same afternoon "providing his wife relieved him at the store."

I telephoned Mrs. C. to tell her Mr. C. would be in to see me at 1:30 P.M. She was surprised and pleased but then began to apologize for what he would look like when he came in. She agreed to leave for the store immediately to relieve him.

[5/22/59]   Mr. C. was prompt for his appointment. He was a fairly tall, well-built man of 38 with ordinary features and dark hair. He was dressed in work slacks and a white sweat shirt that gave the appearance of being an undershirt. When I introduced myself he apologized for his appearance, saying he had come from the store. I said I realized he had not planned to come here today but I was very glad to see him.

Mr. C.'s attitude was controlled, cautious and reserved. At no time in the interview did he raise his voice, and I had the feeling he had decided he was not going to complain but rather he was going to present himself as an observer. I asked Mr. C. what he knew of his wife's talk with me yesterday. He shook his head. I continued, saying I understood their marriage had not been going well. I gathered that at present the situation was quite acute and I guessed that he wasn't too happy about the way things were. Mr. C.'s response to this was a slight shrug of the shoulders and a statement to the effect that his wife probably told me all about the trouble and he felt, if anything, she was a truthful person. I agreed that I knew something of the conflict but I only knew of it from his wife. He was a different person, therefore I was interested in the things he saw and how he felt about their difficulties. It was obvious that, beyond telling Mr. C. she was here, Mrs. C. shared none of the content of the interview with him. I referred to the unhappiness I felt in his wife and which I was also feeling very strongly in him. He acknowledged this but continued to be withdrawn. I commented generally on the agency's interest in families and said that I felt pretty sure he must have hoped for more out of this marriage than he was getting. He replied that it takes two to make a marriage, and I agreed to this wholeheartedly. He then responded by saying that he knew there were things he did that aggravated his wife but he was himself and that was that! When I said I was interested in what he was like, his voice was mixed with bitterness and sarcasm as he said, unfortunately, his wife wants him to be a "Charles Boyer," sweeping her in and out of doors, handing her compliments, etc. I said it obviously felt to him as though what *he was,* she didn't like. Mr. C. did not react to this except to say doggedly he was the way he was and that was that! If his financial condition was better and he could support two households he doubted that they would be together. I said I was sure there were moments when he wished for this and yet it was hard for me to believe that, even as bad as things were, he was ready to give up his wife and children. Mr. C.'s eyes filled suddenly and he looked down at his hands. I went on to say that in my experience, even when a marriage wasn't very good, husbands and wives found breaking it up pretty difficult. Mr. C. finally looked up and said that this was true and he guessed this was why he was here this afternoon. I said gently that this was probably why his wife came too.

From this point on Mr. C. began to talk about himself, telling me that life has always been a battle for survival for him and speaking of having come from a family of thirteen children where there was continual deprivation. His father was blind, and his mother eventually suffered a mental breakdown necessitating institutionalization. He contrasted this with his wife's background of being the only girl among four children. She was sheltered and cherished, so he guessed she expected a great deal from life. In response to my question, he said he had to admit she did not demand a great deal from him in material things. I said lightly that perhaps the things that do not cost money are harder for him to give. He flushed slightly and said this was true as she expected him to be somebody he couldn't be. He acknowledged that this is an area that causes them to argue and asked if I thought there could be any help for them. I discussed what I thought counseling could offer, provided they were concerned about the problem and were willing to work on it. Mr. C. looked thoughtful and then said carefully that he wanted me to know he felt better about being here now and he wanted to give this a try. I suggested we use an exploratory period of five weeks, which this agency often found helpful, and Mr. C. grasped this quickly. I had suggested an interview between the three of us, but Mr. C. objected on the grounds that someone had to be at the store. I did not press this. A fee of $1 an interview was set based on income and size of family. We arranged our next appointment for 5/27, and I said I would see his wife before that date. As he left he said good-bye warmly.

I telephoned Mrs. C. who was obviously expecting me to relate the entire interview to her. I recognized how much she wanted to know but felt the important thing was Mr. C.'s willingness to use the agency's service. Didn't this make her feel more hopeful? I hoped she and Mr. C. could talk about the step they had taken and said that if they were able to share their interviews this would be good. Mrs. C. sounded almost shocked at this thought, saying she didn't even know how she should conduct herself over the week end as she was so tense and worried. I was sure she would find it an uncomfortable week end and maybe she would have to be prepared to "live through" the next few days and we could talk more about it on Tuesday 5/26 when we would see each other again. Quite surprisingly Mrs. C. accepted this.

Mr. and Mrs. C. had now taken the first step toward some resolvement of their conflicted relationship. In committing themselves to help from the agency they experienced some relief, but this also created a new kind of anxiety for them because what was ahead was unfamiliar. In testing out their motivation for help, there was an implied acceptance of the fact that each had something to do with the problem, but considerable ambivalence was displayed as they expressed their doubts about the value of such help (for example, "I don't think you can help my husband"; or "I am what I am").

The two interviews pointed up sharply the isolation each was feeling. Mrs. C. saw her husband's abuse of her as the reason for her unhappiness while Mr. C.'s feeling of dissatisfaction was aroused by what he saw as her refusal to accept him as he was. Each placed responsibility for the marital difficulty onto the other; thus they felt misunderstood by each other, and with communication cut off between them the feeling of isolation had grown and had become unbearable. When the third element entered the picture, a substitute line of communication was set up. The counselor's genuine interest in each of them and offer of help opened the way for them to begin to accept some responsibility for their own behavior and to consider the extent to which that behavior was contributing to the marital disturbance. This takes time and rarely occurs in a couple at the same time. However, this sets the direction and dictates some of the content for the next few interviews with Mr. and Mrs. Cutter.

[5/26/59] When Mrs. C. returned on 5/26/59 she was ambivalent and uncertain. She had to admit that the situation at home had been more relaxed than she had expected and that her husband seemed to be trying. While she gave me an example of a different kind of concern for her on Mr. C.'s part, she also had a great need to negate this by saying on Saturday night they had their usual kind of fight. I acknowledged her disappointment but said I was glad to hear an effort had been made. Mrs. C. thought for a second and almost seemed relaxed as she agreed to this, adding her feeling of surprise that her husband had come to the agency at all, and guessed this was more hopeful. However, the remaining part of the interview contained examples of Mr. C.'s failure to give her warmth and consideration and how she continually needed "to swallow her pride." She was critical of her husband's poor taste in clothes and gifts, and the intensity with which she expressed all this gave me a sharper sense of what Mrs. C. does to arouse her husband's feeling of rejection. I commented on how much Mr. C.'s choice of clothing bothers her and recalled her need to apologize for Mr. C.'s appearance before he came to see me. Mrs. C. launched into a detailed description of the "loud clothes" he wore when he was courting her. I expressed surprise that this was something she knew about prior to their marriage and wondered then what it was that seemed *all right* about him to her. Mrs. C. spoke of her admiration for his ability to fix a leaky faucet and a lamp and his ability to find his way when they were driving to strange places, with no fuss, fuming, or trouble. She thought him generous and impulsive and warmed considerably when she told me of how touched she was when he sent her a corsage of twelve rosebuds on their twelfth wedding anniversary accompanied by a very sentimental message. While Mrs. C. accepted the fact that there was a warm generous side to Mr. C., she rigidly held to her need to have him measure up to a romantic ideal.

[5/27/59] On 5/27/59 Mr. C. arrived, showing obvious efforts to be more neatly attired. He seemed friendly and generally more free with me. He had some need to tell me about himself, repeating some of the deprived background information he had related in his first interview. However, in this interview he affirmed some of what was positive in his early home situation, as he said he thought each child meant something to his mother. He then moved to talk about his daughters for whom he had great affection and pride. It was obvious that he felt his wife was a good mother to them and he approved of her careful training. His eyes became moist when I referred to his love for his daughters and his recognition of the importance of a stable home. He admitted that the trouble he and his wife were having seemed to have become apparent to their oldest daughter and said how disturbing this was to him. We then talked about the incident which led up to the most recent crisis. Mr. C. seemed embarrassed by my reference to his wife's anger over his wearing "sneakers" to church. Mr. C. began to describe them in an attempt to deny that they were "sneaker-like." I expressed interest in his description and recognized that in a strict sense they weren't sneakers. I gathered however that it felt important to him to wear them in spite of their not being acceptable to his wife. Mr. C. sheepishly mumbled something about their being comfortable, which I said I could understand. Yet this incident, like others that were apparently similar, sparked a serious situation, and I was interested in why it did. Mr. C. became quite involved in discussing his feelings when I asked if this was what he meant when he told me last week that "he was the way he was." He admitted that it is his wife's disapproval of his general appearance which angered him and finally admitted he could have worn other shoes, but he didn't. I said then it was her disapproval of him that he found hard to take, so he had to pay her back. Mr. C. struggled with this a bit and then quite suddenly laughed as he said he had to admit it was "spite work." We then considered the end result and whether the temporary satisfaction gained was worth it. Mr. C. was thoughtful and said it certainly wasn't but he wasn't sure he would not do this again. We decided this was one of the questions we would be looking at together, whether or not he can handle himself differently in such situations. Mr. C. thought this sounded good— he wanted to do this.

In these two interviews Mr. and Mrs. C. revealed their reluctance to accept separation from each other as the solution to their problem. While Mrs. C. continued to criticize her husband she was able to acknowledge some of his more positive qualities. Mr. C. expressed appreciation for his wife as a good mother and, while he accepted responsibility for his part in creating tension in the home, he was not sure as yet that he wanted to change. Mrs. C. still believed that Mr. C. was to blame, which meant she had little or no responsibility for the problem. While Mr. and Mrs. C. were more deeply involved in the helping relationship, there was still a tentative quality regarding their full use of the service.

During the next three weeks I saw Mr. and Mrs. C. each three times in separate interviews. Mrs. C. recognized that her husband was trying to be more pleasant and control his criticism of her, but her frustration continued to grow as it became clearer that her expectations of him were still not being met. She explained her feelings about this and became frightened when she realized that her "romantic ideal" would not be possible. She was full of examples of situations where he failed to act in a manner that seemed appropriate to her idealized picture of him. As we recognized the tremendous burden she took onto herself being responsible for another person's behavior, she could admit to how heavy this was. In subsequent interviews some of this compulsive pattern was recognized as being present in other relationships. Eventually she could say that she felt her husband's behavior as a reflection on her and, with some guilt, she admitted being "ashamed" of him. When her own need to dictate and control the behavior of her husband was opened up as a problem, she seemed to find this almost unbearable and began to regress to her more depressed state, which had lifted shortly after the first interview. Some of this feeling became projected on the counselor whom she felt to be on her husband's side; the counselor was not helping Mr. C. to become what Mrs. C. wanted him to be!

She began to speak of her happy unmarried years and saw no disadvantages to being single. Many references pointed to her failure to find much pleasure in being a woman. Again she brought in her fear of becoming pregnant and the whole question as to whether the marriage was worth saving.

Mr. C. in the meantime used the interviews to examine the kind of defenses he had built up and which of these represented distortions that prevented him from realizing a healthier marriage adjustment. He could accept the fact that what felt to him like "being belittled" by his wife stirred up feelings of insecurity, which have always been the part of himself that he disliked. His way of retaliating was to tear her down, be more hostile, more sarcastic. While this gave him temporary release, the pattern was destructive and left him feeling more deprived than ever. While Mr. C. was held to his responsibility in perpetuating the struggle, he was at the same time experiencing a kind of acceptance of himself by the counselor that was new to him, and this support enabled him to make use of the agency's service.

Throughout this period, there was no verbal communication between Mr. and Mrs. C. regarding their interviews in the agency. It was as though each dropped out of existence for an hour each week, with neither one saying where he was going or where he had been. While the degree to which a husband and wife share interviews varies from couple to couple, Mr. and Mrs. C.'s failure to do so seemed extreme. The counselor felt strongly that, unless some initiative was taken in bringing about this communication, she would forever remain the substitute line and they would thereby lose the benefits of the mutual interraction that needed to take place between them. It was at this point in the process that Mr. and Mrs. C. were held to seeing the counselor together. Mrs. C. seemed to welcome this, but Mr. C. struggled to avoid a joint interview, using the "store" as his excuse. The reality of this and the fact that it would represent a sacrifice to him was recognized, but he was held to what the counselor knew was necessary if they wanted help with their marriage. Mr. C. accepted this as inevitable, and an appointment was arranged for 7/1/59. Mr. C. was asked to let his wife know the date and time of the appointment. Characteristically, Mr. C. was unable to share even this much with his wife, and two days before the appointment Mrs. C. anxiously telephoned to ask if an appointment had been arranged. She was advised of the time.

[7/1/59]   Mr. and Mrs. C. arrived at the office separately, with Mrs. C. being first. Both were quite uncomfortable, neither looking at the other. Mr. C. seemed like a little boy about to giggle and Mrs. C. as though the curtain were about to go up at the theatre. I commented on how much they had to put into being here today asking Mr. C. if he had to close the store. He admitted he did but in a genuine tone said he has done this on other occasions if it were important. I referred to this as being important and and briefly outlined my reasons for wanting to see both of them today, emphasizing the fact that individually they had expressed the feeling that they were discouraged and I wanted to hear it from them together. Mrs. C. immediately plunged into a series of complaints about her husband, some of which I had heard and some of which were new but reflected part of the same conflict. One of her annoyances was Mr. C.'s habit of wearing his pencil behind his ear, which he was doing today. Mr. C. sheepishly grabbed the pencil from his ear as she pointed this out to me and put it in his lap but he made no comment. Mrs. C. continued with much determination. At one point I asked Mr. C. if he had nothing to say, and he shrugged his shoulders saying he didn't think it would do much good. However he was unable to resist making a few complaints of his own, all of which reflected his feeling of being henpecked, and said that she only wanted him to do everything she felt to be proper, thereby reducing him to a "nothing." Mrs. C. looked surprised; previously she had complained to me that he wanted her to be a "slave." I made mention of this casually, purposely pointing up the similarity of feelings.

Mrs. C. recovered, but with a hurt tone she turned to Mr. C. asking him to explain to me why he embarrasses her so in public and referred to an incident on Sunday when they went to a picnic. She made a great point of the fact that she didn't like picnics but went to "please" him. She went on to describe his failure to wear an undergarment with his swimming trunks, which she saw as a deliberate attempt to upset and embarrass her. Mrs. C. was near tears as she related this painful incident, while Mr. C. was extremely uncomfortable as he sat with an awkward grin on his face. I agreed this incident might have been avoided but at the same time pointed out how out of proportion the feelings involved seem to be in relation to the incident itself. Mr. C. pulled himself together and said it did seem different to him now and maybe it was kind of childish. As though to take advantage of this admission, Mrs. C. related another incident which she used to point out her husband's failure as a parent. Their oldest daughter Marian was invited to the seashore for the week end by Mrs. C.'s mother who was renting an apartment for the summer. Free automobile transportation was available on Saturday morning, but Marian wanted to go on Friday night, which would have necessitated a bus fare. Mrs. C. felt this was wasteful. In an indignant voice, Mrs. C. related that when she asked Mr. C. whether Marian shouldn't wait until Saturday, his answer was "You make the decision, you will anyway." In a surprisingly angry voice, Mr. C. said that was the way he felt; after all, his wife didn't think it important enough to first ask his opinion as to whether Marian should go for the week end or not. Mrs. C. looked quite taken aback and turned to me asking if I thought that was so important. I said that I thought it was to Mr. C. and that this was the kind of thing parents can decide together; this is what communicating with each other means.

In the remainder of the interview, I helped Mr. and Mrs. C. to examine their use of themselves in each of these incidents. I felt that they almost knew how the other was going to react in a given situation because they knew what touched off certain feelings, and yet they went ahead almost deliberately to hurt each other. I knew unless they were willing to see something more than that the other partner was at fault in such incidents, I had little to offer. Mrs. C. spoke up saying she welcomed "constructive criticism" because she realized she wasn't perfect. I knew that any kind of criticism was hard to take, but if each of them wanted me to agree that the other was all to blame I questioned how much this was going to help their marriage. Mr. and Mrs. C. appeared to think this over, and finally Mr. C. said quietly that he would like to continue. At first Mrs. C. was uncertain but then decided she too would go on. As I would be leaving on vacation the first week in August, this gave us a natural time period to test out the kind of use they would make of counseling in the next four weeks. As Mr. and Mrs. C. left they seemed a bit closer to each other, and there was a sober quality about them.

This interview represented a real turning point in the helping process. Mr. and Mrs. C. were now facing each other with the third person whom they had chosen to help them. The numerous incidents related by both, which represented the old, familiar conflict, could not remain exactly the same because of the inclusion of the agency, which carried for them the hope for a good marriage. It was this new element that held them responsible for recognition that some modification of their behavior must take place if there was to be any change in their relationship. While it is true that self-awareness and recognition of problem does not necessarily bring about behavioral changes, they are a first step toward a reasonable resolvement of conflict. Mr. and Mrs. C. found themselves in familiar roles in this interview as the everyday "drama" was acted out. While they were able to rationalize their behavior to themselves, the counselor's question as to whether anything will change if she too accepts their neurotic defences and distortions presents a choice for Mr. and Mrs. C. They are reminded that the counselor is concerned for their unhappiness but that this does not include agreement with their projections that would tend only to encourage the conflict. They must decide whether they want to give the counselor the kind of place in their struggle that would eventuate in a true learning experience for them as a couple.

The interviews that follow show quite vividly the constructive use Mr. and Mrs. C. made of the joint interview and confirm the necessity for such a meeting.

[7/7/59] Mrs. C. was prompt for her appointment. She seemed uncomfortable as we started off, and I recognized how difficult our last meeting was. She agreed but also said that it had been helpful. I took responsibility for some of the discomfort I may have initiated and added that she could have felt I treated her rather roughly. Mrs. C. denied this, saying they were here to hear the truth. While I agreed that this was probably so, I also was sure she could have felt resentful toward me. Mrs. C. could not respond to this, and I moved on as she seemed uneasy.

As we talked of the past seven days, I felt a new freedom in Mrs. C. She quite positively said there had been a decided change this week. One of the things that pleased her was her husband's offer to manage the store without her the past three days. This had been one of the areas of contention between them, as Mrs. C. felt she could never depend on a full day to do her work at home. When I expressed my pleasure over this, she complained mildly as she explained that he had asked her if she would relieve him today for an hour. I wondered if she was questioning the sincerity of his offer. Mrs. C. recovered quickly and said she felt he had a good reason for asking and went into considerable detail about the particular errand. For the first time she expressed a real interest in the business. She then told me what a pleasure it had been to have all of Monday to do her laundry uninterrupted and other tasks that are important to her. I said I could see that, in spite of having today interrupted, she seemed to be feeling pretty good. Mrs. C. admitted she was. She wanted me to know she was encouraged and went on to give me some examples of how Mr. C. had made an effort to handle himself differently. She spoke of going on a picnic this last Sunday. Usually he makes some cutting remark about her need to have the kitchen cleared before they leave but this time he pitched in and helped her get the dishes done so that they went off in a happier frame of mind. I said this did sound as though Mr. C. was trying and I would think she would be pleased. Mrs. C. flushed as she looked at me and said she guessed she was trying too and this helped. I said quite gently that it did indeed help and I was glad she could say that. Almost as though this was too positive she added that she could tell me a number of things that didn't go right but she guessed things couldn't be perfect. I smiled and asked if she understood that there would never be a completely different Mr. C. any more than there would be a completely different Mrs. C. She looked very sober and nodded her head slowly.

I asked if they had talked over our joint interview. For a moment Mrs. C. seemed to become the counselor's helper as she said she knew I would be interested in this. On Saturday night, when the children were upstairs and things were quiet, she mentioned the interview and bravely asked her husband what he thought of it. Mr. C. shrugged his shoulders and said it was "all right" but seemed unable to pursue the subject any further. I recognized how very disappointed she must have been and how courageous it was of her to initiate the discussion. Mrs. C. admitted feeling some rejection and that it was a disappointment to her. I used this incident to point up what was becoming clearer—that Mr. C. was quite awkward in discussing feelings which touch him deeply. There was some beginning recognition on Mrs. C.'s part that this does not necessarily mean he sees this as not worth talking over but that his discomfort is related to his own personal problems. I expressed understanding of her wish for this to be different but said this may not be a part of Mr. C. that can change. Mrs. C. seemed quite thoughtful as we arranged our next appointment.

[7/8/59]   Mr. C. greeted me in a friendly way and as usual waited for me to start the interview. I had only to mention last week's interview, and he smiled broadly and said he was sure glad it was over. I asked if it still felt that painful to him. Mr. C. responded quickly, saying that I knew he hadn't looked forward to it but now he knew I was right because it was very worthwhile. He went on to describe how good he felt all week and he thought his wife did too. I affirmed the fact that she seemed more encouraged, but I was sorry they couldn't have shared more of this feeling together. Mr. C. quickly said it was his fault because his wife attempted to discuss it at a very inappropriate time. I was glad to know he felt this and I suspect that his wife would have liked to know it too. Mr. C. flushed a little as he told me how he "clams up" when something that matters so is brought up and how he wished he could have done better. I said this was part of his old difficulty and maybe he wouldn't be able to talk as freely as he would like.

He recalled his relationship with his parents, brothers, and sisters and said that talking things out was not their family pattern. For instance, his mother was in the State Hospital, and he rarely talked with his sisters and brothers about this. I recognized how difficult it was to break a lifetime pattern and yet I felt he wanted to do more than keep his feelings to himself. We talked about some of the incidents they brought up in the last interview and his feeling of being hurt and left out when his wife didn't consult him regarding Marian's trip to the seashore. Mr. C. felt I had understood this. While I stood by what I had said, I thought Mr. C. could take a look at whether he could handle his feelings better than he did. Mr. C. appeared puzzled, and I wondered if he could begin to express feeling appropriate to the actual situation rather than work it all up in his mind so that his only reply was a sarcastic blast at his wife, which was often far from what he originally felt. Mr. C. looked up responsively and said he surely recognized himself from my description.

We talked about his problem in verbalization at some length, and he said that maybe he could try to express a hurt or left-out feeling before it reached such a great proportion that only a battle could relieve it. I said this was exactly what I was talking about and maybe this could be a real start for him. I mentioned his wife's pleasure over having some "free days" from the store and I thought it was a fine gesture on his part for I knew he would have to work harder. Mr. C. was embarrassed but pleased as he said he felt this was worth trying.

As we arranged the appointment for next week, Mr. C. rather self-consciously pushed an envelope toward me saying he didn't want the bill to come as a big shock. The envelope contained a check paying for the interviews to date. I said I had just asked the bookkeeper to send out a bill and to ignore it. I felt very strongly that payment was a concrete way of saying he had been helped by me. I would see that the bookkeeper received the check. He looked pleased as he turned down a receipt, saying he would have the cancelled check. He left cheerfully saying he would see me next week.

There was no question that the joint interview had considerable impact upon Mr. and Mrs. C. and represented a meaningful experience that both of them were able to evaluate to some degree. More important was the fact that each had acted upon the questions posed by the counselor in this interview, and, as a result, considerable movement in relation to each other took place. At this point in the helping process the counselor was quite cognizant of Mr. and Mrs. C.'s complex personalities. Mr. C.'s deep feeling of insecurity and Mrs. C.'s difficulty in accepting herself as a wife were the results of early life experiences and relationships. It was recognized that neither Mr. nor Mrs. C. could go back in time to relive their lives in order to effect a basic personality change through casework counseling. However, their strong desire to strengthen the marriage relationship in order to maintain a home for their children provided sufficient motivation for them to want to change the *status quo*. For this reason, counseling was based, not on the premise that these two people could be reborn, but on their wish to live together with a reasonable degree of satisfaction. The counselor's goal was to help them accept themselves and each other. As this took place, they relinquished the idealized version of the other partner, thus making it possible for them to relate to each other in a more constructive and satisfying way.   ＇

It was quite clear in the above interviews that a change in the behavior of the one energized the other toward change. As they experienced satisfaction in their improved relations and expressed it tentatively to the counselor, the value of seeing man and wife concurrently was confirmed.

As counseling continued, Mr. and Mrs. C. sustained their good feeling for each other. Although subsequent interviews were not without incident, their new awareness of themselves and of each other made communication possible in a way that they had not believed could happen. Marian requested permission to use her earnings from baby-sitting jobs to take horseback riding lessons. Mr. and Mrs. C. discussed this, and a mutual decision was reached; this held great significance for both of them. Mrs. C. found increased pleasure at being able to have three days "at home" and spoke of her satisfaction in being "like other housewives." She was amused and surprised when she found herself looking forward to her husband's return home from the store. Mr. C. was "floating on a cloud" as he recognized his wife's efforts to do things for him without acting the martyr. At the same time, Mr. C. seriously discussed his need to reassure himself of his own value and wished this could be different. Mrs. C., too, expressed this wish but in time accepted that this may not be attainable through counseling help. They both hoped that they could develop, to a greater intent, their ability to discuss some of their deeper feelings. In this connection, psychiatric treatment as a source of help was touched upon, but neither Mr. nor Mrs. C. was ready to give this serious consideration. As the month drew to a close, Mr. and Mrs. C. continued to gain confidence in their ability to attain their goal, for they "saw a new value in their marriage." Prior to their last appointments the counselor suggested a follow-up interview in mid-September. The purpose of this was to evaluate Mr. and Mrs. C.'s ability to sustain the gains they had made. Mr. and Mrs. C. welcomed this suggestion. However, on 7/30/59 Mrs. C. telephoned to cancel her final interview with the counselor, as she and their youngest child Barbara were both feeling ill. In a worried tone, Mrs. C. disclosed the suspicion that she might be pregnant. The counselor expressed concern about this, as Mrs. C. had been so fearful of this possibility. While Mrs. C. admitted she was not "overjoyed," she felt better able to accept this than she would have been two months earlier and added, "If there are three, there might as well be four." Mrs. C. expressed disappointment about not being able to arrange another appointment but made reference to the follow-up interview in September. Mrs. C. added that "Harry and she were doing well" and expressed appreciation for the counselor's help in these words: "It has helped us to find a new respect for each other and to handle ourselves in a grown-up way." Mrs. C. wished the counselor a good vacation and said that her husband would be in for his appointment as planned.

In his final interview on 8/3/59 Mr. C. referred to his wife's possible pregnancy and felt that this would create a strain for them but, like Mrs. C., he was sure that if the baby arrived it would be welcomed by them as a family, a fact he would not have been sure of two months ago. He then expressed his appreciation for the counselor's help in his way as he said his "trust in the counselor had been justified." The date for the follow-up was left open.

On 10/13/59 the counselor sent a letter to Mr. and Mrs. C. asking them to call for an appointment. Mrs. C. telephoned on 10/20/59 and sounded friendly as she asked about the counselor's vacation. The follow-up interview was referred to, but it was apparent Mrs. C. saw no particular need to see the counselor at this time. Mrs. C. wanted the counselor to know that she and Harry were getting along well. Her pregnancy was confirmed and, while she was experiencing some discomfort, she was doing well "for her." She thought she would be in town some day soon and asked about "stopping at the agency." The counselor accepted this.

The Cutter case has been presented here to illustrate how casework counseling service was used by one couple whose emotional problems were many but who, through a helping relationship, found a more effective balance between their personal needs and those of the marriage. The service was brief, but the personal investment of Mr. and Mrs. C. was considerable. The question as to how lasting this help will be cannot be answered. The stresses and strains in family living are many, and it is not unlikely that Mr. and Mrs. C. may return to the agency when another crisis threatens. On the other hand, the help they gained through counseling was valid and if it continues to grow, the crisis may very well be one which they can manage on their own. While this case illustrates the limits in casework counseling, there is no attempt to place a limit on the extent to which the client can make use of the new found maturity to work toward future goals.

7

SERVICES
IN LOCAL
WELFARE
DEPARTMENTS

Contemporary public welfare

Previous chapters have traced the development of public welfare services from Elizabethan times, through our colonial days, and up through the Depression of the late 1920s and early 1930s. The impact of that Depression committed the federal government to the provision of some support for welfare services and obliged it to work out a system of federal-state and then federal-state-local relationships. Such developments produced marked changes affecting both the organization and the administration of public welfare services. Public welfare departments, where they existed in states, had to face some fundamental questions respecting both structure and function of agencies. Should these newer and "emergency" services be incorporated into existing agencies, or should a separate agency be established for "the duration" and then, hopefully, expire when the "emergency" was passed? Was public welfare to be a continuing function of government, or would the country ride out the Depression, prosperity return, and people again look after themselves and their families?

A fact of no mean importance was the size of the job to be done. Financial assistance to large numbers of needy individuals or families increasingly became a public agency function with public funds. By 1939, with federal work relief and public assistance programs in effect, the money payments reached into the billions of dollars. For example, according to the fourth annual report of the Social Security Board for the fiscal year July 1, 1938 to June 30, 1939 (p. 273), payments in excess of $3,750,-000,000 were made. A further substantiation of the size of the public job is to be found in the record of the number of recipients. In the month of June 1939, according to the same report (p. 280), there were more than 8 million recipients of public assistance, general relief, and work relief.

On June 30, 1943, the WPA program came to an end. War production had lessened employment. The public social services task was taking form consisting of (1) the traditional institutional services and general relief, (2) public assistance (aid to the aged, aid to the blind, and aid to dependent children, including other specialized children's services), and (3) social insurance (old-age and survivors insurance and unemployment insurance). These services were sizable whether measured by sums expended or individuals served.

A Department of Health, Education, and Welfare

Reference has already been made to the creation of the United States Public Health Service as far back as 1798. In the more than a century and a half since then there had been a slowly accumulating concern about certain aspects of health, education, and welfare, but it remained for the Depression of the 1930s to dramatize the necessity for a continuing implementation of government's responsibility in these areas. The Federal Security Agency was a step in that direction, but the creation of a department at Cabinet level signalized a firm and sustained commitment. In April 1953 the Department of Health, Education, and Welfare was created and placed in the President's Cabinet.

Like local and state units, the federal government operates some welfare services directly for those persons who are within its jurisdiction. For example, the District of Columbia Public Welfare Department, through funds provided by congressional appropriation, offers welfare services very much like those of any local county welfare department. Administrative relationships to the Social Security Administration, Department of Health, Education, and Welfare resemble those of a state department of public welfare to the federal organization.

There are other welfare services that are provided directly by the federal government, such as those to offenders of federal laws—in federal prisons or through federal probation and parole officers. The Veterans' Administration, through its social service departments of veterans' hospitals and regional offices, offers services. The Bureau of Indian Affairs in the Department of the Interior as an auxiliary function must offer welfare services to Indians who are under federal jurisdiction even though Indians

qualify for public assistance payments in the counties and states in which
they have residence.[1]

Aside from those welfare services under its immediate administrative jurisdiction, the contribution of the federal government is essentially
financial, advisory, and supervisory. Many of the acts of Congress provide
for grants to states upon certain conditions so that the task of the appropriate federal agency is to maintain relations to the state governments to see
that these conditions are fulfilled. The provisions of the Social Security Act,
the Barden-La Follette Act of 1943 (Vocational Rehabilitation), and the
Public Health Service Act of 1944 are cases in point. It will be recalled
that federally appropriated funds are available each year to states for
public assistance, child welfare, maternal and child health, and vocational
rehabilitation on condition that the state laws under which the services are
provided are consistent with the requirements of the federal statute. Relations are established and maintained between the Department of Health,
Education, and Welfare and the state welfare departments not only to see
that legal requirements are being met but, just as importantly, to render
help to the state agencies and to effect a useful interchange of experience
and knowledge.

The state and public welfare

The pre-1929 machinery for handling welfare problems of considerable magnitude proved to be inadequate. A number of states that had
provided some welfare services through commissions or bureaus in time,
through the encouragement of federal authorities as well as according to
the informed judgment of its own citizens, established departments of
public welfare. By now, and for some years past, each of the fifty states
functions through state welfare organizations. While the majority of these
are called departments of public welfare, there are various titles signifying
the same thing: social welfare, social security, public aid commission. In a
few instances a new department has been set up along side the earlier welfare department, the former concentrating upon public assistance and the

---

[1] While the old-age and survivors insurance program is essentially a retirement
program, nevertheless there is sufficient relation to welfare by reason of its survivor-
ship provisions to receive at least mention here. In not a few instances beneficiaries—
widows and children, and sometimes the retired worker even—are obliged to apply for
public assistance at the present time because their benefits are so low. For example,
in February 1961 there were 715,000 persons receiving concurrently old-age and
survivors benefits and old-age assistance grants. The services of the United States
Public Health Service should be mentioned also. At core, these are services in the
area of health; nevertheless, there are welfare aspects to be considered, as in mental
health and in certain research grants.

latter upon the traditional welfare services, mainly institutional. Not infrequently, however, these have been merged into one state department of public welfare. In no two states are all the welfare functions integrated into a single department. This is true not only because of lack of agreement as to what public welfare includes, but also because certain services may already have been allocated to other departments before the welfare department was established. Then, too, there is also the belief that many services that could be considered welfare in nature should be administered in units separate from the welfare department.

There are many examples of this tendency to scatter welfare functions. In some states probation and parole may be in the welfare department; in others it may be in a separate department of probation and parole. In some states crippled children's services may be in the health department; in others in the welfare department; and in still others in the education department. In some states, correctional institutions are under the direction of the department of corrections; in others they are directed by the department of state institutions; and in still others by the department of welfare. All of this points to the conclusion that while the range of services constituting welfare are found within most state governments, there is no consistent pattern of departmental allocation.

In the counties the welfare services are furnished directly to the applicant; that is, there is no additional person or organization that stands between the eligible applicant (assuming funds are available) and the public welfare worker. This is not so true with services furnished by the state organization, except in those rare instances of a state-executed assistance or relief program. Usually the state supervises the local administration of services such as public assistance or serves in an auxiliary and facilitating capacity to local administrative units.

The functions of state welfare departments are concisely stated by Marietta Stevenson.[2] She groups these as:

1. Administration or supervision of state institutions
2. Public assistance, child welfare, and other direct care
3. Development and supervision of local public agencies
4. Supervision of private institutions and agencies
5. Research and educational programs

No attempt is here made to amplify these points, a task already well executed by Miss Stevenson. It must be said, however, that current

---

[2] Marietta Stevenson, *Public Welfare Administration* (New York: The Macmillan Company, 1938), pp. 79–84; see also Arthur P. Miles, *An Introduction to Public Welfare* (Boston: D. C. Heath & Company, 1949), pp. 267–295, 363–382, and Wayne Vasey, *Government and Social Welfare* (New York: Holt, Rinehart and Winston, Inc., 1958), pp. 377–428.

public welfare practice operates with the state department in the pivotal position in relation to local units on the one hand, and to federal units on the other. This is the unmistakable and compelling development of the first two and one-half decades of the Social Security Act, offering further promise of mutually productive operation in all three areas.

The county and public welfare

Today most of the counties in the United States have a public welfare department. In some states, even though counties exist as political units, they are not necessarily the operating and administering unit for welfare purposes. Welfare services may be provided on a district or area basis, on a town or township basis, or directly out of the state welfare office. Despite these variations, however, it may be said safely that the bulk of welfare services provided locally is through county public welfare organization.

Many of these were begun during the FERA days and, subsequent to the passage of the Social Security Act, developed substantial programs. Some of these services, such as providing public assistance, are links in the local, state, federal chain. Others, such as foster home care or adoptions, are part of a local-state interrelationship. Still other services, such as general relief or aid to transients, may be entirely local.

The services performed by local welfare departments (counties, and cities within counties) vary considerably in different states and different areas. For example, the returns from a questionnaire sent out in 1937 to cities with populations over 100,000 revealed an amazing assortment of services. Marietta Stevenson, who reported this in 1938, classified them under the nine headings of: public assistance, social service and other special services for adults, child welfare services, licensing and regulatory functions, institutional responsibilities, work relief activities, public works responsibilities, health services, and other functions which included public recreation and administration of employment service. The actual count under these headings was fifty-five. Obviously, no one department provided all these services, but the assortment gives some idea of the spread and variety of services in local departments.[3] Twenty-five years later the substance of these services still holds; if anything, the list is now greater since additional programs—homemaker service and foster care for the aged, for example—have come under public auspices. The history of public welfare is a history of expansion of services as communities express their needs

---

[3] Stevenson, *op. cit.*, pp. 92–95; Vasey, *op. cit.*, pp. 137–251, 429–470.

and call upon their established governments for help in dealing with increasingly complex problems.

The Social Security Act—public assistance

Besides establishing a precedent for a system of old-age and survivors insurance and unemployment insurance, the Social Security Act of 1935 for the first time in history provided for financial aid to the states in a federal-state cooperative program of public assistance. Three groups were differentiated from others to receive these services: the aged, the blind, and dependent children. In 1950 a fourth category, aid to the permanently and totally disabled, was added. A decade later, in 1960, an additional provision was written into the law, making available federal assistance to the aged who do not receive old-age assistance but who are unable to pay medical bills (commonly referred to as the medically indigent). The same amendment also increased the rate of federal financial participation in old-age assistance medical payments in behalf of old-age assistance recipients. Heretofore the individuals composing these various groups had received what institutional or noninstitutional care was made available by the state or the local community, but it was not until the crisis of the late 1920s and early 1930s settled on this country that a newer concept of care came into being. The FERA, the CWA, the NYA, the CCC, the WPA had turned more and more attention to the federal government as an agency to meet problems beyond the province of any one community. At the same time the tradition of local responsibility, the undue (though necessary) emphasis upon federal control during the emergency period, and finally, the very honest conviction that certain values inhered in local participation all pointed toward a rejection of complete federal assumption. Yet the way was open to utilizing federal funds and leadership while still retaining a degree of local administration and financial contribution.

Grants to states for old-age assistance, medical assistance for the aged, aid to the blind, aid to dependent children,[4] and aid to the permanently and totally disabled are made subject to acceptable state plans submitted to the Social Security Administration. In every instance of an award by a state or county to a recipient, certain eligibility requirements must be met. Need is the eligibility factor common to the five programs. Depending upon the type of assistance applied for, certain other eligibility requirements must be met, such as age, blindness, and deprivation of

---

[4] The *Public Welfare Amendments of 1962* changed the term to "state plans for aid and services to needy families with children."

parental support or care because of the death, continued absence, unemployment or incapacity of a parent, or disablement (for persons over 18 years of age). With respect to the latest program, medical assistance for the aged, the person must be 65 years or over and medically indigent.

The state plan for these categories must each provide: (a) that it shall be in effect in all political subdivisions of the state, and if administered by them, be mandatory upon them; (b) for financial participation by the state; (c) for a single state agency either to administer the plan or to supervise the administration of the plan; (d) for granting an opportunity for a fair hearing before the state agency to any individual whose claim is denied or is not acted upon with reasonable promptness; (e) for proper and efficient administration, including the establishment and maintenance of personnel standards on a merit basis; (f) for regular and correct reports; (g) that the state agency shall, in determining need, take into consideration any other income and resources of individuals claiming assistance; (h) safeguards that restrict the use or disclosure of information concerning applicants and recipients to purposes directly connected with the administration of the public assistance programs; [5] (i) that all individuals wishing to make application for public assistance shall have an opportunity to do so, and that assistance shall be furnished with reasonable promptness to all eligible individuals.

Besides these requirements, which apply to all of the public assistance categories, there are other provisions—some mandatory, some permissive—applicable to each. The state plan for aid and services to needy families with children must provide for prompt notice to appropriate law enforcement officials of the furnishing of aid in respect to a child who has been deserted or abandoned by a parent. There is also provision that if the funds are not being spent for the well-being of the child, or children, other arrangements known as protective payments may be made—with appropriate safeguards. Along with this goes the requirement that efforts shall be continued to help the child's relative, usually the mother, to develop the capacity to manage adequately for herself and her child or children. Another provision permits a state plan to include assistance payments to those children who are in need because of the unemployment of their parent or parents. This was included in 1961 as a temporary measure but was extended for a five-year period from July 1, 1962. The state plan may also include in the grant a payment for both parents as well as for the chil-

---

[5] A modification of this was effected by an amendment in October 1951. Under Public Law 183, 82nd Congress, states were permitted to make available for public inspection records of the disbursement of public assistance funds or payments. To permit public inspection the state must enact a law specifically authorizing such public access to records of disbursements. Such a law must prescribe the conditions under which access may be had and, also, must establish and enforce safeguards to prevent the use of the information for political or commercial purposes.

dren. In determining the amount of the grant it is now possible to take into account the expenses attributable to the earning of the income, as well as to take note of the income that a child may earn, and which may be put aside for his future needs, such as education or preparation for employment. The state plan may now use payments under this program for children who have been placed in foster care by court order. This too was a temporary provision enacted in 1961 but was made permanent by the 1962 amendments. Another recent provision stemming from the 1962 legislation permits the federal government to share in payments made for a child placed in a private child care institution. This applies for a two-year period starting October 1, 1962. An additional provision of the 1962 legislation calls for individual planning for each child in relation to his particular needs and home conditions and the coordination of this program with the state's child welfare services plan toward providing the services that will best promote the welfare of the child and his family.

With respect to the state plan for aid to the blind there is provision, in determining need for an exemption of the first $85 per month of earned income plus one half of the next $85. In addition (effective July 1, 1963) for a period of one year limits on income and resources could be completely removed if the blind person has a plan for achieving self-support that is approved by the state agency. The state plan must permit an examination to determine blindness or degree of blindness by a physician skilled in diseases of the eye or by an optometrist (whichever the individual may select).

The state plan for old-age assistance permits the agency, in determining need, to disregard the first $10 of earned income plus one-half the remainder of the first $50. This provision, made possible under the 1962 amendments, becomes effective January, 1963.

With respect to residence the federal legislation makes specific reference to the state plans for the program of aid and services to needy families with children, and to old-age assistance. No state plan for aid and services to dependent children can be approved by the Secretary of Health, Education, and Welfare if it imposes a residence requirement that renders ineligible any child residing within the state who has resided within the state for one year immediately preceding the application, or that renders ineligible any child who was born within one year immediately preceding the application if the parent or other relative with whom the child is living has resided in the state for one year immediately preceding the birth. Likewise, no state plan for old-age assistance can be approved if it (a) imposes a higher age limit than 65 years, or (b) imposes a residence requirement that excludes a resident who lived in the state during five years of the preceding nine and who lived in the state for one year immediately preceding application, or (c) makes any citizenship requirement that excludes any citizen of the United States.

In those states whose plan includes medical assistance for the aged there must be the following requirements applicable to such assistance: (a) provide for some institutional and some noninstitutional care and services, (b) prohibit any enrollment fee, premium or similar charge as a condition of eligibility, (c) provide for furnishing assistance to residents of the state who are temporarily absent, (d) include reasonable standards for determining eligibility of individuals for medical assistance and the extent of such assistance, (e) provide that property liens will not be imposed during an individual's lifetime on account of benefits received, and limit the recovery to the estate of the individual after his death and the death of the surviving spouse. A plan may not impose a residence requirement that excludes any applicant for medical assistance for the aged who resides in the state. Persons 65 years or over who are not recipients of old-age assistance but whose income and resources are insufficient to meet the costs of necessary medical services are eligible for grants. The care and services available to them are: (a) inpatient hospital services, (b) skilled nursing-home services, (c) physician's services, (d) outpatient hospital or clinic services, (e) home health care services, (f) private duty nursing services, (g) physical therapy and related services, (h) dental services, (i) laboratory and X-ray services, (j) prescribed drugs, eyeglasses, dentures, and prosthetic devices, (k) diagnostic, screening, and preventive services.

Federal public assistance payments are not to be made to individuals in institutions, except when the needy individual is a patient in a public medical institution. A 1960 amendment makes it possible for federal financial participation in those state plans for old-age assistance and medical assistance for the aged that provide medical care in a public mental or tubercular hospital, this participation to be limited to a forty-two-day period. An earlier amendment provided that, after July 1, 1953, if a state makes payments to an individual in a public medical institution or in a private institution offering medical or domiciliary care, the state must designate the state authority that shall be responsible for establishing and maintaining standards for such institutions. Applicable to all five public assistance categories is the provision permitting federal participation in payments made by state public assistance agencies directly to medical practitioners and other suppliers of medical services and remedial care.

The foregoing requirements of the Social Security Act as amended are set up as a condition for receipt of federal grants to the states for public assistance purposes. There is a prohibition that underlies each of them to the effect that no person may receive payment from more than one of the assistance programs. Administrative costs are shared with each state by the federal government. The act as amended to date specified the extent to which the federal government will participate in payments to qualified persons, setting a limit with respect to each category. Within recent years the federal share in assistance payments has been well over 50 percent, with states and counties being responsible for the remainder. However, even though the federal share is specified, each state may pay its recipients as high as it chooses beyond the federal matching.

Because the federal matching is related to the payment that each state (including its counties) makes and because states differ in their wealth and capacity to make such payments there is considerable variation between them. This is reflected in the following analysis:

PUBLIC ASSISTANCE PAYMENTS, PER RECIPIENT, BY STATES
APRIL 1962

	High	Low	Average U.S.
Aid to the blind	$124.55	$37.82	$ 77.41
Aid to dependent children [a]	47.87	9.17	31.68
Aid to the disabled	131.41	34.49	71.39
General assistance	68.88	4.10	27.55
Medical assistance to the aged	416.95	22.62	229.66
Old-age assistance	111.83	35.06	72.24

Source: *Social Security Bulletin* XXV (August 1962), pp. 28–32.

[a] It will be noted that the Public Welfare Amendments of 1962 change the terminology of "aid to dependent children" to "aid to families with dependent children"; likewise, "State Plans for aid to dependent children" becomes "State Plans for aid and services to needy families with children."

Some idea of the number of people reached by these six public assistance programs may be gained from the following tabulation:

NUMBER OF RECIPIENTS OF PUBLIC ASSISTANCE
APRIL 1962

Aid to the blind	101,002
Aid to dependent children [a]	2,889,077
Aid to the disabled	408,604
General assistance	960,000
Medical assistance to the aged	93,146
Old-age assistance	2,245,080

Source: *Social Security Bulletin* XXV (August 1962), pp. 28–32.

[a] It will be noted that the Public Welfare Amendments of 1962 change the terminology of "aid to dependent children" to "aid to families with dependent children"; likewise, "State Plans for aid to dependent children" becomes "State Plans for aid and services to needy families with children."

Two additional items are necessary to round out this picture of the extent of the public assistance program in this country: the total dollar expenditures per month and per year. In April 1962 expenditures from federal, state, and local funds totalled $374,536,000. For the year ending December 31, 1961 the sum was slightly over 4 billion dollars—$4,099,790,-000. Of this amount 53.1 percent was federal funds, 35.1 percent state funds, and 11.8 percent local funds.[6]

Maternal and child health and welfare services

In addition to the social insurance and public assistance features of the Social Security Act, there is a third part providing for maternal and child health services, services for crippled children, and child welfare services. The appropriation of federal sums for maternal and child health services is for the purpose of enabling states to extend and improve services for promoting the health of mothers and children, especially in rural areas and in areas suffering from severe economic distress. Each state plan must provide for: (a) financial participation by the state; (b) administration of the plan or supervision of the administration by the state health agency; (c) establishment and maintenance of personnel standards on a merit basis and proper and efficient administration; (d) reports; (e) extension and improvement of local maternal and child health services; (f) cooperation with medical, nursing, and welfare groups; (g) demonstration services in needy areas and among groups in special need. The state plans are subject to the approval of the U.S. Children's Bureau.

Another appropriation under the Social Security Act as amended to date is for the purpose of enabling each state "to extend and improve services for locating crippled children, and for providing medical, surgical, corrective, and other services and care, and facilities for diagnosis, hospitalization, and after care for children who are crippled or who are suffering from conditions which lead to crippling." The state plan must conform substantially to the same requirements as the maternal and child health plan, except that the administration or the supervision of the administration need not necessarily be under the state health agency; nor is there any requirement in the act for local services or for demonstrations. As in the case of allotments for maternal and child health, there is a federal requirement for state matching of a portion of the federal funds and provision as well for a flat grant to each state.

---

[6] Adapted from *Source of Funds Expended for Public Assistance Payments, Calendar Year Ended December 31, 1961* (Department of Health, Education, and Welfare, May 18, 1962).

A third provision is for child welfare services. Since the inception of the Social Security Act, Congress has consistently broadened and deepened its concept of child welfare. Not only has it increased the appropriations for child welfare services but also it has been specific in its revised wording in the statute. The most far-reaching of these rewordings expressed the unmistakable intent of Congress in the Public Welfare Amendments of 1962 as follows:

> Child welfare services means public social services which supplement, or substitute for, parental care and supervision for the purpose of (1) preventing or remedying, or assisting in the solution of problems which may result in the neglect, abuse, exploitation, or delinquency of children, (2) protecting and caring for homeless, dependent, or neglected children, (3) protecting and promoting the welfare of children of working mothers, and (4) otherwise protecting and promoting the welfare of children, including the strengthening of their own homes where possible or, where needed, the provision of adequate care of children away from their homes in foster family homes or day-care or other child-care facilities.[7]

General assistance

The foregoing completes the analysis of the provisions of the Social Security Act, but it seems necessary here to mention another form of public assistance that is not included in the act. This is known as general assistance, a modern euphemism for what used to be called poor relief, and consists of aid in cash or in kind (groceries, goods, etc.) for those persons who are in need and yet are not eligible for the categories of assistance discussed above. Like these assistance programs, it is administered by the local department of public welfare. The funds may be provided by the local county (or city, town, township), or by the county and the state, or entirely by the state. There is no federal contribution towards general assistance payments. There are some states in which no payment whatsoever is made for general assistance. In a number of states there are some

---

[7] The foregoing description of the Social Security Act as it was passed in 1935 and subsequently amended is designed to provide the beginning student with a simplified view of the Act as it stands now. Many details have been omitted, purposely. Wayne Vasey's *Government and Social Welfare* provides a more complete analysis up to 1958. However, the reader is urged to examine for himself the *Public Welfare Amendments of 1962* or to secure excellent analyses prepared by and obtainable from the Social Security Administration, Department of Health, Education, and Welfare, Washington, D.C.; an additional resource is the monthly issue of the *Social Security Bulletin,* which contains a wealth of material including statistics on the financial aspects of state and federal programs.

counties that provide for general assistance payments while other counties do not.[8]

Vocational rehabilitation

In Title V of the original Social Security Act there was provision for appropriation to the states for vocational rehabilitation of the disabled which furthered the program initiated by the Federal Vocational Rehabilitation Act of 1920. The incorporation of these services in the Social Security Act in 1935 further stimulated federal-state cooperation so that by the middle of 1943 all forty-eight states, the District of Columbia, Hawaii, and Puerto Rico had legislated in this area. In July 1943 the substance of the social security provisions along with strengthening amendments were brought together into separate legislation known as the Barden-La Follette Act (Public Law No. 13, 78th Congress). However, by the amendment of 1954 (Public Law 565, 83rd Congress) a great advance was taken, which has been characterized as "a new era in the vocational rehabilitation of handicapped men and women."

As with the other appropriations that have been discussed, there must be acceptable state plans as a condition of receipt of federal monies by the states. The vocational rehabilitation state plans must:

1. Designate the state board of vocational education as the sole agency for the administration, supervision, and control of the state plan (exceptions relating to commissions for the blind or previously designated vocational rehabilitation commissions are noted in the act)
2. Designate the state treasurer as custodian of funds
3. Specify the policies and methods under which the plan is to be carried out
4. Provide that the services shall be available only to employable individuals
5. Provide for the establishment and maintenance of personnel standards
6. Provide reports
7. Provide that no federal sums be used for repair or rental of buildings
8. Make rules governing on-the-job training, medical and hospitalization fees, and prosthetic devices
9. Provide vocational rehabilitation to any civil employee of the United States disabled while in the performance of his duty and to any war-disabled civilian

This legislation permits federal funds to be used by the states for all regular administrative costs as well as for matching of state funds on a dollar-for-dollar basis.

---

[8] Vasey, *ibid.*, pp. 167–170.

The vocational rehabilitation services made possible under the 1920 to 1962 legislation are for handicapped civilians and war-disabled civilians, including merchant seamen and former members of the armed forces whose disabilities are held to be nonservice connected. These services include corrective surgery, hospitalization, occupational tools, prosthetic devices essential to obtaining or retaining employment, subsistence maintenance during training or retraining, guidance and placement of disabled persons. The Office of Vocational Rehabilitation, like the Social Security Administration and the U.S. Children's Bureau, is in the Department of Health, Education, and Welfare. Rehabilitation of persons having service-connected disabilities is the responsibility of the Veterans' Administration.[9]

This recital of provisions of the Social Security Act was necessary to bring the account of public welfare services up to date. The activities beginning with FERA and culminating in the Social Security Act have defined a new area and given a new tone to the public services. It now becomes imperative to take stock of where public welfare organization and administration are during the second half of the twentieth century.

The offer of services in county welfare departments

While it is difficult to generalize with respect to over 3000 counties and 50 states and the District of Columbia (Puerto Rico, and Virgin Islands could be included), nevertheless there are enough consistencies running through their welfare operations to attempt a description of public welfare as people encounter it in their home communities. These services may be classified as follows: public assistance (financial), caring and placing, counseling, regulation, services performed for other agencies, and referral.

The bulk of the local county welfare job—in number of people reached and amount of money expended—is public assistance, that is, old-age assistance, medical assistance for the aged, aid to the blind, aid to families with dependent children, aid to the permanently and totally disabled, and general assistance. The common denominator of each of these is need—financial need. The distinction between them is the qualifying factor of: age, health, blindness, childhood, disability, unemployability, according to the various categories.

---

[9] Some of the possibilities for cooperative effort on behalf of the physically handicapped (and the crippled child as well) are detailed in Caroline H. Elledge, *The Rehabilitation of the Patient* (Philadelphia: J. B. Lippincott Company, 1945). References at this point to Chapter 10, "Medical Social Work," may prove useful; see also Vasey, *ibid.*, pp. 207–217.

Persons who apply for public assistance may file an application at a local welfare office—county, city, or district within city. Eligibility is based upon proof of need as well as of on the other qualifying factors just mentioned. Let it be assumed that a man and wife, each 65 years of age, feel they are in financial need and hence entitled to, as they call it, their "pension." Whether they are eligible or not will depend upon their being 65 years or older and with insufficient resources. The applicant carries the major responsibility for ascertaining proof of his age, but the public assistance worker stands ready to be of help, particularly since birth records were not always recorded officially six or more decades ago. The other aspect of eligibility is the determination of need. Usually this is based on a calculation (a joint enterprise of applicant and worker) of resources and the computation of a budget based on minimal needs. Resources may consist of income of any kind, whether cash or its equivalent, with consideration given to ownership of real estate, as well as personal property, insurance policies, and other assets that could be considered of value. Over against this is placed a fairly standardized budget, usually prepared by the state department of public welfare. If the resources exceed the budget items, the applicant is ineligible. If the resources are less than the budget items, the applicant is eligible for a cash grant monthly, provided there are sufficient funds available and the authorization has been made by the appropriate person or persons (that is, director of public welfare and county welfare board). Not infrequently, only a percentage of this difference between resources and needs is granted because of lack of funds. For example, there may be a budgetary deficit, as it is called, of $60 per month and yet only 75 percent of this or $45 may be granted. Appeals are permissible both from applicants who are found ineligible as well as from persons to whom grants have been made and who may question the size of the grant. This appeals procedure is required by the Social Security Act and is provided for by the state department of public welfare. It is the responsibility of the public assistance worker to keep in touch with the clients at reasonable intervals and to make recommendations with respect to the grants if the original situation changes. He should also be available for such help as the clients may request that is within the function of the welfare department. This applies with equal effect to all of the public assistances even though the provision for general assistance may be locally financed and locally controlled.

A second group of services offered in the local welfare department may be called caring and placing. Receiving a child into foster care, securing a foster family to meet his needs, helping the child and the foster parents with the difficulties that sometimes arise are instances of the caring function. Somewhat the same may be said for foster family care for the aged (or older) person. Perhaps even what is termed home-maker service, whether for children or for aged persons, may be included in this concept of care. On the other hand, the placing service is characterized by the role that the department carries in adoption—the receiving of the child, the search for an adoption couple, the services involved in effecting the adoption. Increasingly, public welfare departments are engaged in caring and placing—functions that until recently were performed by many agencies supported by voluntary contributions.[10]

A third group of services consist of helping persons with difficulties of a rather serious nature, such as the unmarried mother, or the parent who is abusing or neglecting his child, or the youngster who is placed on probation by the juvenile court. These various persons may need financial help or they may not; their essential difficulty is in the area of behavior, and help offered to them must be directed toward assisting them to assume a greater responsibility for their behavior. In many parts of this country the only resource for helping, in any measure, such persons may have to come from the local welfare department—with all of its limitations as to number of staff, training of staff, size of caseloads, multiplicity of duties.

The regulatory services constitute a fourth area: for example, the licensing of foster homes (actually it may be the examination of them and recommendation to the state department of public welfare), the determination of permits to solicit, whether granted to persons or to organizations, or recommendations to the court regarding adoption petitions.

In addition to all of the foregoing, the local public welfare department performs services for other agencies. It has a considerable task of certification, of doing the necessary preliminary investigation, and screening for admissions to tuberculosis sanatoriums, institutions for the feebleminded, state mental hospitals, and institutions for the aged. It may be called upon to certify with respect to financial capacity prior to hospital admission or to other institutions that provide services related to ability to pay for them. It may conduct the intake interviews for institutions or agencies within or outside the immediate area of the county. It may also conduct the out-of-town inquiries for other public welfare departments as well as private agencies such as Travelers Aid Societies. In addition to all of these, it may carry out cooperative arrangements with the appropriate state agencies by providing services to parolees from correctional institutions. The director of public welfare may even perform the school attendance officer job for the school system.

A final grouping to services of the local public welfare departments are referrals—usually to agencies for such other services that are not within the public welfare function or that other agencies are better qualified to provide. Instances are referrals to child guidance clinic, to family service

---

[10] Also see Chapter 8, "Welfare Services for Children."

agency, to hospital social service, to Veterans' Administration hospital or regional office, to vocational rehabilitation facilities and services, to specialized institutions (such as those for the blind, the cerebral palsied, etc.), to legal aid clinics.

Social casework as a method of offering public welfare services

From Elizabethan and colonial days onward very little attention was given to the individual needs of persons asking for public relief. The poor were poor because it was their own fault. If relief was to be given them, it was to be so unattractive that they would be deterred from asking again, and the example would discourage other would-be askers. An approach to persons in need upon another basis came with the development of private social work, particularly of family casework. So long, however, as public welfare in the state government concerned itself largely with institutional care and management, and so long as public welfare in the local community consisted largely of pauper relief, there seemed little occasion or opportunity to use casework services. So long as private agencies could select their clients, and so long as the public institutions and poor boards had to take the rest, there was little sharing of this newer point of view that was called social casework. Today, the situation is changed. The public agency is empowered to administer a service to all who are eligible. Can this be done on a mass basis and still insure a high quality of service to individuals who can make use of it?

To the uninitiated person all this talk about social casework may sound like the lingo of an esoteric cult. Could not anyone who learned the language be a caseworker? What is there to casework that could not be done by, say, a board member, a pastor's assistant, the chairman of the welfare committee of the woman's club? Whoever has read this far must realize that the practice of social casework is based upon a skill in working with people in difficulty and that this skill is related to one's native endowment, one's own personality development, training, and experience. Casework demands infinite skill.

The process of social casework and its usefulness rests upon a conviction of accepting people as they are, respecting their rights to live their own lives according to their best lights, and a willingness to work with them on their plans rather than to make the plans for them. The worker's effectiveness lies in *what* he does in helping people and *how* he does it. He does not take over their difficulties nor their own share of responsibility; rather he helps them to face their difficulties and to carry what is their part of the load. Casework is a skillful way of working with people in trouble. It is not the only way. It is one way that has proven its value by helping people to develop their own capacities for useful and satisfying living.

Does all this have pertinence for the public assistance job as we engage ourselves in the administration of the Social Security Act? Do public assistance workers operate on the basis of what Mrs. Rosa Wessel terms public assistance *as* casework. Indeed, we answer immediately, can public assistance workers operate on any other basis? Do workers see themselves as granting public assistance to an applicant and then undertaking to provide "service," or do they see *what* they do and *how* they do it in the process of determining eligibility or reviewing grants as the very essence of helping? [11]

The Social Security Act in both its insurance and public assistance features marked a break with a three-hundred-year past. No longer were workers and their family members to lose their respectability because they grew old or were temporarily out of work. Not only were many of them to be eligible to receive financial benefits, which bore a relation to previous wage deductions, but others not so covered under the social insurances were entitled to assistance, as a right, when certain eligibility conditions were met. This newer concept of the dignity of the human being has provided a valid basis for casework in the public assistances as well as in the other public welfare services.

The rules of eligibility for the public assistances are laid down by state statutes and federal enactment. Applicants who meet these eligibility requirements are entitled by right to assistance through money payments. The lack of public funds may mean an inadequacy of grant or no grant at all, but that lack in nowise invalidates the individual's right to application or his eligibility. Furthermore, the law guarantees the right of appeal of any applicant. This appeal may proceed through local welfare department, state welfare department, or courts according to the provisions of the various state laws.

Another instance of the respect for human personality embodied in this twentieth-century legislation is the legal provision that limits the use by the welfare agency of information about the applicant or recipient. Whatever information is developed in the course of establishing or maintaining eligibility is to be used for the service of the individual, remaining

---

[11] Rosa Wessel, ed., *Method and Skill in Public Assistance. Published as Journal of Social Work Process*, II (December 1938), p. 6 (Pennsylvania School of Social Work); see also the extraordinarily perceptive pamphlet, so useful for the worker with or without professional training, entitled *Some Casework Concepts for the Public Welfare Worker*, by Alan Keith-Lucas, 1957; another pamphlet, prepared essentially for workers in social insurance field offices, *Interviewing in Social Security*, by Elizabeth and Karl de Schweinitz, 1961, has especial relevance for public welfare workers.

the joint concern and property of the client and the agency, and not to become public property.[12]

These requirements in the laws fortify sound principles of agency administration in the development of policy. Such policy expressed through practice provides assistance on a fair and considerate basis. The needs of individuals are seen as varying just as individuals themselves vary from one another. The capacity of individuals to use money according to their needs is respected. The ability of individuals to manage their own affairs according to their lights is acknowledged. The desire of most individuals to improve their situation and to quicken their incentives is recognized and strengthened wherever possible. The *way* of the worker in dealing with the client is the measure of the casework job.

Casework in a public agency is related to the service for which the agency exists. Service begins with application for assistance. At this point the worker meets the applicant with the conditions of eligibility as defined in the law and agency policy. These must be clearly presented, in language that the applicant understands and in a manner that reveals a willingness to be helpful. Establishing eligibility then becomes a joint enterprise with the applicant producing the data to which he has access and the worker relating that to the agency requirements. In some instances the worker may be called upon to assemble other pertinent data that is more accessible to the agency than to the applicant. All of this is a shared experience, not a tug of war or a game of matched wits.

Throughout this, the worker must understand how vital money is in our lives. The "our" means all of us—applicants, social workers, teachers, lawyers, plumbers, farmers. Money may mean status and independence; it may mean holding up one's head and walking surely. It may mean courage and resolution to face new demands; it may mean security. The lack of money—no matter the reason—may mean denial of one or all of these. The establishment of eligibility and the continuing payment of assistance signifies, not a gift or sweet charity, but the faith of the state in the capacity of the individual to manage his affairs and to do so responsibly. It betokens also a practical as well as a philosophical conviction that whatever serves the welfare of the individual serves the welfare of the community too.

All of this is relevant to another aspect of casework in public assistance, namely, the conditions of continued eligibility. The use of public money requires a knowledge on the part of the agency and the worker that the facts supporting original eligibility are sustained throughout the period of assistance. Changes in the client's condition will affect his assistance payments, and when eligibility is no longer valid, then payments are

---

12 Even with the so-called Jenner Amendment, October 1951, permitting public inspection of disbursement records there still remains intact the confidentiality of the worker-client relationship.

terminated. This in no way compels a recipient to conform his life to the dictates of a governmental agency or permits an agency to use the assistance payment as either a lever or a threat. Throughout the period of eligibility the public assistance worker needs constantly to be sensitive to the dignity of the human personality, the wish of most people to manage their own affairs, as well as the capacity of people to improve their lot to become self-maintaining and self-determining.

Another area of usefulness calling for the worker's skill is that of bringing to recipients knowledge of the resources in other agencies of the community. These resources may be medical, educational, vocational, or recreational and readily known to the worker but not so to other persons. Here again, in the process of referral there is real skill involved. The understandable hesitations of people to expose themselves to other agencies or to unpredictable and possibly uncontrolled situations must be taken into account by the referring worker. Frequently more than information is needed. To information must be added understanding.

The Aid to Families with Dependent Children Program as a case in point

The remarks in the foregoing section, of necessity, have been of a general nature, but it would be more helpful to particularize with respect to one of the assistance programs, Aid to Families with Dependent Children. For centuries there have been children whose normal and major source of support has been curtailed or withdrawn, witness the earlier provisions of the Elizabethan Poor Law. Perhaps in earlier times it was the death of the father that may have been responsible for the child's exceptional dependency, but more recently this has been a decreasing factor while other circumstances have far exceeded it in importance and severity. So serious have been these other dislocations that the one nation-wide program that ministers to these broken families is by far the largest family-oriented program in the country. During the year 1961 there were over 3 million children receiving help through this program. This is a larger number than is being helped by the old-age assistance, or the blind, or the permanently and totally disabled programs—indeed it is larger than the combined total of all three of these.

Why are more than 3 million children receiving public assistance? The technical qualifications specify: a needy child who has been deprived of parental support or care by reason of the death, continued absence from the home, physical or mental incapacity or unemployment of parent.[13] But what are the individual situations back of these legal specifications? Perhaps the child—or most children—can come to terms, emotional terms, with the fact of a father's death more readily than with a father's imprisonment, commitment to a mental hospital, the fact of desertion, or his unemployment.

As one looks at these situations, inevitably the question must be asked: What of the community's attitudes, the self-attitudes, and even the worker's, the social worker's attitudes? Is the community, at least the unthinking members of the community, inclined to look upon families and children in need as being sorry folk? When such need has existed previously in the parent's childhood the community seems all the surer that such persons are hopeless. Doesn't the community, unthinkingly, believe that the least help—money—that can be given the less of the taxpayer's money will be wasted? What of self-attitudes? Do people in such circumstances, whether as parents or as children, tend to regard themselves as they believe the community, unthinkingly, regards them? If so, does such self-image tend to perpetuate them in their helplessness? Does the social worker tend to share in these attitudes—community and client—or does the worker share the profession's belief in the dignity and the worthwhileness of the individual and of his potentiality for change and self-improvement?

This latter is the crucial question insofar as public welfare work is concerned and especially with respect to the Aid to Families with Dependent Children program. It is only as the professional social worker introduces difference into this situation, using a skill that facilitates rather than hinders, that he begins to achieve the purposes for which the services were originally established. The public assistance provisions of the Social Security Act did not aim to keep people on relief or to attract them to it; rather the intention was to help them achieve a more satisfying and useful life. Indeed, the 1960 and 1962 amendments emphasize the strengthening of family life, the movement toward self-support, and the greater utilization of opportunities for self-development of those who find themselves obliged to ask for help from welfare departments.

This is no simple task for the public assistance caseworker. The conventional and time-dishonored approaches of exhortation, of castigating, of demeaning, of pressuring are ineffectual and usually produce deterioration, self-pity, and confirmed hopelessness. Another attitude and another skill on the part of the caseworker enables the client, whether parent or child, to take hold of something positive and to use it toward genuine self-realization and productiveness. The many careful studies that have been

---

[13] In 1961 a change in the Social Security Act permitted federal funds to be available for payment to those needy families in which the parent was unemployed. This temporary provision from May 1, 1961 to June 30, 1962 was extended for a five-year period beyond the June 30, 1962 date.

made, as well as the daily working experience of caseworkers, furnish unquestioned proof of the effectiveness of such approach.

To accomplish such a helping service there must be many elements:
a firm statement in the law, a leadership in federal and state departments,
a staff in the counties sufficient in numbers, and, above all, caseworkers
with conviction about the worth of each individual and possessed of a skill
in helping persons to develop to the full their capacities for constructive
living and working. While these essentials are vital to all welfare programs
they have especial pertinence for a program that profoundly affects the
lives of millions of children, of these children as they become parents, and
of their children as yet unborn.[14]

Trends in public welfare

In our time and in this our country we can see evidences of attitudes and practices that have prevailed throughout three centuries of public welfare. At the same time, even though we stand in the midst of contemporary operation and are inextricably a part of it, we can still discern
some of the more pronounced trends. Without any question the most outstanding is toward an expanding service. This may be measured by dollars,
by staffs, or more importantly, by the range of services and the number
of persons whom these services reach. Welfare still assists the individual
or family of limited means of subsistence, and that is a tremendously important service. But it also undertakes to provide many other services as
instanced by social security developments, veterans' services, vocational
rehabilitation, child welfare services, to mention only a few. This expansion of service has been associated with a changed concept of the public
welfare services. Assistance of whatever kind is to be considered not as a
palliative or a stopgap, but as an investment in human beings, a means
whereby, with help, individuals may discover and develop their capacities
for satisfying and useful living. This applies to services for the aged, for
children, for offenders, for the mentally afflicted, for the otherwise handicapped, in short for all those who look for help beyond themselves and
their family.

Within recent years more and more attention is being paid to services for the aged. The enlarging proportion of the aged in the total population is, without question, a determining factor in this development.

---

[14] Doubtless the many criticisms of welfare programs and the many instances
in which constructive help was not forthcoming were important considerations affecting the 87th Congress as it prepared the Public Welfare Amendments of 1962. Many
of its enabling provisions make it possible for properly qualified personnel to offer,
increasingly, helpful services. Other public officials and entire communities also share
in this opportunity.

Money grants to eligible aged persons are on the increase, accompanied by liberalization of eligibility requirements. Recreational and group work services related to the needs of the aged are on the increase. Counseling services for the aged are coming to the fore. Increased and improved institutional services—in public and private homes—are evident, together with specially adapted programs in them. Planning in the housing field, particularly low-cost housing, is beginning to take into account the needs of older persons. While not related exclusively to the aged, nevertheless the problem of chronic illness has been receiving increasing attention; developments in this area take the situation of the aged as a point of departure for expanded services for all chronically ill.

A third discernible trend is the increasing provision for more adequate medical services for all the people. With the extraordinary progress of medical science it becomes clear that efforts must be directed toward distributing medical services wherever they are needed, and that financial provision also must be made for any interruption of earnings during illness. Many foreign countries have demonstrated the possibility as well as the desirability of such expanded services. The proposals in the last several Congresses looking toward health insurance as an integral part of a social security program have not been enacted, but they are unmistakably affecting the former fixed positions of those favoring the preservation of the *status quo*. Even the efforts to head off health insurance compel the enactment of programs that will provide more extensive medical service than heretofore. Because of the delays in the provision of a more equitable distribution of medical services, state and local departments of public welfare have had to formulate medical care programs for assistance recipients. In some instances there may be inclusion in the recipient's budget of a sum for medical care; in other cases the services of a county physician may be made available, while in still other instances there may be what is called vendor payments by the state or local department to the provider of the medical services.

While there is still considerable controversy about the extension of medical services the issue has become sharpened recently with respect to the aged. It is known by most reasonable people that the necessity for medical care is greater with older people. It is also known that the earnings of most older people decline, especially of course if they retire or are retired from employment. The situation thus confronts most older people of having to meet greater costs of medical care at the very time when their personal financial resources are lessening, or of having to go without adequate medical care. It is not unnatural or unreasonable to see these situations multiplied so many times—yes, millions of times—as to constitute a problem of national importance. With a public assistance system and a social insurance system for older persons the question perforce must rise:

Should medical care provision for the aged be related to the assistance or to the insurance programs? A temporary answer was given by the 86th Congress by the addition of medical aid for the aged to the public assistance program. It is not inconceivable that a succeeding Congress may incorporate a more adequate program with the old-age survivors and disability program—OASDI. In this connection it may not be inappropriate to refer to an earlier attachment of disability to the assistance program—when the same issue, assistance or insurance, was being debated—to be followed a short time later by an addition to the old-age and survivors insurance program.

A fourth trend is reflected in the expansion of the social insurances within the over-all social security program. Not only have survivors been added to the original old-age insurance group but also the disabled, so that a program that began as OAI became OASI and now stands as OASDI. Additional workers have been brought within OASDI so that today practically the only employed persons not covered are employees of the federal government, self-employed doctors of medicine, and persons with quite small amounts of earnings from self-employment, from domestic work in private homes, or from farm work. Ever since the time the number of aged persons receiving old-age insurance had exceeded the number receiving old-age assistance, 1951, there has been an acceleration of those respective trends.

A fifth trend is in the direction of regarding services in public welfare, especially in public assistance, as being offered to persons as members of the family group. Because we have accustomed ourselves to what are called the categories (developed as part of the social security program in 1935 to facilitate state legislation and federal financial participation) we have tended to fractionate families. However, as we have offered casework services as the basic method of helping, including the granting of money, we have realized that children are members of families, brothers and sisters are members of families, parents are family members, and that our approach increasingly must be to the family as a living, interacting group. This but serves to emphasize what we have always known but too often have taken for granted—that the family is our basic human grouping. The wise use of tax money and the effectiveness of casework services must be so premised.[15]

Perhaps the most hopeful of recent developments have been the demonstrations carried on in various parts of the country in reducing the caseloads of public assistance workers so they may do a more intensive job with the troubled families seeking financial aid. Not infrequently pub-

---

[15] See reference in Chapter 6 to the action of the Secretary of the Department of Health, Education, and Welfare in changing the name of the Bureau of Public Assistance to the Bureau of Family Service.

lic assistance workers will have as many as 300 to 500 families to work
with, and experience has shown the impossibility of providing a genuinely
helpful service to all but a few of these families. By reducing the number
of these families to 35 to 50 per worker, convincing proof has been established of the usefulness of the worker to the family members. Rather than
being an extravagant way of doing the public assistance job this has been
highly economical—of money, of the worker's time and skill, but, most importantly, in the conservation of human potentialities. An analysis of ten
demonstration programs produces this conviction:

> We can safely conclude when we study the result with care that given
> time to explore the obstacles to independent living, a concern about helping
> families to overcome those obstacles, a community atmosphere in which
> minority groups are employed during times of stress on somewhat equal
> terms with majority groups, and given day care facilities so that low-income
> mothers can work without neglecting their children, substantial social and
> economic savings could be effected.[16]

Another trend is in the direction of greater integration of welfare
services, national, state, and local. This means a bringing into more effective coordination the various services that minister to the welfare needs
of people, whether this be social security measures, rehabilitation, correctional, institutional, veterans, etc. No longer can we afford the questionable luxury of each welfare service being operated without relation to the
other. Not only does sound administration demand this coordination, but
more importantly, the needs of the people for whom welfare services
exist dictate it.

Finally, let it be said that the day of the Elizabethan Poor Law, if
not entirely gone, is at least going and is being replaced by a positively
oriented welfare based on the conviction of the worth of the individual
and of the value of constructive public services.

The Public Welfare Amendments
of 1962

The most recent and convincing expression of these claims is contained in the Public Welfare Amendments of 1962. For years unfriendly
critics of public welfare have taken it to task for its shortcomings. These
have been seen as ranging from the bumbling ineptness of workers to the
ill-conceived and misguided programs that encouraged chiseling and per-

---

[16] Memorandum dated April 20, 1961, by Elizabeth Wickenden, director of the
Project on Public Services for Families and Children, sponsored by the New York
School of Social Work, Columbia University; see also Elizabeth Wickenden and
Winifred Bell, *Public Welfare: Time for a Change* (New York: The New York School
of Social Work of Columbia University, 1961).

petuated dependency. Others, its discriminating supporters and its professionally qualified workers, have been keenly aware of public welfare's limited effectiveness. These have seen its limitations in the lack of enabling legislation, the inadequacy of federal, state and county appropriations, the indifference or hostility of public attitudes, and the short supply of trained personnel. Foes and friends, while disagreeing on practically all points, at least were in agreement that something was wrong and something had to be done about public welfare. The changes made possible by the Public Welfare Amendments of 1962, Public Law 87–543, while not fully satisfying to all parties, at least make it possible to move forward toward increasingly useful services to those who are obliged to ask for help of public authorities.

The pervading emphases in this newer legislation are: incentive, prevention, rehabilitation—applicable to children, to parents, to families, to the blind, the disabled, and the aged. For the aged the services to be provided are aimed toward attaining or retaining capacity for self-care; for the needy blind and disabled toward achieving self-support or self-care; for needy parents and children toward strengthening family life. There is also the intent to provide constructive social services to those applying for or receiving medical assistance to the aged. Perhaps the aim of this legislation is nowhere more pointedly expressed than in the statement by President Kennedy when he signed it into law July 25, 1962:

> This measure embodies a new approach—stressing services in addition to support, rehabilitation instead of relief, and training for useful work instead of prolonged dependency. This important legislation will assist our states and local public welfare agencies to redirect the incentives and services they offer to needy families and children and to aged and disabled people. Our objective is to prevent or reduce dependency and to encourage self-care and self-support—to maintain family life where it is adequate and to restore it where it is deficient.

Consistent with the concern for strengthening family life is the significant change of the program title from "Aid to Dependent Children" to "Aid and Services to Needy Families with Children." This is not unrelated to an earlier administrative change in title from "Bureau of Public Assistance" to "Bureau of Family Services." Further evidence of this family focus is the provision for payment to a family in need on the basis of unemployment of the parent. Under the 1962 amendments this may apply to both parents; and the temporary 1961 provision has been extended for a five-year period. Formerly the needy child and his family (usually mother) were not eligible for a grant unless the father was absent. This had the effect of encouraging the father to be absent, in short, to desert. As a further incentive toward keeping the family together, there is now provision for federal financial participation in state programs of community work projects with training and retraining opportunities—these to be available to a relative 18 years of age or older with whom a needy child is living. An additional incentive is to permit the family to set aside funds for the future needs of the child, such as education or vocational training, which funds may be disregarded in the calculation by the welfare worker of the budgetary requirements of the family.

The amendments also authorize federal funds for day care centers so that children may be cared for during the day while their mothers, who formerly received welfare grants, are working and becoming self-supporting.

Other incentive features are embodied in provisions relating to the aged and the blind whereby a certain amount of earnings may be disregarded in calculating the welfare grant.

With respect to increasing the quality of services there is authorization, subject to congressional appropriation of funds, for training public welfare personnel. It has been recognized for years there is a severe shortage of personnel not only in numbers but also in the professional training of the workers providing the services. The 1962 amendments aim to assist the states in meeting this critical situation.

While the 1962 amendments are a considerable legislative advance, facilitating much needed improvements in public welfare practice, it must be recognized that still more progress must be made and that as conditions change welfare legislation must respond with alertness and resourcefulness. It was three centuries before we moved much beyond the Elizabethan or the colonial Poor Law. In a world that in less than one generation is moving from electric to nuclear power we may never again be permitted such a three-century lag. Indeed, even the three-decade progress since the Social Security Act of 1935 may prove too halting. In social welfare, as in other areas of modern living and working, we may have to move at an accelerated pace.[17]

----

[17] No attempt is made to discuss in detail the many other provisions of the 1962 amendments, such as protective payments, foster home care, child care institution arrangements, changing in matching formulas, administrative regulations, demonstration projects, etc. For such details, important as they are, the reader is referred to Public Law 87–543 or, preferably, to the director or commissioner of public welfare of the state in which he resides.

Bibliography

Ball, Robert M., "Social Insurance and the Right to Assistance," *The Social Service Review*, XXI (September 1947), pp. 331–344.

Blackwell, Gordon W., and Raymond F. Gould, *Future Citizens All*. Chicago: American Public Welfare Association, 1952.

Chevigny, Hector, *The Adjustment of the Blind*. New Haven: Yale University Press, 1950.

Cohen, Wilbur J., "The First Twenty-Five Years of the Social Security Act, 1935–1960," *Social Work Year Book*. New York: National Association of Social Workers, 1960, pp. 49–62.

Cohen, Wilbur J., and Robert M. Ball, "The Public Welfare Amendments of 1962," *Public Welfare*, XX (October 1962), pp. 191–198, 227–233.

de Schweinitz, Elizabeth and Karl de Schweinitz, *Interviewing in Social Security*. Washington, D.C.: U.S. Department of Health, Education, and Welfare, 1961.

Faatz, Anita, *The Nature of Policy in the Administration of Public Assistance*. Philadelphia: University of Pennsylvania School of Social Work, 1943.

Farrell, Gabriel, *The Story of Blindness*. Cambridge: Harvard University Press, 1956.

Foster, Helen B., *Services in Public Assistance: The Role of the Caseworker*. Public Assistance Report, No. 30. Washington, D.C.: U.S. Department of Health, Education, and Welfare, 1957.

Hoey, Jane M., "The Lack of Money: Its Cost in Human Values," *Social Casework*, XXXVIII (October 1957), pp. 406–412.

Homemaker in Public Welfare, The. Chicago: American Public Welfare Association, 1962.

Illegitimacy and Its Impact on the Aid to Dependent Children Program. Washington, D.C.: U.S. Department of Health, Education, and Welfare, 1960.

Keith-Lucas, Alan, *Decisions about People in Need*. Chapel Hill: University of North Carolina Press, 1957.

———, *Some Casework Concepts for the Public Welfare Worker*. Chapel Hill: University of North Carolina Press, 1957.

Leyendecker, Hilary F., *Problems and Policy in Public Assistance*. New York: Harper & Row, Publishers, 1955.

Manning, Helen C., *More Than Bread: Social Services in Public Assistance—A Community Resource*. Washington, D.C.: U.S. Department of Health, Education, and Welfare, 1958.

Marcus, Grace F., "Changes in the Theory of Relief Giving," *Proceedings of the National Conference of Social Work*, 1941, pp. 267–279.

———, *The Nature of Service in Public Assistance Administration*. Washington, D.C.: Federal Security Agency, 1946.

Meriam, Lewis, *Relief and Social Security*. Washington: The Brookings Institution, 1946.

Peters, Mary Overholt, *The Caseworker: Person with Value*. Chicago: American Public Welfare Association, (no date).

Public Welfare, XVIII (July 1960). (Entire issue on Twenty-fifth Anniversary of Social Security Act.) Chicago: American Public Welfare Association, 1960.

Schottland, Charles I., "The Nature of Services in Public Assistance," *Casework Papers, 1959.* New York: Family Service Association of America, 1959, pp. 5–19.

Smith, A. Delafield, *The Right to Life.* Chapel Hill: University of North Carolina Press, 1955.

Social Security Bulletin, XXIII (August 1960). (Entire issue on Twenty-fifth Anniversary of Social Security Act.) Washington, D.C.: U.S. Department of Health, Education, and Welfare, 1960.

Stevenson, Marietta, *Public Welfare Administration.* New York: The Macmillan Company, 1938.

Towle, Charlotte, *Common Human Needs.* Washington, D.C.: Federal Security Agency, 1954; also, New York: American Association of Social Workers, 1952.

U.S. Advisory Council on Public Assistance, *Public Assistance: A Report of the Advisory Council on Public Assistance,* 86th Cong., 2d Sess., Senate Document 93. Washington, D.C.: Government Printing Office, 1960.

U.S. Department of Health, Education, and Welfare, *Report of the Advisory Council on Child Welfare Services,* 86th Cong., 2d Sess., Senate Document 92. Washington, D.C.: Government Printing Office, 1960.

Vasey, Wayne, *Government and Social Welfare.* New York: Henry Holt and Company, 1958.

Wickenden, Elizabeth, and Winifred Bell, *Public Welfare: Time for a Change.* New York: The New York School of Social Work of Columbia University, 1961.

Wiltse, Kermit T., "Aid to Dependent Children: The Nation's Basic Family and Child Welfare Program," *The Social Welfare Forum.* New York: Columbia University Press, 1960, pp. 218–231.

———, "Social Casework and Public Assistance," *The Social Service Review,* XXXII (March 1958), pp. 41–50.

MRS. WILHELM; MISS WEBB

KERMIT T. WILTSE, D. S. W.
School of Social Welfare, University of California
Berkeley, California

The Eighty-fourth Congress of the United States in its second session in 1956 enacted into law the most important additions and extensions to the Social Security Act relating to public assistance since its inception in 1935. Among the various amendments the one that may have the most far-reaching effect was an addition to the purpose clauses of each of the public assistance titles to include the encouragement of self-care, self-support and strengthening of family life. Substance was given to the renewed emphasis upon services to public assistance recipients to help them achieve self-care, self-support or stronger family life where appropriate to the individual instance through the requirement that each state develop a plan to improve the service aspect of its program; and the federal government would pay 50% of all administrative costs including the extension of additional services to public assistance recipients by states and localities.

The emphasis upon services, implied by the addition of these new clauses to the purposes set forth for each of the public assistance programs, added a new direction and principle. The base is thereby laid for the development of a public social services program that could depart completely from an exclusive emphasis upon eligibility determination as the whole purpose of public assistance administration. Only through many years of diligent effort can states and localities gear their welfare agencies actually to deliver the kind and quality of services envisioned by those who best understand the implications of the service emphasis. It should also be emphasized that welfare agencies in many areas of the nation had already made substantial progress toward implementing a service emphasis in the administration of the various public assistance categories before 1956—indeed such an emphasis has been present wherever sound social casework is practiced. Everyone is aware from a reading of the daily papers, magazine articles, and newspaper editorials of the increasing public concern with two major groups in our society that are the object of the two major public assistance categories, namely, the aged and the dependent children. There is much discussion of the importance of social services to all aged people, but particularly of the necessity of services to aged recipients of public assistance to maintain self-care and self-dependence, and conversely, to prevent the too frequent decline of the aged person into a state of frustrated dependence and withdrawal from active participation in the life of his community. The first example is drawn from a local welfare department that is actually giving social services to the aged. The second example is of a mother whose child is dependent and receiving assistance because of the absence of the father. This example raises many of the complicated questions that are being raised in increasing volume about the Aid to Dependent Children program and its effect on family life.

This first example is drawn from the Old Age Assistance program and illustrates the kind of constructive service that can be given to aged recipients of this category of assistance. The case of Mrs. Wilhelm demonstrates how the promotion of self-care as a program objective actually can be carried out to the benefit of the individuals involved and ultimately to society. This case example should be studied in the light of this program objective plus the question: "What is the attitude, knowledge, and skill the public assistance worker must possess to effectively carry out this objective?"

Mrs. Wilhelm

Mrs. Ophelia Wilhelm had applied for old-age assistance in 1954 when it became difficult for her children to continue the full support of their mother. The OAA grant makes up the budgetary deficiency over and above the regular contributions of the one son who was able to make a regular cash contribution and the one daughter who contributed a small cottage on the property owned by her husband and herself. The amount of the grant varies therefore in accordance with Mrs. Wilhelm's varying needs as the record progresses, depending upon how much or how little housekeeping service is necessary in any given month.

This case record is from a county welfare department in California that is experimenting with intensive short-term services to selected OAA recipients. The services are directed to enhancing self-care and maintaining self-dependence, and selection for these services is made by a continuing perusal of all OAA records to select those cases in which there are indications that intensive services are needed and that such services would yield tangible results. Hence there are two kinds of OAA caseloads: small caseloads carried by certain workers to which they are giving a great deal of concentrated attention, and very large caseloads on which the essential service is the monthly grant plus continued surveillance to detect those instances in which there are indications of a need for additional service, illustrated by the record reproduced here. Transfers back and forth between these two types of caseloads, or we might say, these dramatically different levels of service, are frequent and uninhibited. The efficacy of this plan of differentiated caseloads depends upon careful attention to clues indicating the need for additional service beyond that of a monthly check plus medical care and open channels of transfer back and forth.

Mrs. Wilhelm is a petite, serious widow of 75 years. Her standard of living had been adequate but gleaned through hard work and maintained by frugality. She established a high moral code for her family, which was supported by strong spiritual beliefs. Her spouse died in 1942 after a long illness from cancer. Client did practical nursing in the home of friends for a brief time. The rest of her life has been spent in her own home. There are three children, Frances, now Mrs. Ames, with whom client lived at the beginning of our record, Frank Wilhelm, and Amelia, now Mrs. Fred Hanes. The two older children absorbed the fundamental teachings of the mother and took over the father's duties after his death, supporting the mother, including making the payments on the mother's home. The bulk of this responsibility rested upon Frances, who was the eldest, because the brother later contracted cancer, which resulted in an iliostomy. The younger sister paid $8 a week for room and board, which was a token payment, and contributed $100 towards the payment on the home in one payment, and this her husband demanded be returned to her at the time she was married.

Our client and her daughter Frances and son Frank moved to Oakdale, California in 1944, selling the family home and reinvesting the money in a home. This home was sold in 1954 when Frances and Mrs. Wilhelm moved to Ridgewood, using the amount of their equity in the sale of the home in Oakdale for a down payment on another in Ridgewood. The son and daughter felt that, because of their complete support of the mother for over ten years and the fact that they have made subsequent payments on the home, she no longer held the equity, and the home was put in the name of Frances, who had by this time been married to John Ames. Mrs. Ames stated that she felt that should this home be sold she would return a portion of the money derived to her brother as he was rightfully a part owner because of his contributions. This brother has also made contributions to his mother and at the time of this record is paying $40 a month plus certain payments on outstanding medical bills. At the present time, Mrs. Hanes is unable to contribute because of her family demands and the serious arthritic condition of her own husband.

The daughter Frances was married to John Ames in 1952. This proved to be a very happy marriage in itself, but it produced many overtones to others. Mr. Ames was previously married and, subsequent to the death of his first wife, his mother came into his home to live with him. She stated that no other woman would come into the home except over her dead body, and it was with this welcome that Frances took over her new home. This animosity on the part of Mrs. Ames, Sr., still exists and was only intensified when it became necessary to place her in a nursing home with a contribution from Mr. Ames of $100 a month.

Without fully realizing it, Mrs. Wilhelm suffered a severe psychological shock when her main source of security, Frances, was married. She had nothing but sincere praise for her son-in-law and reviews endlessly his desirable attributes. However, no one could give her the care or service that Frances had given.

On several occasions she became suddenly and seriously ill when Frances had gone away with her husband on business trips, necessitating Frances' immediate return. There was substance to her illness in that she suffers from a heart condition and Parkinson's disease; however, too frequently for it to be coincidental, a crisis arises when Frances is away. It would appear that she is unable to release her daughter and that she is using her illness to make demands upon the daughter's services and attention.

[3/15/57] After reviewing the living and relationship problems of Mrs. Wilhelm, worker decided to endeavor to help her and her daughter achieve greater independence of each other through a combination of discussions at periodic and strategic intervals with each of the persons involved, plus possibly auxiliary nursing and housekeeper services if and when indicated. One of the earliest steps was to hold several discussions in her home with Mrs. Ames concerning her mother's emotional dependency upon her. In the course of these discussions, Mrs. Ames gained a new perspective on her relationship to her mother. Gradually she was able to recognize that her own anger toward her mother, which she largely repressed, subtly communicated itself to Mrs. Wilhelm and only increased her mother's largely unconscious fear of losing her daughter. The crises occurred at those times when Mrs. Wilhelm's anxiety was heightened by the actual physical absence of her daughter. Through these discussions Frances gained additional insight into her own feeling-reactions and was better able to handle her negative feelings toward her mother and give her mother a more secure feeling of her daughter's love for her even though she must go with her husband.

The summary type of recording represented by this case record does not fully reveal all the steps in the process. However, we do see the worker assessing the problem situation, and forming the tentative hypothesis that Mrs. Wilhelm is made so anxious by actual or imminent separation from her daughter that crises occur in her otherwise chronic physical conditions. There is no implication that this is conscious on her part or that she could control the anxiety that wells up. The worker sees two people, in this instance a daughter and her mother, entrapped in a relationship that is handicapping to each of them. On one hand, the daughter is unable to separate herself sufficiently to devote herself fully to her new marriage and to achieving a new identity as a wife; and on the other, her mother is clinging to her daughter rather than finding new avenues of expression and relationship appropriate to her age and situation. The worker includes discussions with both mother and daughter to help each better to understand and hence manage their own feelings and to offer environmental services, specifically housekeeping service at strategic times to give Mrs.

Wilhelm the care she must have, which will substitute physically and
partly psychologically for her daughter.

"Why should the public assistance agency give this service?" Why,
in other words, should the agency concern itself with the relationship
problems of this elderly citizen and her daughter? Two kinds of answers
can be considered. First, the very practical one is that by doing so more
expensive medical or nursing care may be avoided, since it is quite obvious
Mrs. Wilhelm would so easily become a permanent bed patient. From our
knowledge of aged people we know that undoubtedly many thousands of
instances of permanent invalidism could have been avoided or at least
delayed by effective social services. The other answer goes to the point of
services to help aged people and those around them achieve a more personally satisfying pattern of living. Mrs. Wilhelm, as an example, seems
deeply involved in behavior destructive to her own and her daughter's
opportunity for personally satisfying and independent functioning. If there
is to be a service emphasis in the administration of old-age assistance, the
service illustrated by this example must be built into its administration of
the Aged program.

The remainder of the record shows the worker continuing and
enlarging her services to this family.

[8/28/57] Mrs. Ames was secretary for a small philanthropic fund
with offices located in a building at the rear of the Ames home but still on
their property area. The increased demands and serious condition of Mrs.
Wilhelm has required her to give up the work, and the foundation found
other quarters. The situation in the home became more complicated when
Mr. Ames, who holds a very responsible position as vice-president of the
Benevolent Insurance Company, had a stroke and heart attack with leg complication. Mrs. Ames also developed a kidney condition and had an accident
that required hospitalization. She was no longer able to meet the demands
made upon her, and the services of a housekeeper were required. Mrs. Wilhelm became practically a full-time bed patient, and the doctor ordered the
Ameses to get away for at least a month.

The services of the doctor, who was constructive in the psychological as
well as the physical field, together with the aid of a housekeeper and the
firm standing statement to the mother by Mrs. Ames that she and her husband would not return before the expiration of the month recommended,
served to be a challenge to our client. She began to believe that she could
improve, whereas on previous occasions when her daughter went away she
expressed fear she was not going to live and might go at any moment. Gradually she has become more emotionally independent.

Mrs. Wilhelm established her own home in the attractive house in the
rear of her daughter's home. She does her own cooking and stays alone at
night. Mrs. Ames is available when needed, as there are bad days, but the
present over-all picture is one of improvement far beyond anyone's expecta-

tions. Mr. Ames has been instructed by his doctor to have extended and frequent vacations, and each time a housekeeper becomes necessary. The entire program with the requirement of reporting need and income in the month it is indicated or forthcoming was reviewed with Mrs. Ames, who handles her mother's business, and she was admonished to follow this procedure to avoid complications with eligibility.

[1/22/58] Since our last contact with the client she has been doing remarkably well. The daughter has made the house in the rear, which formerly served as an office, into a very comfortable little apartment for our client. Here she is able to live as she wishes under the supervision of the daughter, but with a definite plan of remaining as independent as possible as long as possible. Mrs. Wilhelm is more distressed and upset at night than she is in the day so that she is up and about and disturbs others. When she is in her own quarters she is able to do the things that please her at the time, which gives her a complete freedom of action. She does not have to exert herself beyond a desirable point because the daughter is available to lend the hand and the service needed.

Mrs. Ames, the daughter, is planning to leave April 9th to go on an extended trip with her husband, which will be a mixture of business and pleasure. This should terminate around May 9th. In the meantime and upon the doctor's recommendation, someone will have to be available for Mrs. Wilhelm. Mrs. Ames has been able to obtain the services of a woman in her church, who will live in the home of Mrs. Ames at nighttime since there is no room in Mrs. Wilhelm's quarters and will do the shopping, cleaning, and supervising desired.

[5/15/58] Worker called several times in the home during the daughter's absence. The purpose of this was to keep up a contact in order to maintain the independence of Mrs. Wilhelm during her daughter's absence. Previously it had been the pattern of Mrs. Wilhelm to become ill either psychologically or physically during her daughter's absence, thus necessitating return home prior to the intended time. Each time worker visited, Mrs. Wilhelm had several complaints, which are talked out and prevented from becoming crises. She did have one little flare-up, which the housekeeper covered by calling for her doctor who was on vacation. The substitute doctor, Dr. Carter, proved so much more satisfactory to Mrs. Wilhelm that she changed to him as her permanent doctor. He has asked her to come in for an examination. This in itself will be therapeutic as she is getting some attention and someone professional is hearing her complaints. She is very enthusiastic in anticipation of each visit.

The housekeeper, Miss Christensen, is warm and understanding and has strengthened all the aspects of independence that have been carefully built by the daughter and the Department.

Worker was pleased to have Mrs. Wilhelm tell her of a long-distance call that the daughter had made at the home of a friend in the East where old associates were gathered and to whom client spoke in turn. She was encouraged and delighted over this experience, which proved to worker the strength of her independence. She might well have developed a physical reaction as has happened several times before during her daughter's absence.

[11/23/58]   During each of the absences of Mrs. Ames, the daughter, it had been necessary to have someone come to help Mrs. Wilhelm with the housework and to look in on her every day. However, about the first of September Mrs. Ames learned that her husband was being transferred to Miami. This was quite a blow to Mrs. Wilhelm. After considerable discussion of the matter with her daughter, worker and interested friends, she was able to accept it, at least on a thinking basis. It will take the doing to establish whether she will be able to accept it on a living basis. Mrs. Wilhelm has a very difficult time in relinquishing her daughter to the daughter's husband although there is no resentment over the marriage. She is quite proprietary in her relationship to them, but from their angle it is very fortunate that they are able to have this freedom and enjoy a home of their own for the first time in either of their lives.

Mrs. Ames worked out a plan to rent their home, which is in front of the client's, and in so doing, she found an interested family of three in which the wife was a trained nurse. The son of this couple suffers from multiple sclerosis, and the mother must care for him at all times. Since her presence at home was constantly required, it was felt that she could also look in on our client. A plan was worked out whereby she would see the client every day, be on call in case of the need of any professional service whatsoever day or night, and provide transportation, shopping and everything but cleaning. She stated she was not physically able to do the cleaning, and a cleaning woman, Mrs. Kineman, was obtained for four hours a week. Mrs. Kineman received $15, which included her transportation, and Mrs. Olgerson, the tenant and nurse, received $85. This amount was largely met by county supplements.

[3/16/59]   The daughter left January 31st for Miami, and the plan went into effect. As usual, Mrs. Wilhelm had a very difficult time in relinquishing the home of the daughter to a stranger. She worried over the lawn because the people had a dog, she felt that they were not watering it just the way her daughter had watered it, and she had many criticisms in many areas. Worker talked with her about the fact that perhaps no one would care for her daughter's property as she had herself and endeavored to help her not to notice these many discrepancies. With each discussion she would recognize that both she and Mrs. Ames were perfectionists and it would be the rare person who would carry on as meticulously as they.

From Mrs. Olgerson, worker received complaints that Mrs. Wilhelm was quite demanding in her requests. She even called one night at 10:30 and asked Mrs. Olgerson to ask her husband to go to the drugstore and get her some magnesia since she had found she was out. This was refused. On another occasion, at 9:00 or so, she called Mrs. Olgerson and asked her to come over and comb her hair. Mrs. Olgerson was afraid not to answer every request Mrs. Wilhelm made because of her severe heart condition and her Parkinson's disease with complications.

Things became so acute that Mrs. Olgerson discussed with the doctor on the case, Dr. Carter. Dr. Carter told her she was not a nurse on the case and that if the client had attacks in the night, which she began to claim and so inform Mrs. Olgerson, it was he who should be contacted and not Mrs. Olgerson. He would decide whether it was an acute thing, and if so, he would go. Worker feared that Mrs. Wilhelm was working herself up to a place where it would require the presence of her daughter, Mrs. Ames. Worker feared that the efforts to help Mrs. Wilhelm and her daughter to reduce their dependence upon each other were in great danger of being lost.

Just at this critical moment Mr. Olgerson was transferred by his company to a different city, and Mrs. Kineman, who was doing the cleaning, was requested by worker, after a discussion with Mrs. Wilhelm, to take over full care. Mrs. Wilhelm was very pleased about having Mrs. Kineman all of the time. Mrs. Kineman is able to see the basis of some of Mrs. Wilhelm's complaints and has a rather unusual ability to help her handle them in a positive way. Mrs. Kineman is known to the department from previous cases. It is expected that Mrs. Wilhelm will be able to live more peaceably having only the one relationship to maintain.

[8/27/59] Mrs. Ames is returning to the home briefly to rerent their house. Mrs. Wilhelm is feeling better in anticipation of her daughter's visit. Worker plans to suggest to Mrs. Ames that she encourage her mother to disregard the care of the property by the new tenant. If the relationship between Mrs. Wilhelm and the tenant can remain on a formal neighborly basis she will be less involved in their conduct. A situation could develop in which it would be difficult to keep a tenant. Perhaps Mrs. Kineman can help to anticipate and head off trouble between Mrs. Wilhelm and the new tenants.

[7/15/60] During the last year Mrs. Wilhelm has had severe heart attacks and had to be hospitalized. During the time that she was ill she had extra care at home, but more recently it has been possible to reduce this service in the housekeeping area to around two hours three times a week. According to the physician, she is able to do most of the routine work connected with housekeeping but she is unable to do anything of a heavy nature, and there are certain tasks that she cannot perform due to her Parkinson's disease. It would appear that the plateau she had reached in this area has been surpassed, and the disease is on the ascendancy.

Mrs. Wilhelm has been able to enjoy her home with the exception of some days when she is not up to par, but it has been remarkable how she has accepted the absence of her daughter.

Even during a period when Mrs. Wilhelm was in the hospital she did not demand the presence of her daughter by accentuating her condition. She seemed to accept it on a very realistic basis, and when the daughter phoned from Miami to inquire about her, she was glad to hear from her but she did not break because of it. This is quite in contrast to the way she likely would have behaved when first known to the agency. It will be recalled that it was the feeling not only of the worker but also of the doctor on the case that she dramatized her condition in order to get the daughter to come home.

A very interesting side light on the strength of her independence was given worker recently. Mrs. Wilhelm told of the inconsiderate attitude of Mrs. Ames, Sr., the mother of her daughter's husband, who is in a nursing home in another county. Mrs. Wilhelm had occasion to call Mrs. Ames, Sr. Mrs. Ames, Sr. was very upset because Mr. and Mrs. Ames, Jr. did not come from Miami for the holiday season. Mrs. Wilhelm chided her for expecting them to make such a long, expensive, and strenuous trip when the highways were so crowded and dangerous. She told Mrs. Ames that for her part she was glad they did not come because she would have been anxious for their welfare had they tried to do so under the existing circumstances of the season. Furthermore, she went on to say that they were both well and comfortable and she was glad to know that they were happy and she did not want to be selfish as far as she was concerned. This is certainly a new approach for Mrs. Wilhelm to be the one who is able to see the other's position and to chide the senior Mrs. Ames for being selfish. It certainly shows a switch in attitude.

When Mrs. Wilhelm told worker this incident, worker commended Mrs. Wilhelm for being understanding and independent. Mrs. Wilhelm seemed to appreciate being given this commendation and went on to say that she was interested in Frances enjoying herself and that as far as any comforts or needs were concerned she personally had no complaints.

Mrs. Wilhelm is more than satisfied with the housekeeper, who in herself is a stabilizing factor and has no doubt assisted in giving Mrs. Wilhelm such a sound and balanced attitude in addition to all the other efforts which have been exerted in that direction.

At the end of this record we see Mrs. Wilhelm moving purposely toward a new level of self-dependence. It is quite inspiring to see an elderly person, though faced with progressive and irreversible physical deterioration, achieve an inner integrity and an outer harmony at a higher level than perhaps any time in her previous living. Social workers who work with the aged frequently have this experience and sometimes can identify how their efforts contributed to the elderly person's achievement. It is a great satisfaction to have been part of such an experience, one that compensates for the many frustrations of being a social worker.

The case of Mrs. Wilhelm, illustrating services within the Old Age Assistance program, offers considerable contrast to the succeeding example, which is drawn from the Aid to Dependent Children program. The general purpose of services as expressed in the Social Security Act is to promote self-care and self-dependence with reference to the aged, while services with reference to families receiving ADC are intended to "strengthen family life." Certainly promoting self-care has many subtle and complex facets, as illustrated in the case of Mrs. Wilhelm, but the term is more precise than the phrase "strengthening family life." We cannot think about family life as a whole; we must first divide it up into aspects of family living, which then might become the focus of a social worker's attention. For example, we might focus upon child care, upon the marital relationship between the parents, money management, vocational and educational planning, or relationship of the family in its neighborhood and community. The particular focus of the social worker on a case at any particular time depends upon his perception of the problem as communicated to him by the client's behavior and by his verbal statements of the problem.

In the Webb case, which follows, the inability of Miss Webb to obtain employment may be the surface problem as the agency sees it, and beneath, Miss Webb's lack of motivation. Only if we are willing to think much more deeply about motivation and what contributes to its presence or absence with reference to a particular person in a specific situation can we gain the understanding for perceiving Miss Webb's problem in motivation. One danger is that of oversimplification, in this instance assuming that Miss Webb's only problem is lack of employment, and the social worker's task is to find her a job or exhort her to find one herself. If we study this example carefully, we gradually realize that Miss Webb's financial dependency is only a symptom of an underlying complex of feelings and attitudes, which may be partly described as attitudes about herself, feelings of lack of self-worth, and attitudes towards authority figures, meaning social workers in this instance. We can also speculate about how feelings about racial difference and discrimination are involved. The important point to remember, however, in studying this record, is that a human being always responds as a totality. We may be able to factor out certain of his attitudes and pieces of his behavior for closer study and to develop diagnostic hypotheses, but we know that each facet of his behavior is related to every other facet. For example, if Miss Webb's conception of herself and her own value as a human being improves more or less directly as a result of this social worker's genuine interest in and concern for her, we know this will probably affect positively her relationship to her child, tend to diminish her impulsive acting-out behavior, as well as help her mobilize herself more positively to think of her future with reference to employment.

Miss Webb

Miss Bessie Webb, a twenty-five-year-old Negro girl, has received ADC for her one child, Sandra, age six, for nearly four years covered by the span of this record. The record begins in January 1956 with her application for assistance on behalf of her out-of-wedlock child and shows continuous assistance through December 1960, the month this record was selected for inclusion in this chapter. The entries in the case record show repeated efforts exerted by a succession of workers to force or to "persuade" Miss Webb to secure employment—all without success. In late 1959 the agency decided to carry on intensive work with a group of cases, and Miss Webb was one of a random selection. The caseload that included Miss Webb numbered thirty, in contrast to the more usual several hundred.

This worker begins by summarizing all available knowledge of the case as a first step to understanding Miss Webb and her social and personal problems.

[12/10/59]   Preliminary Case Review. Bessie Ann Webb, age 25, is the ninth of ten children born to Jonas and Bertha Webb. She was born in Madison, Mississippi, 2/18/35. Her father, Jonas Webb, was married twice before, and there were two children of the previous marriages. Miss Webb lived with her family during childhood and, after completing high school, she worked on her brother's farm where she met Zachary Johnson, father of Sandra Webb, age 5. Shortly after Sandra's birth in 8/54, Miss Webb moved to Los Angeles and lived with her father, Jonas Webb, until she applied for Aid to Needy Children. She now lives with her daughter in a three room apartment. Miss Webb's parents are apparently separated, as Mr. Jonas Webb first established residence in California in 1944 or 1945. Mrs. Bertha Webb did not come to California until 1955. She lives in the home of her son. Mr. Jonas Webb is in his seventies, and an application for old age security was denied because of income from social security benefits. He was formerly employed as a shipyard worker, construction laborer, and was a member of the Hod Carriers Union. Mrs. Bertha Webb made an application for general relief in 1958, which was denied because she had not established three years residence. She now supports herself by baby-sitting. Several of Miss Webb's brothers and a sister live in Los Angeles. Brother James was Aid to Dependent Children recipient for several years, due to his being incapacitated (amputee). James Webb's son, Julius, was arrested in 1956 on a robbery charge and served one year sentence under the California Youth Authority. Sister Julia Webb is currently receiving Aid to Dependent Children for herself and three children. There was no legal marriage to any of the three fathers nor a home established. Sandra is presently suffering from anemia and frequent nosebleeds. She also appears to have frequent colds. When she was an infant her mother thought she had worms and treated her with home remedies. Miss Webb also suffers from frequent colds and nosebleeds. Miss Webb's only employment history has been in farm labor in Mississippi while working on her brother's farm. She has had a high school education and attended city business school for approximately two months before dropping out. She has expressed interest in various occupations, such as laundry work, vocational nursing, and restaurant work. However, she has not been able to follow through with definite plans for training or education courses. Recently she was refused a job because the prospective employer did not want "welfare workers" calling all the time to verify wages. Miss Webb appears to have some problems in income management. The

Welfare Department has been contacted frequently by clothing store and grocery because of delinquent accounts. Housing and housekeeping appear to be adequate. Case records indicate there has been steady improvement in this area over the past three or four years. Very little is known about Sandra's father, Zachary Johnson. Miss Webb knew him only as a farm laborer in the Madison, Mississippi area and knows nothing of his family background. He has not been located by any investigations, and the possibility of finding him and of obtaining support for the child seems remote. The primary problems seem to be Miss Webb's inability to plan constructively for herself and her future and to accept the responsibilities that this would involve. She has shown increasing apathy toward self-support and increasing hostility toward the agency on which she is dependent. She has made sporadic but unsuccessful attempts to find work, but without adequate plans or definite goals. She has been unable to use her education or profit from further training or follow through with anything she undertakes. She has also been unable to manage her financial resources adequately. The health problems that she and Sandra have could possibly be the result of poor nutrition and sanitation, indicating poor home management. It appears that every effort should be made to help Miss Webb make constructive and realistic plans for herself and the child, emphasizing goals that can be reached and that would give her a satisfying sense of achievement. Miss Webb may be able to become self-supporting if continued encouragement and help are given in this direction.

It is evident at the end of his summary that this worker is beginning to think of Miss Webb and what might be of concern to her and solutions to her problems as she sees them, rather than being concerned only with the agency's objective of getting Miss Webb off assistance. Actually it is incorrect to state this last as an agency objective because truly the agency's objective is a much broader one, typically stated as "strengthening family life." It is a tragic fact, however, that in California public pressure has combined with the prejudices and inadequacies of public welfare administrative personnel to produce a "climate" in which all too often workers behave as if the agency's only interest was to get its clients off assistance and to become self-supporting. Certainly this is an appropriate goal in many instances, and one that most clients seek for themselves. Space does not permit us to explore here the complexities of the "to work or not to work" dilemma that harasses public assistance worker and client alike. Turning again to the case of Miss Webb, we see how the worker helps this client to begin the process of breaking out of the social and psychological trap she is in and move toward a better way of living for her own, that is, Miss Webb's sake, not for the sake of just getting her off aid.

[1/7/60]   A home call was made this date with Miss Webb and her daughter Sandra. Miss Webb is a very tall, slightly obese and robust looking woman. Her personal appearance is quite untidy, her clothes are seldom buttoned or pressed, and her hair uncombed. The home appeared to be nicely furnished and well kept, but very dark and gloomy. The Webb's apartment is in the basement of the house, and there are few windows and very little light. All the curtains were drawn so that no light entered the house nor were there any electric lights turned on. Sandra seemed to be a very bright, active and alert five-year-old girl; her intelligence seemed normal or above. She talks quite easily and well for her age and seems to enjoy talking about school and the kindergarten activities, which she enjoyed. She was nicely dressed. Her clothes were very neat, and her hair was combed and neat.

When I arrived, Miss Webb took several minutes to answer the door. She said that she was sorry but she had not been feeling well and had been lying down, asleep. I asked if she had been ill, and she said that she had recently been in the hospital because of something that was wrong with her throat. She had some kind of an obstruction or a tumor pressing there, and it was very difficult for her to breathe. When she went to County Clinic they decided she should be admitted to the hospital. She stayed two days, but they were unable to discover what the trouble was. She is going to make another appointment in the next two weeks to go to the clinic again for further tests. She stated the doctor had told her it might be necessary for her to come back to the hospital for an operation on her throat. She was quite worried about this because she didn't know how Sandra would be cared for if she had to be hospitalized again. Her mother had fortunately been able to come to Los Angeles from Seattle when she was in the hospital in November, but she did not know if her mother would be able to do this again. She said that there were no relatives or friends in this area who could care for Sandra if she had to be absent from the home. I asked her about Sandra's health. Miss Webb replied that she was much better than she had been, now that they were going to Dr. Holcomb, on 20th Street. She did not know what was wrong with Sandra but thought the doctor had told her that Sandra had a preluekemia condition. However, the doctor had prescribed medicine for Sandra, and she now seemed to be doing much better and didn't have the frequent colds and nosebleeds she had previously. Miss Webb then said that the medicine was something of a problem because it had to be kept under refrigeration, and her refrigerator was now broken and couldn't be used. I asked if the refrigerator could be repaired or if she thought she was going to need a new one, and explained that we would be able to help with monthly payments for either repairs or replacement of the refrigerator. Miss Webb said that in that case she would get a repair man and see if the refrigerator could be fixed and, if not, try to find a replacement and let me know what the price was. I explained what the maximum price allowance would be so that she could keep this in mind while looking at refrigerators. I also explained that we would try to help financially if it was necessary to find some one to care for Sandra while she was hospitalized again. I also explained to Miss Webb that I would be able to see her quite frequently, as often as once a week, if she would like this, to talk over any problems that she might have or any plans for the future with which we could be of some help. Miss Webb then said that she had been very discouraged in the past few years about finding a job and ever becoming self-supporting again. She said that every time she tried to look for work or thought she had found a job, it seemed as though this agency had prevented her from being able to follow through on this because of the regulations and things that the social workers wanted done. She explained that she had applied for a job at Jones Department Store, and it had been offered to her until she told them she had received aid from the Welfare Department. They then told her that they would not hire anyone who was receiving assistance because it was just too much trouble with social workers calling all the time and asking about wages. She also stated that her last social worker had told her that if she did go to work, she had to know where it was and who her employer was so that he could call there to verify her wages. She felt this was unreasonable and felt a great deal of resentment at having this demanded of her. I explained to her that this would certainly not be necessary now and if she wished to find a job it was not necessary for her to tell her employer that she was receiving public assistance if she did not wish to do this. We would, of course, have to have some idea of what her wages were, but she could arrange with her employer for a statement of her wages or might possibly receive an itemized wage stub, which would give us all the information which we needed.

Miss Webb seemed to be somewhat reassured by the help that I offered during this visit to meet various problems she and Sandra had. However, she still seemed deeply suspicious and resentful of the agency in general and anyone who represented it. She appears quite anxious to regain some measure of independence but too discouraged over the situation in which she finds herself to be able to make any plans or really constructive efforts to help herself.

Notable in this worker's first home visit with the client is his concern with the problems that are facing Miss Webb and the offering of concrete help to do something about these problems. It is also most remarkable that Miss Webb brings up the subject of employment but in quite a different way and at a point in the interview after she had felt this worker was truly interested in helping her. Her bitterness toward the agency comes out around this point, and the worker's sound and unruffled handling of Miss Webb's feelings were most reassuring to the client.

[1/20/60] Home call with Miss Webb. The home appeared much the same as it had been on my first call, with the curtains all drawn, no light in the apartment, and everything appearing very dark and gloomy. Miss Webb had also been lying down and had to get up and dress before she could come to the door and let me in. She again said that she had not been feeling well, in fact she had not even felt well enough to keep her appointment at County Clinic or to make a new one. She has apparently avoided returning for another check up for one or two months. We discussed briefly again possible plans that she might make for Sandra's care if she should have to be hospitalized. Miss Webb again said that there was no family in the area who could care for Sandra, nor did she have any friends who might be able to take care of the girl, nor anyone who she knew of that she could even hire to stay with Sandra for the time that she might be gone. I explained again that we would be able to assist financially if it were necessary to find someone to live in their home to care for Sandra, but that it might be a problem to find a person without a few days notice. However, we would do whatever possible to help in finding a suitable person to care for Sandra if this were ever necessary.

Miss Webb said that she had sent in estimates for a new refrigerator to me a few days before and was most anxious to know if she could go ahead and buy the one she wanted. The cost was within the price we could allow, and I suggested that she try to arrange for monthly payments right away so that the extra money could be sent to her as soon as possible. Miss Webb said that she hoped it would be soon as she was worried about not being able to give Sandra the medicine that she needed and did not want her to be sick again. Sandra had not shown any ill effects so far and was not having any health problems at the present time.

Miss Webb then brought up the subject of going to work, and that she would like to find a job. I asked her what she thought she would like to do and what her previous experience had been. She said that she had completed high school in Mississippi but had only done farm work before she came to California; for a brief period she had worked in a laundry and in a cafeteria after coming to Los Angeles; but she thought what she would really like to do would be vocational nursing or something similar. I agreed that this was a very good field and asked if she had ever done this kind of work. She said no, but she thought she could do it. I suggested that perhaps she would be able to find a school that would give her some training in this work and help her find a job as a nurse or a nurse's aid. She thought this would be alright too, if it didn't take too long. She had become very discouraged once before when attending Franklin Trade School taking secretarial and clerical work. She had dropped out of the school because of illness and the feeling that she was not accomplishing anything. The one obstacle, she felt, to finding employment was the child care problem. And she had no idea how Sandra could be cared for. She did not know about the state child care centers, so I explained what these centers were and how Sandra's care could possibly be arranged for there. I asked her if she thought going to the employment office might be helpful too. Miss Webb said that she had become very discouraged with the State Employment Office. They never seem to offer her any encouragement or be of any help in referring her to any kind of job. She said that she did not want to do domestic work, that she didn't like it and didn't feel it was something she could do permanently and successfully, and other than this, she had not found the employment office very helpful. She said it was also difficult even to find a job as a domestic without any previous experience. She also said that she was thinking of looking for a laundry job as she had also done this work briefly at one time. She was worried however about the cost of this since she had to join the union if she did get a job, and it was sometimes expensive. She then talked further about her discouragement in general, with looking for work, and the apparent hopelessness of ever finding anything that she could do and that she would like. She then expressed her resentment and feeling that the Welfare Department had never helped her in this regard but always prevented her from finding employment and made it impossible to find something to do.

I found during this interview that Miss Webb was even more apathetic and hostile in her reactions to me and the agency and that it was quite difficult to talk to her without asking repeated questions about previous jobs and what she would like to do and what plans she had made. She would seldom talk for long on any one subject without looking down without any apparent interest or desire to discuss these problems. She did however seem interested, slightly, when I offered to get any information I could on vocational nursing and nurse's aid courses that might be available to her. I said that I would bring the information with me on my next visit so that she could decide if she wished to try to take advantage of further education or training.

In this interview the full force of Miss Webb's discouragement comes through, and it even seems that the worker is momentarily thrown by it. The drawn blinds, the dark apartment, and the unkempt personal appearance were suggestive of her discouragement and depression. Only at the end of the interview, after she had felt the security of this worker's acceptance and concern for her, was she able to plumb the depths of her depression. Is it necessary, we might ask, for a person to "hit bottom" as it were, before he (Miss Webb in this instance) can start the long climb up again? Do we see her courage and strength begin to reemerge in the next home interview?

[2/10/60]   Home call to Miss Webb. She said the refrigerator had been delivered, and every thing was much better now. She had also received the supplementary check for January and February to make her first payment. She felt that Sandra had no real health problems now, especially since she was able to have her medicine regularly, and the only thing she was concerned about was finishing Sandra's polio shots, which had been started several months before. She asked if I could tell her where she could get the shots for Sandra, and I said that I would find out the nearest public health clinic and hours that they were open and bring her the information on my next visit. We talked a little more about Sandra and how Sandra was doing in school and what kind of care she would like for Sandra if she did go to work. I said that I could see that Sandra was very important to her and that she would certainly want to know that Sandra was being well cared for if she couldn't be there. Miss Webb said, yes, Sandra was very important to her, probably the most important thing in her life. She realized that in many ways she had made a mistake in having Sandra but she

said this was "the best mistake I ever made." Miss Webb went on to talk
about problems and discouragements she had had in looking for jobs and
her hopes for finding suitable employment or training in the future. She was
not really sure she still knew what she wanted to do or what she would like
to try to aim for. One of the reasons she felt so discouraged about the future
was the problem of racial discrimination, which she felt quite keenly about.
She felt there was really so little hope and so little reason to try to find a
good job, since so very few of these were open to Negroes. We talked further about this problem, and Miss Webb expressed a lot of her feelings of
resentment and hostility over treatment that she received because of
her race and talked about the hopeless feeling she had about trying to do
anything for herself. However, at the end of the interview she did say that
she guessed you just had to keep trying, that you couldn't sit back and do
nothing because of all these things. She also said that perhaps if people like
social workers would only help a little instead of just making it harder for
people to do things, she thought she would also have a better chance of getting somewhere. Then she said, "You know I really can't quite trust you, I
have had so many disappointments. So far you seem much nicer than all
the others but I just can't be sure." I said that I realized this must be difficult for her because of many of the experiences that she had had but that
I hoped she could believe that I would like to be of some help to her and
that she could learn to trust me in the future.

[2/24/60]   Home call with Miss Webb. She said that both she and
Sandra had had the flu this month and been quite sick; however, she feels
much better now, and Sandra seems to be alright and is back in school.
Miss Webb then asked about insurance for Sandra. She said she would like
to have some protection and a policy on Sandra's life. I explained the allowances that we could make for insurance protection just as we now included
the premium on Miss Webb's insurance on her ADC budget. She said that
she would talk to her insurance agent and see about taking out a policy to
be effective about May, when the refrigerator payments were up and she
would have room in her budget for some other additional needs like insurance.

Miss Webb said that she was still anxious to find work and that, whenever she had an opportunity, she went looking for any jobs that might be
available. She had been particularly applying for laundry jobs and waitress
work, in which she had had a little experience. She also felt these might be
fairly easy things to find work in; however, she hadn't yet been successful.
She said that she felt she had to do something, that she was becoming so
depressed just sitting around the house all day. I asked about the courses
that she had mentioned earlier that she had been taking at Franklin Trade
School and if she had enjoyed these and had attended school long enough
to be able to use what she had learned. She said that she had been taking
secretarial courses, including filing, arithmetic, and typing but had become
pretty discouraged and had not really been doing too well. She had enjoyed the filing course very much and thought that she would really enjoy
doing something in the clerical field but because of her discouragement she

had quit going to school. This was when she had gone back to Mississippi on a visit and had become pregnant and Sandra had been born. She had gone back to Franklin Trade to see about getting admitted to school again but something had gone wrong. They had said that they would notify her about her application, but she had never heard anything more from the school.

Miss Webb said one of her other problems was in being able to save enough money out of her check each month for transportation to just look for work. There never seemed to be enough left over after she had paid her rent and put aside enough money for food and perhaps for clothes, which Sandra needed, so that she could make more than one extra trip a month. I said that perhaps this was one way that we could be of more help to her and that we were able usually to make extra allowances in her budget for transportation that was needed. I suggested that we plan to discuss this on my next visit and decide how much she was going to need for transportation each month so that we could add this to her budget for the future.

[3/9/60] Home call with Miss Webb. When I first came in on this visit, I felt that something was wrong. Miss Webb seemed to have returned to her earlier strongly hostile and suspicious attitude, which had been missing the last two or three visits. She hardly replied to my first questions of how she and Sandra were feeling, and I finally sat quietly with her without talking for several minutes, hoping that she would explain what was troubling her. She finally looked up and said, "I wish you would tell me why you keep coming out here all the time. Are you investigating me?" I said no, but perhaps I had not explained well enough on my first visit the purpose of this special project and why I would be coming to see her so often. I explained all this again to Miss Webb, answering any questions that she had. She finally asked, "What do you think you are going to prove with all this?" I said I did not know if we were really going to or even attempting to prove anything but that we were interested in her and in knowing about her feelings toward the ANC program and in knowing from her what ways we could be helpful to her. This seemed to be a satisfactory answer to her questions because she then went on to other subjects in a much more relaxed manner. Miss Webb talked about possibly investigating some further training for herself. She said she thought she would go down this week to City College and see again about enrolling in some courses since she had heard nothing further from them. We also discussed child care possibilities, and she asked for more information about child care centers and if there might be any nearby for Sandra.

Suddenly Miss Webb has to test again the genuineness of the worker's concern for her. It comes out as suspicion expressed around why the worker is seeing her so often, something she has realized is unusual in the light of her previous experience with the agency. This incident should be seen for what it really is, a vigorous reassertion of Miss Webb's old fear and doubt that anyone could really be interested in helping her for her own sake. However, the worker handles it in a straightforward fashion, and Miss Webb's fear seems put at rest, at least temporarily. In the next interviews, we see the quality of this worker's relationship to Miss Webb begin to have real substance as Miss Webb is able to talk about her feelings about Sandra's father, the meaning of Sandra to her, and many other important facets of her life. We can clearly sense the way she is using the worker to "put things in place" in her life, so that she can start living it more freely and effectively. It is noteworthy that immediately after this interview Miss Webb makes her first positive and successful move toward self-support. Then when she loses this job we see the discouragement emerge again, particularly because she did not know why she was discharged. Perhaps again the old fear and suspicion were awakened by this experience, but with calm and concerned handling from the worker she moves on in a new direction to the end of this record.

[3/23/60]   Miss Webb said that Sandra had been home sick for a week and she expected that she would be out of school for another week or possibly two. She would have to wait to go to the Prosecuting Attorney's office until Sandra was back in school but she would try to go as soon as possible because she knew this was something that had to be done every year. Miss Webb then went on to talk about her feelings at having to go through this referral each year and going down to the prosecuting attorney's office. She said this was terribly hard for her to do. She didn't like their attitude and all the questions they asked. She couldn't see why they had any right to ask her the kind of things that they did. She said, "Why do they want to know what my relationship to him was and number of times we had sexual relations and other things like that?" She also said, "I don't like the way they talk down to me. I know what is right and what is wrong, and everyone is certainly entitled to one mistake. I knew what I was doing and I knew it was wrong, but everybody can make a mistake once. Why do they have to keep bringing it up? I see other women with eight and ten children and at least I only have one." She also felt it was wrong to try to force a father who doesn't love his child to contribute to the child's support. She felt this would only hurt the child to know that his father was being forced into doing something like this. I asked if she felt the father shouldn't be held responsible, and she said, no, she felt the father should be, but women always end up having to take the responsibility anyway, so what was the use in trying to make things any different. She said obviously Sandra's father didn't love her because he had never even seen her and never attempted to. She doesn't think he had any feelings for her or the baby. She believes that he is married now with a family of his own, but she doesn't know where he is and really doesn't care. She thinks he would probably deny paternity anyway even if they could locate him. She also said that she thought the prosecuting attorney's office could probably locate him if they wanted to and really tried, but what was the use of trying to locate him when they only put him in jail anyway. I asked her about her own feelings about Mr. Johnson and if she had thought about marriage at the time. She said that she was glad that they hadn't married because it wouldn't have worked out for either of them, and she really didn't think she wanted to marry him at the time. However, it didn't mean that she didn't want to get married someday because "doesn't every woman want to do this?" She went on to talk about her feelings about everyone needing some kind of social life and a life of one's own. She thought this was necessary to be a real person and important in being a good mother to Sandra. If she wasn't satisfied with her own life, she didn't think she could be a very good mother to Sandra. There were lots of times when she felt very irritated with her little girl and got tired of her complaints and all the things that she had to do for her and felt that she just had to have some outside interests; however, she wouldn't change anything, and it had certainly been worth having her. In fact she didn't know what she would do without Sandra. She has been her whole life and her only reason for living. Miss Webb said that she thought she would have gone mad or become something horrible without Sandra and she thanks God every day for her because she has given some meaning to her life and something to live for. I asked why she felt this way and if there hadn't been other interests in her life as well or relationships with other people or family that had been important to her. She said she didn't know, she had just been so desperate at the time and had to have something; she thinks this is what made her go out and have Sandra.

She went on to talk about her family. She said she had gotten along pretty well with all of them, although her father had been away quite a bit of the time. She got along well with her brothers. Her mother had had six boys and then had wanted a girl very badly, and they had been very happy when her older sister was born. I asked if then they weren't pleased that she was a girl too. Miss Webb said she didn't know, at least not so anyone would notice. She said her sister lived in this area. I asked if she saw her much and if they got along pretty well now. Miss Webb gave a little laugh and said only a psychiatrist could help straighten out their relationship. I asked if she could explain what she meant by that, and she laughed again and said she didn't know, they just didn't seem to get along well and went on to talk about other things for the rest of the interview.

[4/14/60] Phone call from Miss Webb. Miss Webb said that she had been unable to be home for the appointment the week before because she had heard about a job and had to go see about it, and she was going to start work this week. She was going to be working for the American Motel in San Fernando as a motel maid. Her earnings would not be high at first because she was only going to be the relief maid. She hoped that I would not call her employer because he did not know that she was receiving any kind of assistance and usually would not hire anybody who was receiving welfare aid; not only she but also the friend who had helped her get the job would be in trouble if he found out about this. I assured her that I would not contact her employer, but explained again that we would have to have some way of verifying her wages regularly and that, if she did get a check stub when she was paid, she should keep these so that I could see them on my next visit. I also made an appointment to make a home call on 4/18/60 to discuss anything she might need to start the job.

[4/18/60]   Home call with Miss Webb. Miss Webb explained more fully about the job, which she now has. Three weeks out of the month she expects to be working five days a week, and one week of the month she will work three days. She expects to get between $18 and $30 a week but she was not sure just exactly how much it would be until after her first few pay checks. She has a friend who is going to baby-sit with Sandra while she is working and who will charge her $12.50 a week for this. She will take care of her in the morning and see that she gets off to school in the afternoons and also will pick her up from school if Miss Webb is not through work in time. Her hours are usually 9 to 3:30 but sometimes she has to work a little late. Miss Webb said that she is also going to need uniforms for work. She has been able to borrow one from a friend but is going to need at least two to continue working. We made arrangements to include the cost of two uniforms in her budget. Her transportation expenses were also discussed so that this could be deducted from her wages.

[4/21/60]   Phone message was received from Miss Webb saying that she had gotten her first pay check today and that she had a wage stub, which showed what her earnings were and the deductions from her earnings, and that she would keep this for my next visit.

[4/25/60]   Home call with Miss Webb. Miss Webb had her first wage stub for her employment from April 14 to April 21. The amount of net earnings was $27.90. We discussed what her total income from the month would be and her total expenses and decided that she would probably have no actual income for the month of April so that there would not have to be any adjustment in her check for the following month. Miss Webb said that she was really feeling very good about starting to work and it had certainly made great difference to her in how she felt about things. The work was pretty hard, and she found she got pretty tired, but even so it was worth it. She had real feeling of being useful again and of accomplishing things. She even felt that her health was much better and she thought that maybe a lot of things that had been wrong with her were really due to the depression that she felt over sitting around the house all the time. She thought that maybe the only cure that she needed was to go to work and get back a little self-respect.

The rest of the interview was taken up with discussing what her future earnings and expenses were going to be and figuring how this was to affect her budget and the amount of her check so that she would be able to plan her monthly expenditures.

[5/11/60]   Home call with Miss Webb. Miss Webb had more wage stubs to show me of her earnings for the past two weeks. We again spent some time discussing her earnings and expenses and what the budget changes would be for June and July. Miss Webb said that she was still finding work very satisfactory. She liked her employer very much because he left everyone alone to do their work and never bothered anyone if they did a good job. She liked to work for someone like this because she hated to have someone standing over her all the time telling her what to do; she was always willing to work and worked very hard if she was just given a chance. She was also not discouraged by the actual amount of money that she was earning each month. With all the expenses of transportation and baby-sitting, she really earned very little but she felt that, if she proved herself and kept working hard, she would probably get a raise in a few months; there was also the possibility of becoming a permanent employee and not just the relief maid. This would mean more hours of work and a higher rate of pay, which would also help. She did not know if this was the kind of job that she wanted to have permanently but she felt she was getting good experience and was at least working at something, which was the important thing for her right now. She thought that, if she were able to continue working like this, she might be able to go to school afternoons or evenings and take some courses, which would help her get a better job in the future. In the meantime, she was content to just be doing what she was and liked the feeling of accomplishment it was giving her.

[5/16/60]   Phone call from Miss Webb. She said she had been quite ill for the past week and had not been able to work. She had had a bad infection, and the doctor had wanted to send her to the hospital, but she had finally gotten over the worst of it by staying home and in bed for a few days; she was now up and going to start back to work again. However, she wanted to let me know that her earnings would be less in May because of the time while she was sick.

[5/25/60]   Home call with Miss Webb. Miss Webb said that she had started back to work; however, she still was not feeling too well. She had had a bladder infection, which was extremely painful, and she had really been quite sick. She was going to the doctor still for shots and seemed to be clearing up, but it had made working pretty difficult; however, she was determined to keep on with this job and not lose it. We discussed changes in income in May because of her sickness. She said that she had had the same expenses for baby-sitting because the woman had kept Sandra all the days that she was sick because she was really quite unable to take care of Sandra during that time. She had also had to pay someone to come in and do a few things around the house and get a few meals for her and Sandra and she hoped that this could also be deducted from her wages this month. I said that we would try to consider all these things in her budget and that on my next visit, when she would know the total amount she had earned in May, we could see definitely what the changes would be.

[6/8/60]   Home call with Miss Webb. Miss Webb said that her health was much better and, although she did not feel completely well, she was continuing to work and felt she was making gradual improvement. She continued to be under the doctor's care and was taking medicine that he prescribed for her. We discussed her earnings and new budget in view of the numerous expenses that she had had in May. Her May wages were also verified. There were no net earnings. I explained the budget changes and resulting increase in grant. Miss Webb said that Sandra was getting along well, although she still had some problems in getting her to eat enough and keeping her weight up to a reasonable level. The little girl is quite thin and still tires quite easily. She thought that Sandra did miss her quite a bit now that she was working and this might be even worse when school was out and Sandra would be free all day. However, she thought she was adjusting fairly well to the new situation.

[6/30/60]   Phone call from Miss Webb. She said that she had gotten the appointment date confused and had not realized that I would be visiting her yesterday. She had been at her brother's, as her mother had come from Seattle on a visit. She reported her June earnings and we made a new appointment for a home visit.

[8/3/60]   Home call with Miss Webb and Sandra. Miss Webb said that she had not been working quite as much lately and her earnings were considerably lower. We reviewed her June and July wage stubs and discussed budget changes and the changes that she would have in her ADC grant for those months. Miss Webb said that she was feeling much better in general and about the only health problem had been an occasional recurrence of the difficulty in her throat, which made it hard for her to breathe. The doctor had still not been able to decide what the trouble was although he was giving her some medicine, which made it easier for her to swallow and eased the pain. She said that Sandra had been quite well and was not having any health problems at the present time. Miss Webb said that she was still enjoying her work and the feeling of independence that it gave her, but she has now definitely made up her mind that she wanted to better herself and try to get some training that would fit her for a better job. She said she thought she would try to go to night school beginning in the fall, as she thought that City College had evening courses. She did not want to give up the job that she had, so she felt night school would be preferable to enrolling in an all day course. We also discussed the possibilities there might be in the various adult schools. She thought commercial subjects, typing, bookkeeping, and possibly business machines, would be the best field for her to pursue. We discussed possible costs that she might have and ways of budgeting for these, such as tuition and books, transportation, and additional child care for Sandra. She thought that the woman who kept Sandra might keep her for the evening hours when she would be in school as well.

Miss Webb said that she felt that she had gained a great deal of confidence in herself in these few months of working and that she would have no difficulty with school and could accomplish things. She does not think she would like to be just a motel maid for the rest of her life but would really like to try to learn to do something better and to make an enjoyable and satisfactory life for herself and Sandra.

[8/17/60, 8/24/60, 8/31/60]   Home call with Miss Webb.

Summary of Case Contacts in August 1960

Miss Webb reported that she had been laid off from her job the week before. She said she was disappointed about this naturally but was not going to let herself be discouraged. Her employer had not given her any real reason for dismissing her quite abruptly; since she had done her work, she felt, quite well, she did not believe that it was her fault. She had made some kind of an error, which she had used as an excuse; but since she had apparently always done her work well, and he had never found fault with her before, she thought there must be some other reason. In spite of the disappointment of losing the job, she felt even more determined to go ahead with her plans for school in the fall. She now felt that perhaps a full-time course at Franklin Trade School would be the best plan. We talked over all the things she would need to do, and she said she would go down and take the entrance examination this week and find out what her costs would be. We made arrangements for another home call in a week to discuss her plans further.

At the next visit, Miss Webb was rather discouraged. She had taken the entrance examination and was quite sure that she had flunked it and would not be able to enter Franklin in the fall semester. However, since she had not heard the results yet or talked to a counselor, things were not definitely settled. In spite of her discouragement over the test and the probable result, we proceeded to make plans for her return to school. We discussed various things like the transportation costs and baby-sitting costs if she did have full-time classes. There was also the matter of clothes for starting school. Miss Webb has a very difficult problem because she is quite tall, close to six feet, and wears an extremely large shoe size, and she practically always has to pay extra for shoes and clothes. We worked out a plan to add the cost of a pair of shoes and a skirt and sweaters to the grant so that she would have some clothes with which to start school.

Miss Webb seemed quite encouraged by these offers of concrete help with her plans, and said at the end of the interview that for the first time in many years she felt someone was really helping her, and she did appreciate it. She phoned at the end of the month and said that she had just heard from Franklin and had been accepted for the fall semester. Her test score had been low; she would be on probation for the first six months but she felt she could make it because she was going to try very hard. We made arrangements for her to come into the office to make verification of her expenses for books and fees and to fill out the GA application form, which was necessary so that a supplement could be arranged for.

[9/6/60] Miss Webb phoned to say that she started school today, and had found out that most of her classes would be in the afternoon for the first semester. She would come in to the office in the morning to complete the forms we had talked about.

At the office visit of this date we mainly discussed Miss Webb's expenses and changes in the ANC grant. She had brought two receipts for her registration fees and her books and a statement from the baby-sitter on the cost of child care that would be charged.

[10/19/60]   Home call with Miss Webb. Miss Webb mainly discussed the experiences she had been having in her first month and a half. She spoke about the differences between going to Franklin several years ago and going to school now. She feels that she is doing much better and has much more interest in what she is doing. She said that she had gotten a "C" on her reading midterm and is not sure what her math grade will be, but feels that she is doing much better than expected. She is making very good progress in typing and is very pleased about this. Her other class is in psychology, which she is finding interesting. We talked further about her progress and accomplishments and about her goals for the future.

Miss Webb also asked about the project and the differences that existed between social workers and the treatment that she had had in the past and the type of help she was getting now. I asked her why she felt that there was a difference, and she talked about all the things that had happened in the past few months and the ways that she felt that I had been more helpful and had encouraged her to do things for herself. She felt that her feelings about the Agency had changed somewhat and that she was losing the feeling that everyone was against her.

We also talked briefly about medical needs that Miss Webb has. She still has trouble with her throat occasionally and feels that she should go back to the hospital or to a doctor for a checkup. She is also in need of some dental work, and possibly an eye examination.

[11/15/60]   Home call with Miss Webb. Sandra was also home at this visit, having just come down with chicken pox. Miss Webb said that she was not feeling too well as she had had a very bad cold, but had not had to miss any school over this. We continued our discussion of the week before about school and the things she was doing, and Miss Webb said that she continues to be very encouraged by her grades and things that she was learning. She said that she was on the honor roll in typing and one of the top ones in the class. She also felt that she was doing well in math and her reading was improved. We talked a little about her goals for the future and the kind of courses she would take in the next semester. She felt that she might have to transfer to the City College campus, as Franklin only offered typing and none of the more advanced courses in office practice.

[12/6/60]   Home call with Miss Webb. We continued to talk about her progress in school at this visit, and Miss Webb reviewed the progress that she had made in this first semester, which would be ending in January. She was doing so well in her math class that her instructor had told her he wanted to put her up into the next group, since she had reviewed practically the entire course. She had just about doubled her reading speed since entering the reading lab course but felt a little discouraged about this, as she still did not feel she was doing well enough. Her typing class continued to be interesting and she was now typing fifty words a minute and was very pleased with this progress. She was also enjoying her psychology class and was getting to write a paper and had been doing research for this, which she found very enjoyable. She said that Sandra was almost as excited as she was about going to school and they both study together. Frequently Sandra would come home from school and want to do lessons too and would insist upon reading whatever she had read in school that day and doing lessons just like her mother. Sometimes Miss Webb felt that she simply couldn't get everything done in one day with all the schoolwork and studying and care of Sandra that had to be accomplished. However, she was so pleased with the progress she was making that she really felt that the future held something for her and that she would be able to get ahead. She felt for the first time in her life, that she actually could make plans for the future and could achieve them.

At the end of the record we see quite a different Miss Webb than the person who less than a year before was suspicious and hostile toward the public assistance worker, discouraged and angry with herself, and who had minor physical problems, probably exacerbated by her emotional tension. Again we can speculate about the satisfaction it must be to this daughter of a poverty-stricken sharecropper to acquire new knowledge and learn new skills that mean raising herself above her background. Generalizing from this one example, we can hypothesize that perhaps one of the most important ways public assistance workers could help individual ADC mothers reduce repeated illegitimate pregnancies is to help them gain an appreciation of their own value and worth as persons. The worker's consistent interest in and concern for the individual is a first step; helping her acquire new goals, new skills, a new opportunity to be a "somebody" who has something important to offer society and a chance to achieve a status within that society—these are the ingredients of ego strength that add up to improved impulse control.

It is left to the reader of this chapter to consider the many questions that are stimulated by the cases of Mrs. Wilhelm and of Miss Webb. It can be a rewarding experience to think deeply about the panorama of human behavior revealed by just these two examples of actual case records drawn from public assistance agencies, changed only enough to disguise their true identity.

8

WELFARE
SERVICES
FOR CHILDREN

The child in his family and group

Anyone who gives thought to the welfare of a child or of children must realize, inevitably, that what affects the interests of children affects the well-being of the entire group of which the child is but one member. To give some substance to these observations, let us examine certain situations involving the welfare of children to see how interrelated the world of the child is with that of the adult in the total community in which they both live. A child is born. Simply from the aspect of physical health, many antecedent conditions must exist in order to insure the child a decent start at birth. How healthy his parents are, how healthy other people are, how much public health there is in the community, these and many other factors determine what the newborn's start will be. The child grows up and begins to acquire an awareness of the world around him. We impress him into a school system. The kind of education he receives is determined not so much upon his native endowment as it is by the amount and quality of education which people unrelated and unknown to him possess. He enters the labor market. The kind of job he gets depends to some extent upon his innate capacity, but more largely is related to the economic organization of his own or other communities. Nor are his opportunities unaffected by such things as the state of the labor market, depression, and prosperity. His prior health experience and vocational training, or lack of it, determine his present availability for a low-pay or a high-pay job, a dead-end job or one that offers a chance for advancement and personal development. What is stressed here is the fact that a child comes into a world already made by other people, that his chance of survival in it and the possibilities of his own effective participation in it are matters usually beyond his control. The immediate bearing of these remarks is to make clear that child welfare services are not services for the child alone, but are part and parcel of the organization of community resources for the well-being of the whole group. They reflect the value the community places upon the child.

Apprenticeship and indenture

By the time Queen Elizabeth had come to the throne of England in 1558 feudalism had given way to the early stage of capitalism. It was Elizabeth's statute in the forty-third year of her reign that set the precedent for modern states in the definition of responsibility for certain disfavored groups within the community, among them certain classes of children. The system of indenture and apprenticeship by which a child was bound over (that is, indentured—the legal instrument was called an indenture) to another person or family was a pronounced development following 1601. As was so characteristic of much of the Elizabethan experience, this system spread to America. Indenture and apprenticeship as a means of dealing with children without support seemed a natural transplantation to colonial soil on this side, and it was quickly adopted, for the earliest record indicates that in 1636 little Benjamin Eaton was indentured by the Governor of Plymouth Colony to Bridget Fuller, a widow. Widow Fuller was to keep him in school for at least two years and to employ him in work for which she saw he was fitted.

Tender age was no bar to apprenticeship, for there are instances of the binding over of children hardly out of the cradle. For example, the court records of New Castle on the Delaware River for the years 1678–1679 show that the widow of the late William Hodges put out her son Charles, aged 5 years, to Thomas Jacobs for a period of twelve years. Thomas Jacobs in turn agreed to provide the boy with sufficient fare, apparel, washing, and lodging, to instruct him in the trade of wheelwright and at the end of twelve years to give the boy a cow and a calf. Incidentally, it was further agreed that Mr. Jacobs' son shall "larn ye sd boy to Reede as much as hee can teach him."

Apprenticeship of children whose parents were unable to support them continued beyond colonial days and well into the nineteenth century, even though alternative forms of child care had been developed. Homer Folks, as far back as 1902, observed that "the old-fashioned indenture or apprentice system passed largely into disuse, if not into disrepute, by

1875." [1] On the other hand, Lundberg, citing the repeal of a law in Mississippi in 1946, remarked, "care of children in almshouses and by binding out or indenture belonged to an era long past, although vestiges of these archaic methods were still to be found in a few communities not so many years ago, and some may still be in existence." [2]

Public institutional care— the almshouse

Almshouse care for children had no great vogue in the early days of the colonies. Not until after the year 1700 did this method of child care appear, and for many years it was outranked by apprenticeship and indenture. The first almshouses developed, naturally enough, in the larger cities, and later the movement spread to the others. New York, Philadelphia, and Boston early had their almshouses into which were herded helpless children who were without means of support. These children received hardly more than what might be termed a residual care. Inadequate diet and lack of proper sanitation took their toll in high sickness and mortality rates. A minimum of educational facilities and instruction did much to render them ineffective when they reached the labor market upon their discharge. The deprivation of the normal developmental experiences of home life crippled their capacity to make subsequent adjustments to other individuals and to community life.

One of the early developments that had some effect in breaking up such devastating situations was the gradual withdrawal of various groups of handicapped children from the poorhouse and the provision for them in specialized institutions. With the opening of the Hartford Institution for the Deaf in 1817 there was available a specialized service for the child as well as the adult. For the blind this service began with the Massachusetts Institution for the Blind in 1831–1832, and for the feeble-minded the way was opened through the Massachusetts Institution for the Feeble-Minded in 1848. For another group, delinquent children, specialized institutional care was signalized by the opening of the New York House of Refuge in 1825, which received both boys and girls. Within a year a second institution for juvenile delinquents was opened. The significance of this was that it was the first such institution to be established under municipal auspices— the House of Reformation of the city of Boston, 1826. As years passed,

---

[1] Homer Folks, *The Care of Destitute, Neglected, and Delinquent Children* (New York: The Macmillan Company, 1902), p. 41.

[2] Emma O. Lundberg, *Unto the Least of These* (Des Moines, Iowa: D. Appleton-Century-Crofts, 1947), p. 299; see also p. 50.

there was a further growth of these specialized institutions, both publicly and privately supported.

A further break with the system of mixed almshouse care was the step taken by the state of Massachusetts to place children in an almshouse solely intended for children at Monson in 1864. Two years later this institution was designated as the State Primary School, and the children therein were no longer to be designated as paupers. Another institution that served to deflect children from the mixed almshouse—and hence provided a welcome alternative—was the soldiers' orphans' home established after the Civil War. These were supported by public funds. Most made provision for children of any soldier or sailor rather than restricting admission to those children whose fathers had lost their lives in active military service. Later, in some states, these homes were authorized to receive other dependent children. About the same time that Massachusetts was instituting its State Primary School, another state, Ohio, was working out a variation known as the County Children's Home, with emphasis upon county initiative and financing. A few other states permitted counties to develop separate children's institutions, but the trend was more along the line set by Massachusetts, that is, state homes. In Michigan the State Public School (opened in 1874 with its legal enactment in 1867) was intended to serve as a temporary home and school until the children could be placed in family homes. Other states, such as Wisconsin, Minnesota, and Rhode Island, within a decade followed the Michigan pattern. Some of the county homes, lacking other than local supervision, tended to degenerate into local poorhouses, but many of the state homes approached a high standard of child care. They were aided in this development not only by the fact that they were on a state-wide basis, but also because they were in a position to profit by developments within the larger national area of child care. Especially toward the latter part of the nineteenth century increasing emphasis was being put upon placing children in private homes, and some state schools came to regard themselves as functioning solely for short-time institutional care. A number of states went so far as to require that no child was to be kept in the state home for as much as sixty days without adequate evidence that every effort had been made for placement in a private home. Such laws further stipulated that the retention of any child beyond the sixty-day period should call for a monthly report of reasons why there was such a delay. Both Massachusetts and Michigan, who in the 1870s, originated the state school plan, did much to extend the principle beyond their own borders.

Another movement that contributed to the reduction of the almshouse care for children was the introduction of the principles and practice of foster home placement during the last half of the nineteenth century. This work will be treated in another section of this chapter, but it is well to remind ourselves that even though all these factors tended to render the almshouse obsolete, nevertheless it continued to house children well into the twentieth century. By now it must be clear that the almshouse has been the most deeply rooted of all our American social welfare institutions.

Private institutional care—
orphan homes

Institutional care of orphans began in the Colonies in the early part of the eighteenth century. While the first orphanage is usually attributed to the Ursuline Convent in New Orleans in 1727, providing care for children whose parents had been massacred by the Natchez Indians, it is necessary to recognize that other services were offered by the Sisters of the Ursuline Order such as teaching (what today would be termed day and resident students) as well as caring for the sick, whether orphaned children, Negroes, or Indians.[3] For the sake of accuracy it would be well to term Bethesda as the first orphanage created solely for that purpose. Opened in Savannah, Georgia, in 1740, it owes its origin largely to the zeal of the celebrated English preacher, George Whitefield. Several other children's institutions were begun before 1800, but it remained for the nineteenth century to lay an unprecedented number of orphanage cornerstones. The number of orphanages supported by public funds remained surprisingly small, in part perhaps because the almshouse still received children and in part because of alternative methods of care, such as apprenticeship and indenture, outdoor relief, and toward the end of the century, foster home care. In addition, the fact that private funds had so largely preempted the institution field made it less imperative for the public orphanage to appear.[4]

By far the greater number of orphan asylums, as they were not infrequently called, were denominational in origin and management. In 1929 it was estimated that some 1500 children's institutions had been established in this country, of which about 60 percent were denominational. Other orphan homes that were nondenominational in origin and control have been established for a variety of reasons. One consideration, particularly in the early days, was to avoid the mixed almshouse care so prevalent for destitute children. Another was the substantial satisfaction an

---

[3] The writer is indebted to Martin Gula of the U.S. Children's Bureau for information on this point gained from Father Chambon's book published in 1908 entitled *In and Around the Old St. Louis Cathedral of New Orleans.*

[4] The first orphanage to be established under public auspice was the Charleston (S.C.) Orphan House in 1790. This institution, which is still in existence, is known as Oak Grove and is located in North Charleston.

individual or group of individuals derived when a memorial in brick and stone was raised. A third motive undoubtedly sprang from a sincere conviction at the time that institutional care was the best method of providing service for children. Furthermore, buildings and staff and children were tangible and gave concrete evidence of monies expended. These, and other motives as well, undoubtedly influenced the founders of orphan homes. Certainly during the first half of the nineteenth century the orphanage was as much a part of the folkways and the mores as foster home care and aid to dependent children are today.

One further point needs to be noted here. Free public education as we know it today was hardly known a hundred years ago, nor well developed until within the past fifty years. Early orphanages that included schools in many cases actually excelled the schooling facilities of many communities from which their children came.

In addition to the denominational and nondenominational institutions, there were orphanages established for special groups such as infants, or Negro orphans, or orphans of soldiers and sailors (when not publicly provided). Few of these have survived to the present day. They have become extinct perhaps more quickly even than the usual run of orphan asylums.

Public subsidy of private institutions

During the last century the abundance of privately supported institutions for children, coupled with the disinclination to use tax money to build children's homes, produced a public subsidy system that turned out to be anything but a blessing. The state of New York early granted public funds, in lump sums, to private institutions and continued the practice until it was legally outlawed in 1874. Thereafter the subsidy appeared in a new guise. Instead of an outright grant, a per capita sum was paid for maintenance of state wards in private institutions. This appeared to be an economy to the state because it obviated the building of state institutions, but in the long run it meant an increasing annual drain on the public treasury. The situation was further aggravated by the fact that seldom did supervision and control by the state follow the grants. The inevitable result was that private institutions ran their establishments their own way largely with public funds. Such a system also made it difficult to get children out of the institution since maintenance ceased as soon as placement in a foster home resulted. When one realizes further how zealous denominational orphanages were to retain children in their own faith, it is understandable that the system of public subsidy was tenaciously defended and managed to persist despite legal handicaps. Prevailing opinion in social work is definitely opposed to the subsidy system.

Foster-home care

Until 1853 indenture, institutional care, and outdoor relief were the chief services available to children in need in this country. It was the pioneer work of Charles Loring Brace that initiated foster home care by means of which a child could be placed in another home when conditions in his own home were so inimical to his welfare as to make removal from the home or giving him up necessary.

It was during the period of his training for the ministry that the opportunity came to Charles Loring Brace to head a children's mission in New York City. The mission in 1853 was renamed the Children's Aid Society, and almost at once Brace began to carry out his idea of withdrawing vagrant and destitute children from the streets of the city and transplanting them into suitable homes in another environment. As originally conceived, the plan was based upon the assumption that the child was to carry a share of work in his foster home, that the foster parents would be relieved of some cares, and that the society would bear the expense of getting the child to the home and returning him if that were necessary. This latter point was of considerable importance because eventually the society transported children as far away as Michigan, Wisconsin, and Minnesota. It all likelihood, these mass emigrations consisting of hundreds of children were founded more upon a desire to remove the children from city streets than upon a certain knowledge of the intricacies of child care. For the leaders of the movement the chief problems were those of gathering children, transporting, housing and feeding them rather than the problems of separation of children from kin and friends and the readjustment to a different home and strange people.

Despite all the shortcomings of the scheme, which were due to ignorance rather than to design, the fact remained that thousands of children were removed from city streets (largely from the eastern seaboard) and given an opportunity to start life again elsewhere. What was equally important was the beginning of a movement that approached the needs of children from a more promising point of view than had ever characterized indenture or almshouse care.

The Growth of Children's Aid Societies

Other private societies followed the New York Children's Aid. In 1860 an agency was founded in Baltimore for the purpose of finding homes for destitute children. Within three years two other organizations were formed, one in Philadelphia, which sought to board Jewish orphans in the homes of relatives or some other worthy family, and the other in Boston, which began rather uncertainly to place children in foster homes, in temporary homes, or in their farm school. Other societies were organized in Brooklyn in 1866, in Buffalo in 1872; a decade later the Pennsylvania Children's Aid Society was established, and in 1895 the one in Rochester, New York. These societies were for the most part privately financed, although in some instances, as in Pennsylvania where the society accepted children from local counties, payment for board was made from public funds.

Another group of societies that formed part of this expanding movement of foster home care for children calls for separate mention. According to the evidence, the establishment of the first state children's home society in Illinois does not seem to have stemmed from the work of Brace with the New York Children's Aid Society but to have had an independent origin in the work of Martin Van Buren Van Arsdale. Van Arsdale, like Brace, had left the ministry for work with children, making a vow to himself during his first years of preaching that he would deliver all children from the poorhouse. In execution of that vow, he organized in 1883 the American Educational Aid Society for the twofold purpose of placing children in family homes and helping girls to get an education. Later this organization was termed the State Children's Home Society, not because it was publicly financed or sponsored, but because its coverage was statewide. After the title was changed to the National Children's Home Society, it began to grant charters to agencies in other states. Iowa was the first of these, to be followed by Minnesota, Michigan, Missouri, Indiana, California, Wisconsin, Tennessee, North Dakota, and South Dakota.

Public Sponsorship

While the pioneering work of developing foster home services for children was privately initiated and directed, it was only a decade or two before a number of states had recognized their responsibilities for the welfare of children and were looking toward other means of care than indenture and institutions. Massachusetts was the first state to make a beginning in that direction when in 1869 it provided a visiting service to all children released from state institutions. This supervision led the way to the state paying board for many of its children who had been placed in private homes. Ten years later the practice of depositing children in city and town almshouses was outlawed, and in 1882 provision was made for the payment of board for children under 10 years of age and, in place of retaining them in the State Primary School, it was required that they be committed directly to the state board of charities itself. The most important step in this development of home placement service was the abolition of the State Primary School in 1895 and the further extension of the principle of caring for children in foster homes instead of in institutions.

In 1899 New Jersey followed the example of Massachusetts by the establishment of a state policy of foster home care for destitute children. The creation of a state board of children's guardians centralized the control and placement of children and made possible the use of private homes as boarding homes until such time as free homes could be found for the children.

Pennsylvania's approach was a recognition of the principle of foster home care implemented by the services of a private agency. When a state law, passed in 1883, threw upon the local communities and counties the care of children, no provision was made for adequate service for these children. Fortunately, the Pennsylvania Children's Aid Society had been organized the year before as a private child-placing agency, and it immediately offered to assist local authorities by working with them on a program of boarding or free homes. Many of the larger counties availed themselves of the society's services, and in such instances payment was made out of county funds for those boarding homes which the agency secured.

Mention has also been made of a number of states that followed the Michigan state school plan and of other states (Connecticut and Indiana) that patterned their programs after Ohio's county home plan. In these instances, whether state home or county home, there eventually developed systems of placement that at first supplemented and later supplanted the institution. Thus by 1935 Michigan had adopted a state-wide system of child placement and had surrendered its institution at Coldwater to another agency of the state government, as Massachusetts had done with its State Primary School forty years before. In Michigan the institution became a training school for mentally defective children, in Massachusetts a hospital for epileptics. In Ohio and Indiana the emphasis still remained upon the county functions in child care and placement, but in both instances a state-wide child-placing agency has been established to handle those cases that could not be provided for by the local authorities. Every effort was made by the state agency to have the local communities develop their own resources and facilities.

Relief for children in their own homes

The system of providing assistance in the home of the applicant has, since its origin in Elizabethan England, been known as outdoor relief. This assistance has generally been allocated to members of family groups and as such we are justified in speaking of outdoor relief for children. Homer Folks wrote many years ago that outdoor relief of pauper children as well as of adults was the predominant method of public care in early colonial days. Its constant rival was the almshouse; and as almshouse care increased, outdoor relief decreased. Indeed in 1823–1824 Mr. Yates, secretary of state for New York, upon the basis of his investigations into the care of the poor, was convinced that almshouse care for children was superior to relief in their own homes. In describing children receiving relief outside of almshouses he spoke of their education and morals being neglected, their health impaired, their living in filth and idleness and likely to become "early candidates for the prison or the grave." At his recommendation outdoor relief for children was curtailed considerably and houses of employment were built in every county, in which paupers were to be maintained and their children to be carefully instructed, later to be put out in trade or business.

Despite this experience in New York, most other states continued outdoor relief to children. Even New York, when years later it realized the vicious effects of the mixed almshouse, reconsidered outdoor relief and reestablished it along with institutional and foster home care for children. These systems continued in operation up to within recent times with relatively little change.

The first separate recognition of the dependent child in the home as substantiated by payments out of public funds came with the adoption of widows' pension laws beginning in 1911. Even though the laws in different states were variously known as widows' pensions, mothers' pensions, mothers' assistance, they all held in common the conviction that it was a valid use of public money to enable mothers to continue care of their children in their own homes. It was not until 1935 that the federal government participated in the financing as well as in the policy formulation of such programs. The Social Security Act contained provisions for federal contributions to states to assist them in what was termed Aid to Dependent Children. This money appropriation, as noted in Chapter 7, was contingent upon certain minimum specifications to be written into the states' public assistance, or welfare, laws.

The White House Conferences

Six White House Conferences during the present century have served to focus the attention not only of social workers but also of the whole nation upon the needs of children and of the responsibility of an enlightened people to meet these needs. President Theodore Roosevelt, who personally dispatched on Christmas Day, 1908 some of the invitations to the first Conference, remarked at the opening session January 25, 1909,

> There can be no more important subject from the standpoint of the nation than that with which you are to deal; because, when you take care of the children you are taking care of the nation of tomorrow; and it is incumbent upon every one of us to do all in his or her power to provide for the interests of those children whom cruel misfortune has handicapped at the very outset of their lives.

The basic guiding principle of the Conference was expressed in a concluding report made to President Roosevelt to the effect that;

> Home Life is the highest and finest product of civilization. It is the great molding force of mind and character. Children should not be deprived of it except for urgent and compelling reasons. Children of parents of worthy character, suffering from temporary misfortune and children of reasonably efficient and deserving mothers who are without the support of the normal breadwinner, should, as a rule, be kept with their parents, such aid being given as may be necessary to maintain suitable homes for the rearing of the children.[5]

This principle that children should not be removed from their own homes for reasons of poverty alone was the expression of a conviction that had been gaining acceptance for some years. A second principle embodied the thought and progressive practice since the days of Charles Loring Brace that, in those instances in which for sufficient reasons normal children must be removed from their own homes or given up by their parents, the carefully selected foster home was the best alternative for the natural home. Additional principles that were expressed in the conference recommendations were to the effect that institutions for children (where they were necessary) should be on the cottage plan; that child caring institutions should be incorporated with state approval and be subject to state inspection; and that the causes of child dependency should be studied and so far as possible be ameliorated or removed.

---

[5] *Proceedings of the Conference on the Care of Dependent Children,* 60th Cong., 2nd Sess., Senate Document No. 721 (Government Printing Office, 1909), p. 9.

At least three outgrowths of this conference have made it outstanding in the history of child welfare in this country: the passage of the first state law providing financial aid to children in their own homes; the establishment of the U.S. Children's Bureau; and the organization of the Child Welfare League of America, a voluntary nationwide agency. The first state widows' pension law was written in Illinois in 1911. It accepted the proposal of the conference but broke with the method advocated, that is, through private charity.

The endorsement of the conference as well as that of other organizations and individuals, including President Taft, of the proposal to establish a federal children's bureau resulted in its creation in 1912. Congress directed the Children's Bureau "to investigate and report . . . upon all matters pertaining to the welfare of children and child life among all classes of our people." In pursuance of this instruction, the Children's Bureau, the first public agency in the world whose function was to consider as a whole the conditions, problems, and welfare of childhood, has developed a staff and a service that has nationwide coverage. It has extended its investigations into the field of child development, child labor, juvenile delinquency, and into the community's provisions for children in need of special care, whether they be in institutions, foster homes, or their own homes. The reporting of these investigations has followed naturally so that the bureau has made its findings accessible to a national audience. A third function has been added from time to time by Congress, namely, the administration of certain federal laws affecting child welfare, such as the first federal child labor law (1917–1918); The Federal Maternity and Infancy Act (1922–1929); and in 1935, the maternal and child health, the child welfare, and the crippled children's provisions of the Social Security Act, and, during World War II, the EMIC—Emergency Maternity and Infant Care program. In addition, consultation and advisory service is rendered to states, localities, and organized groups concerned with the health and welfare of children.[6]

The Children's Bureau, which in 1912 was the child of the first White House Conference, became the parent of the second. In 1919, at the request of President Wilson, the bureau organized the second conference which directed its attention toward the advancement of minimum standards of child welfare. Included in such standards were those relating to children entering employment, protection of the health of children and mothers, and protection of children in need of special care. These latter standards reaffirmed the conclusions of 1909 in all essentials.

---

[6] Originally placed in the Department of Commerce and Labor, it was transferred in 1913 to the newly created Department of Labor. In 1946 it was transferred to the Federal Security Agency. Since April 1953 the Federal Security Agency has been the Department of Health, Education, and Welfare.

A number of striking developments followed this second conference. One year before, only eight states had established child hygiene or
child welfare divisions, while within the year that ensued thirteen states
had laws providing for such services. Another milestone in cooperative
effort to reduce unnecessary loss of maternal and infant life was the passage in 1921 of the Sheppard-Towner Act for the "promotion of the
welfare and hygiene of maternity and infancy." By 1929 forty-five states
and the territory of Hawaii were cooperating under its provisions. Although permitted by Congress in 1929 to lapse, it was upon the foundation of the work done under the Sheppard-Towner Act that the program
for maternal and child health was based and is now carried out through
the provisions of the Social Security Act of 1935 and subsequent amendments.

The third conference, known as the "White House Conference on
Child Health and Protection," was also organized by the Children's Bureau in 1930. It brought together what was probably the largest group
ever assembled in Washington up to that time to consider the needs of
children. Enjoined by President Hoover "to study the present status of the
health and well-being of the children of the United States and its possessions; to report what is being done; to recommend what ought to be done
and how to do it," some 1200 committee members brought together the
latest findings of science as they bore upon the welfare of the child. Since
then, thirty-two reports covering every conceivable phase of child care
have been issued and have proved to be a monumental record of the conference, surpassing the achievements of any other conference on children's
problems ever held. The conference also produced a document known as
the Children's Charter, which enunciated so clearly and compellingly the
needs of children as well as the responsibility of parents, schools,
churches, the community, and governmental agencies to meet these needs.

The fourth conference, 1940, fittingly titled the "White House Conference on Children in a Democracy," was opened by President Franklin
D. Roosevelt, who reminded the delegates that a succession of world
events had shown us our democracy must be strengthened at every point.
Specifically, he charged, ". . . if anywhere in the country any child lacks
opportunity for home life, for health protection, for education, for moral
or spiritual development, the strength of the Nation and its ability to
cherish and advance the principle of democracy are thereby weakened." A
general report, upon which there was substantial agreement and which
was adopted at the conference, stressed a number of topics. Among these
were the following: the child in the family, religion in the lives of children, educational services in the community, protection against child
labor, youth and their needs, conserving the health of children, children
under special disadvantages, and public administration and financing.

In addition to study and discussion before and during the conference, it was decided to take steps to carry out the findings of the
conference. Accordingly, a nongovernmental National Citizens Committee was formed to carry the responsibility for follow-up activities, and a
Federal Inter-Agency Committee to coordinate the work of federal departments whose work touched on matters affecting children. The National Citizens Committee immediately began plans for developing a
long-range program as well as one to meet present and emerging situations. Emphasis was placed on cooperation with federal agencies, on dissemination of information, on stimulation of state and private agency
programs and "consideration of the special needs of children growing out
of emergency conditions, and cooperation with other organizations engaged in conserving and advancing the health, education, home care, and
social protection of children under such conditions."

Hardly was the committee formed than America faced a tremendous defense program and state of national emergency. At once the
health and welfare of a recruited army became a pressing concern. The
large number of selective service rejections brought out, more forcefully
than anything else could have, the damage, sometimes irreparable, done
to a nation's manpower through neglect of children's health and welfare.
Every man turned down by an Army doctor was once a child. It was too
easy for a nation of businessmen interested in reducing taxes to scrimp
on maternal and child health programs. Now that these war babies of
World War I were needed for defense, the sedate *New York Times* could
remark editorially, "If all that could have been done for them after 1918
had actually been done, they would now be in better physical shape, not
merely for a year of soldiering but for the battle of life." The closing sen-
tences of the same editorial must express not only the sentiments of the
hundreds of White House Conference members but of people elsewhere
who have a concern for child life: "We may pray fervently that today's
children will not be in 1960's mass army, and just as fervently that more
than 60 percent of them will be in sound physical condition. To make this
certain more attention must be given now to the health of all our children.
If the cost is equivalent to that of a few bombing planes or even that of
a flotilla of destroyers it will still be worthwhile."

The fifth conference, with President Harry S. Truman as honorary
chairman, met in December 1950 and was called the "Midcentury White
House Conference." While its chairman and secretary were governmental
officials and it drew upon the thirty-seven departments of the federal
government whose work touched the lives of children and young people,
in a very real sense, the conference was a citizens' movement. The preparations for the conference, its execution, and the follow-up programs involved upwards of 100,000 persons, some 464 voluntary organizations,

with the bulk of the financing being supplied from voluntary sources. For the first time in the history of the conferences, young people were represented on the various working committees, and about 500 persons under 21 years of age served as delegates to the meetings.

The stated purpose of the conference was "to consider how we can develop in children the mental, emotional, and spiritual qualities essential to individual happiness and to responsible citizenship, and what physical, economic, and social conditions are deemed necessary to this development." All of the work carried on by professional and lay persons before the conference, joined to the deliberations during the days of the conference, produced not only enunciations on behalf of children and youth but actual on-going programs through organizations and agencies following the close of the conference. These programs are still underway and are intended to be increasingly effective on behalf of children and youth in America in the troubled times ahead.

Just as the 1930 conference produced the Children's Charter so the 1950 conference produced an equally epochal Pledge to Children. This Pledge to Children is not only a reaffirmation of the principles of the 1930 Children's Charter but a dedication to the end of securing for children those essentials of growth due children everywhere.

As was the case with the fourth White House Conference, the Midcentury White House Conference on Children and Youth took steps to translate the recommendations into action. The extensive preparation and planning by hundreds of organizations and thousands of persons not only insured the success of the conference, but gave impetus to the formation of the National Midcentury Committee for Children and Youth. National, state, and local committees, with participation of agencies and persons concerned with children and youth, are carrying on active programs to move the words of the conference into the deeds that will insure better opportunities and services for the present as well as the future generations of young people.

The sixth White House Conference, called by President Dwight Eisenhower, brought together in March 1960 some 7600 delegates. Of these, 1400 were youths of high school and college age and 500 foreign visitors. In contrast to the modest, though fundamental, proposals made by some 200 delegates in 1909, there was a total of 670 recommendations —the 670th urging that the 1970 conference should serve as a prelude to a world conference on children and youth. The avowed purpose of the 1960 conference was to promote opportunities for children and youth to realize their full potential for a creative life in freedom and dignity.

With so large a representation and with a determination on the part of adults as well as youth to seek for a fuller life, it is understandable that the range of discussion and recommendation touched every phase of modern American life—citizenship, the family, education, employment, military service, leisure, law enforcement, health and welfare services. Likewise, no condition of youth was overlooked—the gifted, the slow learner, the drop out, the delinquent, the handicapped—physically, mentally, and emotionally—the dependent and neglected, children born out of wedlock, the migrant, and members of minority groups.

As with the recent conferences, there was ample organization on a state-wide and nation-wide basis in planning for the meetings as well as postconference planning for carrying into effect the recommendations and the taking of steps toward the next decennial conference. It must be evident by now that the White House Conference on Children and Youth has become a firm part of our life—local, state, national, and international.

Contemporary social services for children

At least three aspects of children's services at the mid-point of the twentieth century must be underscored: the range and diversity of services, the considerable use of tax funds for many of the services, and the emphasis upon the desirability of the child remaining in his own home and with his own family. In the ensuing pages the effort will be made to examine some of these diverse services, to gain some notion of the public expenditure on behalf of children, and to deal with services to children in their own homes as well as to children whose homes for a variety of reasons are no longer available to them. Discussion will center upon the financial service, child caring services, child placing services, other casework services, and homemaker services.[7]

---

[7] For another classification of the range of child welfare services reference may be made to that proposed by the Child Welfare League of America in its valuable booklet entitled *Child Welfare as a Field of Social Work Practice.* The three large areas of services are (1) those designed to support or reinforce the ability of parents to meet the child's needs, such as casework in the child's home, protective services, and services to unmarried parents; (2) those designed to supplement parental care, such as homemaker and day care service; (3) those designed to substitute for parental care, such as foster family care, group care, and adoption.

For a broad, and certainly the latest definition of child welfare services the recommendation to the Congress made by the Advisory Council on Child Welfare Services should be noted: "Child Welfare services are those services that supplement, or substitute for, parental care and supervision for the purpose of: protecting and promoting the welfare of children and youth; preventing neglect, abuse and exploitation; helping overcome problems that result in dependency, neglect or delinquency; and, when needed, providing adequate care for children and youth away from their own homes, such as care to be given in foster family homes, adoptive homes, child-caring institutions or other facilities." *Report of the Advisory Council on Child Welfare Services,* U.S. Department of Health, Education, and Welfare, 86th Cong., 2nd Sess., Senate Document no. 92 (Washington, D.C.: Government Printing Office, 1960), p. 3.

Financial services

It is well to recognize at the outset that, even though we hold that a child's own home and family are the best place for him to be, there are clear and compelling reasons at times why other services need to be offered to help him with some of the difficulties he and his family are experiencing. These other services must be offered, not in the spirit of extremity as a last desperate resort, but rather as a vital contribution to his needs and as essential to his welfare. They are to be considered as services designed to keep him in his home, and the decision must turn upon usefulness in the child's present situation and his future development.

A review of the foregoing pages reveals, despite an early and continuous emphasis on institutional care, an equally early and continuous concern to provide such support to the child's home and family as to enable him to remain there. This took the form of pauper (outdoor) relief, supplanted later by mothers' pensions, mothers' aid, etc., and, with the passage of the Social Security Act in 1935, provision for aid to dependent children. The act now defines a dependent child as

> . . . a needy child under the age of eighteen, who has been deprived of parental support or care by reason of the death, continued absence from the home, or physical or mental incapacity of a parent, and who is living with his father, mother, grandfather, grandmother, brother, sister, stepfather, stepmother, stepbrother, stepsister, uncle, aunt, first cousins, nephew or niece, in a place of residence maintained by one or more of such relatives as his or her own home (section 406a).

Besides cash payments under the AFDC program (federal, state, and in some instances local contributions), children may receive on their behalf payments under the old-age and survivors insurance program in those instances in which the deceased father was in covered employment and the orphaned child or children are entitled to payments until the age of eighteen. There are also cases in which payments are made in behalf of children in families where the father has had coverage under the old-age disability insurance program. However, there are still other children who are in families in which assistance payments are made when the adults qualify for old-age assistance or disability assistance grants. Thus, by way of recapitulation, it may be observed that cash payments may be made in behalf of children under the public assistance program, the social insurance program, and sometimes concurrently under both programs.[8]

---

[8] During each year the *Social Security Bulletin* carries an article dealing with

Child-caring services

The financial services just mentioned have made it possible for many children to remain in their own homes (or in "eligible" homes within the definition of the Social Security Act) and for the family to be kept together. There are other children for whom other forms of care must be provided. These services will be called child care services where the emphasis is upon care, as distinct from the placement services where the emphasis is upon placement.[9] Despite efforts to keep members of the family together there are situations in which the best plan calls for care of the child in a foster home. Some children are deprived of their parents through death, desertion, or separation. Others may be without suitable care in their homes because of the continued incapacity of both parents due to permanent illness or mental disability or because of the inability of a surviving parent to carry the burden alone. Some children may need specialized care, occasioned by their own serious health or behavior problems, which may be beyond the resources of their own homes to provide. The decision as to removal or receiving of a child from his home cannot be undertaken lightly. No matter how unfortunate the family situation may have been, it must be borne in mind that the child has already put down some roots. The family still has meaning to the child: the child is bound to it by birth, by blood, and by relationship. In all these instances, and in others as well, provision must be made for a foster family home with parents who can give to the child the love, the care, the understanding, the guidance so essential to developing within the child his own potentialities for useful living.

Before the child enters into the care of a foster family, certain data must be known so that there may be a mutual basis of understanding. The child's physical condition and his health history is vital. The foster family must know what to provide or what not to provide in reference to diet, clothing, exercise, medical care, for example. Likewise the foster family should know something about mental capacity so that it will know what to expect of the child and of what help it may be in school and vocational opportunities. Another item of particular importance is a knowledge of the emotional nature of the child, his background, his previous experience in family life, his relation to parents, brothers, sisters; his

concurrent receipt of public assistance and old-age survivors and disability insurance; in addition, each month it records statistics relative to these matters in its *Current Operating Statistics*.

[9] The writer is indebted to Alan Keith-Lucas for suggesting the distinction between the child caring and the child placing services. Access to Professor Keith-Lucas' manuscript has proven an enriching experience.

attitudes, habits, and behavior. This information about the child enables the agency to work with the child, his own family, and his prospective family toward living arrangements that will have usefulness for all concerned. This does not assure a perfect home for a perfect child (even if, as is unlikely, they each existed), but rather produces a situation in which foster family and foster child can live naturally and with mutual satisfactions.

Numerous child caring agencies use a temporary foster home prior to a more permanent placement. When a child leaves his own home for any of a number of reasons, it is a wrench for him emotionally. Since birth the child has been establishing roots. These have served to help him feel he belonged somewhere and to somebody. It gives him stability and security. Yet the child who runs away, is recalcitrant, is even delinquent, is showing by those very signs his need to belong to somebody, somewhere, and to be accepted and helped. Now, for reasons usually beyond his control, he is threatened with the loss of or is losing his home. Instead of needing less he needs more care, affection, and understanding. Frequently the experience is so upsetting that he is in no way able to take on another home immediately, particularly a long-time home. He needs an interim period and experience during which he can get over some of his fear, rebellion, and resistance to help. Most of all he needs help in dealing with his own feelings of being rejected by his parents. While this struggle is going on in him, he needs to be in a situation where he can work out many of his feelings and at the same time be accepted for what he is and where he is in his difficulties. The temporary foster home does not necessarily demand the return or response from him that a more permanent home would demand. He is freer to test out for himself the kind of relationship he can take on. He can even express his inability to find a satisfying kind of relationship. At the same time he must meet the ordinary requirements of any home and is often able to feel a stability that lets him move toward a new pattern of living. In a temporary home the child needs to feel he has time "to come to himself," to try to say or express what it is he really needs and wants. A temporary foster home with foster parents who understand him will usually help the child and the agency to find out the kind of home of which he can best become a part. When he is ready to leave his temporary home, there will be a more permanent foster home waiting for him.

Knowing the Child's New Home

The job has only begun with the study of the child. Another assignment calls for just as much skill—the finding of the foster home. Some of the things the agency must know are the financial status of the prospective foster family, housing and housekeeping standards, make-up of the family group, the background, intelligence, education, and interests of the prospective foster parents. Equally essential is the willingness of the prospective foster family to share with the agency in the responsibility and care of the child. Foster parents, like all other people, look for satisfactions in their way of living. They expect foster home care to be a mutually satisfying experience. They know, or should know, it will have disappointments, "tough going" at times, struggles, recriminations, and sometimes heartbreaks. But so does any home. Foster parents need to face all this, to realize their responsibilities and the many demands that the care of any child makes upon them. They also have a right to hope for the joy that comes of having a child or children in their home and for the solid satisfaction of having a part in the growth and unfolding of another's life. The most important consideration is: What does this home have to contribute to the normal, healthy development of a prospective foster child? What is there in the adjustment of these family members to each other, to people outside the home, and to a foster child that will make this a mutually satisfying arrangement?

Service to the Foster Home

In addition to its study of prospective foster child and prospective foster family, the agency fulfills a third essential function—a continuing service to the foster home, which means to foster child and foster parent. This, basically, is a helping function to both the child and the foster parents. While the agency still carries responsibility to the parent or to the court for the child, actually it delegates the daily care and many attendant decisions to the foster parents. After all, it is with the family that the child lives and grows and not with the agency. However, the agency stays in the picture with the foster family, owing a responsibility to the child to assure a stability in the home so essential to his development. The agency also has a duty to be on hand in the event the foster home sustains a disintegration damaging to the child. The agency may furnish some direct service to the child such as that related to medical needs on a long-time planning basis (not the ordinary medical care, which any family normally handles without outside consultation), or involving contacts with the child's own family. In most instances, however, the worker's prime concern is helping the foster parents with their relationship to the child. This in no sense implies that the worker tells a foster parent how to raise the child, but it does mean that the agency stands back of or alongside of the parent to help the parent over difficult places. The aim of the agency is to provide as natural a home environment as a foster home permits and to interfere as little as possible, if at all, with the mode of life of this new family grouping. What so frequently happens is that the child brings all his fears, sullenness, resistance, obstreperousness, and other symptoms of insecurity and that the foster parent needs help in dealing with the child. What just as frequently happens is that, as the child finds in this new home love, security, and opportunity for fulfillment, many of his emotional difficulties give way before the normality of living.

In the course of this service every effort is made to keep alive the child's contacts with his own family and vice versa, since in the large majority of cases foster children need to feel that they still are a part of their original family, and for the further reason that they will return eventually to their own homes. This is consistent with the principle that the agency service is *to* the parent *for* the child. The agency will arrange visits of parents to their children and children to the parents under such circumstances that the contacts will not disturb the relationships within the foster home. Workers need to be sensitive to the feelings and attitudes of members of each of these groups and to be guided always by the principle that the welfare of the child is the paramount good in foster family care.

Ending the Service

A final function of the agency is proper termination of service. This ending may come with the attainment of the legal age beyond which the committing court does not assume jurisdiction. It may come when the original home is ready to receive him. It may be when the child, now grown, is ready to leave of his own accord. In all these cases, the underlying service that the agency still has to offer is the working out with all parties concerned of constructive plans for the future. Necessarily central in all these arrangements is the child himself. Plans may require adjustments within his own home, educational, and even job adjustments. There will need to be preparation for a person's standing on his own feet and making his own way alone. Nor is this an abrupt process, but one in which the foster family, child, own parents, and agency participate over a period of time. After the child returns to his own home, there may be difficulties of one kind or another. These may be the difficulties that arise in any home, or they may be so accentuated as to require outside help. As always, the agency stands by, with parents knowing where again to turn for help. In all cases of helping the agency deals with the parents as responsible people and people who can ask comfortably for help of an agency that has meant something to them before in a tight spot.

Institutional care

As a reaction to the predominance of institutional care for children throughout the nineteenth century, and in response to other forms of child care, and especially due to the impact of the 1909 White House Conference, there was a swing away from institutional care in the second, third, and fourth decades of the twentieth century. In all honesty, it must be admitted that the earlier institutions did tend to become too self-contained, too detached from the findings of progressive child care, and furthermore resistive to change. The reaction was expressed through a skepticism about the value of all forms of institutional child care.

All of this was not without its effects upon the institutions. Many of the forward-looking ones had been demonstrating by their programs that institutional care had its contribution to make to child care. These and others participated increasingly in the newer knowledge and newer practices, and by the midcentury it had become clear that institutions did have a valid service to offer. This was a service in its own right and not solely something to become reconciled to or justified only when all other services were tried and exhausted. Rather, today we find institutions for children taking their places alongside other services: as valid a function as exercised through foster home care, adoption, and financial services in the home. To approach this present status, many institutional leaders have had to do some serious thinking and to have effected some substantial changes. To maintain it, requires constant study, self-examination, and resourcefulness in improving existing institutional services based on increased insight and understanding into human behavior, especially behavior of children. In not a few children's institutions, and especially in some of the church-supported institutions, there has been a daringly progressive attitude that has carried over to practices and that has placed such institutions in the van of child welfare services today.

The Caseworker in the Institution

One of the many evidences of these progressive developments has been the increasing use of qualified caseworkers on the staff of children's institutions. In such institutions the caseworker is a regular staff member offering services encompassing admission, the child's stay in the institution, and discharge. The caseworker is governed by the admissions policies of the institution, and it is within these limits that he works with the applicant—it may be the parent (or parents) or the court. He explores with the applicant the child's needs as well as the family needs. He also clarifies what the institution offers. In addition, he and the applicant together consider available resources within the community. The conclusion to which they each come, and come together, is that in the light of the needs presented and the resources available, the institution is the service best suited for the child under consideration. It will be noted that this marks a decided shift from an earlier emphasis of the institution as the only service or the institution as the last desperate resort. As mentioned in the preceding pages, the modern institution is recognized as offering a valid service in relation to others on behalf of children.

A second area in which the caseworker functions is with the child during his living experience in the institution. Upon admission, the caseworker helps the child in his movement toward the cottage and the cottage parent (or houseparent). Sharing material with the houseparent about the child and the family may be helpful, but in all instances must be subject to the administrative policies of the institution—as indeed must all the professional activity of the caseworker. Likewise, the caseworker is of use to the child by serving as a resource to the administration and to the houseparent as the child enters into and becomes a part of the living situation in which he finds himself. The caseworker can be helpful around some of the difficulties that the child is experiencing in everyday living with other children and with houseparents. His helpfulness is in relation to the realness of the institution—its regulations, its staff, the purpose it is designed to serve—and also the reality of the child being there for his needs to be served. Throughout all of this, the child must be free to relate himself to other members of the staff, including the caseworker, but primarily his relationship should be with the houseparent. The caseworker carries responsibility for maintaining relationship between the child and his family. The child will need to feel that even though he is away from his family, they still stand back of him. This may be a decided factor in his own efforts to make the necessary adaptation to institutional life. The maintenance of family relations and the improvement of the environmental situation will prove a real influence in hastening the day of the child's return, an objective that is to be desired by the institution, the child, and the family.

A third aspect of the caseworker's services revolves around the return of the child to his family. This step on the part of the child requires help from the worker in preparing both the child and the family for the reunion. It means the joint consideration of educational and vocational plans as well as of the demands that the outside community will make upon the child. In some instances return to the child's own home may not be possible at the time the child is ready to leave the institution, and other arrangements for a family living situation in the community may have to be worked out. Following the preparation and the planning will come discharge from the institution and the necessary help of the caseworker in making adjustments to family, to community, and to a different kind of world. The service that the worker offers may extend for a long or a short period of time depending upon the capacity of the child to make the essential adjustments. Its intensity will be related to the nature of the child's problems as well as to his ability to develop his own resources within himself. It is as important for the worker to know when to withdraw from such service as it is to know when to offer help. To continue supervision beyond the point of the individual's real need may serve to perpetuate his dependence as much as if he were still in the institution.

A word remains to be said for the institutional setup and staff. By common agreement the children's institution that is composed of cottages where children live in small informal home-life groups under the care of cottage mothers (and fathers) is to be preferred to the old regimented barrackslike institution. Any institution involves deprivations of some individual expression and demands subordination of the individual to the group more than is true of life outside of an institution. What so frequently happens is that after a time much of his individual expression is surrendered, and he yields what is more dear to him, his own unique personality—that personality that holds within itself his capacity for creative living. In the older institutions with their entire domestic arrangements and economy centered around conformity this was especially true. In the newer-minded institutions, especially in those with the cottage system, there is far more opportunity for individual expression. At the same time, the child can assimilate many of the values that accrue from the experience of making adjustment to group situations. It is in this combination of individual and group expression that the institution can make its most valuable contribution to the development of the child, provided the staff is alive to the functions of such an institution. In order to assure competent staffs familiar with the way human behavior is motivated and expressed, it is desirable that staff members shall be persons of personal maturity and fulfillment, shall have led reasonably satisfying lives according to their capacities and opportunities, and shall have an understanding of the emotional development of children. One does not demand that a cottage mother be a graduate of a school of social work (any more than one demands the same of parents!), but that she embody understanding, sensitivity of feeling, and spontaneity and naturalness in her relations with people. Likewise, the same is to be expected of other staff members who come into contact with the children. Especially is this so for the superintendent or head of an institution. In addition to all of these desired qualities, one can fairly expect nowadays that he have the professional competence to operate a children's institution so that it becomes a constructive chapter in the lives of the children who, much against their wishes, are obliged to live for a period within it.

The Modern Role of the Institution: As a Way of Living

Many, if not most, of the children's institutions of the last century were known and operated as orphanages with admissibility of the child turning on the death of one or both parents. In contrast to this procedure, today orphanhood is almost the last, rather than the first, criterion for admission, and should never be the sole determinant. Families today break up for many reasons other than death. Families are smaller, and there are fewer relatives able, or for that matter inclined, to provide alternate care for the child. More and more children's institutions are providing care for children whose parents for one reason or another can no longer provide the rearing so necessary for wholesome development. The following are some of the more important purposes for which these services are offered.

Some children have had such disastrous emotional experiences in their own families that they are not ready to take on a new set of intimate relationships immediately, but instead can benefit by the less personal tone of the institution. They are not ready for foster home care, certainly not until some of the pain has gone out of their hurt. Oftentimes the combination of skilled staff and the socializing effects of group living has value for such children.

Other children not as emotionally damaged, but who are obliged to leave one foster home before another is ready may find the temporary security of the institution a real boon and a valuable preparation for a placement to follow later. Some of these children may have had several unsuccessful foster home experiences and may be needing the institution to get a sense of being able to relate to others but without the degree of commitment so essential to foster family living.

In the case of the child whose parents are recently divorced or separated the institution may afford a kind of breathing spell, allowing the child to get some perspective on his relation to one or both of these parents. It is hardly likely that such a child will be ready for a foster home so soon after his own has come tumbling down.

Sometimes families break up in which there are three, four, or five children. Seldom can arrangements be made quickly enough to place these children in the same foster family or even in contiguous foster families. To locate foster parents who can meet the needs of such children requires not only time but infinite ingenuity and persistence. An institutional placement can be made more readily, which will come nearer to meeting the needs of these children temporarily.

Despite what has just been written about the role of the institution, it is becoming increasingly difficult to be categorical about the use of children's institutions. As community resources develop, as institutions themselves modify their programs, and as more is learned about human behavior, we are less sure of our characterization of children's institutions and more inclined the see the needs of each individual child. When we do this we are more likely to relate that child's needs to those resources that assure him the maximum opportunity to realize to the full his unique potentials. The institution as it changes, just as other services change, will find its useful place in the full range of child welfare services in this twentieth century.

As a Treatment Center

It must have been evident in the foregoing paragraphs that the emphasis was on the institution as a way of living. This was predicated upon a temporary stay and as approaching, insofar as practicable, the ordinary "livingness" to which the community feels every child is entitled. True, problems are bound to arise in such institution living, just as problems arise in living in foster homes or in one's own home, and it is expected that the institution will be so staffed as to help children with the difficulties incident to growing up. However, within recent years an increasing demand has arisen for a kind of institution for children that is treatment centered. The institution with a properly qualified staff may serve a valuable purpose for those children who are so emotionally disturbed as to require residential and sustained treatment in other than their own homes or their foster homes. For this, there is required not only competent casework service, but available psychiatric consultation (or full-time service, depending upon the size of institution) as well as psychological testing service. The entire staff (professional and administrative) must be oriented to the problems presented by the disturbed child, and the program must be designed to provide the maximum opportunity for study and treatment. Along with the focus upon individualization, there must be an opportunity for experiencing what group living has to offer.[10]

Group homes

One further word needs to be said, and that is to refer to the occasional use of what are called "group homes." They have been in use in Great Britain for some years and in this country are beginning to claim attention. These homes provide care for six, eight, or ten (usually unrelated) children living under one roof with a couple who serve as the parent persons of the group. In Great Britain provision is made for such group

[10] Joseph H. Reid and Helen R. Hagan, *Residential Treatment of Emotionally Disturbed Children* (New York: Child Welfare League of America, 1952).

homes in the architects' drawings as part of the public housing projects carried on by the Local Authorities (local governmental unit). In the United States a number of privately supported agencies have experimented with such homes, which have the advantage of offering a degree of group living—a development somewhere between the foster home and the congregate institution.

These listings by no means exhaust the varied uses to which the modern children's institution is put, but they do give some notion of the changed use of the institution within recent times. It must be noticeable, by omission, that no mention is made of the service to babies and preschool children. Almost without a dissent anywhere, child welfare workers will insist that the institution is no place for babies or preschool children. The findings of psychiatrists substantiate the thesis that nothing can take the place of the one mother person during those early years. Physically, emotionally, educationally (in a broad and basic sense) the baby and young child need the warmth, the spontaneity, the devotion, and the "humanness" of the mother or the mother person. The institution, no matter how well intentioned its staff, cannot provide these indispensables or furnish an adequate substitute.

Part-time care: Day nursery and foster day care

Another expression of the conviction that children should not be removed from their own homes solely because of poverty is the service of the day nursery. This service, first introduced into the United States in 1854, aims to provide care in a day nursery for children whose mothers are unable to look after them during the day. It is the usual practice for such mothers, generally working mothers, to leave their child or children, usually under 3 years of age, in the day nursery and to call for the child after the day's work. This care may be either free or at low cost, and is designed to allow the mother who is obliged to work to do so and at the same time to provide care for the child during her working hours. Other resources for care and for keeping the child in his home should be explored before day nursery care is granted. Once day nursery care is provided, then every step is taken to insure adequate care for the child. This service will include attention to the educational and recreational needs of the child, as well as his physical needs. Many day nurseries provide a casework service to the family with a view toward utilizing the family resources in the best interests of the child and the family. Such day nurseries have integrated their programs with other social service agencies in the community, particularly with child welfare and family welfare societies.

An experiment known as foster day care has given promise of some interesting developments. Instead of providing day care for children within the institutional nursery, the agency seeks to place, by the day, children needing care in carefully selected foster homes. The child returns to his home at night and stays with his family whenever his mother is home, but when she is working, he is part of another home or family. In this way it is felt that the home ties may be preserved and at the same time the child permitted the freedom of individual expression, which in the day nursery group, must so often be subordinated to the group. As with other forms of child care utilized by social agencies, it is essential to have available to foster day care parents the services of qualified caseworkers.

Adoption

Another area that focuses upon the needs of the child is adoption. Many of the children who are born of unwed mothers are brought to the attention of reputable agencies. These agencies undertake to plan with the mothers the services that will best meet the needs of the child. Other adoptions may be made of children born of a married mother, but in which case the father—the putative father—is other than her husband. In other instances the family may be broken—perhaps catastrophically—and adoption may be the most fortunate solution of a tragic situation. In other cases legitimate children may be adopted by relatives, or they may be placed for adoption by agencies.

By whatever means children become candidates for adoption, there are actually three basic considerations: the needs of the child, of the own parent (or parents), and of the adoptive parent. If it may be assumed that a child is a possible subject for adoption, it is tremendously important to ascertain all the information available about the child and his background. The purpose of such knowledge is to facilitate the location of a family that will as nearly as possible meet the particular child's needs. Usually agencies will utilize a temporary boarding home for a period of time to provide him affection and security and also to gain additional understanding of him. In such a temporary home the child must experience acceptance of others and be helped to be ready, when the time comes, to move into the adoptive family. By the same token, the parents in this temporary boarding home must not only provide the warmth of human relationship while the child is with them but must also be emotionally mature enough to enable the child to leave them at the proper time.

Just as something must be known about the child, it is equally essential to know about the persons who wish to become the adoptive parents. Agencies must satisfy themselves not only about their physical, financial, and intellectual resources—to whatever degree—but their emotional needs and motivations as well. Again, it must be stressed that the primary concern is the child and his needs. Persons, for example, who want to adopt a child in hope that such a step will solve their marital difficulties are hardly likely to contribute to what the child requires. Indeed, they are likely to use the child for their own ends to the disadvantage of the child. On the other hand, there are couples who can provide a normal, healthy, and emotionally satisfying living relationship in which a child can grow and in which he can realize whatever potentialities he has within him. Such a living experience will further the child's growth in all aspects—physical, intellectual, emotional, and spiritual.

After a child has been placed in an adoptive home, there is a period of time ranging (depending upon state laws) from six months to one year before the adoption is final. During this period the agency worker offers help to the adoptive parents as well as to the child to surmount the quite understandable difficulties in the situation. All of us are aware of the strains and stresses in the own-parent-child relationship and of the necessity, at times, for parents to turn outside of the family for help. If anything, the situation is accentuated in the case of an adoptive family for at least two reasons: (1) the effects upon the child of what he may have been through earlier and (2) the disadvantage of not having the experience of dealing gradually with the child's problems that emerge. As the child and the adoptive parents increasingly work out their ways of living together, the worker withdraws so that when the adoption becomes legally final, the worker and the agency are ready to conclude their service to the family. From then on they enter the home only upon the call of the family, as is the case with other families in the community. Once the adoption becomes final, the (new) parents and the child have the same rights, duties, and privileges toward each other as if the child had been born to them.

Not every child born out of wedlock becomes a subject for adoption, nor is every adoption that of an illegitimate child. However, since so large a percentage of children born out of wedlock and who come to the attention of reputable public and private agencies are considered for adoption, it seems pertinent to carry forward at this point the discussion of services for unmarried mothers and their children.

Every situation of illegitimacy involves the welfare of at least two people, mother and child. Others undoubtedly are involved, either legally or as relatives of the mother, but the needs of the mother and the child are paramount when they come or are referred to an agency. The first questions that arise are: What are the needs of this child? What are the needs of this mother? And what does the agency have to offer either or both of them? If the prospective mother comes before confinement and delivery, the agency works with her and what plans she may have, if any. It has been found that an agency can be useful in many instances before birth has taken place by talking with the mother and helping her to arrive at what she thinks she really wants to do for herself and her child. Even though she may be facing a crisis, she is at least likely to be able to consider with some calmness and judgment what is the best thing to do. It is then that the agency can work out plans with her for keeping the child with her, placing the child with relatives or friends, or for adoption. At the same time the agency can help her to decide her own subsequent actions. There is always the possibility that plans made at this time may not always be carried out after the birth of the child because the birth itself may have changed the mother's entire feelings about her previous decision. Again, the casework skills are the same: to help the mother arrive at the decision she really wants to make.

If the mother does not come to the agency until after delivery, the same questions will need to be faced: What will serve the best interests of the child? What of the mother? It must be emphasized that there is no one absolute rule of what is best because every situation is unique and because every situation has a new and different constellation of personalities in it. In some instances it is well for mother and child to remain together, in others the child may be placed with relatives or friends while the mother seeks to earn her living. In still other cases it may be well to seek foster home care or adoption for the child.

An adequate understanding of the situation confronting an unmarried mother and a child born out of wedlock leads to the conviction that such a child needs affection and security just as does any other child. He needs it, not because he is an illegitimate child, but because he is a human being. The accident of his birth merely places upon his mother and anyone to whom she goes for help the responsibility of seeing that he has the opportunity to secure that love and that feeling of belonging. Without that start the child is handicapped from the outset in his emotional development, which may be as crippling as any physical illness. Consistent with this attitude is the practice of children's agencies of first attempting to help mother and child to remain together whenever that is possible. It may be that interviews with the putative father will reveal what possibilities there are of marriage of the parents, but in no instance is a marriage to be forced when there is every indication that such a move is contrary to the basic wishes and feelings of either or both parents. Many agencies have found that more is to be gained by a frank conference with both parties than by the use of force. Where, however, marriage is not agreed upon willingly, consideration must be given to support by the father, and in cases of extremity the mother may be obliged to seek court action. This is usually done upon her initiative rather than by the children's agency.

We know it requires two persons to produce a child and yet we become so preoccupied with helping the mother and the child that we frequently, almost always, overlook the father of the child. Whether he is married or unmarried, he is more than a biological transmitter. It is not inappropriate here to suggest that there is much work to be done by case-workers with putative or acknowledged fathers and that such services may be focused on the needs of the mother, the child, and the father as well. It is not improbable that such an offer of help, skillfully made, could be a constructive force in the lives of all three concerned.[11]

Other casework services

Protective Services

Other services to children, particularly within recent years, have focused upon help to the parent on behalf of the child. A particular instance of these services is to be found in those cases in which action is initiated by someone other than the parents where the parents have been unwilling or unable to provide the care for the child that the community considers desirable and essential. The child (or children) may have suffered neglect or abuse, and someone has had to intervene in order to call a halt to such experiences for the child as well as to help the parent (parents) to use himself otherwise than in ways destructive to his child.

Traditionally, the origins of such a service go back to the period when England passed Dick Martin's Act (1822) for the prevention of cruelty to animals. A similar act was passed in America in 1866, when the American Society for the Prevention of Cruelty to Animals was chartered in New York, and for a while the society (SPCA) was called upon to intervene on behalf of children as well as animals. Miss Emma Lundberg's remarks are sufficiently revealing to bear repeating:

> The New York Society for the Prevention of Cruelty to Animals had been in existence for eight years when it was discovered that "with all the law there was no legal way of protecting a child." It is related that a mission worker had discovered a child called Mary Ellen who was being cruelly beaten and ill-treated by a man and woman who had taken her in infancy from a charitable institution. Unable to gather evidence necessary to obtain court removal of the child, the mission worker appealed to the society for the protection of animals. The society held that "the child being an animal" it would act, and Mary Ellen was taken to court and complaint was made against the guardians. The child was removed from their custody, and those

---

[11] See "The Unmarried Father," Chapter 8 in Leontine Young, *Out of Wedlock* (New York: McGraw-Hill Book Company, Inc., 1954), pp. 131–148, especially p. 148.

who had mistreated her were sent to the penitentiary for one year. When it became known that the animal society would interest itself in children who were ill-treated, numerous complaints were received, and it was decided that a separate society should be formed.[12]

Similar societies were organized in other cities. In many places the humane societies created for the protection of animals added to their activities the prevention of cruelty to children. More recently through legislation the state has added this as one of its court or welfare services.

In earlier years the emphasis was largely upon apprehension, trial, conviction, and punishment of the person by whose actions the child suffered abuse or neglect. This frequently—almost always—resulted in the removal of the child from his home, to be followed by institutional care or foster home care. Today, we are more likely to see as the purpose of our services the protection of the child and to regard as the object of our services the parent. This shift emphasizes the conviction that some, perhaps not all, persons can be helped with their difficulties—even those difficulties that find expression in undesirable actions toward their children. It also involves a recognition that even if all homes are not perfect, there may be a great deal of attachment between parents and children that should not be too peremptorily or too thoughtlessly broken by agents outside of that home. What such parents are showing so many times are their distress signals that they need help in managing with the many problems they have. Caseworkers approach such parents with the offer of help, and, despite the community's attitude of indignation and hopelessness, in many instances have enabled such parents to come to a greater sense of their responsibilities and capacities. Such workers operate on the expressed premise that change must come about. The actual steps and action leading toward change must be taken by the parent as the responsible person. In no case can the worker take over for the neglectful parent, nor alter the family pattern of parental rights and responsibilities. There has been enough evidence of success of this approach (for example, The Protective Services, Baltimore City Department of Public Welfare) to believe in its soundness of helping parents, rather than allowing children to grow up with warped and unhappy lives. It is also a far better investment of the taxpayer's dollar to provide the kind of help, through qualified personnel, that makes it possible for families to stay together and for family members to learn to trust each other, experiencing the joys, sorrows, and satisfactions that are a part of everyday living.[13]

---

12 Emma O. Lundberg, *Unto the Least of These* (Des Moines, Iowa: Appleton-Century-Crofts Company, 1947), p. 103.

13 Elizabeth and Karl de Schweinitz, "The Place of Authority in the Protective Functioning of the Public Welfare Agency," *Bulletin of the Child Welfare League of*

Probation and Correctional Institution Services

When youngsters get into serious enough difficulty to come to the attention of the juvenile court, probation service will be necessary for those cases in which the court believes the child warrants continued help in his own home. In those jurisdictions where the juvenile court is of sufficient size, the casework services to the youngster will be provided by its own probation staff. This is to be preferred to other arrangements, but the reality must be faced that in so many parts of the country due to the small size of the court the county department of public welfare is called upon to furnish such casework service. This is usually accomplished through specialized child welfare workers who undertake to help the child, and his family, with the difficulties that have found expression in his unacceptable behavior. Regardless, the service (whether provided by the court's probation officer or the county child welfare worker) is nonpunitive and is focused upon helping the child to face and to accept, increasingly, responsibility for what he is and does. The place of the other family members as they contribute to the child's difficulties must be taken into account, but the child himself must be the person to whom the service is offered and the one who must remain the essential and primary client.

In all fairness it must be admitted that the juvenile industrial school receives its charges only after all other agencies in the community have failed or given up the job. Furthermore, it may be questioned whether the job of preparing youngsters for participation in a free society can be done in an atmosphere so unlike a free society as is inevitable within an institution. Admitting these two limitations apparently inherent in an institutional framework, it may be well to examine the task which any correctional institution has in adapting itself to the needs of the individual child.

Acting on the premise that the institution exists for the child and not the child for the institution, it becomes imperative that the two basic needs of the child must be met: the need for security and the need for growth. In many instances the denial or thwarting of one or both of these needs has driven the child to such a pass that commitment seemed, to the community, the only way out. So the child comes to the institution with not less but more need for security and growth. This places upon the institution personnel the responsibility for affording to the child the opportunities for obtaining these satisfactions. He must be allowed to feel that

---

America, XXV (September 1946), pp. 1–6; Claire Hancock, "Protective Service for Children," Child Welfare, XXVIII (March 1949), pp. 3–9; Barbara Smith, "Helping Neglectful Parents to Become Responsible," The Child, XIV (September 1949), pp. 36–38, 45–46.

he belongs, that he finds stability in the group in which he is thrown, that, in turn, he means something to someone else, that his home ties are maintained, that he can look forward to a return to his family, that his present experience enables him to carry more and more of his own responsibility for himself, that he can retain enough of his individuality to be himself when he returns to the community. If these opportunities are denied him in the institution, he will either fight his way through, possibly doing damage to himself and others, or he will become resigned and submissive so that, while he conforms, he is in nowise equipped to act as a free personality in the world outside. Adequate trade training within the institution may help him to earn his living, which is mighty important, but unless the institution has made other conditions possible, he will leave severely limited in his capacity for successful adjustments or creative living.

Within recent years foster home care of delinquents has been tried and found to be successful. The practice of today is far removed from the early efforts of Charles Loring Brace, yet it bears a distinct relation to his dictum in 1859 that "the family is God's Reformatory." Many juvenile courts have sought to provide foster home care for children who have been adjudged delinquent. It is not uncommon for such care to be in the homes of relatives in order that family ties may be maintained, but the primary concern of the court and the agency is for the quality of the foster home. It has been learned from experience that successful care depends upon careful selection of foster home and child to be placed. It is generally recognized that all foster parents have a seriously demanding task, which is all the greater when the foster child has been damaged or deprived of security and opportunity for growth and responsibility. This requires first an understanding of the child, then a thorough knowledge of the prospective foster home selected. Once the care is undertaken there is need for continued supervision of a helpful nature so that over a period of time the child achieves security in his new home and the foster parents gain satisfaction in the feeling of doing a constructive job. By common agreement, a child has a much greater chance of development under such circumstances than in any other short of his own home.

If the child returns from the correctional institution to his own home—as is to be preferred in most instances—continued casework service is essential to help him to deal responsibly with his own limitations as well as with his capacities. Here, again, if the institution does not have its casework (or parole) staff that can reach out to him in his community, it will have to look to the local county welfare department to provide the needed services.

Homemaker service

Occasionally situations arise in families in which the mother (sometimes it may be a foster mother) is obliged to be out of the home temporarily and the children and the father are faced with decisions as to how to manage. This is a particularly critical problem where the children are of school age or younger and where the father must continue with his regular employment. There may be a number of such situations with varying degrees of urgency. The mother may be confronted with a serious operation that will require not only a period in the hospital but perhaps a carefully regulated recuperation afterward. Or the mother may be on the verge of another confinement; or of commitment to a mental hospital or to a tuberculosis sanatorium; or there may have been death, desertion, or divorce. These are emergencies in which family (and sometimes friends) may help temporarily, but there may not always be family members available and within reach, or in a position to leave their own children. Increasingly services are being set up by both public and private agencies to minister to such needs. These are called homemaker services because another person comes into the home—temporarily—and undertakes to provide many of the services that are customarily the mother's in order to permit the family to remain together. Such a person may work an eight- or a twenty-four-hour day. The father may take over at the close of a day when he returns from his work, or the demands of the family may be such that even though the father is present there is need for the homemaker's skills and presence throughout the entire twenty-four-hour period. Such homemakers carry on the usual duties of the mother—cleaning, cooking, sewing, washing, and the care of the children. Someone has described this as a service that tides over without taking over.

The homemaker is employed by the agency (a public welfare department, a family agency, a family and children's agency), recruited by the agency, trained by the agency, and paid by the agency. A fee is paid by the family receiving the service, usually on a scale based on the earnings and the size of the family. In addition, there is available to the homemaker, and particularly to the family, a caseworker whose service is to help with the various problems and difficulties that may arise.

Most agencies offering this service do so for a limited period of time, since such a service is to help in an emergency in order to keep the family together. In those cases in which it appears, after a reasonable time, that the emergency will continue indefinitely it will be necessary for the agency and the family to work together toward a more lastingly realistic plan. The contribution of the agency to the lives of the family members has been to help them to live through a critical period and to develop the resources to reconstitute their lives with satisfaction.[14]

Other services for children

Several important services relating to child welfare have gone unmentioned. One of these—crippled children's work—is considered more appropriately as part of the chapter on public assistance and social security. The same may be said for aid to dependent children in their own homes, another service available under the Social Security Act. A consideration of the juvenile court and of probation will be presented in the chapter on probation and parole.

There are many other services that touch the lives of children that might have been treated in this chapter. Hardly any phase of social work can be considered as an entity unto itself, and this is especially so of children's services. However, the selection in this chapter has been directed toward those services that, primarily, are designed to aid the child, either in or outside of his own home. There are many other services that incidentally benefit the child, but in this chapter the emphasis and discussion has been on those services where the child is the primary consideration.

The rights of the child—All children

The third White House Conference wrote a Children's Charter, which, using a Washington place line and date line, addressed itself to children in America. Since then a world-wide depression, a world war, and a world organization have affected the lives of children everywhere. Quite appropriately the General Assembly of the United Nations spoke for all children—the children of the world—when, on November 20, 1959, it proclaimed the following ten principles in the Declaration of the Rights of the Child, calling upon individuals, parents, voluntary organizations, and governments to recognize these rights and to strive for their fulfillment.

PRINCIPLE 1   The child shall enjoy all the rights set forth in this Declaration. All children, without any exception whatsoever, shall be entitled to

---

[14] Homemaker service is not restricted to families with children, although the priority may be granted in their favor. The service has been adapted to the aged—again, in order to enable them to remain within their own homes rather than to be institutionalized or shunted elsewhere. See Chapter 13, "Social Services for the Aged."

these rights, without distinction or discrimination on account of race, colour, sex, language, religion, political or other opinion, national or social origin, property, birth or other status, whether of himself or of his family.

PRINCIPLE 2   The child shall enjoy special protection, and shall be given opportunities and facilities, by law and by other means, to enable him to develop physically, mentally, morally, spiritually and socially in a healthy and normal manner and in conditions of freedom and dignity. In the enactment of laws for this purpose, the best interests of the child shall be the paramount consideration.

PRINCIPLE 3   The child shall be entitled from his birth to a name and a nationality.

PRINCIPLE 4   The child shall enjoy the benefits of social security. He shall be entitled to grow and develop in health; to this end, special care and protection shall be provided both to him and to his mother, including adequate pre-natal and post-natal care. The child shall have the right to adequate nutrition, housing, recreation and medical services.

PRINCIPLE 5   The child who is physically, mentally or socially handi-capped shall be given the special treatment, education and care required by his particular condition.

PRINCIPLE 6   The child, for the full and harmonious development of his personality, needs love and understanding. He shall, wherever possible, grow up in the care and under the responsibility of his parents, and, in any case, in an atmosphere of affection and of moral and material security; a child of tender years shall not, save in exceptional circumstances, be separated from his mother. Society and the public authorities shall have the duty to extend particular care to children without a family and to those without adequate means of support. Payment of State and other assistance towards the maintenance of children of large families is desirable.

PRINCIPLE 7   The child is entitled to receive education, which shall be free and compulsory, at least in the elementary stages. He shall be given an education which will promote his general culture, and enable him, on a basis of equal opportunity, to develop his abilities, his individual judge-ment, and his sense of moral and social responsibility, and to become a useful member of society.

The best interests of the child shall be the guiding principle of those responsible for his education and guidance; that responsibility lies in the first place with his parents.

The child shall have full opportunity for play and recereation, which should be directed to the same purposes as education; society and the public authorities shall endeavour to promote the enjoyment of this right.

PRINCIPLE 8   The child shall in all circumstances be among the first to receive protection and relief.

PRINCIPLE 9   The child shall be protected against all forms of neglect, cruelty and exploitation. He shall not be the subject of traffic, in any form.

The child shall not be admitted to employment before an appropriate minimum age; he shall in no case be caused or permitted to engage in any occupation or employment which would prejudice his health or education, or interfere with his physical, mental or moral development.

PRINCIPLE 10 The child shall be protected from practices which may foster racial, religious and any other form of discrimination. He shall be brought up in a spirit of understanding, tolerance, friendship among peoples, peace and universal brotherhood and in full consciousness that his energy and talents shall be devoted to the service of his fellowmen.

Bibliography

Baker, Inez, "Uphold the Rights of Parent and Child," *The Child*, XIII (August 1948), pp. 27–30.

Bowlby, John, *Maternal Care and Mental Health*. New York: Columbia University Press, 1951.

Burmeister, Eva, *Forty-Five in the Family*. New York: Columbia University Press, 1949.

———, *Roofs for the Family*. New York: Columbia University Press, 1954.

Einstein, Gertrude, "The Homemaker's Role in Prevention and Treatment of Family Breakdown," *Child Welfare*, XXXIX (May 1960), pp. 22–25.

Folks, Homer, *The Care of Destitute, Neglected and Dependent Children*. New York: The Macmillan Company, 1902.

Freud, Clarice, "The Meaning of Separation to Parents and Children as Seen in Child Placement," *Public Welfare*, XIII (January 1955), pp. 13–17, 25.

Gordon, Henrietta L., *Casework Services for Children*. Boston: Houghton Mifflin Company, 1956.

Hagan, Helen R., "The Child-Caring Institution as a Casework Agency," *Child Welfare*, XXXIII (June 1954), pp. 3–9.

Hancock, Claire, "Protective Service for Children," *Child Welfare*, XXVIII (March 1949), pp. 3–9.

Hopkirk, Howard W., *Institutions Serving Children*. New York: Russell Sage Foundation, 1944.

Keith-Lucas, Alan, "Status of Parent during Placement," *Child Welfare*, XXXII (June 1953), pp. 3–5.

Konopka, Gisela, *Group Work in the Institution*. New York: Whiteside, Inc., 1954.

Lundberg, Emma O., *Unto the Least of These*. Des Moines, Iowa: Appleton-Century-Crofts, Inc., 1947.

Maas, Henry S., and Richard E. Engler, Jr., *Children in Need of Parents*. New York: Columbia University Press, 1959.

Overton, Alice, "Serving Families Who 'Don't Want Help,'" *Social Casework*, XXXIV (July 1953), pp. 304–309.

Polk, Mary, "Helping Children in Foster Care to Cope with Separation from Parents," *Child Welfare*, XXXIX (June 1960), pp. 12–17.

Raymond, Louise, *Adoption and After*. New York: Harper & Row, Publishers, 1955.

Scher, Bernard, "Specialized Group Care for Adolescents," *Child Welfare*, XXXVII (February 1958), pp. 12–17.

———, "Work with Parents in a Placement Agency," *Journal of Social Work Process*, V (1954), pp. 81–99.

Schulze, Susanne, ed., *Creative Group Living in a Children's Institution*. New York: Association Press, 1951.

Studt, Elliott, "Therapeutic Factors in Group Living," *Child Welfare*, XXXV (January 1956), pp. 1–6.

Taft, Jessie, ed., *Social Casework with Children*. Philadelphia: Pennsylvania School of Social Work, 1940.

Thurston, Henry W., *The Dependent Child*. New York: Columbia University Press, 1930.

U.S. Children's Bureau Publication no. 346, *Standards for Specialized Courts Dealing with Children*. Washington, D.C.: Government Printing Office, 1954.

Wires, Emily, "Some Factors in the Worker-Foster Parent Relationship," *Child Welfare*, XXXIII (October 1954), pp. 8–9, 13–16.

Young, Leontine, *Out of Wedlock*. New York: McGraw-Hill Book Company, Inc., 1954.

Christopher Allen

LOIS BENEDICT,
General Secretary and Director of Casework,
Children's Home Society of Virginia
Richmond, Virginia

The Children's Home Society of Virginia provides an adoption service throughout the state. It is licensed by the Virginia Department of Welfare and Institutions; governed by a citizen board of directors; and supported by individual contributors and monies raised by community chests and united funds in Virginia. It serves three groups of people; natural parents, children, and adoptive parents, for whom it provides a caseworker for the mother, a different caseworker for the baby, and a third one for the adopting parents.

A mother who is pregnant out of wedlock has to decide on a way of life for herself and her child. It is not simple to decide between giving up forever one's own baby or rearing him with the economic and cultural hazards that follow when there is no husband and father. The pain inherent in this may invite a quick, blind decision but this is dangerous. To live at peace with the decision, it is important that it be made not on advice or pressure but according to personal conviction. Sometimes, in deciding about her own future, a mother has to look back and understand why she got into the situation, as a means of being self-determining in the future. It is the responsibility of the mother's worker to help her to a decision that, insofar as possible, will not leave her haunted by worries, nor literally searching for the child, nor full of hostility to be taken out on the world and herself, but convinced of its validity.

It is the responsibility of the baby's caseworker to see that he has a constructive experience from the time he leaves his natural mother until he goes to adoptive parents; to know something of his unique qualities so that he can be placed with people who, as years go by, may feel to him like people who speak his own language. Most babies are "normal," and that is all that most adopting parents ask. But "normal" includes extrovert and introvert, the plodder and the pioneer, the poet and the athletic champion. Even in a hospital newborn nursery some individual differences are observable. Life experiences will greatly influence what the child does with his innate qualities, but the agency hopes to give each one an opportunity to realize all of his potential.

The caseworker for adopting parents works with adequate people unaccustomed to using social services; people who have suffered thwart-

221

ing and deprivation of the basic biological and spiritual experience of parenthood. The worker wants to know whether they have had their grief and left it behind and are now healthy, happy people. She wants to learn and help them learn whether a child born to someone else can become fully and satisfyingly their own; whether they can deal constructively with the problems of normal parenthood plus the additional problems inherent in parenthood by adoption. She wants to know what specific factors are important to them in the child they adopt.

Service in the supervisory period is intended to help the new family lay a strong foundation for a lifetime relationship together. Like other relationships, adoption is not achieved in a moment, and rarely does the family experience a static storybook ending of "they lived happily ever after." Like marriage, there is a period of getting ready, a joining, and then a new adjustment to be achieved.

On February 23rd the agency received the following letter from Lucy Carter: "Mrs. Henley, the social worker at the maternity home, suggested that I make an appointment at your convenience to discuss plans for the adoption of my future child. I shall be available at any time that is suitable with you. I shall appreciate hearing from you as soon as possible."

In this agency there is an interview, sometimes more than one, in which the client learns what is involved in the service and decides whether she wishes to begin it. If she decides to file a formal application a permanent worker is assigned. The application worker acknowledged Miss Carter's letter promptly, made an appointment, and saw her at the maternity home on February 29th.

Miss Carter proved to be a charming and sturdy young woman of twenty, who last June finished her sophomore year at college. She volunteered almost at once that the baby is now expected on April 15. She hopes he can be received by the agency as soon after birth as possible, since she wishes not to see him. We talked a little about how the agency receives a new baby into care and she decided she would want us to receive him seven days after birth.

Miss Carter was open and steady in letting me know how the baby happened. The father had been visiting her home. There was only one time when conception could have occurred, and she considered it "more my fault than his." She did not realize she was pregnant and returned to school. She let her parents know before the Christmas holiday. In his first shock her father was furious with the boy and intended to take him to court to get support. After they talked it over, they put their energies instead into arranging maternity home care. She was relieved, for the baby's father had been working several years, saving for further education, and she would hate to see his plan interrupted. She herself planned to get a job in the city for a while and then go on to another college as a junior next fall. Her parents were standing back of her, and this felt very good. It was very different from what she saw some other girls experiencing.

Miss Carter considered thoughtfully what I told her about what we would need from her, what the usual steps are for a baby, and related these in practical fashion to her own plans. She said clearly this is what she needs and asked for an application. I gave it to her with confidence and told her that Miss Reid would be the person to help her carry out the plans we have been discussing.

Miss Reid's work with Miss Carter began following this and continued until the legal release of the baby.

On March 21 I telephoned to make an appointment for the next day. Other work had made it impossible to call sooner. Miss Carter was very responsive and friendly on the phone. She explained she is known by her first name at the maternity home. (This is the policy of the Home; last names are not used for reasons of confidentiality.)

The next day I visited Miss Carter, and again she was responsive, attractive, and poised. She had prepared for the interview by being well groomed, and presented herself as a capable young woman with some sparkle and a sense of humor. She recalled her interview with the applications worker and said that right now she doesn't have any questions she needs to discuss. So I asked if she can help me understand why she is asking for adoption. She did this readily. Her manner showed adequacy and independence but several times she also conveyed a helpless feeling; for instance, through frequent references to the caseworker at the Home and how much their talks together mean.

Lucy was convinced that adoption is the only fair thing to do. If she could provide for the baby practically, he would still need a father and the acceptance of a family and the community. In their community they are considered "a good family," and a baby out-of-wedlock would not be accepted. But her baby has "a good heritage." All her family are in good health; she herself has never been in the hospital before. This leads her to talk about the hospital she will soon be going to and her dread of delivery. She has been talking with the nurse and getting ready by understanding it. I thought her expressing her feeling, and my accepting it, was another way of getting ready.

I reminded her that we need to know in detail about her health and offered the medical form. She accepted it readily and will take it to the doctor to be filled out by him at the next clinic day. She asked me to come back the day after clinic, and we made a definite appointment. As she thinks back over the pregnancy, she admits now she really knew it before she returned to college. It was terribly hard to bring herself to tell anyone. When she finally did confide in her parents it was pretty hard to stand the things they said as she already felt so bad about it. Her father was furious and raved about taking the young man to court to make him pay expenses, and she had to work hard to talk him out of it. Her father is paying the full Maternity Home fee, but she intends to pay him back every cent and has her plans all made.

I asked Lucy if she plans to see and take care of the baby. Frankly she had not yet made up her mind but thought she could get through the experience better with not too much contact. She thought, though, she would see him at least once. I accepted this.

Lucy referred to her baby's father and with resignation said, "I suppose you are like Mrs. Henley and want to know all about him." I explained that this information helps know her baby and the kind of home he might be happy in. She took hold to describe the father's appearance, his work and education, his present attitude. It was a struggle for her to admit that he was not helping her at all. His last letter almost doubted her pregnancy. She did not answer him, and for her the relationship ended when she knew he wasn't going to stand by her.

Our time had ended before we had finished family history, and she chose to write it up herself before we met again.

On April 10 the maternity home worker phoned. Lucy's baby was born on the 8th. He is a big boy, active and handsome, on a Lactum formula and takes it with gusto. Lucy has seen him once and now plans to be the one to bring him to us but not to see him in the meantime.

On April 11 I visited Lucy in the hospital building at the maternity home. She said she was glad to see me, and the determination and effort she showed in walking to the interviewing room certainly indicated that she wanted to see me. She had her medical report with her and six pages of family history which she had written. She said she wanted to go over these papers first and then tell me about her experience and her baby. She was very well organized and could make several jokes. First we looked over the medical form together and recognized her good health and what it means to her and to the baby. Then she showed me the family history, which she had written so carefully. She started it in pen, then she had her baby, then she completed it in pencil. She used the form that another adoption agency gave one of the other girls, and in her opinion this is a good way to pull one's thoughts together. She went on to talk about what is particularly important to her for us to know about her baby's heritage and with feeling concluded that she so much wants her baby to have the right parents.

With deep feeling but without dramatics, Lucy reviewed the experience of the baby's birth. She remembered asking the nurse to see him but hardly remembered anything except that he had lots of dark hair. She has named him Richard for her father, Martin for his (the baby's) father, and gave him his father's last name. I explained that it would be necessary to correct the birth registration to show his last name the same as hers and I would help her with this. After we had discussed this, she concluded in a moving way by saying, "Yes, I'll claim him—he is really and truly mine." She was determined to see him every day and to take full part in bringing him into care.

Lucy did not like the fact that there were so many different girls on nursery duty. Five different people had fed him so far. I asked if she meant she was thinking of feeding him herself. She shook her head and her eyes filled but she did not cry. She wanted to get clear on the details of his coming into agency care, eagerly accepted the form to get medical information about the baby, and reviewed with me the agreement she will sign authorizing the society to give him foster care and medical care. I asked when she wants him to come into care. She wanted him to come soon, wondered if Tuesday, his ninth day would be possible, and we agreed on this. She wondered how we will travel if it is bad weather. She had questions about what boarding homes are like. When would he go to his adoptive family? She said simply she feels responsible for making good arrangements. She sees that I care about her and that I have been dependable, so concludes she can trust him to my agency. She did not notify the father of his birth for she feels satisfied that she can make arrangements herself.

Lucy arranged for me to see the baby but she herself could not bear to see him today and left hastily. Richard was an appealing baby, rather handsome, round face, almost chubby. His abundant straight dark hair was sticking up in all directions. When he was disturbed he began to cry and used his whole body in protest. The nurse said he is an unusually enthusiastic eater and is doing well.

On April 16 I received Richard from his mother at the Maternity Home and took him into agency care. Lucy had decided to give Richard his last feeding herself. He spit up most of it, but she was not dwelling on this; she was ready for the agreement placing him with the society and for the forms to correct the birth certificate. She was very steady and self-controlled as she placed him in my arms.

On April 17, as planned, I visited Lucy at the hospital. She had a high temperature and was in bed, but we could have privacy on the ward. She had concluded she was even more upset yesterday than she realized. She was anxious to hear how he traveled and was reassured at hearing that he demanded, and got, another feeding soon. She wiped tears from her eyes saying she cried all last night and thought she was over it by now. She was sure about the rightness of her decision for adoption, even though it hurts now, and went on to hope that she could leave the hospital soon. She will call me when she gets back home.

On April 22 Miss Carter telephoned that she was back in town, busy about getting a job and getting into college next fall; she was not worried about the baby but had a couple of things on her mind and wanted to plan an appointment.

On April 29 Miss Carter was in the office, well groomed but rather pale. She brought me up to date on developments about a job, an apartment, examinations for college. She wanted to hear about Richard, and I told her that he is doing well in his boarding home. With a sigh, she repeats her conviction that adoption is the best plan for him, adding "and under the circumstances it is the best thing for me too."

The birth certificate was now corrected, but she did not want to keep it, and we agreed she would mail it to me. She asked if he will be told he is adopted. Together we recognized that the answer is *yes* and considered what it means to her. She wondered what he will think about her. She would like his adoptive parents to understand her situation; though she was irresponsible in becoming pregnant, from that point on she planned for him in a responsible way and she loved him.

Miss Carter had been talking with her sister about whether she should tell that she has had a baby if she marries. Her relationship with Richard's father was not the full kind of relationship she hopes for in marriage. She and the father had not been in touch now for several months. She believed he could find her; she did not intend to initiate contacts and did not expect that he would try. We concluded that what she would tell in the future would depend upon how she felt then and on the person with whom she was considering marriage. Right now she did not see marriage in the foreseeable future. The immediate need was a job and we discussed the openings she was considering. Dejectedly, she said here she is 21 years old and still in need of clarifying what she wants to do with her life. As if thinking aloud, she wondered whether to go back to college if she should have a good job by summer. I supported her working now on the present need of a job and recognized the effort she is putting into it.

In getting ready to leave, Miss Carter said again she really did feel right about her plans for the baby but sometimes she got to thinking and needed to talk about it all. She knew from me that I would be ready to talk with her at any time and that we would keep in touch about Richard's readiness for legal release. She said that for his sake, she will be ready when he is.

In the next few weeks she telephoned in a number of times "just keeping in touch."

On June 4 Miss Carter was in the office by appointment and got to business quickly with the assertion that she now feels ready to complete legal release as soon as possible. She gave me the birth certificate, which she no longer wanted to keep. She asked for confirmation of her belief that he was getting along all right. I gave her this with conviction, but she did not ask for the details, which I could have given. She said she had not entirely "gotten over" having had Richard but felt she was "coming along." There had been little incidents where she was able to maintain a balance. For instance, someone made a joke about Mother's Day, and she was jolted for a second. Then she remembered that this person did not know she was a mother. She had been accepted at a state university next fall and was proud of it. She talked a little of her present living and her job. She had begun dating again about two weeks ago. She was going with a young Frenchman, but his temperament was too much for her. While she was eager for college, one of the things she had learned this last year is that when it is necessary to wait, she can. I was impressed with Miss Carter's own progress.

A few days after this Richard was ready for legal relinquishment, and I told Miss Carter this by telephone. Her response was, "Good," and she was ready to make plans for ending. She arrived promptly, looking well groomed and very well. She volunteered she had been waiting for this day, saw the papers on the desk, and said she was ready for them. First, though, she wanted to hear how Richard was and how he looked. I gave her this information, and she was surprised that his eyes were brown. Then she remembered that his father had brown eyes too.

With a half smile Miss Carter repeated she was glad Richard could have his permanent family. She felt no doubt that this was the right decision. Briefly she had to ruminate and orient herself to the past and future. It was almost a year ago that she became pregnant, and at that time she really cared about Richard's father. Now she hoped not to see him again. For herself, "I certainly don't want to sell dresses for the rest of my life," so she was looking forward to a new college in a new place and "really making something of my life."

Slowly we read the final relinquishment papers aloud together, and the meaning of these dignified, final words touched her. A notary was called in, and Miss Carter completed her part with conviction.

Miss Carter sat back quietly after signing. When I asked how she felt, she laughed and said she was surprised at how finished and "at peace" she felt. She thought she would go home and do the ironing. Her thanks to the agency are gracious but quickly finished; she was really ready to leave all this behind her and go on.

What of Richard as a person? In the maternity home Miss Reid was aware of the handsome boy whose every hair stood alone; the sturdy little fellow who ate with gusto and protested with his whole body when his sleep was interrupted. She had studied his mother's medical report and Richard's own birth history and neonatal medical report. She could bring him into agency care for preadoptive study with belief that he could contribute to a good life with adoptive parents.

A different social worker received him into care and took him to the Bates boarding home. The family consisted of Mr. and Mrs. Bates and a son of high school age. The two older children had married and gone, and Mrs. Bates reached out to give warm temporary mothering to one agency child after another. Each child was treasured for himself, and when each one went to his adoptive parents there was sadness, but also rejoicing, for his sake. Mrs. Bates, the caseworker, and the pediatrician watched Richard's development closely. The pediatrician studied carefully the record of events at the time of the birth that might affect Richard's later development. Of course, Richard could be adopted if there were some problem, but in that case he would need an unusually wise or courageous family. The caseworker also watched something of his emerging alertness and temperament so as to choose for him a family who would value and claim the boy that he is. Before he was ten weeks old, the worker could say he was ready for a home, and her record presents:

Richard is an appealing boy, both in physical appearance and personality. He is unusually large, falling within the 90th percentile range for weight and height. Because he is well proportioned and above average in motor ability, he gives the impression of being older than he is rather than exceptionally large for his age. His heritage includes a variety of heights but mostly above-average.

Richard is a good-looking little boy with a well-shaped head and regular features. His eyes and hair are dark brown. The bridge of his nose is wide, and on the first medical examination his eyes appeared to cross. On the last examination the pediatrician again saw his eyes cross, but until he is about seven months old it cannot be known whether this is a genuine problem. It may simply be due to the wide bridge of the nose. Other than this, his medical examination was negative. Psychological examination given when he was nine weeks old indicates that he is "near the top of the average range or possibly above-average in rate of psychomotor development."

This little boy's rapid development was noticed by Miss Reid (the mother's caseworker), the pediatrician, the psychologist, and myself. At ten days his eyes appeared to focus, he made little gurgling sounds, his smile seemed to be meaningful, he distinguished between known and unknown persons. His physical strength and control now appear above the average. He uses his hands well, supports weight on his feet, and is physically active. He is an enthusiastic eater. Usually he appears happy and contented but when he exercises his will it is with strength and determination. I believe this boy has considerable strength of body and spirit. He seems to need parents of equal strength who can set limits, give a variety of opportunities, and relate with warmth and openness.

The Allen home was chosen for Richard. Mrs. Allen's first letter on November 10 said they had been married four and a half years and had no children. Their doctor had suggested that they consider adoption and recommended this agency. They asked for information about procedure.

The Allens were immediately sent a printed booklet telling something about the kind of families the agency can serve and the procedures involved. Their letter in response said, "We found it very informative and helpful in its clear explanation of what we can expect. After reading it, we feel we would like to adopt through the Children's Home Society." Following this they gave factual information about themselves, which showed no impediment to their being served by the agency. It was some weeks before their first interview, as the society sees only the number of people each month that it is likely to be able to serve, and others had inquired before the Allens.

The application interview serves as a preliminary sifting. It helps a family to know whether adoption, as practiced in this agency, seems likely to fill their need, and this implies some looking at the need itself. It also helps the agency to learn whether this family is one it can probably use as parents to an agency child. Neither aspect can be known finally at this time, but the filing of a formal application blank, if it occurs, signifies a mutual wish to go further and an expectation of moving toward the placement of a child.

On January 14 Mr. and Mrs. Allen came for an application interview. Mr. Allen looked like a bright young executive, a bit stuffy at first, but as we got related this impression was quickly dispelled and a quality of humility emerged. Mrs. Allen was a lovely looking young woman, informal in dress, and she did not accentuate her good looks. She was the one to begin the interview, explaining how long she had wanted a child, the long series of medical tests and treatments, the frustration of knowing no physical reason for childlessness. They had wanted children while they were young. Their doctor concurred in their decision to come here, and they took this as an indication he thought they could not have their own. They are finding relief in giving up the hoping and frustration about a child by birth and turning to adoption. I pointed out that in their situation they would have to think how it would be if they had a child by birth after adopting; how it would be for them as parents and what it would mean to two children. Mr. Allen gave a rambling story of boys he has known in a nearby institution, how much he respects them, and how much they have to give. They knew other adopted children in their neighborhood whom they admired. The possibility of children by birth was now so remote to them that they found it hard to work on the possible difference of feeling between the children; they did not block it out, but their emphasis was on giving themselves to children, and the problem they anticipated was avoiding spoiling. A recent magazine article saying a child should not be told of his adoption had challenged their thinking and made them aware it is not an easy subject, yet they came out with a conviction of their own. They liked the idea of thinking more about such subjects during home study. They were pleased that service might be quicker than they had expected. Application was offered and accepted with a feeling of rightness on both sides.

Application was returned by mail a week later. It showed that Thomas Allen was 30 years old, blond coloring, 6 ft. 3 in. tall, American of English and French descent, Episcopalian, a college graduate employed with a leading bank at $8000 a year. He owned his home, and carried life, health, accident, and hospitalization insurance. Nancy Allen was 29, 5 ft. 6 in. tall, with dark hair and eyes, American of Scotch-Irish descent, Episcopalian, college graduate. Neither of them had been married previously.

On March 28 Mrs. Parks, the Allen's caseworker, wrote that she could begin home study if they were ready and offered a choice of times when they could come to the office. They telephoned immediately and enthusiastically accepted the earlier appointment.

The interview on April 4 began with my suggestion that they might like to consider what home study and supervision would be about. The Allens expressed an idea we would be measuring them against a norm of what we expect of all families. We discussed this, and I made the point that each couple is different, that they bring different strengths and weaknesses to adoption. I spoke of our interest in knowing them as individuals and as a couple and outlined what we would do together.

They were eager to offer their experience about children. Before they married they planned a large family. Then there were several miscarriages, treatments, and finally the doctor's recommendation of adoption. Mr. Allen said with a grin that there doesn't seem to be much probability of children by birth, and I responded to the grin saying that although he was smiling about it, it probably hurt pretty deeply. He guessed it did but had gotten resigned to it. I said the way one feels about childlessness has a lot to do with the way he is as an adoptive parent. If an adopted child always reminded him of something that was still painful, it wouldn't be very good. If they adopt, other people will draw their own conclusions. Mr. Allen said people are always asking questions about why they don't have children. He thinks I would be surprised how nosy they have been. He recalled so vividly a man who asked all kinds of questions on the very day after the last miscarriage. It was the last thing he wanted to talk about then, but by now it has fallen into place and can be talked about if it needs to be.

The Allens believed there was little likelihood of a child by birth after adoption. Anyhow, she thought she would feel more special toward the adopted child you had to work so hard to get, and also the first child in any family is something special. He said all children are special and got very earnestly involved in discussing how you should treat all children alike. Of course, you can't because each one is different; finally he got it clear that he wants to give each one the understanding and affection and opportunity that will enable him to be himself. He was concerned that they might spoil their children because they want them so much. I asked what he meant by spoiling and he defined it briefly as "unreasonable indulgence." Mrs. Allen looked at him with great warmth through this part of the interview, and he beamed and blushed under her approval. She started teasing him about spoiling his hunting dogs, but he did not appear to be uncomfortable under her teasing. Apparently she has the same enjoyment of them; she said, "Every time these dogs come in I have to wipe eight muddy paws and I can't see that taking off children's galoshes would be more of a chore than that." I could see that the way they react to one dependent living creature could give some indication of how they might react to a little child, and Mr. Allen expounded his thinking about consistency of discipline, understanding what the rules are for, giving a lot of affection along with limits. He said there are neurotic dogs like neurotic humans and the cause is the same—"unreasonable and unloving discipline." They are thoroughly enjoying visualizing giving themselves to bringing up a baby; Mrs. Allen said realistically, "I wonder how these far-flung theories are going to work out when we actually have a child."

The Allens had given little thought to the aspects of adoption that are different from biological parenthood. Their thoughts on telling the child that he is adopted were somewhat naive. They knew someone who learned about adoption when she was 19, and, as they analyzed her reaction, they found in themselves a comfort in meeting this problem with their child. Not that the telling would necessarily be easy. Mrs. Allen assumed that the baby would probably be born of an unmarried mother, but she could not see how anyone would give up a baby. We examined this, and she was able to see that she was seeing herself in the mother and could try to understand why the mother might be different. Mr. Allen thought probably the mother "just got into deeper water than she expected." I spoke of loneliness or unmet needs, and he recognized that we all feel lonely at times. She was inclined to turn off his earnestness with teasing, but he responded with good humor.

As the interview ended I suggested a book they could read that would provoke some discussion between them, and we could discuss it together later. As they were leaving, he said, "Boy, I feel a lot better now." He admitted he was scared to death about coming today, not knowing what to expect and wanting a child very much. In a disarming and boyish way he said he is going to put his mind on adoption now and come up with some more ideas, and she thought both of them now will be looking forward eagerly to the next interview.

I offered medical blanks with conviction as the Allens were investing themselves in this interview with warmth and openness, and I felt no serious problem. I explained the blanks could be filled out by a doctor of their choice and that our next interview could be when they had been returned.

The medical reports were returned in a week, and I telephoned Mrs. Allen to make another appointment. She said they are wondering now why they were so frightened last time; now they see they were given an opportunity to discuss adoption and had someone listen to them, for a change, and hear them out. Mr. Allen particularly had told her that I seemed to value their opinions! They were ready for the next appointment as soon as I could arrange it.

At the next appointment on April 16 we talked first about the fact that they had been so worried about home study, why they had been so worried, and how they feel now. They said that although we covered some intimate things, they did not feel that it was horrible. For one thing, I was not mean about it. They had had the impression they would be judged and now they saw the purpose is understanding them and helping them become parents. In fact, they had begun to act like prospective parents. They had decided to use the den for the baby's room, to move the den furniture into the garage, to move the dogs out of the garage, and to reroof the doghouse. There was humor in this story, but recognition that they are getting ready. Mr. Allen said he had suddenly begun to take himself very seriously, seeing that he is going to have the responsibility of being a father. His job had taken on new meaning, and he had begun to think about advancement in the future. This surprised him as he usually takes things casually, but when you are thinking about being a father, you look at the whole world differently.

Mrs. Allen said this has been her experience too. She was now forever asking what age some child is and is interested in its sleeping and eating patterns. I asked how she felt about babies before, especially when she was having trouble having one. Mrs. Allen looked at the floor and braced herself and told me she really had had a hard time; there for a while it was almost impossible to look inside a baby carriage. It hurt way deep inside to think that someone else could have a baby and she could not. It was so good to get over this feeling that "I can't be a mother." Both said they now see they can be parents in this different way and there is every reason to think it can be a satisfying family life. She said again that the first child will be very special, but said it is not the way the child comes to you nor the position in the family, but the child himself. He felt everybody has something special and it is up to you to make the most of it. They were noticing more carefully how other parents handle their children, thinking what they won't do in similar situations.

To tell the truth, Mr. Allen said, he has been spending a lot of time thinking what fathers should be like. This takes him into his own experience—a happy relationship with a father who died when Mr. Allen was nine, then a period of unhealthy closeness to his mother, then a stepfather who became a heavy drinker and whom ultimately the mother divorced. A half brother had been born, and Mr. Allen became something of a father person to him. He is flattered that this boy still looks to him for guidance. I said it looked as though Mr. Allen had some pretty tough experiences, but he thought they made him a better person in that he is more understanding of others, and certainly from it he has a real recognition of the importance of fathers to children.

During this interview we talked some about their relationship with each other. I told them I had the impression that probably their disagreements took the form of good-natured kidding. He said this is right most of the time, but once in a while they have a real blowup. They consulted together and decided they had had four real fights. All of these had been when she became angry with him for something rash he had done, and they gave examples. During some of this, she sat rigidly in her chair, looking ready to blow up, shaking her head as though to say, "Sometimes I think he's just a big boy." They agreed heartily he is the impulsive one of the two, and he considered how this would be for a child. There was mutuality in their deciding that you can't expect parents to be perfect, any more than you can expect children to be just right. However, he wanted me to know that he can take a firm hand with himself and his children. He felt sure he could keep himself under control. She said she had already guessed she will be the disciplinarian of the family. His discussion of this seemed to be defending himself, and I said one cannot generalize about the father and the mother role. Sometimes the mother is the disciplinarian, but the important thing is how comfortable the couple themselves are with it. It is not so much a matter of fitting in with a stereotype as adjusting to a three-way relationship in a way that is satisfying for all three of them.

We talked a little more about husband-wife relationship, and Mrs. Allen blushed and, looking straight at her husband, said, "I've never told you this, but one reason I wanted to marry you was because of how wonderful you seemed to be with children." I let them know I valued the depth of feeling they were bringing to getting ready for parenthood.

We talked some more about the painful aspects of adoption, and the Allens had done a great deal of thinking since last time. They are developing a comfort and realism about this. At ending, Mrs. Allen said one reason for home study was so you could prepare yourself and she thought someone receiving a baby from a hospital wouldn't be nearly as ready as they are going to be. Shyly, she offered examples of how real parenthood is becoming to her.

In the following week the Allens arranged for Mr. and Mrs. Anderson, their reference, to come to see me. These were the Allen's contemporaries and they had been friends for many years. They said they had been noticing with amusement the Allens beginning to act like other parents, for instance, deciding between diaper service and buying a washing machine. They told me how good Mrs. Allen is with children in general, especially with the Anderson children, and how Mr. Allen is so easy-going and steady and kind. This, too, was backed up by incidents. They were impressed with his easy relationship with people at all levels of society and his varied interests. They could think of no couple who would be better parents for a child.

On April 30 by appointment I visited the Allens in their very attractive suburban home. It was distinctive in their imaginative use of color and their mixing of fine antiques with modern furniture. I told them of the Anderson's warm endorsement of them as parents and the broader understanding of them I had through talking with their reference. As they talked about their interest in antique furniture, antique cars, guns, boats, I could really see how they lived together and settled their differences. Mrs. Allen's humorous cracks at him, which once had a sharpness, now seemed to express admiration as well. He named the feeling of adequacy and self-assurance he gets through being able to do these many various things, and she volunteered that this is another of the things that attracted him to her. Together they agreed it will add richness and meaning to a child's life too.

I told them, too, that the Anderson's statement that Mr. Allen was so easy-going made me wonder if he could be such a paragon, and with humor he told me about once having punched his boss in the nose; he can get angry, but this isn't his usual way. In fact, he is inclined to identify with a person who has anger directed against him. Mrs. Allen said freely that she gets riled over little things; she thinks each of them has provided a balance for the other.

We discussed the child whom they could claim most fully. Their original request for a girl was because they thought they might harm a boy by overindulging him. Now they are more confident about themselves as parents and would feel equally good about a boy or girl. I thought it would be good to know any particular fears, and Mrs. Allen blushed and finally said, "Well, I think I should tell you something that has been in

the back of my mind all the time"; that is, she would be concerned at receiving a child from a "messy situation," meaning parents of limited ability and markedly unsocial behavior. Having gotten this out and said it
would be hard to take a child like that, she turned thoughtful and said,
"No, if a baby like that came to us we would love it, and it would probably
turn out like us just the same." We talked again about the way most babies
come to us and what a family knows in making their decision to take a
child. We looked at special problems a child might have, and they recognized that they have some too and they could keep this in proportion.
They knew from friends that the process of claiming a child to become
their own is not always immediate and that they might find some unexpected response in themselves on meeting a baby. At the same time, they
knew that the baby might be sensing some unusual tension at the point
of meeting new parents.

We have gone forward so steadily together that it was no surprise
to the Allens when I said I was ready to offer them a child when we have
one who needs their home. They are equally ready, and the interview concluded with gay excitement about arrangements.

When the Allen home was suggested for Richard, the workers who
had responsible knowledge of him and of the Allens studied the records
Mrs. Parks, the Allen's caseworker, had a visit to get acquainted with
Richard, and a conference was held in which the positive and negative
factors were weighed. It was decided this could be a very good home for
Richard, but the final decision, of course, would depend on the Allens'
conviction. Then on June 21 Mrs. Parks telephoned and told Mrs. Allen
there was a little boy just over ten weeks old whom she would like the
Allens to know about. The response was, "Oh, no. Let me sit down. It
seems like a miracle. How soon can we see him?"

The next day Mr. and Mrs. Allen came to the office to hear about
Richard. Already they were emotionally exhausted, yet in a high state of
excitement, and it took them the first part of the interview to settle down
to responsible consideration. They had spent last night putting the last
coat of paint on the nursery, finishing at eleven o'clock but were too excited to sleep so they stayed up and talked about themselves as parents.

The Allens could not choose what they wanted to hear first, "Just
tell us everything about him," so I started with the boy's heritage, describing the mother's qualities, the nature of her relationship to the baby's
father, and her responsibility in making plans for the baby. I mentioned
that Mrs. Allen's feeling about "a messy situation" had been taken into
consideration, and Mrs. Allen nodded saying quietly, "Thank you." The
appearance, interests, education, and employment of both parents was
described, but anonymously. The Allens steadily laid claim to likeness to
themselves in all this, even when the likeness was farfetched.

I made clear that we were not thinking of heritage alone in suggesting this baby and described his vigorous attachment to life, his ability to protest and his individuality. The possibility of a crossed eye was named clearly. In all probability there will be no problem but there might be; if so, it is treatable or correctible by surgery. The Allens were somewhat sobered by this reality, yet felt it was an entirely normal problem and one they could deal with. Other than this, his health history is excellent. They got some sense of his vigor and the demand it will make on them and have acquired a regard for his first parents.

The next day the Allens came back to see Richard, arriving a half-hour early. Their first question was "What is his name?" When I told them "Richard," they responded that it will soon be Christopher, which is a family name. They were again under emotional strain. Mr. Allen jokingly asked if we had ever lost a father and then asked her, "Are you sure you are ready to be a mother?" Seriously, she feels a great sense of humility in the face of this wonderful thing. They wanted to talk again about some of the things we discussed yesterday, not because of doubt, but savoring the goodness of it and wanting to be sure to remember.

When the Allens entered the nursery to see Richard he was crying hard, and the caseworker had been unable to comfort him. The eye was noticeably out of alignment. Mrs. Allen's first words were, "Boy, no one will ever say that you are beautiful," and she burst into tears too. There was strong emotion in all three of them. When she had picked him up and started rocking him and all three of them were oblivious to the caseworker, I left them alone, but because of the tension I made it a short visit.

Afterwards I recognized how much meaning this could have for two sensitive people and asked if they were ready to talk about their feelings. Both of them said they were startled because he did not fit their preconceived notion of what their child would look like. We had talked about this before, but still they were surprised. They thought there was no use fooling themselves, there might be trouble about the eye. They were also intrigued that such a tiny baby could be so aggressive and demanding, and Mrs. Allen said, "We said we wanted an individual, and we are certainly getting one." I recognized some hesitation in them. Without denying it, they went on to admire the fact that this little boy is so masculine, "an opinionated little rascal," and presently they discovered with surprise that Richard had all the qualities they admire in people—strength, uniqueness, firmness—and discovered in themselves a wish to direct this little boy's native capacity into good channels. In fact, Mr. Allen thought he and Mrs. Allen were "just what the little rascal needs." She was aware of what the first few days would be like with a little boy who feels things this strongly; there was nothing facile in the Allens' claiming Richard, but step by step through the interview it became a strong, dependable claiming.

The next day when Mr. and Mrs. Allen came to take their baby home they were eager and happy. Overnight they had decided a baby of their own might have had far worse medical problems than a possible crossed eye. They joked about the battle of wills that would go on in the first week, or perhaps for the next fifty years, but had decided that grit to face the world is a tremendously important thing to them, and he has it. Mrs. Allen was frankly uncertain about physical care but had taken some steps to prepare herself and knew she could call her caseworker if necessary. Looking at their feelings, they knew they wanted very much to have Richard for their own, and an agreement defining mutual responsibilities was signed. They also received a statement of medical history to give to their pediatrician and a statement of the daily routine Richard had been accustomed to.

When the Allens went to the nursery for Richard, who was again crying lustily, Mrs. Allen picked him up confidently and put his sweater and cap on more competently than many new mothers do. Then they turned to say, "There aren't any words to say what we feel."

The Allens took their baby home on June 24. Within a week, Mrs. Allen telephoned to say that Christopher was doing just beautifully. Mother and daddy had trouble getting enough sleep until they decided to change their schedule to fit the baby's, and now all is going beautifully. I suggested a late afternoon appointment for the first supervision visit, and Mrs. Allen's answer was, "Don't be late because I want you to have plenty of time to see my baby."

The first supervision visit was in a little over two weeks, and I found Mr. and Mrs. Allen bursting with eagerness to show "our baby." They find him utterly beautiful; his eye has not looked crossed since they got him home. The grandmothers think he is not only beautiful but a genius. For the first few days they were not only inexperienced but also so overcome with awe at this wonderful child that they just stood around stupidly. Christopher got his trouble expressed in the placement process and has not been as hard to live with as they expected. They admit he is an opinionated little fellow who knows what he wants, primarily food on time. Already they can hardly remember back to the time before they had him. They are having a feeding problem because, "We can't seem to give him enough to fill him up." Holding him lovingly, Mrs. Allen says this baby couldn't be any more right for them and every day they feel they are so lucky that he is theirs.

Another visit was made on September 12. Christopher was by now a big, heavy boy developing rapidly. He was secure enough to join in the gaiety and to enjoy letting me hold him. Before long Mrs. Allen said,

"Don't you think he is the most unusual baby you have ever seen in your life?" They looked back on the experience at the time of placement, marveled that they could have worried at the possibility of crossed eyes, and wondered how the agency trusted them when they burst into tears. I explained I knew people express tension in varied ways and I was glad to see it expressed instead of bottled up. Even now they do not fully understand their feelings at that time. There was no doubt of their claiming of Christopher now, and they were quite perceptive in noticing his different relation to different people and were not asking too much of him.

On November 25 another visit was made to Mr. and Mrs. Allen and Christopher. They were immediately eager to show their lovely baby. All their actions show confidence in the agency that gave him to them and pride in all the details of his development. Christopher was obviously flourishing.

The Allens then discussed, seriously at first and then with increasing sparkle and humor, that they had come to know themselves better. They used to think all parents had to live in the suburbs. Now they know they really prefer the convenience and hustle and bustle of the city. Before buying, they have worked out problems of getting Christopher transported to the school they want him to go to, a yard for him and the dogs, and other children in the block to play with. There was some undercurrent of wondering what the agency would think, which I recognized, saying I thought children are raised best where the family feels comfortable and that we trust them to make proper decisions and plans. Their conclusion was that it had taken them a while to find out what they want in life and where they want to live. Christopher's grandfather had already given him a lot on the River Road, but they have decided on living in a city residential neighborhood.

On February 14 I visited the Allens in their new home, an old house completely and charmingly renovated. They were full of their change of home and what it has meant to them. There was a good bit of humor about the "do-it-yourself" aspects and great enthusiasm for the easy companionship with good neighbors. Christopher stayed with his grandmother during the move and was thoroughly spoiled, but was now back to normal family living and finding things to enjoy.

Christopher had grown tremendously and at ten months of age was wearing three-year clothing. Spontaneously, the Allens brought up that there will be some problems in raising this youngster who is so large and so advanced. Adults expect too much of him, and children his own age cannot cope with him. For themselves, they were thrilled with these qualities and knew for sure why he was placed with them. I recognized the part of this that is not easy, but together we concluded they had good capacity to help him develop.

Numerous times during the interview Mrs. Allen had to get Christopher out of trouble. He tried to climb the stairs, play the piano, hang from the dining room table. I saw a definite setting of limits with him, and she exclaimed, "You have to be pretty definite with this fellow."

On May 27 I visited the Allens for the last supervisory visit. Christopher continued to be his big, alert, mischievous self. He was using a number of words, and his language development appeared very good. There was nothing new with the Allens. They continued to have the normal ups and downs of happy parenthood.

As we turned our discussion to ending, the Allens wanted to involve themselves in a time of rumination. Looking back over the process they remembered their fear at beginning, fear whether they would be accepted and also fear whether a child born to someone else could really become their own. Now they knew for sure that Christopher was theirs.

This led into discussion of Christopher's original background. They recognized that after the adoption they will be on their own, responsible for making it understandable and right to him. They had quite good memory of the facts that were given to them and still felt comfortable about them. They believed they could help him respect the people he came from and also understand that that was ended and gone. Occasionally something brings them up short. Once a neighbor's child asked why his first mother couldn't take care of him. Once a waitress was very interested in him, and suddenly Mrs. Allen wondered if it could be his mother. Then she realized, of course, it could not. With tears in her eyes she told me how hard it must have been for this woman to give her baby up and she thought of her on Christopher's birthday. I spoke firmly about the mother's having other plans for herself and going ahead to something new, and this seemed to have meaning to Mrs. Allen. She recognized she was thinking of it from the standpoint of one who wanted a child so much and was unable to bear one. Adoption is complicated sometimes, but it is so enriching! They wondered why they were so frightened of the home study when actually we had spent our time talking together about what taking a child would mean to them and how they could help the child in his future life.

We discussed the legal steps. The Allens have chosen a lawyer to represent them, and I told them the steps that are involved and the approximate time it will take until they get their final order and later the birth certificate in his new name and theirs. We parted lingeringly, and Mr. Allen said it seemed strange to be saying good-bye, as my visits seemed to be a part of Christopher for them. This was my opportunity to say that they will now go forward as a family together alone; Christopher's future is in their hands and I probably will only hear of him again when he becomes valedictorian of his high school class. There was solemnity in our shaking hands and saying good-bye.

Nearly three months later, the judge signed an order "In the matter of the adoption of Richard Martin Carter, an infant," an order that ended "and the Court being fully satisfied as to the fitness and propriety of such adoption, and as to the ability of the said petitioners properly to bring up and educate the said child, does declare and adjudicate that from this date the said child to all legal intents and purposes is the child of the said petitioners and that the said child shall be named Christopher Allen."

9

PSYCHIATRIC
SOCIAL WORK

Extent and cost of mental illness

Within recent years there has developed an increasing awareness of the existence of mental illness, some acknowledgment of its extensiveness, and even some efforts to calculate costs. Institutions for the mentally ill have existed in this country, under private or public auspice, since our colonial period. However, it has not been until the last several decades that the American public has become alert to mental illness. In part, this more recent recognition has come about through concern over the amount of money that state legislatures and the federal government (including Veterans' Administration) were called upon for institutional and noninstitutional care. Another factor has been the knowledge that came from the Selective Service and the military experience of World War II as civilians were screened out of military service—before and after induction. This number, as reported to the Congress, was a shocking figure. Translated into peacetime figures a decade and a half after the war's close, this comes to more than a million persons hospitalized and another million receiving services in mental health clinics and psychiatrists' offices. Still another consideration that made the American public more aware of mental illness were the spectacular developments in treatment, principally chemotherapy, which markedly reduced the period of hospital residence. The combination of all these factors, and others, has required us to look realistically at the size of this contemporary problem and to be willing to face the $3 billion per year that we must pay either directly or indirectly. At the same time, we have been obliged to look at the services provided and, for the purposes of this volume, to examine the area of psychiatric social work.[1]

---

[1] Robert H. Felix and Morton Kramer, "Extent of the Problem of Mental Disorders," *Annals of the American Academy of Political and Social Science,* CCLXXXVI

Earlier notions of mental illness

Before there was ever a knowledge of mental hygiene or a mental hygiene movement, there were centuries of misguided, or unguided ignorance about the nature and causes of mental illness. Despite our contemporary concern over the unprecedented apparent increase of mental cases, a little reflection or, better yet, study will reveal that mental disorder was not uncommon among earlier peoples. Among preliterate cultures and in the civilizations that followed, the person of disordered mind was variously conceived of as a madman, a fool, or one who had outraged the gods. Such a person may have been deemed to be possessed of a demon, or to be the victim of magic wrought upon him, or as one being punished for his sins. It has only been within relatively recent times that any light has been shed upon the origin of mental disease. It has required the scientific investigations within the larger field of medicine to prepare the way for inquiry into causation.

The emerging concept of causation within modern times helped to effect a changing practice in the care and treatment of mental disease. When demons or spirits were believed to possess the body of a man, the common practice was to exorcise or drive them out by incantations, ceremonials, and other ingenious devices, thereby releasing the affected person from supernatural influences or freeing him from the power of magical spells. At another time prayer and sacrifice served as propitiation for the sins that had invited mental disorder. The fancied potency of herbs and drugs very often supplemented other propitiary exercises. During the Middle Ages persons possessed of evil spirits were physically scourged and tortured, and in many instances were burned, hanged, or drowned because of the conviction that they practiced witchcraft and sorcery. Our own experience during colonial times, hardly more than two centuries ago, stands as a mute testimony to our nearness to such beliefs. Even within the nineteenth century, when a limited knowledge of causation provided no answer to the eternal "why," we oscillated between punishment of the insane as criminals and indifference to them as baffling enigmas. When the answers were sought in physical disorders during that same century, our "treatment" emphasis was entirely custodial for all victims and restraint for violent cases. Not until the ferment that is psychoanalysis quickened our thinking and enriched our insight did we understand the psychogenic factors in mental disease. Then only could we supplement and, in many

---

(March 1953), pp. 5–14; see also Rashi Fein, *Economics of Mental Illness* (New York: Basic Books, Inc., 1958).

cases, replace custody with therapy. The organized efforts to translate this realization into action is the story of the mental hygiene movement.[2]

The impetus from psychiatry, psychoanalysis, and psychology

Throughout most of the nineteenth century emphasis had been placed upon improvements in custodial care of the insane. What study there was of mental disease concerned itself largely with descriptions, climaxed in the classification system of Kraepelin based upon symptoms rather than causes. At about this same time Sigmund Freud was beginning his studies of hysteria, which were to eventuate in psychoanalysis and to provide a far more fruitful approach to the phenomena of mental illness. Freud's analysis of the unconscious opened up the possibilities of a wholly new orientation to the human mind and personality. A dynamic conception of personality appeared, which was to modify forever, if not eventually to replace, the old static view. There were many American psychiatrists who, although not psychoanalysts in any sense of the term and certainly not Freudian, came to express the psychoanalytic point of view. These men, such as Adolph Meyer, August Hoch, C. Macfie Campbell, Thomas W. Salmon, affected the development of psychiatry immeasurably. William Alanson White and A. A. Brill were perhaps the only avowed Freudian psychoanalysts among this early influential group.

Developments within the field of psychology were also spreading into the field of human behavior. The many researches into the problems and processes of child growth produced increasing evidence of the vital importance of the early years of the child's life. It was becoming clear that early emotional experiences as well as their resultant attitudes had lasting effects upon the personality. Psychometric studies made of individual differences showed the wide variations of human intelligence and abilities. The growth of psychological clinics, of which Witmer's in Philadelphia in 1896 was the earliest, made possible the accumulation of considerable knowledge about the nature of these individual differences and their role in the development of the individual.

Thus, by the first decade of the twentieth century, there were signs upon the horizon that presaged a new departure in the study and treatment of mental disease. Psychiatry was turning from preoccupation with custody and classification to a concern with causes; psychoanalysis was introducing a dynamic approach; while psychology was tracing the growth of the child and stressing the nature of individual differences. The cumu-

---

[2] Albert Deutsch, *The Mentally Ill in America* (rev. ed.; Garden City: Doubleday & Company, Inc., 1949), Chapter 1.

lative effect of these varied approaches was the emergence of an entirely new outlook upon mental (personality) mechanisms, health, and illness. Essentially, it consisted of a recognition that the human personality is basically emotionally motivated and that behavior can be understood better by taking into account the forces that lie beneath the threshold of consciousness.

Clifford Beers and the mental hygiene movement

When it is remembered that the preventive ideal had already begun to find expression in medicine and public health, it is understandable and even predictable that a movement embodying this principle in the field of mental health would develop eventually. The mental hygiene movement is an illustration of this. There might be some honest difference of opinion as to when this would have taken place but there can be none about Clifford Beers being the precipitating factor. Without Beers the movement might have been delayed for years, but that it would have been started eventually is beyond question.

What then was the contribution of Clifford Beers? To understand something of its uniqueness, it is necessary to bear in mind that it was hardly more than a hundred years ago that the French alienist Pinel struck the chains from the insane at the Salpêtrière. Throughout the succeeding century, abroad and in America, asylums had continued to emphasize custodial care with little insight into why patients were what they were. Despite increasing refinements in asylum care and despite some knowledge of classification of mental disease, practically all institutions, public and private, were still pervaded with the densest ignorance concerning proper care and treatment of patients. For those innocent and harmless inmates who created no disturbance there was such care as met the necessary standards of decency and fairness. However, obstreperous victims, whose disease expressed itself in disorderly and violent ways, were exposed to the degree of harshness and brutality that their disorder aroused in attendants. It was not unusual for patients to be beaten, choked, placed in isolation or in the strait jacket for days at a time.

It was into this situation that Clifford Beers (1876–1943) came as a patient. Beers had entered upon a business career during the three years following his graduation from college in 1897. For six years he had carried around with him a fear of epilepsy that by 1900 had become an obsession with him. His attempt at suicide was unsuccessful, and for the next three years he was a patient in three different institutions of the state of Connecticut. The first was a privately owned asylum run for profit, the second a private nonprofit-making institution, and the third a state hospital. In all three the treatment was equally harsh and brutal, consistent with an ignorance that shrouded the very origins and nature of mental disease. Beers' treatment was not unusual for the day; if it had been, perhaps his life subsequently would not have been given over to the mental hygiene movement. It was just because it was so characteristic of institutions of the day that upon his recovery and release Beers wrote, at white heat, of his experiences while under institutional care. What spared the book from being just another "exposé" of asylum conditions was its sincere conviction and the author's foresight in having his manuscript examined and criticized by a number of outstanding psychiatrists and psychologists. A *Mind That Found Itself* appeared in 1908 with an introduction by William James, the outstanding American psychologist and philosopher of his generation. Within the same year the first state mental hygiene committee was formed in Connecticut, followed the next year by the National Committee for Mental Hygiene.

Mental hygiene emphases

The originating driving force of the movement was Clifford Beers. In the face of repeated discouragements, financial and otherwise, he persisted, with the aid of his book and his organizing abilities, in his efforts to bring about improvement in the care and treatment of the mentally ill. The brutalities he had experienced in three institutions were not peculiar to him alone. They were recognized as the inevitable product of the almost universal ignorance of the very nature of mental disease. It was realized that even though individual instances of brutality might be dealt with by discharge and punishment of the offending attendant yet more than that had to be done to overcome the prevailing attitude of the entire personnel. This attitude in turn reflected the beliefs generally held throughout the country.

While this first approach, improvement of institutional care, held constant, the attack was proceeding along other lines. The nature of mental disease and the process by which it develops were being studied. This called for an understanding of mental disorders that went far beyond the traditional concepts of classification and etiology that had been in vogue for over a generation. An analysis of causative factors demanded a positive approach that went to the roots of the disorder rather than a mere exercise in classification based on certain well-defined symptoms. The study of mental disease had to pass out of the realm of categories into the dynamics of personality development and personality adjustment.

A third essential in the early aims of the mental hygiene program was the recognition of the importance of prevention. Desirable as it might be to have institutions more humane, and valuable as theories of causation were, nevertheless it seemed just as imperative to be able to prevent the addition of millions of new recruits or potential recruits to the already large army of mentally disabled. Prevention was obviously predicated upon a knowledge of causes and had to wait for developments in that field. Stress was placed upon the positive ideal of prevention, not merely upon its negative aspects. It was just as vital, perhaps more so, for a person to be helped to attain and maintain a healthy, functioning personality as it was to be reminded perpetually of what not to do in order to avoid commitment to an institution. This concept of prevention had taken its place in medicine, especially since the beginning of the twentieth century, and had furnished an example which the mental hygiene movement quickly made its own. This was consistent with the pattern of moving from cure of the patient after he is sick to assisting the well person to stay in health.

A fourth and indispensable emphasis of the mental hygiene movement was the dissemination of knowledge concerning causes, treatment, and prevention. It was not sufficient that psychiatrists alone be acquainted with the nature of mental disease; it was just as necessary to have the general public informed. The National Commitee for Mental Hygiene, with Clifford Beers as its secretary and backed by most of the outstanding psychiatrists of the country, carried on a campaign of enlightenment through the medium of books, pamphlets, public meetings, and study groups. State committees for mental hygiene materially assisted in carrying on these labors with individuals and groups. That such efforts were not without their appreciable effects was reflected in the increasingly widespread acquaintance by large segments of the population of the general concepts of mental hygiene and of their utilization in everyday living. Perhaps for the first time in history a people had become conscious of what mental health meant and were implemented in some degree to attain it.

A final guiding principle of the mental hygiene movement has been the search for those ways and means by which people may be helped to live constructively and to realize their own capacities for living. Prevention may very well revolve around what should not be done to such an extent that mental health becomes a preoccupation with the negative. It may be very much like the man who is so careful not to get sick that he has no opportunity to enjoy health. While an original concern of the mental hygiene movement was a consideration of the psychoses and neuroses, attention has shifted more and more to all forms of maladjustment that the individual is experiencing within himself or with the larger groups of which he is a part. This has resulted in a renewed interest in helping to release individuals not only away from the disabling disorder but also toward the direction of positive mental health. The ultimate goal is the enrichment of human experience so that individuals may live creatively and be free fully to develop their potentialities.

The development of psychiatric social work

The shift in emphasis, around the beginning of the present century, from custodial care to individualized study and treatment prepared the way for a new departure in the kind and quality of care accorded mental patients. This first found expression in the newly opened psychopathic hospitals, neurological clinics of hospitals, and hospital social service departments. Psychiatrists were becoming increasingly aware of the crucial importance of the effect of emotional experiences upon the personality development of the individual. They were at the same time taking into account that environmental pressures upon the individual were factors to be reckoned with in any form of mental disability. The early psychopathic hospitals, of which the first was established in Michigan in 1906, concentrated upon the study, diagnosis, and treatment of the earlier and more hopeful forms of mental disease. As part of this study and diagnosis, the psychiatrist gathered material on the life histories of patients. Gradually, however, this assignment was delegated to field workers who functioned under psychiatric direction.

The first instance of the actual employment of a social worker in a hospital occurred in 1905 in the neurological clinic of the Massachusetts General Hospital under the direction of Dr. James J. Putnam. In the following year, a social worker was employed in the psychopathic wards of Bellevue Hospital, New York, for the purpose of assisting patients who were recovering from mental illness. The New York State Charities Aid Association, through its committee on mental hygiene, had in 1910 secured the appointment of an "after-care worker" to supervise patients discharged from two of the state hospitals of New York. It was not until the next year that the first social worker was placed upon the payroll of a state hospital for mental diseases, the Manhattan State Hospital. In 1913 two Massachusetts hospitals, Danvers State Hospital and Boston State Hospital, each placed a social worker upon the staff.[3]

The real impetus to the development of this work came when, in 1913, the Boston Psychopathic Hospital began its social service depart-

---

[3] See Roy R. Grinker, Helen MacGregor, Kate Selan, Annette Klein, and Jane Kohrman, "The Early Years of Psychiatric Social Work," *Social Service Review,* XXXV (June 1961), pp. 111–126; see also by the same authors *Psychiatric Social Work: A Transactional Case Book* (New York: Basic Books, Inc., 1961).

ment under the leadership of Dr. Ernest Southard and Miss Mary C. Jarrett. Hardly had this project started than World War I began. By the time
the United States was drawn in, in 1917, it had become clear that the
developing social service in civilian hospitals would be just as necessary,
if not more so, for army hospitals. The practical difficulty that needed to
be faced was that there were not enough specially trained social workers to meet emergency needs. Accordingly, plans were made to enlarge the
training facilities at the Boston Psychopathic Hospital, and eventually an
arrangement was effected whereby an emergency training course was
given under the joint auspices of Smith College, the National Committee
for Mental Hygiene, and the Boston Psychopathic Hospital, with Miss
Jarrett in charge. It is generally believed that the term describing this new
specialty, psychiatric social work, was coined by Dr. Southard and Miss
Jarrett. In their book *The Kingdom of Evils*, they expressly state that this
branch of social work was a new emphasis rather than a new function,
having grown out of ideas and activities that already existed in scattered
forms. In this respect, its development is not unlike that of medical social
work.

Out of these first training courses of eight weeks' duration in 1918
there came the establishment, within a year, of a permanent graduate
school of social work training at Smith College. Other schools, already
established, such as the New York School of Social Work, the Pennsylvania
School of Social and Health Work, and the Chicago School of Civics and
Philanthrophy, continued their interest in the field of psychiatric social
work and added to its rapidly enlarging area, which already was going
beyond the bounds of the hospital. Within a decade there was not a school
of social work that did not pay its respects to the psychiatric point of view,
and for some it constituted the cornerstone of the curriculum. Nor was
there a single agency or a phase of social work that escaped the impact
of its principles or implications.

During this period, that is, from World War I to the early 1960s, all
schools of social work in the United States and Canada have strengthened
their training programs not only in psychiatric social work but also in public assistance, child welfare, family service, school social services, the
correctional services, medical social work, group work, community organization, administration and research. By the same token, there has been a
strengthening of the services that the trained worker was equipped to
offer to the clients who came to the agencies asking for help with their
troubles. The caseworkers who trained in these many schools drew upon
a common and generic base (in the casework area) and utilized these
basic knowledges and skills in the variety of settings in which services
were offered. In the case of the psychiatric social worker the skills were
offered to clients who came to state mental hospitals, Veterans' Adminis-

tration hospitals, mental health clinics, child guidance clinics, psychiatric sections in general hospitals, residential treatment centers, and schools or hospitals for the mentally retarded. In these psychiatric settings the worker is an essential member of a professional team—psychiatrist, psychologist, psychiatric social worker—all of whose services are directed to the alleviation of mental illness and the restoration of mental health.

Psychiatric social work in hospitals for mental illness

When hospitals for the mentally ill moved beyond a preoccupation with custody and classification to a felt concern for treatment, it naturally followed that adjustment of the individual upon discharge assumed considerable importance. This "after-care" program Dr. Adolph Meyer traces back to the Switzerland and France of a century ago and then to our institutions in America for the mentally ill.[4] By the end of the first decade of the twentieth century, a number of "after-care agents" had been employed, and psychiatric social work in the hospital for mental disease was well underway.

This early interest in after care has continued with increasingly effective programs being developed in both parole and foster care. A working distinction is frequently made upon the basis of the patient returning to his own home in the case of parole while the arrangement whereby the patient goes to a home other than his own is referred to as foster care. Some workers are inclined to characterize the patient in foster care as one who is not well enough to take his place in his former environment or to earn his living, but this differentiation is by no means commonly accepted. To most workers the test is: Is the home from which the patient came able to receive him, and is there a reasonable prospect of a satisfying adjustment? If the original home is no longer available or would be seriously prejudicial to the welfare of the patient, then an alternative home should be found for him. This decision is an especially crucial one in all those instances where a living experience outside the institution will assure not only what the institution has to offer but much more by way of satisfying usefulness.

Before amplifying these remarks about after care, it will be well to trace the points at which the social worker encounters the patient. Admission to a mental hospital is a medical decision usually based upon the sworn statements of two physicians. Occasionally, there may be descriptive material about the individual, his family, and his community, which

[4] Adolph Meyer, "Historical Sketch and Outlook of Psychiatric Social Work," *Hospital Social Service,* V (April 1922), p. 221.

has been prepared by a county welfare worker in those states and counties where such arrangements have been established. Psychiatric social workers may see, at intake, relatives who have brought the patient to the hospital. Here there may be received material, or additional material, about the patient. The emphasis at this point, however, will be to assist the family with some of the problems arising from the fact of the patient's admission, to deal with some of their fears and anxieties, and to try to make understandable the hospital facilities and programs. This contact with the patient's family is important because it sets the tone and the nature of the continuing link between the hospital and the home. The quality of this early contact may have a great deal to do with whether the patient's family leaves thinking this is the end or thinking this is the beginning. Because of the usual stereotypes about mental illness and mental hospitals, there is a real service to be performed that will help the family to see the possibilities of treatment and restoration rather than to continue to regard commitment as an irrevocable doom.

When the patient is in the hospital, the psychiatric social worker continues contact with the patient, the family, and the community. The actual medical and psychiatric treatment is carried on by the physician and the staff associated with him, but there are many instances in which the social worker will be called upon to work with tangible as well as intangible matters as they affect the patient. In the realm of feeling, for example, there may be occasion to deal with the meaning of illness—with the patient as well as with family members; there may be matters to be handled affecting the marital partner. Or there may be very practical problems with which help must be given—legal matters, insurance, housing, clothing, etc. These services of the social worker are performed as a professional operation and as part of the treatment team whose existence is solely for the patient. The psychiatrist is necessarily working with the illness of the patient, with those aspects of illness that interfere with resolution of the patient's inner difficulties. More usually the social worker works with those areas of wellness that can be directed toward participation in the reality of everyday living and working. These two—the psychiatrist and the psychiatric social worker—are but a part of the total institutional process that is offered to the patient to be used according to his capacities.

As the psychiatric team members observe improvement, steps are taken toward modifying the treatment program. There may be presentation of the patient's progress at a staff meeting. It may be agreed that other forms of care should be explored, whether return to own family or foster care family. The social service department will be working not only with relatives around their resources and responsibilities but will be reviewing other possibilities. Here again the worker will face fears and anxieties on the part of patients and relatives; fears, this time, not about entering but about leaving the hospital.

The extraordinary results, within the past decade, associated with the use of drug therapy (also termed chemotherapy and pharmacotherapy) have affected the psychiatric social worker's services, especially as the patient returns to the community. Even though hospital admissions have not decreased or have decreased only slightly, there has been a marked shortening of the residence period inside the hospital and a pronounced increase in hospital releases. Social workers have been called upon to begin working earlier with the patient while in the hospital so that the patient may be more ready to meet the outside world. Much of this preparation, for example, such apparently simple, yet vital, matters as table manners, attention to clothing, handling money, etc., must take place within the hospital and with the help of other hospital personnel. Then steps must be taken to provide trial visits to the community, the use of common transportation, the purchase of clothing, and many other experiences that the rest of the world takes for granted. With so many exhospitalized patients continuing with drug treatments, either through private physician or local health department, it is important that contact be maintained. Living arrangements as well as employment are of fundamental importance, and these are matters to which the social worker keeps related far more than was true heretofore. Furthermore, the social worker, whether from the hospital or the community, has a considerable task in helping the family and the community to participate in the care of the person seeking to reestablish himself as a useful and productive human being.[5]

In addition to recognizing the mental hospital as a community agency, there have been further developments looking toward eventual rehabilitation of the patient who is ready to leave or who has left. Suggestions have been offered for a day hospital, for a halfway house, for after-care clinics at the hospital or the community level, for homemaker services, for social therapeutic clubs, and for protected workshops.[6]

---

[5] For pertinent examination of these recent developments see: Irene L. Hitchman, "A Follow-Up Study of Patients Treated with Tranquilizing Drugs," *Social Work*, 4 (October 1957), pp. 61–62; Else Jockel, "The Challenge of the New Therapies to Social Work," *Social Work*, 4 (October 1957), pp. 63–64; ———, "Hospital Social Work and Mental Health," in Robert H. Felix, ed., *Mental Health and Social Welfare* (New York: Columbia University Press, 1961), pp. 192–203; ———, "Social Recovery—the Focus for Social Services," *Release* (publication of the Maryland Department of Mental Hygiene), Winter 1962, entire issue; Else B. Kris, "New Drug Therapy and the Rehabilitation of Mental Patients," *Social Work*, 4 (October 1957), pp. 57–60; M. Genevieve Slear, "Psychiatric Patients: Clinically Improved but Socially Disabled," *Social Work*, 4 (April 1959), pp. 64–71.

[6] For an elaboration of these possibilities, see Milton Greenblatt and Benjamin Simon, eds., *Rehabilitation of the Mentally Ill: Social and Economic Aspects* (Washington, D.C.: American Association for the Advancement of Science, 1959).

Psychiatric social work in
psychiatric clinics

The psychiatric clinic is a second area in which the psychiatrist and social caseworker are associated. The child guidance clinic, to be discussed in the section that follows, is a third area.

The clinics that shall be dealt with here bear such titles as: neurological clinic, neuropsychiatric clinic, mental hygiene clinic, and psychiatric clinic. Some of them are connected with general hospitals, some with mental hospitals, some with courts (criminal or juvenile), and some are community-sponsored in the sense that voluntary contributions are made to provide psychiatric services under the auspices of one social agency or on behalf of all agencies.

Regardless of the affiliation or the sponsorship, the essential relationship of psychiatrist and psychiatric social worker is there. As in the case of the mental hospital, there is considerable variation in the nature of the service offered. In most clinics the intake interview is conducted by the psychiatric social worker. As with all initial contacts wherever sound casework is practiced, there exists the opportunity for engaging the client in a dynamic process. The application interview enables the troubled applicant and the social worker to explore what appears to be the difficulty, or difficulties, to examine the possible resources of the agency, and to come to a sense about the usefulness of the clinic. As treatment is undertaken, the psychiatrist carries medical and psychiatric responsibility. The psychiatric social worker keeps himself related to the reality problems of the client, concentrating upon the concrete aspects of day-by-day living, such as finances, living arrangements, family members, job, etc. Not infrequently, the worker may be in contact with other members of the client's family or with resources within the community. However, as with the mental hospital, there is a complementary role of psychiatrist and psychiatric social worker, each focusing on his particular area and each coming into conference and collaboration the one with the other on behalf of the client who asks for help.

With the heightened interest in mental hygiene during the post World War II period, the increased appropriations by state legislatures, the availability of substantial federal funds for mental health purposes to states and local communities, and the larger number of trained psychiatrists, psychologists, and psychiatric social workers, there has been a considerable expansion of psychiatric clinics throughout the country. By far the largest grouping of these is what has come to be called the all purpose clinic (outpatient). As these all purpose clinics have developed, there have been increasing demands placed upon psychiatric social workers, not only to perform their traditional roles of caseworkers but also to reach more and more into areas of clinic administration, research, and work with communities. There is every indication that greater emphasis will be placed upon the establishment of all purpose clinics in communities throughout the country with the basic function of treatment and prevention at the family and community level.[7]

Child guidance clinics

Although it was not until 1922 that the first child guidance clinic was established, there had been anticipations of such development for several decades. As early as 1896 Lightner Witmer had begun a psychological clinic at the University of Pennsylvania, the primary interest of which was educational. In 1909 Dr. William Healy began his notable work with delinquents referred by the Juvenile Court of Chicago to the Juvenile Psychopathic Institute, of which he was the first director. Serving as physician-psychiatrist, he was assisted in his researches into criminal behavior by psychologists who made mental tests and by field workers who gathered information pertaining to the delinquents' background. The work of both Witmer and Healy produced overwhelming evidence of the vital importance of the relation between the child's emotional life and his maladjustments and delinquencies. This was entirely consistent with the earlier findings of American child psychologists and was being reaffirmed constantly by the contributions from the more dynamic field of psychoanalysis.

By the time World War I had ended, steps had already been taken toward the professional education of its personnel. Likewise, the war had made possible the expansion of our knowledge of mental abilities through the unprecedented opportunity to test millions of men who had been called to arms. The specialty of psychiatry had been going on apace as well and by 1918 had accumulated a valuable store of information not only about war neuroses and psychoses but also about the adjustments that the human personality makes under stress. This was added to the already existing knowledge gained from psychiatrists in mental hospitals and others who had been working with children's disorders. All these developments and more besides were being incorporated into the mental hygiene movement and pointed the way, by the beginning of the third decade of the present century, to a new synthesis to be achieved by bring-

---

[7] This challenging assignment is described in Luther E. Woodward, "Changing Roles of Psychiatric Social Workers in Out-Patient Clinics," *Social Work*, 6 (April 1961), pp. 74–81.

ing these various specialties—psychiatry, psychology, social work—into a new combination.

The Commonwealth Fund

The new combination proved to be the child guidance clinic which took form in 1922 under the auspices of the National Committee for Mental Hygiene. The means by which this step was undertaken was the support given the National Committee by the Commonwealth Fund, a private foundation established in 1918. What stamped the child guidance clinic as unique was the fusing of these different specialties into a new whole with all of the attendant possibilities of developing a body of knowledge and skills in dealing with children who presented behavior or personality difficulties. It may be a matter of historical interest, in view of the changed emphases of the present-day clinics, to observe that the original purpose of the child guidance clinic was to reach the problems of juvenile delinquency by concentrating upon the child referred by the juvenile court. Evidence of this is reflected in the fact that it was through the Division of Delinquency that the National Committee for Mental Hygiene conducted the first demonstrations of child guidance clinics.

In accordance with the original purpose of the leaders of the movement, a five-year experimental program was adopted in November 1921 and initiated in the spring of 1922. According to the 1922 annual report of the Commonwealth Fund, the program was designed:

1. To develop the psychiatric study of difficult pre-delinquent and delinquent children in the schools and juvenile courts; and to develop sound methods of treatment based on such study.
2. To develop the work of the visiting teacher whereby the invaluable early contacts which our school systems make possible with every child may be utilized for the understanding and development of the child.
3. To provide courses of training along sound lines for those qualified and desiring to work in this field.
4. To extend by various educational efforts the knowledge and use of these methods.

A number of organizations already in existence were utilized to help carry into effect the first three of these purposes. The New York School of Social Work was placed in a position to offer additional courses for psychiatric social workers, to provide fellowships for training students in this new field, and to establish a psychiatric clinic for the study and treatment of children presenting special problems and for the field training of students. The National Committee for Mental Hygiene, through its newly formed Division on the Prevention of Delinquency, was to carry on the demonstration child guidance clinics; while the Public Education Association of New York, through its new organization known as the National Committee on Visiting Teachers, was to conduct demonstrations of visiting teacher work in different areas of the country. To attain the fourth objective the Fund set up its own agency, the Joint Committee on Methods of Preventing Delinquency, to act as a coordinating agency for the program as a whole and as an interpreter of the work through published articles or special studies.

Early in 1922 the first demonstration child guidance clinic was initiated in St. Louis with a staff consisting of one psychiatrist, one psychologist, and one psychiatric social worker. Children with behavior difficulties were referred by schools, institutions, private homes, and the juvenile court. Three fourths of these were via the juvenile court, and it was soon realized that if a preventive service were to be offered, it would have to be done, in a great many instances, long before the child was brought to the juvenile court. If the purpose of the newly established clinics was to give meaning to the title of the committee on the Prevention of Delinquency, it—the clinic—was doomed to ineffectiveness because so much of the responsibility for preventing delinquency rested with other agencies than the clinic. Throughout the remainder of the demonstration period in the cities of Norfolk, Dallas, Minneapolis and St. Paul, Los Angeles, Cleveland, and Philadelphia this fact became more and more self-evident. It was realized that the community services, such as those of the school and of social agencies, particularly children's agencies, were valuable because they helped the child to achieve a constructive objective for himself and because they furnished a more natural medium for approaching the child. At the same time, it became apparent that more stress in the clinic setup would need to be placed upon social work, and accordingly the ratio of workers was changed to one psychiatrist, one psychologist, three social workers.

The clinic in operation

The study and treatment process in a child guidance clinic is initiated when referral is followed by application for service. In most instances the clinic prefers to have the parent come for the application interview without the child. During this interview the parents—it may be both together or either father or mother—present to the psychiatric social worker the nature of the difficulty that they are having with their child. At the same time, the social worker gives the parents some idea of the clinic, the kind of service it offers, and the arrangements under which the clinic

appointments are carried out. During this interview the parents are turning over in their own minds whether this is the place to bring their child
for treatment, while the clinic person is also considering whether this is
the kind of difficulty that is within the scope of the clinic's service. If a
"meeting of the minds" results, each side agreeing this is a matter with
which the clinic may help, then appointments for the child with the psychiatrist, and the parent with the psychiatric social worker, are discussed
as well as the fee, which is adjusted according to the income of the applicant. If either a medical or psychological examination of the child is
indicated, arrangements are made for such service either within or outside of the clinic. Since every child guidance clinic has a psychologist, the
testing is usually done in the clinic, while in most cases the medical examination is either performed outside of the clinic or by a physician on the
staff, but usually not by the psychiatrist who will see the child.

Once appointments have begun, the usual procedure is for the child
to be seen weekly by the psychiatrist and the parent by the psychiatric
social worker. Throughout the course of treatment there are frequent conferences between psychiatrist and social worker by means of which each
is kept informed of the progress, or lack of progress, of the other. In those
instances in which the referral has been made by another social agency or
by a school it is customary to keep them apprised of developments in the
treatment interviews and to bring them into a joint conference at the
clinic. For the clinic, it is important to know of changes taking place in
the life of the parents and the child, while the social agency or school also
needs to know what is happening in the clinic. The conferences with the
psychologist are more likely to be held following application in order to
clear the ground as to whether the child under consideration falls within
the intelligence group with which the clinic can work most effectively.
Experience has shown that the child of decidedly subnormal mentality
cannot profit as much by clinic treatment, and it is customary not to accept
such children. During treatment there may be occasion for other conferences with the psychologist in order to have an interpretation of the child's
capacities as they are stacked up against his use of them in the clinic, in
school, or at home. Another conference that is usually held, although not
necessarily for every case, is the staff conference, which brings together
psychiatrists, psychologists, and psychiatric social workers. Such a meeting furnishes occasion for an exchange of point of view and an opportunity
to bring out the varying differences between these specialties from which
there may eventuate a new approach to the problems presented in the
case. Such interprofessional group thinking is one of the valuable contributions which the child guidance clinic has been able to make in working
in the field of personality and behavior.

In many instances, clinics offer a diagnostic and consultative service to schools, social agencies, and parents pertaining to school problems, matters touching upon intelligence and special abilities or the lack thereof. The clinic may be able to indicate where some of the difficulties seem to lie and to suggest referrals to appropriate agencies or community facilities. The opportunity to consult with the clinic sometimes obviates the long treatment period. Clients often take help best through infrequent contacts with the clinic.

Function and Process in the Clinic

In the early days of the child guidance clinic the title was accurately descriptive of its approach. The assumption was made, quite naturally, that the parent came for advice about guiding his child's life, and that if only he were told what to do, he could then proceed to do it. At a later period the clinic concentrated upon the parent, seeing him as the focus of the problem, his own or his child's. What was simpler, then, than to remake the parent! No sooner, however, had the error of this way been perceived than there occurred a swing to the opposite extreme. The child became the object of direct treatment and the parent was relegated to a secondary role, to be considered, as the law would have it, as an accessory before the fact.

Time and experience demonstrated the limitation and ineffectiveness of all three of these approaches. Just as futile were the alternations of clinic philosophy that sought to eliminate undesirable behavior either through changing the child by means of moralizing, or with sweet reason, or by means of changing the environment. It was no wonder that many people, including the clinic workers themselves, began to question the value of the clinic. So long as the clinic undertook to wave a magic wand that superficially changed the child, just so long could parents evade facing their own problems that bore some casual relation to the behavior of the child. It was not until fuller account was taken of the role of emotional factors in the development of personality and behavior that any perceptible progress was made. Basic to all of this was the belief that there could be no change in behavior without a change in those elements that had produced the behavior.

The more recent emphasis takes into account the interrelatedness of the child and parents in their life outside of the clinic as well as during treatments in the clinic. While the clinic still retains the title of "child guidance," it realizes that its help is offered to both child and parent. Indeed, the clinic has learned by now that if the help that is offered is to have any meaning for either child or parent, it must be directed to both parties as integral parts of the clinic function. Consistent with this newer orientation, the primary function of the child guidance clinic is conceived to be helping of a child in his emotional development so that he can realize more the capacities that he has for attaining an adequate adjustment within himself and to his environment. All this applies to the parent as well, with the added qualification that the help is directed toward his relationship with the child. Adjustment is usually a matter of definition and of standard, but the clinic continues to insist that the criterion of adjustment is the use that the individual makes of his abilities in his relations to other people and within himself. Most children are normal mentally and physically and manage to adapt themselves to the ordinary demands of life with little apparent difficulty. It is, however, in the realm of their emotional relationships with other people—parents, brothers, sisters, playmates, schoolfellows, teachers—when demands are made upon them, or they are faced with prescribed limitations, that many of their difficulties become evident. When this situation becomes serious enough to be threatening to the parent or is impeding the emotional development of the child, the clinic stands ready to help. The clinic, as a community agency, is willing to have its services used by parent and child, but it leaves the responsibility for coming to the clinic entirely to them and also the decision as to whether this is the kind of help they need and want.

The Child, the Parent, and the Clinic

This interrelated movement of child and parent in a clinic is basic to the clinic process. Two people such as a child and a parent—mother or father—comes to a clinic because something has gone askew in their relationships or because of some blocking in the growth or experience of either or both. If the clinic is to be of any service, it must take them as they are and offer to each the help which they need and are able to use. The clinic can in nowise take away the individual's responsibility for living his own life. The capacity of the client to work on his own problem must be respected. This helping process goes on between psychiatrist and child, and between social worker and parent. Change, if it takes place at all, generally comes slowly and is related to what is happening with the other person. For example, despite the mother's initial insistence that the clinic make over her child, no real change takes places in the child until the mother herself realizes she is a part of the situation and undergoes change too. The necessity for this mutual modification of behavior responses is made all the clearer if a hypothetical situation is illustrated. Suppose the clinic by some magic could alter the child's behavior and leave the mother untouched. It is extremely doubtful whether the child's difficulties would remain cleared up for any length of time for the very important reason that his mother (family, etc.) is a part of the living world to which he reacts. It was from this situation that he was brought to the clinic, and it is this situation to which he returns; and if all the other factors remain the same, the chances are excellent that he will revert to his original use of self, since personality seldom changes in a vacuum. Much of this would be just as true if it were the mother and not the child who changed by reason of the clinic experience. Nor is this a matter of allocating blame. The clinic is concerned not so much with who is at fault as it is with helping where there is need. It recognizes that children and parents are different, that children come into the world with certain potentialities, that children build on these potentialities a personality that is considerably affected by the persons in the environment. It also realizes that parents have developed their personality patterns over a period of years and continue to do so in their adjustments to the developing personalities of their children and of the world about them. This dynamic concept of human personality affords the clinic a working premise in its services to children and parents.

At no point is it the purpose of a child guidance clinic to order the life of a parent. The clinic recognizes the uniqueness of the human personality and the differences that distinguish individuals. From such a belief there follows logically the proposition that a life plan can only be set up by the individual himself and not by an outside agency. The individual comes to the agency, in this instance the clinic, not to be turned upside down, inside out, and made over into another person, but rather for help in living with the kind of self that he is. A mother asks for help in one or two little areas, and will resist, almost to the death, any effort to remake her. She comes to the clinic of her own accord, takes what help she can use, and leaves when she feels her needs have been met. Even though she may, ostensibly, ask for advice either for herself or for a child, actually that is the last thing that she wants or needs. The clinic has long since learned that advice is entirely gratuitous unless it is related to the movement that is taking place in the client. What the adviser is doing, in effect, is saying, "If I were you, this is what I would do." Actually, nothing could be more false. How can one person ever predict what he would do if he were someone else and in another situation? Furthermore, whose life is it?

It is necessary to dwell a moment longer on what it is that brings a parent to a child guidance clinic as well as to make clear the role of the clinic. The parent in coming with some problem with a child is giving expression to a vital impulse that arises from what seems an impassable and impossible situation with a child. This impulse, and those subsequent impulses that find expression in the treatment situation in the clinic, carry more of the fears, hopes, dreads, loves, and hates of the parent within herself and in relation to the child. In coming to the clinic she has admitted the need to take these feelings outside of her normal sphere, to take them to a neutral, understanding person. In many instances she must do this in order to be able to face them and to resolve some of her ambivalence about herself, her child, and his need for help. The worker recognizes and meets the mother's feelings and works with her in furthering her capacity to take help and eventually to leave the clinic more secure in her ability to deal with her own problems and her child's difficulties. The agency realizes that this is not done all in a day. It requires time for the parent to take on the clinic experience as a growth experience, to be able to accept help and yet not to be overcome with the fear of losing her own identity in the process, and at the same time to get a sense of her own capacity for living.

This idealized description of the child guidance clinic does not overlook its many shortcomings. The clinic, with all its specialized knowledge of human behavior and personality made possible by the combination of psychiatrist-psychologist-social worker, does not have all the answers to the riddle of personality. Nor has it developed sufficient skills to be of help in every situation with which it is faced. In the light of our present knowledge and skills there are many children and parents who present difficulties that the clinic simply does not reach. Because of the highly individualized character of the helping process, there are no two clients to whom the same specific therapeutic skill can be applied. At the present time there are many people whom the clinic is unable to help. There are cases in which the clinic cannot assist because a parent or child has resolutely set itself against accepting any help from the clinic, or from anyone. In other instances the power to help is limited by the training and experience of the clinic staff. During its four decades of existence, the child guidance clinic has demonstrated its usefulness and at the same time has acknowledged its limitations. It has performed what at times seemed like miracles and at other times has failed abysmally. It has made significant contributions to the understanding of behavior and personality, yet stands today upon the threshold of a still greater knowledge that waits to be born.

The experience of two world wars

While World War I did not initiate psychiatric social work, nevertheless we have noted in another section of this chapter the tremendous impetus that it furnished. Yet despite the developments in the mental hygiene field in the quarter century between wars, the nation was shocked with what Selective Service rejections showed about the mental health of our people. The record was still sorrier when we realized the volume of discharge from the armed forces for mental and personality disorders. One cannot but wonder whether all of the mental hygiene efforts in the period between these two wars had been of any avail. On the other hand, one cannot but speculate what our situation might have been without those years of psychiatric advance.

By 1941, World War II was upon us. What did psychiatry and what did psychiatric social work have to contribute to the successful prosecution of the war? Psychiatrists were used in many places, such as induction centers, general and station hospitals in this country, and in general, station, and evacuation hospitals overseas. They were placed in specialized neuropsychiatric hospitals here and abroad; in outpatient units, called mental hygiene consultation service; in basic training camps where they aided recruits in their adjustment to army life and advised the command on matters relative to morale and mental health. They were assigned to all large transports and hospital ships that carried psychiatric patients. They were stationed in disciplinary barracks and in the centers for the rehabilitation of miltiary prisoners. Psychiatrists served in combat divisions. They were a part of the examining team in distribution centers and separation centers. They served as consultants to theaters of war, service commands, armies, and air forces.[8]

Military psychiatric social work

For the first time in American military history the army psychiatric social worker was granted an occupational classification—SSN 263, Social Worker, and MOS 263, Psychiatric Social Worker. As Elizabeth Ross pointedly states it, a military psychiatric social worker "is a soldier with social work duties, assigned to a psychiatric unit, under the administrative and professional direction of a psychiatrist." [9] What was the job of this worker? Again, the answer is simple and direct: to help win the war by increasing fighting manpower. To quote Mrs. Ross again:

> Army administered social services are provided to help produce first-class fighting troops to vanquish the enemy. They exist to serve the army group purpose, as does army medicine and psychiatry . . . in principle, the army is deeply concerned with the growth and development of each person . . . as a soldier. It is to speed up and to maintain effective soldier

---

[8] William C. Menninger, "Psychiatric Experience in the War, 1941–1946," *American Journal of Psychiatry*, CIII (March 1947), pp. 577–586. The confirming experience of the Navy is reviewed by F. J. Braceland, "Psychiatric Lessons from World War II," *American Journal of Psychiatry*, CIII (March 1947), pp. 587–593. The Air Force experience is presented by J. M. Murray, "Accomplishments of Psychiatry in the Army Air Forces," *American Journal of Psychiatry*, CIII (March 1947), pp. 594–599. See also William C. Menninger, "Psychiatry and the War," in *Modern Attitudes in Psychiatry* (New York: Columbia University Press, 1946), pp. 90–115.

[9] Elizabeth H. Ross, "What's So Different about Army Psychiatric Social Work?" *The Family*, XXVII (April 1946), p. 70.

development that the military has provided, more in this war than in any other, services for the individual.[10]

In concert with the psychiatrist, the psychiatric social worker shared the aim of helping to restore to active service soldiers who were experiencing mental and behavior difficulties. For those individuals who could not be returned to duty the maximum benefit was to be provided before return to civilian life.[11] Generally speaking, army psychiatric social workers worked wherever army psychiatrists worked, except for special assignments of surveys, administration, and research. In the period since the end of World War II an extensive bibliography of army psychiatric social work services has appeared. This is material prepared very largely by the workers themselves as they were in the midst of their war assignments, or since as they evaluate what the experience has meant to them, to psychiatric social work, or to the profession of social work as a whole.[12]

Psychiatric social work service was available following induction and on through training, classification, reclassification, replacement, rehabilitation, discharge. This statement does not imply that it was everywhere available, and at any time, or always with adequately trained staffs. It does mean that by the time we entered World War II there was a quarter century of psychiatric social work skill that could be used to further the end for which our armies existed—that is, to win the war. Despite the difficulties encountered in having psychiatric social work recognized as a useful specialty in the army organization, there is now no doubt about its valid place alongside an infinite number of other services in contributing to the successful prosecution of the war.[13]

---

[10] *Ibid.*, p. 64.

[11] William C. Menninger, "Psychiatric Social Work in the Army and Its Implications for Civilian Social Work," *Proceedings of the National Conference of Social Work*, 1945, p. 78.

[12] No attempt is here made to present the mass of published material on psychiatric social work in World War II. However, the reader who is interested in any or all phases of such work is referred to a number of useful bibliographies that have so far appeared. Several of the more useful references are: Minna Field, *Bibliography of the Development and Practice of Military Psychiatric Social Work*, July 1945, made available by the Josiah Macy, Jr., Foundation, New York: Dorothy L. Crow, *Selected Bibliography on Psychiatric Social Work*, May 1945, American Association of Psychiatric Social Workers. The bibliographical references of Saul Hofstein are worth noting: Saul Hofstein, "Differences in Military Psychiatric Case Work Practice," *Journal of Psychiatric Social Work*, XVI (Winter 1946–1947), pp. 74–83. The substance of the experience of psychiatric social work as adapted to the military setting is recorded in Henry S. Maas, ed., *Adventure in Mental Health* (New York: Columbia University Press, 1951); see also Leslie J. Shellhase, ed., Bibliography of *Army Social Work: The First Twenty Years, 1942–1962*. Department of Psychiatry, Walter Reed Army Institute of Research, 1962.

[13] The contribution of the American Red Cross to the development of psychiatric social work during World War II calls for special mention. Not only did the

Having successfully contributed to the war, does psychiatric social work have a valid place in this postwar world through which we are all struggling so desperately? Yes, perhaps with nothing quite as spectacular as followed World War I, but nevertheless tremendous potential contributions in helping individuals (and even nations) to achieve a more satisfying use of their capacities for creative living. The need for these services and contributions is recognized in the widespread demand for trained psychiatric personnel. In an effort to provide the services and the workers a national program supported by tax funds has been started. The United States Public Health Service has been charged by the Congress with responsibility for furthering and developing a nationwide mental health program. According to the terms of the National Mental Health Act its purpose

> . . . is the improvement of the mental health of the people of the United States through the conducting of researches, investigations, experiments, and demonstrations relating to the cause, diagnosis, and treatment of psychiatric disorders; assisting and fostering such research activities by public and private agencies, and promoting the coordination of all such researches and activities and the useful application of their results; training personnel in matters relating to mental health; and developing and assisting States in the use of the most effective methods of prevention, diagnosis, and treatment of psychiatric disorders.[14]

The stimulation and substantial support furnished through the United States Public Health Service, according to the intent of the National Mental Health Act, has given tremendous impetus toward the encouragement, initiation, extension, and enrichment of programs throughout the country. These programs include not only the training of personnel in psychiatry, clinical psychology, psychiatric social work, and psychiatric nursing but also research projects and the development of mental hygiene services in states and local communities.

Nor did the use of psychiatric knowledge or personnel within the military organization cease with the end of the war. The lessons learned through the use of psychiatric knowledge in the stressful situations of war were just as essential in the maintenance of a peacetime military establishment that might be called upon again to defend the liberties of the American people. Provision has been made for the training of officer personnel

---

American Red Cross make available to the military establishments hundreds of highly qualified social caseworkers, but the standards of performance required of and executed by that personnel did much to contribute to the well-being of our military men. See Imogene S. Young, "American Red Cross Psychiatric Social Work," in Maas, *ibid.*, pp. 228–238.

14 Public Law 487, 79th Cong., Chapter 538, 2nd Sess. HR4512, signed by the President July 3, 1946, p. 1, section 2.

and for the use of officer and noncommissioned officer personnel throughout the armed services.

There are a number of specific and concrete evidences of the values
placed by the Army on military psychiatric social work. With a standing
peacetime army, provision already has been made for the officer position
classification of psychiatric social worker. A regular Army officer has been
appointed as Chief of Branch, in the Neuropsychiatric Consultant's Division, Surgeon General's Office, Department of the Army. Furthermore,
psychiatric social workers in the Army are included in the Medical Services Corps, and programs are under way for the training of enlisted
personnel to assist the officer psychiatric social workers.[15]

The Veterans' Administration program has also developed psychiatric services to an extraordinary extent. Such services are available not
only in general hospitals and regional offices but are the core services provided in the neuropsychiatric hospitals distributed throughout the country.
In addition to providing a high quality psychiatric social service through
the facilities of the Veterans' Administration, the veterans' hospitals have
assisted in the training of hundreds, if not thousands, of students in schools
of social work by means of field work placements and supervision furnished by staff members. The tie-in between the Veterans' Administration
hospitals and adjacent medical schools through the device of a Dean's
Committee has helped to insure a consistently responsible quality throughout the Veterans' Administration facilities.

Individual therapy and group therapy

Practically all of the foregoing discussion was based upon the one
to one relationship that exists between the client and the psychiatrist or
the client and the psychiatric social worker. Increasingly, however, it is
becoming clear that help can also be offered through a relationship involving the psychiatrist or psychiatric social worker and a group of clients
or patients. This is not to be confused with the usual range of activities
carried on with groups by workers in group work agencies. Rather it is a
recognition that the lives of most of us are lived in groups, and that what
is termed socialization of the individual takes place essentially through
group activity. Likewise, when difficulties within any one of us become

---

[15] Elwood W. Camp, "Psychiatric Social Work in the Army Today," in Henry
S. Maas, op. cit., pp. 202–220; also Military Psychiatric Social Work, Technical Manual, 8–241, Department of the Army, March 1950; and Daniel E. Jennings, Jr., "The
Social Worker in a Military Setting," Social Casework, XXXVIII (May 1957), pp. 246–
250.

serious enough as to require outside help there is a substantial resource through group participation and the services of psychiatrically specialized personnel.

Group therapy, or group psychotherapy, is a relatively recent development, having been pioneered by S. R. Slavson of the Jewish Board of Guardians in 1934. By World War II enough had been learned out of the experience with disturbed children and parents to adapt the essentials to the military experience. It must be recognized here that in addition to the basic values inherent in group therapy another virtue so far as the military forces was concerned was the opportunity it provided to reach a large number of soldiers who needed and could use such a service. Group therapy was provided in practically every military hospital where psychiatric patients were treated in large numbers. It was also offered to military prisoners in various rehabilitation centers, in mental hygiene clinics operated at various camps, at clearing stations near the front, as well as in "exhaustion centers" and convalescent hospitals further to the rear of the fighting lines. Since the end of the war and with an expanded Veterans' Administration program, group therapy is an integral part of the hospital—inpatient and outpatient—care offered to veterans.

In addition to its use in the military setting, there is an increasing application in state mental hospitals, child guidance clinics, prisons, and occasionally in residential treatment centers for emotionally disturbed children. It must be made clear that group therapy is not used as a substitute for or a replacement of individual therapy. Rather it is serving a useful purpose in its own right and for the values inherent in it. At the same time it becomes evident that there is an interrelationship between the two, for a number of agencies and institutions use them complementarily, that is, persons in the group therapy sessions also have access to the psychiatrist for individual service as well. The relation of the psychiatric social worker to the psychiatrist is maintained as in all the services previously described in these pages with the ultimate medical and psychiatric responsibility residing on the psychiatrist.[16]

Conclusion

Psychiatric social work as described in this chapter has dealt with the use of social casework in the clinical team of psychiatrist, clinical psychologist, and psychiatric social worker. By the very nature of its origins in relation to the fruitful developments in psychiatry, psychoanalysis, and psychology there has been a tendency to worship psychiatric social

---

[16] For a distinction between group therapy and the utilization of social group work in a psychiatric setting see chapter on "Social Group Work."

work as the alpha and omega of social casework. No competent case-worker indulges in this erroneous presumption; yet there is enough loose thinking abroad to require these few words of explanation. Social case-work existed before there was a specialization known as psychiatric social work. As psychiatric social work developed, it borrowed from and added to social casework. Today wherever and under whatever auspices social casework is practiced, it utilizes the richnesses that have come from psy-chiatric orientations. What realistic caseworkers have come to recognize is the validity of the various emphases and settings in which social casework is practiced. They also realize that there is a helpful interchange between areas of practice. The family caseworker draws from the psychiatric case-worker and vice versa. The probation officer utilizes some of the contri-butions from psychiatric casework just as the psychiatric caseworker utilizes some of the contributions made by caseworkers with the convicted offender.

In addition to the foregoing, it is important to recognize that contri-butions from mental hygiene have reached almost every area in which human beings undertake to be of help to others. Where these services tend to get well defined and to be offered to individuals by social work agencies they are called casework services. Where, however, they remain under nonsocial work auspices, they nevertheless have very real value and con-stitute important services within our culture. Thus the pastoral and coun-seling services of the ministry are a case in point; or the consultative services to parents around problems of child rearing and family life; or the services with individual children in nursery schools.

These are all valuable services, but they should not be confused with the essential elements of social casework practice in conjunction with psychiatric services. Psychiatric social work, too, has its important part to play in helping people with their difficulties. It should be recognized as one, and only one, of the many services that people require.

Finally, it should be reemphasized that extraordinary developments have taken place in the institutional aspects of the care and treatment of the mentally ill. It is not yet ascertainable whether the drug therapies have reached fundamental factors in mental illness or have dealt with symptom modification only. Even though the final answer is not yet given, nevertheless, psychiatric social workers have had to respond to these changes and to adapt their social work skills accordingly. Perhaps this has happened more dramatically than in other casework areas, but the re-sponse that has been made has demonstrated the capacity of the profes-sion to adapt itself to the realities of the changing world in which it is functioning.

Bibliography

Ackerman, Nathan, *The Psychodynamics of Family Life.* New York: Basic Books, Inc., 1958.

Allen, Frederick H., *Psychotherapy with Children.* New York: W. W. Norton & Company, Inc., 1942.

Alt, Herschel, *Residential Treatment for the Disturbed Child.* New York: International Universities Press, Inc., 1960.

Caplan, Gerald, ed., *Prevention of Mental Disorders in Children.* New York: Basic Books, Inc., 1961.

Crutcher, Hester B., *Foster Home Care for Mental Patients.* New York: The Commonwealth Fund, 1944.

Davies, Stanley Powell, *The Mentally Retarded in Society.* New York: Columbia University Press, 1959.

Deutsch, Albert, *The Mentally Ill in America*, rev. ed. New York: Columbia University Press, 1949.

DeWitt, Henrietta B., "Family Care as the Focus for Social Case-work in a State Mental Hospital," *Mental Hygiene*, October 1944, pp. 602–631.

Felix, Robert H., ed., *Mental Health and Social Welfare.* New York: Columbia University Press, 1961.

French, Edward L., and J. Clifford Scott, *Child in the Shadows.* Philadelphia: J. B. Lippincott Company, 1962.

Grinker, Roy R., et al., *Psychiatric Social Work: A Transactional Case Book.* New York: Basic Books, Inc., 1961.

Gurin, Gerald, Joseph Veroff, and Sheila Feld, *Americans View Their Mental Health.* New York: Basic Books, Inc., 1960.

Hitchman, Irene L., "A Follow-Up Study of Patients Treated with Tranquilizing Drugs," *Social Work*, 2 (October 1957), pp. 61–62.

Hollingshead, August B., and Frederick C. Redlich, *Social Class and Mental Illness—A Community Study.* New York: John Wiley & Sons, Inc., 1958.

Jockel, Else, "The Challenge of the New Therapies to Social Work," *Social Work*, 2 (October 1957), pp. 63–64.

Joint Commission on Mental Health, *Action for Mental Health.* New York: Basic Books, Inc., 1961.

Knee, Ruth I., ed., *Better Social Services for Mentally Ill Patients.* New York: American Association of Psychiatric Social Workers, 1955.

Kris, Else B., "New Drug Therapy and Rehabilitation of Mental Patients," *Social Work*, 2 (October 1957), pp. 57–60.

Krugman, Morris, *Orthopsychiatry and the School.* New York: American Orthopsychiatric Association, 1958.

Lippman, Hyman S., *Treatment of the Child in Emotional Conflict.* New York: McGraw-Hill Book Company, Inc., 1956.

Maas, Henry P., ed., *Adventure in Mental Health: Psychiatric Social Work with the Armed Forces in World War II.* New York: Columbia University Press, 1951.

Ridenour, Nina, *Mental Health in the United States: A Fifty-year History.* Cambridge: Harvard University Press, 1961.

Robinson, Reginald, David F. DeMarche, and Mildred K. Wagle, *Community Resources in Mental Health.* New York: Basic Books, Inc., 1960.

Rockmore, Myron John, "A Psychiatric Social Worker in Community Mental Health," *Social Work*, 3 (October 1958), pp. 86–92.

Slavson, S. R., *The Fields of Group Psychotherapy*. New York: International Universities Press, Inc., 1956.

Slear, M. Genevieve, "Psychiatric Patients: Clinically Improved, but Socially Disabled," *Social Work*, 4 (April 1959), pp. 64–71.

Stevenson, George S., *Mental Health Planning for Social Action*. New York: McGraw-Hill Book Company, Inc., 1956.

Woodward, Luther E., "Changing Roles of Psychiatric Social Workers in Outpatient Clients," *Social Work*, 6 (April 1961), pp. 74–81.

RICHARD ROBERTS; JAMES KERN

ELSE JOCKEL, D.S.W.,
Chief of Social Services
Department of Mental Hygiene
State of Maryland

As our state mental hospitals have become modernized treatment facilities it has been recognized, increasingly, that medical intervention in disease processes is only a part, however important, of a psychiatric treatment program. If the goal of therapy—the recovered patient's return to productive functioning in society—is to be achieved, the social aspects of psychiatric institutionalization will need to be dealt with as well. It is out of this kind of thinking over the past twenty-five years that the psychiatric social work program described here was able to develop.

The mental hospital that provides the setting for the program is Springfield State Hospital, one of six psychiatric facilities of the State of Maryland. Springfield was the first of Maryland's state institutions to enlist the services of a social worker. From the very beginning the primary objective of the hospital's psychiatric social work program has been the social recovery of patients. To achieve this, social services have been developed to assist patients and their families at those phases of hospitalization where social problems most frequently interfere with progress.

The social services are based upon sound casework principles not the least important of which is that of positive participation. By involving the persons concerned in doing the things that their situation demands, the caseworker engages them gradually in a process of action in their own behalf, and helps them experience their own resourcefulness and use the resources of the hospital and community for dealing with the problems that hospitalization brings to them.

The following material illustrates these services in action. The case of Richard Roberts describes a group of social services called intramural services. These services have grown from the recognition that social obstacles to rehabilitation can often be obviated if the patient's social relationships are purposefully strengthened when he enters the hospital. The case describes the caseworker's efforts to involve Richard's parents in the patient's hospital experience at the earliest possible time. Through preadmission counseling, admission assistance, and interim service to the father, the caseworker helps the patient and relative to experience the hospital as a source of therapeutic help for the patient. Simultaneously, the worker endeavors to strengthen family relationships in order to keep these

269

natural resources alive for the boy's eventual return to his home and community life.

The case of James Kern portrays the part the social worker plays in the restorative process to overcome problems of chronicity and social crippling. Here, we see the social worker helping a patient who is psychiatrically ready to leave the hospital, but whose social resources will have to be rebuilt before he can leave because he lost them during his prolonged hospitalization. Excerpts from the record describe how through preparole counseling, followed by preplacement assistance and foster care, the social worker helps this patient rediscover his own, the hospital's, and the community resources with which to rebuild his life and functioning in the community.

Intramural services

Underlying this group of services is the belief that the restoration of mental health, not stigma and social crippling, can result from psychiatric hospitalization, provided the persons concerned are helped at the earliest possible time to make responsible plans in the patient's behalf for his hospital experience and his convalescence. Accordingly, because the resources of social work equip him to assist individuals at times of decision, it is the social worker on the hospital's staff who takes responsibility for this helping function. The social worker meets new applicants in what is known as preadmission counseling, provides reception assistance to patients on admission, and introduces to the family the idea that hospitalization is not a final solution to problems but a treatment experience during the acute phase of the patient's illness. And it is again the social worker who, through interim and preparole services, helps the patient and the family to prepare for after care outside the hospital, once the patient can no longer benefit from continued hospitalization.

Richard Roberts

Richard Roberts, a 15-year-old boy, was being considered for rehospitalization at Springfield. He had been in the hospital once before when he was 13. At that time, slight retardation, together with convulsive disorders and uncontrollable behavior, had led to trouble at home and at school. His parents, unable to accept Richard's difference from their other more gifted children and entirely dependent upon the advice of others, had been to all available public and private welfare agencies in their suburban, highly sophisticated home community in an attempt to be spared having to plan for their own boy. Finally, Richard was committed to the state institution. Emotionally unprepared for the experience, Richard benefited little from hospitalization and, before therapy could really take effect, his guilt-ridden parents took him out of the hospital.

Over the next two years, outpatient therapy, special schools, and other community services were extended to the patient and his family without success. Richard became sick again, was expelled from school, and rehospitalization was recommended. The worker from Pupil Personnel Service telephoned Preadmission Service at the hospital.

In preadmission counseling, the caseworker ascertains what the inquiring person expects of the hospital and thus helps him to find out what the hospital is actually like. A part of preadmission interviews usually also calls for a consideration of alternatives to hospitalization. Through this procedure, the applicant is helped to think of hospitalization as only one of several possibilities and to concentrate on the patient's need for the best possible help. If hospitalization is decided upon, the applicant is encouraged to prepare the patient frankly for the necessity to enter the hospital, and a convenient time for admission is arranged.

Aware that another kind of involvement on the part of Richard's parents had to be expected if hospitalization was to be more helpful than before, I [1] said to the worker of the referring agency that the hospital would expect the parents' participation in planning. I suggested that she ask the parents to initiate the new contract with the hospital themselves. When Mr. Roberts telephoned later I suggested an interview during which we would discuss his and his wife's expectations of the hospital and also the hospital's ability to meet these.

Mr. Roberts began the ensuing preadmission interview by going into a detailed description of all the things that had been tried, of his and his wife's feelings of failure, of Richard's behavior problems at home and at school, of things having gone from bad to worse. As I listened to him without comment, he became defensive and ended up by saying that it was their family physician and representatives of the many interested agencies rather than he and his wife who wanted Richard to be rehospitalized.

I gave recognition to what they had been through and added that this was the right kind of place to come with problems such as his. Nevertheless, we did need to clarify some things before going much further. Could it really be only other people rather than he and Mrs. Roberts who could decide about rehospitalization for Richard? Maybe the agencies had nothing to offer Richard, but how could anyone know at this point whether the hospital has what he needs? What we could do today was to help him explore what this hospital has to offer Richard. As he knew, it was only one of many different sources of help and, as he also knew, Richard's previous hospitalization here had not helped him very much. Mr. Roberts remembered this.

---

[1] The psychiatric social worker on the hospital staff.

Yet, as he thought about the last few months, it seemed to him that even bringing Richard back here for the second time could not be harder. I asked if hospitalization seemed the lesser of two evils. This did not seem quite good enough; Richard and they would have to have some hope that the outcome could be better than last time, or why try again something that had no prospect of success?

Mr. Roberts had never thought of things quite this way. I could understand that Richard's relapses were discouraging to them. Still, Richard did stick it out for two years. Did a relapse have to mean total failure? Mr. Roberts thought for a moment and then said that he supposed they had not given Richard enough of a chance while he was in the hospital last time. He thought that they could do better this time. I agreed and pointed out the need for better preparation and the importance of their staying close to Richard while he was in the hospital to prevent his feeling abandoned by his parents.

I asked Mr. Roberts whether he and his wife wanted to talk things over once more before deciding on rehospitalization. He said that his wife was leaving it to him, and he was ready to decide now. We then decided on a day and time when they would bring Richard. When Mr. Roberts left, I reminded him once more of the need to have Richard prepared for his coming to the hospital.

In the reception interview the caseworker secures face-sheet information, encouraging as much as possible the patient's and his relatives' participation. The caseworker helps them to get a sense of the institution, explains its routines, and introduces the patient to the admitting physician. Again it is the caseworker who stays by the relative during the ordeal of waiting for the admission examination and who helps the patient and his family through the experience of having to part from one another.

When I met father and son in the reception room at the appointed time, Richard told me that he felt relieved to be back here. We settled ourselves in the admission office, and I suggested that we take a little time before the doctor would come to talk over the recent happenings and go over the questions Richard and his father might have. They had little to say except that last night had been very rough. I reviewed our admission procedures, reminding Richard that new patients always begin here with a bath and a shampoo in a closed ward. Richard nodded, saying he did not mind.

While the admitting physician interviewed the patient, I talked with the father about the next steps for the parents and also about the necessity for them to begin now to prepare themselves for Richard's return home. I said that when this time comes social service can be made available to help them work through the problems they will then have to face.

With the trend toward shorter hospitalization, preparole service, formerly used chiefly by patients who had to leave the hospital without help from their families, now is frequently offered to patients soon after admission to prevent them from becoming chronic patients.

If preparole service is offered to recently admitted patients it becomes a part of the intramural continuum. Through the preparole service the patient is assisted in tackling the social problems that interfere with his way of readjustment to community living. He is asked to demonstrate his readiness for outside living, while still in the hospital, by activities that show promise of his increasing self-responsibility. He is helped to find ways to participate in the recreational, occupational, and industrial therapies in the hospital and to explore the services open to him in the community.

An integral part of this service is the relationship with the patient's family, to whom both patient and hospital look before any alternate aftercare plans can become feasible. Frequently, the family needs substantial help with their own conflicting feelings before they and the patient can move forward constructively.

Richard's case was rereferred to Social Service about two months after his admission. When I conferred with Dr. T., the patient's physician, about the referral, I learned that he had made quite satisfactory progress in the hospital so that continued residential treatment was no longer indicated. However, Dr. T. was very concerned about the poor outlook for the patient's convalescent care. His use of individual psychotherapy had been promising, but the parents had not been able to participate helpfully in our therapeutic efforts. When approached by the physician about possibilities for convalescent leave they had been hesitant and quite ambivalent about whether or not they could plan for their boy. Dr. T. thought that Mr. Roberts might actually want to care for his son were he not influenced by Mrs. Roberts' attitude. From what the doctor had seen, the mother continued to be very rejecting of Richard, seeing him as a burden to her personally and to her management of her family and the home. Apparently she had done nothing to check the other children's rejection of Richard, but instead was saying that he was awkward to have around the house when the daughter's college friends dropped in.

I agreed with Dr. T.'s feeling that both Richard and his family were very much in need of help in planning for the patient's release from the hospital. I added that I thought planning might actually have to be a later step, following some direct help to the parents with their conflicting feelings about their son. It was agreed that I would enter the case in the usual preparole manner, that is, to offer Richard a chance to explore possibilities for leaving the hospital and to involve the parents in this kind of helping situation. If it was found that they needed help themselves before they could give their support to the patient's movement toward the community, Interim Service could then be provided for them.

Interim service

This service is defined as a short-term casework service to the relatives of hospitalized patients who are handicapped by social problems in moving forward constructively. While the service is always provided in the patient's interest, it is intended as help to the relatives with their problems about the patient, his hospitalization, and his approaching convalescence. The service is to enable relatives to find what they can contribute to the patient's psychiatric and social rehabilitation and then to take appropriate action. This action may be preparation of the home for the patient's return or the decision to free the patient to plan with the hospital for convalescent care.

When I visited him on the ward, Richard looked much better than I remembered him from admission. He had obviously experienced hospitalization as something positive for himself, feeling accepted and emotionally nourished by the attention he was receiving through both formal and indirect therapies. Therefore, I was not too surprised about his cautious, rather tense response to my coming, which in final analysis represented a reminder that his present protected situation was not to be his way of life. Having experienced relatively little prior to hospitalization that could be compared with protected institutional living, Richard saw me as an intruder. When I introduced myself and my purpose for coming he told me that he did not remember me and could not recall my saying on admission that we might work together again later.

He shook his head to my question of whether my coming bothered him, but with further help he brought out that he was afraid my coming meant that he would not be permitted to go home. I said that he was really miles ahead of me. I was here today to ask if he would like to talk with me about what might be on his mind for the future. Richard relaxed enough to tell me that from his experience the appearance of social workers usually meant that something had gone wrong again. While giving recognition to the good reasons for his feeling this way, I asked if he did not think he could do better than this. Had he not found while he was here that the worker's visit did not necessarily mean that something was wrong but rather that people came to help things get better? Could he think about this? Today, we would just set a time when it was convenient for us both to talk together in case he decided on a talk with me. He could sleep over it and send me a message.

Richard sized me up for a few seconds and, with a shrug signifying "what have I got to lose?," asked about when and where. We went to my office to look at my calendar, and I showed him where he and I would sit and how to ask for me when he came to the department.

One notes how the patient's life experiences are playing into his melancholy outlook and his lack of belief in people, and how the case-worker endeavors to stimulate a different way of thinking. By relating to and challenging the stronger elements in the patient and by reducing for him the risk involved in starting a relationship with her, she establishes a climate for the relationship in which the patient can become engaged in a new venture and yet feel safe enough to take the risk.

Richard followed through on the invitation. He came for two successive interviews, which he used primarily for checking his continuing progress in the hospital. In his very first interview he reported that he had been given ground parole,[2] was thinking about applying for an Industrial Therapy assignment,[3] and also made inquiry about the hospital's part-time school for hospitalized youngsters. He came in gay and exuberant for the second interview, reporting that he had been transferred to a con-valescent cottage during the week and was to go to work under Industrial Therapy within the near future. He had done nothing further about school, however, fearing that our school would be like the special school he had had to attend prior to coming to the hospital.

On the surface, the patient's use of the preparole experience was very promising since all of the opportunities mentioned are intended as preparatory experiences for community living. However, Richard did not seem to use them in terms of these purposes. Instead, it became increasingly apparent that he withdrew from any discussion that even remotely connected his present activities in the hospital to the possibility of his future functioning back home.

Week-end visits to his family, intended as trial experiences for the patient and his family and meant to eventuate in longer and longer spans of time at home, became nothing more than hospital routines to be lived through once a week. And for the family these week-end visits became a substitute for the inconvenience of their visiting the patient at the hospital during the week.

Moreover, the worker's contacts with the various community agen-cies revealed that neither they nor the family were making much progress toward expecting Richard back from the hospital.

Following an interdisciplinary conference at the hospital, the worker, therefore, took steps toward initiating Interim Service for the par-ents and toward raising questions with the various agencies involved. The response from both groups was anything but enthusiastic at first. How-

---

[2] The privilege of moving about the hospital grounds without escort.

[3] Patients are encouraged to engage in purposeful activity at the earliest possi-ble time in order to reduce negative by-products of institutional living. They move from purely recreational pursuits in the beginning to occupational therapy and from there to industrial therapies, which are part-time work assignments that resemble outside jobs as much as possible.

ever, as the worker was able to convey the hospital's continuing readiness to share with them the responsibility for meeting the patient's many different needs during his convalescence, she was able to enlist their participation in joint efforts to help Richard.

During this period, it was necessary also to reintroduce into the patient's thinking the expectations of the hospital. The social worker's record continues as follows:

Prior to my third interview with Richard, in which I wanted to prepare him for his parents coming to see me, Dr. T. saw the patient to tell him that he had recovered sufficiently not to have to live in the hospital any longer. Similar to anyone who is given good news about his health, the patient's first reaction was positive. However, before the interview was over, Richard became very apprehensive and began to ask questions about where he was to live, who would care for him, whether he would be going to school. While giving reassurance, the physician reminded him that he had me to help him explore possibilities and develop a plan that would be right for him. In the patient's presence, Dr. T. telephoned me to confirm the fact that I was expecting Richard at the appointed time.

Richard displayed the kind of behavior that said that the hospital had become a place of refuge for him. As he spoke of his progress there, comparing it with his failures outside since early childhood, I realized how much he had already rationalized that a mental institution was not too bad a place in which to live. I gave him my understanding of what it must have meant to him when he came in sick to find that the staff here could minister to his needs, and also what it must have meant when he started to improve and could find so many interesting things to do. Could he believe enough in the abilities he had discovered in himself here at the hospital to know that these abilities were his for keeps? Could he think of trying to use them back home as he had learned to do here at the hospital? Richard's first responses to my questions were filled with expressions of fear and of resistance to change based on his memories of personal and social failures before he came to the hospital. However, his greatest battle was actually no longer so much with the fact that he had to give up the hospital but more with the problem of having to face going home. With help from me, he spoke of his past difficulties with his family, his friends, the neighbors, the people at school, saying that he did not think he had much of a chance, no matter what he thought of himself.

After going on in this vein for some time, I asked if he did not think these people were just as able to improve as he had proven to be. Or had he thought that he was expected to do all this alone? In fact, I had been meaning to tell him that I would be seeing his parents in a few days to find out what help they might need to prepare themselves for his homecoming. Did this make any sense to him?

Richard nodded tearfully. After he composed himself, he became quite active, asking me many questions about his parents' coming visits to the hospital, whether he could see them too, what we would be talking about. While I was unable to satisfy his curiosity, I could tell him that we would be talking about him, his parents' relationship to him, the sources of help available to him and to them back home. Another thing I was sure about was that he would be included when it came to making definite plans. He left in an animated fashion, confirming his next appointment and saying that he hoped he would hear from his parents in the meantime.

During the week I had a telephone interview with Mr. Roberts in response to my letter. Mr. Roberts hoped that I would not expect his wife to participate in the interim contact but agreed with me that, since Richard was the son of both, our planning for Richard should be done with both present.

Mr. and Mrs. Roberts came promptly. It was my first meeting with Mrs. Roberts, who approached the interview cautiously. Mr. Roberts, on the other hand, greeted me as one would an old acquaintance. Although inner discomfort was quite evident, he spoke in a jovial manner about the fine spring weather, which made their ride here so pleasant, and his pleasure over finding Richard living in the most attractive convalescent cottage and looking so well.

After returning Mr. Roberts' cordiality, I picked up on his statements about Richard's progress, confirming the fact that he had used the hospital well and was considered ready to leave. After a pause, which was broken by one more superficial expression of pleasure on the part of Mr. Roberts, I said that I thought we should come to the purpose of this conference. Richard no longer needed residential treatment, as they knew, and the hospital was looking to them to make living plans for him. Realizing that the hospital's expectations might create some problems for them, I had suggested this conference to see if I could help them in any way. My directness was obviously hard for them to take. There were some denials of problems and some complaints about the slowness of the various agencies that were to provide some sort of service for Richard, until I asked why it was so hard for them to accept that they might need help with planning for Richard. After all, some special things were necessary for him, and people frequently had to learn how to provide these. Besides, there was the problem of them getting used to Richard's being around the home again. As they experienced my acceptance Mr. and Mrs. Roberts could admit that they felt at a loss on how to begin, and we agreed on setting up a few interviews during which we would work together on these problems.

I suggested that the first step would probably be an interview that included Richard so that we all could start off together with a common understanding. This idea appealed to Mr. and Mrs. Roberts.

Before they left, I suggested they talk with Dr. T. and also with some of the welfare workers since it seemed that Richard might need them later.

Mr. and Mrs. Roberts came at the appointed time for the joint interview. During the preceding week, I saw Richard briefly to invite him
to the interview with his parents. I had also alerted the Pupil Personnel
worker of the possibility that the Roberts were on their way to talk with
her about Richard's readmission to school and told her that we were offering Interim Service to the parents in an effort to help them take on the
responsibility for their son.

Mr. and Mrs. Roberts had had a few minutes with Richard before they
all came in. Mrs. Roberts took the initiative this time, reporting on her
conversations with the Pupil Personnel worker, who thought that some
vocational training would be available to Richard through the public school
now that he was 16. After expressing my appreciation, I encouraged
Richard to tell us about his preparations for going home and back to school,
which he did with considerable help from me. Mr. and Mrs. Roberts
listened quietly for a moment. However, it looked increasingly as if Mrs.
Roberts was under considerable strain, and Richard stopped talking. Noting
their discomfort, I suggested that we had better look also at the other side
of the coin while we were together. All was not well yet, and many things
to be done still lay ahead. Mrs. Roberts then asked bitterly why Richard
could do so well here and not at home. Mr. Roberts wanted to stop her,
but I suggested that this conversation was within the family and Richard
might want to tell his mother something of his reasons for the different
kinds of behavior. Richard could only speak after his father encouraged
him. Then, while beginning to cry, he blurted out, "Everything is always
all my fault."

I broke the awkward silence that followed, acknowledging that it was
hard for everyone concerned to have not only the pleasant but the bitter
feelings come out. Didn't we have to know, as a family who deep down
really cared, how what anyone of us does affects the feelings of other members of the family? Isn't this how things begin to get better? After a number
of face-saving devices on everyone's part, all three said, each in his own
words, that they wanted Richard to come back home.

After Richard had left the interview, the parents and I reviewed what
today's experience was telling us. Both seemed together in the wish to
provide a home for their son, despite all the problems, and Mr. Roberts
said that he would want to come back to talk with me before they took
definite steps. I said that we could try it this way for a while and see.

Mrs. Roberts did not come for any more interviews until the day
when both parents came to the hospital to take the patient on regular
convalescent leave. However, Mr. Roberts continued to talk with me until
he had seen things through to the point of Richard's return home. While his
ambivalence and frequent indecision prevented rapid progress, Mr. Roberts was able to sustain a good enough relationship with me to grow in his

sense of responsibility and to help his wife deal with her bitter feelings toward Richard. With his help, Mrs. Roberts started to make some friendly gestures, such as fixing up Richard's room, and also to arrange for outside services, such as outpatient therapy, school enrollment, and application for summer camp.

Richard seemed to thrive. He used his rather brief interviews with me primarily to tell me about his very much happier week ends at home and about his growing eagerness to get really started there. As time went on, it seemed that his stays at the hospital were becoming visits. He continued to participate as before in activities, but his true center of interest had moved to the community several weeks before his parents took him on convalescent leave. On the day when the leave papers were signed, Richard and his parents stopped in to see me for a brief farewell visit. After each in his own way had expressed appreciation for the help received, they affirmed their own achievements. Over the last few weeks, school, clinic, and camp plans had been completed, and Richard had already made his connections with the people involved. What seemed best to them, however, was the fact that the family had talked things out together on several week ends and all were eager to try on a new basis.

Preparole service for long-time hospitalized patients

With the advent of chemotherapy, psychiatric improvement in chronic mental patients has become for the first time an ever-increasing reality. Yet the miracles of these modern treatments would remain doubtful blessings for the long-time hospitalized individual without psychiatric social work. When, after years of institutionalization, an individual rouses from his self-absorption he faces a severe social crisis. Usually, his memories of life in the community prior to hospitalization are vague and unrealistic. Frequently he thinks of home as it was many years ago and he cannot conceive that the world has moved on without him. To add to his problem, he is out of touch with the people who once were meaningful figures in his life, and the only familiar experiences for him are hospital routines and the simple recreational and work diversions that the hospital provides. Often such people do not even realize the problems ahead of them should their return to the community be considered. To help them with these problems, they may be offered Preparole Service.

In essence, this service is similar for both short-time and long-time cases—assistance in tackling the problems that are in the patient's way of readjustment to community living. While the recently admitted patient usually remembers failing experiences prior to hospitalization and, therefore, fears having to face the world where he failed before, the old-timer has forgotten his unhappy past and thus is likely to encounter many disappointments. While the loss of meaningful social connections can often be prevented for the short-time hospitalized patient, for the chronic patient these connections are lost. A social world will have to be rebuilt if he expects to venture into the community.

James Kern

When Mr. Kern was originally referred by his physician to Social Service he was 51 years old. For the past fifteen years he had been a patient in several mental hospitals—first in veterans hospitals and finally in Springfield. A veteran of World War II, twice divorced and father of two married children, Mr. Kern had not roused from his delusions over all these years until drug therapy resulted in a remission. On the surface it seemed that the patient had sufficient resources left to rebuild his life. He was living quietly on an open ward, worked in the hospital's mechanical storeroom as a janitor, and both his first wife and his children from that marriage thought that they would be able to make a home for the patient after he left the hospital.

While both the patient's physician and his social worker recognized his need for help with some intermediary step before he and his family could hope to move on together again after so many years of separation, neither Mr. Kern nor his people were ready to accept this necessity. The record opens as follows:

When I began with Mr. Kern he was not able to understand the help available through Social Service, nor was he aware of what he needed. He turned down all offers of assistance, saying bluntly that he knew his son would take responsibility. I accepted that he had a right to refuse help, especially since he was not aware of problems, and gave support to his wanting to try things out in his own way. On the other hand, I hoped he would not wait too long before letting me know if some things did not turn out the way he hoped they would.

Before the patient could find his way back to his physician and to me, I received a number of telephone calls and letters from the first Mrs. Kern and the son. Despite the fact that Mr. Kern had divorced her prior to going overseas during the war, Mrs. Kern had retained a warm, protective attitude toward the patient throughout the years. She even confided that she was convinced Mr. Kern always loved his first family and that his divorce was due to his beginning mental breakdown. Similarly, the son, principal of a private religious school, felt warmly related to the patient although he had not even visited him for twelve years. The family's attitude seemed so unusual that I suggested they stop in to see me if they should come to the hospital for a visit with the patient. In the face-to-face discussion mother and son finally clarified their true feelings. They really were fond of the patient, or rather of their memories of him. Never expecting him to get well again, Mrs. Kern had seen no reason for facing the fact that he had once divorced her or for informing Mr. Kern that she could not possibly provide a home for him. Apparently, she had brought up her children to think in these terms too.

I could understand their dilemma. Mr. Kern was well enough to leave the hospital and, no matter how glad they were about his improved mental health, it was becoming a problem for them now because he assumed that they would help him pick up life with them where he had left off fifteen years ago. I could not help but feel that Mr. Kern needed some preparation for the experience of finding out the truth. In her quiet way Mrs. Kern assured me that she would find a way to handle this if it was clear that Mr. Kern was really to leave the hospital.

The patient never shared with me that the family told him where things stood. However, soon after my interview with them, Mr. Kern renewed his contact with me and asked quite directly for a chance in foster care. When I mentioned my surprise, he told me that he had done a lot of thinking in the meantime. It would be nice to visit back and forth, but living together— no. He did not want to be taken care of. He could not stand being that dependent and he also knew that the friendly feeling between them would disappear. He had heard that you can get independence through Social Service and this is what he wanted.

Mr. Robert Kern, the patient's son, was obviously using in his father's interest the thinking expressed in his and his mother's interview with me. He started to visit his father regularly, establishing gradually a more mature and realistic father-son relationship. Both shared with me, as they came to see me individually over the next three months, the content of their discussions. From their reports it appeared that they talked increasingly about the kinds of matters that two adult men, deeply aware of a family bond but neither overly dependent upon the other, would talk about. With my support, the younger Mr. Kern became very active in enlisting resources for his father's vocational rehabilitation. Finding that our patient could not be reinstated in government service, he initiated for his father the necessary contacts with the rehabilitation program of the Veterans' Administration and assisted him in seeing through the necessary applications. In the beginning, the younger Mr. Kern still had the dream of being able to manage the home-finding for his father, hoping that the older man could live near him, somewhat like an annex to his own family unit. He was disappointed at first when he did not find his father too responsive to this idea and needed some more help from me before he could let the older man rebuild his life in his own terms, using what the son had to give as contributions to this.

About a month after Mr. James Kern had begun in preparole, the younger Mr. Kern came in to see me following a visit with his father. He said rather unhappily that the patient did not seem to want to take what he was so willing to give and what would mean so much to his mother. However, before I could even respond, he was already getting to work on the idea that the rediscovery of a sense of independence in a person usually meant also emancipation. I said that I thought he was on the right track and added my question of whether he had not been the one who had helped his father start to move in this direction. Looking tearfully pleased for a moment, somewhat like a mother who discovers suddenly that her child is grown-up, Mr. Kern said that his father's getting back on his feet this way after all these years was still quite unbelievable to him. Meeting him in feeling, I commented on the indestructability of human growth.

In the meantime, the patient's progress became more distinct and purposeful. During the week following my interview with the son, Mr. Kern asked me quite directly when I would let him make application for foster care. I expressed my pleasure over his clear-cut expectations of me and then reminded him of the need for us to take his request to the Social Planning Staff.[4] I thought that in preparation for coming to this staff, we would have to go over the events since he started to work with me and evaluate his progress in preparing himself for living in the community. I mentioned that this staff did not expect a "finished product" since he would be asking for continuing help, but that the staff would want to know how useful my help had been to him so far since it would be a similar kind of help he would be asking for while in foster care. In response to this, Mr. Kern became very active both verbally and in practical demonstration of his progress. He asked his doctor for transfer to the rehabilitation ward of his unit, where all patients not only have a job in the hospital but also are working actively with a social worker and usually with a rehabilitation therapist on plans and preparations to leave the hospital. His work habits and the quality of his performance at his job assignment in the mechanical storeroom became increasingly those of a skilled worker in industry. In his interviews with me, Mr. Kern demonstrated awareness and quite a bit of objectivity about evaluating his progress and estimating what he could expect of himself in the future in the light of recent experience.

In his last interview with me prior to staff, Mr. Kern and I reviewed the course of our relationship. He recalled how he had begun: waiting for his

---

[4] This staff is a regular hospital function. It is presided over by the clinical director and attended by representatives of all the disciplines. After hearing the reports of the patient's physician and preparole caseworkers, the staff determines the patient's psychiatric and social readiness for a try in the community under Social Service supervision.

doctor to tell him that it was time to leave the hospital, waiting for his son to plan his life, waiting for me to direct his course. We then spoke together of how he came to gain understanding of his true needs as a convalescing patient who had been sick for a long time. We reviewed how he refused to believe that he was no longer 36, but 51, and he explained to me that this had to do with his hoping against hope that he could start again in the community where he had left off fifteen years ago. As I gave him my understanding of how very hard it was to believe that one could start again, even later in life, he acknowledged this and added warmly that he had to "borrow" my belief in this sort of thing for the time being, but now he knew that it was true.

I said that he could not have said a more rewarding thing at this, our last interview. Mr. Kern was very pleased with himself for a few minutes and then moved into the ups and downs of the next level of his spirallike progress. We discussed his natural apprehension about his coming to Social Planning Staff and, if he passed, the meeting with and getting used to his new caseworker. As I shared with him the bit of sadness we both felt because he was moving on to someone else, he could affirm that it was his moving on and that he wanted to. He could also hear my saying that he would doubtlessly encounter further obstacles or even temporary setbacks. We ended with his reminding me that he had been very sick and would need time, but that he had learned "If I can do it once, I can do it again."

Foster care

The Maryland Plan for Foster Care of State Hospital Patients is defined as a psychiatric casework service, operating within the framework of public psychiatry, which offers convalescing mental patients without suitable homes of their own the opportunity to live out their social recovery in the home of a family in the community.

Following Social Planning Staff, patients are transferred to a new caseworker who helps them explore the resources in the community. During this early exploratory period, the preplacement period, the social worker takes the patient on trips to look for a home and, if he is employable, a job. When the patient has selected his home, and the selection meets the program standards and the physician's requirements, the patient moves into foster care.

Following Mr. Kern's acceptance at Social Planning Staff, I made an introductory visit to the patient and found him very eager to begin with me. Realizing that the ending with the preparole worker, the Staff experience, and meeting me was as much as should be expected at this time, I suggested an appointment three days hence. This postponement and the fact that, according to foster care regulations, he could not leave the hospital for a minimum of two weeks, disappointed him at first, but he took it in his stride.

Mr. Kern came for his first appointment, commenting that he had thought he could appear today "all packed," but he realized all over that neither I nor he could go that fast. I agreed that what he said was certainly true. However, I wondered whether, even if we could speed up things like this, it wouldn't be wise to give more thought and planning to an important decision like finding a place to live. While Mr. Kern needed to argue this point for a few minutes, he settled down to the job of our looking over the prospects I had on hand and of deciding whether any of the situations were worth investigating. I explained that all of the families provided homes that met our standards and all had had some people from the hospital living with them at one time or another. I added that this was not saying though that the homes would be right for him. I could, therefore, not think of anything else to do than for us to go out together so that he could look things over, talk with the prospective careholders, come back and sleep over what he had seen, and go out some more if the first group of homes were not suitable. The thought of that much choice seemed to be almost too much for Mr. Kern. While looking slightly pleased, he blurted out that he wished I would just settle it and get it over with. I understood his pressure but had to tell him that it would be he, not I, who would have to live in the home we found. While he certainly could change homes while in Foster Care, provided he gave proper notice just as we expected his careholder to do, I felt that a lot of trouble and setbacks could be avoided when people were starting out if their home was a comfortable place to begin the day's activities from and to return to in the evenings. Could he try it this way? Mr. Kern admitted that he really liked this idea, but he warned me with a smile that it would be slow if he had to do so much of this business himself. I said that I was willing to take that chance, was he?

Mr. Kern was correct with his predictions. It took more than the usual amount of time, the usual number of visits to prospective careholder families, and the usual number of office interviews with the patient and with his son before placement plans were completed. Both patient and son were quite disappointed at first about the external limitations of the available homes, and at one time the son thought again of taking his father home and getting him a job in his own neighborhood. The younger Mr. Kern admitted that the questions he had about the homes his father had been shown were partly due to his own discomfort with the thought that his friends and business associates might look down on his father and on him. With more help from me, he was able to lift this extra burden from the patient, who subsequently asserted his independence and settled on a small, private boarding home. Here he could eat and socialize with the family but could also meet his social needs elsewhere. He finally moved into this home three months after Social Planning Staff.

In retrospect, this less intimate, yet homelike and very flexible situation appears to be a good first experience for Mr. Kern. As a person who has just discovered that he still has some family resources left after many years of institutionalization, he may not need or want to develop a substitute family life for himself. Moreover, since his vocational interests have become very strong and future jobs will undoubtedly be in industry, there should be less need on his part for becoming a significant figure in the family of his careholder.

The patient got settled very nicely in the Price home and when I came to see him one week after placement, he behaved very much like an old-timer there. While he was waiting for word from Vocational Rehabilitation, to whom he had been referred by the Veterans Administration, he got himself a door to door shoe-selling job. "It wasn't so much the money," he said, "but the desire to keep busy," that prompted him to try some sort of work. I commented on how busy he seemed to be, wondering whether with all this he had had the time to catch up with the more personal matters. I asked particularly about his relationship to his son, who up to now has been managing his finances and had agreed to pay his board out of the patient's estate. I mentioned that money matters did not appear quite as important when one was in the hospital. It could feel quite different now that he was out to have his son handle these matters for him. Had they talked about this? Did he feel like talking with me about this?

Mr. Kern told me that it was his hope to begin taking over his affairs again. His son knows this, but they haven't really had a good talk about these matters recently. He would feel better if he could pay his board himself, but he guessed that committee arrangements like that do not get dissolved that quickly. We then discussed his medication and the need for visits at the outpatient clinic at regular intervals. While Mr. Kern grumbled a little about so many errands, which interfered with his job-hunting, he acknowledged that his medication was a "must" and was willing for me to arrange for clinic appointments.

Throughout the next month, I saw Mr. Kern each week and found that he was making quite steady progress. He was getting acquainted with the careholder family, taking most of his meals with them, and chatting with them a little after dinner. Once a week he went to see his Vocational Rehabilitation counselor, who usually expected him to go for an interview or two in connection with his pending application for retraining. In addition, he went to the clinic twice monthly, stopped in at his son's home occasionally, and was trying to sell shoes. While I felt some concern over the possibility of Mr. Kern overdoing it, his improved appearance, good spirit, and the careholder's reassuring reports seemed very good evidences of a satisfactory convalescence.

On my fifth visit, I asked Mr. Kern how he would feel about my starting to come less frequently. His response was that of a gentleman who feels
indebted because of help received in the past, still enjoys the friendly
association, and feels assured by the thought that an interested person is
around. He could not think of any pressing problems just now and added
that he thought it was only fair to have me give some newer patients more
attention. Besides, he felt that he had really learned how to make it known
when things began to bother him.

I said that he was really making his own way fast. I was willing to go
along with him though because it felt very right to me to see him need us
less and less as he was taking on new things in the community. We arranged for a monthly visiting schedule for the time being with the understanding that he could call me if this was not enough.

During the following month Mr. Kern's application to the Vocational Rehabilitation training program in electrical motor work was accepted, and an apprenticeship job placement was arranged for him. Since
then, he has established an almost full-time vocational routine, going to
classes and the work placement. He continues his bimonthly visits to the
clinic for regulation of his medication. His monthly visits with me are
becoming self-evaluating and in terms of his objective to earn his discharge from the hospital at the end of his year in foster care.

Summary

These selections of case material are intended to illustrate: (1) the
kinds of social problems with which mental patients and their families are
confronted when hospitalization for a psychiatric illness becomes necessary, (2) the type of social services that must be developed in order to
prevent or alleviate the negative effect of such problems on the patient's
convalescence, and (3) the nature of help provided by psychiatric social
workers so that patients and their families may discover both the inner
and outer resources necessary for the restoration of the patient's functioning in society.

The case of Richard Roberts was chosen to illustrate psychiatric social service to patients and family prior to and during the early phases of
hospitalization. Aware that understanding on the part of the family and
the home community of the patient's need for acceptance had to replace
the existing patterns of rejection, the caseworker first initiated a helping
relationship with the patient's parents. This required the worker's acceptance of them and their need for help and a willingness to begin with them
where they were at the time—exasperated, confused, helpless. It required
further that the worker engage them in a relationship process wherein

they felt accepted and sustained until they could discover whatever they had left in themselves to give to their boy. Finally, it meant that the worker had to help them bring this to the building of a new relationship with Richard. Only when it was clear that some parental caring would be forthcoming could the worker begin to engage the patient in fruitful pre-community activity. Like his father, Richard had to begin where he was—fearful of moving back into a world where he had failed before. With the worker's sustaining help, which included opportunities to experience his parents' new kind of receptiveness, the patient's dependency on the hospital lessened, and his center of interest shifted away from the hospital back to his home and community.

The case of James Kern was chosen to illustrate social service help to patients who, during prolonged periods of hospitalization, have become socially crippled. Basically, the nature of casework help to the persons involved was the same as in the Roberts case. However, while the emphasis in the Roberts case could be largely preventative, in the Kern case it was necessary to resort to restorative measures. Mr. Kern's social resources were far less accessible despite continuing family bonds, and his long institutionalization had disconnected him from real life. Contrary to Richard Roberts, Mr. Kern had forgotten, or blotted out, his unhappy past so that his fear over leaving the hospital was less due to memories of past failures in the community than to the fact that the institution had become the only home he knew. Accordingly, if Mr. Kern was to be helped to function outside again, the caseworker's activity had to be directed first toward helping Mr. Kern discover the personal resources left in him with which to rebuild the essentials of his life and to reconnect with other resources for the more peripheral social needs. A supportive, as well as challenging, relationship was developed to help the patient experience a series of social successes, as well as to increase his adequacy for dealing with obstacles. The patient's reawakened need for an independent existence, his request for and later use of foster care, and the surprisingly mature way in which he planned to reconnect with family members, illustrate the restorative process in which the caseworker helped him to become engaged.

10

MEDICAL
SOCIAL WORK

Formal beginnings in 1905

In the foregoing chapters the development of social casework has been presented together with applications to specific kinds of needs and within specific agency settings. Thus, social casework is seen as the basic skill and method of the caseworker while the differentiated application according to needs and settings marks the child welfare worker, the psychiatric social worker, the public assistance worker, etc. Now we come to the use of social casework in relation to other needs and, correspondingly, in another setting. The needs are illness and medical care, the setting the medical institution with its wards, laboratories, and clinics.

In her informative volume, *Social Work in Hospitals*, Miss Ida M. Cannon traces in considerable detail the forerunners of medical social work: (1) services provided for the aftercare of the insane in Germany, France, England, and America; (2) services furnished by lady almoners in London hospitals; (3) nursing, especially visiting nursing service begun by Lillian Wald and Mary Brewster in New York City; and (4) the field work training of medical students at Johns Hopkins Medical School and Hospital.[1]

These developments furnish the background for the more formal beginnings in 1905 when two Boston medical institutions introduced social workers on two successive days in October 1905. From one point of view, this may have seemed mere "happenstance." From another point of view, that is, analysis of the cultural antecedents, there was a kind of inevitability that medical social work would develop at about this time. This does not rule out the importance of the men and women who shared in these

---

[1] Ida M. Cannon, *Social Work in Hospitals* (New York: Russell Sage Foundation, 1923).

beginnings, but it does give some much needed corrective to the too commonly held opinion that a particular individual is solely responsible for a new development. Miss Mabel Barkley at the Berkeley Infirmary and Miss Garnet Pelton at the Massachusetts General Hospital in October 1905 were instrumentalities through whom medical social work came into being. According to a former member of the Board of Managers of the Berkeley Infirmary, the idea of establishing the Infirmary and the social work accompanying it were the outcome of Dr. Samuel Breck's experience in his office practice and his contacts with women and children in the Floating Hospital, of which he was one of the founders. He felt the need for wider follow-up work. Dr. Richard C. Cabot wanted to know more about the patient in order to help him use to the full all available medical care. It was he, a member of the staff of the Massachusetts General Hospital and associated for years with the work of the Boston Children's Aid Society, who envisioned the need to bring to the hospital an additional service from another field to enable the sick person to utilize more effectively what the physician and the hospital had to offer. What Dr. Cabot effected was not a numerical adding together of after care, visiting nursing, hospital admittance, and the supplemental training of medical students. This is not medical social work any more than the numerical addition of wheel, internal combustion engine, differential gears, and brake is the automobile. The automobile is a product in which the wheel, the engine, the gear, the brake and other parts are integrated into a new creation that is something more than the sum of its parts. Likewise with medical social work. It was a combination of after care, nursing, admission, training medical students, and social casework integrated into a new service for the sick person.

So much for relating medical social work to its cultural setting. It will be well at this point to recall Dr. Cabot's experience. A 10-month-old baby suffering with stomach trouble was brought to the Massachusetts General Hospital. Five weeks of care restored the child to its mother, without any instructions as to diet or care. Within a few weeks the baby was back in the hospital as sick as ever. Again, $30 worth of care was expended on the baby and again it was turned over to its mother "cured" and without instructions. Once more the trouble occurred, and to Dr. Cabot the performance promised to approximate perpetual motion: "Baby goes out, baby gets sick, baby comes back, baby goes out and so on forever." Dr. Cabot's answer to this was to place on the staff of the hospital a social worker to study the conditions under which patients lived and to assist the patient to carry out the treatment recommended by the medical staff. From such early steps medical social work expanded, slowly at first and then with increasing acceleration, until at the present time there are probably few, if any, first-rate hospitals that do not have a medical social service department.[2]

The institutional setting of medical social work

One of the unmistakable characteristics of the development of medical care in this century is the increased utilization of hospital treatment. Hospitals have grown in numbers and in beds—from 4359 hospitals with 421,065 beds in 1909 to 6845 hospitals and 1,612,822 beds in 1960.[3] Undoubtedly, this has reflected a change in attitudes about the hospital—from a previous fatalism about it as a terminal illness institution to a more recent regard for it as a resource to use in getting well.

Likewise, within the present century the hospital, which is being increasingly patronized, is also becoming increasingly compartmentalized. Dr. G. Canby Robinson in his volume *The Patient as a Person* mentions the experience of Dr. Dochez

> . . . who contrasted the records of two patients with heart disease, one admitted to the hospital about twenty-five years ago and another to the same hospital in 1938. The first patient was cared for by a visiting physician, an intern, and one specialist, the pathologist-bacteriologist, and the completed record covered two and a half pages. The second patient had been observed and described by three visiting physicians, two residents, three interns, ten specialists, and fourteen technicians, a total of thirty-two individuals, and the uncompleted record of the case covered twenty-nine pages.[4]

Today there are departments of medicine, surgery, neurology, psychiatry, obstetrics, gynecology, orthopedics, cardiology, pediatrics, oto-

---

[2] In previous editions of this volume the writer drew heavily upon Ida M. Cannon's invaluable record *Social Work in Hospitals*. The debt to Miss Cannon is increased further by virtue of the usefulness of her later (1952) book *On the Social Frontier of Medicine*. The latter work traces in revealing detail not only the early struggles to have medical social work introduced into hospitals but also the sure growth of this service as an essential part in the total operation of the modern hospital. The thoughtful, daring, and pioneering work of Dr. Richard C. Cabot is frankly appraised and appreciated. In his foreword to Miss Cannon's volume, Dr. James Howard Means refers to Dr. Cabot as the man who "had the genius to introduce social workers to the Massachusetts General Hospital for the purpose of improving the over-all medical care of patients. Social work already existed at that time, but not in hospitals. It was in its extension to medical care that Dr. Cabot's great contribution lay."

[3] For late figures see *Hospitals*, 34, part 2, Administrative Guide Issue (August 1, 1960), p. 359.

[4] G. Canby Robinson, *The Patient as a Person* (New York: The Commonwealth Fund, 1939), pp. 7–8.

laryngology, ophthalmology, X-ray. These reflect and formalize the increasing specialization in medicine. The result has been, as frequently pointed out, that as medical science learns more and more about disease the practitioner knows less and less about the patient. In an earlier day when the sick avoided hospitals as a place where people died, the problem of knowledge concerning the person was not what might be called acute. Likewise, when the general practice of medicine was the prevailing mode, there was little question of the physician's knowledge of his patient and surroundings. He treated, not a case of pneumonia or diabetes or malaria, but rather a sick person. Nothing stood between him and his patient; he required no one to interpret the patient to him nor to interpret his findings to the patient. His recommendations for treatment took in the patient as a person.

Institutionalization and specialization in medicine have changed much of this. When a hospital becomes highly departmentalized, when it adds clinic to clinic, multiplying specialist by specialist, and ends up with elaborate equipment and an endless line of patients, the point is reached where the sick person is in danger of being lost in the maze.[5] The best equipment in the world seldom proves an adequate substitute for the all-around knowledge of the patient that the physician needs. It is into this institutionalized, specialized, depersonalized mass situation that the medical social worker comes primarily to aid the patient, secondarily the physician.

The original reasons for the introduction of medical social work in 1905 still obtain to some degree. For Dr. Cabot, medical social work served to assist the physician in diagnosis and treatment through study of the patient in his social situation and by interpreting the patient and his environment to the physician. In addition, the medical social worker was to assist by organizing resources in the hospital as well as in the patient's family and the community at large for making medical treatment effective. For Dr. Adolph Meyer of Johns Hopkins Hospital, casework in the hospital was for the purpose of securing facts about the patient while he was in the hospital, insuring healthy conditions in the home in preparation for the patient's return, and maintaining such conditions after the patient's return home. Throughout all of this, the social worker was to be in constant contact with the physician.

---

[5] Dr. Henry B. Richardson lightly but tellingly deplores this tendency to think of the patient as a structural defect in some vital organ by such references as "the metral stenosis in the second bed on the left," "the gastric ulcer in the fourth bed on the right." See Henry B. Richardson, *Patients Have Families* (New York: The Commonwealth Fund, 1945), XIV, 209; see also the incident of the patient who was labeled so easily as "Dr. S.'s submucous resection" in Helena Willis Render, and M. Olga Weiss, *Nurse-Patient Relationships in Psychiatry* (New York: McGraw-Hill Book Company, Inc., 1959), p. 75.

For Dr. Henry B. Richardson, a more recent student of the role of social and emotional factors in sickness, medical social service has as its immediate objective the relief of inner and outer pressures, whether these arise from external realities and illness or more from personal attitudes and feelings. "The ultimate objective is to enable sick people to draw on their own capacities in seeking or using medical care, in preventing illness or maintaining health." [6]

Another physician, Dr. H. M. Margolis, late in 1946 in speaking of the medical social worker as an integral member of the medical community of effort, observed:

> In order to insure integrated help for the patient, the physician shares professional thinking and planning with the worker. We depend on her largely for an objective picture of the patient's social setting, his relationship with the family group, its socio-economic as well as its emotional resources. . . . We see her as having capacity for helping the patient to participate more fully and comfortably in the doctor-patient relationship and in the processes of medical diagnosis and treatment. From her must come the specialized knowledge of community resources for vocational job placement and for meeting the other social needs of the patient related to his illness. [7]

Most medical social workers will bear witness to the distinction in function that Drs. Richardson, Margolis, and a host of other physicians have emphasized in recent years. In the Memorial Lecture at Johns Hopkins Hospital in honor of Margaret Brogden (one of the pioneer medical social workers), Miss Cockerill recognized that the physician has primary concern and responsibility for symptomatology and treatment. To her, the focus of the medical social worker was upon "the social factors which have helped to make the patient ill, the social problems which his illness creates for him, and the obstacles which may limit his capacity to make use of what medicine has to offer." In another part of her address she emphasized the point that the primary objective of the medical social worker's services is "to enhance the usefulness of medical care to the patient and to help the hospital to achieve its purpose in medical treatment." [8]

---

6 *Ibid.*, p. 212.

7 H. M. Margolis, "The Psychosomatic Approach to Medical Diagnosis and Treatment," *Journal of Social Casework*, XXVII (December 1946), pp. 298–299. For a specific instance of this "medical community of effort," see Bessie Schless, "Achieving Maximum Adjustment in Chronic Illness" *Journal of Social Casework*, XXVII (December, 1946), pp. 320–325.

8 Eleanor Cockerill, "The Use of the Psychosomatic Concept in Social Case Work." *Bulletin of the Johns Hopkins Hospital*, LXXX (January 1947), pp. 86–97; see also Doris Siegel, who insists that social work in the medical setting is an important and valuable service for the patient as well as for his family. She adds: "In some instances, social service makes it possible for medical care to begin. In others, it speeds recovery and may be helpful in preventing any further or additional deterioration or

Another medical social worker, Minna Field, moves one step beyond this—actually beyond the hospital—as she draws upon her experience in dealing with patients with prolonged illness. She emphasizes social service as part of total medical care and insists upon relating the ill person to his family and his community:

> In this process of helping, the social worker, as part of the medical team, utilizes the same basic skills which characterize casework in general, namely, an understanding of human behavior and an ability to apply this understanding constructively to help in difficult situations. As in all casework, and particularly in dealing with those whose illness and incapacity tend to undermine their feelings of worth and status, the primary prerequisite is an appreciation of the dignity of the individual and a respect for his rights as a human being, regardless of the stage of his illness or the degree of his impairment.
>
> Since we recognize the significance of the close emotional ties which bind members of a family group, and the importance of satisfactory family relationships for the welfare of the patient, the social worker must of necessity be ready to render whatever help may be needed by family members. They may need assistance in meeting the problems which the patient's illness creates for them, or help to see the person behind the illness, to have regard for his intrinsic worth, to gear their demands to the limitations imposed by his illness, to utilize imaginatively his remaining potentialites, and to draw him into active participaton in family living.[9]

The social worker in the hospital

When a sick person enters the hospital the entire machinery is set in motion to get him well. All that medical science knows and all the skill it has is directed toward restoring him if that is possible, or of effecting such improvement that he can function outside the hospital as he is helped to make an adjustment to partial restoration. The tests and analyses that are made and the treatment programs that follow from them are the major concern of the physician, but a well-rounded service will demand that the skill of the medical social worker be joined with that of other hospital personnel. It is the physician's job to provide medical care, it is the social worker's to help the patient to utilize medical care so that health will be achieved. To do the latter job the social worker must first know and understand the patient, how and why he feels as he does, what his capacities

---

handicap. In still other situations, social service is what is needed by particular patients and their families and is the treatment of choice." "Social Work in the Medical Setting: An Instrument for Health," *Social Work*, 2 (April 1957), p. 73.

[9] Minna Field, *Patients Are People*, rev. ed. (New York: Columbia University Press, 1958), pp. 260-261.

are for assuming his share of the responsibility of getting well. He, the worker, will need to know where the patient is blocked and why and what can be done to help the patient move on from there. He will want to learn what meaning this illness has for the patient and how it affects his feelings about himself and also how it affects or is affected by his social relationships. In short, the worker will be dealing with the medical problem without being the physician; he will be dealing with the emotional elements without being the phychiatrist. But he will be dealing with both of these in relation to the social situation and the social relationships of which the patient is a part. It is this strictly defined function of medical social work that cannot be emphasized too often if medical social workers and hospital staff are going to continue to work harmoniously.

The patient as a person

Throughout this chapter, the expression "the patient as a person" is used. It is not an original statement. Yet it is perhaps the most succinct and arresting of those many expressions that have gained currency within recent years, emphasizing the essential "individualness" characteristic of each human being. The stress upon the individual in the field of education and in all forms of social casework are other instances of the same trend. Educators speak of the student who is first of all a person who learns. The probation or parole officer or the social worker in a correctional institution conceives of an offender who first of all is a person who commits a crime. The medical social worker sees the patient first of all as a person who is sick. The consistent principle that runs all through these is that the human being who needs help, whether he be a student, a probationer, a parolee, a prisoner, or a patient, has as his core his own unique personality. This personality distinguishes him from every other human being.

All of this is pertinent with respect to the person who is sick. What he will do about his illness, about getting himself to a doctor or a hospital, how he will be able to face the diagnosis and all that it may mean to him, how he will carry out recommended steps in treatment and make the necessary adjustments in his life are decisions that every sick person must face. No two persons will react the same way, not even to the same disease, if for no other reason than that a disease never means the same to any two people. The crucial point involved here is: What is the meaning of this disease to this person at this time?

Not only must the hospital staff, including medical social workers, consider the patient together with all of his attitudes about disease and about himself, but that same staff, especially the medical social worker this time, must see him as part of a configuration of social relationships.

This configuration would include especially his family and job. No individual manages to live unto himself, and what a particular person may mean to his family and what his family may mean to him are entirely relevant whenever anything goes wrong, whether it be in the field of behavior, such as delinquency and crime, or in the field of health, such as tuberculosis or syphilis. Much the same may be said for the job. For most people "the job" means not only status that comes from being able to provide for oneself and one's family but also the personal satisfaction of accomplishing something. In addition, the job makes possible a stability that becomes a factor for strength in the development and expression of the individual. What the loss or surrender of that job because of illness may mean to the individual is essential not only to diagnosis but also to treatment.[10]

The psychosomatic approach

Within the past two decades considerable attention has been given to what is rather frequently referred to as the psychosomatic approach. Essentially this expression means a taking into account of the emotional as well as the physical factors in disease. Actually this is not a new concept, for it goes to the very basis of diagnosis and treatment and has had to be reckoned with ever since there was an art of healing. However, as Dr. H. M. Margolis points out, the phenomenal discoveries of modern medicine tended to obscure the interrelatedness of mind and body.

Medical discoveries in bacteriology, pathology, surgery, biochemistry, and biophysics, with their potentiality for help to the sick, came as an overwhelming avalanche of medical progress. These advances were stirring; they had a mathematical precision that was unknown before; they literally swept away the existence of certain infectious diseases and created specific cures, hitherto undreamed of. All of them focused on the physical constitution of man and his ills and emphasized the accomplishments that could be achieved by physical means. Actually, medical literature dropped the word "man" and began to speak of the human organism, which was being studied so precisely and which could be manipulated so mechanically. In time, medical students and physicians came to regard this human organism as a biological unit not different from the amoeba or the turnip. They forgot

---

[10] A number of excellent treatises have emphasized the points mentioned in this and other sections of the chapter. The student who wishes to explore further these concepts and to find substantiation through a variety of illustrations is referred to the following: Minna Field, *Patients Are People* (rev. ed.; New York: Columbia University Press, 1958); Henry B. Richardson, *Patients Have Families* (New York: The Commonwealth Fund, 1945); G. Canby Robinson, *The Patient as a Person* (New York: The Commonwealth Fund, 1939).

that the individual was more than a turnip; he was a biologic unit, it is true, but endowed with a highly sensitive nervous system that held in delicate balance a highly complex emotional apparatus with a storehouse of memories, loves, hates, fears, feelings of security and anxiety.[11]

It is because these loves, hates, fears, feelings of security and anxiety are related to the precipitation of illness, the duration of illness, and the recovery from illness that the practitioner needs to be aware of both the emotional and the physical factors. There is an increasing literature being made available to the practitioner that emphasizes the emotional components in what used to be thought of as only physical ailments. The impressive 2300-item bibliography in Dr. H. Flanders Dunbar's volume *Emotions and Bodily Changes* (1935, 1938, 1946) constitutes substantial evidence of the increased interest in the psychical and physical factors of illness. Dr. Dunbar's presentation of the gist of these studies in her more recent publication intended for the layman *Mind and Body: Psychosomatic Medicine* contains many illustrations of the interplay of the *psyche* and the *soma*. Case histories are given of the emotional elements of such ailments as: appendicitis, arthritis, asthma, cancer, colitis, diabetes, eczema, hay fever, heart diseases, migraine, pneumonia, rheumatic heart, skin diseases, tuberculosis, and ulcers. The further work of Drs. Weiss and English in their text on psychosomatic medicine, of Drs. Alexander and French in their published studies in psychosomatic medicine, and the recent volume of case histories by Miles, Cobb, and Shands bear further testimony to those developments. To all of this must be added the quarterly journal *Psychosomatic Medicine,* which has been appearing since 1939.

A balanced judgment is necessary here lest the assumption too readily be made that psychosomatic medicine is a new and radical departure in medical practice. Dr. Weiss, whose textbook has been mentioned, denies the validity of the either/or concept; that is, that an illness is either functional or organic. Instead it is necessary to deal with the interrelatedness of the two. He then observes that as psychiatry is established on a firm scientific basis and is integrated into general medicine "we will no longer need the term psychosomatic because good medicine will be psychosomatic." [12]

In much the same vein with the emphasis upon the wholeness of the person Dr. Robinson observes: "Man is a unity of mind and body and medicine must consider this unity. Physiology, chemistry, and biology

[11] H. M. Margolis, *op. cit.,* p. 291.

[12] Edward Weiss, "Psychotherapy in Everyday Practice," in *Modern Attitudes in Psychiatry* (New York: Columbia University Press, 1946), p. 117; see also Franz Alexander, "Present Trends in Psychiatry and the Future Outlook," in *Modern Attitudes in Psychiatry*, pp. 83–84.

cannot alone or together explain all the intricacies of illness. The disturbances of mind and body cannot be dealt with separately; they form two phases of a single problem." [13]

The patient's reaction to illness

It is necessary to realize what a threat illness can be to the personality of the patient and how it may affect the whole manner of living or way of life. Illness sets one off, accentuates one's differences or establishes other differences that may be hard to bear, especially in the face of illness. It may accentuate or establish an inferiority, an inferiority that perhaps one could get along with while well, but which is too overwhelming during illness when one is robbed of the usual devices of defense. Other individuals may cling to illness because of what it gives them. With illness they amount to something, they get attention; without illness they are mediocrities who somehow get along without much notice. All of these possible reactions must be borne in mind by the medical social worker when he offers help to the sick person. No two of them will act alike. One patient will go so far as to deny illness and by this denial manage to spend the energy that otherwise would go into getting well, in keeping sick. Not admitting illness, of course, means taking no responsibility about getting well. Another person may acknowledge he is sick and not care to do anything about recovering. Actually such a person may get more satisfaction from being sick than in being well, the person we all know who enjoys ill health. Still a third person may positively admit his illness and by accepting what limitations inhere in his illness is able to release his energies toward getting well. Others may react differently at various stages of their illness or recovery. Some who start by affirming their illness may find the going too tough, may relapse and not have the will to go on. Others who began by denying illness may suffer such reverses as to be willing to face death or permanent incapacitation before they can come to grips with themselves and admit their need for help. Still others can take help so long as another stands by but are utterly incapable, seemingly, of carrying their own load. With all of these patients the medical social worker deals and must adapt his skills accordingly.

Most medical social workers learn early in their careers that, medical science notwithstanding, the patient has a good deal to do with whether or not he gets well. Some workers have gone so far as to say that no one can "cure" the patient but himself; that no matter how strongly the physician may want to cure, the real desire must come from the patient,

[13] G. Canby Robinson, *op. cit.*, p. 10; see also Leland E. Hinsie, *The Person in the Body* (New York: W. W. Norton & Company, Inc., 1945).

not primarily from the physician or the social worker.[14] The realization of this truth early in his career spares the medical social worker many fruitless hours of trying to get over to the patient someone else's plan. This realization may be a bit discouraging, but its sobering effect does much to keep the patient-worker relationship centered around the problem of illness, its relation to the patient's social and social-psychological needs, and finally to the capacity of the individual to take help.

Probably the first step in this casework process of offering help is an understanding of the patient, of the disease and what it means to him, and of his ability to cope with the situation in which he finds himself. If the medical social worker is to be a part of the hospital and yet differentiated from it, if he is to bring something new into the hospital setting, it is this very difference that approaches the patient upon an individual basis, that understands him in relation to his disease, that expresses its concern with return to health, but which at the same time leaves the decision with the patient. To come upon this offer of help, to realize one is free to accept or to reject it, to know that there is someone to "go along with" him in the steps toward recovery may give the patient some understanding of what a social casework service is.

That the patient has come to the hospital and to the social worker upon referral by the physician or nurse means that he has moved in the direction of doing something about whatever is bothering him. He may not have as clear a notion of what he wants to do or of what the hospital will do to him as, say, the parent who takes a child to a child guidance clinic. Yet the very step of coming to the hospital—as the mother's steps to

---

[14] Dr. Flanders Dunbar very dramatically illustrates this in the following passages:

"Two men lay side by side in the hospital ward, both advanced stages of cardiovascular disease. The seriousness of their condition is typical of hospital cases, since these victims generally do not arrive for anything they or their physicians regard as trivial. They wait until they require major treatment of some kind, and congratulate themselves upon their fortitude in holding out so long. They might have been cured easily at an earlier stage, but would not have showed so much courage. The two lying side by side were rather extreme examples. Each was pathetically eager to get well. Each watched the physician breathlessly during his examination. Each spoke his uppermost thought at the end.

" 'It's up to you now, Doc,' said one.

" 'I've got to do something to get well,' said the other.

"These patients were on opposite horns of a common dilemma. They were not quite sure of what their own role should be in working out their restoration to health. They had similar past histories and similar symptoms, which probably resulted in the acquisition of essentially the same disease. The personality of the first, however, was not so well integrated as that of the second. The result was that the response of the first to treatment was to leave it all to the doctor. The response of the other was: What can I do to get well? The first died, the second recovered, although laboratory tests and clinical examinations failed to show any real difference."—H. Flanders Dunbar, *Mind and Body: Psychosomatic Medicine* (New York: Random House, 1947), pp. 65–66.

the child guidance clinic—indicates the possibility of movement. All that can be asked at this point of the medical social worker is that he understand the patient's feeling about his disease, acknowledge the steps he has already taken, and indicate his willingness to work along with him on the things that lie ahead. He must meet the patient where he is, not where he thinks the patient ought to be; take him for what he is, not what he ought to be; and start moving with him at his pace and in his direction rather than at the worker's own speed toward a preconceived goal. This does not mean the worker adds nothing to this relationship; he does, but he adds what the patient needs, not what he, the worker, needs.

The patient's use of help

Before people can use help they must want help. This may sound commonplace enough, but certainly social caseworkers have had sufficient experience with the helping process to appreciate the fact that individuals, no matter how badly off they are, still have their own wants, wishes, wills, and need to work out their lives accordingly. To those who are well it must seem absurd to speak of sick people without the will to get well, just as absurd as it must seem to speak of sick people not accepting the fact that they are sick. Yet such is the case, and it is frequently at this point and for this reason that the medical social worker is called upon. A person may be diagnosed by the doctor as having heart trouble, a kidney disease, tuberculosis, syphilis, or cancer. The mere diagnosis does not make the person want to get well; it may actually arouse so many fears that he is unable to act. Even repeating the words of the diagnosis is not tantamount to accepting the fact of the disease. There is such a thing as intellectual acceptance of the disease, which is an entirely different acceptance than an emotional one. Emotional acceptance means admitting the disease is a part of oneself, then expressing a will to do something about the disease, and finally beginning to do something about it. Here is an area in which the medical social worker functions. The patient may need to be helped to understand the disease, what its course is likely to be, what it may do to the patient, the adjustments it will necessitate, temporarily or permanently, in the life of the patient, the kinds of limitations it will set and how these can be handled. The patient knows he is taking help when he comes to grips with his illness, when he feels freer to work and live within its limitations than to spend his energies fighting it. The very acceptance of the disease and the necessity of adjusting to it may actually prove to be a growth experience never before known to the patient.

The responsibility the patient
carries

Feelings, emotions, and ideas eventually get expressed, in one way or another, in action—action being another word for behavior. The behavior with which the patient and the medical social worker are concerned is directed toward adjustment to illness and handicaps, or toward restoration to health. Not all sickness turns toward absolute health, yet an individual may need help in adjustment to a more or less permanent incapacitation or at least handicap, as well as to the happier movement toward recovery. The services of the medical social worker, which consist of interviewing and counseling with patients, are directed toward action on the part of the patient in making the accommodation to the limitations of illness or the step toward health. For either the doctor or the social worker to take over the patient's responsibility would be to rob him of the opportunity to take hold of his own problem. For them to allow him to carry his share of responsibility means that he is freer to move into action on his own behalf. It leaves him free to do something about himself. The social worker, by enabling him to express his fears, by taking him for what he is, by instilling confidence in him, by thinking out some of his difficulties with him, by being there to help him work out plans further if need be, provides releases that enable him to take his own next steps. Perhaps he cannot see far enough ahead to work out the whole problem alone, very few of us can, but he can relate himself to one small part of it and as he gains a feeling of sureness there, he can go on to larger areas. This step toward action very often is the answer to fear; for if a patient can only make a decision to act and then act, many of the fears that have beset him are dissolved away. Certainly the feeling of helplessness is not so great. There is no freer medium in which to express feelings without condemnation, to face fears, to feel accepted and understood than the relationship with the patient that the medical social worker is enabled to set up. Out of this relationship should come a freer use of the patient's self, his creative energies, his capacities to take on responsibility for his own life.

A sick person is part of the web of social relationships and a member of a social group in a community situation. He is a member of a family, he affects and is affected by the other family members, he has job responsibilities and community contacts of various kinds. His illness may remove him for the time being from that family and that community, but eventually he must return there. The adjustments he must make, the limitations he must bear are in relation to his social setting. This the medical social worker must constantly bear in mind. Sick people, like others, make their adjustment to a reality situation, not to a ready-made or ideal one. No matter what the skill of the medical social worker is nor how profound the personality needs of the patient, the central job is to relate the patient and the medical plan to the social situation. The ultimate test is whether, in the light of the capacities of the individual, the nature of his disability, and the demands of the social situation, the medical social worker has helped to effect such an adjustment of the patient to the community as will most satisfactorily meet his own needs and at the same time the requirements of the community.

Medical social work outside of the hospital setting

Medical social work has operated traditionally within a hospital setting. Within recent years there have been developments that have used the medical social work approach to deal with problems outside the hospital. The components of these problems are essentially those with which medical social work has always dealt: people, illness, a social situation. The more spectacular of these newer medical social work services has been in the crippled children's program and in vocational rehabilitation.

Under the provisions of the Social Security Act of 1935 and subsequent amendments, funds are made available by the federal government for crippled children's services throughout the states, territories, and insular possessions. States, territories, and insular possessions submit an acceptable plan to insure service to the crippled children, which must provide among other things financial participation by the states, administration by a state agency, and cooperation with medical, health, nursing, and welfare groups in the state.

Pediatricians and orthopedists have welcomed the services of the trained medical social workers in the carrying out of a crippled children's program. Thus far the demand for service has been so great, despite the many years of excellent service that a score of private groups have rendered, that the physicians have been swamped and able to look into only the medical aspects of treatment. The necessity of seeing the patient as a person is as marked here as in the more conventional areas just described. If anything, the requirement is all the more urgent because of the disfiguring, disabling, and handicapping effects under which crippled children have suffered or do suffer. Here certainly is a place where the medical social worker must understand what illness and defect mean to the child, the accent on difference from other children, the loss of status in the home and in school, the feeling of not being wanted, of feeling oneself a burden, of feeling inferior to whole children. Here, too, even though the patient is a child, he must be helped to accept his crippled condition, to make decisions for himself, to work within limitations, and if cured to leave behind many of those compensations that inevitably accompanied his defect. Here, too, the child must be helped to share in community life. In short, the ordeal of crippling and the restoration from crippling may afford as excellent an opportunity as life will ever again allow to know what a real growth experience is. To be in a position to enable a child to realize his potentialities is one of the enviable opportunities few others can know.[15]

Another service in which medical social work has been utilized increasingly is vocational rehabilitation. This service has been available on a federal-state basis since the Vocational Rehabilitation Act of 1920, but it remained for the Social Security Act of 1935 and the Vocational Rehabilitation Act of 1943 (Barden-La Follette) and as subsequently amended to provide it with its greatest impetus for usefulness. In the preceding pages emphasis has been placed upon illness and adjustment in relation to it. Everything said on that score would be just as applicable to the handicap that disease or accident produces. Indeed, the vocational and emotional adjustment to handicap may be, and usually is, a lifelong one. Effective vocational rehabilitation requires not only medical diagnosis and treatment but physical and occupational therapy, vocational training and retraining, financial assistance, job placement, and casework services. Here are at least three professions involved: medical, educational, social service.[16]

Medical social workers are being used, increasingly, in public health. Traditionally, and with greater emphasis within recent years, public health has concerned itself with preventive aspects. There has come to be a place for using the knowledge and skills of medical social work in local county health departments as well as on the staffs of state health

---

[15] In a useful pamphlet "Medical Social Services for Children" prepared by the medical social work staff of the U.S. Children's Bureau emphasis is given not only to the core of casework services in the maternal and child health and crippled children's programs but also to auxiliary services as essential to the medical social work function in these areas. Such auxiliary services were suggested to be: program planning, policy making, standard setting, community planning, educational activities, planning and participating in medical studies and research. See "Medical Social Services for Children" (Washington, D.C.: Children's Bureau, U.S. Department of Health, Education, and Welfare, 1953), pp. 10–31; see also Elizabeth P. Rice, "Medical Social Work," *Social Work Year Book* (New York: American Association of Social Workers), 1954, pp. 339–346; and Eleanor Cockerill, in *Social Work Year Book*, 1960, pp. 375–382.

[16] It is also pertinent to mention several recent volumes bearing on medical social services in relation to rehabilitation and prolonged illness. For the former see Caroline H. Elledge, *The Rehabilitation of the Patient* (Philadelphia: J. B. Lippincott Company, 1948); and for the latter see Minna Field, *Patients Are People*, rev. ed., (New York: Columbia University Press, 1958).

departments. Schools of public health, especially in those universities in which a school of social work is located, are tending more and more to use medical social workers on their teaching staffs.

Public welfare departments, more usually at the state office level, are utilizing medical social workers in relation to disability determination in the public assistance disability programs (APTD or AD as they are usually designated). Likewise, as public welfare departments are becoming more and more involved in using tax funds for medical care for public assistance clients and for those termed "the medically indigent" they must draw upon the resources of the professionally trained medical social worker.

A still further use of the medical social worker is by national health and welfare associations that are referred to as private agencies. The financial support of such organizations is largely by private contribution. The American Red Cross, the National Foundation (formerly for poliomyelitis), and the American Public Welfare Association are examples of such agencies. However, even though they may not minister directly to ill persons, nevertheless, they use the knowledge and skill of medical social work in such a way that a more effective service is ultimately available to more patients and in more places.

Conclusion

Medical social work, like other specializations within the casework field, has been responsive to the fundamental changes in philosophy and practice within the present century. The early emphasis was upon changing the environment so that there would be as ideal a situation as possible in which the patient was to live. Gradually this gave way to an approach that recognized the emotional factors involved in illness, and the necessity to explore the psychological needs of the patient and to reorient him to his illness in the light of his inner needs. More recently the focus has been upon the helping function to the ill person in relation to his social situation. This newer trend recognizes the important role of environment, but includes within it the much larger area of social relationships. With the followers and disciples of the psychoanalysts of the second period, it sees the part which the emotions, past experiences, etc., play in individual behavior, but it also sees those as related to other factors and to present situations. The medical social work of today is not to be regarded as a compromise of the first and second eras. Rather it is to be considered as a progressive movement which has retained their contributions but has fused them into a richer service, a service stressing the essential dynamics of the patient-physician-worker relationship and the greater possibilities of realizing the patient's potentialities within his particular social situation.

Bibliography

Alexander, Franz, *Psychosomatic Medicine: Its Principles and Applications.* New York: W. W. Norton & Company, Inc., 1950.

American Public Welfare Association, *The Medical Social Worker in the Public Welfare Agency.* Chicago: American Public Welfare Association, 1955.

Bartlett, Harriet, *Fifty Years of Social Work in the Medical Setting.* New York: National Association of Social Workers, 1957.

Bell, E. Moberly, *The Story of the Hospital Almoners: The Birth of a Profession.* London: Faber & Faber, Ltd., 1961.

Brown, Esther Lucile, *Newer Dimensions in Patient Care.* New York: Russell Sage Foundation, 1961.

Cabot, Richard C., *Social Service and the Art of Healing,* rev. ed., New York: Dodd, Mead & Company, Inc., 1928.

Cannon, Ida M., *On the Social Frontier of Medicine.* Cambridge: Harvard University Press, 1952.

Cockerill, Eleanor, "New Emphasis on an Old Concept in Medicine," *Journal of Social Casework,* XXX (January 1949), pp. 10–15.

Cooley, Carol H., *Social Aspects of Illness.* Philadelphia: W. B. Saunders Company, 1951.

Dockhorn, Jean M., "The Influence of Social and Emotional Factors in the Treatment of Tuberculosis," *American Journal of Respiratory Diseases,* 82 (August 1960), pp. 223–231.

Dunbar, H. Flanders, *Mind and Body: Psychosomatic Medicine,* rev. ed., New York: Random House, Inc., 1955.

Elledge, Caroline H., *The Rehabilitation of the Patient.* Philadelphia: J. B. Lippincott Company, 1948.

Field, Minna, *Patients Are People,* rev. ed., New York: Columbia University Press, 1958.

Goldstine, Dora, ed., *Expanding Horizons in Medical Social Work.* Chicago: University of Chicago Press, 1955.

———, *Readings in the Theory and Practice of Medical Social Work.* Chicago: University of Chicago Press, 1954.

Hinsie, Leland E., *The Person in the Body.* New York: W. W. Norton & Company, Inc., 1945.

Miles, Henry H. W., Stanley Cobb, and Harley C. Shands, *Case Histories in Psychosomatic Medicine.* New York: W. W. Norton & Company, Inc., 1952.

Rice, Elizabeth P., "Social Work in Public Health," *Social Work,* 4 (January 1959), pp. 82–88.

Richardson, Henry B., *Patients Have Families.* New York: The Commonwealth Fund, 1945.

Robinson, G. Canby, *The Patient as a Person*. New York: The Commonwealth
    Fund, 1939.
Siegel, Rose, "Social Work in the Medical Setting: An Instrument for Health,"
    Social Work, 2 (April 1957), pp. 70–77.
Simmons, Leo W., and Harold G. Wolff, *Social Science in Medicine*. New York:
    Russell Sage Foundation, 1954.
State Charities Aid Association, *The Changing Pattern of Illness*. New York:
    State Charities Aid Association, 1960.
White, Grace, "The Distinguishing Charactreistics of Medical Social Work,"
    Medical Social Work, 1 (September 1951), pp. 31–39.

MR. W.; MR. F.

MRS. BEATRICE PHILLIPS, DIRECTOR,
Social Service Department
Beth Israel Hospital
Boston, Massachusetts

In this chapter the history and concepts of medical social service have been presented. It is readily apparent from the description that there are a variety of settings in which medical social service functions, for example: a hospital for long-term care, a general hospital, a public health department, a hospital for specialized services, such as an orthopedic hospital. The manner in which each department functions reflects the specific setting and personality of the institution of which it is a part. Departmental purposes of necessity must be related to the broad goal of the institution offering medical service in order to be an effective part of the whole. Since this general statement allows for wide interpretation of the ways in which help may be offered sick people in psychosocial difficulty, the following description is that of a specific Social Service Department in a general hospital, the Beth Israel Hospital in Boston, Massachusetts.

Beth Israel Hospital is a general hospital of 365 beds, located on its present site since 1928. Its financial support is, in the main, derived from voluntary contributions and grant funds. Medical care is offered with no geographical restrictions and on a nonsectarian basis. Although it is a community hospital, it is also one of that special group of hospitals in this country, the teaching hospital group. Beth Israel Hospital, affiliated with the Harvard Medical School, the Tufts Medical College, and the Simmons College School of Social Work, has always stressed educational goals along with its service aims. The hospital operates its own school of nursing, program for postgraduate dietitians, dental students, laboratory technicians and dental hygienists. These give additional scope to the educational aspects of the institution.

The service goals of the hospital are given breadth and depth by the inclusion of an Outpatient Department, Emergency Ward, and a Home Care program. This latter program, established only a few years ago, in actuality extends the services of the hospital by approximately fifty beds. Patients are admitted to the hospital on referral by their private physician or through referral from the Outpatient Department or Emergency Ward. Although the hospital does not have beds for patients needing only psychiatric treatment, it does have a large and active psychiatry service offering both in-hospital and ambulatory psychiatric consultation and treatment to adults and children. An approved child guidance clinic within the hospital setting is open to referral from schools, social agencies, and parents in the community, and thus, further extends the services of the hospital.

The Social Service Department, considered by the hospital from its beginning as an integral professional arm of the institution, has as its purpose the broad goals of the institution to promote the health of those who seek its help, whatever their economic circumstances. The department's special contribution is concern for those factors within the patient's social and emotional situation that contribute to his illness or prevent him from using, optimally, the care given him. Each patient is considered in relation to his own interpersonal, physical, emotional and cultural make-up. Services of the Social Service Department are available for all patients using the hospital.

Both medical social workers and psychiatric social workers are employed in the department in keeping with the present trend toward the generic in social work. However, there are certain specifics that require special knowledge and skill. In the medical field the very real pressures that may call for a worker to assist patients in preventive services, in severe long-term illness, or fatal illness point up the need for this specialized knowledge and skill. Carefully supervised practice for at least two years following postgraduate training helps to incorporate the knowledge of the specific field. In working with physicians and other paramedical personnel, the worker's understanding of illness and its effects on the patient, his family, and his community requires her to have a high degree of interpretative skill, as well as collaborative ability. Scope to practice quality casework in the areas of specialization in a general hospital makes a departmental, on-going education and supervisory program imperative. This too is in keeping with the hospital tradition, which emphasizes the need for medicine constantly to evaluate its program and to be alert to progress.

It is implicit that the social worker is considered and used as a member of the treatment team. Therefore, all workers are encouraged to attend clinical teaching and administrative rounds, to participate according to their assignments in patient care rounds on a regular, weekly basis on the medical, surgical, obstetrics, and pediatric wards. Daily discussion with the doctors involved in the joint care of patients is probably the most effective way of ensuring service and one of the most useful mechanisms for the informal interpretive teaching that is the responsibility of the well-trained medical social worker.

In the medical setting, the Social Service staff is usually allocated according to the services. Accordingly, workers are assigned to ward, Out-patient Department, Emergency Ward, Home Care, and Private Patient services. Essentially, their functions are the same since, regardless of age or financial status, illness creates problems for many patients with which neither they nor their families can cope alone. Often, before medical treatment can be initiated, there may be a need for social adjustments. Likewise, before the plan of treatment advised by the physician can be carried through, problems of a social nature may come to the attention of the doctor. Medical social service has been developed in the hospital to provide such service to patients and thus assist the physician in the care of the patient.

Although referrals to the social worker may be made by any hospital personnel, the patient, his family, or community member, the majority of referrals that the social worker receives are from the doctor. The social worker assigned to ward responsibility receives most of her referrals from the house officer (intern) during medical-social ward rounds (preferably known as patient care rounds). These rounds occur at a specific hour each week and are carried out by the visiting physician, resident physician, house officer, and social worker. The ward charge nurse, medical students, dietetic interns, and occupational therapists attend as their time commitments permit. At these rounds the house officer presents a statement of each ward patient's medical situation and also certain basic social facts pertinent to the patient's total situation, which he has secured during his history taking. The patient's attitude toward his illness, family attitude, the patient's home situation, his economic stability, factors for consideration of his after care, as well as the patient's specific needs, are carefully discussed. During these rounds, it is the responsibility of the social worker to raise questions regarding the meaning of the illness to the patient in relation to his usual activities, or questions regarding the integration of the social and emotional factors in conjunction with the patient's physical situation. This kind of discussion leads to referrals to the social worker in which she may offer preventive casework services, as well as supportive, palliative and therapeutic—all dependent upon the individual situation.

In addition to the ward worker helping the house officer to carry out an effective program of total medical care, her role during medical-social ward rounds is also a teaching one. Through skillful questioning and interpretation, the worker helps the house officer to perceive and understand the influence of the patient's environment and personal problems on his physical condition. This also helps to prepare the house officer for his future practice by enabling him to become acquainted with the community and the resources that are available and necessary to make medical care as effective as possible.

If referral to the social worker is made by a doctor, the worker will usually request that the doctor discuss the referral with the patient as part of his medical recommendation so that the patient immediately sees the social worker as a member of the medical team. If referral is made by other ward personnel, family, or members of the community, the worker discusses this with the attending doctor so that there is mutual understanding of the problem and plans for medical and casework treatment. After the patient is seen and the situation evaluated by the social worker, the latter informs the referring person and the doctor of her decision to accept or reject the referral. This is an important point since, in the medical setting, the doctor is the person in authority and the social worker must relate her services to the over-all medical plan and work within the medical recommendations. However, the medical social worker must have conviction about her own role and aims and be prepared to communicate this clearly and concisely. She must be equally clear and have conviction when rejecting a referral, interpreting carefully why the particular referral may not fall within the orbit of the medical social worker. If the patient is accepted for service, the progress of the patient's treatment and after-care planning usually will require conference with the doctor; thus, planning and treatment are carried out in teamwork fashion. Often, the medical social worker will be called upon to work with one or more medical specialists in conjunction with the referring physician. This may include the surgeon, the orthopedist, the psychiatrist, the physiatrist, the occupational therapist, or the physical therapist. In order to function as effectively as possible, it is required that the social worker have understanding and knowledge of each team member's role. She must be able to share pertinent data with the others, to follow or to lead, depending on the individual circumstances. She must keep in touch and communicate clearly with the other team member or members in order to ensure the fullest benefits for the patient. Frequently, it is helpful for both the social worker and the doctor jointly to interview relatives of patients with exceptionally complex problems. The following case illustrates a typical referral in the medical setting.

Mr. W., a 44-year-old man, was referred to the ward social worker during medical social ward rounds for medical social evaluation in connection with his resistance to a proposed gastrectomy (partial removal of the stomach). In the course of rounds, the doctors had stressed Mr. W.'s emotional unwillingness to undergo surgery. After considerable urging from the doctors and Mrs. W., he had agreed to accept the proposed surgery, but it was obvious that he was still reluctant. The doctors felt that the medical social worker could be a valuable aid in medical treatment here. Her training in the implications of the surgery, as well as her training in interviewing skills, might help to elicit material around the patient's resistance. The patient's ease of mind in undergoing surgery is almost as important a factor in the successful outcome of the procedure as the skill of the surgical team. A mass had been found in the patient's stomach and the doctors felt that the mass should be removed. Casework with a patient like Mr. W., who is involved in an acute or crisis situation, presents very special problems for the patient as well as the caseworker. Because of the acute nature of this referral, definite limits are set on time within which the worker can evaluate the situation, make a social diagnosis, and carry out some form of treatment. This kind of situation usually has great emotional impact on the patient, as well as on those around him. However, this kind of problem highlights another aspect of the values of social work training and skill, as it enables the worker to remain objective; not that the worker is oblivious to the intensity of feelings, but her training makes her aware of her own feelings. While it is important to empathize, it is also necessary to understand that the emotional elements can obscure what is going on underneath and thus add to the difficulties of the evaluation.

When surgery had first been presented to Mr. W., he had threatened to sign out against medical advice rather than undergo the operation. The doctors felt that that would be a dangerous step for the patient to take. In the discussion of the case with the house officer prior to seeing the patient, the worker learned that the patient's wife also had had a serious illness. However, her illness was now in remission.

From the medical record it was learned that the patient lived with his wife, aged 40, his son, 19, a daughter, 15, and son, 13, in a two-family house. Mr. W. was employed as a skilled laborer.

The social worker first approached Mr. W., a slight, attractive man, on the ward two days before the proposed surgery. He was very nervous and tense, gripping the bed with both hands and appearing almost rigid. The worker introduced herself explaining her function as a member of the medical team and said there might be something he would like to talk about. His initial response was an explosion of nervous hostility, replying with, "Well, like what? Anything in particular?" He said he did have some thoughts about the operation. There was a pause, and then he said in an outburst that this is always what you read about in books and magazines and never believe could happen to you. Worker asked what sort of things these were he had read about, and he said that they were operations and diseases and things like that. Worker questioned how he felt about the operation, and he said that he felt better now. At first, he said, he had been completely against it, but now everyone had made up his mind for him that he would go through it. After worker asked him what he thought would happen in connection with the operation Mr. W. responded that he did not know, that if he did, he would be a lot happier. He commented that he felt it would be all right if only he could see the operation. Worker asked why he felt this, and Mr. W.'s response was that he felt helpless and afraid if he did not know what was going on. He commented that when he had had a bone marrow sample taken, "they" had covered his face with a cloth while they did the operation. He had asked to have the cloth removed, and it was. He had watched the whole thing, and when worker queried whether it had bothered him, he answered that it might have bothered some people, but he had been much better because he could see. He would much rather see than be in the dark, adding that he was afraid of the dark, preferring the light. Worker asked what he thought would happen in the dark, and he said that he felt completely defenseless and afraid. Mr. W. said, "I would always rather be told everything and know one way or the other than to be unsure and in the dark."

Worker asked how long he had known about the operation, and he said that his private doctor had told him about three weeks previously, suggesting that he come here. He had gone to his doctor thinking that he had flu, and this whole business has been a shock to him. Mr. W. said that doctors in the hospital had started to lead up to the fact of the operation on Friday and then had told him on Saturday. He had had a hard time from Saturday to Tuesday because he wanted to leave and not have the operation, and everyone else was trying to talk him into it. Worker asked him if he had made up his mind on Tuesday, and he laughed and said that that was when his mind had been made up for him. He had been ready to leave the hospital since he had felt the operation would do no good, and he would rather live with the mass than have it removed and die in the process.

The doctors and his wife "got in a huddle" and convinced him that it would become much worse if left alone. He said that the doctors had told him that, while they could not say whether the operation would help or not, they could definitely say that he would be back in a week as an emergency case if he left the hospital and went home. There was a chance of things being better with the operation, but not at all without it. He repeated this several times throughout the interview, as well as that he was not so much scared of the operation as of the doctors finding that the mass had spread and he was a hopeless case.

Worker questioned what the doctors had told him. Mr. W. said that he had been told that he had a mass in his stomach that might be malignant or benign, but which "they" would not know about until they could get it out and see. He went on to say that if you kidded yourself, you were living out of reality and that you would come back to it with a bang; therefore, he had to face facts. He said he was pleased that the doctors were not kidding him but were telling him "straight." He had asked for a guarantee about the operation, but the doctors could not give him any. Mr. W. said he was grateful for this, and when asked why, commented that he knew then that any encouragement that came from the doctors was genuine. Worker questioned whether doctors had given him any encouragement, and Mr. W. felt they had, as they had taken tests in every part of his body and so far there was no sign of spread. The doctors had told him there was a good chance of its being localized, and he said he could agree in that case that it would be good to get it out.

Worker asked if any one else in the family had had the same kind of thing. Mr. W. said, "Yes, that's the trouble" and went on to tell about his sister who had had an operation four years ago and "did not come out."

Worker asked if sister had had the same thing. Mr. W. admitted this was
not exactly the same. However, his sister had been ill for about six months
before her death and had had a pain in her left side, which he also has.
Worker asked Mr. W. to tell her about sister's illness and operation. There
was a long and very tense pause during which Mr. W. stared at the end of
the bed with his face muscles working and his hands gripping the side of
the bed. He finally said that his sister had luckily taken out a very heavy
life insurance policy about a year and a half before her death. She had been
checked by the insurance doctor who had found nothing. Shortly after this,
the sister started feeling ill and went to a doctor who told her she was neurotic and nothing was wrong. (It is important to emphasize that this is the
patient's version of his sister's illness, not necessarily a factual account.)
Later she was much worse and was admitted to a hospital. This time "they"
did a biopsy on some lumps she had on her breast and found that they were
cancerous. "They" then did an exploratory operation, "opened her up,"
and found cancer everywhere. She died during the operation.

Worker asked if Mr. W. felt that this might happen to him. He said that
he did, that once "they" opened him up they would find cancer everywhere,
and that it would be better to live as long as possible without dying in the
operation. Worker asked if it did not make a difference that his tumor was
localized. He said that this was encouraging. Worker asked if his sister had
ever talked to him about her illness. Mr. W. answered, "No, not really. You
see she did not really know herself." (It is apparent from this comment that
the description of sister's illness was, in truth, the patient's version.) Worker
said Mr. W. must feel better at having done something early, although it
was not the same as his sister. Mr. W. agreed that he actually did.

Mr. W. showed more fear of the hospital and illness in general in
his first interview by such statements as "If and when I get out," but when
worker said that in a way it was a shame that the operation could not be
that afternoon, Mr. W. commented that things did not look as black as
they had. "They're just a brownish color now," he said smilingly. He rationalized that "an operation such as this" could not be performed on the
week end because the full quota of staff would not be available on the
wards. He worried about the fact that it was necessary for him to have
blood donors to give transfusions before he could have the surgery. Mr. W.
had interested a friend who was active with the local Red Cross to give
more than the required amount of blood. However, he himself had
checked with the blood bank and had learned that the blood had not
arrived, and he remarked he was sure it would come, "Otherwise, they just
can't do the operation," he said with a smile. Actually, this was Mr. W.'s
anxiety, as the necessary operation would be performed even if no blood
could be secured from donors. It is usually possible to pay for needed
blood or to make future arrangements for replacement of blood used. If

neither of these solutions is feasible, this hospital provides the necessary surgery anyhow.

Worker asked how long he had been in the hospital, and he said two weeks. He said that he would be here another two weeks, and it probably would be some time before he could return to work. "I can't start standing on my head right away." Worker asked if he had ever had an operation before this time, and he said "No, I'm brand new at this game" and "That makes it rougher—that's another thing." He went on to say that he had noticed that everyone on the ward was greeting the new ones coming in with "You here again?" He said that everyone he sees seems to go out only to come back in again and he thinks "What have I started?"

At one point he stated, "I'm no hero, and I certainly don't pretend to be." Worker asked what he meant by being a hero, and Mr. W. said someone who took everything without a word. Worker commented that she did not think any of us were heroes when it came right down to it. We might be in the small things, but in bigger things most of us were not. He agreed, but went on to say that he could be a hero in some other things. Worker asked what some of these other things might be, and Mr. W. said "Oh, like other people or . . ." and would not say anymore.

Worker assured him that he should not feel that he has to say anything that he does not want to. There was a long pause as the worker said it sometimes helps to talk about things and share a worry, meaning about the operation. Patient responded that there was nothing to say. Worker wished him good luck with the operation on Monday and told him that she would see him after this. Mr. W. said he hoped so.

It may be noted here that the worker gave no unrealistic encouragement about the results of the surgery itself, but did promise to stand by when she indicated that she would be seeing the patient following this surgery. The worker's first step in attempting to reach her casework goal of helping Mr. W. allay his anxieties in order that he might undergo the surgery in as optimum a condition as possible was to indicate interest in Mr. W. as a person. She helped him discuss his fears and gave him realistic reassurance in such a way that he would not feel inadequate. The establishment of this relationship would be essential in any on-going casework treatment with Mr. W.

Following the operation, the decision was made not to tell Mr. W. what the findings were but to tell his wife. In every situation, a responsible family member is told. If Mr. W. had asked the surgeon a direct question, the surgeon would then have had to decide on the basis of his knowledge of Mr. W. as an individual how much and what he was to be told. This is a highly controversial matter, and it can be noted from the popular literature, as well as the technical literature, that a rigid rule cannot be employed.

There is reason to believe that patients may ask direct questions not wishing to know the answer, or wishing for actual denial of the answer. Therefore, before one makes the decision of how much to tell a patient, it is important to understand the patient as an individual. In any situation, it is important that the medical social worker see the patient not only as an individual but also in the context of the family situation. The social worker's training and skill manifest themselves by her ability to see beneath and through the presenting problem and give her the perspective needed to help the patient follow medical recommendations. The skill of the interviewer lies in her understanding the meaning behind words, as well as the reality circumstances described by the patient. With Mr. W. the worker had an idea of the stresses that had precipitated the acute crisis in his mind.

Surgery is threatening to most patients. Many fears and old conflicts may be aroused at this time and produce anxiety. In a situation like Mr. W.'s there are many areas of concern for the patient, and the worker has to decide where to focus in order to be most helpful to her patient. Since the immediate prospect in this instance was that of helping the patient face this surgery in as hopeful a manner as possible, the worker collaborated with the medical treatment team by helping the patient to follow medical recommendations. The worker enabled Mr. W. to discuss the operation, how he saw it, and his reactions to it.

During the first interview after the operation, Mr. W. said that he had learned a great deal since he had been in the hospital. When he first came in, he had kidded himself and had taken the easy way out by saying there was nothing wrong. Then he had learned that it was better not to do this. He went back over the whole operation and the preceding period. He said that, just as the doctors could not be sure until they saw the mass, so he could not be sure until he saw the laboratory report, which he knew he would not be allowed to see. He then said, "So, I might as well stop here. They have given me a nice cover and I'm going to take it and hide under it." He guessed he was just a coward.

It was in the second interview that Mr. W. questioned worker's role asking if she was anything "like a head-shrinker"? Worker explained that sometimes people want to talk and have a chance to say what they are feeling to someone else. The doctors had been "talking at him" for so long that he should have a chance to talk too and say what he was feeling about it it all. He agreed that it was sometimes good to talk with someone else and that if you had something bottled up inside it helped to get it out and share it. The worker continued in later interviews to help Mr. W. express his fears. She was aware that in so doing he would become more comfortable in facing these fears. She then could use her relationship with him in a purposeful manner to set further goals as his situation changed.

At first it was natural that Mr. W. concentrated on himself and the environment of the hospital ward. He volunteered no information about anything outside himself and his anxiety until this was asked for. His world was the ward, the other patients, the medical staff—and the operation two days away. It would have been helpful and important to know Mr. W.'s previous life history and his past adaptations to stress as a means of more fully understanding his current reactions. The patient facing major surgery is concentrated on the ordeal ahead of him, and the anxiety is usually at such a level that this is the only area with which the caseworker can deal. Ambivalence was one of the most striking aspects of Mr. W.'s personality during his hospitalization. He wanted to know and he did not want to know. He wanted to sign out against medical advice and he wished to stay. The caseworker identified with the positive aspects of the patient's ambivalence in order to help him follow medical recommendations.

Another important factor to keep in mind when working with patients in a hospital setting is that a patient in the hospital, and particularly on the ward, is in a very different environment from his normal one. He is in a bed in a room with many other patients and is cared for in a dependent way by numerous medical personnel. This dependent position is an issue often raised by hospitalization and enters into casework done in a hospital setting. The patient is put in a dependent position whether he likes it or not. He is under orders from figures in authority just as he was as a child. This raises many problems. It may reactivate old problems or dependency needs that have been repressed, and patient may use his illness to prolong the state. This may impede his recovery rather than facilitate his return to the degree of independence needed to function in the world outside the hospital. This may be one reaction of a dependent person. Another may be an overreaction of independence due to a terror of falling back into the dependent state he desires but must avoid. An overly independent type person may fret so much against the enforced dependencies that he is unable to follow the medical regimen. Both aspects are serious and are familiar problems confronting the medical social worker.

Outpatient service

Earlier it was mentioned that workers are assigned to various parts of the hospital—one of these may be the Outpatient Department. The social worker in the Outpatient Department receives those requests for service that concern patients who come, or who are about to come, to one of the clinics for medical care. Referrals come to the intake worker from a wide variety of sources, originating both from within the Outpatient

Department and from the community. The former may include referrals made by clinic, doctor, or other hospital personnel. Those originating outside the hospital may come from doctors, community agencies, or patients themselves.

Outpatients vary as to age and medical diagnosis, and the kinds of situations facing the social worker also vary. For example, the social worker may be asked to evaluate a patient's family, home, financial, and vocational situation in order to enable the doctor to make feasible recommendations for continued medical care. Helping the patient to find a job within his physical capacity, to secure housekeeping help, and to change one's living arrangements are reasons for referral to the Social Service Department. Implicit in these referrals is the fact that the worker sees her role as helping the patient to understand and accept the need for these environmental changes. Likewise, the social worker is often called upon to help the patient make arrangements for admission to the hospital by relieving him of certain responsibilities at home, such as the care of children or ill family members. Evaluation of the situation may reveal that such arrangements can be worked out with the help of other family members or other agencies; the social worker may then find her role is to help the patient "work through" certain fears pertaining to hospitalization, surgery, anesthesia, death, or dependency due to a disabling illness. The role of the social worker can be that of liaison between the hospital and a social agency, a school, an employer, or the family of a patient as part of a therapeutic plan. It is not enough for the social worker to transmit medical information and recommendations. The skill of the social worker is shown by her ability to interpret the plans and recommendations in relation to the patient's social and emotional situation.

Referrals from the department of physical medicine at the Beth Israel Hospital go to an assigned worker who is a member of the physical medicine team. These patients, as are all patients in the hospital, are evaluated and treated from the point of view of physical and psychological rehabilitation. Workers are assigned to the Obstetrical and Pediatric Service where the emphasis is largely on preventive casework service as a way of ensuring healthier mother-child relationships. Some clinics, such as the Tumor and Cardiac Clinics, are singled out for special coverage by assigned workers because they represent major areas of illness with significant social implications and because they receive support in part from special grants made available to the State Health Department by the U.S. Public Health Service.

The psychiatric social worker in a general hospital has most of her contacts, and is in closest collaboration, with the doctors whose specialty is psychiatry. Patients may come to the attention of the psychiatric clinic by special referral both within the hospital and from the community.

However, in the general hospital, medical social workers are also working with psychiatrists as patients known to them are referred for psychiatric consultation and treatment.

Home Care Programs

In the last few years with reawakened interest in the meaning of continuous, total care for patients, there has been an increase of Home Care programs. Through Home Care, coordinate services are set up to fulfill individual needs such as medical, social, economic, and vocational needs of patients who can be adequately treated at home. Chronically ill patients or long-term care of patients in their own home puts considerable strain on families. However, with the support of this program, care given in a coordinate, continuous, and complete way helps many patients to maintain their positions in their own families and function as members of the community within their own limitations. Families also respond to the support gven by a team approach and are thus able to participate in the care of the patient more effectively.

Home Care, as it functions at Beth Israel Hospital, is set up to meet the needs of long-term or chronically ill patients. The program is considered an extramural arm of the hospital for patients who do not need all of the inpatient services, but who are too ill for ambulatory care through the clinics. An integrated team representing the variety of specialties contributes to the over-all management of the patient. The team at Beth Israel Hospital consists of the administrator, internist, surgeon, psychiatrist, medical social worker, public health nurse (on the hospital staff), occupational therapist, physiatrist, and administrative assistant (secretary).

Referrals to Home Care come from ward services, Outpatient Department, affiliated agencies, and physicians of the hospital staff. Selection of patients for care under the aegis of the program is based on established criteria. Correlated with these is the current medical nursing and social evaluations of each patient in his or her family demonstrating need for coordinated medical care. Included in the criteria are the following: patients who would benefit both psychologically and medically from care at home and who need the services of a coordinated group; patients who live within the geographical limits covered by the program; patients who are unable to afford long-term private medical care. The Home Care team meets weekly to discuss any referrals and current problems concerning ongoing situations. The maximum number of patients on the Home Care program in this hospital is approximately fifty. The social worker's chief function is to offer casework treatment to the patient and his family in order to maintain the patient at home; this may be tangible assistance such as a homemaker service, referrals to appropriate social agencies, etc. Case-work is geared to prevent any breakdown in the home situation that might interfere with the patient's on-going progress. A good deal of anxiety is alleviated for patients when they learn about Home Care and realize that it is possible to contact the Home Care physician any time during the day or night. It is also reassuring to know that the same physician will be available.

Mr. F., a 49-year-old married man, was referred to the Home Care program by the medical ward service. Mr. F. had been in the hospital for six weeks because of a severe heart attack. While he no longer needed the twenty-four-hour care of an acute hospital, he would continue to require very close medical supervision since part of his therapy was treatment with long-term anticoagulants. Mrs. F. wanted very much to have her husband at home following his discharge from the hospital. (Whenever possible, care at home with one's own family is most desirable. It is of utmost importance that a patient still feel an integral part of his family, and that he maintain his position in the household despite his illness. This is especially true in long-term illness, where the patient away from home feels displaced. Simi-larly, return to the familiar environment usually lends reassurance.) Since Mr. F. needed very close medical supervision, and as the family could not afford private medical care, it was felt that Mr. F. could be helped by the Home Care team.

Medical-social evaluation of the F. family revealed that Mr. and Mrs. F. and their only child, an 18-year-old son, lived in a large, six-room apart-ment, paying $95 a month rent. Mrs. F. worked part time at home earning $45 weekly. Since Mr. F. had no savings and would be unable to return to work for at least three months, application for disability assistance was made during Mr. F.'s hospitalization to support the family. This was a severe blow to Mr. F., who prided himself on his independence and his ability to care for his family. The social worker, recognizing the emotional and personal problems that this illness and hospitalization created for Mr. F., skillfully directed her casework goals toward helping Mr. F. in his feelings of inade-quacy aroused by his illness.

In the beginning, the doctor visited Mr. F. twice a week. As he im-proved, visits were made weekly and finally biweekly. It is apparent that the physician was initially the key member of the team involved upon Mr. F.'s return home. Mr. and Mrs. F. needed to be reassured that the doctor was really available, and early in their contacts with the Home Care team they telephoned frequently to ask questions or request the doctor to visit. (This is typical of many patients who come to Home Care. To alleviate as much anxiety as possible, both the doctor and the social worker visit within forty-eight hours of the patient's return home.)

Concurrent with the doctor's visits, the social worker visited, seeing both the patient and his wife. Social worker learned that the family had come to the United States in 1939, having lived through extremely difficult times in Europe during World War II. Their only child was born just after their arrival here, and both parents had striven to give him opportunities they had missed. Until a year before his illness, Mr. F. had worked as a skilled laborer in several factories. Mr. F.'s strong feelings about independence made it possible for him to save enough money to begin a small business of his own in which he sold products to small concerns. He was proud of his ability to set up his own business and was optimistic that he would succeed in his venture when suddenly he suffered the heart attack, which brought him to the hospital.

Complicating the situation was the fact that Mrs. F. had been ill with duodenal ulcer about the time Mr. F. went into business, and therefore she had to give up her full-time job. The son, who had worked at a local gasoline station, had injured his shoulder at work and was incapacitated for several months. He was now attempting to help his father by keeping up his contacts with Mr. F.'s customers so the business would survive. In addition, he was planning to attend the local university night school in order to obtain a degree.

The social worker's role here was centered around helping Mr. F. face his illness realistically. Although Mr. F. found it extremely difficult to be inactive even in the hospital, he worried constantly about the possibility of a second heart attack if he attempted any activity. He avidly read articles about cardiac illness and applied them to himself. It was only as the social worker enabled him to express his feelings, pointing out that it was not unmanful to be concerned that he could accept realistic answers to the many questions that he had. Mrs. F., an important member in the family constellation, was feeling the impact of her husband's illness. She was apprehensive about her husband, as well as exhausted from working late at night. The medical social worker offered casework assistance to Mrs. F. too, particularly when she began to have a recurrence of her ulcer symptoms and became fearful that she might also be having a heart attack. Considerable time elapsed before the worker could help Mrs. F. express and face her fears. She was afraid of coming to clinic because she felt that the doctors would want her to stay in the hospital, and this would eliminate the source of income for the family. Worker's focus with Mrs. F. was on the interpretation of Mrs. F.'s need to obtain medical care for herself as insurance for her family's benefit as well as her own. It was important to help Mrs. F. maintain her health as otherwise the family's ability to sustain itself would be further impaired. The social worker's role here is a delicate one, as Mrs. F.'s problem must be handled without further damage to Mr. F.'s feelings of adequacy.

While at home Mr. F. developed an acute arthritic pain in his leg. After complete evaluation by the physiatrist, physiotherapy was instituted. The physiotherapist visited the F. home three times weekly, giving exercises to the patient and instructions to the family. The occupational therapist on the Home Care team also visited, giving Mr. F. occupational therapy, which was both therapeutic and diversional. As Mr. F.'s condition continued to improve, the medical social worker helped him discus the various job possibilities within his range of activity as prescribed by the doctor. Social work aims to help people use their own strengths in overcoming their problems. The medical social worker must have a similar goal, but must help the patient relate this goal to the realities or the limitations of the patient's illness. It is important that, within the limitations of the patient's illness, he receive the gratification in getting well that makes it possible to give up dependency. Mr. F. was eager to return to his own business, and since his son expressed willingness to accompany him for a few months and to lift and carry supplies as necessary, the doctors felt this would be feasible. The worker therefore used her relationship and casework skills to help Mr. F. regain his independence. Mr. F. began to work on a part-time basis, gradually increasing his activity as he improved.

Since Mr. F. had used up his savings on medical expenses and had had no income for four months, the worker knew that it was difficult for him to start again. Knowledge of the community and its resources is imperative for the caseworker. A referral was made to a community agency that provided small loans to businessmen who are attempting to start a business. Although Mr. F. was both excited and eager to use this opportunity, he was also apprehensive about beginning work. The social worker, with her awareness regarding the meaning of illness and her understanding of this particular patient, was able to accept Mr. F.'s ambivalence. Most patients struggle between their desire to be independent and dependent. The worker used her skills to foster Mr. F.'s feelings of independence to help him return to work. The worker offered further service in referring Mr. F.'s son for counseling and possible scholarship help. Presently the caseworker is working with Mrs. F. attempting to aid her to come into clinic on a regular basis for thorough checkups. Mr. F. is now well enough to come to the Outpatient Department and therefore has been discharged from Home Care.

The situation just discussed exemplifies how various members of the Home Care team work together in attempting to give total care to a patient and his family in their own home in order to achieve optimum rehabilitation. In this particular situation, the primary team members were the doctor, the social worker, and the physiatrist. There are times when other members of the team are utilized, and it is possible that in some situations the key members may be the psychiatrist, visiting nurse, or the social worker, depending upon the individual needs of the patients.

Research

The Social Service Department includes two social workers assigned to research projects. These social workers have the same training and background as other staff members and bring to the medical team their own particular skills and experience, as well as knowledge of the principles of research. In broad terms, their goals and philosophy are identical with those of other social workers in the same setting, but their activities are focused within the design of the research project of which they are a part.

The way in which the research social worker functions on any particular project depends on the kind of research that is being undertaken. Some projects have their major emphases upon service while others stress research. The latter involve studying certain phenomena about human relations, about cultural or ethnic practices, or about the social adjustment of particular groups of people, such as those with physical handicaps.

The two projects in which research social workers are currently engaged at Beth Israel Hospital are service-oriented. The focus of the research in one project is directed toward a study of the emotional factors in pregnancy. Its purpose is to study a selected sample of women coming to the prenatal clinic and pregnant for the first time. The social worker is responsible for the collection of certain data relating to the patient's social adjustment, her interpersonal relationships, and the reality problems with which she is confronted as a result of pregnancy. The other members of the team, composed of psychiatrists, psychologists, and medical personnel, collect data in their respective areas of competence. These data are brought together in such a way that a full picture is obtained of the patient and the complexities of her situation. Treatment plans are suggested by members of the research team, and the research social worker offers service as part of the over-all treatment program.

The second research project relates to the development of social services for private patients on a fee for service basis. The hospital was interested in knowing why social services were not used more widely by private doctors for their patients, and what steps might be initiated to encourage the use of social service for these patients. Since this was a newly formalized program, it seemed advisable to study the extent of use of the program as set up and to determine its proper scope through compilation and analysis of data about patients served. This is a study of current practice as it develops—built-in evaluation rather than retrospective research.

The above are two specific research projects in which social workers in the medical setting are engaged. However, research is a continuing function of all social workers in the Social Service Department, and each worker is periodically engaged in a research project or a service of an administrative nature.

The foregoing illustrations of inpatient, outpatient services, Home Care programs, and research have served to emphasize the conviction that the social service department of a hospital is identified with the aims and objectives of the hospital as a whole, although it derives its strength as a special discipline from a defined body of professional knowledge and skills. It is the ultimate purpose of the department to use its special knowledge and skills in such a way as to contribute significantly to the hospital's five-point program of: patient care, teaching, research, interhospital policy and program formulation, as well as community planning for health and welfare services. The growth and development of a social service department must, therefore, reflect the growth and development both of the hospital and of social work as a profession.

11

THE
CORRECTIONAL
SERVICES

Individualization and the court

Criminal courts existed before institutionalized social services. Long before the time of the Elizabethan Poor Laws English courts had been dealing with the offender. By the time social work had begun to be a profession in this country the courts already had established a fixed pattern of administering criminal justice. If the charity organization movement of the last quarter of the nineteenth century is taken as the starting point of professionalized social work, it at once becomes clear how late, comparatively speaking, it appeared on the scene.

It is important to recognize this late appearance of social work in order to understand the slow headway it made in its approach to the court. The criminal court is essentially, and perhaps necessarily, a conservative, slow-changing social structure. It is little wonder then with over a thousand years of precedent and practice behind it that the court resisted the introduction of any new ideas or new ways from a profession just beginning to emerge. Furthermore, the very eagerness of the newer workers to insist upon the welfare of the individual as well as society as a whole must not have sounded very convincing to judges and lawyers, who felt the court had always done that very thing. It may be said, by way of explanation, that in this early period social work had crystallized neither its philosophy nor its practice. Fervid convictions and enthusiasms, coupled with an evangelical zeal to help, were hardly tangible or impressive enough to be of much use to the court, which heretofore had managed to get along alone. It is not surprising, therefore, in view of the lack of concrete contributions

323

by social workers and the tendency of the court to hold to an ancient groove, that very little resulted from this early contact.

An approach that proved more fruitful following this early period was the one that directed the energies of the sensitively minded lay person and the professionaly interested social worker toward the establishment of a specialized service for the juvenile delinquent. When these two groups joined with court and administrative officials who were seeking a way to avoid the rigors of the conventional criminal court, the way was opened to a new departure in dealing with the offender. This did not happen suddenly. For the better part of a century, the handling of younger offenders had been undergoing change. The establishment of houses of reform for juveniles was an early instance, as was also the modification of penalties for acts committed by minors. Later provision was made for separate hearings for juveniles, and later still the use of probation.

The Juvenile Court

Illinois enacted the first juvenile court law in July 1899. As early as 1891, a juvenile court bill had been introduced into the Illinois legislature, but it required eight years of effective education and support before the final measures drafted by Judge Harvey B. Hurd emerged as the world's first juvenile court law. The new law, which provided for separate detention, separate and private hearings, and probation, brought under one jurisdiction all cases involving delinquent, neglected, and dependent children. This was not the first time that the child had received special consideration. For years there had been a variety of services available for those children who were so readily grouped into the categories of the dependent, the neglected, or the destitute. The Courts of Chancery in England long had stood, whenever necessity demanded, in the place of the parent to safeguard the interests of the growing child and the future citizen. However, the child over 7 years of age who was delinquent or criminal did not share this protection. Let him commit a criminal offense, and the law quickly seized him and dealt with him as with any other offender.

All of this was true until the establishment of the first juvenile court in America in 1899. Under the common law of England, children under 7 years of age were deemed incapable of entertaining the requisite criminal intent, between 7 and 14 years of age this presumption could be rebutted, that is, established by the prosecution that the child was capable of entertaining a criminal intent, and over 14 years of age the child stood trial as an adult offender. These rules of law applied in the American Colonies and later in the states as they were formed, either as part of the common law or of the statute law, which was based upon the common law. However, with the creation of the juvenile court, the chancery or equity principles (as they are more commonly called) were applied not only to the dependent, the neglected, or the destitute child, but also to the delinquent child under 16 years.

A socialized court, of which the juvenile court was the earliest example, concerns itself with the individual. It wants to know before court hearing by objective examination what kind of person the offender is. This becomes an essential part of the court process in arriving at a full understanding of the individual, the offense, and the present situation in order to determine what is the best plan to follow. This end is referred to as treatment rather than punishment and is a service that the individual can use in effecting his own adjustments within himself and in relation to other people and the community in which he lives.

The juvenile court has not been without its effect on other courts—the family court and even the criminal court. Within recent years there has been an increasing recognition of the interrelatedness of persons within the family grouping and especially the problems that beset them. Family courts have been instituted in which a more individualized consideration can be given to family members and their problems by the judge and his probation staff. Much more emphasis can thus be placed upon understanding the difficulties within the family and of the skills needed to help. At the same time none of the conventional safeguards bearing on the legal rights of persons is in any wise sacrificed or jeopardized. These legal rights have been fought for during a thousand years and should not be abandoned or seriously modified through well-intentioned efforts to help. Individuals (and that means juveniles as well) need to have assured to them all of the rights to which they are entitled and at the same time have available to them services which will strengthen their wills and capacities to do something about the troubles that brought them to court. Likewise is this true insofar as the court for the trial of the adult criminal is concerned. No matter how well intentioned the court staff may be in wanting to help the offender, it is fundamental that all his legal rights be assured to him. All of this must be borne in mind in the discussion that follows concerning social services within the correctional framework.

Probation

Although the use of probation has been associated most closely with the juvenile court, actually it antedated the court by many years. As early as 1841 a Boston shoemaker, John Augustus, had begun as a sort of volunteer probation officer when he served as surety for a confirmed drunkard. In 1878, twenty-one years before the first juvenile court, adult probation was undertaken officially in Boston, and within two years the authorization was state-wide. From that time until the present each of the fifty states has authorized adult probation, and since the initiation of the juvenile court in 1899, every state has made provision for juvenile probation. The federal probation service, begun in 1925, has developed into a national service for adults and juveniles involved in federal offenses.

The basic elements in the probation process are presentence investigation and supervision. These in turn are based upon an adequate understanding of and insight into human personality and behavior. Indeed, the indispensable equipment of the probation officer, as of all social workers, is this knowledge and awareness of the human being as he is, with all of his feelings, attitudes, ideas, motivations, strengths, and weaknesses.

What is the worker's understanding of delinquent or criminal behavior? How purposive is the behavior of the offender? What are the individual's basic needs and what satisfactions is he seeking? To what extent is his behavior symptomatic, and symptomatic of what? Does the worker realize the necessity for understanding the uniqueness of each individual personality and of the attempts of each individual to make his adjustment in line with his own capacities and the environment in which he happens to be? By whose standards does the worker judge the offender? Is there an arbitrary, fixed standard applicable to all? Does the standard of the worker as it has developed under different circumstances and in a different personality become the standard that must be imposed upon other people? Can the worker differentiate himself sufficiently from the group of which he has always been a part and proceed to function in a helping relationship with individuals who have broken with the mores of that group? These are real questions to the worker in the probation, parole, or the correctional institution field. The attitude toward such questions and the working answers made to them determine to a large extent the approach of the probation officer to people and his effectiveness in working with them.

There is another aspect to this matter of understanding criminal behavior that may be overlooked too easily in our desire to reach deep into the personality of the offender. After all, the individual does not live in a vacuum; he has his relations with other people, he lives in a certain neighborhood and house, he has a job or he hasn't a job, but nevertheless he lives in a workaday world, he has leisure-time interests, clubs, hangouts. All of these may be spoken of as influences outside of or external to the individual, but which nevertheless may have their effect upon him. The lack of a job, particularly over a long enough period of time, may have a good deal to do with whether a man suffers enough deterioration to turn to other ways of securing satisfactions or what he considers his rightful share of the world's goods. The prevalence of boys' predatory gangs in a neighborhood may not be without relation to the inclination of a given youngster to follow the crowd to gain some satisfaction otherwise denied to him. Living in a slum neighborhood in what is blithely referred to as substandard housing may have nothing to do with the formation of attitudes toward criminal behavior; on the other hand, it may. What must be obvious from these remarks is the interrelatedness of both the personality and the environmental factors. Individuals develop personality characteristics on the basis of their innate physiological equipment, the experiences that beset them from birth on and the relationships that they establish with other human beings and social institutions that surround them. After all, it is an individual, not a house or a neighborhood, that commits an offense, and to understand the offender one needs to comprehend the individual in his social setting.

The "How" of the Presentence Investigation

What is the purpose of a presentence investigation? How does a probation officer go about making it, what does he look for, and what does he do with what he has obtained? These may seem simple enough questions, but it is only when the probation officer is clear about his function that he can act responsibly in this very important and critical stage in the probation relationship. It must be recognized, for instance, that probation can prove most helpful when it is conceived of and executed as a casework service. If this is understood, then it follows that the first interviews with the offender are vitally important and may do much toward setting the tone and quality of the subsequent worker-client relationship. The process of probation begins with the first interview of the presentence investigation and continues until final discharge from probation.

Granting that this becomes a working conviction, importance attaches to *how* the investigation is conducted. A presentence investigation might otherwise be an inquisition, a cross-examination, an extension, or a refinement of the prosecuting attorney's tactics. What it can be is an exploration together of the situation in which the individual finds himself. What are his personality needs, what relation do they bear to the trouble he got himself into, what potentialities does he have within himself to go to work on his difficulties or to avail himself of what probation has to offer? What are the factors in his environmental setting that may have had something to do with the delinquency or crime, what of his marital and family relationships, the kind of neighborhood he lives in, his employment experience, his associates, his connections with church, club, or other activities? What does clearance with the social service exchange show of this individual or of his family?

After data concerning the individual and his situation has been gathered, it must be evaluated. At this juncture the probation officer is face to face with the question: Is this man probation material? The answer is not to be undertaken lightly. It is not a matter of whether there is an ailing wife or baby at home, or of a job hanging on the outcome, or of repeated pledges to sin no more. There may be sickness at home, a job may be waiting, conscience may have struck the man sore; but unless the probation officer can convince himself that, in the light of the potentialities of the individual and of the situation, the offender can utilize what probation has to offer, he is in nowise justified in recommending probation. For the probation officer to act otherwise would be to do a disservice to the offender, to be unfair to the court, to betray his profession, and be untrue to himself. So much of this depends in turn upon what it is that probation has to offer. For a probation officer to recommend probation must mean a faith in his own skills and in the essential helpfulness of his profession. In short, he must have a conviction of probation as a casework service and security within his own competence as a social caseworker.

If the probation officer recommends probation, he should do so if he feels the man can profit more by supervision in a free society than by imprisonment. The probation officer should also feel that the man has begun to come to grips with himself and with the world of people and things around him, and that the man is willing and able to do something about his difficulties with the help of the probation officer. The officer must recognize that some individuals are not able or ready to do this, and that for them there may be no alternative but imprisonment. Some offenders may only be able to profit during a prison experience or afterward. Imprisonment need not of itself be an unmitigated evil.

After the investigation is made and the probation officer's reports are in, the judge exercises his judgment in deciding whether to grant probation. If a juvenile court hearing has been held, the judge probably gets a fairly well-rounded picture of the child and of the situation, but this is unlikely if there has been a trial of an adult offender. The prosecuting attorney has presented the facts with a view to conviction; the defense, to acquittal. The judge is thus left in the anomalous position of supposedly knowing all about the offender when really he has nothing but contradictions with which to work. The probation investigation preserves what must otherwise be an arbitrary, no matter how well-intentioned, judgment. The better the probation officer has done his job the more enlightened a decision the judge can come to consistent with the needs of the individual. The probation officer owes this service as much to the court as to the offender, because it is only through the court, at this point, that the individual is reached.

Authority in Relation to Probation

The worker who knows what he is doing, recognizes that authority has real value in a casework relationship with the offender and that it is a necessary part of the judicial and probation function. He will really need to have more than an intellectual acceptance of this; he will need to "feel it in his bones" and have it be a part of the way he works with probationers. How otherwise could he reconcile for himself or the probationer the modern concept of individualized treatment with the age-long traditional attitude of vindictiveness against the offender? Without it how could the probation officer explain in language that made sense the imposition of requirements by the court?

From the very outset the competent probation officer will realize that authority defines the area within which he and the probationer will work. There are certain requirements set up by the court that the probationer will have to live up to,[1] and if there is too great a deviation from these rules, the court may use other more drastic means of control. The probation officer sees himself as an agent of the court. The probationer sees him as the delegated authority of the court. It is here that the worker will want to be clear on his own role. Is he the court? Is he distinguishable from the court? Does he embody the total authority of the court? Is he so caught in the web of authority that he is helpless to aid the probationer? The answer to these questions reaches to the very core of the probation function.

The Use of Limits

To simplify the analysis it will be well to examine the situation presented by a 15-year-old boy who has committed an offense. The very act of delinquency has reference to this matter of limits, for it may well be an expression of the inability of the boy to accept any kind of limits. Or it may indicate the need of some limits in order to achieve a working balance between the impulses within him and the demands that the community makes upon him. The overt delinquent act may signify the child's need for help with those limits. The child comes to the attention of the juvenile court and the probation officer. How can the court with all of its power, authority, and awesomeness for the child help with the problem that the child is presenting? If we are perfectly honest with ourselves and with all due respect to the court, we are obliged to doubt whether the

---

1 These rules may require regular reports from the probationer, regular work, regular hours, no operation of an automobile without pemission of the probation officer, no marriage without permission, staying within the district or state unless granted permission to leave, etc.

court can be very useful were it to impose its total authority upon the child and compel him to be good. The child already has known the total authority of the community and has not been able to make his adjustment, nor will the imposition of the total authority of the court accomplish what the community has failed to do so far. This is not to deny the utility of the court but merely recognize its limitations without the right arm of probation. Basically the child cannot make use of the total authority of the court because the court seeks to impose too total a restraint upon the child for the responsibility for his act. The court in effect says: "You have broken the law of this community; the community has charged this court with the duty of dealing with you; we therefore command you to be good." The child's answer to this is to slough off any responsibility for improving himself and to defy the court to change him.

When, however, the court breaks up this totality and places a part with an agency and an agency that it has created for the purpose, a situation is produced whereby the child can begin to take help. Here is where the probation officer comes forward. The probation department is part of the court structure, it has certain duties to perform, it operates within certain statutory and functional limits. If probation is to serve the child helpfully, it must break up this totalness and separate itself from it and yet be a part of that authority. This is more than a mere playing with words. When probation has achieved that separateness, it can let the child know that the court has referred him to the probation officer for help that the child is free to accept or not. This places the decision squarely where it belongs—upon the child. The child may reject the offer of help and defy the probation officer to make him good. The probation officer may exercise all of his skill, but the decision whether to take help or not is still the child's. The child can so act as to have his probation revoked and be committed to an institution for more restrictive treatment. If, on the other hand, the effect of the worker's definition of help has been to enable the boy to make the choice to accept responsibility for his conduct, then the two of them together have started work on the boy's difficulties. The delinquent act is a putting outside of the self of the child the responsibility for himself. Refusing the offer of help still keeps it outside. Accepting the probation officer's challenge may for the first time in the boy's life mean admitting his own share in what he is, and what he does, and why. Once the decision is made, the worker's task consists, not in making the boy good, but in helping the boy to face and work through his share of the problem. Having really faced authority and accepted what it means, the delinquent is freer to work within it constructively rather than to be blindly fighting it all the time.

This extended discussion has aimed to develop the thesis that probation functions within a definite framework of authority; that authority is positively and creatively useful as it provides an occasion for and a way of dealing with limits; that genuine change comes from within when the individual is ready to take responsibility for himself. Basic to all of this is the quality of service the probation officer offers, which is functionally related to his conviction that many individuals in trouble can be helped to achieve an adjustment within themselves and to the demands of the community in which they live. This implies a belief on the part of the probation officer in the capacity of individuals to change and to assume some responsibility for their own lives.

All that has been written here, while illustrative of the probation procedures of working with a juvenile delinquent, is just as applicable to the adult offender. The chief difference may be that the process seems more difficult with the older offender because he is more set in his ways and less amenable to suggestions. He seldom has the frankness and directness of the child or his uninhibited responses. The process may be much slower with the adult, and there may be fewer dramatic transformations, but once the adult takes hold of himself, it is likely to be more lasting because of his greater stability and the reality of the everyday demands put upon him.

The Worker's Awareness of Himself and of His Service

The probation officer who possesses an awareness of the needs of the probationer and of the process by which those needs are met will already be familiar with the importance of the early probation interviews. This he will have demonstrated in his presentence work. However, the very fact that probation has been granted, introduces an element of difference into the situation. The authority that probation expresses has defined and set a limit to the relationship. The probationer will need to know the nature of that relationship and what are its bounds. This the probation officer gets over not so much by what he says as by what he does and how he does it. The worker, for example, who approaches the offender with a punishing or vindictive attitude can put into words all the things probation should be, and yet by his very acts undo everything he has said. This is related very definitely to the worker's understanding of himself, of his emotional responses, his philosophy of casework, and the standards he has set for himself. Nowhere does this come out more clearly than in his authoritative relations to others. The worker who in his own developmental experience has not made his peace with authority can be of only limited help to the individual whose struggle is so largely with authority.

Likewise, the worker, let us say, whose own childhood suffered because of a father's desertion, may find it difficult, unless he has undergone the discipline of training, to deal understandably with a probationer who has deserted or is on the point of deserting his family. Another worker, who has never achieved the security of his own personality because he has never been able to make the emotional break from his family, may not be of much help to the individual who has already established his emotional independence. By contrast, the worker who is still going through the process of emancipation may identify himself so closely with his probationer who is undergoing the same experience that for all practical purposes the two of them are engaged in the same struggle. The one who is supposed to be exercising a helping function has become as helpless as the one he was to help. Instead of there being a worker and a client, there are now two clients and no worker. The individual who has never struggled through to a comfortable affectional relationship with another person may transfer his self-torture to the probationer who has not achieved any more balance in that struggle. All of this is a bit on the heavy expository side, but it is pertinent to a casework relationship because so much of the worker's effectiveness depends upon the degree to which he has attained satisfaction in working out his own difficulties, personal and professional.

The Person and the Environment

It is necessary to emphasize the need for a balanced service to the probationer. Not every individual who commits a crime is engaged in an acute personality conflict within himself. Social workers will do well to acquaint themselves with the important role which cultural factors, material and nonmaterial, play in our everyday lives. Sociologists and anthropologists for years have been studying the interrelationships of personality and culture and have accumulated a tremendous wealth of knowledge that has real pertinence for workers whose jobs bring them into touch with people's lives under every situation. Sociologists have long since established a case for the relativity of standards and values. They have shown over and over again that what the mores dictate to be "moral" or "right" in one place may not obtain elsewhere. Students of human culture have made a clear distinction between folkways and mores that would be helpful to some social workers who are only too willing to set up moral standards for other people or for other communities.

Some probation service may be directed toward help for the individual offender with his personality difficulties, and some may be directed toward environmental factors. A probation officer may learn early in his interviews that the probationer needs psychiatric treatment and will make a referral to the proper agency, if such exists. If no psychiatrist is available, the worker will nevertheless need to stay within his own probation function, giving such services as he can and that fall within the function of the court. In many instances, the probation officer will deal with tangible services—jobs, for instance. Most workers know that obtaining a job for which the probationer is qualified means much in helping him to get on his feet. It often gives him a sense of belonging, of accomplishing something that furnishes the stability to carry on. The worker may need to keep in touch with the employer from time to time, or he may decide that it is better to keep out of the way. Most probation officers and probationers find it best to make clear to the employer the status of the employee rather than to let him carry around the weight of possible disclosure at any time. There may be other services to render, such as helping with living arrangements in a suitable neighborhood, or helping to establish leisure-time or recreational outlets, or with church, school, or vocational training contacts. Very frequently there may be occasion for referral to other social agencies, such as a family society, a child guidance clinic, the social service department of a hospital. The worker may also need to bring to the attention of the probationer or his family the services of governmental agencies, such as departments of public welfare. These services are offered not because the probation officer must always be doing things *for* people, but because he, rather than the probationer, is the one who should be acquainted with all of the facilities of the community. The final decision to avail himself of these services is the probationer's, not the worker's.

Interviews and Interviewing

Every probation officer, whether he has a small or a large caseload, must develop his own way of conducting interviews. Much of the effectiveness of the interviews depends upon the worker's approach. A not uncommon practice of untrained probation officers is to direct the lives of their probationers. What seems to give sanction to such a practice is the obvious fact that the individual by his very act of transgressing the law has shown his inability to manage his own life, and hence what is more natural than to tell him what to do, to make the decisions for him that will oblige him to conform? Furthermore, the very injunction of the court to report any serious violation of probation seems to make it all the more imperative to keep the offender good. Despite the plausibility of this position, there is a fundamental contradiction inherent in it. The one unmistakable conclusion about the offender is that he needs help in accepting responsibility for his behavior. For someone else to direct his life means that the worker has robbed the client of the decision for his own life. This might be very well if probation officers supervised the offenders throughout their lifetime, but the real fact is that all probationers finish with probation at some time either successfully and by discharge or by failure and commitment. Some day the individual will need to make his own decisions, and the surest way to prepare him for that day is to help him while he is under supervision. Another aspect of this question pertains to what is happening to the individual when another person makes his decisions for him. Instead of the probationer carrying the responsibility for his decisions, he can always shift it over on the probation officer who made them. Thus the very opposite of the probation objective is accomplished; instead of helping the individual to do more for himself the probation officer makes it possible for him to do less.

Although there are general principles of helping the individual effect adjustments within himself and to the community in which he lives, there exists no formula for probation interviews. What goes on in the interview is governed by the help which the probationer needs and can use and the capacity of the worker to meet those needs. No doubt there are many instances in which the client will avoid his share of the interview by keeping it at a superficial level. According to him, everything is all right, the job is fine, affairs at home are fine, etc. All of which may be true, and the probation officer does not search for mountains where there are not even traces of molehills. On the other hand, everything may not be all right, and the statement that all is well may be simply a refusal to face his difficulties. At this point the probationer will need more help.

Interviews may be held either in the probation office or in the home of the probationer. There are certain advantages to an office interview; it affords privacy, it places the interview in a professional setting, and it calls for a certain amount of initiative and exertion on the part of the probationer as something that he puts into the occasion. A home interview enables the supervisor to get a view of the man in his home setting and may make possible a more comfortable relationship for the client. This latter, the comfortableness of an interview, is not always determined by the setting. No matter how hard a supervisor may try, there are probationers who can never be made comfortable; the capacity must be within the person. Continued home visits may relieve the probationer of some of the responsibility that attaches to probation. Probation is not simply a *doing to* someone else, it is a *doing with,* and a probationer may feel that all he needs to do is to wait for the worker's visit in order to be told what to do or what not to do. Most probation officers find a combination of home and office visits to be desirable, possibly alternately.

A third kind of reporting, besides office and home interviews, is common to probation supervision: monthly reports by mail. If the worker sometimes has reservations about his knowledge of what is happening with the probationer whom he sees in the office or in the home, how much more must he be skeptical of monthly reports that consistently affirm that all goes well? What probationer who has only a one-way contact with his worker is ever going to report anything else? This comment does not overlook the regulations, local, state, and federal, that require such a system of reporting, but it does look to the matter of its effectiveness. Suppose the individual were in difficulty, how would he get help from the supervisor? The offender who needs help seldom can communicate it by mail. A long-continued practice of mail reporting hardly encourages or justifies an appeal for help. If a probation department holds to its rule of mail reporting, let it not delude itself, the workers, or the probationers. It is never a satisfactory substitute for a personal interview.

Revocation of Probation

Not all probation is successful. Sometimes the probationer does not make the grade. At least two people are involved, the worker and the probationer, and whether success attends their efforts depends upon many factors, some within and some outside of their control. In the first place, there is the probationer himself and his suitability for probation as revealed in the presentence investigation. Assuming for the moment that probation has been granted with a reasonably hopeful prognosis, there may still be other items that are essential to helping the offender. Without question the most vital of these is the quality of casework service that the probation officer can render. The resources within the community, the job opportunities, the presence or absence of recreational, cultural or social outlets, the attitude of relatives, friends, employers, and the community may have a good deal to do with whether the probationer can get hold of, and keep hold of, himself. The individual's adjustments do not happen of their own accord. They are earned within a reasonably helpful community setting with the combined efforts of the worker and client. Sometimes there is not enough help from the community, sometimes not enough from the probation officer, or sometimes there is not quite enough material to work with, especially in view of how little we know about human behavior.

Unquestionably, the probation officer must face several questions such as: What help have I been able to give the probationer? What help has he been able to take? What help does probation still have to offer this individual? In short, has he made sufficient progress on probation so that even in the face of a defection, he could still profit by the probation experience? So much of the answer to this question depends upon the faith that the worker has in probation. If probation is merely a prelude to imprisonment and a kind of club to be held over the head of the probationer, then the worker can force a certain degree of conformity without reaching to the problem at all. If, therefore, the probationer violates probation, the obvious step to take is to revoke. It may too easily be over-looked that the very failure of the probation may be not so much the probationer's as the worker's. Or, it may be that the individual has not been able to use what the probation officer has to offer, and the decision to revoke will have to be made on that basis. The important point that must be borne in mind is that the probation officer must understand the basis of the decision to revoke; whether it is his own lack of professional skill, or the inability of the probationer to benefit by probation, or the lack of community facilities, which may militate against successful probation.

Community Attitude toward Violation

A very real situation, which every probation officer encounters at one time or another, is the attitude of the community toward the violation, or more particularly, the violator of probation. There may be instances in which the nature of the violation may be especially reprehensible to the community, and yet in the opinion of the probation officer not of such a kind as to preclude a successful outcome. Specifically, a juvenile delin-quent may have been placed on probation following some rather spec-tacular escapades, which were shocking to the community. He is having a hard time on probation, but in the opinion of the supervisor he is beginning to take hold. However, sometimes the struggle becomes too hard and during one of those spells he backslides and commits another offense. The probation officer still feels the boy can profit by probation, but the public is demanding swift retribution. Shall the probation officer yield, or does he really have a conviction the boy can still take some help? Indeed, the worker may see the relapse as rather naturally related to the growth process that is taking place in the individual's struggle with proba-tion. In such a situation the worker may be willing to stand by his profes-sional guns, admitting that his primary consideration is the welfare of the probationer, which means protecting the progress he has already made. At this point the probation officer should submit an objective report, evaluating the recent criminal offense in the light of the probation experi-ence as a preliminary consideration for the court.

One might just as well be realistic at this point and admit that a probation officer who differed with the court constantly would advance neither the cause of probation nor himself. The same dilemma springs up here as it does in every phase of social casework. The caseworker has developed by training and experience a certain competence in the field of human relationships, as well as certain convictions about the values of social casework for the individual in need. Occasionally there is the making of a conflict between that point of view and a lay or community point of view as reflected, let us say, in the agent of the community, in this instance the court. The worker may choose to surrender all principle and run, or he may see his job as holding to his convictions, using his skill in trying to make clear his position, and then accepting with good grace the final verdict if it goes against him. No one can ask more of him, and professionally he has permitted the decision to be made where it belongs. If trained workers do not stand by professional principles, who will? Or who will bother to advance them? In few areas is this truer or more clearly illustrated than in probation, parole, and in correctional institutions where the worker is already dealing with society's scapegoat.

Casework in a correctional institution

It is recognized that the present state of knowledge of human behavior does not permit the abandonment of any of the three most common correctional institutions: the reform (or training) school, the reformatory or industrial school, and the prison. Despite the many enthusiasms for the ideal of probation, neither community opinion nor professional practice has yet succeeded in outmoding institutional care and treatment of the offender. Social workers, realizing that the institution will be here for a long time and convinced that casework has real utility wherever there is a human and social need, have pressed for the use of casework in an institution setup. Instead of being willing to relegate the offender to the dump heap, they have contended that offenders who have not been granted probation or those whose probation has been revoked have perhaps greater need than ever for an individualized help. Without any illusions about the institution furnishing an ideal setting for casework, the social worker recognizes that there is still a valuable service to render within the limits of a correctional framework. Limits are recognized as a part of the reality situations facing both worker and client, and yet those very limits within an institution can be used constructively as a part of the casework process.[2]

Provision has been made for casework services within some state

---

[2] For a penetrating analysis of the use of limits and of the larger area of the use of social casework in correctional services see: Kenneth L. M. Pray, "The Place of Social Case Work in the Treatment of Delinquency," *Social Service Review*, XIX (June 1945), pp. 235–244; ———, "The Principles of Social Case Work as Applied to Probation and Parole," *Federal Probation*, IX (April–June 1945), pp. 14–18; ———, "Social Work in the Prison Program," *Federal Probation*, VII (October–December 1943), pp. 3–7; see also Mazie F. Rappaport, "The Possibility of Help for the Child Returning from a State Training School," *Journal of Social Work Process*, V (1954), pp. 21–46; Arthur E. Fink, "Authority in the Correctional Process," *Federal Probation*, XXV (September 1961), pp. 34–40.

reformatories and prisons and in most of the federal reformatories and prisons. In these institutions the usual plan calls for a social service department or at least a social caseworker whose work is coordinated with that of the other departments. The services of these departments, medical, psychological, educational and vocational, religious, parole, and social service, are in many instances considered vital to the functioning of the institutional organization. Wardens and superintendents have learned, as judges have with probation officers, that the social caseworker instead of being a necessary nuisance may actually have something useful to contribute.

By the time the offender has come to the institution he has had his brush with the law, that is, the police, jail, and the court. He is not exactly anxious to hear the final clamp of the gates behind him, signalizing his separation from family, home, friends, neighborhood, and possibly job. He comes very often with feelings of hatred that may either lie smoldering during his incarceration only to flare up vindictively upon his release, or that may burst out uncontrollably once imprisonment is a fact. It is early in his institutional career that he meets the social worker, possibly during his thirty-day quarantine period and as a prelude to the first classification clinic. He may carry bitterness and antagonism into his early interviews, much of it directed at the social worker and indicating inability to face the authority that crowds all around him and with which he never managed to make his peace when he was free. Or he may bury his feelings, distrusting any member of the prison staff, and refuse to let the worker gain any entrée into his real self.

The competent social caseworker is aware that he cannot force the inmate to get out his feelings, that it may take time for the individual to realize that the social worker is there to help him with his difficulties. In the initial interview the caseworker may be able to help the prisoner to express some of his feelings that have been pent up within him—to permit even the hostile explosiveness against all forms of authority. It may not be until he has faced some of his own projections that the prisoner can begin to make some constructive use of the time he has ahead of him. The reassurance that social casework is a helping service may need to be more than verbal. The person who has gotten as far as prison is rather distrustful of people who are supposed to help. He mistrusts everyone connected with authority. On the other hand, for the first time in his life the individual, in view of what seems his hopeless plight, may actually face his need for help. Part of the worker's job will be to determine how much help the inmate needs, how much he can take, and, just as importantly, how much the worker and the institution can offer. Not infrequently the worker may misjudge any or all of these and so overwhelm the inmate with the offer of help as to make it impossible for him to take anything.

Perhaps the essential role that the social worker exercises has never been put as clearly or as arrestingly as by Richard Farrow when he wrote: "The most important discovery I have made about my job as a private agency social worker operating in prison is that if I am to be of help to prisoners, the main focus of my job will be not in getting them out of, but rather helping them get *into* prison." [3] The facing of the fact that he is in prison, and why, and then moving on to using that time and experience constructively are the areas in which the prisoner needs help. It is here that the social worker can be of real usefulness.

In many instances the inmate is likely to express his needs about concrete situations, such as the way he left things at home, or the job he left behind, or some detail of institutional life, such as change of work assignments, or living quarters, or a suspected discrimination against him in privileges. The basis of these complaints may be real and may furnish a specific issue upon which the caseworker and the inmate can work together. After this is cleared up, there may still remain the basic need which brought him to the worker. This may be some difficulty he may be having within himself, as evidenced by his inability to get along with his fellows, or with the guards, or to accept the authority of the institution. Or it may be related to his difficulties at home, of his struggle for independence, which becomes all the clearer as he sees in retrospect a connection between the trouble he got into and the conflict that has been going on at home between him and his parents. It may require an experience in a reformatory or prison to bring close to him what is really happening.

The caseworker can rarely indulge in the energetic manipulation so often possible to the worker in outside agencies, who manages, as Gordon Hamilton puts it, to confuse effort with effectiveness. Instead he works with such intangibles as the inmate's attitudes and feelings toward his crime, his sentence, his presence here in the prison. The worker directs himself to a clarifying of the problem to the point where the individual is able to do something about it and to cease putting the blame for his difficulties on to other people. What holds the worker to bedrock is the conviction that his function is to help the client with his problem without taking it from him.

The classification clinic, where such exists, affords an opportunity for the caseworker to be of help to the inmate. In the steps from arrest, to detention, to trial, to imprisonment the offender seldom meets with any individual consideration. All along he is one of a mass of criminals. Perhaps for the first time he comes to learn inside the institution that a

---

[3] Richard G. Farrow, "The Basic Problem of Penal Administration," *Prison Journal*, XXII (April 1942), p. 202.

worker exists who can help him with some of his difficulties. The individual interview, which the caseworker has with each new inmate for the purpose of learning what program may best be worked out with him, may open the possibility of further interviews. At least it indicates that there is available a worker to whom he may go. This is especially important in relation to the inmate's adaptation to the institution. The classification system sets as its object the fitting of the individual into the institutional scheme, and, so far as is practicable, the adaptation of the institution to the individual. It is an attempt at individualization in a mass situation, to offer proper job placement, educational training, housing and recreational facilities, and contacts with home. As such it must take into account the equipment of the inmate as well as his personality needs, and it is in this area of assisting the inmate in making the institutional adjustment that the social worker functions.[4]

Preparation for Release

Not the least important of the social services of a correctional institution is helping the prisoner to move toward release. In view of the variations in commitment and release practices, there is considerable leeway as to the uses that the institution may make of the indeterminate sentence. It may use it destructively as a threat, compelling the inmate to submit to the institutional regime, or it may use it constructively as a means whereby the individual works on his own problem and prepares himself for release. Destructively used, the institution undoubtedly will get conformity, perhaps only after the individual has rebelled, been quelled, and then has decided to play the waiting game. The inmate can conform, he can deny his part in making use of the institution, he can throw the responsibility for any change in him upon others, in short he can put everything outside of himself and refuse to get anything out of the experience. Nor is this reaction to the reformatory or prison regime surprising because it is only too common for such institutions to produce good prisoners but not well-integrated personalities. This may show up in the overwillingness with which an inmate "accepts" plans made for him as part of the classification and reclassification scheme or as a prelude to parole but which leaves the bases of his difficulties untouched.

Constructively used, the experience permits the individual to be faced with his share in the difficulty which brought him to the institution

---

[4] See Kenneth L. M. Pray, "Parole in Relation to Classification and Case Work in Prison," *Yearbook of the National Probation Association*, 1944, pp. 182–195; also William G. Nagel, "Modern Trends in Institutional Care," *Journal of Social Work Process*, X (1958), pp. 57–70; "Some New Areas for Casework Activity in a Correctional Institution for Young Men," *Journal of Social Work Process*, IV (1953), pp. 29–45.

and to take some part in assuming responsibility for his own change or self-improvement. This unquestionably is a much harder job than conformity, for it may need to be done in spite of the institutional regime. It may also be done in the face of the distrust and disapproval of fellow prisoners to whom taking help may be interpreted as a "squealing" or a "selling out," a "breaking of the code." It requires extraordinary courage to be willing, within one's self, to change when those all around want to help in effecting that change; it calls for much more when such willingness to change is not supported and is even aggressively challenged by persons in the environment that is as closely lived as in prison. A competent social worker will recognize that although the decision as to how long he will stay is to a large degree the inmate's, nevertheless it is a decision that carries a degree of responsibility with which the individual may need help. Some inmates who have looked toward freedom from the day they entered prison actually when faced with freedom within a short time may feel unable to bring themselves to it without assistance. To the average citizen this must sound like sheer nonsense, but to the individual who has fitted too easily into the comfortable and relatively effortless regimentation of the institution it may be a rather threatening prospect to contemplate the insecurity of the outside world with all of its demands upon initiative, decisions, and responsibility.

Not only may the social worker help the inmate with his decisions but he may enable the offender to use in a positive way the experience of imprisonment and of leaving. There is a certain amount of pain that goes with such an experience that no one can take away from the individual, nor would. There is also a certain amount of frustration that comes of the blocking of normal impulses in an abnormal environment. This, too, no social worker can take away from the individual. But there is also a certain strength that may have been gained through the experience, and it is the realization of this that enables the individual to go on, to face the realities of life outside the institution, to endure the inevitable pains of readjustment and growth.

Despite the setting—indeed accepting the reality of it—the far more important factor is the quality of the relationship set up between the worker and the prisoner. William Nagel expresses the essence of this and its relevance to preparation for parole as follows:

> Those of us who work in a treatment relationship with the men who are sent to our institution, try to provide him with an emotional experience in which he can grow. We let him struggle with us, hate us, love us, test us, reject us, and as he does he works out some of the conflicts which have been so destructive to him. Some knots in his emotional being begin to get untangled, and after a while he begins to react more maturely to situations

which previously he would have met in ways which were unacceptable to the community. He seems to have changed. Indeed in a very real way he has changed, and we consider him ready for parole.[5]

Parole

It has been said frequently that preparation for parole begins before an offender ever gets to a correctional institution. The treatment he gets at the hands of police, jailers, prosecuting attorneys, and judges leaves its impression with him and may have a good deal to do with his attitude when he leaves prison toward such officials and the agencies they represent. A more specific preparation for parole begins when he enters the institution, for despite all the strictures we pass upon reformatories and prisons, they are designed to discharge offenders, presumably improved. This preparation commences with quarantine, proceeds first to classification, then to reclassification and to the program that is worked out with the individual.

How ready the individual is for parole may depend in large measure upon how carefully these details have been shared with the individual. Who wants parole, the inmate or his people, wife, mother, etc.? Whose initiative is it, the inmate's, his family's, or the social worker's? Who arranges for the sponsor? What part does the inmate have in locating a job; if simeone else makes the contact, does the inmate have any choice in the matter? Trivial as these questions may seem as a person stands on the threshold of freedom, they may bear some relation to this subsequent adjustment. The eagerness of other people to get an individual out of prison may so deprive him of decisions and responsibilities that are his that he may be crippled in more ways than one when he is actually freed.

The man who is being considered for probation usually has not been robbed for years of his opportunities for decisions, nor has his life been interrupted as is the case with the parolee. But in practically every instance the individual who has been imprisoned has a more difficult readjustment to make. For one, he may be the more serious offender or one whose difficulties were so deeply rooted that the court thought probation inadvisable. In addition, he has lived in an unnatural environment and has lost many of the normal human contacts that most people find essential. Finally he may come out of prison, even the best prison, with feelings and attitudes that he has held inside of himself but that he now must get outside: bitterness, hatred, resentment. He also comes out with

---

[5] William G. Nagel, "Some New Areas for Casework Activity in a Correctional Institution for Young Men," *op. cit.*, p. 40.

fears about his job, fear of failure, feelings of being rejected or persecuted, putting the blame for his mistakes on to other people, feeling dependent and yet fiercely resenting the need to be helped as well as the help offered. This is the person the parole officer is likely to meet no matter how fortunate the parolee's institutional experience has been.

The parole officer's job is not so different from the probation officer's, except that it is likely to be more difficult. Assuming that ideally parole is a continuation of the treatment begun in the institution or earlier, the parole officer is endowed with authority, which remains a part of his relationship with the parolee. While parole is not voluntarily undertaken by the offender, the parole officer recognizes this as part of the situation, but nevertheless offers a helping service, which the parolee is free to accept or reject. Much of what has been written in the forepart of this chapter about casework in probation applies as well to parole. The parolee may be able to use what the parole officer has to offer, or he may not. That in no wise affects the quality of the casework service offered. The worker needs to be aware of what the client is trying to express and to offer such help as the client wants and is able to use. Part of the answer to this latter question depends upon the worker's ability to determine how much responsibility the client can carry.

The parallel with probation proceeds throughout, for both probation and parole involve essentially casework relationships. Help may be needed with external and environmental factors or with internal and personality needs. This may be accomplished by help given the parolee by the parole officer or by referral to appropriate social agencies, public and private. The use of community resources may be just as important in work with the parolee as with the probationer. The matter of parole violation and revocation also will have to be reckoned with. Just as with the probation officer, the parole worker will have to weigh the seriousness of the infraction, the character of the offender, the capacity that the individual has already demonstrated to use the parole service, as well as an estimate of his potentialities if continued on parole or if imprisoned. If these are serious questions for the probationer, they must seem doubly so when affecting the life of the parolee. Many workers feel the parolee needs more help than the probationer, and there certainly is much to support such a conviction. When it comes to the point of discharge from parole, the worker will want to assure himself that the individual is ready to go on his own without help. If the institutional experience has been a constructive one and parole supervision has managed to help the parolee accept his share of responsibility for his own feelings and behavior, then the parole officer may feel fairly comfortable about the individual proceeding under his own steam. Both probation and parole must recognize the inherent ability of the individual to meet life according to his capacity.

Application to the military setting

Many of the lessons that were being learned slowly in peacetime were quickened by the impact of war and the resulting necessity to conserve manpower. In World War II, the Army and the Navy with the assistance of leaders in the correctional field developed programs for dealing constructively with military offenders. There was never the slightest suspicion that the Army or the Navy were in the social work business; nevertheless, the military organization had to contend with thousands of offenders within the ranks. Rehabilitative programs were developed, which incorporated some of the fundamental principles of dealing with offenders of all kinds. Both Richard Chappell of the Navy's corrective services and Austin MacCormick of the Army's described the programs as designed to treat offenders in such a manner that they would be restored to duty benefited rather than damaged by the period of confinement.[6]

Conclusion

Frequently it has been asked whether the principles of modern social casework are applicable to probation, prison work, or parole. Without going into an exhaustive analysis of the pro's and con's, it can be said here that when the essential nature of social casework, as well as the purpose of probation, prison work, and parole, are understood the answer is decidedly in the affirmative. Perhaps the most pointed presentation yet made has been the one by Kenneth Pray. This analysis examines the apparent contradiction between the authoritative character of correctional work and the customarily voluntary nature of social casework. Does an

---

[6] For additional references to services to offenders in the armed forces, see: Irving Brodsky, "Disciplinary Barracks," in Henry S. Maas, *Adventure in Mental Health* (New York: Columbia University Press, 1951), pp. 99–117; Richard A. Chappell, "Naval Offenders and Their Treatment," *Federal Probation*, IX (April–June 1945), pp. 3–7; ———, "What Did the War Services Develop in Correction Technique?" *Proceedings of the National Conference of Social Work*, 1947, pp. 361–368; ———, and F. Emerson Logee, "Training Wayward Sailor Men for Return to Duty," *Yearbook of the National Probation Association*, 1945, pp. 20–29; Albert G. Fraser, "Out of the Travail of War," *Prison Journal*, XXVI (January 1946), pp. 149–156; Austin H. Mac-Cormick, "Some Basic Considerations in the Treatment of Military Prisoners," *Federal Probation*, IX (January–March 1945), pp. 7–11; ———, and Victor H. Evjen, "The Army's Rehabilitation Program for Military Prisoners," *Yearbook of the National Probation Association*, 1945, pp. 1–19; William C. Menninger, "Psychiatry and the Military Offender," *Federal Probation*, IX (April–June 1945), pp. 8–12; Perry V. Wagley, "The Army Rehabilitates Military Offenders," *Federal Probation*, VIII (January–March 1944), pp. 14–19.

individual on probation, in prison, or on parole have a choice as to whether he will accept the worker's services and skill? The answer is "Yes." True, it is a qualified "Yes," because the choice is related to the factors that have necessitated probation, imprisonment, or parole. Within the real and legal limits imposed by probation, imprisonment, or parole, the offender—the client—has the freedom to accept or reject the help of the worker, just as any other client has. If he does not or cannot use the helping skill of the worker, he—the client—will have to carry the responsibility and the consequences, just as any other client.

Does the imposition of limits militate against the use of casework in probation, imprisonment, or parole? The answer is "No." There is no area of casework service that is without limits. There are limits in the situations in which family casework is offered, child placement, medical casework, etc. The differential is the nature of the limits. So, too, with the correctional casework services. Indeed, one is more aware of the limits in probation, prison services, and parole, but one also realizes the very necessity for them. When Mr. Pray asks about these limitations, he answers his own question by saying, "Not only is there room for such limitations upon individual freedom; again, there is positive, unavoidable need for such limits. They constitute the framework within which alone real freedom, real movement, and change is possible." [7]

Does the offender require the limitations that the authority of the court or the prison impose upon him? This question can be answered positively, with very little hesitation. In the article just quoted, Mr. Pray comes to grips with this, and says of the offender in relation to authority: [8]

> It is particularly true of the delinquent that social readjustment must be founded upon the recognition and acceptance of the inherent, rightful, and essential authority that underlies social living. He has rejected or violated that authority in the past. He has to learn anew, through painful experience, that those limits, like his own capacities, are inviolable, and that his real satisfactions are to be found only within them.

Both Albert Fraser and Kenneth Pray apply the same principles to casework within the prison. There is no denying the reality of limitations that the prison imposes upon the offender. Nevertheless, if the prison experience is to be a useful one and the worker's service a genuine helping, these limitations must be frankly faced and dealt with. The offender must know he is in prison, accept it even though he does not like it, and work with himself and the situation as it is. Contradictory though it may seem, the caseworker's skill is to help the prisoner to get *into* prison (as

---

[7] Kenneth L. M. Pray, "The Principles of Social Case Work as Applied to Probation and Parole," *op. cit.*, p. 16.

[8] *Ibid.*, p. 17.

Farrow expresses it), to face why he is there, and to handle himself in relation to it. Fraser well states it when he writes: "He needs to understand that not until he is ready to accept the commitment, to bring *all* of himself into the prison, can he begin to prepare himself for leaving it." [9]

These principles, based upon an understanding of the dynamics of the helping process, hold great promise for useful employment in probation, prison work, and parole.[10]

Bibliography

Anderson, C. Wilson, "Social Case Work in the Juvenile Court," *Prison Journal,* XXX (July 1950), pp. 46–53.

Block, Herbert A., and Frank T. Flynn, *The Juvenile Offender in America Today.* New York: Random House, Inc., 1956.

Bowen, Croswell, *They Went Wrong.* New York: McGraw-Hill Book Company, Inc., 1954.

Bowers, Swithun, "The Application of Social Work in the Correctional Field," *National Probation and Parole Association Journal,* V (January 1959), pp. 16–20.

Burbank, Edmund G., "The Place of Social Casework Service in the Pre-Release Program of a Correctional Institution," *Prison Journal,* XXIX (April 1949), pp. 33–39.

Chute, Charles L., and Marjorie Bell, *Crime, Courts, and Probation.* New York: The Macmillan Company, 1956.

Cloward, Richard A., and Lloyd E. Ohlin, *Delinquency and Opportunity: A Theory of Delinquent Gangs.* New York: The Free Press of Glencoe, 1960.

Cohen, Albert J., *Delinquent Boys: The Culture of the Gang.* New York: The Free Press of Glencoe, 1955.

Deutsch, Albert, *Our Rejected Children.* Boston: Little, Brown & Company, 1950.

Farrow, Richard G., "The Basic Problem of Penal Administration," *Prison Journal,* XXII (April 1942), pp. 202–209.

——, "Prison and the Man," *Prison Journal,* XXII (July 1942), pp. 218–221.

——, "What the Parole Officer Has a Right to Expect From the Institution," *Federal Probation,* XII (September 1948), pp. 30–35.

---

[9] Albert G. Fraser, "The Function and Program of a Prisoners' Aid Society," *Federal Probation,* VIII (July–September 1944), p. 26.

[10] While the emphasis in this chapter has been on the usefulness of casework services, it should be recognized that other services are also helpful in contributing to the redevelopment of the offender. Among the most important of these, although still frankly experimental and demonstrational, are those involving services to the group within the correctional setting. The work in the New Jersey Reformatory described by William Nagel and the work carried on by McCorkle and his associates at Highfields in New Jersey should be given careful study and followed with interest. See Chapter 14, "Social Group Work."

Glueck, Sheldon, ed., *The Problem of Delinquency*. Boston: Houghton Mifflin Company, 1959.

———, *Unraveling Juvenile Delinquency*. New York: The Commonwealth Fund, 1950.

———, and Eleanor Glueck, *Delinquents in the Making: Paths to Prevention*. New York: Harper & Row, Publishers, 1952.

Keve, Paul W., *Prison, Probation, or Parole*. Minneapolis: University of Minnesota Press, 1954.

———, *The Probation Officer Investigates—A Guide to the Pre-Sentence Report*. Minneapolis: University of Minnesota Press, 1960.

McCorkle, Lloyd W., Albert Elias, and F. Lovell Bixby, *The Highfields Story: An Experimental Treatment Project for Youthful Offenders*. New York: Holt, Rinehart and Winston, Inc., 1958.

Meeker, Ben S., "Social Work and the Correctional Field," *Federal Probation*, XXI (September 1957), pp. 32–42.

Nagel, William G., "Modern Trends in Institutional Care," *Journal of Social Work Process*, IX (November 1958), pp. 57–70.

———, "Some New Areas for Casework Activity in a Correctional Institution for Young Men," *Journal of Social Work Process*, IV (May 1953), pp. 29–45.

Peck, Harris B., and Virginia Bellsmith, *Treatment of the Delinquent Adolescent*. New York: Family Service Association of America, 1954.

Powers, Edwin, and Helen Witmer, *An Experiment in the Prevention of Delinquency: The Cambridge-Somerville Youth Study*. New York: Columbia University Press, 1951.

Robison, Sophia M., *Juvenile Delinquency: Its Nature and Control*. New York: Holt, Rinehart and Winston, Inc., 1960.

Rowles, Burton J., *The Lady at Box 99*. Greenwich, Conn.: The Seabury Press, Inc., 1962.

Silverman, Edgar, "Integrating Social and Legal Process in a Family Court," *Journal of Social Work Process*, V (1954), pp. 47–63.

"Social Casework in Corrections," *Prison Journal*, XXXIX (October 1959), entire issue.

Wessel, Rosa, ed., *A Case Work Approach to Sex Delinquents*. Philadelphia: Pennsylvania School of Social Work, 1947.

Wilson, Everett E., "The Nature of Probation," *The Social Service Review*, XX (September 1946), pp. 396–402.

JOE SCHMIDT

NATHAN ZIRL,
Director of Social Work
New Jersey Reformatory
Bordentown, New Jersey

Bordentown is the medium security reformatory in the State of New Jersey. The population is composed of inmates between the ages of 16 and 30 who have been committed for felonies. Approximately 90 percent of the men are given an indeterminate sentence with a five-year maximum. However, in the event that violence is involved in the offense, the maximum sentence may be longer.

Upon arrival, the inmate is processed for identification, and is then confined to the orientation tier where he remains for thirty days. While he is there he is in contact with the Medical, Psychological, Social Casework, Educational, Religious, Recreational, Industrial, and Parole Departments. These departments submit reports on their findings to the Classification Committee, which has the responsibility for making all major decisions regarding the inmate's stay at Bordentown. The committee is composed of the superintendent, assistant to the superintendent (who is a social worker), chief psychologist, director of education, deputy keeper (chief custodial officer), industrial manager, and the classification officer.

At his first appearance before the Classification Committee the inmate is assigned to his housing tier, is given school and work assignments and, where indicated, is assigned to a treatment program. Four months later, after a careful review of his progress within the institution, he appears again in person before the committee and is informed as to how much longer he will have to remain. His progress is periodically reviewed until his ultimate release on parole or maximum sentence.

The casework department has always functioned as an integral part in the total administrative and treatment program at Bordentown. The assistant to the superintendent, who is in charge of the treatment program, is a trained social worker and represents the social service department at the Classification Committee meetings. In addition, there is a director of social service and two trained workers. The department also includes student social workers affiliated with three schools of social work who are there on field work placement.

Along with the casework staff, the treatment staff consists of two part-time psychiatrists and eight psychologists who engage in testing and in individual and group therapy. The educational department is made up

348

of six teachers (including a recreational director), four of whom are engaged in elementary sociology courses aimed primarily at enriching the meager social knowledge of the inmates.

When an inmate arrives at the institution he has been through the long procedure of arrest, indictment, and conviction. His initial contacts with the institution are extremely important in affecting his attitude toward his confinement and future behavior. Social workers are aware of the significance of the beginning process. Having an opportunity to see the inmate at the initial step of admissions and helping him to accept responsibility for the actions that led him to jail enables the worker to render a useful service. While confined to the orientation tier the inmate participates in individual and group sessions at which time the worker imparts information about the rules and regulations. The inmate is told that Bordentown is, not a treatment center, but a reformatory with a treatment program. A considerable amount of time is spent in discussing the program as well as the function of the Classification Committee. Of particular interest to the inmate is information about how the committee arrives at the decision of "how much time" each inmate is to serve—including such matters as past and present offenses, personal attitude, emotional make-up, and even community attitude toward the offense. To this the inmates react very sharply. They cannot understand why this should be so. "I have paid for my past, so why should I have to pay again?"; or, "And anyway, why should the attitude of the community influence the length of my confinement?" They show their hostility, their rationalizations, and they verbalize a great many distortions about their offense, the police, the parole officer, etc. They try to prove that there is no reason for their incarceration and no justification for the community to confine them. The worker accepts their protestations but points out the reality of the situation. The beginning goal is to move them to the point where they accept being in Bordentown.

The worker does not minimize the punitive aspect of confinement but, rather, indicates that while we have to confine the offender we can offer him the opportunity to explore what led to his coming. By so doing, we can also help him learn how to remain in the community when he has earned his release. The simple act of talking to him about preparing his mailing and visiting list affords him the opportunity to become familiar with the worker. This contact often serves as a springboard from which the inmate can become involved in a more intensive relationship. In addition, these initial contacts serve to screen or detect any extremely emotionally disturbed men. These are referred for immediate psychiatric attention.

The most difficult and immediate problem for the caseworker is to establish a relationship. This has to be the vehicle through which the worker enables the delinquent to outgrow his original faulty primary relationship with the parental authoritative figure. Some workers have difficulty in being truly accepting of delinquents because they—the delinquents—are so strongly rejecting of the offer to help and show such little outward signs of remorse. They deny that they need help or want it and verbalize emphatically that "there is nothing wrong" with them. "It is the world that needs changing, not me." Nevertheless, if the worker can persevere enough to convey a real concern for him as a person the relationship may begin to be a helpful one.

The relationship is subjected to constant testing by the inmate to see if it is genuine. This is understandable in the light of the delinquent's attitude of distrust, suspicion, and fear of revealing too much of himself. When the worker says, "I wish to help with your difficulty," his response is, "I will show you how bad I can really be, and then let me see if you really wish to help"; or, "If you really want to help me, you would get me out of this place." It is at this point that the worker has to make clear his identity as being part of the confining authority, that is, the institutional administration, the courts, and even the police.

Two important things must take place in order for a caseworker to function effectively in a correctional setting. First of all, the caseworker must accept and have a belief in the *raison d'etre*, that is, the need for the correctional setting. Secondly, he must be able to identify himself with the agency and its needs, and present himself in this light to the client. If the worker allows the inmate to separate him from the rest of the administration, he allows him to make caseworkers the "good" people and the authorities the "bad" people. When this happens we do not give the inmate the opportunity to come to grips with one of his basic problems. He must be helped to work through his negative feelings with an understanding person who represents "authority" to him. The process that he must go through is one of being helped to be aware of his need for help and of his necessity to change, and then to be helped to do so. While the need to "belong," to "feel a part of," are extremely important, it is a tremendous thing we ask of him. He has put so much of himself into finding some kind of peace between his own inner struggle and the hostile world around him that it is understandable for him to be resistive when we ask him to change.

We must discard the clichéd concept of the delinquent as a mean and arrogant individual who acts in a deliberate manner to inflict pain on the world around him. For, when we come to know him, he often reveals himself to be an inadequate, passive person who feels that the world around him has hurt him. A closer look at the delinquent's life experience will usually show that it has. He was the once "left-over" child, raised through indifference, unwanted or unloved, with feelings that the world really has no place for him. His is the problem of finding a reason to go on living. All too often the job of the caseworker is to breathe back life into these socially and emotionally deprived people. They have seen too much of the sordid side of life. These are the children that did not adjust in foster homes, the out-of-wedlock children, the children of broken homes. We can recognize them immediately by their problems about rejection and separation. The inadequates steal cars, the aggressives break heads.

Many delinquents are the children of minority groups, who have difficulty in securing the benefits of our affluent society. To them the monotonous job, the crowded slums, the fights, the drinking on Saturday nights, the use of drugs, and the hatred of the world around them becomes the norm. They cannot cope with the people who are always there on the first of the month with their hands out for a payment and finely typed installment agreements. It is difficult for us to understand the importance of "saving face" through the showing of "heart," of fighting if one's turf or home ground has been threatened, but to the delinquent that is all that is left to be important.

Joe Schmidt

In Joe Schmidt we have a young man who appears to stem from a stable environment. He does not belong to the deprived minority group nor is he limited in his mental capacity. He suffers from another kind of deprivation. He does not feel that he "belongs." This is as handicapping as any language or cultural barrier. His efforts to find acceptance and to resolve his fierce inner struggles have led to social ostracism and institutionalization. What follows is an attempt by the caseworker to help him to find a place for himself in our world.

Joe was assigned by the Classification Committee to a social worker for individual attention. This being his second admission to the reformatory, the committee felt that Joe had not really come to grips with his inner problems; that there was considerable superficiality in his past good institutional adjustment record. He was given a twenty-four month goal for parole.

Joe is a 25-year-old, good-looking young man with deep set eyes and a slight limp. He is white, single, and of average intelligence. There are two conspicuous scars on his face, an inch scar on his wrist, and, according to the record, an abdominal scar from a bullet. In spite of this external evidence of trouble, he is described as a shy, quiet, and reserved person, who tends to keep to himself but gets along with others.

The record further indicates that Joe comes from an intact and closely knit family. The father, a naturalized immigrant, had provided them with their own home and worked steadily to support his family. He was described as being a strict disciplinarian. The mother, a rather easy-going, overprotective sort of person, took care of the home and children: two daughters and a son besides Joe. He was the only one in the family group to become a public offender.

Joe was said to be of normal birth and development. At the age of seven however, he suffered a serious accident. He fell from a moving bus and was wedged between the curb and the back wheel of the bus, resulting in a crushed pelvis. Although he was not expected to live, Joe pulled through with only a slight limp due to minor shortening of one leg. His school record was poor, and he attended only until the ninth grade. He stopped school completely at 16 when he ran away from home and joined the merchant marine. Coming home after three months, he stayed a while and ran away again.

By the age of 17, Joe first became known to the police on a charge of disorderly conduct. He was given a suspended sentence and placed on probation. Although he later enlisted in the Navy, Joe never seemed to have adjusted and, after repeated AWOL charges and special courts-martial, he was given a bad conduct discharge two years later. The record shows continued infractions of the law, including mugging and robbery, disorderly conduct, and larceny of five cars for which he was ultimately sentenced to Bordentown for the first time at the age of 21. It was during his last attempted car robbery that Joe was shot through the abdomen by a policeman who tried to stop him. Joe's statement at the time was that, "I wanted to drive, so I just took the cars." Both his parents attributed Joe's difficulties to outside influences, particularly his friends and to his excessive drinking habits.

During his first stay at the reformatory all reports submitted by the various departments described him as making a "very good adjustment, was cooperative, had a pleasant manner about him." Eventually, Joe was doing well enough to be promoted to work outside the institution on the farm where he did well. On the record an episode shows where he slashed his wrist but denied that his attempt was at suicide. He claimed that he was being pressured for sexual reasons and that his action was merely a way to get off that particular tier. The psychological and psychiatric examinations that followed did not reveal any severe emotional disturbance, and with a change of tiers his conduct continued to be without incident. Previous and subsequent contacts with the psychologist described him as

> being superficially cooperative, but with little or no insight into his delin-
> quent behavior. He minimizes the importance of what took place, or at-
> tempts to place the blame on the situation, is immature, has strong feelings

of masculine inadequacy, and believes that aggressive and delinquent behavior is an expression of masculinity. The current clinical impression is of a passive aggressive dependent individual who harbors considerable repressed hostility. He talks of his parents in a positive manner and claims harmonious family relationships. Although with pressure he reveals that he and his father were not too close, he states that he does not like to talk against his parents.

The last psychological report indicated little real change in his overall total attitude. Continued satisfactory adjustment enabled Joe to get released after serving one year and seven months at Bordentown.

Within two months Joe was readmitted. The police reported that he had been charged with aggravated assault and battery. In a relatively unprovoked argument he hit a man and fractured his skull.

[12/7]   Joe had been assigned to the worker by the Classification Committee and came up to see me at his request. We discussed his assignment to me for individual attention. I informed him that I had made an appointment for him on Monday at ten o'clock.

[12/10]   Worker began by asking Joe how he felt about being back in jail. He said that he didn't like it, that he felt lousy about it. He doesn't feel he should be here at all. They should have given him another chance and not sent him back to Bordentown. There were many racketeers on the outside who did worse things than he, and they were not in jail because they had money. He hadn't meant to fracture the guy's skull and was only protecting himself when he hit him. The same thing could have happened to the worker. At least, he said it was not impossible that this could have happened to me. Worker replied that it might well be true, but the fact was that it had not happened to myself; it had happened to him. How did it happen to him after he had been outside for so short a time? Joe lowered his head and seemed to have difficulty answering the question. After a while, he answered that he had felt it coming. He somehow knew he was going to get into trouble again. He had wanted to escape from his "environment" so that he could have prevented it. He wanted to go to Florida where he could have started things "fresh." He wanted to get away from the people and places that got him in trouble, but didn't because of his "family ties." His mother and father were against it, and it would have meant breaking parole to go to Florida anyhow. He added that he wasn't trying to push all the responsibility on other people,—he was also responsible for what he did. What really bugged him was the kind of thing he was back here for. He just lost his head and punched this guy. With a little will power he knew he could have avoided the whole thing. He hadn't stolen anything at all.

At this point Joe tried to involve the worker in a theoretical discussion of why people steal. He commented that all kids at one time in their life stole and wondered if worker thought this was a "proven fact" as he did. Worker indicated that he was more interested in how Joe felt about the judge sending him back. After some hesitancy he said that he felt especially bad about it because the whole thing could have been prevented if he had just avoided getting involved in the fight. He has now been here for five months and thinks this is sufficient time for such an offense.

The worker chooses to begin around Joe's return to Bordentown to which Joe responds by attempting to negate his being confined and tries to minimize the importance of his confinement. Joe says this could happen to anybody, and the worker focuses this back on the role he played in his being returned. In his own immature mind, Joe sees leaving his community and going to Florida as an escape from his problems. He also tries to involve the worker in an intellectual discussion that is really a rationalization of stealing; but, the worker sticks to Joe's feelings about being recommitted. Joe asks that the Classification Committee reduce his length of stay, knowing that they are going to refuse him, but he still has the need to test. It also reveals his unreadiness to face the seriousness of the offense and its true implications for himself.

[12/14]   Joe begins by talking about his visits, preferring to discuss what he feels to be the brighter side of his stay at Bordentown. His mother had come to see him, and although she came alone this time he expects his father to come with her next week.

Worker focuses the talks to Joe's reaction to the Classification Committee's refusal to cut his time. He replies, "Well, what can I do, they make the decisions; all I have to do is wait to be released." Worker asks him whether this is not a way of ducking his responsibility in doing something for himself. He reacts saying that it may be so, but he hates all authorities, and begins a hostile verbal tirade against the Classification Committee, cops, judges, parole officers. He felt that he had been shanghaied several times and did not trust anybody in an authoritarian position. He continued for several minutes, then stopped, cast his eyes upon the floor, and became silent.

The worker encouraged Joe to continue, but he tries to start an intellectual discussion about authority. It was as though he felt that he had revealed too much of himself and was fearful of the consequences. The worker raised the question of Joe's feelings to his father. At first he talks of his father as being "a good old man." They had their difficulties in the past, but now everything was fine. Worker asked about their past difficulties.

Joe said that it was hard to explain. His father has never once called him "son." When he was younger his father had not accepted him at all—he completely rejected him. Joe recounted how he had once told his father how he felt about him. At the time he had been in the county jail for disorderly conduct. When his father came in, Joe called him all kinds of vile names, one of which he knows his father will never forget. His younger brother was always treated like a "son." His father always favored him to the exclusion of Joe. Worker wondered about this, and Joe answered that it made him feel good. He was glad to see his brother make it where he didn't. When worker asked how he really felt he admitted that he was jealous, hurt, and angry because his father favored his brother who was given all of the material things—toys, clothes, etc. His father never took him fishing, to the movies etc., like the other kids' fathers did. Worker asked what this did to him, and he said that it made him feel hurt and sorry for himself. He said, "I had everything but love, and that's what I wanted the most."

At the beginning Joe tries to deny what has happened between himself and the Classification Committee, but the worker stays with this and helps him to bring out his negative feelings towards the committee and other authority figures. Then worker connects these feelings in a discussion of Joe's relationship with his father. Although at first he is superficial, when pressed he does reveal more of his true feelings.

[1/4] Joe continues to express feelings of hostility and resentment of authority. When worker tries to help him discover the source of these feelings, Joe replied angrily that he had them because he was in jail. He added that, when he was on the outside, the cops around the neighborhood used to tell him that he would wind up in jail. Worker wondered how long he had these feelings of bitterness and resentment. He said that he had felt this way his whole life. Worker commented that these feelings didn't begin after he had come to jail. Joe lowered his head at this point, paused a while, then said, "they come from my father." He spoke about his father and expressed his hostile feelings towards him and somewhat to his mother. He used to pray often, he said, that his father would die. He described incidents when his father beat his mother and himself. His father used to drink heavily and would usually do these things when he was drunk.

Worker asked how he felt about this. He said that he felt bad, that he had reached a point where he just didn't care. He said that he never had a normal happy childhood. He used to envy the other kids in the neighborhood whose fathers took an interest in them and did things with them. His father never did any of these things with him. He thought that he never was really loved by either his mother or his father. His mother always treated him O.K., but he never had the feeling that she really loved him. His two sisters and one brother seemed to get most of this love.

Worker commented that things must have been really tough for him when he was a kid. It must not have been easy to have grown up in such a way. Joe agreed, saying that things were always that way for him. He wondered if I thought he was ready for parole. To my inquiry about what he meant, Joe at first said he was curious, but then clarified himself and said he wondered if worker could do anything about getting his parole. At first he had been very "skeptical" about talking with me because he didn't know what my job was in relation to the Classification Committee. When worker told him about his part insofar as the committee was concerned, he seemed to accept it.

The discussion was once again focused on Joe's readiness for parole. He said that he didn't really know. Sometimes he thinks he is, sometimes he doesn't. He still believes he got a raw deal in being returned here, and to that extent he feels that he should be paroled. He realizes, however, that he still has the same attitudes about authority that he always had. He doesn't like anybody to tell him anything. Worker wondered how he felt when anybody told him what to do. He said that these old feelings of hostility and bitterness returned. When he is paroled no parole officer will tell him not to drink, not to stay out late, etc. Worker commented that this seemed to be the same way he reacted to his father and asked him if he could see the pattern. Joe replied that he did. As a matter of fact, when people tell him what to do they remind him of his father. He continued to feel hostile to his father and was even thinking of writing a letter to his parents telling them how he really felt about them. He asked what worker thought about it. Worker replied that they could discuss it and work it out in the next interview. Joe replied that it was o.k. with him, he was not in a hurry and wanted to talk about it before making a decision.

Joe at first tries to appeal to the worker's sympathy by telling him of his difficult childhood. When he feels that the worker has responded he asks for help in securing an early release. In typical delinquent fashion he sees the worker as a "mark"—someone to be manipulated into doing something for him. The worker instead focuses the interview back to Joe's readiness for release and indicates to him the kind of help that he really has to offer. Instead of Joe losing interest in the talks, he is really able to start to make use of them. We see this in the next interview.

[1/11] Joe picks up from his previous session. He states that he had written that letter to his parents last week. He just explained to them that he felt that he would like to go out on his own after he was released. His parents wrote back saying that maybe this is a good idea, that it was time that he began taking on responsibility for himself. Worker wondered about this. He said that he was glad his parents agreed with him, that he had been afraid that they would take it to mean that he was going to have nothing to do with them. He continued that he just wants to get out on his own. He will visit his parents, etc., just not live at home.

Worker wondered why he really did not wish to live at home. How did he really feel about his parents? Joe replied that he tries not to think about this. Worker agreed that such feelings are sometimes painful and that it is natural to try not to think about them. Joe then said that he guessed he really didn't hate his parents for, after all, they were his parents. How would he feel about them if they were not? He hesitated and then answered that he would hate them, that he would have nothing to do with them. How long had he felt this way about them?

Since he was seven years old, after the accident, he began feeling this way. At that age a bus had crushed him between itself and the curb. He was in the hospital for many months and was in very bad shape. One leg consequently is shorter than the other. He commented that he doesn't even remember that his father visited him in the hospital. All he remembers is that when he came home things began to change. He got no sympathy at all from his father. He seemed to blame him for the accident. His father kept telling him that he did everything wrong; that he was bad. His father never took time out to be with him or to explain things to him. All he did was to make promises. One time when Joe was about nine he asked his father to take him to a major league ball game. His father kept promising that he would but never really did. Sometimes he even wondered if he was really their son. He didn't know exactly what made him feel this way. He felt different from his brother and sisters; they seemed to do everything right. He remember that he asked his parents about this a couple of times. Although they reassured him that he was, Joe thought that it was the difference he saw in the way that his brother and sisters were treated that accounted for his feelings. Worker wondered if he had this feeling now, but Joe stated that he didn't, that it was just the way he sometimes felt when he was small. He has no doubts now; he knows he is their son.

In discussing his parole plans, Joe reveals his ambivalent feelings towards his parents. He still yearns for the love that he feels he never received as a child. He sees himself as being different from his siblings and other children. In spite of the fact that he is 25 years old, he still shows some immature and childish fantasy about his father and mother not being his real parents. He continues in the next interview to talk about his love for his mother and hatred for his father. When the worker succeeds in helping Joe to talk about his own concept of himself, he reveals an incident that has been eating away at him and has been causing him endless inner turmoil and tension. After Joe is able to talk about the incident he needs a rest from the sessions and almost immediately receives a disciplinary report, which curtails their contacts.

[1/18] Joe started the interview by talking about his father, who had come to visit him. Each time Joe is able to express hostility about his father he becomes quite depressed and emotional. Tears frequently come to his eyes. He feels that he shouldn't hate his father—because he is his father. He even sends him $20 a month. He can't help, however, hating him the way he does. Worker remarked that it must be difficult and confusing for him to have these feelings and at the same time to have to be nice and perhaps even grateful to him. Joe agreed, saying that it wasn't easy to live with all this hate. He supposed that after all his father wasn't such a bad guy. He is looked up to in the community. The community, however, didn't see his father as he saw him. If they only knew the other side of the story. His father never cared about him, never explained things to him, never took him places, etc. Worker wondered how all these things made Joe feel about himself. He hesitated and asked worker what he meant. Worker rephrased the question. What kind of a guy did he feel he was; how did he see himself? Joe paused at this point and seemed to have difficulty answering. He finally answered that he hates himself as much as he hates his father because of the things he has done. When worker wondered what these things were, Joe said that he was afraid to tell me. Worker was encouraging, stating that he wasn't going to be shocked by anything he had to tell him, was not going to judge him, and reminded him of the confidentiality of our interviews.

Joe then told worker something that he "did" when he was only ten years old. There was a sixteen-year-old guy in the neighborhood who was the leader in the gang. Joe always tried to be part of the gang and always wanted to make an impression on him since he was older and was the leader. He continued that one day this guy made him do something that he would never forget or never forgive himself for as long as he lives. When worker wondered what it was that happened, Joe said that he has never been able to tell anybody this. He has kept this hidden in himself for a long time—since it happened. Worker was supportive, and Joe then described how this boy had made him engage in a homosexual act with him. He remembers how degrading he had felt about this. To make matters worse the guy spread the word all over the neighborhood. It seemed that every guy in the neighborhood knew about what had happened.

This is one of the reasons that he used to fight so much. The other kids used to kid him about being a "fag" (homosexual). When they found out he could fight they let him alone. Worker said that this must have really been tough for him. He must have been quite hurt and confused about all this considering that this happened to him when he was so young. Joe agreed, saying that he didn't know much about sex. He continued that he came to have doubts about himself because of the incident. When worker asked what these doubts were, Joe said that sometimes he felt that maybe he was not a man. He found that he used to fight because it made him feel that he was tough and was a man, not a girl.

After telling the worker these things, Joe sagged in the chair as if he was glad to have gotten all this out of his system. Worker reassured him that he understood how difficult it was for him to express this and could appreciate how confusing it must have been. Worker stated that things like this sometimes happen to kids through no fault of their own, and that he didn't think he should blame himself for this. Nobody had realized what he was going through, and it must have really been upsetting when people didn't see his side of the story. Joe responded by saying that he was glad that worker understood how he felt about these things. He knew that worker would understand or he would not have told him about it.

[1/25] Joe was locked up in G-3 segregation this week for taking extra food from the kitchen. Worker visited him today on G-3. He seemed to be taking this disciplinary action quite well and admitted that he had been wrong. He expressed disappointment because he wouldn't be able to keep his appointments for a couple of weeks. He realizes that worker can only see him for a few minutes at a time while he is here.

[2/29] Joe in office on time for scheduled appointment. He appeared to be quite despondent and bitter today. He had a very defeated appearance, as if the whole world was against him. In response as to how he felt, he simply answered, "o.k." Worker remarked that he didn't act as though everything was o.k.

Joe replied that prison was getting him down and expressed his feelings about being in prison; how difficult it was to be doing the same things day in and day out; how difficult it was to live with some of the other inmates. It really upsets him to have to put up with all this just because he hit a guy. He feels that he was railroaded. Worker wondered if Joe wanted to talk about this. What really happened that caused him to be sent back to prison? Joe described what happened the night he was arrested. He and some friends had been out on the town drinking in some bars. They came out of one bar and began to get into one of the fellows' car when another car backed into their car. Joe explained that they all thought this was funny. The guy who owned the car they were in had been in another accident earlier in the week and had smashed the whole side of his car. All the guys started hooting and hollering to make it seem as though the present accident was worse than it was, hoping that the driver would think he was responsible for it. When the other driver got out of the car he was upset, and as he went to the rear of the car to inspect the damage he shoved Joe. That's when Joe hit him, knocking him to the ground. Joe continued that this was justified, that he had to protect himself. Worker wondered how he had felt when the fellow pushed him. Joe replied that it was hard to explain. After it was all over he had thought about it. He thought it was like a guy who was at a party and who was laughing and having a good time. Suddenly somebody makes a fool of him in front of everybody else. The guy had to prove himself. He has to show everybody that he isn't a fool. If he doesn't do this, he really will be the fool.

The worker wondered how many times Joe had felt this way in the past. He hesitated and said he couldn't remember. After some silence, he said quite despondently that he has felt this way quite a few times in the past. He referred back to the homosexual incident and to the fact that he was the only one in his family who had ever gotten into trouble. He was the black sheep in the family, and his parents never let him forget it. He explained that his relatives are "society people" and because he is in jail, they don't have anything to do with his parents anymore. All these things made him feel like a fool. Worker wondered what happened to somebody when he felt that everybody was trying to make a fool out of him. Joe answered that they get mad and begin to protect themselves. Worker agreed, commenting that he had been reacting this way for a long time, hadn't he? Joe agreed, and when worker asked him how something like this made him feel about himself he said o.k. When he got out he would be the one on top. He was going to get a good job, his own place, his own business, etc.; that's what he means by being on top.

Worker tried to elucidate this in the light of his being the black sheep, everybody trying to make a fool of him, etc. Joe at this point was able to say that he felt he never had a chance, that everybody picked on him, etc. Worker pointed out that all this seemed to have something to do with his hitting the guy and with the way he handles his feelings. Joe stated that he could see this now. He realizes that he strikes back, which only gets him into trouble and back in jail. He would never come back. Next time he would just talk it over instead of striking back. He didn't think it would be too difficult, and worker remarked that it might not be as easy as that.

Joe is despondent and depressed. He has some question of the worker's acceptance of him but does not show it. He articulates the unpleasantness of "pulling time" and the difficulties he has to live with. He says that he was "railroaded." Although this may not be so, it is important for Joe to be able to say, "I did not bring myself here, 'they' did." The worker does not challenge this directly but chooses to explore with Joe the incident that led him to Bordentown. Joe reveals how important it is for him to prove again and again that he is a man, not a fool. He discusses his feelings about his family, himself, and his wishful thinking about being on top. He claims that next time he will know how to handle his feelings. The worker questions whether it will be as simple as Joe feels. The relationship has developed to the point where the worker can challenge some of Joe's defenses.

[3/21]   Joe in office on time for his appointment. His parents had both visited him, and the conversation continued about them. His mother and father almost got a divorce a couple of times. It was only because his mother is a Catholic that she never followed through on it. Joe described how he started to run away from home at the age of 15, and stayed away for months at a time. He went to Florida, got a job in a banana boat, and sailed for South America. He had been West and had worked on a farm in Maryland for a couple of months. The worker wondered how his parents felt about this. Joe answered that they didn't like it very much. When he left, he would just pack up and go without saying a word to anyone. The worker asked him what he was running away from, but Joe denied this, saying that he had just been curious about the world like any other kid. Worker questioned this. Joe smiled and said that he supposed he was running away from something, but he didn't know what it was. Worker commented if this wasn't the story of his life; that it seemed as though he had been trying to find something for a long time now. Joe said, yes, that he had been trying to find himself. He hasn't been able to find it yet. Worker wondered what he meant by this. He couldn't explain it; he just seemed to be looking for something and hasn't been able to find it.

We often see parents who will choose to reject one child. The other children then seem to escape and can almost live normal lives. Joe tells of being placed in an orphanage and how terrifying this experience was to him. He reveals his feelings of rejection and the origin of his wanderlust. He leaves home each time to see what the other side of the mountain will look like. Each time he returns home expecting and hoping that something will have changed. It never does. He keeps looking for something, a place for himself in the sun, a place where he can be different and where things will be different. All he ever finds is another place where he still has his problems, so home he comes, problems and all.

[4/11] The worker begins the interview by telling Joe that he has written a report on their talks for the Classification Committee, before which Joe has to appear next week. Joe responds by saying that he has read the report. He hoped the worker would not say anything about it since it might cause someone trouble. Worker says he was aware this information got out once in a while and wondered how Joe felt about the report. The more we discussed the report, the more apparent it became that he had not seen it.

Joe instead preferred to talk about feeling different from most people. He said that he didn't quite know how to explain it, he had just felt that way, ever since he can remember. Even before he began to get into trouble, he felt that he was somehow treated different than other people. Joe began to describe how he was treated when he was a kid by his father. He had always looked up to his father and wanted to be like him. He tried to please him, and if he made any money he would take it home to him. His father, however, just never treated him like a son. Although he made promises that they would go places together, the promises were never kept. It used to make him feel really bad. He had the feeling that his father never trusted him and went on to describe how he had been placed in the orphanage, etc. He could remember to this day how terribly rejected he had felt then. Worker remarked that he must have really been scared that his father had given him away for good. Joe agreed and continued by saying that his father had always treated him this way. When worker wondered how this had made Joe feel about himself, he said that he began to feel as though he was different. Sometimes he felt that something was the matter with him. Worker asked him what he meant by this, and he replied that he sometimes felt as if he were crazy or something. Then he believed that perhaps he was "just born bad." This was after he began to get into trouble.

Worker wondered how this had affected him, and Joe explained that he had always been looking for acceptance from somebody. When he succeeded in finding it with someone else he would "destroy" it. For example, he would just back up and leave without saying a word. He would go home again feeling that maybe his father would give him acceptance, but it would be the same thing all over again. Finally he just got so he didn't give a damn. He supposed he did feel bitter and hostile about it all. Worker commented that he could understand that Joe would feel this way, but wondered how he handled these feelings when he was on the outside. Joe replied that he got into trouble, fighting and things. Worker wondered why all his offenses were violent and aggressive ones. Joe supposed that it was because of this hostility and bitterness that he had in himself. He was taking it out on other people. Worker pointed out that perhaps he had to find a way to handle his feelings so that they would not get him into trouble.

[4/18]   Today's interview was geared to helping Joe see how he felt when he acted out violently against someone and what really happened to him when he felt this way. Worker attempted to do this by having Joe recall how many times he had acted in this manner. He encouraged him to tell about each incident and how he felt during each one. There were three such incidents: once when Joe had hit the manager of a theatre, once when he had punched a janitor in a dance hall, and the last incident when he hit a man on the street. Each of these times Joe described that he felt "insulted" or that the person was "trying to make a fool out of me." Joe was able to see that he felt the same way in each of these incidents. The worker then attempted to help him see the reality of the situation; that in each of these episodes the parties concerned were not making a fool out of him, but that this was his own feeling, which he had projected onto these people. Joe looked surprised as he seemed to become aware of this. He recognized that he actually had felt that he was a fool himself and that he felt that everybody else saw him this way too. He commented that "the way my father treated me had a lot to do with the way I felt." He always felt as if he got the wrong end of the stick—like a fool. During the first few minutes of the interview we discussed Joe's feelings and what part they had in his violent acts. He was able to see that he would not get rid of these feelings; that there would be times when he would feel the same way again. It would be up to him to handle these feelings. Worker tried to help Joe to see the pattern of his way of acting and indicated that it is what he will do with these feelings that will be the important thing.

The worker had to begin to prepare Joe for his—the worker—leaving the reformatory. When the topic was first mentioned, he took it very matter-of-factly and wished the worker luck. In the next interview, however, the worker became aware that Joe was not responding as he usually did and picked up with him the unfinished topic of his leaving.

Separation for many clients is an extremely traumatic experience. It reawakens in them a great many unexpected separations, experiences that they have known before. If it is not handled properly, it can undo a good deal of the progress gained. A great many men on leaving Bordentown will minimize their going home but will react very strongly to the worker's leaving. It is almost as though it is permissible for them to reject the worker, but the worker cannot ever reject them.

[5/2] Worker focused today's interview on handling Joe's feelings about his (the worker) leaving Bordentown. Worker had begun preparing him for this last week when he first informed him that he was leaving the agency. During the first part of today's interview, worker lost sight of this and began to pick up on the area of Joe's social relationships and feelings about himself. It soon became apparent, however, that Joe was not responding to this at all. He appeared a little depressed and responded on a "yes" or "no" basis. Worker refocused consequently on Joe's feelings about his leaving, believing that this was the underlying factor in his poor response. As soon as worker did this, Joe became spontaneous. At first he was hesitant to express himself, but after a while he responded.

Joe was able to tell worker that he felt badly about his—the worker— leaving. The same old thing was happening to him again. He felt that everything that they had accomplished up to that time had been "thrown out the window." When worker wondered how he felt about him in the light of his leaving he admitted that he felt the worker was giving up on him, just as everybody had given up on him in the past. Worker attempted to handle this first by letting Joe express his feelings about this. Next, worker conveyed to him that he could understand them and had anticipated them. This was one of the reasons why he had raised the issue of his leaving. Worker explained why he was leaving and reassured him that he was not rejecting nor did he feel that what went on before had to be thrown out of the window. Worker also attempted to show him how these feelings were connected to what had happened to him in the past. It was understandable that he should feel this way in the light of his past separations and rejections. From here worker showed him that he did have the capacity for social relationships. He had made one with the worker and perhaps he could begin with his parole officer. Joe responded to this by verbalizing that he could see this a little better now. Worker's leaving was tough for him because he liked him and he had helped him. Worker remarked that this kind of thing was tough for him also, that it worked both ways.

What the worker has been trying to achieve with Joe is to help him to begin to understand himself. He has not allowed Joe to escape from the part he played in his returning to Bordentown. Neither does he allow Joe to wallow in hatred of his father or in his own self-pity. The worker helps him to bring these feelings to the surface so that he can see what they have meant to him; to see them for what they really are. The repeated discussions about his resentment towards his father and people in authority show how much he has had to repress. Although he may never quite get over these feelings, the fact that he can talk about them and "see" them will enable him to do something about them. Joe has always felt alone and unwanted, filled with anger against the world for what it did to him and for what he has done in return. Now he has had a living experience of revealing this to himself and to someone else. He has found that in spite of what he feels to be so hideous a life experience the worker still cares and does not change in his desire to help.

The worker leaves, but Joe will have a new worker and later on will have to deal with a parole officer. Hopefully, he will have learned that he can trust a person in authority. Periodically he may still have his moods of depression and feel as though the world is making a fool of him. We hope that these moods will not last as long and that they will occur with less frequency. More important, we hope that they will occur on the street and not in institutions.

12

SCHOOL
SOCIAL WORK

Early developments

The use of social casework and social caseworkers within the school system, usually the public school system, affords another illustration of the value of such services in helping the child to profit by what the school has to offer. Here again, there is the application of casework within an agency that is set up for an entirely different purpose. The school is not a social service agency; its purpose is educational. But in the process of offering educational opportunities, the school finds there are difficulties that prevent some children from making maximum use of what the school offers. The teacher finds she has plenty to do in conducting a classroom and inculcating the knowledge geared to each grade level. Likewise, the principal has his share of administrative duties, together with problems that teachers bring to him. Yet some of these problems that teachers and principal are confronted with require the skills of another professional person, and it is at this point that the school social worker comes upon the scene.

School social work, like so many other aspects of social casework, is a product of the first decade of the present century. In a very real sense it was a social invention, much as was the juvenile court, workmen's compensation, social insurance, or the city manager plan. Like so many other inventions, enumerated by the late Professor Ogburn, it developed in response to a felt need; and, like some of these inventions, arose at about the same time but in different places.[1]

In 1906–1907 the beginnings of school social work were discernible

---

[1] William Fielding Ogburn, *Social Change* (New York: The Viking Press, Inc., 1922).

in three different cities: New York, Boston, and Hartford.[2] The simultaneous upspringing of this social invention indicated a common culture base that these cities shared. It also indicated there were fundamental conditions, as well as changes, which had taken place or were taking place. The response of these three cities to identifiable needs was school social work. In New York, the immediate impetus came from two social settlements that had assigned visitors to school districts in order that the settlement house and staff might keep in closer touch with the teachers of the children who lived in the settlement neighborhood. The initiating group in Boston was the Woman's Education Association, which established a home and school visitor in one of the city schools for the purpose of insuring a closer tie between the home and the school. In Hartford, the suggestion came from the director of the Psychological Clinic. At first the worker was known as a "special teacher" who assisted the psychologist by gathering case histories and later by carrying out the recommendations.

The school child individualized

What were some of these conditions and changes? A fundamental condition was a school population. Not only was this school population enlarging because of a rising total population but also because of an increasing measure of compulsory school attendance. These changes necessitated shifts in educational philosophy and practice. Before the days of compulsory school attendance there was no great concern expressed for the child who did not keep up in his class work or who raised too great a rumpus in class. The easy thing to do was to drop him out of school. School was for those who could use it as it was. If there was any changing to be done, that was not the province of the school. However, with the advent of compulsory school attendance (which, significantly enough, placed the compulsory requirement upon the state to furnish instruction) there arose the problem of large-sized classes and the tendency toward regimentation upon a mass basis. The individual child stood a good chance of being swamped in the school system.

Teachers, and teachers of teachers, were not uninfluenced by thinking in other fields. From the realm of psychology there emerged concepts of individual differences, of the varying equipments with which individuals came into the world (confirmed by research in biology), and of their

---

[2] At the time of the first edition of this volume (1942) the terms "visiting teacher" and "visiting teacher work" were the accepted expressions, but since then they have come to be replaced, increasingly, by "school social worker" and "school social work." Wherever possible in this revised chapter, the newer terms will be used. However, there will be instances, for historical reasons, where the earlier terms will be used.

capacity to adapt to the changing demands made upon them. Sociologists were concerning themselves with the nature of the social order as well as the modifiability of the human personality. Social workers, too, in their day-by-day casework practice, were learning something about the capacity of the individual to make the adaptation to his environment, together with a fuller understanding of how that environment in turn might be altered to meet the individual's needs.

During the first decade of the twentieth century, the contributions of these various specialties were focused upon the child in school. Because of large classes and concomitant regimentation with stress upon teaching of subject matter and the compulsion upon the child to fit himself into the mold of the school, a countertendency developed that emphasized the needs of the individual child. The shift meant greater attention to the capacity of each child to make the adaptation to the school; it signalized a departure from the traditional role of preoccupation of the school with the intellectual life of the child to a concern for some of the emotional factors that are related to learning. It veered away from the criteria of successful teaching as the inculcation of a quantity of knowledge to the idea that a teacher's success might be more rightly measured by the growth of the child. The newer approach was finding its ultimate expression in the increasing efforts of educators to adapt the school program to the actual needs of a growing child.

The change was accomplished, not by theorizing alone, but by implementing changing philosophies so that practice exemplified theory. Attendance departments, medical inspections, special classes, psychological departments, and special service divisions were instrumentalities by and through which these changes were effected. School social work brought to the school setting an emphasis upon the individual child and with it a technique that augmented the skill of the teacher in dealing with a classroom teaching situation. Let it not be supposed from these sketchy remarks that social casework came as a fully matured professional skill in the years of the first decade of the century; rather, it developed hand in hand with that of teaching in the joint effort to meet the needs of individual children.

Commonwealth fund support [3]

The subsequent development of school social work in this country gave substance to much of the early promise. Following the pioneering efforts of private agencies, a number of public school authorities intro-

---

[3] For historical reasons the term "visiting teacher" is retained in this section on the Commonwealth Fund. See footnote 2 of this chapter.

duced visiting teacher projects into the publicly supported school systems. Rochester, New York may be cited as an early, if not the earliest, instance of such a development. There, in 1913, school social services were supported and controlled by the board of education. The greatest impetus, however, came from the program inaugurated by the Commonwealth Fund with its fourfold approach to the prevention of delinquency. One part of that program was committed to the National Committee on Visiting Teachers, affiliated with the Public Education Association, composed of leaders in the fields of education and social work. Thirty approved centers located in twenty-three states served as bases for visiting teacher demonstration projects. In each instance the community was selected after application (only 30 out of 270 applications were accepted) with the proviso that there would be local sharing (usually one-third) in the payment of the worker's salary and an understanding that if the project demonstrated its worth, it would be taken over by the local community. For the first five years of the period beginning in 1921, the Commonwealth Fund conducted these thirty demonstrations, while for another three years it concentrated its attention upon training teachers for such work, increasing the understanding of behavior problems on the part of teachers in training, improving the standards of the work by field visits and conferences, and advising school systems that were interested in establishing visiting teacher service. After having thus contributed for eight years to a demonstration of the possibilities of this form of social service, the Fund withdrew from the field in June 1930. As of that date, twenty-one of the thirty demonstration communities continued the work as a permanent part of the school system. The contribution of the Fund, however, went far beyond the boundaries of these twenty-one communities. Within the next decade and a half, as the conviction mounted that what was needed was more, not less, social services in the schools, an increasing number of school systems inaugurated such services. Although, inevitably, visiting teacher work spread throughout the larger cities, nevertheless, many small towns and even some definitely rural areas demanded and were willing to pay the price for this service which was rapidly proving its value. Indeed, some of the best work has been done in these smaller communities, an effect not unintended by the Commonwealth Fund.

The child meets the worker

Throughout the twentieth century there has been not only an expansion of the school population, but an expansion of auxiliary services to the school population as well. No longer was the sole objective of the educational system to inculcate a certain amount of knowledge and information into the student. Increasingly educators came to believe that the school experience was more than just preparation for life, it was life itself. The implications of this concept made clear the importance of understanding the child's emotional life and of meeting those needs. Success in school thus became more than attainment of an arbitrary intellectual standard. It consisted more largely in the adjustment of the child in and to the life experience he was undergoing. The child who made a fairly adequate adjustment in the school setting was likely to make a fairly adequate adult adjustment later. This did not necessarily mean he would be richer or more famous, but it did mean he stood a fairer chance of getting sufficient satisfaction out of life to keep an even keel.

The acceptance of this point of view meant that greater attention had to be paid to the growth needs of children in school. The developments of social casework in other fields coincident with this evolving educational practice led, quite naturally, to the use of social casework in the schools. Thus the school social worker became a worker in a school setting, a person whose job it was to offer help to a child, a parent, or a teacher with a problem that centered in the school experience and the child's adaptation or lack of adaptation to it. As a social worker in the school, he may be called a school counselor, a visiting social counselor, a home and school visitor, a visiting teacher, or a school social worker. Administratively, the service may be placed in a department of pupil personnel and counseling, in a division of special services, in a guidance bureau, in a division of child welfare, in the office of the superintendent of schools, or in a separate department of school social services. In most instances the supervisory personnel will be trained social workers. In all instances, regardless of the title of the worker or the organizational location of the service, the ultimate administrative responsibility lodges in the superintendent of schools.

There are advantages as well as disadvantages to such close affiliation with the school. It permits a rather natural approach to the worker by the child and the teacher. Frequently the child comes to accept the worker as a staff member long before he may have occasion to visit or be referred to him. Being on hand to help when things happen or during emergencies (or what seem at the moment to be emergencies) has its strong point. Then, too, the association between the school and the home is a natural situation that very often affords an easy entry into the home, or a comfortable visit by the parent to the office of the school social worker.

On the other hand, there is the likelihood that some of the value of the worker may be sacrificed by too close an identification with the teacher and with the school system. Not infrequently the school social worker will be associated with the authority of the school and the authority of the teacher. The worker must realize that most, if not all, school children are still trying to find themselves in relation to authority—authority in any form: parental, societal, legal, educational. If what the worker offers is indistinguishable from other manifestations of authority, the child may not be able to use school social services. On the other hand, the worker as an integral part of the school system is inevitably and properly related to its authority. Hence, the worker must feel comfortable with the school's authority in order to use it constructively on behalf of the child. There is a fine balance to be maintained here for the worker to be of maximum use to the child, a balance based on the worker's clarity about relation to the authority of the school and on clarity about the worker's professional difference and attendant skills. His usefulness lies in his likeness to the school as well as in his difference in ways of working. As a member of the school staff he shares certain educational objectives with the rest of the staff, but at the same time brings a different professional skill.

Children come to the attention of the worker through referral by teachers, principals, social agencies, occasionally by parents, once in a great while by other children who know the visiting teacher, or by self-referral. The difficulties may be those centering around the child's personality and behavior, or around school adjustments, or detrimental home conditions that have their effects upon the child in school. The service may be rendered to the teacher, the parent, or the child. The quality of the service is the same as that demanded in any other social work agency, that is, according to the best practice in the field of social casework.

All of these points need elaboration. Experience has shown that principals and teachers make most of the referrals. This is understandable, since it is to the teacher that the child presents a problem or is troublesome. The teacher may either attempt to deal with the situation herself or take the matter up with the principal or the school social worker. Should the matter be placed before the principal by the teacher, then it is the principal who makes the referral to the worker. Parents are next most likely to make referrals, followed by social agencies. The attendance department, the medical department, and the psychological testing department are also sources of referrals.

Children are referred for various reasons. The problem that the child presents may not be his fundamental difficulty, it may merely mask it, that is, be a manifestation of some feeling within himself that is expressed in certain kinds of behavior. Scholarship troubles may indicate either lack of mental equipment (which a psychometric test will help to reveal), or they may refer to still more fundamental difficulties not reached by tests and measurements. A child may be failing because he is expected to perform at a level beyond his capacity, or he may actually be working far below his ability because he is emotionally blocked, frustrated, or so torn with inner conflicts as to be unable to organize himself. The boy of 14 years with an IQ of 119 may be failing his first year in high school in large part because of his struggles at home with a tyrannical father and an overindulgent mother. Besides those cases of children failing because of lack of ability or failing although possessed of above-average ability, there are other children of ordinary ability who are failing, or doing very spotty work, or children persistently failing in one subject, or other children with profound lack of interest.

Other children are referred because of health or physical defects. A child, for example, may have been referred for years to the medical service for diseased tonsils and defective hearing. For years the school nurse may have gotten nowhere with the parents and have finally thrown up her hands in dismay and discouragement. Ultimately, this child may come to the attention of the school social worker because of low grades, inattentiveness, and general mischievousness. The worker may immediately discern some connection between deafness, inattention, low grades, new school situations and later find back of them all a father who has stubbornly refused medical care for his child's growing deafness and who, at the same time, has set an enormous premium on high grades. Many cases of this type may first turn up with the school nurse and eventually find their way to the school social worker.

Personality or behavior troubles may also bring a school child to the worker. A discerning teacher may be quick to spot the child continually obsessed with fears and phobias, or the child who is always friendless and unable to mix with his fellows. More usually she may be aware of the child who is continually fighting, or stealing, or truanting. Parents may come to the school and to the worker asking for help for their child who resists staying in school or for the child who has developed habits or practices with which the parents feel powerless to deal, such as enuresis, masturbation, or stuttering.[4]

---

[4] An unusually useful analysis of referrals, especially by school principals, was made by Mildred Sikkema in a study under the joint auspices of the National Association of School Social Workers and the American Association of Social Workers. Principals in the twelve communities in which school social work practice was examined made referral as follows:
1. Children whose behavior becomes progressively more difficult, or whose behavior has become chronic
2. Children who differ considerably from the group over any length of time, who are isolated, won't talk, won't come to school, are unhappy, can't get along with others
3. Children who are not making normal progress within their capacities
4. Children showing sudden change which can't be readily understood and is something more "sensed" than seen
5. Children who, having trouble in school, come from a home situation known to be complicated

What the worker does

While the worker may follow the general procedures of any case-work agency, she necessarily adapts them to the school situation. Even though the child has not asked directly for help and may begin as an unwilling client, nevertheless, the worker may sometimes want to have an interview or interviews with him. Seeing the child may not necessarily be the first step. Very often children, particularly those in the lower grades, are better helped by working through the adults who are already around them as a natural part of their environment. To have another adult, the school social worker, come into the picture would in many instances be too confusing for the child. On those occasions when the worker does see him, he will want to learn from the child something of what he sees of his difficulty, if he sees it at all, and of how or where he feels he needs help and how and where the worker can give it. If the teacher or principal has mentioned the child to the worker, he will want to hear a clear story of the situation as the principal or teacher sees it. Should the parent do the referring, the worker will want to talk with him in order to help to define the problem and to explore with the parent where help is needed. As in any caseworking agency, the application interviews are for the purpose, as Gordon Hamilton puts it, of creating a condition of mutual confidence, of permitting a tentative exploration and diagnosis of the area of difficulty, and of furnishing a preliminary estimate of the applicant's and the agency's capacity to deal with it. As part of the beginning steps, the worker may want to examine school reports, medical reports, psychological tests, but he will always understand that these are supplemental to and not substitutes for personal interviews. If he is to work with the child, he will want to have it clearly understood at the outset whether the interviews are to be regular or occasional. He will also want to clear with the teacher and the principal the distinction between interviews with the child or his parents or with the school people. He will probably need to

---

6. Children who need special class placement
7. Children with attendance problems which are chronic—after teacher and principal have first tried to solve them
8. Children found by the nurse to need help she cannot give

Emphasis is given to the importance of distinguishing between the symptom for which the child is referred and the problem back of the symptom. See Mildred Sikkema, *Report of a Study of School Social Work Practice in Twelve Communities* (New York: American Association of Social Workers, 1953), pp. 16–17, 21–22, 23. Many of these symptoms were underscored by a group of school social workers as recorded in *A Summary of the Workshop on School Social Work Practice* (School Social Work Section, National Association of Social Workers, July 1–6, 1956), p. 3; see also Virginia Quattlebaum, *School Social Work Practice: Proceedings of the Lake Forest Workshop* (New York: National Association of Social Workers, 1958).

arrange for appointments of various kinds for examinations, medical and psychological.

Early in his contacts the worker will determine the basis upon which service will be rendered. In one instance he may decide that the child requires some intensive treatment, which a child guidance clinic is in a better position to offer. This infrequently may involve help for extreme behavior disturbances owing to a physical cause, postencephalitis, or glandular dysfunction, or more likely it may call for protracted therapy with a child whose difficulties are deeply seated with in the personality. The school social worker will continue with the case, but will carry it co-operatively with the clinic, or he will probably arrange for parent and child together to go to the clinic. With another child or in another situation the worker may leave the responsibility of the child's problem with the teacher and reach the child indirectly by reason of the help which he gives to the teacher. A still further possibility is for help to be offered upon a short service basis for those needs that can be met through the medium of the school services, such as special coaching. Much of the effectiveness of such help depends upon the capacity of the individual child, parent, or teacher to change. The essential of the short service contact is an awareness of need, a willingness to change, and a capacity to accept responsibility for the growth which takes place.

Relation to teachers

There has been a distinct reorientation of the school social worker-teacher relationship since the early days when the worker was in reality a "visiting teacher," that is, a person who visited children's homes and brought such information to the classroom teacher as she had managed to uncover. After passing through various stages of trying to educate and then "casework" the teacher, present-day workers have arrived at a working philosophy that regards school social workers and teachers as two different professional people who are working together on a common interest —the child in a school situation—each sharing a mutual goal, which is the development of the child through the medium of the school experience. The worker is of service by helping the child to get more out of the classroom experience or by helping the teacher so that she feels more capable of handling the situations with the child in it. There is a complementary professional relationship involved. The teacher with a class of thirty to forty or fifty children cannot always sacrifice the movement of the group because of a small number of nonconformists. Her primary concern is with the group as a group. On the other hand, the school social worker is dealing with individuals with their own unique needs. If the classroom situation resolves itself into a stalemate between teacher, class, and non-conforming child (or children), then some dynamic will need to be introduced, that is, change either in the child, the teacher, or the situation. This is a legitimate area within which the worker functions. But it must be recognized that change does not come to people unless they are willing to have it. This applies as well to teachers, who are just as much individuals as the children in their classrooms.

Teachers may ask for help of various kinds and for various reasons. They may want help for a child who needs to get over a tough spot in his own development. Even though teachers in training today are getting a great deal more knowledge of mental hygiene than formerly, they still find there are areas in which a more specialized skill needs to be summoned. This recognition of inability to handle certain involved emotional difficulties is as much a part of the teacher's job as is her handling of the subject matter that sets a bound to her teaching field. In most instances of this kind of referral the teacher and the caseworker will need to work together closely, with the focus being kept constantly on the child's adjustment to the school situation.[5]

Working creatively with the teacher

Throughout all of this discussion of the use of the caseworker in the school system there has been an implicit assumption that the two roles of teacher and school social worker are different. No school superintendent and no teacher wants a caseworker to come into a school system and show him how to teach. School officials, teachers, and school social workers realize that what is helpful for the school is a caseworker who will not undertake to usurp the teaching function but will work with teachers to help them handle their own classroom problems more effectively and at the same time will render a service to the children who compose the school.

Much of the caseworker's effectiveness depends upon the way he works with teachers. In the first place, the caseworker recognizes the

---

[5] In this connection, the study of children's behavior and teacher's attitudes by Wickman is revealing. What to the teacher is a serious behavior problem may be rated entirely differently by the mental hygienist. To the teacher defiance of authority, truancy, untruthfulness, and disobedience are serious offenses. To the mental hygienist there are other offenses that rank far higher on the scale, such as shyness, sensitiveness, unsociableness, fearfulness, and dreaminess. The shy and fearful child may never give the classroom teacher any trouble, but he may be on the way to some serious difficulties later on. The disobedient and impertinent child may be an annoyance to the teacher, but he may be making a far more natural adjustment to the school situation than the dreamy or unsociable child.

teacher's feeling about the problem she is bringing. This is especially important since very often some of the problem may be with the teacher, and help can begin only after the teacher has been assisted to an understanding of her part in the situation. The teacher, however, remains the teacher and in no sense becomes the client. Teachers may have a suspicion and fear of a person from another profession on the staff merely because the worker is there. To handle the teacher without the insight and understanding that is expected in any professional relationship is to invite resistance and open antagonism. The reality with which they both work is the problem as the teacher sees it and her feeling about it.

Some teachers are very reluctant to bring notice of classroom difficulties to another person, whether it be principal or caseworker. To do so seems to the teacher a reflection upon her own professional capacity and a confession of failure. Nothing that the caseworker can say will relieve these feelings or invite the teacher to come. Only as the worker carries on his day-by-day job, unthreateningly, and comes to be accepted by the rest of the staff, can teachers feel comfortable about bringing their troubles. The caseworker who recognizes that a teacher may not want to come, by that very attitude, may leave the teacher freer to work with the difficulty alone or eventually to come for help.

In contrast to this situation are those occasions in which the caseworker, through his way of working with the child and the teacher, has made it possible for the teacher to use the experience creatively. Many teachers can take such help, whether they ask for it only casually or deliberately seek it, and use it for their own professional development. In this sense they add not to the teaching content of their courses, but rather to their own capacity to understand more of themselves, their relation to children in the classroom, and their capacity to function more effectively. The objective toward which the worker is striving with the school staff is to assist in such a way that the teacher herself is better able to go on from that point in helping the child. This may consist of helping the teacher to see another side of the child, or to see him as he is, or to accept him as he is. If the teacher can feel that someone else has an interest in her concern with the child, it may release her enough actually to bear some of the heretofore impossible behavior. A child who at one time presented such behavior as to outrage the teacher may become to that same teacher a person whom she can endure and even work with. Likewise, the child who carries the brunt of the teacher's feelings because of what the teacher cannot endure within herself may actually seem to change into a person acceptable to the teacher. On the other hand, the help the worker gives the teacher may be simply to provide the teacher with enough self-confidence and stimulus to work out her program in relation to her students and the classroom situations. Strange as it may seem, the worker's purpose is to be of such help to child and teacher that they can proceed on their own ways alone and under their own power. The worker does not do it for or to them, he does it with them and then withdraws to let them realize their own growth potentials.[6]

Relation to parents

From time to time children evidence in school some of the difficulties in their homes, which hinder them in making normal adjustments. These come to the attention of the school social worker because they have a bearing on the use which the child is making of what the school has to offer. Practically speaking, what happens in the home is almost bound to carry its effects over into the school, if for no other reason than that the child spends so much of his time and his life in the modern school. Within recent years so many of the functions traditionally belonging to the family have been taken over by other institutions, such as the school, that the school bears a much heavier responsibility for the development of the child than it did in those days when its sole task was to inculcate a certain amount of rote learning. In token of this, many parents turn more and more to the school for help with the children. When this happens, the school social worker is in an excellent position to help because the client— here the parent—comes willing to put something of herself into the experience. The worker is also fortunately placed because of his very association with the school because he comes to stand for, for the words of Edith Everett, "an expression of the school's interest in, and concern for the happiness and success of the child who seems at the time not to be fitting into the school regime."

There may be occasions when the parent either does not understand what is going on in school or is indifferent to what is happening to her child by reason of her treatment of him at home. Reference here is not to those flagrant cases of cruel or vicious treatment of the child, which are matters that very often come to the attention of other community agencies, but to the more subtle, and in many instances, unconscious practices that interfere with a child's growth. The parent who shields a child from all responsibility for his schoolwork or for his conduct may be crippling him just as much as, if not more than, if she were indulging in the grosser and more readily condemned cruelties. A child who neither knows nor accepts responsibility for himself is definitely limiting what he can get out of the developmental years of school life. Such a child may be helped by

---

[6] Dollie R. Walker, "Use of the Knowledge of the Casework Process in Collaboration with School Personnel," *Social Work*, 3 (July 1958), pp. 97–103.

the worker if he can work with the child, his teacher, and his parents. He must be allowed to plan part of his program, his teachers must assist in those efforts, and his parents must be helped to realize their share in permitting the normal opportunities for the child's growth. No child can grow to responsible adulthood if other people always make his decisions. Sometimes even well-meaning parents fail to comprehend that.[7]

The burden the child carries

Another child may be compelled to carry too heavy a load. Some parents may feel that this generation is entirely too soft and that what was good enough for them when they were 10 or 12 years old is still good medicine for their children today. Such parents may not always appreciate what this is doing to the child in making him timid and fearful of accepting any responsibility for fear of failure. The heavy load may be the expectations that a brilliant father has built up for his average-ability child, whose brothers and sisters by the roll of the dice of heredity are as brilliant as the father. This child may be haunted by the fear of failure until he actually experiences the marvelous relief that comes of failure under such circumstances. Still another load that is rather heavy for youngsters to carry derives from the instability of a family in which parents are incompatible but still preserving the outward forms of the family, or from a situation in which a child has lost one home and not yet gained foothold in another. Much of the insecurity that stems from such experiences will be reflected in the child's adjustment or lack of it in school. Few children can compartmentalize these two areas of their living.

Still another instance in which the worker functions in the school-home area is to be observed when questions concerned with the child's health are raised. The child, previously mentioned, who was hard of hearing had presented a problem of diseased tonsils and adenoids and running ears to the school nurse for a number of years. Despite the unquestioned fact that the child's condition was actually getting worse, the school had been able to get nowhere with the parents. While the mother was willing to try something, the father was adamant, declaring that no doctor was going to poke around his daughter's ears. To make his case still stronger, the father had convinced himself that the body needed every organ that

---

[7] Dollie R. Walker, "Parents as 'Enablers' in Helping the Child with a School Problem," *Child Welfare*, XXXVIII (March 1959), pp. 11–16; Virginia Quattlebaum, "The Parent as Client," *Child Welfare*, XXXVIII (June 1959), pp. 22–24; Florence Poole, "The School's Professional Responsibility for Casework to Parents," *Child Welfare*, XXXVIII (June 1959), pp. 24–26; Dollie R. Walker, "More on School Social Work," *Child Welfare*, XXXVIII (October 1959), pp. 30–33.

was there, otherwise why did the good Lord put them there? As for his daughter's ears, he was certain that when they stopped running her hearing would be better, but you could not keep them from running as long as there was something there to run.

The handling of a situation of this kind sheds some light on the contribution that a caseworker has to make in the school. After the school nurse and the teachers had given the child and her parents up as hopeless, the worker was called in. A visit to the home revealed that these parents set a tremendous store on high grades. Unfortunately, or fortunately, their child was failing in school. Her increasing deafness made it difficult for her to follow her teachers, and she had been getting more and more inattentive and mischievous. The fact that the next report card would show her deficient in most subjects was more than the parents, particularly the father, could stand. He was not yet ready, however, to do anything about those ears until he had some assurance from the caseworker that the head doctor at the clinic would examine his daughter's ears—"no student was to fool with them." By clearing with the hospital the worker was able to give them this reassurance. At no point, however, did the worker force them in their decision. He recognized that the child was still theirs, that all the force of the school and of the school nurse had come up against a stone wall. The more that pressure was brought against them, the more determinedly they resisted it, until after a while even the daughter was lost in the struggle. It was not until the worker could interpret the matter in the light of what meant so much to them—their child's school record—and could do it not so much by words as by his feeling that this was ultimately their decision, that they could really take the step toward getting help for her. Again and again this same principle of social casework comes out: people still have a right to make their own decisions. What a caseworker does is to assist in the clarification of the question and then help the individuals come to the decision they really want to make.

Relation to the child

The child is the person for whom school social work exists. He may not come to the worker for help as an adult does, and he may not be willing to put as much into taking on help as an adult might. Yet the very fact that he is a child, that he is getting into difficulties, that he would not, voluntarily, come asking for help (even if he knew a social worker when he saw one or understood casework, which he does not), creates a responsibility for adults to make help available to him. The one thing a child has an inalienable right to ask of adults is the right to grow. A necessary corollary to this is the right to be helped when he is having difficulty in growing.[8]

When a question comes up in school about a child's developmental difficulties, it is imperative to keep the service centered in the school. Outside agencies, such as a child guidance clinic, a boys' club or a settlement house, may be used, but the core of the job is still with the child in the school setting. Hardly is this said than one realizes how important the teacher is in such a concept and in its execution.

A caseworker quickly recognizes the differences between children. One aspect of this matter of difference is the response of various children to the referral by another person and an offer of help. Some exhibit fear in diverse forms. This experience faces the child with a new situation and summons up the fear expressions that most of of us employ when we are brought near to the unknown. It may also arouse his fears over loss of control of a situation by appearing to pass under the will of another person. Or he may evidence all kinds of resentment and hostility, which are an attempt to keep another person out. A still further reaction may be to deny the difficulty all together, which serves to limit the entry of a person who wishes to help, while the opposite to this is for the child to admit fully his involvement in the difficulty, which becames an open invitation for the worker to take over the problem.

There are many occasions in which the social worker is dealing with concrete matters pertaining to the child. Service may call for changing a child's class either because he is too far behind or too far ahead in relation to the age and school rank of children around him. A child may need to be transferred to another school or to a special school, depending upon his needs and the availability of other facilities. Perhaps another child requires special tutoring, or a psychological examination, or medical or dental care. Sometimes conditions may be so damaging at home that either home conditions will need to be changed or other arrangements will have to be made. Once in a while the services of other agencies will be called upon, either caseworking or group-working agencies, that is, family society, a child welfare society, a social settlement, Boy Scouts, etc. Within recent years school social workers have become alive to the services of public agencies for children as well as, incidentally, for other members of the child's family. Such public welfare services come to mind as aid to dependent children, aid to the aged, child welfare services, unemployment insurance, and old-age and survivors insurance.

Despite all these services—and one should never underestimate what they mean in the lives of those in need—the fundamental fact remains that the worker is dealing with a human personality. That person-

---

[8] Ruth E. Smalley, "The School Social Worker Helps the Troubled Child," *Social Work*, I (January 1956), pp. 103–108.

ality is contained in, in fact is, a child, with all his hopes, his fears, his likes, his dislikes, his "cussedness," and his likableness. The caseworker can help to change a child's environment and still leave the child in as much trouble as before he appeared on the scene. If any change is to come, it will be because the child (and the teacher and the parent) is willing to have it come, and furthermore, is willing to put something of himself into the changing. A starting point in this process is to be found in the attitude of the child: his attitude toward himself, his home, his school, his difficulties. That in many cases is the most tangible factor the caseworker has to work with. Once attitudes change, other developments follow. It is often said that human nature does not change. Perhaps we are not in agreement upon what human nature is, but this much is certain, that attitudes change. The school social worker is content to work in that area of change, and the change in behavior that follows.

Trends

One very pronounced trend in school social work has been the vertical and horizontal extension of the service. Formerly, the work was restricted to the lower grades; since then it has been extended upward through the high school. Formerly, only the older and more difficult cases were brought to the school social worker, while today efforts are directed more and more to getting help for those youngsters who are just beginning to show signs of trouble. Formerly, the worker was located in schools in the underprivileged parts of the city, today, increasingly, school social services are being made available to the total population in a given city or area. Formerly, the worker was used on an emergency basis—after all other agencies had failed the child, he, the child, was brought to the worker for the purpose of holding off commitment to an institution. Today, the worker's skills are used earlier and more and more as a preventive service.

Consistent with this shifted emphasis has been the change in the school's attitude toward "problem" children and toward the school social worker. No longer does the referral of a child imply failure, no longer is it a negative reflection upon the quality of teaching. Rather it is a recognition that there are certain difficulties in the classroom that the teacher knows to be more within the province of a specialist, and a realization that good teaching requires a yielding of the problem to another rather than a jealous guarding of it. Furthermore, the teacher remains active by sharing with the caseworker the helping service for the child. More and more teachers are developing a responsibility to the child that goes beyond his intellectual needs. Under such conditions the child (a hundred or a thousand of them) is actually better equipped to utilize what the school has to offer, and a higher level of performance is inevitable. For the child there is no longer the stigma attached to referral to the school social worker, particularly since all children at one time or another evidence difficulties in school that they are having around growing up. Referral may mean that this is the first specific offer of help that has come to him.

One token of the increased acceptance and usefulness of the service is the demand for consultative service by principals, teachers, and parents. Principals desire consultation not only about children's behavior problems but also about some of the perplexities of dealing with a school staff. Frequently the worker will be used in staff conferences to help in staff development projects. Teachers, themselves, very often will bring to the caseworker some of their problems. These may be beyond the ken of the worker and he will suggest the proper agency, or, if it pertains to the school situation, the worker may give what help he can. Parents, too, have come to talk over a child's difficulties or their difficulties with a child, just as they would consult as freely and as easily another social agency.

Group work and community relationships have received an increasing share of attention within recent years. School social workers have met with groups of teachers or groups of parents in order to help with problems centered in the school. Active participation in parent-teacher associations have, in many cases, been considered a part of the role that the school social worker plays in the community. By reason of his strategic position as a social worker and as a school person he frequently has occasion to interpret each field to the other. In many communities he is the one person upon whom the responsibility falls for making known the unmet needs of children and for furnishing the stimulus to meet those needs. Thus he not only interprets the school, its philosophy, and its practice to the community but brings firsthand notice of what is lacking in the community in order that the schools may be enabled to do a still better job.

School social work traditionally has been rather closely associated, if not in practice at least in thought, with truancy and attendance work. Some of its early connections with the school were through the attendance department. In other places, school social workers resisted being tagged along with "hooky cops" and maintained that theirs was a social casework, not a legal or compulsive service. Nevertheless, the school social worker as a part of a school system that has compulsory attendance laws is obliged not only legally but by his very profession to accept the realities and the limitations that attach to his job. He is a part of the authoritative setup of the school. The child who is truanting, for example, needs help. That help is offered by facing up with the child the rules under which they both operate. The youngster needs just that sureness, that definiteness, from a person who is in a helping role.

Within the last decade or so there has been a trend toward co-

ordinating these and other school services, including the medical, psychological, and guidance. Some school systems have no provisions for caseworkers but have for attendance officers. The tendency has been to employ
caseworkers wherever vacancies occur in order to strengthen the service
of the school. In such a coordinated scheme the school social worker has
insisted upon a clear definition of casework function that sought to give
help to the individual whether truant or not. The worker is interested in
truancy, not for the sake of instituting court action, but because truancy
may so often be but a symptom of an underlying maladjustment either
within the child or in his home or school environment.[9]

Another trend is in the direction of setting up the service on a state-
wide basis. Heretofore, school social services were associated with particular cities—Rochester, Minneapolis, Philadelphia, Pittsburgh, San Diego,
Cleveland, Los Angeles, Portland, being a few of the several hundred.
However, within the past few years Virginia, Louisiana, Michigan, and
Georgia have instituted provisions for such services throughout all school
districts. The programs that have been legislated in these four states differ
according to definition, method of state-wide coverage, integration into
school systems, qualifications of workers, and basis of payment. Despite
these understandable and inevitable variations the significance lies in the
movement toward a casework service to reach all children during their
critical school years.

---

[9] Martha Perry very pertinently observes: ". . . Compulsory education laws, and
attendance departments to enforce them, were an early reflection of a need for protection of neglected and exploited children. With the growth of the mental hygiene
movement, visiting teachers with social work background became increasingly valued
by the schools, but they deliberately divorced themselves from attendance departments
because of their connotations of authority and compulsion. As child guidance clinics
developed in the schools, with a dual responsibility to help the individual child and to
further the schools' understanding of all children, a changing concept of attendance
work has also occurred in some places. But a recognition that handling truant children
is a case work job requiring a diagnostic rather than a legal approach has lagged sadly
behind a recognition of the symptomatic nature of other types of behavior problems.
As a paradoxical result, the child whose personal or home difficulties lead him to
truancy is treated as a violator of the law; but if his difficulties lead him to other kinds
of atypical behavior, he is treated as a clinical problem requiring expert professional
diagnosis and treatment." Martha Perry, "Truancy Is Not a Crime," *Better Times*,
XXVII (December 7, 1946), pp. 1, 14.

For a valuable exposition of the integration of school social work and attendance
services in four communities—Indianapolis, Minneapolis, San Diego, Pittsburgh—see
the entire March 1951 issue of *The Bulletin of the National Association of School Social
Workers*.

School social services in Charlotte, North Carolina, developed out of an earlier
attendance program. School social work is now an integral part of the Division of
Special Services of the Charlotte-Mecklenburg School System. For a clear and percep-
tive presentation of the essentials of the service see the pamphlet prepared by Anne
Hausmann, Director of the Attendance and Social Work Department, entitled "School
Social Work: An Instrument of Education," 1961.

A glance at the forepart of this chapter will reveal the impetus that was given to visiting teacher work by the Commonwealth Fund. The early emphasis, it will be recalled, was upon the prevention of delinquency. Two decades later the primary emphasis is to provide a constructive treatment for all children. It has turned from a negative to a positive role. Undoubtedly it can truly be said that its possibilities are unlimited once that objective is implemented in practice. Perhaps this is nowhere better stated than in an article by Edith Everett entitled "The Dynamic of Case Work in School Counseling." Using the terms "school counselor" and "school counseling" for visiting teacher and her work, she wrote:

> For the child himself, the counselor offers the opportunity to experience for a time a school relationship which is different from that with the group. He finds in it respect for him as a person, a new awareness of himself as an individual and the beginning at least of an ability to accept the requirements of the school as just and right for himself and others. For the majority of children this comes naturally, as part of their growing up. But in the classroom as in society as a whole there are always some who are unfortunately caught at some point in their development and are "flying blind." Help for them at the right moment to clear some of the fog and get a straight course set, is as much the business of the school as is their attention to the educational process set up for the entire group.[10]

Bibliography

Benedict, Agnes, *Children at the Crossroads*. New York: The Commonwealth Fund, 1930.

Boston, Opal, "School Social Services," *Social Work Year Book*, 14, pp. 517–523. New York: National Association of Social Workers, 1960.

Conant, James Bryant, *Slums and Suburbs: A Commentary on Schools in Metropolitan Areas*. New York: McGraw-Hill Book Company, Inc., 1961.

Culbert, Jane F., *The Visiting Teacher at Work*. New York: The Commonwealth Fund, 1929.

Everett, Edith, "The Importance of Social Work in a School Program," *The Family*, XIX (March 1938), pp. 3–8.

Johnson, Arlien, *School Social Work: Its Contribution to Professional Education*. New York: National Association of Social Workers, 1962.

Lee, Grace, ed., *Helping the Troubled School Child: Selected Readings in School Social Work, 1935–1955*. New York: National Association of Social Workers, 1959.

[10] Edith M. Everett, "The Dynamic of Case Work in School Counseling," in Jessie Taft, ed., *Social Case Work With Children* (Philadelphia: Pennsylvania School of Social Work, 1940), p. 184.

Nebo, John C., and Jane Wille, "Children with Social and Emotional Problems," *The Illinois Plan for Special Education of Exceptional Children*, rev. ed. Illinois Office of Public Instruction, 1960.

Nesbit, Elsie, and Florrie B. Still, *The Visiting Teacher in Georgia*. Atlanta, Georgia: The State Department of Education, 1955.

Oppenheimer, J. J., *The Visiting Teacher Movement*. New York: Public Education Association, 1924.

Poole, Florence, and Mildred Sikkema, "An Analysis of the Structure and Practice of School Social Work Today," *The Social Service Review*, XXIII (December 1949), pp. 447–459.

Quattlebaum, Virginia, *School Social Work Practice: Proceedings of the Lake Forest Workshop*. New York: National Association of Social Workers, 1958.

Ryan, W. Carson, *Mental Health through Education*. New York: The Commonwealth Fund, 1938.

Sikkema, Mildred, *Report of a Study of School Social Work Practice in Twelve Communities*. New York: American Association of Social Workers, 1953.

Smalley, Ruth E., "School Counseling as Social Work," *Bulletin of the National Association of School Social Workers*, XXX (June 1955), pp. 21–34.

Walker, Dollie R., "Direct Work with Children in a School Setting," *Journal of Social Work Process*, 8 (1957), pp. 61–72.

Wille, Jane, "The Relation of the School to Protective Service for Children," *Bulletin of the National Association of School Social Workers*, XXIV (June 1949), pp. 19–26.

MICHAEL KATZ

MRS. DOLLIE R. WALKER
Specialist in School Social Work
Division of Special Services for Pupils
Baltimore Public Schools, Maryland

When a normal, intelligent child is offered the opportunity of a sound education, the chances are that he not only welcomes this school experience but finds ways to enjoy it. On the other hand, if he resists school, fights the authority invested in principal and teacher, and if he is rebellious in his attitudes, it is safe to say that an examination of those factors in the school and in the home that affect his learning is in order.

By and large it is the teacher [1] who is first to realize that the child is in trouble with school, and it is this trouble that cuts across her efforts to teach him to use and develop his mind. If he is physically ill, the teacher, without apology or sense of failure, will refer him to the school nurse or physician. If he is troubled and troublesome, a teacher alert and sensitive to the needs of children, will refer him to the school social work service [2] with the same degree of ease and comfort.

School social work in both the elementary and high school is for the purpose of assisting the school in reaching its goal of educating children by giving a needed specialized service to the individual child. This means that the focus is on helping the troubled child resolve his basic conflict in relation to school. The presence of a social work service in a school gives the expectation and hope that the individual child can give up some of his fight, resolve some of his conflict, and relate to the values the school offers him and others. If a social worker can help one child to relinquish his unacceptable behavior in the school, it may open the way for him as well as for others in his group to receive a more comfortable and a more rounded education.

In the case material that will follow, the school social worker finds a human connection with a junior high school pupil through the use of casework. Her help is given within the framework of a school and is geared to helping the troubled child utilize his basic urge to grow and change [3] in relation to his particular school problem. This material will at-

---

[1] This does not exclude the principal, counselor, nurse, or some other school personnel.

[2] Or to some other specialized service for help.

[3] Change as used here is seen as a process, a movement back and forth, a sorting out of alternatives that have not proved satisfactory against reality exigencies. It may be conceived as a giving up of something (in this instance, inner conflict) in order to reach a given goal.

tempt to show the use of casework as a method of helping a child to become involved in changing his destructive behavior and in using his ability to learn. No description of a troubled child's growth and change in relation to a school problem would be complete without at least a brief description of the involvement of the teacher and parent in helping the child.

Let us look at Michael.[4] Here is a boy who very much needs specialized individual help if he is ever to utilize his opportunity for an education and find his rightful place in the community. The school social worker begins with the counselor.

Referral conferences with school personnel—March 1960

Mr. Brown, counselor, spoke with me about Michael for the first time on 2/16/60 stating that he believed a referral to me should be considered. Michael, who would be 14 years of age on 5/3/60, had achieved above grade level in reading and arithmetic when he was tested in February 1959, and was failing every subject. Mr. Brown had talked with his parents and tried to encourage Mike to study. His "pep talks" had not helped, and Mike continued to be a nuisance to his teachers. Although he had very interested parents, they had not been able to help him to improve his conduct or effort. His mother had asked for the referral. I agreed that a referral to me seemed in order, and Mr. Brown said he would discuss it with the Coordinator of Special Services as usual.

On 3/1/60, Mr. Bernstein, vice-principal and Coordinator of Special Services, Mr. Brown, counselor, and Mrs. Jones, the teacher who had first called the matter to the attention of the counselor, and I evaluated the school problem that Mike was presenting.

Mrs. Jones, who came to me before I had a chance to tell her about the conference, repeated on 3/1/60 an account of her effort to help Mike to make some effort to do his math assignments. He was a regular "class clown" and tried in every way he could to get the attention of the class away from what she was teaching, it seemed. Mr. Brown had a good bit to say about the effort he had made but to no avail. Mr. Bernstein remembered Mike as a good-looking, well-dressed boy, who had been sent to the office for being a disrupting influence in the class. Mrs. Jones said she had sent him there too because he seemed unable to sit still more than five minutes at the most. Mr. Bernstein stated that he would inform Mike's

---

[4] Michael Katz, born 5/3/46; 8th grade; Kuhlman-Anderson 2/58, IQ 108; Otis 9/58, IQ 115. Reading 10.8, arithmetic 8.1. His referral form filled out by the counselor indicated that he came from a seemingly nice family; had above-average intelligence yet receives D's (deficiency) in all subjects. His parents are very worried about Michael. The father is recovering from a serious injury sustained in an accident. The counselor worked with Michael but with little success. The mother asked for help.

parents of the school's decision to refer the matter to the school social work service. Mrs. Jones, a probationary teacher, was blaming herself because she could not get him to learn, but her learning that other teachers, especially the Spanish teacher, were having problems seemed to give her some feelings at least it was not all her fault. Mr. Brown repeated that Michael was failing every subject.

The teacher wanted to know from me right away what was wrong and how to correct it. I was sorry I did not have a ready answer but emphasized my feeling that Mike had a lot to do with whether or not we could help him improve his achievement and conduct. I would need her cooperation and would let her know my opinion as to what I might be able to do to help when I conferred again with the three of them on March 10. In the meantime, I would see Mike and his parents and evaluate the situation with them.

Here we see three disciplines together in a large junior high school finding their relationship to each other and to the purpose of the institution they serve. They are concerned about Michael's getting an education. Planfully they begin by combining their efforts to see whether or not the child can be helped by them.

This worker began with the teacher by recognizing her as a professional colleague who could justifiably find Michael's behavior as a class clown difficult to take. She recognized the difference between helping the teacher and displaying knowledge as she answered truthfully that she did not know what was wrong with Michael or how to correct his behavior. The worker did not make a prediction for she operated with the knowledge that she could not control what the child could do with her or determine the outcome of the casework process. She could only try to help him. Mike, however, must be willing and able to assume some responsibility for seeking and accepting help for himself in order to get rid of his undesirable behavior in school. There was an awareness that she could not help a child adjust to school if there was no teacher for him to relate to and that she and the teacher needed each other in this job that was jointly theirs to do.

Mike's situation had to be explored with his parents as well as with him.

Summary of interviews with parents—March 1960

Mr. Bernstein, the coordinator, informed Mrs. Katz of my presence in the school and of his referring Mike to me. Mrs. Katz had asked that he do anything he could to help her son. She told him of her husband's having had an auto accident as she had told Mr. Brown, the counselor. Although she knew she would hear from me within the week concerning an appointment, Mrs. Katz came in on the afternoon of March 1st—immediately after she learned of the referral. I was not free to see her; she went to Mr. Brown, who telephoned me, and I talked with her as soon as I could find a few minutes. We arranged an appointment for March 8. I wanted to talk with Mike before seeing her again.

She was a rather youthful woman to have a son nearing 14. Mr. Brown had described her as "Mrs. Hollywood"; the slightly excessive amount of make-up for daytime use, the fancy hair style etc., made it easy for me to understand his description. Even though Mrs. Katz was rather extremely dressed, she was stylish and quite attractive. Her anxiety was obvious as she rushed on to tell me about her thankless effort, her husband's illness, her son's failure to achieve or to have acceptable conduct.

She emphasized how glad she was that Mike had been referred to me and refused to consider the other side of her feelings in the matter; namely, her embarrassment for her child's being referred to the school social worker when she knew he had enough intelligence to do what was being expected of him. She described him as a likable boy who resembled her and warned me of how he "can pull your leg." Mrs. Katz was under a great deal of pressure because she had more responsibility for the family business since her husband suffered a concussion in an auto accident in December 1959. I felt she must have been expecting even more of Mike now that his father could neither give to the business nor to her what she had been used to receiving. She denied this, stating that Mike was not learning long before her husband became ill. I thought she really had her hands full.

When Mrs. Katz came in for her appointment on March 8, she was more ready to look at the situation from all points of view. Mr. Katz was willing to see me as soon as he was able. It was very obvious that Mrs. Katz felt very injured by her son's lack of achievement. When she described a typical evening at home, it sounded as if she were nagging Mike to death. We discussed her feelings at some length with my emphasizing the fact that I would be trying to help him to understand how he could improve the situation at school and how I could help him. She accepted my feeling that unless she found a way to help him begin to want for himself what she wanted for him, there would be little hope for improvement. She thought she understood what she could do at home. She really had not tried to control the nagging. The mother could say that Mike's behavior deteriorated as the months went by. She told what he was like after one of these sessions. "What is he like when you don't nag?" I asked. There was a long silence, and then she said she really did not know as she always nagged. Neither Mrs. Katz nor I tried to visualize what it would be like if she tried to control her impulse to ride him about his schoolwork, and she said quietly that she would like to try. We agreed to keep in touch regularly as planned.

The worker respected the rights and responsibilities of the mother, Mrs. Katz, in relation to her child with the school problem. There was identity with the mother's hope and despair and an acceptance of the parents' rights to standards different from her own. She knew that it would not be helpful to Mike to diagnose his problem in terms of Mrs. Katz's nagging, pressuring, and her husband's illness. The question gently put but very telling, "What is it like when you don't nag?" helped Mrs. Katz to organize herself into considering whether there was some way she could refrain from nagging and whether a different experience with her son would yield a larger return. It also placed value and expectation on the parent, an expectation that she could change. There was a willingness to relate to the mother as she was rather than to the way the worker would like for her to be. Thus, we know that without a doubt some of Mike's problem is in the home, but the worker who is there to help him did not lose sight of the fact that the problem was also inside of him.

Interviews with the child—early March 1960

Michael Katz is an attractive, tall, well-developed, well-dressed boy with wavy brown hair. He seemed quiet, almost shy, as I began with him by telling him who I was and what I did in the school in relation to trying to help pupils to realize what they and I could do to alleviate their school problems. It was hard for me to imagine him the "class clown" as he fumbled with his hands and squirmed around in his chair. When he became aware of my noticing his discomfort, he made a decided effort to pull himself together and talk in a grown-up manner. He struggled to find the words that he seemed to think I would accept as he admitted he was failing every subject. He at first denied being a behavior problem to teachers but had to admit this too when we discussed his not paying attention and how this affected the other pupils.

I believed him when he told me, after I said something of my understanding how hard it was to talk to a stranger and a grownup at that, how much he really wanted to pass. He would like to please his parents and teachers but he did not seem able to bring himself to getting down to work and sticking to it.

As he described himself, he sounded like a very lazy boy, and as I said this to him we both laughed. Mike seemed to relax some but continued to emphasize how hard it was for him to keep his mind on his work. He sounded as if he really doubted his capacity to do so. He replied that his teachers wanted to "make my parents feel good," when they said he could.

I asked what he did instead of his work in class, and his reply left no doubt as to the reason for his nickname. I felt that even though the students believed he did not care, I wanted him to know that I was well aware of the fact that the man who is "the life of the party" is not usually the happiest one there. Mike turned away from me as I said it was possibly harder for him to let a woman know how he felt than it was for anyone else. Couldn't he trust anyone to know how he really felt? Mike managed to hold the tears from overflowing but he talked more freely then.

His parents did not understand that he wanted to learn, they punished him when he did not bring home satisfactory marks. He felt like the "family disgrace" on the one hand, but got some satisfaction out of not doing what they wanted on the other. Mike seemed well aware that they could not "make" him learn as I brought this to his attention. We discussed at length the meaning that his choice in the matter had. He had shown all persons concerned that he could refrain from learning if he decided to do so. Did he want to let it remain this way?

Although we could not go very far with this in the first interview, it was no struggle for me to get Mike to agree to three consecutive interviews in which we could go into the situation thoroughly: the purpose I had with him, the choices he could make, and an agreement on how we would go about it. He would then know what help he could expect from me, his teachers, and perhaps his parents as well. If he wanted to work to improve the situation, I was sure he could decide how he could help himself. We would decide by March 25. I would let the school personnel know what I felt to be the problem after our second interview on March 8.

On March 8, Mike seemed to be thinking seriously about what he really wanted to do. Even though I believed him, I told him of my doubt that he would take a chance on studying so late in the term. He could still fail. Mike was very determined to convince me that he meant to try. I thought that by the time he reached home, found that he did not know very clearly what had been asked of him, etc., he would give up his good intentions. Mike assured me this would not happen.

As the worker undertakes to involve Michael in a casework process, there is a belief and conviction on her part that he is the center of his own change. There is faith in the relationship as a means by which Michael, with her help, begins to use himself differently not only with her but in the classroom, with his teachers, and with his peers. Her warmth, her interest, and deep concern were offered to him with skill and knowledge, and from her beginning contact she was there in a realistic way for him. She was clear about her function and stayed within it by keeping a sharp focus on the school problem that brought Michael to her attention. The part that belonged to Michael was brought out into the open and in a way that he could accept accountability.

He tried to justify his failure in learning and his disrupting exhibitions in the classroom by placing the blame on his parents. The worker passed that part that belonged to Michael back to him by saying "He had shown all persons concerned that he could refrain from learning. Did he want to let it remain this way?" To her, he was a boy with will and determination and not a mere victim, powerless in the face of his problem. As she worked with him, she responded to any evidence of strength, will, and creativeness within the child. These were his possessions to be freed and used by him.

Through the social worker, Mike was helped to engage himself positively instead of continuing to use his will to fight her, his parents, and school. She realized that he, too, wanted an education, and he could achieve it, not for the worker, the school, or his parents, but for himself. The worker, understanding the meaning of being the class clown, was able to relate to the way Mike felt about himself (the inner) regardless of how he acted (the outer). It involved knowing Mike's basic assumption not only about himself but about his teachers, his parents, and classmates.

Michael's doubts and uncertainties about wanting help did not escape the worker. In dealing with them, she set up three consecutive interviews for the purpose of enabling Michael and her to know whether or not he could begin moving out of the impasse he had reached at school.

Further interviews with child—
March 1960

In our interview on March 16, Mike began with the same kind of lengthy discussion of how much he wanted to improve his classwork. I reminded him that this was our third interview and that I had no evidence from him or his teacher (I had been in regular touch with Mrs. Jones since Mike and I had agreed that math was a good place to start) that he was making any definite effort to improve. There had been times when he had not brought in his homework nor made any effort to participate in class. He was quiet but out of the activity. Mike insisted that this had not been true in the previous week—just the first one after we met. I said he had always told me he wanted to improve, but unless he had something to show he was trying, I failed to see the difference that our interviews made. Mike agreed. We discussed what he considered to be a "typical school day" and that day was like the rest. We looked at what he had done in the morning before his seeing me. In one class, he had been quite responsible about his part in what was expected. We came to science, the class Mike had told me earlier he liked best. He did not know where his textbook was and used this as an excuse for not knowing his homework assignment. I told Mike that I thought I understood what had been said to me about his being able to "pull my leg." I assured him that I would not permit him to miss classes to continue interviews with me when he did nothing about our reason for seeing each other. It was not up to me to decide whether he would try to do his work or not and I knew that I could not "make" him. From March 2nd, when we had our first interview, to March 16th, when we were ending our third, he had done nothing but say what he wanted to do.

Mike became very upset when I asked how he had lost his science book.

He could not be sure when or where he was when he missed it. I learned that he had lost books before; his parents had paid for one recently. He found it later but was not concerned enough to return it to get his refund. I told him that I felt a boy who was failing every subject could ill afford to waste time "enjoying" interviews with the school social worker. I had spent considerable effort making sure he saw me at times when he had his minor subjects and could easily make up the time he lost from class. I considered his time precious. Since he was doing nothing but talking, I said I thought it would be better for him to spend his time in class now that he was no longer keeping the other children from learning as he had been doing with his clowning.

Mike stood up to leave, his face reddened, and he started for the door. As he turned, he pointed to the calendar on my desk, while saying something about trying to find his science book. I said that having the equipment with which to work might convince me that he meant to try. If he could not find the book, he at least could get his refund on the other lost book and purchase the missing science book. Otherwise, what was the point? Mike's eyes filled with tears. I said that I had told school personnel on March 10th I felt I could help him to help himself. Perhaps I had made a mistake. Nevertheless, I would be there if he decided to make the effort immediately.

Mike came back the same afternoon and told me that he had found the book in one of the shop classrooms where he had left it on a shelf. He had his science homework—the teacher had been willing to help him. Also, he had his refund from the school office. He would take it to his mother. It was about four o'clock, and all of the other children had left the building. I asked Mike to sit down for a few minutes, which he did willingly. He had made this step in the direction of being able to improve the situation. I wanted to know what he thought we could do from that point on.

He told me he had felt there was no point in trying to do what his parents wanted. No matter what he accomplished, it would not be enough for them. They punished him by not allowing him to attend his fraternity meetings whenever he brought home marks that did not satisfy them. I knew Mike was aware of my seeing his mother and of my plan to see his father as soon as he was able to talk with me. If they were expecting too much of him, I would discuss it with them and I was sure they would consider how he felt. If he received more satisfaction from punishing his parents, by not doing what they knew he could do in school, than from what he gained by putting forth his best effort, then it was up to him. I was not there to persuade him to do what all of us felt he could do. As I had said to him before (and this time Mike understood), my job was to help him to decide what he wanted to do about his lack of achievement. Mike smiled as he said he supposed there was no point in my trying to help him to do "nothing." I said he was right, he could manage that all by himself.

He looked pathetically humorous standing there with his long arms dangling; his eyes filled with tears while he smiled with the bottom half of his face and stared at the science book, which he had placed on my desk. I said, "Mike you are really a mess, aren't you?" He assured me that things would not stay that way; he would work so hard I wouldn't believe my eyes. I said that what happened between him and me, such as today's interview, did not leave my office. He had hinted about not being able to "live it down" if his teachers or the students knew how he felt, etc.

We confirmed the March 25th appointment, which Mike kept on time and in a very businesslike manner. We evaluated the whole situation, and he showed me what he had been doing meanwhile. I told him I would communicate to Mrs. Jones, Mrs. Brown, and Mr. Bernstein my belief that I would be able to help him after all. He was sure he had convinced his parents that what he was doing in school was different. I had no doubt that Mike and I would be together as we faced his successes and disappointments from that point on.

Here was a chance for Mike to work on his own stake in change in spite of his fear. The element of choice was present in the first interview when the worker risked the relationship in freeing Michael to work with her. In the preceding interview we see Michael in the act of rechoosing. Without a doubt, he understood clearly the grounds on which she would continue to see him. Steady identification with her function put in the difference and focus that Michael needed. By controlling her part in the process, she gave Michael a chance to come to grips with his own desire to change. She held him to doing something about the science book—something tangible that would convince her that he really wanted help.

Interviews with child—April 1960

In the week-by-week interviews in April, Mike showed that he meant to stay with his decision to study and shared with me his difficulties, which were mainly related to his lack of confidence in himself. The spring holiday from the 15th to the 25th cut into our time, but we discussed what he could do on his own, and Mike felt that he had had so much "holiday" all term that he could well use this time to catch up on his notebooks, etc. He asked for extra reports to do, and the teachers willingly obliged.

His actual lack of knowledge in mathematics, which had increased during the weeks when he put forth little or no effort, began to show itself as a real problem. Mr. and Mrs. Katz had offered to get a tutor for Mike in the previous semester, and he had said he would not work with him. At this point, however, he was asking whether they would still consider it.

Mr. Brown, the counselor, saw Mike with my knowledge as soon as he returned after the holiday. He had to consider with him his placement for the term, which would begin in September. He was so impressed with the difference in Mike's attitude and what he was able to show him in the way of definite improvement that he mentioned the possibility of summer school and a trial in ninth grade, instead of his repeating the eighth as he had been sure would be necessary just a month earlier. Mike's being in the middle of his junior high experience gave him a better chance for "the benefit of the doubt" than he would have had if he had been in his third or last year. Mike left Mr. Brown knowing that if he passed all subjects except two (he knew he would fail Spanish), he could attend summer school.

Mr. Brown recommended a math tutor whom he knew. Mike's parents made the arrangements for him to begin on May 1st. Mike's insecurity about what he was able to do when he began to be aware of how much academic work he had missed became very obvious during the month of May 1960. We continued our interviews each week during this month since a less frequent schedule was not indicated even though the school term was near the end. Somehow he managed to speak with me almost every day in the hall or in the yard, except when we had planned interviews. On two occasions, he knocked on my door while changing classes to say he was going to take a test. One day he was positively trembling as he stood at my door saying "Mrs. Todd, I've got to take a test in math." I thought if he did not hurry he would be late. He did not know whether he could make himself remember anything he had studied. He knew he would surely not pass the test. I told him if he did not take it, I knew he would get a zero and even a low mark was better than that. What did he have to lose by taking it? Possibly he would gain something! I assured him the world would not end and that one test would not make all the difference between passing and failing or knowing and not knowing. I expected him to go and take it and live with the "butterflies" in his stomach. I knew he could do it.

Mike rushed on to class, and when the test was over and he was on his way to his next class, he stopped back and told me he had been surprised by how much he had been able to remember. He was sure he had not done very well, but at least he thought he had passed. In our interview the following week, Mike began to look back at the time when he believed his lack of knowledge had begun to pile up. He spoke of elementary grades and how he had not had to work very hard in order to make quite satisfactory marks. He supposed he had never really learned to study. The teachers had liked his parents and often they had been friendly. He was quite relaxed in his classes and never really felt he was "on the spot" so to speak. I assured Mike that he must have learned just the same. I doubted that a boy in seventh grade could do as well as he on his achievement tests if he had not been learning. It was possibly true that he had been so relaxed that the work had not seemed difficult for him. I was sure that junior high school had presented quite a different picture and that the situation had grown worse since he began in 1958. This was obvious from the slowly decreasing grades that Mike had received. There was a great deal of difference between elementary school with one main teacher and junior high with seven.

Mike's report card for the third quarter showed no improvement over the previous one at the end of January 1960. He was still failing all major subjects with the exception of two. This was disappointing to him, but as we had discussed it later, he was able to see that the increase in his effort could not possibly have shown on the report card that he received in April. He was now willing to accept the opportunity to attend summer school and possibly have a "trial" in the ninth grade, or to get nothing more out of this than the relief of knowing that he could learn again and had the willingness to repeat the eighth grade if necessary. At the point where Mike was not working just for passing, it seemed to me he began to take in much more of what was being taught.

Mrs. Katz, Michael's mother, gave him a rather rough time about the deficiency cards. The following day I saw him during the first period walking down the hallway giggling with other children and seeming to be as disorganized as he had been when I first met him. I called him aside and spoke with him, saying his mother had telephoned me and I was sure he was feeling pretty badly this morning. Mike looked away and reminded me about our interview that afternoon.

When Mike came in for his interview, he went through what had happened between him and his mother. I shared with him something of what she had said to me on the telephone and something more of what I knew it was like for parents, when children they loved as much as his parents loved him failed to live up to their expectations. Mike assured me he was no longer trying to make marks for his mother or refusing to make them because of her or his father. He wanted (for himself) to pass eighth grade and have a chance in ninth grade. He was "scared to death" that what he would be able to do would be too little and too late for him to make much progress this term. He thought that if by this time they could not realize how he felt, there was nothing more he could do. He was willing to give up all over again. At the end of the interview, however, I believed that Mike realized he could not stick with his best studying effort each period each day and that I did not expect that he would be able to do this. He was surprising himself each day he received a compliment from a teacher, and their encouragement was increasing.

At our interview of May 15th Mike insisted, "Mrs. Todd, if I ever get through this, no one will have to worry about me again." I knew Mike was thinking also about my not continuing with him after I left school on June 10. He was not ready to end with me and wanted assurance that I would see him again in September. I told him that even though it was very near the end of the term, I would be sticking with him and his school situation to the last minute. We did not need to decide that day whether I would end with him then or when it would be. It was true that we would not have very long to work toward ending, but the plans for him for next term would be settled before I stopped seeing him. This was all he really needed from me I thought, and he agreed.

In the middle part of the process, one can see how tensions mounted in Mike and how much he needed more than ever the support and encouragement of the worker. It must have been a relief to him when the worker took the attitude she did regarding the deficiency card and his mother's reaction to it. There was no shame nor sham shown in his need for the worker to help him accomplish his own purpose. There were deeper levels of confidence shown as he found the courage he needed to take a test by merely looking in on her and hearing from her, "You can do it." This child, who had struggled with his lack of self-esteem, began overcoming his self-doubts but needed the worker's continued involvement in his efforts. This was equally true in her continued contact with his parents. They too, needed to believe in Mike's change and in his efforts to help himself.

Further planning with parents—
April and May 1960

Mother

Mrs. Katz had a difficult time, she told me, trying not to nag Mike after she had discussed with me her feelings about the situation. At that time we agreed she was helping to perpetuate the vicious circle of his wanting to punish her by not doing what she expected while she punished him by denying the privileges he thought he deserved. Now she was closing herself in the bathroom and covering her mouth with her hand, etc., when she felt like screaming at him, but she felt he was truly trying now. She knew he could "not change over night."

I was impressed with what Mrs. Katz was saying to me concerning her effort to be of help to Mike at home. She had encouraged him to go out at least on a Sunday afternoon instead of doing nothing but schoolwork. She was afraid he would not be able to stick to it. Mike had asked permission to attend school on a Jewish holiday, and she had agreed. If he would only let her help, even if it were no more than arranging a more suitable light for him or something. He was eating less too; she guessed that was good, for he used to be fat. "Maybe that was why he felt so insecure." It was hard for her to be on the outside at times, I knew, but she agreed he was the one who had to do it.

When deficiency cards were issued in May 1960, Mrs. Katz had not understood that they took into account a child's average for the entire school term up to the date of their issuance. She had forgotten all of our well-laid plans for her leaving Mike free to choose the rate of speed at which he would move in his learning or chose to involve himself in studying. She went back to her old nagging, threatening, and denying him privileges. Mike had been hurt, but he said nothing to her, and she seemed stunned by the difference in his attitude. The following day after he left home for school, she telephoned me and said, "Mrs. Todd, I really goofed." She knew from his facial expression after she had scolded him that he was even more hurt by the deficiency cards than she. When I told her what I knew about the deficiency cards and how teachers were obligated to notify parents when there was any possibility for a child's failure in June of a school year, Mrs. Katz understood how Mike could not possibly have avoided getting it. I told her too that many children had questions about bringing home a deficiency card when they knew their parents would not understand, and sometimes they signed the parent's name and returned the card without their parents knowing they had received it. Mrs. Katz then felt very "humble" to her son for being willing to let her know what was happening with him. She supposed that a few months back Mike would have done just the thing I described. She had truly let him down. I said she would have plenty chances to help.

Mrs. Katz told me that Mike and his father were getting along better and how pleased she was about it.

Father

Mr. Katz's concussion had improved. He talked with me twice by telephone in April and made an appointment at the school for May 2nd. In the beginning, he expressed the opinion that "children these days have no sense of responsibility." From his tone, I knew that he did not want me to agree with him. He did a lot of talking to convince me that Mike had had every chance and there was no reason for his lack of achievement. All he cared about was "cutting up" and "wearing clothes." The money he spent on those "Ivy Leagues" was enough to dress two boys his age, etc.

He listened finally when I emphasized my feeling that Mike and he wanted the same thing out of the school situation—good grades. I said Mike was very insecure about what he might be able to achieve and I knew that it was one thing to act as if one did not care and not try, but it was something very different to invest all one had when he had a good chance of not achieving what he wanted out of it. Mr. Katz knew what I meant and that he had to find a way to help Mike believe in himself. He reminded me that our appointment was the day after he and Mike would talk with the math tutor for the first time. It was so late in the term, would it do any good, etc.? I felt that if Mike found he could achieve satisfactorily, even at the end of the term, and even if he had to repeat the eighth grade because it was not enough, it could be worth it. He guessed he had to agree with that.

Mr. Katz was on time for his May 2nd appointment. He was young looking and very well dressed. He responded warmly to my bringing him up on the elevator instead of allowing him to walk the one flight to my office. He felt as if he knew me already and, frankly, he had said at first that he would not waste his time talking to any social worker. But he knew I had been "real hard on the boy"; he did not know why Mike liked me so much—he talked of nothing else. I learned that he had taken Mike to the tutor the day before and had felt closer to him than he had since "the boy was a little kid." He was so scared "inside"—did not want the tutor to know how "dumb" he was. I was sure he did not want Mr. Katz to know either. Mr. Katz made no response. That was when Mike had told him about several of his upsetting interviews with me. Mr. Katz seemed to know I had little doubt that Mike could "make the grade." He wished he could be as sure. He knew the "spot" he was in though and related a personal experience to prove to me he understood. I believed him.

He was encouraging Mike to talk to the tutor and be honest about his lack of knowledge. After all, he was paying him $5 per hour and he knew it was cheap as the prices for tutors went. I told Mr. Katz that my seeing Mike work so hard now was a real pleasure. He was surprised that the school would put this much effort into helping anyone, and I told him something of the many special services that the school and community provided.

I was aware that Mike might not sustain his present effort; I was sure he would reach a slump somewhere. I tried to prepare Mr. Katz for the day when he might behave as if he had given up again. He did not take very much out of what I said, I felt. Mr. Katz said he still had a great deal of doubt that Mike would not have to repeat the grade, but I would have his full support, and he knew that helping the boy to believe in himself was paramount. He had been slipping back in his achievement ever since he entered junior high school, I reminded him. He thought perhaps they had not realized how very different the situation was from elementary school.

Later when Mr. Katz telephoned me to bring himself up to date on what was happening at school and to inform me of what he was learning in relation to Mike and the tutor in mathematics, he told me, too, how helpful Mike had been to him in his store and how he believed the boy was "really growing up." I tried to get both of them to realize that there would be times when Mike would not seem to be putting all he had into it. I tried to help them understand that he was still very fearful about taking tests at times and about giving oral reports in class, but his conduct was much improved. There were rare occasions when teachers needed to make a complaint. He was no longer the "class clown."

Mr. and Mrs. Katz and I agreed that the three of us would have an evaluation conference together toward the end of May, for at that time school personnel would know more about the possibility of future plans for Mike.

One can see how essential it is in cases such as this for the school and parent to work together. Unless both are a part of the process, one might well destroy the good work done by the other. Certainly this was true in regard to Mrs. Katz's reaction to the deficiency card. The worker realized that Michael's strained relationship with his parents was a source of distress and that he did not want it to be that way. Yet she refused to become enmeshed in his casting off of their standards while searching for his own. Her job as she saw it was that of staying with Michael and his strivings, helping his parents to see his problem as he saw it and to appreciate the trial and error aspect of his solution of it. To say the obvious, Michael belonged to his parents "both of them," and the worker knew this. Excerpts from further work with the school people speak for themselves.

Evaluation with school personnel
—May 1960

When I met with the school personnel I spoke about my interview of May 23rd with Mike. The one class in which he had very little idea of how he was getting along was his English class. He seemed to stand more in awe of the English teacher than any of the others at this point. Mr. Sawyer, the science teacher, and Mike seemed to be getting along well, and he seemed fairly sure that he would pass. Mrs. Jones, the math teacher, did not agree with some of the things the tutor was doing with Mike. She and I had discussed this, and she thought she could talk directly with the tutor. She had had tutoring experience herself and thought perhaps she could say something to him about what she was teaching that would make it possible for him to be more helpful to Mike. We agreed the two of them might handle this better if I were not involved. Mr. Brown, Mike, and I had agreed that it was impossible for Mike to pass in Spanish this term and this was one of the subjects he had just as well let go. He would continue to go to class and see what he could learn out of his own interest in the subject. Mike had agreed, in planning for next year's program, not to take a foreign language but to begin again in senior high school if this seemed to be a good plan at the time. That left him to continue working hard on his other major subjects since he was passing the minor ones.

A few days later, I sent notes of appreciation to the teachers who had been working closely with me, and Mike helped me to word them. He was so clear about how he stood in each class that I did not need to ask anyone but the English teacher whether he was making noticeable progress. Her reply may be seen in the record; she stated that if Mike continued the way he was working he would be able "to pass English."

Ending interviews with child and
parents—June 1960

Michael

We had a full interview on June 1st and kept in close contact until school closed on June 17. Mike had moved to the point of feeling that he was well aware of what it took from him to have satisfactory achievement. He was no longer angry with his parents because he believed them to be ashamed of his lack of school progress. He did not blame them, he could do better. He did not want teachers to "give" him grades and even though he did not know on June 1st whether he would repeat the grade or go to summer school, he was completing his work in a most responsible manner. He expected to fail math and knew that he had failed Spanish. He thought he had done fairly well in all of his other subjects since it was easier to "pull up grades" when extra reports could be done. Math and a foreign language were different for obvious reasons.

He was so afraid that teachers would feel sorry for him and give him more than he had earned that he hoped I would not talk with them further. This was a real switch—he had wanted me to see them every time he did the least bit of work at first. I had to admire his attitude and reminded him that our notes of appreciation had been my last contact. He had no trouble deciding that he would not need to continue with me in September. He was even more aware than I had expected him to be that he was responsible for his own progress and that this was a beginning only.

Mike was concerned about his parents and their being willing to accept our decision. From what they had said to him, on June 1st, they were where he "had been last month," Mike explained, meaning they were giving me credit for his improvement altogether and could not trust that he would begin in September without me. I thought I could handle this with them, for they really wanted him to be able to do his work on his own, I knew. My greatest concern was about Mike. He could have some very anxious days, even weeks, in September. He could feel so pleased about what he accomplished this term that he might forget that he was able to get his "trial" in ninth grade (if he did) by the skin of his teeth. Mike was determined to pay for his continuing with the tutor if he were not allowed to go to summer school. He could earn the $5 by working with his father. If he went to summer school for math, he would work hard and pass, he knew.

He felt he knew how to get over his feelings of being "scared inside" by making himself do what he was afraid of trying, instead of clowning to try and hide them. Mike said his mother had never realized how he cried with one-half of his face and laughed with the other until I had called this to her attention. I was pleased to know that they were talking more these days.

I used this with him as another reason he did not need to work with me in September. He had his parents, and if he did not let his ability to truly communicate with them (even though it was fairly recent) begin to slip back to the point of their fighting again, the three of them would be able to work out a way to cope with most of the problems that he would have in the future. Mr. Brown, the counselor, would be able to help him with the others.

Following the interview on June 1st, Mike simply wanted to share with me the success he was having with final assignments. He was getting back reports for extra credit, test papers, etc. When I knew from the counselor that he had passed all subjects he was working on except math and therefore had to go to summer school, I tried to reach him by telephone to spare him additional anxious moments. I was not successful, and the next day he called me. He was so happy over the "opportunity to attend summer school" that he could hardly contain himself. He thanked me over and over but did not give me complete credit. He had "worked so hard and worried so much" that he knew he would pass the math test this summer and would stop in to see me to let me know about it when I returned in September.

I said I would be expecting him to do that. He then caught me, as I was putting down the phone, to ask, "If I find that I'm in a spot then, will you help me?" I said I was sure he did not need me to answer that, and he agreed.

The description of what happened to Michael, a troubled junior high school pupil, whose problem was that of not learning and being the class clown, depicts school social work as one of the services designed to help educators in their efforts to educate each child in accordance with his capacity. It shows the use of casework as a method of helping a child to become involved in changing his destructive behavior in school and in using his ability to learn. To say it simply, a casework process was established for the purpose of assisting Michael to help himself in the school setting. There was a negative beginning for this unhappy boy filled with ambivalence regarding whether he wanted to change. But the warm, yet firm, professional stand taken by the worker created an opportunity for him to clarify, to formulate an alternative and arrive at a choice as he became increasingly able to take some responsibility for his plight in school. This in itself was a tremendous hurdle but small in comparison to the turbulent conflict he experienced in the days that followed, in being held yet helped by the worker to sustain his growth in the on-going casework process.

Into this free-flowing process the worker integrated the contribution of the counselor, the teacher, the principal, and that of both parents. In numerous ways, she communicated to school personnel her awareness of their caring and concern for Michael, her appreciation of their knowledge of human behavior. In working with the child and his parents, the worker did not get caught up in the entanglements of family problems—sick anxious father, nagging frustrated mother—knowing that her help to Michael lay in keeping focused on his school problem as she worked with him and his parents. She was able to achieve her goal with the parents by getting a mutual concern going in a way that enabled her and the parents to carry their respective responsibilities, thus helping Mike to find a new concept of himself, which he needed in order to bring about the needed change in the school situation.

Although it is not recorded here, the parents, who were valued and respected by the worker, had a part in the ending as well as in the beginning. They, as well as Michael, were able to affirm his growth, as felt by the school personnel. Michael, who had been "shaken down to his boots" in experiencing this psychological growth, was a little fearful of it. He had been helped to do something constructive about his school problem and felt the need to act on his own strength. He understandably still wanted to be sure that the source of help would be there for him if he needed it again. His father showed the same need. The worker, aware of these conflicting feelings, was able to reassure them that she would be there for Michael if and when the need arose. It was Mrs. Katz, the mother, who clearly stated that she and her husband would have to hold onto this "new satisfaction" of having Mike confide in them and that they must remain firm in saying what he could and what he could not do. This is an affirmation of the help parents can give. It seems to imply casework service to Michael helped him find a new set of values; helped the school to mitigate its unhappiness over his poor use of its facilities; and in addition the mutual search with the parents found a way for them to give Michael the needed acceptance and approval so vitally important to any child's growth in school.

13

SOCIAL
SERVICES
FOR THE AGED

Emerging interest in the aged

The United States of America, which is often referred to as a young country, only within recent times has come to a realization that it is growing older. From our colonial beginnings up to the first decade of the twentieth century and the eve of World War I, ours had been a "youngish" people. An almost unrestricted immigration, chiefly of persons in the childbearing age group, had served to keep our population weighted with the young rather than with the old. Related to this was the high birth rate that, despite a high infant and childhood mortality rate, tended to increase the total population at the same time that it increased the percentage of younger persons in the population. It was not, perhaps, until we began to be conscious of the plight of the aged following the ending of World War I and through the frenzied 1920s that we began to look at the proportion of various age groups in our population structure. Not until then did we, as a nation, begin to face some of the problems with which we had to deal. Only slowly did we note some connection between an almost standstill immigration, a shift from rural to urban concentrations, a decreasing birth rate, and improved mortality and morbidity (sickness) rate, a fiercely competitive, highly organized, industrial system, an aging population, and the problems that seemed to beset from all sides the older persons in our midst. It is the purpose of this chapter to present something of our population changes, to examine the financial dependence or independence of the aged, to analyze some (not all) of their needs, and to discuss the range, variety, and helpfulness of

403

the social services that are available or are being developed by, for, and with the aged.[1]

Age groups in the population

In the preceding section refernce was made to our late recognition of population changes. Other nations—in existence longer than ours—have, before us, been conscious of the increasing proportion of their aged. Great Britain, for example, at least a generation earlier than we not only presented a demographic pattern such as now characterizes us but also undertook considerable research and planning in relation thereto. The Report of the Royal Commission on Population (1947) showed that the age group 65 years and over had increased between 1891 and 1947 from 4.8 percent to 10.4 percent. During this period the total population of Great Britain had increased 45 percent. By 1961 the percentage had risen to 11.6, and it has been estimated that by 1977 those over 65 years of age would constitute 16 percent of the British population.

The figures for the American population follow the same general pattern. Between 1900 and 1960 the age group 65 years and over increased from 4.1 percent to 9.5 percent of the total population. In the decade 1950 to 1960, the increase of persons 65 years and over was 34.7 percent, in contrast to the total population increase of 18.5 percent. The 1960 census recorded 16,559,580 persons 65 years and over (in 1840 the total population of the United States was 17,069,453 persons). On an average throughout the 1950–1960 decade more than 1 million persons reached the sixty-fifth birthday each year. It is estimated that by 1975 approximately 11 percent of the population will be 65 years and over; and that between 1960 and the year 2000 the aged population will double, meaning there will be more than 30 million people over 65 years.[2]

---

[1] The recency of our concern for the aged, remarked upon by many writers, is reflected in the many beginnings of programs and confirmed by the analysis of social work literature. For over seventy-five years there have been annual conferences of social work, but it was not until the 1930s that any serious discussion pertaining to the aged was recorded in the published proceedings. See Frank Bruno, *Trends in Social Work as Reflected in the Proceedings of the National Conference of Social Work, 1874–1946* (New York: Columbia University Press, 1948). Ewan Clague also remarked upon the interest in the aged as being expressed during the first half of the present century—first with the attacks upon the condition in poorhouses and almshouses, then proposals for pension aid assistance, and finally for social insurance and supplementary programs. See chapter on "Aging and Employability" in Clark Tibbitts, ed., *Living Thorugh the Older Years* (Ann Arbor: University of Michigan Press, 1949), pp. 141–153.

[2] P. K. Whelpton, *Forecasts of the Population of the United States, 1945–1975* (Washington, D.C.: Bureau of the Census, 1947), pp. 39–51; *New Population Facts*

Hold old is old? Who are the aged? Why 65?

Is age a chronological fact readily ascertained by calculating the years since birth? Are all persons who are born in the same year of the same age? Are the aged to be considered as a group, a category? Do individuals of identical chronological age behave alike, think alike, feel alike, work alike, play alike, have needs alike? It must be obvious from these questions that older persons, in common with all persons of all years, are still individuals, each with his or her own biological history, family influences from birth on, educational and work experiences, and emotional life. All these constitute a uniqueness that differentiates one from all others. It is a trite but nevertheless accurate observation that one person is old at 50, while another is young at 70—recalling, perhaps, the remark attributed to the late Justice Holmes in his ninety-second year, "Oh, to be young and 70 again." Likewise, two persons of 70 may vary tremendously. What then is the measure of "oldness" or age? For whom are the programs that are being developed on all sides intended? Why is 65 years seized upon so automatically?

Whether one is old at 65 years of age does not seem to be so important as the unthinking and "unthoughtout" prescription that workers should retire at 65, that eligibility for old-age assistance begins at 65, and that old-age benefits under our federal social insurance program may be obtainable at 65 years. In this connection it may be pertinent to recall the pressures during the Depression of the 1930s for older workers to make room in the labor market for younger workers. Nor was it accidental that as the Social Security Act was being written during that same decade (signed August 14, 1935) the number 65 came to be fixed as the standard for old-age assistance and old-age insurance. One cannot but wonder, if the Social Security Act were being written today (1962), whether the age might have been fixed at 70 rather than 65 years. The practice for many years of insurance companies stressing endowment policies to mature at 65 years also helped to fix that age as the time for retirement. For the purpose of this chapter and this volume, and without further discussion of its merits, the commonly accepted age of 65 years will be used—

---

on *Older Americans, 1960,* Staff Report to the Subcommittee of the Aged and Aging of the Committee on Labor and Public Welfare, United States Senate, 86th Cong., 1st Sess., May 24, 1961 (Washington, D.C.: Government Printing Office, 1961); see also *Chart Book,* prepared by the Federal Council on Aging for the 1961 White House Conference on Aging (Washington, D.C.: Government Printing Office, 1961).

with, however, a reservation about its validity as a sufficient criterion for old age.[3]

Financial resources of older persons

It is common knowledge that the financial resources of older persons are quite limited. This is to be expected when one considers that many persons over 65 years are no longer gainfully employed; that most workers earn modest wages throughout a working life; that persons who have raised families on modest wages seldom are able to save except on a limited basis; and that as one grows older medical expenses take an increasing proportion of one's income. Statistics from many sources substantiate this generally held knowledge. The most reliable data are those made available to and for the 1961 White House Conference on Aging. These data show that the great majority of persons 65 years and older receive money from old-age survivors and disability insurance (OASDI) or old-age assistance (OAA), or both. In February 1960 there were 675,000 persons over 65 years of age whose OASDI benefit payments were so inadequate that they qualified for and were receiving old-age assistance grants. Others had monies that came from veterans' payments or public employee retirement systems, including railroad retirement. A relatively small number had income from savings, investments, annuities, or rents. About one-fourth were still in employment.

When this is expressed in another way the limited resources are still more disturbing. More than half (57 percent) of persons over 65 years had money incomes of less than $1000 per year; almost four-fifths (79 percent) had less than $2000.[4]

---

[3] Before leaving this section, it may be well to see in historical perspective the changed position of the aged person. In an earlier age and in a patriarchal state the aged person was considered the embodiment of wisdom and authority. This status continued, without fundamental modification, through the feudal and medieval years, as well as through agricultural and early industrial economies. With the impact of modern industrialization the individual was less able to provide for his late-life needs, has been increasingly dependent, and his position within the family, as well as within the larger social group, is affected accordingly. No longer is he the patriarch and final arbiter. Quite likely he is tolerated, sometimes respected, and not infrequently pitied. See Leo W. Simmons, *The Role of the Aged in Primitive Societies* (New Haven: Yale University Press, 1945). Abraham Epstein, in commenting upon the changed status of the aged, goes so far as to declare that "The progress of a nation may be marked by the care which it provides for its aged." See Abraham Epstein, *Facing Old Age* (New York: Alfred A. Knopf, Inc., 1922), p. 2.

[4] See *Chart Book*, 1961 White House Conference on Aging, *op. cit.; Background Paper on Income Maintenance*, 1961 White House Conference on Aging; also Lenore A. Epstein, "Money Income of Aged Persons, Mid–1960," *Social Security Bulletin*, 24 (January 1961), pp. 12–17.

Employment and the aged

Just as income, or lack of income, is related to the aged person's independence or dependence, so too is employment related in a marked degree to income received. To what extent are persons 65 years of age and older gainfully employed? In 1958 there were more than 3 million persons over 65 years of age who were in the labor force. Stated another way, about one out of every five (21.3 percent) persons over 65 years of age was in paid employment. This is in marked contrast to the year 1890 when almost two out of every five (39.9 percent) of persons over 65 were in the labor market. For male workers the decrease was from 70 percent in 1890 to 34.7 percent, just about half, in 1958. Another salient point to be noted here is that even though life expectancy at 60 years has increased from 1900 to the present time the years of working after 60 have not. In 1900 the male worker of 60 years had a life expectancy of 14.3 more years, of which 11.5 years were likely to be in employment. By 1955 the male worker of 60 years could look forward to 15.9 more years of living, with only 9.2 of them in the labor force.[5]

Looking realistically at the employment situation affecting the older worker, it is essential to examine some of the difficulties that confront him in an economy that is dominantly industrial and urban centered. What stands in the way of utilizing the labor and skill of the worker who is moving on in years? Is there a supportable case for automatic retirement at a designated age? Does the older worker have a useful place in the modern industrial system? Can or will industry make an adaptation to the reality of an aging working population?

The barriers that the older worker faces may be those imposed by industry, which might be termed external, and those that he, the worker, places upon himself, which might be termed internal. Foremost among the former are those that derive from the unmistakable fact of the dominance of the machine in modern industry. In a simpler economy, agriculture, the individual was to a far larger degree in control of production and his part in it. Not so with increasing mechanization. Now the machine seems to determine the pace of production, and increasing reliance is placed upon it. Indeed the processes of production are geared to the

---

[5] *The Aged and the Aging in the United States: A National Problem,* a Report by the Subcommittee on Problems of the Aged and the Aging to the Committee on Labor and Public Welfare, United States Senate, 86th Cong., 1st Sess. (Washington, D.C.: Government Printing Office, 1960), pp. 27–63; also statement by Wilbur J. Cohen before the Subcommittee on Problems of the Aged and Aging, Committee on Labor and Public Welfare, United States Senate, 86th Cong., 1st Sess. (Washington, D.C.: Government Printing Office, June 16, 1959), pp. 3–32.

speed of the machine, and it is the human being that must fit into this scheme of things. The younger worker is in greater demand because of his supposed adaptability to the speed as well as the uninterruptedness of the machine. The greater emphasis upon piecework as it relates to the time factor and the greater capacity of the younger person to work under pressure tend to favor the employment of the younger rather than the older worker.

Another aspect of this dominance of the machine is the belief on the part of the managers of industry that the skills of the older worker tend to become obsolete with newer changes in machine production. According to this assumption, the machine is modified or replaced by a newly invented one, but the older worker does not make as rapid an adaptation to the change as the younger man. He—the older worker—is less likely to be considered as productive as the younger one.

Other beliefs or assumptions affect the employability of the older worker. He is thought to have higher accident and sickness rates. Since he is not as nimble as a younger man and since the machine does not slow up to account for human fallibilities, the older worker is regarded as the victim of the machine to a disproportionate extent. Likewise, because he is growing older and because it is commonly assumed that older men are more sickness prone, the conclusion is unthinkingly come by that the older worker is a far greater sickness risk than the younger worker.

A still further barrier to the employability of the older person is related to the practice of many firms of providing pension plans and the disinclination of those firms to weight the working force with too large a proportion of older workers because of the effect upon premium rates. In many instances these pension plans antedated the Social Security Act, and in some they have been instituted because of the very shortcomings of the federal old-age and survivors insurance program. In either case the individual firms have wanted to hold their premium payments as low as possible, and this has emphasized the advantages of a younger working force.

A concluding consideration (the foregoing are but a fraction of the total) has been the decision on the part of many employers—particularly the larger companies—for a compulsory retirement age for all employees. Usually, but not always, the age has been set arbitrarily at 65 years regardless of individual factors of good health, alertness, productiveness, etc.

The greatest and usually most defeating self-barrier has been the attitude and feeling of the worker himself: he has often lacked the conviction about his own usefulness. Affected by general opinion for a number of years and then overwhelmed by the actual realization of his 65 years (to use the commonly accepted figure), he has not had the confidence to "sell" himself. Failing that, he too readily may accept commonly held stereotypes and in time may actually evidence many of the ailments and disabilities attributed to people of his years.

What are the facts?

Many of the traditionally held beliefs as stated in the preceding section have had a deterring effect upon the hiring as well as upon the retention (except when insisted upon by labor union policies) of the older worker. Very little effort has been made until quite recently to test many of these assumptions. Surprisingly enough, few of the assumptions are sustained by investigation. For example, absenteeism is less among the older workers than among the younger. There are fewer accidents among older workers than among younger (although the older injured worker requires a longer period for recovery). The older worker is characterized by a greater reliability and dependability. His performance may not be as speedy; yet in most operations involving judgment and stability, he is a more efficient worker than the younger man and usually a more productive one. Perhaps the clearest comment concerning our admitted incomplete knowledge in this area was made by Ewan Clague of the U.S. Bureau of Labor Statistics when he pointed to the following conclusions:

> (1) Many older people retain their full faculties and vigor to an advanced age and can successfully hold a job or practice an occupation far beyond the arbitrary time of retirement; (2) Many other old people experience some accident, disability, debility, or simple decline in powers which lessens their capacity for their previous jobs but which does not make them at all unemployable; (3) Some old people (an actual minority) become permanently ill or disabled (not at any fixed age but at varying ages) so that they cannot or should not be required to earn their own living.[6]

---

[6] Ewan Clague, "Aging and Employability," in Clark Tibbitts, ed., *Living through the Older Years* (Ann Arbor: University of Michigan Press, 1949), pp. 149–150; see also Albert J. Abrams, "Barriers to the Employment of Older Workers," *Annals*, CCLXXIX (January 1952), pp. 62–71, and his "Industry Views Its Elderly Workers," *Birthdays Don't Count* (Albany: New York State Joint Legislative Committee on Problems of the Aging, 1948), pp. 141–162; Milton L. Barron, "Employment Practices for Older Workers," in *The Aging American* (New York: Thomas Y. Crowell Company, 1961), pp. 150–162; "Employment Security and Retirement," in *The Nation and Its Elder People: Report of the White House Conference on Aging* (Washington, D.C.: Government Printing Office, 1961), pp. 142–150; "The Employment Status of Older Americans," in *The Aged and Aging in the United States: A National Problem, op. cit.,* pp. 27–63.

Arbitrary retirement?

Within recent years there has been lively discussion of the relative merits of withdrawing workers from the labor market at a fixed age— usually 65 years. Many of the larger industries maintain that a fixed retirement age is the fairest and most democratic. It is contended that where the retirement policy is settled and known to all employees, it has the effect of treating all employees alike and without discrimination. Such a policy also enables employee and employer to do the necessary planning for retirement. It permits the retired worker a number of active years, which he may devote to useful community activities as well as pursuing his own hobbies and interests. The clinching argument is usually the one that retirement at a definite age makes way for and furnishes incentive to the younger worker. One retirement at or near the top of a large organization may mean promotions affecting ten to twenty persons in the various subsidiary echelons of the company, with attendant improvement in morale.

The opposing contention is that the readiness for retirement is so highly individualized as not to lend itself to an arbitrary policy applicable to all. Some individuals should retire at 50 years, some at 55 years, others at 60 years, while others are still useful to themselves and to industry at 70 or even 75 years.

Many factors, such as health, variations in job requirements, family situations, etc., need to be taken into consideration rather than reliance being placed upon age alone. Employers, whether in industry or government, who act on these premises insist that "functional" age furnishes a more valid basis for decisions about employability than does "chronological" age (indeed, most students of aging insist upon the usefulness of the concept of "functional" age in all matters affecting older persons). Policies based on functional criteria do not require compulsory retirement at a fixed age; workers may be assigned lighter or less demanding work (with or without a change in compensation rates); there may be a tapering off of a full working load through lessened hours or fewer days per week or with longer vacation periods; workers may be permitted to work beyond the usual (but not compulsory) retirement age and thus accumulate larger credits toward their eventual pensions. Many thoughtful employers favor a preretirement counseling program so that the worker may be more ready for retirement when it actually comes and able to retire usefully and, hence, satisfyingly.

In not a few instances, resources are available for the retired worker through what is known as a sheltered workshop where the work program is geared to the worker's limitations of health as well as age. In some communities, philanthropic and nonprofit employment agencies have stimulated the interest, as well as the initiative, of some employers in the potentialities of the older worker. Many older workers can still carry on usefully part-time employment as a means of supplementing rather limited social security benefits. (By reason of the 1961 amendments, it is possible for the retired worker to earn as much as $1700 per year with only a $250 deduction from his annual benefit; after 72 years of age there is no deduction on account of earnings.)

One fundamental consideration persists throughout this entire question. The gross national product of goods and services is distributed each year among the total number of persons who compose our population. In view of the increasing proportions of our older age groups in the total population, together with the decreasing proportion of older workers in the labor force, it appears that a smaller percentage of the working population is being called upon to produce the goods and services for the total population, which includes a larger percentage of older persons who are nonproductive. If persons are not contributing to the total product of goods and services by reason of being out of the labor force and yet are sharing in the consumption of the product, there will be a heavier load placed upon the producers or there will be a smaller total product to be distributed. This observation is especially pertinent when it is realized that many of the workers arbitrarily pushed out of the labor market still have considerable productivity for years to come either as full-time or as part-time workers—nor should these statements be interpreted as arbitrarily holding in the labor force any older workers who choose for their individual reasons to leave it. The essential issue involved here is a plea for decisions and policies to be based upon the realities of the situation affecting our total economy as well as the welfare of the individuals who compose our society.[7]

Age and health

In a previous section of this chapter, reference has been made to changes in our population structure—that is, an aging population—by reason of an almost unlimited immigration up to World War I and its

[7] Solomon Barkin, "Organized Labor Says No," *Annals*, CCLXXIX (January 1952), pp. 77–80; Wilma Donahue, ed., *Earning Opportunities for Older Workers* (Ann Arbor: University of Michigan Press, 1955); Eugene Friedmann, and Robert J. Havighurst, *The Meaning of Work and Retirement* (Chicago: University of Chicago Press, 1954); George B. Hurff, ed., *Economic Problems of Retirement* (Gainesville: University of Florida Press, 1954); Geneva Mathiasen, *Criteria for Retirement* (New York: G. P. Putnam's Sons, 1953); Geneva Mathiasen, *Flexible Retirement* (New York: G. P. Putnam's Sons, 1957); Irving Webber, ed., *Aging and Retirement* (Gainesville: University of Florida Press, 1955).

practical cessation thereafter. It is now appropriate to list several other factors responsible for an aging population. These are a declining birth rate and an increasingly effective control over certain diseases. The latter—control of disease—is particularly pertinent in this section not only for what has been done but also for what still remains to be done.

Despite a declining birth rate in this country, there is considerable evidence that a larger proportion of conceptions eventuate into births than was formerly the case. Likewise, the chances of survival are greater than ever before. Babies who attain one year of life have increasingly better chances of attaining the second, the third, the fifth, the tenth year, etc., than ever before. The conquest of childhood diseases—especially the communicable diseases—has increased the statistical chances of children surviving into adulthood. By the same token the attendant elimination of many of the previous *sequelae*, or consequences of these diseases, the impaired heart or kidney, etc., have enabled more people to reach maturer years.

The practical effect of all this is that as people reach the years of the late forties, the fifties, and into the sixties they are likely to fall before the as yet unconquered ills—the degenerative diseases. An examination of the leading causes of death of persons 65 years and over during the year 1945 illustrates this point: heart disease (39.1 percent), cerebral hemorrhage (12.9 percent), cancer (12.8 percent), nephritis (8.1 percent), and pneumonia (4.0 percent) account for more than three-fourths of deaths. This becomes clearer when one notes the shift in causes of death over the last half century. In 1944 heart disease ranked first among total population as cause of death, while in 1900 it ranked fourth; cancer was second in 1944 and eighth in 1900; cerebral hemorrhage was third in 1944 and seventh in 1900; diabetes was eighth in 1944, and twenty-seventh in 1900! arteriosclerosis was tenth in 1944 and thirty-fourth in 1900.[8]

The most recent studies of the United States Public Health Service (1957–1958) showed that while persons 65 years and over have a lower incidence rate of acute illness than younger age groups, the older person's rate is much higher for chronic illness and disability. For the population as a whole, 41.4 percent had one or more chronic conditions, whereas for those 65 years and over the percent was 78.1. Again, it was the group 65 years and over that had the highest percentage of activity limitation, 36.8 percent—over 6 million persons. With respect to other measures, the group 65 years and over had higher incidences: number of bed-disability days per person per year was 16.3 in contrast to 7.8 for all ages; and 14.7

---

[8] Louis I. Dublin, "Significant Trends in the Health of the Aging," in *Birthdays Don't Count* (Newburgh, New York: New York State Joint Legislative Committee on Problems of the Aging, 1948), pp. 189–194.

days average length of stay in hospitals per year in contrast to 8.6 for all ages.[9]

The experience of public health officers, of physicians in general practice, as well as specialists, including those in geriatrics, confirms the foregoing data. These persons and all others whose interests take them into the larger area of the study of aging and the aged—known as gerontology—realize there is as great and useful a task on behalf of the aged as was present a half century ago on behalf of the child. Persons who have had years of useful experience are still a considerable asset to society. The best that medical practice and medical research can make available should enable older persons to continue to be useful to themselves as well as to others. Medical science should be used not only to relieve or ease the pains of the aged, not only to treat the large numbers of the chronically ill, but to emphasize prevention. It should also promote a healthier old age, thus furthering the satisfactions that accrue with a lifetime of satisfying living. These premises can rest upon an humanitarian base, or a base of realistic common sense that keeps people productive and independent rather than nonproductive and dependent. In a very substantial sense, society has an investment of education, training, and experience in every older person, and it should be able to count on a return on that investment through the older years.

The significance of this material descriptive of the health of older persons is related not only to the present situation, but also to the future as an increasing proportion of the population is distributed through the older age brackets. This is important so far as health services and facilities are concerned, and also with respect to employment, housing, recreation, and the community's social services.

Aging and the personality

Throughout life all of us are called upon to make adjustments. The aged are no exception. Each period has its identifiable demands—in babyhood, childhood, adolescence, early adulthood, maturity, later maturity, early aging, old age. As human beings, we express in one way or another our basic needs for emotional security and a sense of adequacy. Perhaps in some period—say, during adolescence—the difficulties involved in assuring such satisfaction may seem overwhelming, but somehow most persons manage to survive the experience. While not intending to allege that old age is as complicated and baffling as adolescence, nevertheless one brings to it whatever resources living has made possible, and one is

---

[9] "Health Status and Programs," in *The Aged and the Aging in the United States: A National Problem, op. cit.*, pp. 85–89.

faced with the very finality of life itself. That very finality may endow the late years with satisfaction and happiness or with pain and despair.

What the person does with those last years or what those last years do with the person are related, basically, to how one's life has been organized in the preceding years. How has one met change, adversity, success, accident, ill health? What has been the nature of one's relationships to other persons—to one's family members, fellow workers, friends, even to one's enemies? Have one's responses been those of aggression or submission, dependence or self-sufficiency, rigidity or flexibility? With these remarks in mind, it may be well to examine three areas in which changes take place—family, job, health.

Families come into being, children grow up, enter upon careers, marry, move away, lead their own lives. Each of these changes in the family constellation asks different things of the family members. For the parent or parents moving on in years it may be possible to permit the children to lead their own lives—their reconstituted lives—or control may be attempted through overt domination or through subtler forms of emotional absorption. For the children to go may be interpreted as rejection, at the very time that parents feel the need for acceptance all the more. Attempts may be made, directly or indirectly, to have the married children live near by, or to visit at regular intervals, or to consult on all matters requiring decision—major and minor. On the other hand, the parents may welcome the establishment of a separate life for their children and feel in the release an opportunity to undertake many tasks and activities heretofore denied them by the exacting demands of family rearing. Parents with creative capacities within them may be able to go into a differently satisfying mode of work and living.

Another change in the family situation—the loss of the spouse—may call for quite another adaptation. Assume for the moment it is the husband who dies first (statistics reveal that women outlive men). There will be serious decisions to be made about housing arrangements—should the widow stay on in the same house, should she have her married child live with her, shall she live with a married child, shall she board, or shall she go to an institution? Can she continue activities she and her husband shared, or can she resume earlier ones that were put aside while the children were growing up? Or doesn't she have any interests now? Will the loss of a spouse so overwhelm her that life no longer seems to have meaning? Can she begin a new life of her own or is it simply a matter of hoping for this one to expire? Many of these same questions obtain where the surviving spouse is the husband.

A third aspect of this matter of relationship must be mentioned, and that pertains to the loss of close personal friends. These friends may no longer be on hand, either because of having moved away or because of death. Here again it will make some difference if one is with or without spouse, but in either case there are difficulties in adapting to other persons as the years advance. Loneliness is little comfort, especially when the younger generations crowd the older.

Throughout this chapter there have been repeated references to the question of whether 65 years should be an arbitrarily imposed retirement age. It must be obvious that the conviction of the present writer is on the side of flexibility and individualization. This is based on more than sentiment. There are personal considerations involved as well as matters of broad public social and economic policy.

Work in modern society has fundamental meaning for the individual. Not only does it involve the use of time, but it provides an outlet for abilities and furnishes an income for support of oneself and one's dependents. It gives status—the work as well as the income. When employment ceases at an age usually fixed by someone else, the person is confronted with a situation that demands considerable adaptability. People vary in their responses to such a situation. Some may fight retirement, trying to convince themselves and others they are not through. Others may fold up and completely give in, having no resources within themselves to see themselves through this difficult period of readjustment. For others it means the surrender of a previous commanding and respectable role. For some, particularly when income is drastically curtailed, it may signify helplessness and an accentuation of one's dependence on others. For not a few, certainly in the early years of the Social Security program, it means a slender financial benefit and, not infrequently, a supplement from public assistance. This is felt to be an ignoble end of a lifetime of struggle.

There are others, however, for whom the cessation of customary employment may not be a catastrophe. There may be sufficient income to permit one to hold up one's head. There may be a leisure, hoped for throughout previous decades, that permits the development or the furthering of hobbies and avocations. There may be both time and occasion to busy oneself with community activities. There may even be opportunity for creative pursuits to climax the few days vouchsafed to all of us upon this planet.

Throughout life most of us are aware of the importance of good health. Perhaps at no period are we more mindful of this than in the later years. By then the natural processes of the body have "caught up with us," as it were, and we find ourselves obliged to run (or walk, limp, or crawl) our course with whatever equipment we still possess. For some, old age may mean chronic illness and disability, with life literally a burden. Others cannot accept the physical failing of the body and consume themselves with denials of the reality of old age. For others, aging is a welcome time of slowing down, an acceptance of the inevitability of the human mechanism wearing out, and an adjustment of one's tempo and habits accordingly. As is true of so many of the adaptations required of the aged, the clue to them is usually within the individual's own life history of adjustments in the previous active decades.

Individualized services for older persons

Too frequently, and unthinkingly, old age is referred to as a problem, or a social problem. It is questionable whether a process as natural as aging should be called a problem, any more than other natural processes such as birth, growing up, or dying should be called problems. This is not to deny that there are difficulties associated with these natural processes, but to make it clear that these difficulties derive from our ways of meeting—or not meeting—the needs that are inherent in the natural processes. It is upon these needs—and particularly our ways of meeting them—that our thinking and our services should be focused.

Do not the aged share with other people the need for security and the need for love? Do they not want to be needed, to be useful? Do they not require to be related to other people and to feel themselves an essential part of the on-going world around them? These questions could be extended indefinitely, and to all of them an affirmative answer could be given. What would be more useful would be to consider some of the difficulties that develop or that are accentuated because of what happens to persons as they move on in years and as they are affected by what happens to those around them.

Adults marry, have children, raise families. During this period the wage earner is the main provider, and while children are in school and preparing for their careers there is a dependency relationship existing between the two generations. The children marry, raise their own families, and support themselves. The two generations have moved, usually and normally, to a basis of equality relations between them. In time the original parent has moved out of the labor market, voluntarily or involuntarily, and has found the range of human contacts considerably restricted. Increasingly the relationship between the two generations is that of dependency of the original parents—a reversal of the original pattern.

These changes, and many others, develop feelings in older people that need to be understood, not only by family members but especially by social workers. There is little question but that some of these shifts in role and status do produce a loss of self-esteem at the same time that they accentuate dependency feelings. Fears of all kinds, many of them vague and diffused but nevertheless threatening, are released. Feelings of isolation—not always a matter of distance—may be devastating in their effect.

What do older persons do with these feelings and with the situations in which they find themselves? What is the helping service of social work? In so many instances, and of course this is not characteristic of older people only, the adjustment and the efforts exerted toward such are definitely related to previous life experiences. Persons who have lived satisfying lives, who have both given and received love and security, who have made adaptations to people and to life situations, and who have developed a maturity with it all—these persons will be able to face the limitations placed upon them by aging with equanimity and without panic. They will not be without their difficulties, but on the other hand they will not be consumed by their frustrations and continually taking refuge in various defense mechanisms.

Social work's most important contribution to the older person is its recognition of him as an individual and its insistence that all programs shall embody this conviction in practice. This may seem an utterly obvious and nondisputable position, but an examination of much current thinking and practice evidences a too facile grouping of everyone over 65 years of age and a too ready assumption that decisions and programs must be made for them. The nub of the controversy about arbitrary retirement, for example, is largely that of dealing with persons of 65 years (or 60 or 70 years) as all of one group, and as a group *for* whom the decision must be made. Likewise, if we are candid with ourselves, we, too often, are inclined to lump all of the retired—voluntarily or involuntarily retired— as a group and to prepare and carry out programs *for* them. We do this, of course, with the best of intentions, failing however to conceive of them as individuals and as persons capable of working *with* rather than *for*.

What are some of the basic convictions upon which social work strives to operate? First, is the belief in the worth of the individual. True, this is not original, nor peculiar, nor exclusive with social work—what may be unique are the methods or processes by which its convictions are translated into action and into actual services. Second, is a regard for the right of self-determination, for the individual to make his decisions concerning himself that seem to meet his basic needs. This is contrary to a widely held supposition that individuals cannot make wise decisions for themselves; instead decisions must be made *for* people. Third, is a consideration for the privacy and the feelings of the other person. This privacy and these feelings are not surrendered because an individual asks for help or as a price for receiving help. Fourth, is a respect for the individual's capacity for change, for with change can come growth and adjustment in relation to other persons as well as to situations.

Educational services

Using the concept of education in a broad sense, it can be said, with considerable accuracy, that its purpose is directed not only to the present but to the future as well. Thus, in the early school experience education aims to educe native capacity, to develop it, and also to prepare for the next steps in growth. Likewise is this true for each stage that follows so that by the time later maturity or old age is reached there will have been adequate preparation for useful and satisfying living. When one realizes the importance of the kind of adjustments that the individual has been evolving throughout living and how they bear on the adjustments he makes in older age, the continuity of the learning and the living process becomes evident.

It seems necessary to evoke the foregoing remarks because of the too easy assumption that educational services to the aged begin when age 65 is reached. Actually, education as we know it in this country has a life-span responsibility, with its greater contribution to the aged being placed upon the opportunities it affords for continuing exercise of the individual's capacities and for continuing as a participating member of society.

The degree to which education (or more properly educators) has expressed this responsibility has been related to the leadership that has been available in many areas. Sometimes this leadership has stimulated industry to help prepare the older worker for retirement (hopefully a flexible retirement system) or even for retraining for a larger period of usefulness. Sometimes the leadership has manifested itself through community agencies—churches, clubs, libraries, museums, welfare groups—with resulting vital programs. Not infrequently, but not frequently enough, educational institutions have taken literally their responsibilities to all age groups and have ventured their facilities and personnel for experimental and serviceable programs. Such institutions as Cleveland College, University of Chicago, Illinois, Michigan, and Syracuse are among the most enterprising in this field.

At the present time there is some difference of opinion as to whether the educational programs offered under university auspice should be restricted to the older age group. If account is taken of the wishes of older persons that they be not segregated but dealt with as a part of the total population, then the program offered by the University of Michigan commends itself to favorable consideration. At Michigan the offerings have been on a noncredit basis and have been open to any interested person. While the majority of the attendees have been older people, there has been an age range from the second to the eighth decade of life. Professional workers, members of families that have aged parents, as well as older persons, have constituted the group. Professional workers have wanted to know more about aging in order to increase their usefulness. Family members have wanted help in understanding the needs of older persons who are living with them. The older enrollees have wanted knowledge, understanding, and direct help with some of the adjustments that are facing them. A glance at the course description will give some idea of its range and usefulness:

> The broad fields of information covered in the course include the biological aspects of aging, maintenance of physical and mental health, psychological changes, living arrangements, religion, creative activities, social and economic security, legal problems as related to wills and inheritances, and responsibilities of the community in providing citizenship, recreational, and other types of suitable activities.[10]

The section on Education of the White House Conference on Aging favored educational programs—essentially adult education—that cut across all adult age lines but that also met the particular needs of the older age group. It stressed the importance of offering broad and diversified educational programs, and urged leadership from the U. S. Office of Education, state departments of education, universities, libraries, and community groups, including full participation by older persons, in shaping such programs. Such opportunities might call for continuance of or reentrance into formal education as well as the expansion of informal educational programs.[11]

The role of the church

Whether or not older persons have been consistent churchgoers, there is a substantial contribution that churches can make to their lives. This does not imply a deferred conversion or a specific preparation for a future life, but rather an acceptance of what people are and a willingness to help them realize more fully and satisfactorily their capabilities.

---

[10] Wilma Donahue, "Age with a Future," in *Social Work in the Current Scene* (National Conference of Social Work, 1950), p. 78; ———, "Education's Role in Maintaining the Individual's Status," *Annals* CCLXXIX (January 1952), pp. 115–125.

[11] *The Nation and Its Older People, op. cit.*, pp. 197–204; also *The Aged and the Aging in the United States, op. cit.*, pp. 161–170; Wilma Donahue, ed., *Aging in Today's Society* (Englewood Cliffs, N.J.: Prentice-Hall, Inc., 1960).

This is not too different from that which can be asked of other community agencies, but it can be more specific because of the personnel and facilities which the churches have. Thus the fellowship of worship may have very real meaning not only for the persons who have always known it but also for others, to whom it may be a rewarding experience as it comes later in life. This is especially true for those persons who are surviving their kin and accustomed friends and for whom loneliness is a present reality.

Pastoral counseling, which is a normal part of the pastor's work, may be a source of encouragement and satisfaction to the older person and a welcome supplement to the congregational meetings. Another recent development has been pastoral psychiatry, which draws substantially upon many of the findings of modern psychiatry and makes them usable to the pastor in his service to his disturbed and troubled communicants. There has been an increasing number of institutes on pastoral psychiatry, which hospitals have set up to help clergymen in their ministrations to the ill—among them older persons. Friendly visiting with older persons may also be developed as part of the church's program, with this taken on by other persons within the congregation and involving some of the older persons themselves as visitors.

The church's physical plant lends itself to many kinds of group activities. Increasingly, the meetings rooms of churches are being put to use throughout the greater part of each hour of the day and evening and of each day of the week. In some instances the church may have staff to assist with group activities, in other cases its rooms may be used with staff provided by other community agencies. Here, too, is an area in which many of the older persons themselves can exercise leadership and example in order to facilitate a larger and more effective participation.

Church programs may be accelerated because the older parishioner has free time available and flexibility in the use of such time. This may be especially true in some communities whose resources lend themselves to retirement. However, it is essential to keep such programs properly balanced to serve all age groups rather than to develop an exclusively old-age-centered operation. While older people may enjoy other older people they also want to be with people of all kinds and of all ages.

Some, but not many, churches may be of such size and possess such resources as to have social service staffs of their own, which may offer services directly to older people. In most communities, however, social services are available through the public welfare departments as well as voluntary social agencies, and churches will make referral to them rather than set up parallel or competing services.

One of the increasingly important services of the church has been the support of homes or institutions for older persons. This development has been not unlike that in the children's field of a century ago when so many institutions—particularly for orphaned children—were offered under denominational auspices. Within recent years children's institutions have had to take stock of their purposes and programs and have redefined their services in the light of newer understanding of children's needs and of changing conditions and times. Today, as we know and learn more of the needs of older persons as well as of the variety of services available, there is a more thoughtful approach to the place of the institution for older persons. Increasingly the admission policies are being carefully defined as we become surer of what the institution has to offer and of the value of noninstitutional services that are available throughout the community. There is a tendency in many quarters not to let the institution for older persons become a general depository but rather to encourage public and voluntary (including church) agencies to develop appropriate services and programs outside the institution so that there is a range of services available, each to meet appropriately the specialized needs of older persons. In this way the church exercises its role as one of the essential and cooperating agencies working on behalf of all people.[12]

Housing—Including group care

Among the many adjustments that older people frequently encounter is the one relating to housing. Even when an older couple own their home, possibly the one in which their children were born and reared, there may come a time for decision as to whether to remain, or to move to smaller quarters, or to live with the children. These questions are not always simple ones with an open or shut answer, but are complicated by many pertinent factors such as income available, state of health, accessibility of children and friends, and even climate. Another decision may involve possible institutional living and demands most careful consideration.

There seems to be a preference, which older people express in many ways, for remaining in their own and familiar surroundings as long as possible. Their abiding interest is in noninstitutional living. They wish to remain a part of the life they have known rather than to be shunted into an institution and separated from active age groups. It may be claimed that these are very broad statements, and example may be given of the increase in number of institutions and of the persons residing in

---

12 Geneva Mathiasen, "Role of Religion in the Lives of Older People," in *Charter for the Aging* (Albany: New York State Conference on Aging, 1955), pp. 423–437; Paul B. Maves, and J. Lennart Cedarleaf, *Older People and the Church* (Nashville: Abingdon-Cokesbury Press, 1949).

them throughout the country. To this the answer must be given that even though some do exercise the choice to enter an institution, the overwhelming number prefer other arrangements.

Living alone is not without its difficulties: this is true whether it is a couple who is living together or a surviving spouse. For the older couple who has raised a family and in the process has dissolved many of its differences, it may come as something of a shock to realize how irritating and even unbearable some of these differences are when only two people are involved. The unremitting daily association without the relief of children's troubles may so accentuate difficulties as to put substantial strain upon the living relationship. On the other hand, years of living together may have developed an understanding of and a tolerance for the other person. This, together with the joys and sorrows commonly shared in the rearing of children, may have resulted, by later years, in the mutual affection and respect that surmounts most minor irritations. The sufficiency—or lack of it—of income is not without its effect as couples deal with the various aspects of living together.

Living with one's children may have its satisfactions, but it also has its problems if the arrangement is an involuntary one, that is, of necessity. Many of the difficulties may be accentuated to the point of mutual exasperation or even destructiveness. Generations do not easily adapt to each other, especially when over a span of years the roles are reversed. Not infrequently, there are sufficient antagonisms carried from childhood to adulthood for the struggle and tension to be well-nigh intolerable between former child, once in dependent role, and parent, who is presently in dependent role. Likewise the relationship between mother-in-law and daughter or mother-in-law and son may be less than amicable in many, if not most, instances. Somehow the father person seems to come off somewhat easier in this process of adaptation of the generations to each other, although the mother may be a more useful person insofar as household tasks are concerned.

When a third generation arrives, many of the difficulties in the child-rearing process may be reactivated as the (now) grandmother and mother relive many of the struggles that engaged them years before. It is not easy for a parent who has reared one generation to refrain from imposing the lessons learned therefrom upon the next two generations of child and grandchild. Nor is it always possible to escape the guilt or the expression of that guilt for what, as a parent, one did or did not do.

As is true with so many other matters related to the aged, there are varying points of view as to how specialized a particular program or facility shall be or to what extent the aged shall not be partitioned off from the total population. This is certainly true of housing. In those instances where housing for the aged is being considered, the question arises: Shall this housing segregate the aged or shall it be for all age groups, but with definite provision for the aged? Most opinion favors housing developments that make provision for older people—but as part of an over-all population. Some housing projects may set aside a certain proportion for the aged. It is questionable whether any housing project should be established solely for older persons. Despite the existence of some colonies catering entirely to the aged, the weight of opinion is against them, whether such projects be on a commercial basis or under labor union auspice. As has been said many times in this chapter and elsewhere, most older people do not want to be set apart.

Certain lessons have been learned in connection with housing that includes the aged. For example, older people want to be near adequate public transportation; they want to be near shopping facilities, near recreational centers, accessible to hospital and medical care, and away from serious traffic hazards, or excessive noises, smells, or smoke. They do not want to be close to slums or swiftly deteriorating areas. Like everyone else, they want to be near friends.

Consideration also should be given to the safety and comfort aspects of housing. Living arrangements, including bathroom, should be on one floor, and that floor should be reached by few, if any, steps. There should be no thresholds or tripping hazards; surfaces should be nonslip; there should be adequate handrails, and sufficient illumination of all passageways; heat should be provided from a central source and should be fully automatic.

Despite considerable recent discussion (largely in national and state conferences on the aged) of alternative living arrangements, the institution remains still another way of dealing with housing for the aged.[13] The institution may be a nursing home with primary focus on the medical care and treatment of the aged person, or it may be the home for the aged in which admission turns on the age factor and in which the medical services are provided as a part of the operation of the institution—in the same sense in which medical services would be provided in a children's institution. The institution for the aged may range anywhere from the county poor farm or county old folks home, through fraternal, charitable, or denominational homes, to privately supported homes for which fees of varying amounts are paid. Obviously it is hazardous to characterize institutions of such variety, but aside from the medically

---

[13] For two informed and succinct presentations of housing developments here and abroad, the reader is referred to: Charles Abrams, "Housing the Elderly Here and Abroad," in *Birthdays Don't Count* (New York: New York State Joint Legislative Committee on Problems of the Aging, 1948), pp. 247–252; Hertha Kraus, "Housing Our Older Citizens," *Annals*, CCLXXIX (January 1952), pp. 126–138; see also Geneva Mathiasen and Edward H. Noakes, *Planning Homes for the Aged* (New York: F. W. Dodge Corporation, 1959).

specialized institution for the aged (for those persons who could not receive the service otherwise) there is considerable doubt about the wisdom of multiplying indefinitely the number of institutions for the aged under whatever auspice. There seems to be a far stronger case to be made for exploring alternative forms such as residence clubs, senior apartment hotels, modified dwelling units in housing projects, etc. A still further possibility will be elaborated upon in the sections on nonresident and on foster home provisions.

The question raised about institutions for the aged might be dealt with upon the basis of the human personality factor or upon the financial aspect. As noted in some of the preceding pages, the preference of most aged persons is to be in familiar surroundings, with people whom they have known, and not to be segregated and treated as a group apart. Even though they are old, or possibly because they are old, they still want to be in the stream of life. Their movements may be slower, but they are more adapted to their physical and emotional needs. Even though older, they still want the contact with the young and the younger. The institution represents shelving, a getting put out of the way, an isolation, an accentuation on the end of life with death the immediate exit. No matter how comfortable the appointments may be, how palatable the food, how adaptable the visiting hours, how convenient the medical services, nevertheless one can never forget that one is in an institution for the aged, surrounded by the aged, and expected to act accordingly.

This is not to overlook the experience that some older persons may prefer institution living. Institution living may be less demanding psychologically. It may be less threatening to the older person since he can submerge himself in the group. It may seem to offer "security" as it provides to the end of life a habitation, food, and medical care. It may be the welcome release from a lifetime of unrewarding struggle.

The financial cost of institutions and institutional care must also be considered. This refers not only to the initial cost of construction but also to the continuing cost of operation. The per capita cost of all institutions—children's, educational, medical, correctional, etc.—is high. Institutions for the aged, because of the necessary amenities for the comfort as well as the safety of its clients, may run higher than usual, except perhaps prisons and hospitals. Buildings also tend to become obsolete and do not lend themselves too easily to changes in ideas or practices. There is some prospect that we may as overbuild for the aged in this century as we did for children in the nineteenth century. The very existence of children's institutions, in many instances, impeded newer and more effective programs of child care because of the unadaptability of the institution, or rather of the institution managers, to changed ideas and conditions.

The operating cost of institutions for the aged is considerable, and past experience indicates that operating costs always increase. They never seem to decrease. The better managed an institution is, the better qualified its staff, the more extensive its program, the higher per unit cost there will be. We have learned from two centuries experience with children's institutions that it is no economy, certainly in human terms, to run an institution at a low-quality level. It certainly would not be for the aged, who are a far more vocal group than children, especially where comfort is concerned.

The practical effect of this is: (a) an institution for the aged that holds itself out as low-cost operation is not able to meet the physical, medical, emotional, or social needs of aged persons, and hence, cannot justify its existence before the community; (b) an institution that has too high an admission fee or rates (weekly, monthly, annually) cannot meet the need of most of those who may require its services. Certainly if the figures on the income of older persons are studied (see mention earlier in this chapter), it is evident that few persons have sufficient resources to utilize institutions even if institutions were the answer to their prayers— or the prayers of their children.

The foregoing paragraphs may appear not only harsh but even unfair. That we may challenge the accuracy of these words reflects our sensitive concern with those institutions for the aged that have erred and records our determination that institutions for the aged can serve a constructive purpose in the lives of its patrons. At the same time it expresses our hope that we shall have learned from the two preceding centuries of institution building for children. Denominational and religious bodies, philanthropic and fraternal agencies, labor and industrial organizations faced with the contemporary imperative of wise stewardship, are in a position to develop institutions and institutional programs that will effectively and creatively serve the needs of older people. Such institutions and their programs are focusing more and more upon services for those requiring medical and custodial care. They are also keeping their policies flexible enough so that a "Home Care" service permits applicants to remain in their own homes as long as they are able to, with community agencies providing medical and housekeeping services, and with provision for institutional admission when it is no longer possible for the aged person to remain at home.

A specialized form of housing is the nursing home. This is a home for the older person who requires a degree of medical and nursing care that usually is not available in one's own home, or in the home of one's children, or in those housing arrangements where the older person is living alone. Nursing homes may be under public auspice; or may be under private control, (nonprofit, religious, fraternal, etc.); or may be what is termed "proprietory" (not nonprofit). In most states nursing homes are subject to licensing and inspection, usually by the state welfare or health department. It must be admitted that the ones most likely to be substandard, that is, lack of adequate nursing or medical care, or hazardous and unsafe, are the proprietory ones. Part of this is due to the pressing need for additional facilities of this kind and part of it to the limitations of staff and time of the regulatory authorities. There are some 500,000 physically and socially disabled people residing in the 25,000 homes that may be called nursing homes, convalescent homes, or rest homes. There is need for many more.[14]

Interest and activity programs

As an increasing number of older people have moved into retirement (voluntarily or involuntarily), programs have been developed to provide satisfying expression of interests and abilities. Many persons throughout an active working life may have neither the inclination nor the occasion to discover or express those capacities within themselves that are not job connected. Some may have lived to a period of leisure literally not knowing what to do with themselves. For many persons to whom the job has been demanding, unceasing, and unremitting, a period of leisure—particularly if it is enforced—may accentuate their loneliness, their helplessness, and their lack of purpose. Community programs are designed to offer opportunities to convert much of this aimlessness into satisfying and possibly even useful pursuits.

In a number of instances existing facilities have been used to provide a setting for the various programs. This is especially true in the larger cities where settlement houses are located. True, most settlement houses have always been available to all age groups within a neighborhood, but the emphasis has usually been upon youth programs. However, with older persons having time throughout the day, it has been possible to use the facilities morning, afternoon, and night. Since their beginnings in the late nineteenth century, settlement houses have evidenced remarkable adaptability in meeting the leisure-time needs of their surrounding populations.

---

[14] "Housing and the Elderly," in *The Aged and Aging in the United States: A National Problem, op. cit.,* pp. 117–129; also *The Nation and Its Older People, op. cit.,* pp. 181–196; "Nursing Homes," in *The Aged and the Aging in the United States: A National Problem, op. cit.,* pp. 131–147; *The Condition of American Nursing Homes,* Study by the Subcommittee on Problems of the Aged and Aging of the Committee on Labor and Public Welfare, United States Senate, 86th Cong., 1st Sess. (Washington, D.C.: Government Printing Office, 1960); *Standards of Care for Older People in Institutions* (New York: National Committee on the Aging of the National Social Welfare Assembly, 1953); *A Home in the Later Years* (New York State Association of Council and Chests, 1953).

With few exceptions, they have acted with remarkable alacrity in opening their buildings and with exceptional resourcefulness in developing programs for older persons.

Other community agencies have made their facilities useful: churches, parks and playgrounds, some educational institutions, as well as libraries and museums. Perhaps the most encouraging development has been the day center, as exemplified in the William Hodson Center in New York City. In addition to these agencies, the sponsoring or stimulating agency may range from municipal recreation departments, councils of social agencies, to national organizations such as the National Council of Jewish Women.

A review of the programs will give some idea of the variety of interests and activities that are afforded expression. For those who find satisfaction in working with their hands and with materials, there are the arts and crafts, such as painting, sculpture, ceramics, woodwork, metal work, leather work, sewing. For others who prefer a different way of expressing themselves, there are opportunities for writing, editing the group's newspaper or magazine, acting, folk dancing, folk singing. Others may find satisfaction in group contacts such as afforded by social clubs, of which the Golden Age clubs would be an example. Some few may engage in the physical activity of some of the less strenuous sports.

What must be apparent from the foregoing paragraph is that the activities of older persons are essentially the activities of people of all age groups—with the possible exception of the more active and competitive sports. What this also illustrates is the importance of providing the opportunity and permitting the choice to be made. Older persons prefer to express themselves in their own ways and according to their own decisions. They resent, like most of the rest of us, an overorganization by someone else of leisure-time interests. It may even be that some older persons prefer not to indulge in any activity and may make a choice of traveling at their own pace and using up their energy without too much motion. If such persons prefer to sit quietly and unactively, it may be the better part of wisdom of the program planners to recognize that sitting quietly, apparently doing nothing, may have very real value and satisfaction for some people.

The day center

One of the most promisingly useful of the many developments is the day center. This is literally a center—a place and building—to which older persons come during the day to engage voluntarily in satisfying activities. There are a number of such centers throughout the nation, chiefly in larger cities. The William Hodson Center in New York City may be used to illustrate the diversified program and its satisfaction for the aged. It offers all of the activities mentioned in a previous paragraph and more besides. Among its other group activities are monthly birthday parties, holiday celebrations, lectures, an annual bazaar, boat rides, summer camping, outings to park, and sound movies. Although there is a nucleus of a professional staff, the greater part of the organization is on a self-government basis with the following committees: executive, refreshment, clean-up, shopping, serving, sick-visiting, entertainment, house grievance, editorial, and library. Individual counseling services are also available, with help given for such matters as housing, medical and dental care, convalescent care, terminal care, employment, legal matters, social security, and public assistance. Since the center opened in 1943, there has been an increasing membership so that at the end of its first decade there were 1000 members. Of this number about 300 are in daily attendance, with a year's attendance somewhere between 40,000 and 50,000. About one-half of the operating budget is supplied by the New York City Department of Public Welfare (the center, one of fourteen in New York City, is named after William Hodson, who before his tragic death in an airplane accident, had been director of the Department).

The annual review of the program shows not only participation in the opportunities for self-expression and individual recognition (with new activities added each year, camping being one of the latest examples) but also certain collateral evidences of the value of the center in the lives of its members. Many individuals who used to spend their time in frequent trips to medical clinics and were preoccupied with their ailments, real or fancied, have found the center's activities so satisfying that they have shifted their interests from the medical clinics to an increasing participation in what the center offers. A study showed that there was a 50 to 70 percent reduction in total number of visits to clinics on the part of those who were participating in the activities of the center. "In fact, it is sometimes necessary to prod members to attend clinics if they become over-absorbed in center life." [15] Another noticeable change is the lowering of the age at which persons come to the center. In the earlier days of the center there was a pronounced interval between the older person's retirement and the time he could bring himself to trust the center (or himself) sufficiently to use it. In many instances this signified the lack of adjustment to retirement, the years of loneliness, brooding, self-absorption, a sensitivity to mixing with other people. That interval is now less, and persons are participating earlier in the center's program. Another identifiable value of the center is reflected in the low rate of admissions to homes for

[15] Henry L. McCarthy, *Day Centers for Older People* (Chicago: American Public Welfare Association, 1954), p. 14.

the aged from the membership. At the end of the first five years of operation, it was reported that ten persons, of about 500 membership, sought admission to a home for the aged. Three of these later decided they preferred to live in furnished rooms in the community and have returned to the center. Further confirmation of its value is reflected in the fact that during the same period there was not a single admission to a mental hospital from among the membership. Incidentally, this is corroborated by centers in both Minneapolis and Philadelphia, two other cities that have developed forward-looking programs for older persons. It is otherwise well known that admissions of aged persons to mental hospitals is decidedly on the increase.[16]

Other group work programs

While there are a number of effective programs in various other cities—Chicago, Cleveland, Detroit, Milwaukee, Nashville, Philadelphia, San Francisco, Syracuse, Washington—it is important to mention here the diversified program in Minneapolis and its utilization of group work knowledge and skills. The County Welfare Board several years ago created the position of group work consultant to help stimulate a community-wide program for older citizens. Through the consultant's services it has been possible to encourage a number of organizations such as churches, schools, libraries, industries, and settlement houses to sponsor group activity for older persons; to coordinate the activities of these organizations into an over-all community program; and to establish new services for the older age group as they are needed.

Because the program in Minneapolis is community-wide, it is possible to offer a tremendous range of activities to all groups of older persons according to their many and varied needs. Emphasis is placed upon the helpfulness of group work skills in working with groups of older persons. The role of volunteers is recognized as important. Services in institutions as well as boarding homes are a valid part of the total community program.[17]

---

[16] The range and quality of services at the William Hodson Center have made it possible for schools of social work to place students there for training—this in recognition of the role that such schools must exercise to prepare workers for this expanding field; see Eileen Martinson Lavine, *Learning to Work with the Aged* (New York: The William Hodson Community Center for Older Persons, 1960).

[17] Jerome Kaplan, *A Social Program for Older People* (Minneapolis: The University of Minnesota Press, 1953); James H. Woods, *Helping Older People Enjoy Life* (New York: Harper & Row, Publishers, 1953); for an account of the community organization process, which successfully culminated in a well-rounded program for older people, see Marcelle G. Levy, "The Syracuse Experience in Organizing for Better Services for the Aging," in *Charter for Aging, op. cit.*, pp. 50–66.

While few, if any, homes for the aged can carry on as varied and as extensive a program as the aforementioned William Hodson Center, nevertheless there are signs, here and there, of such institutions increasingly adapting their resources to the fuller needs of the aged. One evidence of this is the shift from a purely sedentarily centered institution to one that lends itself to use by the community. In some instances the facilities of the institution have been opened on a day basis so that activity programs can be developed not only for the residents of the home but for older persons who will come from their own living arrangements and share in the opportunities so provided. This serves not only to vitalize the home's program but to extend its usefulness to a larger segment of the community.

Thus, whether the programs are in institutions for the aged, in settlement houses, in churches, community, or day centers, there is convincing evidence that they are meeting, increasingly, the needs of older people as they undertake to make their own adjustments to retirement and still maintain satisfying and useful lives. Again, whether we call such programs recreation or interest or activity programs, it becomes clear that they make possible what the late Eduard Lindeman said about recreation—that it is an opportunity for a continuing educational process, a development of skills, a participation in esthetic experience, and an engagement in the affairs of the community. All of these have meaning for the older person.

Enabling the older person to remain in the community

It must be obvious that the bias, if it may be called that, in this chapter is toward making it possible for older persons to remain in the community. There is no question about the necessary place for the institution in meeting some of the needs of the aged, whether it is a medical institution, or one for the mentally ill, or the institution that provides residence care upon the choice of the individual. It is equally clear that the institution should be utilized when its unique and specialized facilities are required, but it is imperative that greater efforts be made not only by workers in the field but by all members of all communities to develop the resources to enable older people to remain in the community. The predictable number of older persons in future years will demand this, but even more importantly, the value to each older person of community living should be the determining consideration.

Perhaps ideally the older person should be in his—or her, or their—own home, preferably with a member of his own family. In many cases there may not be a family member available, and other resources must be explored to make it possible for the older person to stay. There may be housekeeping, or homemaker, or home care, as well as home medical and nursing services available.[18] There can be "meals on wheels" services. There can be, if the need exists, financial grants, the most basic of which might be old-age assistance, or there may be temporary grants from private agencies or sectarian agencies. There, of course, can be casework services available, either by the public welfare department, or by a family service agency, or by a church agency.

Life, however, is not always ideal for all persons, and there will be instances in which other living arrangements must be made. Without intending to suggest any system of priorities, it is possible to mention alternatives, such as living with family members in their homes, or with friends in their homes, or in boarding homes. A possible variation, especially in those instances in which a social welfare agency is the facilitating agent, could be a foster home.

A program that reaches out from an institution and into the community and into the habitation where the older person is makes it possible to remain in the community. Such a program is more likely to be offered by a medical institution, the Montefiore Hospital in New York City being one of a number of such institutions. The Home Care program may include complete medical services as well as social services. These are likely to be geared to persons with chronic illness, who may require the in-hospital service for a short time but the out-of-hospital service in the home for a much longer, and unpredictable, period. Casework services are an essential part of such a program.

Social casework services are available to older persons through public welfare departments as well as through the voluntarily supported agencies. In the former instance, the service may be related to old-age assistance or it may be part of the total program of service provided by the public welfare department to persons in the community regardless of age and of financial need. Some county welfare departments may be large enough to use a specialized staff, or so small that service to older persons is provided by all staff workers especially when caseloads are on a geographical basis. An increasing number of state welfare departments—North Carolina is one—offer leadership throughout the state, not only in stimulating quality casework services in the counties but by encouraging the development of additional programs seeking to meet the manifold needs of older citizens. Leadership is also offered to states by the Department of Health, Education, and Welfare through the Bureau of Family Service and the Federal Council on Aging. Additional resources avail-

---

[18] See especially: *The Homemaker in Public Welfare* (Chicago: American Public Welfare Association, 1962).

able on a nation-wide scale are provided by the American Public Welfare Association with its Public Welfare Project on Aging, as well as by the National Social Welfare Assembly with its National Council on the Aging.

The aforementioned resources are not restricted to public welfare agencies, but may also be available through the voluntary agencies that minister to older persons. The casework and other services may be provided by a specialized or unspecialized staff within a family service agency or a sectarian agency, although experience thus far lends support to the value of using a specialized staff within a multifunction agency. As in so many other aspects of social work, there is ample opportunity, indeed necessity, for experiment and demonstration, both in public welfare and in programs under voluntary auspice.[19]

Two items of surpassing importance and not unrelated to each other are the necessity for adequate public assistance grants and sufficient provision for medical care. Both of these matters call for improvement. Monthly cash grants to old-age recipients are shamefully low, and every effort should be exerted at the county, state, and federal level to increase these sums. Likewise, efforts should be directed toward including as part of the OASDI program provision for medical care. True, there may be honest differences of opinion as to whether to expand a fourth category of public assistance, namely, medical assistance for the aged who are medically indigent (but not otherwise eligible for old-age assistance), or to attach it to the insurance part of the Social Security Act. The position taken here is on the side of insurance rather than on the side of assistance. The entire developmental history of the Poor Law since the Elizabethan days shows a desirable progression from relief to security, and security in this sense means social insurance.

The White House Conference on aging

Americans have become familiar with conferences that have been called by the President during the past six decades of the present century to examine the needs of children and to enhance the range and quality of services for them. However, it was not until the year 1961 that the first of such conferences was called for older people. From January 9 to January 12 more than 2500 delegates from states and voluntary organizations came together for that purpose. Their deliberations took place in some twenty

---

[19] See *Aging: Progressive Programming* (Chicago: American Public Welfare Association, 1960); "Casework with the Aging," entire issue of *Social Casework*, XLII (May–June 1961); *Services for Older People* (Washington, D.C.: U.S. Department of Health, Education, and Welfare, 1959).

workshops and found expression in a volume of recommendations, which were transmitted to the President of the United States by the Secretary of Health, Education, and Welfare. This conference document *The Nation and its Older People* will continue to stimulate significant contributions to helpful programs for older people.

In addition to the many recommendations that the conference made, the following Senior Citizen's Charter was adopted, which emphasized both rights and responsibilities: [20]

RIGHTS OF SENIOR CITIZENS. Each of our Senior Citizens, regardless of race, color or creed, is entitled to:

(1) The right to be useful.
(2) The right to obtain employment, based on merit.
(3) The right to freedom from want in old age.
(4) The right to a fair share of the community's recreational, educational, and medical resources.
(5) The right to obtain decent housing suited to the needs of later years.
(6) The right to the moral and financial support of one's family so far as is consistent with the best interest of the family.
(7) The right to live independently, as one chooses.
(8) The right to live and die with dignity.
(9) The right of access to all knowledge as available on how to improve the later years of life.

OBLIGATIONS OF THE AGING. The aging, by availing themselves of educational opportunities, should endeavor to assume the following obligations to the best of their ability:

(1) The obligation of each citizen to prepare himself to become and resolve to remain active, alert, capable, self-supporting and useful so long as health and circumstances permit and to plan for ultimate retirement.
(2) The obligation to learn and apply sound principles of physical and mental health.
(3) The obligation to seek and develop potential avenues of service in the years after retirement.
(4) The obligation to make available the benefits of his experience and knowledge.
(5) The obligation to endeavor to make himself adaptable to the changes added years will bring.
(6) The obligation to attempt to maintain such relationships with family, neighbors and friends as will make him a respected and valued counsellor throughout his later years.

---

[20] *The Nation and its Older People, op. cit.,* p. 118.

Bibliography

The Aged and the Aging in the United States, Hearings before the Subcommittee of the Aged and Aging of the Committee on Labor and Public Welfare, U.S. Senate, 86th Cong., 1st Sess., Washington, D.C.: Government Printing Office, 1959–1960.

Aging—Public Welfare's Role. Chicago: American Public Welfare Association, 1960.

Anderson, John E., *Psychological Aspects of Aging.* Washington: American Psychological Association, 1956.

Barron, Milton L., *The Aging American.* New York: Thomas Y. Crowell Company, 1961.

Birren, James E., ed., *Handbook of Aging and the Individual.* Chicago: University of Chicago Press, 1959.

Breckenridge, Elizabeth, *Effective Use of Older Workers.* Chicago: Follett Publishing Co., 1953.

Burgess, Ernest W., *Aging in Western Societies.* Chicago: University of Chicago Press, 1960.

"Casework with the Aging," Entire issue of *Social Casework,* XLII (May–June 1961).

Charter for the Aging. Albany: New York State Conference on Aging, 1955.

Corson, John J., and John W. McConnell, *Economic Needs of Older People.* New York: The Twentieth Century Fund, Inc., 1956.

Cumming, Elaine, and William E. Henry, *Growing Old: The Process of Disengagement.* New York: Basic Books, Inc., 1961.

Donahue, Wilma, ed., *Earning Opportunities for Older Workers.* Ann Arbor: University of Michigan Press, 1955.

———, *Education for Later Maturity.* New York: Whiteside, Inc., and William Morrow & Company, Inc., 1955.

———, *Housing the Aging.* Ann Arbor: University of Michigan Press, 1954.

———, and Clark Tibbitts, eds., *Aging in the Modern World.* Ann Arbor: Institute of Human Adjustment, University of Michigan, 1957.

———, and ———, *The New Frontiers of Aging.* Ann Arbor: University of Michigan Press, 1957.

Drake, Joseph T., *The Aged in American Society.* New York: The Ronald Press Company, 1958.

Fridemann, Eugene, and Robert J. Havighurst, *The Meaning of Work and Retirement.* Chicago: University of Chicago Press, 1954.

The Homemaker in Public Welfare. Chicago: American Public Welfare Association, 1962.

How Public Welfare Serves Aging People. Chicago: American Public Welfare Association, 1954–1955.

Hunter, Woodrow W., and Helen Maurice, *Older People Tell Their Story.* Ann Arbor: University of Michigan Press, 1953.

Jacobs, H. Lee, *Churches and Their Senior Citizens.* Iowa City: State University of Iowa Press, 1957.

Kaplan, Jerome, *A Social Program for Older People.* Minneapolis: University of Minnesota Press, 1953.

Kaplan, Oscar J., ed., *Mental Disorders in Later Life, rev. ed.* Stanford: Stanford University Press, 1956.

Kubie, Susan H., and Gerturde Landau, *Group Work with the Aged*. New York: International Universities Press, 1953.

Kutner, Bernard, *Five Hundred Over Sixty, A Community Survey on Aging*. New York: Russell Sage Foundation, 1956.

Lavine, Eileen Martinson, *Learning to Work with the Aged*. New York: William Hodson Community Center, 1960.

Mathiasen, Geneva, *Criteria for Retirement*. New York: G. P. Putnam's Sons, 1953.

———, *Flexible Retirement*. New York: G. P. Putnam's Sons, 1957.

———, *Planning Homes for the Aging*. New York: F. W. Dodge Corporation, 1959.

Maves, Paul B., and J. Lennart Cedarleaf, *Older People and the Church*. Nashville, Tenn.: Abingdon Press, 1949.

Moore, Elon H., *The Nature of Retirement*. New York: The Macmillan Company, 1959.

The Nation and Its Older People. Washington, D.C.: Government Printing Office, 1961.

Shock, Nathan W., *Trends in Gerontology*, rev. ed. Stanford: Stanford University Press, 1957.

Tibbitts, Clark, *Handbook of Social Gerontology*. Chicago: University of Chicago Press, 1960.

Toward Better Understanding of the Aging, Aspen Seminar. New York: Council on Social Work Education, 1959.

Webber, Irving, ed., *Aging: A Current Appraisal*. Gainesville: University of Florida Press, 1957.

———, *Services for the Aging*. Gainesville: University of Florida Press, 1957.

Wickenden, Elizabeth, *The Needs of Older People and Public Welfare Services to Meet Them*. Chicago: American Public Welfare Association, 1954.

MR. KANE

HELEN LOKSHIN, DIRECTOR,
Social Service Department
Beth-El Hospital
Brooklyn, New York [1]

The health needs of the aging person represent a commanding challenge to established medical and social institutions. The number of persons 65 years and over, as well as their percentage in the total population, is increasing rapidly. While illness is not necessarily a concomitant of aging, the incidence of chronic illness and disability increases with age.

Although general hospitals, like Beth-El Hospital, are usually regarded as devoted only to the care of the acutely ill, these hospitals find themselves playing an increasingly important role in the care of the chronically ill. The aged comprise a substantial proportion of the inpatients and outpatients of the hospital. While there are no specially designated geriatric services at the hospital, certain outpatient clinics serve mostly older persons. Among these are the Adult Cardiac Clinic and the Clinic for Vascular Diseases, Physiotherapy, General Medicine. A recent one-day patient survey revealed that 31.3 percent of the non-obstetrical hospitalized patients were in the age range of 65 years and over. Since 1957 such older persons have been involved in 35 to 40 percent of the total caseload of the Social Service Department.

Role of the Social Service Department

These older patients frequently suffer from on-going irreversible conditions, with periods of acute exacerbation alternating with periods of remission. It is not unusual to find an older person suffering from the impact of several illnesses or disabilities. When such a person is afflicted with still another illness or an additional handicap, his hospital stay is likely to be prolonged. The functional ability of the older individual depends not only on the nature and degree of his illness but also on the totality of his personal strengths and deficiencies, including his relationship with his family. The personal and emotional stresses of the patient require professional attention if the health care is to be effective. Case-

[1] The contribution of Mrs. Leah Polenberg, Senior Caseworker, is gratefully acknowledged, particularly in the preparation and editing of the case record material.

work services to deal with these psychosocial aspects simultaneously with the medical treatment being rendered are, therefore, particularly important to the health care of the aged. The Social Service Department offers casework counseling and concrete services as part of such a program.

Can the pace of deterioration be retarded? What services may bolster other abilities even where there is irreversible disability so that the limitations imposed by this disability are modified or overcome? These are among the crucial questions with which caseworkers approach the situation of older persons, like Mr. Kane, whose case is presented here. Mr. Alex Kane could be considered one of our "younger" aged clients. He was only 67 years old when we began to work with him. However, he was suffering from a number of serious ailments including diabetes, vascular breakdowns, and a cardiac condition. These conditions are classified among the "degenerative diseases" with a particularly high incidence among older persons. While they may be controlled, they cannot be cured. Mr. Kane had already undergone surgery to relieve conditions that resulted from his diabetes several times. The doctors felt that an amputation of his left leg appeared inevitable. One of the toes and part of the metatarsal bone in this leg had already been amputated. His diabetic retinopathy was likely to lead to further decline in his already severely limited vision. The medical outlook for Mr. Kane was poor, the prognosis indicated a downhill course.

The material presented in this chapter covers a period of close to four years. Mr. Kane's behavior during this time was affected not only by changes in his current situation but by previous events in his life. In order to work with him toward an answer to these problems, it was important that the caseworker include the family. Mr. Kane was living with a daughter, Mrs. Alice Retamo, her husband John, and their three children. James, 19 years old, was the oldest grandchild, then came Jean, age 16, and Edward, age 10. The generational component and the relationship of Mr. Kane's situation with that of his grandchildren also often came into focus.

Early contacts

As is often true, the original request Mr. Kane brought to the Social Service Department in April 1957 did not represent his most important or his total need. Mr. Kane had been attending our Outpatient Department for several months. Prior to this he had been under private medical care, for which he had paid out of his earnings. Although Mr. Kane knew that the Social Service Department did not deal with medications or their costs, he asked for help with the cost of this medication, including help in paying for his insulin and supplies. Because he appeared very upset, an early appointment was arranged. The physician's notes in the medical chart were checked and showed that there were questions as to whether Mr. Kane was following the prescribed diet and if he were taking his medication.

In the early interviews, the worker was able to learn that Mr. Kane's manner of asking for help was a reflection of his struggle and inability to come to terms with his need for help, his changed position in the family, and the limitation imposed by his illness. During these interviews, the worker was sensitive to the clues that suggested that Mr. Kane felt considerable discomfort and distress at home. The caseworker knew such feelings could affect Mr. Kane's attitude toward himself and his desire to care for himself although Mr. Kane had not directly voiced this. It had been found to be contrary to the mores of many members of Mr. Kane's generation to seek solutions for problems related to their personal relationships through the intervention of an outside agency. To admit disappointment in their relations with their children and grandchildren seemed to many like admitting to overwhelming failure. Therefore, Mr. Kane chose to request help for what appeared a more acceptable problem, for which he knew that there was a tangible remedy.

In the first interviews the caseworker conveyed his concern about Mr. Kane's welfare, as well as about Mr. Kane's unhappiness at requiring help. In the initial interview the worker gave him enough recognition of his achievement and contributions to others as a husband, father, and wage earner so that Mr. Kane could discuss his need for a reduced clinic fee. Mr. Kane revealed that he had felt "too proud" to give an accurate picture of his financial status at the clinic where fees were on a sliding scale; instead, he had paid the maximum fee. As a first step to reduce some of the immediate pressure on Mr. Kane, the caseworker helped him secure an appointment with the clinic for a reconsideration of his fee. As a result, the clinic arranged to charge a token fee and to provide his medications free.

During the interviews Mr. Kane was quite upset and cried several times. He had no teeth and when he cried, he tried to hold back his tears by sucking in and biting on his lip and clutching his fist. Mr. Kane told me he was living with his youngest daughter, Alice Retamo, her husband, and three children. His wife and he had had their own apartment when Alice was married twenty-three years ago. Shortly after her marriage, at her request, Mr. and Mrs. Kane and the Retamos moved together into a six-room apartment, set up a joint household, and continued this way.

Mrs. Kane died in 1954 after lingering with cancer for two years. Mr. Kane was upset and grieved at his wife's death. He pointed out that he was even more upset by the sudden death of his brother last year. This younger brother was killed in an automobile accident. He was somewhat prepared for his wife's death, while his brother's came as a sudden shock.

During the past two months medication cost him $50. Even though he was getting money from his daughter and son-in-law, he felt sure they were depriving themselves and their own children in order to help him. At first he told me that he had been to see about his "old-age pension," but "they" told him that he would have to be paralyzed or on crutches to collect any money. He later told me that he was receiving $60 a month as his old-age and sur-vivors insurance benefit, but that was not enough. Until last year he had been able to take occasional jobs, but the continuing ulcerations of his legs made him give up work entirely. It was because he could no longer pay private doctors that he registered in our clinic.

Mr. Kane reiterated his previous statement that his daughter was de-priving her children in order to help him. As an example, he said the children were now sleeping in cramped conditions so that he might have his own room. He could also see a difference in the amount and quality of food and clothing in the family. His daughter maintained an optimistic out-look and shielded from him the fact that she had a hard time in making ends meet.

In the following interviews Mr. Kane still emphasized that he was afraid that the family would divide because of all the burdens he has placed on them. If he could remove the necessity of asking for money, things at home would be "all right." At the same time he continued to point up that his son-in-law as well as his daughter never refused to help him and both tried to make him feel he is not a burden.

I asked about his other children. Mr. Kane told me Mrs. Ehrlich, the older daughter, lives in Houston, Texas. She has been forced to go to work to supplement her husband's small earnings. She has no children. Mrs. Stein is a widow and is working to support her son, who is in his first year at col-lege. She lives in Philadelphia and is able to visit Mr. Kane occasionally. Alice is the youngest child and the closest.

At one point Mr. Kane wanted to know in a hostile tone "why others get whatever they want." When I sought to learn more about what he was re-ferring to, Mr. Kane related he knew other people who get whatever they want from the Department of Welfare. I asked him if he had ever applied to the Department of Welfare for assistance. Mr. Kane thought that he had, sometime in the 1930s. However, his explanation indicated that his prob-lem and reaction were to a much more recent situation. He stated that dur-ing the Depression, unlike other people, he worked steadily. He recalled that he gave part of his income to several families in the neighborhood. He felt that nothing could bring him to the point of applying to the De-partment of Welfare since he would be abused and degraded. Later, how-ever, Mr. Kane told me that he had made a recent application to the Department of Welfare for assistance, which had been rejected. This was one of the reasons that he was so upset and felt so degraded at this point.

I indicated that many people found it difficult when they were in the position of asking for help. I wondered if he had had those feelings when he considered coming to see the Social Service Department. When he made no answer, I said that I understood that it took a great deal of effort for Mr. Kane to come to see me.

Mr. Kane and the caseworker needed an opportunity to know each other better before Mr. Kane could discuss the problems that impinged on his ability to live hopefully and with some satisfaction from day to day. As Mr. Kane continued with his caseworker, it became clearer that his bewilderment at his changed status was a source of unhappiness. Mr. Kane was frightened by such changes in his situation as the turn from wage earner to retiree, from married life to widowhood, and from being the father of young dependent children to the parent of married adults, and a grandfather. When he was younger and the head of his own household he had been in much greater control of the family. Money symbolized an opportunity to regain his former status. After the initial request about the clinic fee had been met, the caseworker continued to see Mr. Kane because he realized that what had happened in relation to the fee was a symptom of other emotional stress even though Mr. Kane actually had limited means. His concern about money was related to other aspects of struggle in the family.

The clinic chart during this period showed that Mr. Kane was attending the Diabetic and Vascular Clinics regularly. In addition, he had been referred again to Cardiac and Eye Clinics. My conference with the doctors confirmed that Mr. Kane could not work.

Mr. Kane let me know that he was pleased with the way the clinic was handling his fee but added that he did not want to fight to get help. He emphasized that when his wife was alive and when he was working, he had a different, more important status in the family. I told him that I could see that he had achieved a good deal in his life through work and raising a family. I had been thinking about the things we had discussed; there seemed to be something more troubling him than a desire to obtain more financial help for his medications. Mr. Kane responded by emphatically saying I was "right." He really wanted an apartment of his own. Then he would not be in the position of cramping the family.

We discussed what it was like at home and how he spent his time. Mr. Kane presented a picture of estrangement in his daughter's house. He spent most of his time in his own room, a good deal of it in bed. Neither his daughter nor his grandchildren obeyed him. He claimed to have no friends and few relatives. Two brothers and two sisters were still living. However, he felt angry toward them because they were "out of my class," because they had money. He hadn't seen them in over a year and talked bitterly about their past visits because they had not inquired as to whether he needed money. The only brother with whom he had been friendly was the one who had been killed.

Mr. Kane said that in thinking about the whole situation, he realized that pride was standing in his way in reapplying to the Department of Welfare. He had never been a skilled worker, always a laborer, a very good and reliable one. For ten years he had worked in a power plant, for some years he had worked on the docks. His last job was in the maintenance department of a railroad. After the onset of the diabetes, he had been able to continue work, but the repeated breakdown in his vascular system with leg ulcers and gangrenous infections resulted in the loss of his last job. After that he had several part-time jobs, and even now he thought that he might be able to do some kind of work. When I went back to a discussion of his health and asked what the doctor recommended in regard to work, Mr. Kane said that he had not asked the doctor, because he "knew that the doctor was not on his side."

Throughout his life Mr. Kane's sense of adequacy had been challenged by the fact that he was a poorer earner than his brothers and sisters. Even when he was younger and while his wife was still alive he sought to bolster his self-esteem by soliciting recognition of his abilities as a steadfast worker. Within the family circle he strove to enhance his own sense of self-worth by trying to control the lives of those about him. But as his physical condition declined and his daughter's children grew older, it became increasingly difficult for him to exercise this control. With this change came a growing sense of frustration and inadequacy. His unhappiness then led him to neglect the physician's recommendations regarding diet and insulin injections.

When Mr. Kane first amplified his request to set himself up in an apartment, he discussed this as something he expected would be done for him entirely by the worker. He saw himself in a passive role, one that would not involve a real consideration of alternatives or positive action on his part. He was obviously impatient and angry with the worker for attempting to draw him into a discussion of what possible changes could be effected in his current situation. He expected the worker to "arrange" a new life for him. His anger at his daughter was not openly expressed, but there was a definite note of his wanting the daughter and the worker to feel sorry for him.

The caseworker let Mr. Kane know that he was concerned that Mr. Kane was troubled and unhappy and expressed the opinion that important changes require careful consideration. A plan for on-going contact was then set up in which Mr. Kane and the worker together could consider the possibility for change and what would be involved in this. Conferences with the doctor were also arranged. Shortly after this interview, Mr. Kane informed the worker by mail that he would not carry through on the plan for continued contact because he was going to visit his daughter, Mrs. Ehrlich, in Houston, Texas. He had suddenly decided to try this plan and see if it could work.

The next contact with Mr. Kane occurred several months later, in May 1958. He had returned to New York and was hospitalized because of an infected leg ulcer. The chart entry by the physician who saw him in the clinic prior to this admission noted that the patient did not cooperate and was told that if he did not follow the prescribed diet the clinic could not take care of him further. During this hospitalization Mr. Kane and Mrs. Retamo were both seen by the caseworker. Mrs. Retamo substantiated much of the information already given by Mr. Kane, stressing that no matter how hard she tried Mr. Kane always seemed angry and resentful. At a joint interview it was decided that because of the tension in the household, a period of recuperation at the Valley Convalescent Home before Mr. Kane's return to his daughter's home would be helpful. This was arranged, and a plan for on-going contact upon his return was evolved. Although the failure of his plans to stay in Texas was a further blow to Mr. Kane, the experience brought him closer to considering how his situation could be improved in New York.

When Mr. Kane returned from the convalescent home in April 1958, an appointment was set up with a new caseworker. He was seen regularly thereafter, the frequency of appointments depending on the nature of the pressures with which Mr. Kane was coping.

At the initial interview Mr. Kane listed a great many complaints about his stay at the convalescent home. The food was very poor, the regime too rigid. During this interview we also considered Mr. Kane's difficulty in changing to a new caseworker. I felt also that at our first meeting it would be useful to help Mr. Kane clarify the purpose of his contact with the Social Service Department and how we could help him.

Mr. Kane asserted that continuing to live with his daughter aggravated his illness. He would like our help in establishing himself in his own apartment. From discussions with the previous worker he believed that we might be able to help him. He was anxious and concerned but didn't know how to cope with the problem.

I expressed my appreciation of his quandary about what he could do. He was unhappy and hurt in his present situation; at the same time, it contained some important satisfactions for him. I suggested that perhaps we could be helpful in thinking through the various possibilities available. In working with us he might clarify for himself what it was he did want. This could mean that he would work out a change in his current living arrangements or he might find a way of living more amicably with his daughter. Mr. Kane said that moving had strong points but admitted rather reluctantly that there were some bad points as well.

Reversal of roles

As Mr. Kane became more aware of his increased dependence on the younger members of the family, he intensified his efforts to become again its controlling figure. Instead of achieving the desired results, his desperate efforts to overcome this reversal of roles only brought about more strife with his daughter, son-in-law, and grandchildren.

Mr. Kane pictured the situation in his daughter's household as one where there was an increasing amount of friction. At the same time he agreed that both his son-in-law and daughter treated him with respect. Much of the stress was about his ideas on how his daughter's children should be disciplined. There was a time when his word was "law." But now, even when he insisted that his daughter should not allow the younger boy out to visit his friends at night, she did so in spite of his protests. Mr. Kane continued to attribute his failure to win his way to his inability to contribute financially.

Mr. Kane presented himself as knowing more about the management of the household than his son-in-law and daughter. He still saw his daughter as someone whom he needed to control and direct. He was especially critical of his daughter's housekeeping, her methods of cleaning, and the kind of meals she planned. He liked cooking and liked his own way of preparing certain dishes so that he often cooked for the family. He differed with the daughter and her husband about the children, their bedtimes, their friends, etc. As the children grew older, friction increased. When the youngest grandchild passed him, he sang out, "Who's afraid of the big bad wolf?"

Mr. Kane related that when he was upset or angry he neglected his diet, then his diabetes went out of control; his leg ulcerations consequently were intensified, etc., etc. The doctors kept warning him that this would lead to an amputation of the entire leg. He confided to me that it had been his own doing when he was admitted to the hospital this last time. He told me that Mrs. Retamo's daughter Jean was "going steady" with a young man who was not Jewish. Mr. Kane felt that his daughter should prohibit this relationship. This boy had been invited to James' wedding. Mr. Kane had insisted that the Retamos cancel this invitation. When the family refused, he began to neglect his diet and his insulin, so that he might become ill enough to be hospitalized and thus avoid attending the wedding.

Knowing that ambivalent feelings were natural, and that it would be important for Mr. Kane to come to grips with this problem, the worker gave him an opportunity to discuss these feelings. Mr. Kane alternated between minimizing the difficulties in the household and emphasizing how imperative it was to move away. He brought up his love, as well as his resentment, toward his daughter and other members of his family.

When he found that the caseworker still continued to be interested in him, Mr. Kane grew more confident in his relationship with the worker. The worker recognized too that since past hurts were often reawakened or intensified by current changes, Mr. Kane needed help to separate the past from the present. For Mr. Kane, his granddaughter's engagement reawoke an earlier difference with his wife and his own conflicting feelings about the fact that his daughters grew up and were married. In reviewing the past with Mr. Kane, he also gained enough sustenance from the worker's recognition of his achievements and strengths, as well as problems, to admit his current explosive behavior. As he felt surer that the worker was desirous of helping him, even if he were angry and had hostile feelings, Mr. Kane was able to discuss his current situation more realistically.

Mr. Kane said he could not control his daughter's marriage. His wife had not told him about Alice's plans even though she knew about them earlier. I commented on the anger that Mr. Kane still showed when he discussed the circumstances of his daughter's marriage and asked whether he could undo something that had happened in the past. I also pointed out that his granddaughter was not his daughter.

Mr. Kane brought out that the Retamo marriage was the best that any of his daughters had made. In the more than twenty years that he had been living in the same household with the Retamos, he could find no fault with his son-in-law, who always treated him well. Even at times when there was an argument his son-in-law never carried over anger or a grudge. When I commented on the fact that he still seemed distressed that his wife had not fully confided in him at the time of his daughter's marriage, Mr. Kane nodded and agreed life was "never simple."

He pointed out his wife was a good woman. During the forty-six years of marriage she tried to keep him happy by concealing facts that upset him. His temper was easily aroused. It was a fault, but he couldn't control himself. He admitted that his original desire to move out of his daughter's household was as much out of a wish to punish his daughter and make her feel sorry as a wish to solve a problem for himself.

Although Mr. Kane was willing to admit that he could not possibly control all situations as he wished, he felt that even when he tried to stop himself, he was unable to do so. It was for this reason too that he felt he would be better off living apart from his daughter. When he did not win his point, Mr. Kane resorted to sulking in his own room or stalking angrily through the house when Mrs. Retamo had guests. Frequently, Mr. Kane was unhappy about his behavior. Sometimes he felt his daughter should make greater concessions to his age and illness. At still other times he admitted that he was asking for too much. He reluctantly admitted that it must be difficult for his daughter too.

The family

Any plan would have an impact not only on Mr. Kane and his daughter but also on his son-in-law and grandchildren and on their relations to each other. It was important, therefore, that Mrs. Retamo also have an opportunity to work with the caseworker.

In the interviews with the caseworker, Mr. Kane had reached the point where he could acknowledge that his distress was a part of the family picture. In the course of these contacts he came to recognize that it was important to discuss openly his discomfort and wish to move. As we shall soon see, Mrs. Retamo had entertained a similar desire but had not voiced it because she felt it would not be "right" and because she feared her father's reaction to such an idea.

An important step in opening up more realistic communication within the family was the involvement of the daughter in the treatment of this family problem. With Mr. Kane's knowledge and consent, the caseworker began to see Mrs. Retamo on a regular basis. It was not as necessary to see Mrs. Retamo at such close intervals as Mr. Kane because she was not as frightened. Although she felt guilty about her anger and distress at her father's behavior, she was bolstered in her self-esteem by satisfactions in her relationship with her husband and children. She had much more to look forward to.

While expressing warmth and concern for her father, Mrs. Retamo also displayed resentment about his temper tantrums. Although she presented the same factual data as Mr. Kane, she considered that it was not she or her family who had changed but rather her father.

When Mr. Kane was working, he had assisted them during those times she and her husband couldn't quite make ends meet. He was generous when he had money. In the past his stubbornness had always been a family joke; he could be won over by joshing. Her father often harped on the fact that his brothers looked down on him because he was a less successful "earner." Actually, instead of looking down on him, his brothers admired him for his aggressive behavior, his forthrightness, and use of strong language. Her father's manner of stirring things up made it interesting to be with him. He was said to be exactly like her grandfather, stubborn and abusive but loving and lovable.

Mrs. Retamo reemphasized that she hadn't changed, but her father had "lost his sense of humor." Still she tried to be patient because the doctors had told her that his diabetes made him irritable.

She felt quite divided in her loyalties: she wanted to be a good wife and a good mother and also a good daughter. She must sometimes side with her children. Her father wished that she would always agree with him. While she insisted that her children act respectfully, she felt that they were entitled to their freedom too. Mr. Kane openly showed his favoritism. The oldest boy was his "special."

In the interviews we recognized together that the situation had changed. The children were older, more grown-up, Mr. Kane was sicker. Mrs. Retamo talked about her marriage and her children with much warmth and satisfaction. Her husband was always ready to help her. Mrs. Retamo felt that her husband was very considerate of her father, and the two had such a long relationship that her father never thought of him in terms of not being Jewish. It was different with the daughter's boy friend. Mr. Kane did not know him. In fact, he refused even to meet the boy.

Mrs. Retamo felt that she had problems in disciplining her children because of her father. She was having the greatest problem with the youngest boy. Because she was afraid to make a mistake, particularly because of the type of disapproval it would bring from her father, she was confused about what to do.

Current happenings reawakened reactions appropriate to the past in the daughter too. Fear of her father reactivated her apprehension of displeasing him, the fear of making a "mistake," when she was a little girl. In going over some of the events in her past life, the worker was able to bolster her "grownupness" and to underscore her real achievements as a wife, a mother, and a daughter, and a potential grandmother. Afterward, Mrs. Retamo admitted that she would like a change and that it would be best for all of them if there were different living arrangements for her father. She showed her guilt at harboring such feelings by retreating from this suggestion and by referring to it as impossible and preposterous. When the worker pointed out that there were a number of possible alternatives that she and her father could consider, such as boarding homes, homes for the aged, an apartment in a housing project, Mrs. Retamo felt freer to discuss her wish to have her father live outside of her home. She believed that her father could never fit into a home for the aged. It was apparent that in addition to whatever her father's wishes were, in Mrs. Retamo's eyes her father could only be the head of a home and a homemaker. Her views were influenced in part by her own guilt and images of Mr. Kane when he was younger, but they were also based on a realistic understanding of her father.

Through the help and encouragement of the caseworker, Mr. Kane and Mrs. Retamo reached a point where they could discuss a change, not as a medium of reciprocal punishment, but as a way of making the future more mutually satisfying.

In my interview with Mrs. Retamo we discussed the desirability of her considering with her father the unhappiness she sensed in him. She could raise the question of his moving out if this seemed the answer. Mrs. Retamo said this would be difficult for her because it was always her father who decided what would be discussed and when. In reply to my suggestion that he might welcome her opening up the question with him, Mrs. Retamo thought Mr. Kane would "explode." Later she reluctantly said she would try to open up the subject only because she could not think of any way of avoiding my suggestion.

Mrs. Retamo telephoned me quite excitedly, after talking to her father, to say that "it was working." Their discussion was not quiet. Mr. Kane did have a slight "explosion," but actually it was nothing worse than what happened during the last year whenever they discussed other, often trivial, things "like what to have for dinner."

She told him she wanted to help make things easier for him. Still, when she said she would cooperate with Welfare Investigation if he needed to apply, he told her he could do it "all on his own." In contrast, however, the next day he told his older brother that he and Mrs. Retamo were "working together" to get him a place of his own. He even began to look around the house for the things he wanted to take with him. She felt the "ice was broken."

Mr. Kane decides to move

Mr. Kane was freer in discussing alternative solutions after he had reached the stage of open discussion with Mrs. Retamo. The only solution that would be in harmony with Mr. Kane's most effective personality aspects and strivings seemed to be an apartment of his own, even though such a plan had serious shortcomings. Although Mr. Kane realized that he would require a special kind of apartment with many other aids, he would not consider a home for the aged or a nursing home, or even a boarding home.

Mr. Kane felt that these plans would make him more dependent. He did not consider himself "old" and felt culturally apart from the "old" people in such homes. While he had been born in Europe, his parents had brought him to the United States when he was only three years old. He had completed elementary school here. He read an English newspaper daily, even if it was with the aid of a magnifying glass. He emphasized that he liked to mix with people of all races and religions. Moreover, he felt that there might be more pressure for conformity to religious ceremonial observance from the orthodox residents than he would be able to tolerate. Mr. Kane expressed strong feelings about his possessions. He could not take most of them along into a nursing home, or home for the aged, or rooming or boarding home. He wanted his own pots and pans, as well as his own routines. Even in his daughter's home he had a room of his own. In all his adult life he had never shared a room with anyone but his wife.

As Mr. Kane expressed his ideas about an apartment of his own, the caseworker helped him to compare his ideas with the possibilities. For Mr. Kane, this plan involved conducting a household all by himself for the first time in his life. It was therefore important to counterbalance advantages and disadvantages in advance so that expectations might not be out of line with reality and plans could be made to minimize the difficulties. It was also important for him to know that he might still change his mind if he wished.

We talked frequently about the vacillations that occur in making such important decisions. I also encouraged Mr. Kane to feel that no decision need be final. If the current plan did not work out after a reasonable trial, one of the other plans could still be considered.

Mr. Kane, in response, discussed some of his worries. He was concerned about being alone at night and about what would happen in the event of a setback in his health condition. He was also worried about how he would manage on a limited welfare budget. Up to this point he had been spending all his social security money for his personal needs. At no time did he evidence any concern about running a household. He was certain that he could arrange the kitchen so things would be easy for him. He knew how to inject the insulin. When he was not upset, he could be careful of his diet. He felt he could benefit from the "quiet" in a place of his own.

He continued to stress the growing incompatability in the household. He related that on one occasion he provoked an actual fight with his son-in-law. Mr. Kane objected to Mr. Retamo's allowing the youngest boy to go out to visit a friend. In the course of the argument Mr. Kane struck his son-in-law. Even so, Mr. Kane pointed out, his son-in-law didn't hold a grudge. Mr. Kane indicated that he felt much relieved after this quarrel because he had proved that he was not a weak person. This incident appeared to help Mr. Kane mobilize his efforts to move out of his daughter's house. He became much more active in filing his City Housing application and plans for moving, also much more realistic in his outlook and expectations.

Mr. Kane applied to the New York City Housing Authority in December of 1958. He obtained the application himself and filed it with the aid of his daughter. At frequent intervals thereafter he came to me with letters to the Housing Authority that he had written and asked me to rewrite them because he had difficulty in spelling. I did this for him, and since the letters included reactions to his home and family situation, it gave me added opportunity to discuss with him what was involved for him and the family in the contemplated move.

In March 1959, Mr. Kane received a notice that he had been assigned a special apartment in the Greene Houses. The apartment he was assigned was one of those specially designed for the handicapped aged in a new federal grant housing project. The interior was provided with doorways wide enough to accommodate a wheel chair, low cabinets in the kitchen, handrails in the bathroom. Ramps that could be negotiated on a wheel chair led from the apartment to the outdoor sitting area.

He came to see me, elated at the news. He was proud of his accomplishment in securing the apartment. Many people waited for much longer periods and still were unassigned.

While he planned creatively and positively for the move, he also continued to evidence his unresolved ambivalence, particularly in relation to his daughter. Despite her genuine interest in helping him, he rejected all her efforts to do so.

Mr. Kane completed his moving arrangements, paying his first month's rent out of his monthly social security benefit. Then he began his efforts to establish his eligibility for supplementary assistance from the Department of Welfare. Their procedure required the cooperation of his daughters in giving information about their finances to the Department of Welfare. Since none of them had ever received public assistance, I helped to interpret this requirement to them.

Collaboration of the health team

Mr. Kane's ability to use his medical care constructively required the close collaboration of the doctors, the nurses, and the social worker. The details of this collaboration, the conferences, and other exchanges of thinking that resulted in the plan to help Mr. Kane try living in a special apartment in a housing project, as well as in securing services for him after he moved into the Greene Houses, are omitted here since Chapter 13, "Medical Social Work," discusses and illustrates this collaborative process. For present purposes those parts of the record have been selected that emphasize the direct contacts with the older person and his family. However, the collaboration of the hospital personnel, for example, doctors, nurses, and social worker, was an essential feature of his health care. This collaboration was involved in the assessment of his medical, social, and emotional situation and in the way these factors interacted with one another, and in the development of the treatment plan.

The doctors who treated him in the Outpatient Department, as well as those who were responsible for his care during the hospital admission, discussed earlier, were rightfully concerned about Mr. Kane's self-neglect, his failure to carry out the prescribed diet and insulin injections. They were frustrated by the failure of their warnings to Mr. Kane about the serious health complications that could result and their threats to discontinue treating him if he did not alter his pattern. Moreover, in the case of Mr. Kane, as in that of other older chronically ill persons, the doctor's interest wavered because they did not find his condition a challenge to their medical skill.

The caseworker's contribution to the health team served to widen the area of concern from thinking only of the treatment of his illness to a comprehensive treatment outlook derived from an assessment of Mr. Kane's strengths, desires, and potentials, as well as his weaknesses and illness. When the doctors' and the social worker's findings were put in relation to each other and when Mr. Kane was viewed as a whole person, he became much more interesting and more of a professional challenge to everyone. Originally the doctors had felt that institutional care in a home for the aged, or admission to a chronic disease hospital, should be presented to Mr. Kane as ultimata without alternative. As one young intern expressed it, "he should be put" where he would get his insulin and where there would be no opportunity to avoid his recommended diet.

A changed attitude toward himself, and a greater interest in staying well became evident. This progress encouraged the doctors to more active participation in the collaborative efforts to help Mr. Kane find a satisfying way of daily living that would stress attention to his medical regime. The doctors' recommendation was an important factor in Mr. Kane's successful application for the special apartment in the Greene Houses. The medical information supplied to the New York City Housing Authority pointed up Mr. Kane's special physical needs in view of his health condition.

Continuing services essential—
Many services required

After Mr. Kane moved, Beth-El Hospital continued to provide for his health needs. He required a whole complex of services to compensate for his handicaps and to make it possible for him to live significantly and effectively from day to day. The assurance that the caseworker was standing by lessened his anxiety, as well as Mrs. Retamo's, about possible snags so that there was greater chance for the plan to succeed.

Many of Mr. Kane's needs might have been served well by a hospital Home Care program, which would bring treatment facilities—medical, nursing, and social services—to his home. Neither our hospital nor any other serving this area of the city had such a program. However, the collaboration of the caseworker with the doctors and nurses at Beth-El made it possible to identify the required services and to secure them from several of the community agencies.

The Department of Welfare met a variety of crucial needs. Under the prevailing subsistence standards of public welfare budgets, the hospital's information about his special needs was essential to establish Mr. Kane's eligibility for a welfare grant to supplement his old-age and survivors insurance benefit. After an initial rejection of his application, Mr. Kane began to receive such a grant on the basis of the special expenditure required for medical care and medications. In addition, he then became eligible for a number of other special allowances. Among those that he was granted on the basis of the information provided by the caseworker and hospital physicians were: allowances for travel to and from the clinic by taxicab, the purchase of specially moulded shoes to make walking safer and more comfortable, and the installation of a telephone. Later, because his condition deteriorated, he was provided with a wheel chair in order to reduce the damage caused by his bearing weight on his feet. The Department of Welfare also assigned a physician to visit the patient's home for periodic checkups during the interval between his clinic appointments.

The Visiting Nurse Association was another source of important assistance. One of their nurses helped Mr. Kane with the proper hygiene for the care of his feet. She visited from one to three times a week as recommended by the clinic doctor.

Seemingly small services may have far-reaching effects. Easy and immediate access to a telephone, for example, bolstered Mr. Kane's ability to carry on for himself and reduced greatly his anxiety about being alone. Not only did the phone provide a means for summoning help in an emergency but it also enabled Mr. Kane to shop and to continue active social contacts with friends and relatives.

Mr. Kane's "success"

It was not long after Mr. Kane moved into his own home that he appeared more contented. He grew more careful in following the doctor's recommendations.

After Mr. Kane moved in April 1959, we discussed the change and his adjustment to living by himself. Most of the time Mr. Kane spoke about the pleasure of being in his own apartment and the relief in not being provoked by the grandchildren. He stressed his satisfactions in being the head of the household and pointed out that all of the things in his apartment belonged to him. At other times, however, Mr. Kane expressed loneliness and sadness and anger at his children for putting him in a position where he was "forced" to move out.

On one occasion, when I commented he might be angry with me too because I also was involved with him in this plan to move, Mr. Kane cried, but on another day he just laughed cheerfully and said that he gets angry at everybody sometimes. I assured Mr. Kane that this would not change my interest in helping him. Mr. Kane told me that no one knew him as I did. He felt that he had been too revealing of his weaknesses and that I might become "disgusted" with him.

Mr. Kane showed satisfaction in having accomplished the move. Although Mr. Kane had found it difficult to apply to the Department of Welfare for help, he later expressed pride for having seen his application through until "justice was done." He responded with increased pride when I pointed out that he had achieved a number of other goals too; for example, he filed the project application, arranged the moving, organized the new household, and paid careful attention to the recommended regime.

In June, Mr. Kane related that on Father's Day his daughters visited him, and each one brought him a present. Then, they wanted to put up curtains. At first he became excited because he didn't want them "to do anything" for him. Then he remembered our many discussions and decided to let them help. He was surprised to find how much better everyone felt; even he felt good. He was proud that he had "controlled himself."

Mr. Kane showed himself to be a competent cook and housekeeper. Through his easy manner he made friends quickly. He made new friends in the project and seemed to know a good deal about his neighbors and their troubles. He compared these to his own with a comment that most people had problems when he got to know them. We recognized together some of the realistic limitations to any mode of living, whether alone or with one's family. Mr. Kane felt that he would not want to change his present situation. The good things far outweighed the negatives.

Still later, Mr. Kane noted that his place had become the gathering place for his family on Sundays. Mr. Kane expressed tremendous satisfaction that he was being consulted more by the family, and that they thought of him as "a more successful man."

Mr. Kane had attained a sense of significance. His satisfactions were improving his relations with his family.

As happened in the case of Mr. Kane and Mrs. Retamo, frequently adult children and aging parents are able to enjoy more mature interrelationships when they live in separate households than when they resided together. After he moved, Mr. Kane even felt friendlier toward his son-in-law and told the caseworker about how much he looked forward to the latter's visits each Sunday. Feeling freer to fulfill her function as a mother, Mrs. Retamo realized that Mr. Kane's presence in her household was not the only reason she had a problem with her children. Some months after her father had moved, Mrs. Retamo began to seek help for these problems.

Mrs. Retamo described how she visited her father several times weekly. Before Mr. Kane's telephone was installed she ran anxiously each morning. Because of her tenseness the visits usually involved some argument.

More recently the visits have become pleasurable. She knew that he could call for help if he needed it and so she was more relaxed. Now her father often urged her to take better care of herself. She had not sensed so much real concern for her on his part when they lived together.

She encouraged some of her friends to visit Mr. Kane too. He was flattered to show off his homemaking ability. Mrs. Retamo was particularly pleased when he allowed her to do some of the heavy chores around the house, without fussing.

Mrs. Retamo asked to see me about a problem with her younger son. He was having difficulty in school. When Mr. Kane was in the household, she blamed her father's stormy scenes for the fact that the boy was moody, depressed, and losing interest in his schoolwork. However, his behavior had not changed even though he had his own room. She didn't feel quite as helpless and such a failure as before and dared to try to get some help. Mrs. Retamo was referred to the Community Guidance Center for this problem.

Needs may change

Mr. Kane has been living by himself for over a year. Contrary to the doctor's original expectation that the gangrenous infection of his leg might not be controlled so that an amputation would be necessary, the medical staff was again able to help Mr. Kane to a recovery without the amputation. He returned to his household and has been able to carry on. The more recent entries in the clinic chart by the physician call attention to the persistent and careful way Mr. Kane was now cooperating with their recommendations. Mr. Kane's appearance reflects a marked change from the earlier period. A nurse noted that he was "a heavy set, pleasant man, seeming much at ease. As a result of his outgoing manner and his sense of humor, he made friends with the other patients and was much sought after by them."

Despite the fact that Mr. Kane was more conscientious about following his diet and taking his medicines and carrying out instructions about his regime, there were occasional setbacks. After spending several weeks in the hospital again in April 1960, he was able to return to the apartment. It is still possible that his physical state might deteriorate to the point where he would require more intensive care and that the apartment would not suit his needs. In the meantime, Mr. Kane has secured so much satisfaction from the current arrangement that his outlook is more positive in relation to the future.

Conclusion

In serving older people the worker's own attitudes are crucial to affording the older person and his family sufficient and timely help. An outlook that recognizes potentials of older people to learn to change and to develop is essential if they are to be served appropriately. To do this, their right to make choices as adults needs to be protected. The work with Mr. Kane reflected this point of view, which has been developed to a great extent during the last fifteen years.

While statistically the life expectancy of an older individual is less than that of a younger one, many changes may take place during these remaining years. The conviction that these years are worth while is basic for a creative approach that leads to the use of services for undercutting limitations and enhancing residual strengths and potentials. Sensitivity on the part of the caseworker to stresses that diminish self-esteem, as well as his understanding of the individual's abilities and established patterns of social adaptation, open the way for rehabilitation and restoration of capacities and more significant daily living.

While persons 65 and over, as a group, have many common needs, it is urgent that each older person be treated as the unique individual that he is with respect to his background, needs, potentials, and aspirations. Should the worker's preconceived notions about the aging and the aged, fears about illness, aging, or death impinge on the treatment of a given older individual and his family, then a rigid and constricted approach is likely to result with possibilities for helping them becoming obscure or diminished.

It is necessary that services be based on the ability of the older person and his family to use them, as well as geared to their changing needs. Since the changes that older people are called upon to make require drastic breaks and separations from long established patterns of living in which there have been deep emotional investments, it is not surprising that the casework relationship needs to allow them a sufficient period of time in which to make such important decisions.

Many older persons, who in former years might have been relegated to more constricted lives in institutions, can now be helped to lead satisfying ones in the community. The collaboration of a number of disciplines in one agency and the cooperation of several agencies may be required to serve the varied and changing needs of any given case. The personal crises faced by Mr. Kane who was ill and disabled, as well as over 65 years of age, were similar to those often faced by the relatively well aged. Casework help to older persons requires comprehensive consideration of a wide range of personal and social factors; the individual's health situation impinges on his emotional and social problems. Conversely, medical treatment may be hampered unless the focus of treatment includes attention to the personal and social problems. Public Assistance, Family Service Agencies, Homes for the Aged, and even Group Work Centers, as well as hospitals, are among those agencies called upon to provide casework help to older persons and their families. Because the older individual's family circumstances are an integral part of his psychological and environmental resources and exert a strong influence on his outlook and behavior, casework services for the aged involve services to the family. Where there is a spouse or adult children, they too are important clients.

New programs and services, geared to prevention and restoration and encouraging people to live in the community, are still needed. Caseworkers serving older people, through the knowledge about such needs gained from their experiences, have an opportunity to lend impetus to the community effort to establish needed social services for the aging and their families. Advances in the situation of older people will reflect the improvement in the welfare of other age groups.

14

SOCIAL
GROUP WORK

Out of the social complexities of our twentieth-century society, the ability to participate in groups has emerged as an essential social skill for responsible and effective citizen participation. No longer is the choice of whether to participate through groups or as an individual left open to many people. The types of groups vary widely. It may be a neighborhood council, a labor union, a professional organization, a businessmen's group, or a civic association, but the ability to make an appreciable impact on one's community outside of some such structure is practically nil. This fact was very clearly pointed up in a document "Autonomous Groups and Mental Health: A Report to the International Congress of Mental Health." It stated

> Individuals are members of groups and through these groups they function-ally achieve whatever actual sense of belonging to society they ever acquire. The individual has no recognizable existence save as a member of social groups, family, church and other associations. . . . The small social groups of compatible individuals who know each other intimately, and are united by interpersonal relationships characterized by love, confidence, intercommunication and mutual understanding, is the most meaningful social unit for the bulk of mankind. In it the individual experiences his keenest sense of being a member of society.[1]

The growing importance of groups in our culture is evidenced by the increasing amount of research and study being conducted in the fields of sociology, psychology, social psychology, and psychiatry, as well as social work. Groups have become a major instrumentality of society's functioning.

---

[1] Autonomous Groups Bulletin, III, No. 4 (no date), p. 22.

It is not this contribution alone, however, that makes the role of groups so indispensable to a democratic society. Groups also play a vital role in the development of a mature social personality. Social maturity is achieved only through a progressively widening opportunity for interpersonal relationships. These may include the nursery school, the gang, neighborhood friends, associations of boys and girls in their own sex groups, the co-ed group, and so on to the establishment of one's own family group. Sociologists have pointed out that no two groups make identical demands upon the individual, and by the same token no two make identical contributions to his social development. Thus, constructive experience in different kinds of groups varying in such factors as formality or informality, size, purpose, structure, and composition all add to well-rounded social growth. No person can become a fully developed social being without a variety of such experiences, which help him identify that which is uniquely his own and that which he holds in common with others. No one can live solely as an individual or as a group member. It is only through the ability to operate freely in both spheres that the individual becomes truly socially literate.

The family group has long been recognized as a major factor in this social evolution. Out of family relationships are developed the tools for building wider social associations. The quality of these tools depends on whether confidence or fear, friendliness or antagonism, freedom or restriction, sympathy or callousness, inward control or revolt against authority are the materials out of which the tools are being forged.

Historical developments in group work

Most social group work activities are carried on in a variety of social, informal education, and recreational agencies. While social group work is now an integral part of social work, it was not always thus. In spite of varying developmental history, both social casework and social group work originated in the same conditions spawned by the Industrial Revolution in England and the United States. The Charity Organization Societies, on the one hand, and the settlements, the YMCA, the YWCA, and similar organizations on the other, not only grew out of the same social ferment but in the beginning also had many leaders and sponsors in common. Jane Addams, Octavia Hill, and Edward T. Devine among many others on each side of the ocean were sensitive to the deep human needs growing out of a social environment that was creating social problems more rapidly than established programs could either meet or recognize. Of necessity these leaders encouraged activities that were broad in scope.

As the complexity of problems grew and the skill required to meet them became more specific and specialized, social organizations began to circumscribe and restrict their services. Through the imagination and courage of common social leaders, these programs arose originally from the same social needs, moved through a period of separate and individual development, then again merged into a common profession more specialized and more adequately defined.

Out of the social milieu mentioned above, a variety of social organizations evolved in the leisure-time and informal education field. The Jewish Center movement started in 1854, and it now covers every major Jewish community in America. Early adult education programs began to take shape at Lake Chautauqua about 1874. Settlements started in this country in 1886. One of the unique contributions of the settlement movement, patterned after the early English experiments, grew out of the fact that many of the staff workers went to live in the neighborhoods they were serving. They became "neighbors" with the focus of much of their work on the family, although in reality they worked with individuals, families, groups, and neighborhoods. By 1911 there was a sufficient number of settlements in cities throughout the country that a need was felt for channels of communication between these organizations, which had a common core in philosophy and methods but had developed in accordance with the particular needs of the community each one served. The National Federation of Settlements was organized in 1911 to provide such a structure for the sharing of vital information and for joint planning that would increase the effectiveness of all affiliate organizations. Recently the federation changed its name to the National Federation of Settlements and Neighborhood Centers, denoting a broadening area of interest, concern, and service.

The first YMCA was established in Boston in 1851, some seven years after the program had been initiated in England by George Williams. By 1866 this movement had developed to a point where a national organization was deemed necessary for the ordered growth of the organization. The first local YWCA was founded in New York in 1858. For a time there were two YWCA organizations, one in the East centered in New York and the other in Chicago. Since 1906, when the two combined, there has been one national YWCA organization. Actually, both the YWCA and the YMCA are now international organizations.

The New York Young Men's and Young Women's Hebrew Association in 1874 was one of the founders of the Young Men's and Young Women's Hebrew Associations. Out of World War I came the Jewish Welfare Board to coordinate the work of Jewish community centers and the Y's.

In 1896 the first Boys' Club was launched in Salem, Massachusetts.

By 1906 the number of Boys' Clubs had increased to the point where they too formed a national organization for consultation and coordination.

The year 1910 saw the initiation of the boy scout program, followed two years later by both the girl scouts and the campfire girls.

The 4-H club program was developed in 1907 under the auspices of the Department of Agriculture in Washington, D.C., and the various state agriculture colleges. Later government-sponsored programs included the Future Farmers of America, initiated in 1928 for agriculture majors in public high schools throughout the country. Supervision and sponsorship is the responsibility of the Office of Education of the Department of Health, Education, and Welfare.

The Catholic Youth Organization originated in Chicago in 1930. This program is found mainly in the larger cities but is spreading rapidly.

This listing is merely indicative of the types of programs that were introduced throughout the country and the relative periods of their development. Some were voluntary, while others were publicly sponsored; some were for boys and young men, while others were for girls and young women; some were family focused; some developed with strong central guidance, which produced relative uniformity throughout the country (such as the scout program), while others were more or less autonomous and free to build their own program emphasis in relation to local needs and interests (such as the settlements); some were rural, most were urban; some were secular, others had religious sponsorship. Through this variety of philosophy, structure, program, and methods there ran a common purpose—to help develop to the fullest extent possible the social capacities and potentialities of the members served.

It has been indicated that the identity or lack of identification of these services with social work has to be viewed through an historical perspective focused on the source and main currents of thought that influenced philosophy and methods. While most of the more familiar programs in the leisure-time field were established prior to World War I or about that time, there were major developments between World Wars I and II that vitally affected the philosophical as well as the scientific foundation of these programs. During this developmental period both philosophy and operating practice evolved from three major sources, namely, (1) public recreation, (2) education, and (3) social work, primarily social casework.

Public recreation

The place of recreation and leisure-time activities in the building of morale was recognized during World War I when organizations such as the YMCA and the Salvation Army were brought into military establishments to conduct activities. By World War II the value of such services was so well established that on military bases leisure-time programs were operated solely by military personnel. During the depression years in the 1930s public recreation programs, such as playgrounds, parks, recreation centers, and programs operated in public schools, were augmented by a rapidly developed work relief program, which included the Works Progress Administration and the National Youth Administration. They supplied staff, and to some extent equipment and supplies, for the necessary enlargement of activities to meet depression needs. Developments in the national parks and forests; wildlife conservation; flood control programs that made available lakes, camping and fishing sites; and the Federal Security Agency buildings and facilities in the vital war production and training centers during World War II were only a few of the governmental activities. These services led to both the expansion of such programs and to the general acceptance of the philosophy that leisure-time services were a legitimate and necessary function of government—national, state, and local—the same as health, education, or police protection are logical responsibilities of government. During this time, development of recreational activity skills progressed rapidly, as well as criteria for planning and construction of facilities, for the training of recreation leaders and the evaluation of programs. Social group work as we know it today drew heavily from these developments.

Education

From the field of education during the 1920s came developments that gave vital impetus to the leisure-time activities, which were growing by leaps and bounds but without essential clarity of purpose and a scientific base. Social psychologists began to identify the interpersonal relations—the interplay that is the essential "social process" within a group, but which is not present in a crowd. This emphasis on the "group," as distinguished from the crowd, the mob, or just people in close proximity, provided a focus for further insight and research.

In the middle of the decade, primarily from progressive education, came the "project method" of providing a variety of learning opportunities through one activity participated in by a group of pupils. From this development evolved an interest and focus not only on *what* people did but also on *how* they did it. The "process" became increasingly important, and with that, an attempt to find out what type of process was most effective in terms of the goals the program was set up to achieve.

Later, workers who were in the field of mental hygiene and guidance began to emphasize the impact of social experience on personalities, values, attitudes, ideas, and behavior of individuals. Out of this growing body of knowledge, education was given an *individual focus*. Attention shifted from group focus only to both the group as a unit and the individual in the group. From these contributions group work found resources to help build up its philosophical and scientific base.

Social casework

In the early years of the 1930s contributions from social casework began to make their impact. The contacts with social casework gave rise to a need for more adequate recording and improvement in referral practices, which helped etch the close identity and the complementary nature of casework and group work services. Through this relationship a growing concern for standards of practice and professional training was evident. Both have been fundamentally affected by the insights and conceptual base of psychoanalysis.

Social work identification

Thus, social group work, as we know it, drew heavily upon the fields of public recreation, education, and social work. For a period of time most workers in group work programs coming from a background in any one of these areas felt their closest identification with the field of their basic training and experience. As a result, there was a genuine confusion and uncertainty as to which of the three major fields represented the logical base for professional identification and professional education for social group work.

Another timely development bearing on this struggle for basic orientation was the formation of a Group Work Section of the National Conference of Social Work, which met for the first time as a separate body in 1935. This strengthened not only the recognition of developments in group work but also its identification with social work.

In the following year the American Association for the Study of Group Work was organized, with many of the same persons active in the formation of the National Conference section participating here also. This was in no way a professional association. It was open to anyone interested in the serious study necessary for defining social group work function, for determining the educational base essential to carry out such goals, and for developing the underlying philosophy and concepts. Membership was still drawn from the fields of public recreation, education, and social work, but those from social work were in a majority from the beginning. For a period of ten years the association operated under this type of organization. During that period other related developments occurred. An association of workers in public recreation [2] was organized, and at the same time professional associations within the field of education [3] were becoming stronger both in membership coverage and in effectiveness of program. With these workers finding closer ties in their own field, membership in the American Association for the Study of Group Work became even more social work based.

Following World War I when the Community Chest movement began to spread rapidly, most of the voluntary agencies offering programs in the leisure-time field became members of the Community Chests and therefore became affiliated with Councils of Social Agencies, further strengthening their associations with social work. By 1946 this trend toward social work identification had reached the point where the American Association for the Study of Group Work membership voted to become a professional association with membership based primarily on educational qualifications. As this was defined, it still left the way open for those trained in social work, education, or recreation, but the large majority came from the schools of social work. In 1952 the American Association of Group Workers, as the professional association was named, voted overwhelmingly to participate in the program to combine five social work professional associations [4] into one social work organization. This move was a final step in social work identification, which resulted in the formation of the National Association of Social Workers in 1954.[5]

Roles of the professional group worker

There are several types of responsibility the group worker may be called upon to assume within the variety of organizations using this skill as part of their professional service. These will be examined under the headings of direct practice, administration, supervision, consultation, and teaching and research.

---

[2] Society of Recreation Workers of America, presently known as the American Recreation Society.

[3] Such as the National Education Association; American Association for Health, Physical Education and Recreation.

[4] American Association of Social Workers, American Association of Psychiatric Social Workers, American Association of Medical Social Workers, American Association of Group Workers, National Association of School Social Workers.

[5] The final organization included also the Association for the Study of Community Organization and the Social Work Research Group.

Direct Practice

Direct practice in social group work consists primarily in leadership responsibility for a variety of different types of groups. The definition of the group worker's function has of necessity been a continually evolving process. The whole field of social work is relatively young as professions go. Group work as an integral part of that profession has a still shorter life span as indicated above. The most widely accepted and comprehensive statement was formulated in 1949 by the American Association of Group Workers.

The Group Worker enables various types of groups to function in such a way that both group interaction and program activities contribute to the growth of the individual, and the achievement of desirable social goals. The objectives of the group worker include provision for personal growth according to individual capacity and need, the adjustment of the individual to other persons, to groups and to society, and the motivation of the individual toward the improvement of society; the recognition by the individual of his own rights, limitations and abilities as well as his acceptance of the rights, abilities and differences of others. Through his participation the group worker aims to affect the group process so that decisions come about as a result of knowledge and a sharing and integration of ideas, experiences, and knowledge rather than as result of domination from within or without the group. Through experience he aims to produce those relations with other groups and the wider community which contribute to responsible citizenship, mutual understanding between cultural, religious, economic and social groupings in the community and a participation in the constant improvement of our society toward democratic goals. The guiding purpose behind such leadership rests on the common assumptions of a democratic society; namely, the opportunity for each individual to fulfill his capacities in freedom, to respect and appreciate others and to assume his social responsibility in maintaining and constantly improving our democratic society. Underlying the practice of group work is a knowledge of individual and group behavior and of social conditions and community relations which is based on the modern social sciences. On the basis of this knowledge the group worker contributes to the group with which he works a skill in leadership which enables the members to use their capacities to the full and to create socially constructive group activities. He is aware of both program activities and of the interplay of personalities within the group and between the group and its surrounding community. According to the interests and needs of each, he assists them to get from the group experience the satisfactions provided by the program activities, the enjoyment and personal growth available through the social relations and the opportunity to participate as a responsible citizen.[6]

---

[6] "Definition of the Function of the Group Worker," *The Group,* XI (May 1949), pp. 11–12.

Since that time, revision and refinements have been a constant concern. In early 1956 the National Association of Social Workers, through the Group Work Section Committee on Practice, sent a comprehensive questionnaire to members. Some 665 members, approximately 25 percent, responded. The answers highlighted one of the situations that has caused concern for the professional association but seems to be an inevitable result of the tremendous shortage of workers with professional education. Only about 10 percent of those who answered were in positions classified as "direct service" workers. A high proportion of those so listed were in the more specialized settings of clinics, hospitals, and institutions rather than the traditional youth-serving agencies such as Ys, settlements, and community centers. The shortage of available staff with professional preparation has propelled graduates almost immediately into supervisory and administrative responsibilities in the traditional agencies, leaving group leadership predominantly in the hands of volunteers and staff without professional education. It is the specialized agencies that are using the direct group leadership skill. It is probable that this situation will continue until available graduates with Master of Social Work degrees more nearly meet the demand. This will not likely be soon.

This same questionnaire made an attempt to clarify the role of the group worker. While there were varied reactions, either to the definitions suggested or to parts of the definitions, it was an additional step toward clarifying social work responsibility as distinguished from that of recreation and educational roles. Essentially, the attempt was to distinguish between "social group work" as the social work responsibility in the leisure-time field and "work with groups." Social group work was defined as:

> . . . a service to groups where the *primary* purpose is to help members improve their social adjustment and the secondary purpose is to help the group (whatever its structure) to achieve objectives approved by society. This includes interviews with individuals for the purpose of helping them in their adjustment to their groups and/or accept referral to other social, psychological or educational services.[7]

This definition assumes that members of the group receiving social group work services have problems of adjustment and that some diagnostic process based on understanding of human behavior and cultural factors is essential if programming is to be made specific to the needs of a particular group's members and that group itself. Most of the discussion and questions were focused on what were the implications of the assump-

---

[7] "The Practice of Social Group Work," Summary of the report prepared by Gertrude Wilson, National Association of Social Workers, New York, 1957, p. 7.

tion that the group members had social adjustment problems. There was some fear expressed that this was an attempt to define social group work primarily in terms of therapeutic services. An elaboration of this concept by the author indicated the context that "In a sense, living life is a process through which an individual is continually making adjustments within himself to fit the many and varied social situations in which he finds himself even within the course of one day. In a period of rapid social change, adjustments are made more difficult." [8] Work with groups was defined as including:

> . . . service to groups as a leader, teacher, advisor or participant where the *primary* purpose is to educate, promote or initiate action in relation to defined objectives. Work with boards and committees, staff meetings, in-service training sessions for staff and for volunteers, community committee meetings, classes in an agency, school, college or school of social work all fall within this category.[9]

All social group workers serve this type of group also, but this is not defined as social work per se just because a social worker is carrying on the work. Although this is an important service of any agency, it is focused on helping the group achieve specific program purposes, that is, production rather than individual and group growth primarily. These results will accrue in some degree as a concomitant benefit but not as the *primary* purpose.

The last word has not been said yet nor will be for a long time, but each discussion is a step along the long road of refinement of this professional service. The fact that this process is still going on adds to the fascination of this work.

Administration

As indicated above, administrative responsibility comes early to graduates of schools of social work. In the traditional agencies it was over 60 percent of those responding to the questionnaire mentioned above. In the larger agencies and those in urban areas, this administrative responsibility is likely to be as a head of a department such as adult or teen-age, or responsibility for a segment of the service such as program director. In the smaller communities or agencies it might be as assistant director or even executive. This reflects the philosophy that in view of the shortage of staff with professional degrees, the best insurance of the qual-

---

[8] Letter from Gertrude Wilson, Chairman of the National Association of Social Workers Committee on Group Work Practice to the committee, March 1956.

[9] "The Practice of Social Group Work," Summary of report prepared by Gertrude Wilson, National Association of Social Workers, New York, 1957, p. 7.

ity of the service is to have it directed and supervised by the most skilled staff available. This situation, as most, has its advantages and disadvantages. On the one hand it means excellent job opportunities for social work graduates, but it also means at times that responsibilities are being assumed without adequate experience. Again, this is a reflection of the stage of development of the profession and is not much different from the history of other professions.

Supervision

Since, as has been previously indicated, the bulk of groups in many organizations are led by volunteers and part-time staff without professional preparation, supervision becomes a major factor in determining the quality of such services. Over 25 percent of those answering the questionnaire were currently in supervisory positions. Supervisory responsibility frequently, and usually for the staff members with social work degrees, includes responsibility for other full-time professional staff as well as part-time and volunteers.

It should be emphasized, however, that the use of volunteers is not based solely, nor in some agencies even primarily, on the shortage of professional staff. It is based also on the philosophy that the opportunity to offer volunteer help is one of the services of the organization. Volunteers have played an important role in group service agencies since the days when there was no professional staff and all work was carried on by volunteers. This is one major difference in the development of casework and group work, for volunteers have practically ceased to exist in the actual giving of direct service to clients in casework agencies. In the group service agencies, volunteers not only lead groups of various kinds but also assist full-time staff, offer clerical service, assist in transportation in special situations, such as helping the aged or crippled to attend activities, and also perform a major administrative service on boards of directors and other committees.

Only a limited number of volunteers are highly skilled when they come to the agency. Many have not developed particular skills useful to the agency but are eager to contribute to the program in meeting individual, group, and community needs. While the key factor is good supervision, jobs for volunteers should be as carefully defined as those for professional workers, and the selection of persons to fill them should be made with the same care. Not all persons desiring to volunteer are emotionally mature enough to lead groups. Each person must be placed in a position where his maximum contribution can be utilized and where growth and development is possible. It is just as important for volunteers to have a satisfying experience as it is for professional staff—perhaps even more.

Recently one of the most exciting developments in the use of volunteers has been the increase in the number of teen-agers offering their services. The fact that this has not happened sooner is a reflection not on the interest of the teen-agers but rather on the willingness and ability of the agencies to offer opportunities and the supervision to make it a helpful experience both to the young people and the agency members alike. Social workers have long expressed the need for this, but a systematic provision for it to take place is recent. To give some indication of what the response can be when the opportunity is offered, in 1959 in a five-county area around Philadelphia, with limited publicity, over 1900 junior and senior high school students from public, parochial, and private schools in urban and suburban communities contributed over 158,000 hours of service, and many schools still had no opportunity to participate. Some did clerical work or filing, collating of materials, typing, reception work, and getting out bulk mailings. Many worked in health agencies and hospitals by making beds, arranging flowers, running errands, feeding patients, assisting in the supply room, helping in the diet kitchen, the laboratory, or doing occupational therapy and recreational work. Some worked in recreation programs as junior counselors, some as teachers' assistants for children under 8 years of age, others on playgrounds or reading to older people or writing letters for them, helping children learn to sew, teaching games, and other tasks too numerous to mention. And this was only beginning to scratch the surface of a vast potential. Schools have become interested and are actively encouraging and helping out such programs.

Consultation

A large portion of positions carrying consultation responsibilities are with national organizations, public and voluntary, which operate through state and regional representatives. Examples would be the national Y's, the National Federation of Settlements and Community Centers, the U.S. Children's Bureau, and similar organizations. There are also organizations that operate on a state-wide basis. They too may be public or voluntary, such as state recreation departments, state welfare departments, or state Y organizations. Consultation might be on interpretation of the organization's policies and procedures, program content and administrative structure, and policies appropriate for specific local situations, services for specialized needs such as the handicapped or aged, public-voluntary agency relationships, or adaptation of programs to institutions and other specialized settings.

There are a number of staff positions in health and welfare councils or community councils, serving city-wide, county, or regional areas that are offering consultation services through a group work and recreation division. While such responsibilities in a council are technically community organization positions, group work education and experience have qualified staff for those positions.

Through organizations such as the United Nations, the federal government, and national voluntary organizations, consultation in group work is being offered increasingly on an international scope. Some of this responsibility is directed to consultation with group workers in various countries and some in assistance with in-service training of local staff groups. Obviously this type of consultation requires a mature experienced person. It is not for beginners.

Teaching

As more and more of the graduate schools of social work include group work, the opportunities for teaching appointments have increased. Faculty assignments include not only classroom teaching but also responsibility for selection of agencies for field instruction, recruitment and selection of field instructors, supervision of field instructors, and occasionally supervision of a student in the field placement. These various responsibilities may be at the Masters or Doctorate level.

The above brief survey of some of the various roles open to the social group worker indicates the breadth and scope of responsibilities that offer opportunities to meet a wide range of interests and ability of any one entering the field. The range runs from neighborhood-centered programs to those international in scope; from direct service to teaching; public or voluntary, sectarian or nonsectarian; large or small; working with all ages and both sexes. To further indicate some of the range, we will look more closely at some of the settings where social group work skills are in demand and some of the services they offer.

Traditional agencies

Organizations such as the Ys, Scouts, Boys' Clubs, settlements and community centers are frequently referred to as the "traditional" agencies because it was largely through the leadership of these organizations that group work was fostered and the process of refinement and development initiated. However, the term "traditional" does not mean that the programs have remained unchanging. One of the tests of a vital program is its flexibility to meet new needs and changing conditions.

One of the problems facing many organizations serving rapidly changing and new neighborhoods and communities is the inability to reach many who need the service because programs have been limited primarily to a building. An increasing number of agencies are emphasizing a more decentralized approach. This means taking the program activities out where the potential members are. It may be a vacant lot, a member's home, a church, a school, a housing development, a library, or any number of available and suitable places. This requires flexibility in program, an imaginative approach to services, and a sense of security and direction. It means the "community" is the service arena, not just the four walls of the agency.

Another indication of this trend is the increasing number of agencies serving neighborhoods and communities offering what in essence is a community organization service. This not only brings activity programs out to the community but also focuses on the identification and development of local leadership so the community people can help themselves, both by conducting some programs for their children under the supervision and encouragement of the agency and also by learning how to obtain other needed services, whether public or voluntary and not limited to leisure-time programs. Many communities are able to get increasing services because they are united; they know how to function as a group and can speak for a block group or the neighborhood. They know where to go for help and how to get results, whether from the city council, the school, the United Fund, the health and welfare council, or city departments. Many group service agencies are multifunctional and offer not only social group work services but recreation, informal education, adult education, individual and community services. This type of approach gives every indication of increasing in scope and volume in the next few years.

Many agencies are facing the problem of serving new, rapidly developing suburban areas. This brings into focus many problems. In some instances the sense of community has not yet developed. It is difficult to develop community support because there is no real "community," just many people living close together. Without a community it is difficult to know who the leaders and the potential leaders are. It is difficult to identify community needs, at least as far as the community recognizes them, since there is no organized community expression.

In other suburban areas a sense of community has developed, perhaps several "communities" within the area the agency is trying to serve. It is sometimes difficult to get "local" interests to be broad enough to plan for activities of sufficient scope to offer the variety and breadth necessary to be effective. Much still needs to be learned about how to be most helpful in situations such as these. The skills needed to understand and work with these situations combine both group work and community organization with some individual service added. More and more it is becoming necessary for a good social worker to be well versed in each method. As responsibilities broaden, so do professional horizons.

Many group service agencies are finding that one of the hardest groups to hold in active membership are the older teen-agers. One approach to this has been an increasing number of coed activities with more responsibility for the programs carried by the young people themselves. Activities run for them have limited appeal, but programs planned by them with adult consultation and help as they need it find increasing acceptance.

Another trend in many places is for smaller agencies to merge with a larger organization or for two or three to unite. This makes possible a staff of adequate size and quality, administrative effectiveness and efficiency, adequate physical facilities and sufficient range of skills and flexibility to offer meaningful programs in the face of shifting needs arising out of an increasingly complex set of community factors.

Institutions and clinics

Some of the best progress in defining and refining social group work services in recent years has been coming out of the institutional and clinical settings. In the hospitals and clinics, the social group worker becomes a member of a team composed of the medical doctor, psychiatrist, psychologist, therapist, nurse, and social caseworker. In such settings with a defined treatment goal, the purpose of the service becomes much more specific than in the traditional agency. As service is more "pinpointed," the methods and evaluation can also become more specific.

In the institutional setting the social group worker makes a contribution through providing opportunities for constructive use of free time, but his contribution is in no way limited primarily to that. It includes the understanding of the group nature of institutional living and makes it possible for many of the institutional residents to make a constructive use of the institution's services. Institutional living is group living. It consists of living groups, school groups, work groups, leisure-time groups, friendship groups, age groups, and a wide variety of other group associations. It is becoming increasingly clear that any successful institution will be so in no small degree because of its skill in making constructive use of these group relations. Some of the types that have made use of the group worker's skill are penal and correctional institutions, institutions for the mentally retarded and the handicapped, homes for the aged, convalescent homes, and children's homes.

By the very structure of an institutional setting, many if not most of the policy decisions, regulations, and programs must be determined and initiated by the administrative staff. This varies with the nature of the institution from a maximum amount of administrative authority in an institution for the mentally ill to a small home for children where much democratic participation is possible. Discussion groups led by group workers have demonstrated repeatedly that the residents of these various institutions have many fears, that they lack understanding of the over-all program and the reasons behind many of the procedures, and that they have many "gripes." Although the group worker is a full member of the staff, the nature of the program activities allows the group members to participate, to the extent of their ability, in the determination, planning, and execution of the programs. Thus the worker develops a different type of relationship with residents than do most of the staff. This makes it possible for these discussion groups to create an atmosphere where the "gripes," fears, and unknown facts can be identified, clarified, and frequently dealt with constructively by the residents. If there is some misunderstanding about the medical procedure necessary, a doctor can be invited in and the matter cleared up. If it is about the meals (and it frequently is), the dietician can be consulted by the members or asked to meet with the group. Through helping to create a frame of mind that is positive toward the total service of the institution, through creating an identification with the program, the members very often are helped to make a much more effective use of the services.

Camping

The skill of the social group worker has been associated with camping since the days group work first appeared in social work curricula. The executive director of the American Camping Association has described camping in the following terms:

> Under trained leadership, it (camping) offers each camper an opportunity for growth, development, and happiness through a program of living and playing, and of learning activities related to the natural surroundings. Organized camping emphasizes group living, broad education, social adjustment, recreation—all with a focus on the individual camper within the group.[10]

Camping is an integral part of the programs of such organizations as the Scouts, Ys, Camp Fire Girls, settlements, and Boys' Clubs, and plays an important part in most leisure-time services, public and voluntary.

---

[10] Hugh W. Ransom, "Camping," *Social Work Yearbook, 1957* (New York: National Association of Social Workers, 1957).

In recent years there has been a very rapid growth of day camping, as distinguished from resident camping where the camper usually spends one to eight weeks in camp. Day camping does not usually include overnight trips. Many day camps are held in parks and other open places within the city limits while others travel to nearby country locations. The American Camping Association has recently developed standards for day as well as resident camps. No day camp can meet these specifications unless it falls within the following definition: "Organized day camping is an experience in group living in a natural environment. It is a sustained experience carried on during the daytime under the supervision of trained leadership." [11]

This definition bars those programs that are completely agency centered. Some programs that remained in the building all of the time had been called a day camp program prior to this. There is no way to prevent an organization from continuing to do so if they are not members of the American Camping Association. However, accepted standards in some detail are now available for anyone who wishes to know the best thinking in the field. Standards for both resident and day camping cover such factors as personnel, program, campsites, facilities and equipment, administration, health, sanitation, safety, and transportation. Renewed interest in using the natural setting to the fullest is being stressed more and more. Bringing the city to the country is being looked upon with less favor by those interested in camping.

Both resident and day camp periods are fast becoming a popular program for senior citizens 60 years of age and over. Some campers are in their nineties! The range of activities in such camps is no different from any other camp. It includes swimming, arts, crafts, dramatics, hiking, nature projects, campfire, and all the rest. The pace may be a little more relaxed, but the enjoyment and benefits are just as rewarding!

Camping is sponsored by both public and voluntary organizations. Many city recreation departments run camps as a definite part of their services.

Some of the trends in camping, as identified by Mr. Ransom, include more emphasis on the growth and development of the individual camper, more careful selection of camp staff, small units replacing dormitory type of living, more flexible programming and more camper participation in planning, more camps with campers from different racial, ethnic, and religious backgrounds, more use of outdoor setting in programs and increasing development of year-round camping.

---

[11] American Camping Association, "Day Camp Standards," (Bradford Woods, Indiana, no date).

Church-centered programs

Many churches have carried on group work and recreation programs for a number of years. Many of the earlier programs were focused primarily on attracting participants in order to get them interested in church services. Leisure-time programs were a means of obtaining church attendance. As the importance of leisure-time in our culture has become more widely appreciated, the trend has become that of offering good programs for their own intrinsic value, in many instances with the activities open to the community in general. As this shift has taken place, the responsibility for these activities has become less and less that of the religious leadership and increasingly that of staff with religious education or social work backgrounds. Some schools offering an educational program in religious education have added courses in group work to their degree programs. Churches have for many years sponsored settlement houses and community centers, which operate for the total community with no direct connection to any one church.

As part of the trend, mentioned above, of decentralized and community-centered programs, the churches have cooperated more and more in making their facilities available for such activities. Scouts have made much use of church and synagogue facilities as well as their lay leadership and sponsorship.

Area youth work

In crowded urban areas especially, gangs have existed for many years. They have been the subject of many sociological and psychological studies especially since Frederick Thrasher's classic *The Gang*. Gangs have long been of concern to many of the youth-serving agencies, but their traditional programs have never been really effective in reaching the more serious gangs. In recent years the activities of an increasing number of gangs have been characterized by activities so violent and destructive that general public concern, as well as that of social agencies, religious organizations, law enforcement agencies, and others, has reached a point where the relatively ineffective customary approaches no longer are acceptable. To meet this serious gap in service, a new program has been developed that is known by various names. It may be called "gang work," "area youth work," "detached workers," or have other similar titles. While the job title may vary, the basic approach used is essentially the same, namely, having a worker, in many instances with a social group work background, spend time with the gangs wherever they are, on the street

corner, in the candy store, or in the hogie shop. Establishing a working
relationship is a long, slow process with the more serious gangs, for they
are suspicious, hostile, and defensive. Gradually as they get to know the
worker he may gain their confidence, at least of some of the members
and hopefully of the leadership. If the leaders of the gang gain confidence
in the worker, the rest of the members usually follow suit. As this happens,
the worker attempts to help them as they are ready and able to use help.
It may be to help them get a job, to find a place to use a gym, to plan and
run a dance, to show up in court for them—to show that someone really
cares about what happens to them as individuals as well as a group. The
worker accepts them as individuals but does not approve of all of their
behavior. They wonder whether he is a cop or not, just who he is, why
he hangs around with them, what he gets out of it. Gradually he explains
to them the organization he represents, why he is there, his relationship
to the police and to other organizations set up by the community. As the
members gain confidence in and respect for the worker, more of their
fears, hates, hopes, and frustrations are laid bare. The goal of the worker
is to alter the antisocial attitudes, values, and behavior, to help them become related to the community rather than fight it destructively. The record at the end of this chapter describes the experiences of such a worker.

The handicapped

More and more the emphasis in group work and recreation in relation to services for the handicapped is toward social integration rather
than social isolation. While there are many special programs such as
camps, clubs, and classes for the crippled, blind, or mentally retarded,
where possible the trend is to help them become a part of regular activities of this type in their own neighborhood with their own neighbors. As
the degree of handicap becomes more serious, this becomes increasingly
difficult to the point where special programs are necessary.

The range of activities include most of those found in any good
leisure-time service. Much ingenuity is needed to adapt the activity to the
physical, mental, and emotional capacity and needs of the individuals participating, but this too is a matter of degree. This adaptation to need is
one of the major skills of the social group worker. Since individuals vary
in such factors as age; cultural, social, and economic background; personality; health; race; religion, and ethnic background, these factors make
their influence felt. As individuals vary, so do the groups they form. Each
change in membership, even one member leaving or a new one joining,
shifts the relations that have been established and makes the relationships,
the demands on the individuals, and the contributions to the members a

little different. To the degree that the physical and emotional factors are exaggerated, to that degree the role of the worker becomes more specific in the goal of helping that group experience become meaningful to the members. To help each individual participate to the fullest capacity is the ultimate goal, never reached perfectly, but new knowledge, carefully evaluated experience, and increasing skill bring each generation a little closer to the goal.

Programs for senior citizens

Chapter 13 has reviewed the problems and services stemming from the increasing proportion of our population over 65 years of age. We will only mention here briefly the rapid growth and expansion of day centers and clubs, whatever name they may adopt. Program activities run the gamut of any good leisure-time program. The club may be open only a part of one day a week or for two or three sessions. The center is usually open all day four or five days a week and offers more than just leisure-time activities. Some include medical, psychiatric, and other services. Many of these clubs and centers have expanded their activities to include service to others, as well as getting something for themselves. This takes such forms as visiting members when they are sick at home or in a hospital, visiting older people in homes for the aged who are less fortunate and can no longer get out to activities, sending cards and letters to older people who are bedridden, and similar services. Some have volunteered their services to organizations serving younger members when they possess a special skill such as wood carving, woodwork, arts, crafts.

Public-voluntary agency
relationships and responsibility

With the time available for the enjoyment of leisure-time activities having increased at a rapid pace in recent years and with the forecast predicting more in the future, there has been much thoughtful consideration of the relative responsibilities of the public and voluntary organizations. There has been in most places a tendency toward more cooperative relationships between the two and more joint planning. This is an essential development for any community contemplating a well-balanced leisure-time program, since this is not possible without the best of both. Whether the money comes from taxes, from United Funds, from direct gifts, from individuals, families, corporation or foundations, it all comes out of the same pockets, so to speak. In most communities and in all large urban areas, public and voluntary funds combined fall short of community needs. Therefore, to insure the most complete and effective coverage of community needs possible, it is essential to have as clearly stated principles as possible for determining the relative responsibilities of public and voluntary funds.

It is generally agreed that the public responsibility is to provide basic recreational facilities, leadership, and a broad, balanced program of services for all citizens of the community. This means services for all age groups, both sexes, all races and creeds. This does not mean, however, that the public programs have the responsibility for providing service for all leisure-time needs of citizens. The activities they do provide must be available to all.

It is generally agreed that voluntary agencies provide specialized facilities, leadership, and services to meet the particular leisure-time needs of that segment of the community the agency is set up to serve. Voluntary agencies can concentrate on meeting the special needs or interests of particular groups, such as a particular age group, a cultural or religious group, a particular neighborhood or community. Voluntary agencies can also offer more in the way of small group experience under highly skilled leadership than can a public agency under ordinary circumstances since the latter have a broader community responsibility and cannot be as selective in their intake. This does not mean that public agencies cannot provide service on as highly a skilled basis as voluntary agencies. In both instances the quality of program is determined by the quality of leadership. In some communities the public services may be of the highest quality in the community, in others some of voluntary services may be the highest. Communities in general get the kind of service they insist upon. As the implications of the new leisure in our culture are more widely understood, communities must be educated to demand the same care in selection of the persons who offer leisure-time services to their families as they do for teachers, doctors, lawyers, or any other professional service that is basic to modern family life.

Because of these differences in basic coverage responsibility, the public agency must concentrate more on the program activity while the voluntary agency can concentrate more on participants' social development and even treatment when necessary. This in no way implies that either type of service is inherently better or deserves more public support. What it does mean is that each offers a distinctive contribution that should not be duplicated by the other, and any community with services that meet basic leisure-time needs must have both. An enlightened community will support both while at the same time insisting upon joint planning and coordination.

Trends and future outlook

More Leisure Time

On the average, our culture provides more leisure time than any other in history. The prospects are for more in the future. A hundred years ago the work week was near seventy hours. A few years ago it was approximately forty; currently it is around thirty-seven hours. Some predictions are that by the year 2000 it will be down around twenty-eight hours a week. This shrinking work week, increased vacations and holidays on a regularly scheduled basis, more long week ends, an increasingly mobile population, and a constantly increasing family income all combine to anticipate both more leisure time available and more means to enjoy it. Since the supply of group work and recreation workers with professional preparation is currently running far short of demands, much will have to be done to recruit the caliber of staff needed over the next few years, plus an increasingly intelligent use of volunteer help. One essential, both in the social work and recreation fields, is for a careful evaluation of the use now being made of professional staff. There are clear indications that professional staff are being assigned many types of responsibility that could be carried by others, leaving them too little time to concentrate on the parts of their responsibility that do require professional judgment and skill. Once this is done, and salary schedules reflect the increasing importance of leisure-time service in our culture, progress should be made toward attracting to the field a more adequate number of staff.

More Emphasis on the Theoretical Basis of the Profession

With the increasing knowledge of both individual and group functioning, group services are being based more on scientific analysis and less on trial and error. Theories of individual and group behavior are being undergirded by scientific research in the fields of psychiatry, psychology, social psychology, sociology, anthropology, social work, and others. While it is true that the individual and group theories have not been integrated into a unified theoretical framework, progress is encouraging, and practice becomes increasingly sound as that takes place. Even though any solid foundation of this sort is still probably years off, it is continually opening new avenues of development that are attractive to those who are interested in improving leisure-time services.

The range of opportunities in group services, already diverse, will continue to expand. Increasing leisure-time is destined to play an ever more crucial role in the shaping of our cultural patterns. Top quality personnel must be the minimal goal.

———

Bibliography

Addams, Jane, *Forty Years at Hull House*. New York, The Macmillan Company, 1935.

American Association of Group Workers, "Definition of the Function of the Group Worker," *The Group*, XI (May 1949), pp. 11–12.

Austin, David M., "Goals for Gang Workers," *Social Work*, vol. 2 (October 1957), pp. 43–50.

Bradford, Leland P., and John R. P. French, Jr., "The Dynamics of the Discussion Group," *Journal of Social Issues*, IV (Spring 1948), entire issue.

Cartwright, Dorwin, and Alvin Zander, eds., *Group Dynamics—Research and Theory*. New York: Harper & Row, Publishers, 1953.

Cogan, Juanita Luck, "Social Group Work," *Social Work Year Book 1960*, New York: National Association of Social Workers, 1960, pp. 540–549.

Coyle, Grace L., *Group Work with American Youth*. New York: Harper & Row, Publishers, 1948.

———, "Some Basic Assumptions about Social Group Work," *The Social Group Work Method in Social Work Education*. New York: Council on Social Work Education, 1959, pp. 88–105.

Cunningham, Ruth, and Associates, *Understanding Group Behavior of Boys and Girls*. New York: Teachers College, Columbia University Press, 1951.

Dyer, Donald B., "The Role and Responsibility of Public Agencies in Building a Total Community Program," *Selected Papers in Group Work and Community Organization*. Raleigh: Health Publications Institute, 1952, pp. 25–27.

Frey, Louise A., "Social Group Work in Hospitals," *New Perspectives on Services to Groups: Theory, Organization, Practice*. New York: National Association of Social Workers, 1961, pp. 92–103.

Gibbs, Howard G., "Camping as a Tool in Social Welfare," *Group Work and Community Organization, 1955*, Paper presented at the 82nd Annual Forum of the National Conference of Social Work. New York: Columbia University Press, 1955, pp. 87–96.

Haiman, Franklyn S., *Group Leadership and Democratic Action*. Boston: Houghton Mifflin Company, 1951.

Hendry, Charles E., ed., *A Decade of Group Work*. New York: Association Press, 1948.

Jennings, Helen Hall, *Leadership and Isolation*, rev. ed. New York: Longmans, Green & Co., Inc., 1950.

Kadison, Sam, "Group Living Experiences in Camping," *Group Work and Community Organization, 1956*, Paper presented at the 83rd Annual Forum of the National Conference of Social Work. New York: Columbia University Press, 1956, pp. 91–100.

Kaiser, Clara A., "Group Work Education in the Last Decade," *The Group*, XV (June 1953), pp. 3–10, 27–29.

——, "The Social Group Work Process," *The Social Group Work Method in Social Work Education.* New York: Council on Social Work Education, 1959, pp. 115–128.

Klein, Alan F., "The Effect of Cultural Variables on Group Work Practice," *The Group,* XV (February 1953), pp. 13–14, 23–26.

——, *Society, Democracy, and the Group.* New York: Whiteside, Inc., 1953.

Konopka, Gisela, "Group Work: A Heritage and a Challenge," *Social Work with Groups, 1960.* New York: National Association of Social Workers, 1960, pp. 7–21.

——, *Group Work in the Institution—A Modern Challenge.* New York: Whiteside, Inc., and William Morrow & Company, Inc., 1954.

——, "Resistance and Hostility in Group Members," *The Group,* XVL (October 1953), pp. 3–10.

——, *Therapeutic Group Work with Children.* Minneapolis: University of Minnesota Press, 1949.

Lindsay, Doreen, "Group Placement of Long-term Mental Hospital Patients," *New Perspectives on Services to Groups: Theory, Organization, Practice.* New York: National Association of Social Workers, 1961, pp. 104–113.

Lippitt, Ronald, "Applying New Knowledge about Group Behavior," *Selected Papers in Group Work and Community Organization.* Raleigh: Health Publications Institute, 1951, pp. 7–17.

Martin, Alexander R., M.D., "Utilizing New Knowledge about Individual Behavior in Work with Groups in the Leisure Time Setting," *Selected Papers in Group Work and Community Organization.* Raleigh: Health Publications Institute, 1951, pp. 18–31.

Meyer, Harold D., and Charles K. Brightbill, *Community Recreation.* New York: Prentice Hall, Inc., 1956.

——, and ——, *State Recreation, Organization and Administration.* New York: A. S. Barnes & Company, Inc., 1950.

Murray, Clyde E., Max G. Bowens, and Russel Hogrefe, eds., *Group Work in Community Life.* New York: Association Press, 1954.

Nash, Jay B., *Philosophy of Recreation and Leisure.* St. Louis: The C. V. Mosly Company, 1953.

Olmsted, Michael S., *The Small Group.* New York: Random House, Inc., 1959.

Pacey, Lorene M., ed., *Readings in the Development of Settlement Work.* New York: Association Press, 1950.

Pernell, Ruby B., "Professional and Volunteer Workers in Traditional Youth-Serving Agencies," *Social Work,* vol. 2 (January 1957), pp. 63–67.

Phillips, Helen U., *Essentials of Social Group Work Skill.* New York: Association Press, 1957.

——, "Group Work Services in Residential Settings," *Social Work with Groups, 1960.* New York: National Association of Social Workers, 1960, pp. 108–119.

——, "Social Values and Social Group Work," *Group Work Papers Presented at the National Conference on Social Welfare, 1957.* New York: National Association of Social Workers, 1958, pp. 20–27.

Polansky, Norman A., "On the Dynamics of Behavioral Contagion," *The Group,* XIV (April 1952), pp. 3–8, 21, 25.

Ray, Florence, "Planning Decentralized Programs," *Proceedings of the National Conference of Social Work, 1955,* pp. 221–230.

Reynolds, Rosemary, "Services to Individuals within a Group Work Setting,"

Selected Papers in Group Work and Community Organization. Raleigh: Health Publications Institute, 1951, pp. 32–42.

Richards, Catharine V., "Finding a Focus with Hostile Youth Groups," *Social Work with Groups, 1958,* Selected papers from the National Conference on Social Welfare. New York: National Association of Social Workers, 1958, pp. 75–86.

Ross, Murray G., and Charles E. Hendry, *New Understanding of Leadership.* New York: Association Press, 1957.

Ryder, Eleanor L., "Some Principles of Intergroup Relations as Applied to Group Work," *Social Work with Groups, 1960.* New York: National Association of Social Workers, 1960, pp. 52–61.

Schulze, Susanne, *Creative Group Living in a Children's Institution.* New York: Association Press, 1951.

Schwartz, William, "Camping," *Social Work Year Book, 1960.* New York: National Association of Social Workers, 1960, pp. 112–117.

Sheffman, Bernard M., "Effecting Change through Social Group Work," *Proceedings of the National Conference on Social Welfare, 1958,* pp. 190–202.

Slavson, S. R., *Recreation and the Total Personality.* New York: Association Press, 1946.

Sullivan, Dorothea F., ed., *Readings in Group Work.* New York: Association Press, 1952.

Trecker, Audrey, and Harleigh B. Trecker, *How to Work with Groups.* New York: The Woman's Press, 1952.

Trecker, Harleigh B., ed., *Group Work in the Psychiatric Setting,* Proceedings of an Institute conducted by the American Association of Group Workers, 1955. New York: Whiteside, Inc., and William Morrow & Company, Inc., 1956.

———, *Social Group Work—Principles and Practice,* rev. ed. New York: Whiteside, Inc., 1955.

Vick, Hollis, "The Role and Responsibility of Voluntary Agencies in Building a Total Recreation Program," *Selected Papers in Group Work and Community Organization.* Raleigh: Health Publications Institute, 1952, pp. 28–32.

Vinter, Robert D., "New Evidence for Restructuring Group Services," *New Perspectives on Services to Groups: Theory, Organization, Practice.* New York: National Association of Social Workers, 1961, pp. 48–69.

Wilson, Gertrude, *Group Work and Case Work.* New York: Family Welfare Association of America, 1941.

———, "The Social Worker's Role in Group Situations," *The Social Group Work Method in Social Work Education.* New York: Council on Social Work Education, 1959, pp. 129–168.

———, and Gladys Ryland, "Social Class: Implications for Social Group Work," *Proceedings of the National Conference of Social Work, 1954,* pp. 168–186.

———, and ———, *Social Group Work Practice.* Boston: Houghton Mifflin Company, 1949.

Wittenberg, Rudolph M., *The Art of Group Discipline.* New York: Association Press, 1951.

———, *On Call for Youth—How to Understand and Help Young People.* New York: Association Press, 1955.

———, *So You Want to Help People.* New York: Association Press, 1947.

THE FALCONS

WILLIAM F. BUSSIERE, DIRECTOR,
Special Services to Youth
Friends Neighborhood Guild
Philadelphia, Pennsylvania

The following report is based on records of a group served as part of a special research project in a metropolitan area. The purpose of the project was to test the effectiveness of a coordinated program of services in dealing with the problem of delinquency within a limited geographical area. The project was initiated in June 1957 with special funds allocated by a federated financing agency. A welfare planning agency was responsible for over-all supervision of the program. The staff of the project included nine persons: a director, community worker, group worker, and caseworker, plus staff workers from Big Brothers, Boy Scouts, a family service agency, Girl Scouts and the Young Women's Christian Association. Staff offices were located in a settlement house within the project area. This report is an account of the experiences of one group, the Falcons, which was served as part of the area youth work program of the project.

Area youth work

"Area youth work" is one of the many terms used to designate programs aimed at providing service to groups-in-conflict. Agencies with "reaching-out" programs initiate the services to such groups on the basis of information concerning the group's membership, activity, location, etc., from neighborhood and community resources. The service is regarded as temporary and supplemental to other agency programs. The agency, through a staff worker, assists the group members with a variety of experiences in which their attitudes and behavior are tested and evaluated. Opportunities are provided for gaining status and recognition that are not dependent upon the values that govern gang life.

In addition to serving as an advisor at regular club meetings, a worker's assignment includes spending some time with the members at their favorite congregating places. In the beginning, group members resent this kind of intrusion, and the staff member's presence is viewed with great suspicion. They assume that the worker's interest is directed toward obtaining information for the police. As the boys become convinced that their cherished secrets, when shared with the worker, do not lead to increased police activity, they begin to realize that the agency's concern is directed toward their becoming more responsible citizens. As they begin to accept this function as part of the worker's responsibility, there is increased discussion and evaluation of their attitude and behavior about their illegal activity and intergroup conflicts. The value of the worker to the group is established when members begin to share information with him prior to their engagement in antisocial activity. As the need for area youth work diminishes, the group members demonstrate increasing ability to make use of various community resources in a positive manner. During this phase of group development, the staff person and his supervisor maintain close communication with the agency and staff that will assume responsibility for continued club program.

The group as seen by the community

Some information about the group and its members was acquired from the community organization worker assigned by the settlement house to a neighborhood council located in the same area as the Falcons. During December 1958 and January 1959, these boys had become the subject of considerable discussion in the Neighborhood Council. Opinions of the group by council members varied. Some persons felt that the youngsters were basically a good group of boys with time on their hands. Other persons complained that the boys were troublesome and often required police attention, especially on week ends. More specifically, council members said that members of the group often congregated in large numbers at Sixth Street and Riley Avenue. Their street corner activities consisted of loud conversation, card playing, and friendly boxing. Some council members believed that the group had engaged in street fighting with a teen-age group a few blocks north of Sixth and Riley. Some of the members were usually near the building in which the council had their meetings, and the community organization worker often exchanged greetings with them.

The Neighborhood Council members, divided in their impressions about the behavior of the boys, were also at odds as to what to do about them. Some members felt that a youth committee of the council should provide programs for the boys. Three council members met with the boys to fill out application forms. Twenty boys enrolled at that session. The repercussions of that enrollment caused a showdown in the council with respect to its responsibility to youth groups. It was decided that the council could not provide direct service to youth groups and that supervision of such programs should be the function of the group work and recreation agencies.

Also, in January 1959, the club advisor of the Young Women's Christian Association reported that some of these same boys were making it impossible for a girls group to conduct meetings. The boys at first had engaged in shouting to the girls from the sidewalk beneath the windows of the meeting room. The exchanges were friendly but distracting. Later, however, some of the boys had entered the building and come into the meeting room. When asked to leave they became rude and defiant. Some of the girls were delighted with this form of attention while others protested on the basis that the interferences would break up the club. Some consideration was given to formation of a coed club, but the girls voted against this proposal as it would only serve to limit their program interests.

Finally the settlement house was asked to provide service to the group. Further consideration was given to the nature of the group in order to determine the kind of service that would benefit the group. Juvenile Aid authorities were aware of the group's existence and believed that they had engaged in street fighting with a group known as the Junior Wildcats. Investigations of these conflicts had not resulted in any arrests, but the group was under surveillance. Five members had arrest records. Other members had been investigated on suspicion of various minor complaints, but no formal charges had been made. Although a number of the members resided in the project area, their congregating place was outside of the project boundaries. In February, it was decided that the group would be identified with the settlement house and staff service provided through the area youth worker of the project. Further evaluation of the group and its neighborhood activity would determine the extent of need for area youth work service.

Description of the group

During the year and a half of service, a total of thirty-five persons became associated with the club program. Approximately half of these persons showed a temporary interest in formal membership. The records show that eighteen persons were active members for at least six months and a total of ten persons of the original enrollment maintained their association for eighteen months. At the point of registration, the age range of group members was 15 to 17 years of age. With reference to school, the majority of the boys were classified by the school as Retarded Educable, which meant that most of them would leave school on their seventeenth birthday. The state law required attendance at school until that age.

A list of the eighteen club members follows with some information about each boy, his relationship to other members and to the group. The age listed is the age of the individual at the time of enrollment. School classification is included, using the terms: Retarded Educable, Regular Class, or Not Enrolled. The boys' names are listed alphabetically.

1. Allen. 16 years. Regular Class. Allen commanded attention by responding loudly and negatively to most club suggestions. His talk was accompanied by dramatic gestures of arm waving. The group never regarded his demonstrations seriously, and he possessed other talents. As a tall, good-looking youngster, he was popular with the girls. He was an excellent athlete and owned a large record collection. His parents were separated, and he lived with his mother and sister. His mother was a self-centered person, unable to be genuinely interested in her children. Allen felt rejected by his father and maintained that his interest in his father was limited to the money he could get from him.

2. Arnold. 18 years. Not Enrolled. Arnold was a tall, well-developed individual who had spent some five years in correctional institutions. He joined the group six months after its formation and worked responsibly on special events. He was a restless and energetic person, unpredictable, and long discussions were impossible for him. He quickly gained a reputation for his ability in street fighting. The group members were interested and concerned about Arnold. His short temper flared in some situations while other members were present and as this became more frequent, there was a risk in associating with him outside of club meetings. He was the eldest of eight children. He did not remember his father. His mother was employed in a garment factory.

3. Charles. 14 years. Retarded Educable. A short, lean, quiet youngster, striving for acceptance with bigger boys. He had been arrested for breaking into parking meters. His 16-year-old brother was the leader of the most aggressive gang in the neighborhood. He had five brothers, two older than himself. He was usually with Pete, Allen and James. He said nothing at club meetings. There was no father in the family.

4. Edward. 16 years. Retarded Educable. Edward was with the group for approximately six months. He was an aggressive and hostile youngster and had great difficulty in adjusting to the club's social setting. He was friendly with a number of the members and tried to be accepted, but he was his own worst enemy. His mother was an alcoholic. His stepfather insisted on high standards for Edward's behavior while he engaged in illegal activity himself. He was committed to a correctional institution because he knocked a man down to steal a bottle of liquor from him.

5. Fred. 18 years. Not Enrolled. Fred joined the group in its fifth month. He was on parole after serving time in a correctional institution in another state. He had known some of the club members when he was younger. Although he had considerable status, he never asserted his influence on the group. He had a great ability in telling stories, which could keep the members amazed and interested. He worked full-time in a warehouse.

6. George. 17 years. Not enrolled. George did not have a strong commitment to the group. He was most often present when the group members congregated at their favorite corner. He eventually left the group and went to work in a nearby community where he lived with relatives.

7. Gus B. 17 years. Regular Class. Phil's brother and by contrast very talkative. He had considerable influence in the group and was respected by most of the members. He was one of three key persons in swaying group opinion toward gang fighting or social programming. While he did not attend meetings regularly, he accepted assignments resulting from the group's decisions. Gus and Phil lived with their grandparents.

8. Hank. 16 years. Retarted Educable. A tall, heavy-set youngster mainly interested in athletics, and his interest in club meetings was limited to the group's interest in athletics. He participated easily in discussion in club meetings and on the street corner. He appeared to be well informed about membership in other gangs and persons recently arrested or released from institutions. Easily influenced by decisions of the majority.

9. James. 15 years. Regular Class. Very quiet youngster; well-mannered and neat in appearance. Spent much of his time with Pete and Allen and supported their point of view in club meetings. Related very well to adults, uncertain in his peer relationships. Mother, dominant member in the family. Father, quiet and reserved.

10. John. 17 years. Not Enrolled. John did not regularly associate with the group except for special programs. He had a very good sense of humor and was well liked. He had a severe case of stuttering, which became a problem when he became excited. The group's reaction to his stuttering depended on the nature of discussion. If John was attempting to make a serious point, the group waited patiently for him to finish. However, as he was seldom serious, the group spent much time laughing at him and with him.

11. Leon. 15 years. Retarded Educable. Leon was the clown of the group and its nonconformist. He distracted others during club discussions through humorous comments or unusual sounds in such a way that the group seldom took action to curb his disturbances. He was friendly with all the members and never became strongly identified with one subgroup. He also avoided forming meaningful relationships with adults. Eldest of six children. Mother of limited intelligence. No father.

12. Morton. 19 years. Not Enrolled. Morton had served approximately two years in a correctional institution for his part in a gang war. He was regarded as a kind of older brother to the group. Because of his age and interest, the agency agreed to have him serve as assistant advisor. His demands on the members to conduct club meetings in a strictly businesslike manner created friction in the group and frustration for Morton. He contributed food, finances, and hard work to the club's first two social events. When he realized the group could not meet his expectations in terms of their interest and conduct, he left the group.

13. Paul. 17 years. Regular Class. Paul was the president of the Falcons. A tall, quiet, and serious youngster. He related well with adults as well as his peers. He was reliable and responsible. While he was respected by the members and could provide strong leadership, he lacked self-confidence. He did well at conducting the meetings, when the agenda was prepared and reviewed with the worker in advance. His close friends were Robert and Fred. During the summer he worked in an ice cream cone factory. His father had been unemployed for a number of years, which Paul silently resented. His mother worked from time to time as a housecleaner.

14. Pete. 15 years. Retarded Educable. Pete was the most popular member of the group. He participated in program with enjoyment and enthusiasm. He was also very outspoken, defiant, and quick-tempered. In junior high school, he was elected president of the student council. He was often asked to serve as chairman at club meetings, although he was never elected to the position. His quick temper often created trouble for his friends with other teen-agers and adults. Mother active in community affairs but unable to set limits for her children. Father's whereabouts unknown.

15. Phil B. 15 years. Retarted Educable. Phil was well liked by the group. Very personable and good-natured. Seldom entered into club discussion but when he did he spoke independently. Responsible in carrying out group assignments.

16. Robert. 15 years. Regular Class. A very good-natured youngster. Tall and well built for his age. Robert was treasurer of the club and leader of the gang. He was honest, reliable, and clever. When the gang first formed with seven members, he presented each of them with homemade pistols. During club meetings Robert made no attempt to dominate group decisions, and he participated as any other club member. He did not participate much in the discussion over gang problems, but when he did speak his words were regarded as final authority. He was very interested in science, and the only member with a hobby. He worked four to five hours each day after school. His family attended church each Sunday as a unit. His father was a craftsman and a union member.

17. Roger. 17 years. Not Enrolled. An isolationist, Roger would appear when there was a special activity. He was considered an alcoholic by members of the group. He was on probation as a result of carrying a concealed deadly weapon. He and Gus were often together when dating. He was often ridiculed by other members for his appearance or condition. While he denied these accusations, in defending himself, he never lost his temper.

18. Roland. 16 years. Retarded Educable. A tall, thin youngster who never participated in formal club discussion. In the beginning he was Hank's close friend, and they were always together. Outside of the club settings he was more communicative, and the boys close to him regarded him as having a good sense of humor. He was somewhat tense and serious with adults. One of eight children.

The first meeting

Some two months had passed between the time that some members had approached the Neighborhood Council with their interest in a social club. A volunteer of the council, well known to some of the boys, served as a liaison between the group and the agency. At their suggestion, the worker met with three of the members at the home of one of the boys. An agreement had been reached by the staff of the project and a public recreation agency regarding service to the group. The recreation agency would make its facility available for group meetings and program activities, and the project would provide the staff worker. The following excerpts from the records indicate reaction of the group members to this plan.

[2/19]   James, Charles, and Allen. At Allen's house. The boys were quiet but not relaxed. Allen did most of the talking. Allen said, "The guys are sure interested in getting a club set up. They want something to do for the summer, but most of all we want a place to have meetings." I asked about the possibility of meeting at the recreation center. Their expressions froze for a moment, and they turned their eyes away from me and to each other. Allen broke the silence with a chuckle. He said, "Oh, no, Bill. That wouldn't work out." I was surprised by his use of my first name as they had gone through great length in our introduction to memorize the pronunciation of my last name.

I explained the advantages of the recreation center as a place for programs. Allen sighed and replied, "I'll tell you the truth. There are some boys who hang around the center and they don't want any company." Charles chirped, "Yeah, 'specially us." I remarked innocently that the only group around the center was the Junior Wildcats. "That's them, Mr. Bill, that's them," shouted Allen. The three of them started laughing, which released some of the tension of discussing this with a new adult.

They finally suggested the auditorium of the housing project as a good meeting place. They were not very optimistic about acquiring permission to use the building, however, and Allen commented that group activities had not been too successful in the past. I said that I would talk to Mr. Morris, the manager. Allen remarked, "Just don't use my name." When I asked for an explanation, he refused to elaborate.

This first meetings with representatives of the group helped to bring out a major factor that was important in providing service to the group. The boys identified the conflict with the Junior Wildcats in terms of geographic location.

In this first meeting with some of the members, the worker became directly informed about the conflict existing between the Junior Wildcats and the Falcons. The boys rejected the recreation center because its loca-

tion was in the other gang's territory. The worker introduced the name of
the other group but he avoided asking specific questions about the difficulties between the two groups as this would have made the boys very
suspicious. He focused his attention on their interest, which was limited
to "a place to meet."

The worker's immediate interest, however, was with reference to
the three members he had just met. He knew very little about them. What
status did they have in the group? How had the group decided that the
first meeting should be arranged with these three persons? In conversations with staff members at the settlement, the worker learned that Allen
had been active in athletic programs two years ago. Charles was known to
the agency through his older brother Dominic. Dominic was the leader
of the Little C's, which was considered the most aggressive gang in the
section. Little was known about Charles except that he was very quiet.
James was not known to any of the staff members.

Following Allen's suggestion the worker made an appointment to
meet and discuss the group and its request with the housing manager. In
the following conferences, further information is obtained about the group
and also about some of the attitudes of adults about the group.

Mr. Morris, manager of the housing project, was not very enthusiastic
about teen-agers using the auditorium. He had received a number of complaints from residents about large groups gathering in the project. He also
reported that Allen and his friends had damaged some of the property
when they used pipes in the basement as chinning bars. We agreed tentatively to experiment with this particular group in the hope that a supervised
program would change their attitude toward the project. He deferred a
final decision, however, until I spoke to Mr. Jones, the custodian. He felt
that Mr. Jones knew all of the families in the project and would know how
much of a risk was involved with this particular crowd.

[2/21] Conference with Mr. Jones, also with James. As I was walking
through the project, I heard someone shout, "Mr. Bill!" I turned and recognized James. He asked me if Mr. Morris had given permission for using the
auditorium. I told him that I had spoken to Mr. Morris who had referred me
to Mr. Jones. He asked if he could come along, and I replied that I preferred it that way.

Following introductions, Mr. Jones listened patiently as I explained the
interest of the group in requesting permission for use of the auditorium.
James, in answering his question, said that he was a member of the group.
Mr. Jones commented that James was a nice youngster and new in the
project. Mr. Jones said that he would let me know his answer in a day or
two, but it would be up to Mr. Morris to make the decision.

As James and I were leaving, Mr. Jones said that he would like to see
me for a minute. I told James that I would see him later. Mr. Jones pro-

ceeded to inform me that I did not know what I was getting into. He said that while he liked James, he felt that most of the boys were hoodlums. They chased girls in the project, sang and made noises until all hours, and they were a general nuisance. He added, "There are a number of nice younger boys in the project, and you shouldn't waste your time with that crowd."

I explained to him that part of the agency's program was specifically aimed at working with teen-agers who caused problems in the neighborhood. While this would take some time and cooperation, we felt the boys could improve. He continued to talk about the hopelessness of today's teen-agers. I asked him if he felt conditions would improve if no program was provided. I explained that the group wanted something; and in order to get it, they would have to be willing to abide by the rules of the project. He agreed that the problem would not get any better if left to itself. He said that the boys could meet in the auditorium on Wednesdays at 7:30 P.M. He said that we would notify Mr. Morris. Then he added, "One wrong move and out they go."

Final agreement was reached by the two agencies when the settlement house made its request in writing to the housing manager and it was approved. Gaining community cooperation in providing service to such groups was very difficult. Certain acts of the group members had helped to form the negative attitudes about the entire group held by Mr. Morris and Mr. Jones. When some of the group members were noisy, the housing personnel phoned the police. This in turn created resentment among the boys toward the project staff. They then planned further ways of harassing people in the project.

Attendance at the first three meetings ranged from ten to eighteen members. Some persons came to one meeting and never returned. The same eight persons were present at each meeting, however, which helped to determine the persons most interested in the club. Prior to the meetings, the worker had opportunity to talk with two or three individuals at a time. The worker noticed that Morton usually arrived earlier than other members. Shortly after Paul and Robert arrived, the majority of the members appeared.

The group had selected a dance for their first program activity. It provided a quick means of presenting their group to other teen-agers, and it was also an activity with which they were most familiar. The worker had explained the conditions for using the building and pointed out that whether or not they continued to have that privilege was determined by their actions. Paul, Robert, and Morton helped to remind other members of the rules, as well as setting an example. There was no election of officers as Paul and Robert had been designated president and treasurer, respectively, prior to any meetings with the worker.

The following record indicates the role of some of the members in planning an activity and how the worker helps to augment the discussion and follow-through on matters with certain individuals.

[3/16]   Present: Phil B., Gus B., Hank, Allen, James, John, Charles, Robert, Paul, Leon, Roland, and Morton. The club dance was a week away, and apparently this accounted for most of the members being present and on time at 7:30 P.M. Robert reported that he had the dance tickets, which were mimeographed on 3x5 cards at the settlement. Robert explained that tickets were 15 cents for members and 25 cents for nonmembers. There was still resentment about this decision. Pete commented that he felt that the members should not have to pay for attending their own dance. Morton stood up and gave an impassioned speech as to the merits of each member contributing his share to the treasury. While some members snickered at Morton's dramatics, there was general agreement to his point of view.

I then announced that Mr. Morris had insisted that a police car be parked near the auditorium. Without exception, all members voiced their disapproval of this. Morton said, "The dance wouldn't look too cool with a red car outside. People would wonder what kind of jitterbug affair was going on inside." I asked for alternatives, keeping in mind that some kind of police coverage was necessary in terms of the housing project's interest. After receiving no suggestions I asked if it were possible to request police coverage through the Juvenile Aid division. Juvenile Aid officers don't wear uniforms or use red cars. There was a positive response to this idea, and Morton and Gus B. volunteered to accompany me to Juvenile Aid headquarters.

The matter of chaperones was discussed, and Robert reported that he had talked to Mr. Clark, president of the Neighborhood Council, who said that three or four council members had expressed interest in attending the dance. Gus B. reported that he had talked to two adults who said that they would serve as chaperones.

Morton agreed to be in charge of refreshments. Robert accepted the responsibility of distributing tickets and collecting money for tickets sold. Allen agreed to get the records and be the disc jockey. My suggestion to have Paul coordinate all three committees was accepted.

As we were leaving, I talked to Gus B. and Morton and asked them to be at my office tomorrow and we would make an appointment with Juvenile Aid. I also spoke to Charles and Leon and said that I knew that they had ideas but the group was not getting the advantage of them because they seldom spoke out. Another significant point was made by Allen as the boys were leaving the auditorium. I overheard him comment that ties should be worn, "because Mr. Morris might come around, Man."

The worker helped Charles and Leon realize that he was aware and concerned about their lack of participation during club meetings. As Allen had a particular problem with Mr. Morris, the dance could serve as an opportunity to show Mr. Morris that Allen was something more than the problem youngster of the project. While the Juvenile Aid Division would have accepted the worker's request for police coverage by phone, the worker was interested in having the boys meet policemen when they needed help.

In general, the formation of a social club by a gang presents some conflicts to a group in terms of their identification as a gang. Their real status in their neighborhood is achieved by gang reputation. There are usually other social clubs in the neighborhood, but to most gang members in the area these clubs are not important. For some members the social club offers an opportunity to escape the risks involved in maintaining a gang reputation. Other persons find it difficult to associate with a social club on any basis as this reflects a conformity to values of the larger society, which they refuse to accept. The following record illustrates some of this conflict in a discussion of selecting the club name. The tension exhibited at the meeting indicated that some discussion on the matter had taken place before the scheduled meeting.

[3/2]   Phil B., Hank, Allen, James, John, Charles, Pete, Robert, Paul, Gus B., Leon, and Roland. Paul was quite tense as he announced that the group had to select a name for itself. Gus B. said that he couldn't see any need for discussion as the "Royal Turks" was the only name for the club. Pete said that it was "jive," meaning that it struck him as being phony. Allen agreed with Gus B., and his action received the nodding approval of Charles and James. Paul said, "I don't know about the rest of you guys, but the name sounds like a fighting gang name to me. Personally, I would like a name that shows that we are a social club."

I said that Paul's point should be considered from the point of view of the club's purpose and how they wanted to be known to others. Gus B. said, "And what does the 'Royal Turks' sound like to you?" I replied that the name of the club would take on meaning as their activities, good or bad, became known. I added, however, that a group called the "Royal Turks" had received considerable attention in New York City last summer as a 'bopping' gang. Gus B. excused himself from the meeting before the discussion was completed. As he departed, he said that he still favored the name of "Royal Turks."

Paul continued, "I, for one, do not want to stand behind a club name with a gang reputation." Pete added, "I'm with you, Paul; I thought we were organizing a social club to get up off that junk." The name "Falcons" was suggested, and with a minimum of discussion the name was adopted by a unanimous vote. Allen said, "Gus won't dig that, Man." Robert replied, "Gus will have to accept the decision of the club."

Prior to this discussion it had been assumed, on the basis of information from the community organization worker, that Gus was the leader of the group. He certainly spoke strongly and with great conviction. The interest in gang identification was indicated by Allen, Charles, and James. Pete supported Paul's point of view, but his action was an independent one. Unfortunately, some of the more uncommunicative members did not express their real feelings on the matter. While Robert did not participate in the discussion, his final remarks demonstrated considerable power. He had, in a sense, approved the group's decision and his authority to do this was unquestioned.

The Falcons at this point had demonstrated their abilities in conducting meetings. They had gone to Juvenile Aid authorities to request help for coverage at their dance. Mr. Jones, while withholding his opinion until the clock struck twelve at their dance, admitted that their affair was "impressive." The worker appeared to have a good relationship to the group. However, it is situations of intergroup conflict that test the extent of the group's acceptance of the worker. In this respect, the Falcons were similar to other groups, and a relationship with the worker had not developed in which information about gang activities could be shared.

The group had been meeting about two months when the newspapers and radio reported that a gang had cornered two boys who were walking their girl friends home. In the process of breaking away from the gang, one boy had been injured by a shot from a pistol. The boy was identified as Pete Robinson. The role of worker in such a situation should be an immediate response to the injured member and his condition. Secondly, he must make every effort to minimize further intergroup conflict in which retaliation is almost inevitable. The worker phoned the Juvenile Aid authorities and learned that Pete had received medical treatment but was not hospitalized. The worker informed the Juvenile Aid authorities that Pete was a member of a group to which the worker had been assigned two months ago but conveyed no further information about him.

[4/12]   Pete, Mitch, and Bubbles. Pete was standing on the street corner near his house with two other boys, neither of them Falcons, when I arrived. Pete had been grazed on the shoulder and the chin by a bullet. His head was also bandaged where he had been struck. In answer to my question, he replied that he was feeling fine except that he had a constant headache. I handed him a book from the library that I thought he would be interested in reading. He thanked me for the book and commented that he had seen the movie based on the story of the book.

Pete then introduced, in a very casual fashion, the fact that he had been taken to the police station last night at a late hour. He explained that he had been asked to identify a person named Perry in regard to the shooting. Perry had admitted being present during the shooting but denied that he ever held the gun that was fired at Pete. Pete said he told the police that he recalled a boy similar to Perry being present but admitted that he did not know who did the shooting. I asked Pete if Perry was a member of the Junior Wildcats. He replied uneasily, "No, it wasn't any of the Wildcats 'cause I know most of them." (Actually, as it was learned later, the Wildcat Juniors and Seniors had been present.)

During the course of this conversation, I could sense a distance between Pete and myself. Our relationship at this point did not permit him to relate exactly what happened. I did have the definite impression, however, that Perry had chosen to tell this particular version of the incident and Pete was willing to support whatever story they (Perry and his friends) chose to tell the police. Mitch and Bubbles appeared to accept the story given for my benefit, although I had the feeling that they both knew exactly what had happened. The rest of the conversation avoided any reference to the incident.

Pete, as the above recorded conversation indicates, fulfilled the requirements of a qualified gang member on a matter in which most adults are regarded as outsiders. The unwritten code regarding intergroup conflict is that gang members cannot provide information that will result in police action against their own members or *members of the opposing group*. Information about the specifics of an incident will eventually be shared with the worker. In the beginning, however, false information is often given to test the worker's reliability. For instance, casual reference may be made about a "neat .38 that Roger keeps locked in his bureau drawer." The comment is made in worker's presence although the conversation is between the members. When the release of such information does not result in investigation by the police, the members become more convinced that the worker's real function is to help them seriously evaluate the meaning of gang activity and its consequences.

Clarification of services and cooperation between various agencies is essential in reducing tension and conflict between hostile groups and creating better understanding. Reports of the activities of the Junior Wildcats continued to come to the attention of the agency, very often through group members who were being served in the area youth work program. In April, the staff of the project requested the assistance of the Youth Services Association [1] in arranging a meeting with personnel of the Department of Recreation. Information concerning the Junior Wildcats was shared. The Recreation Department stated that their facilities and program were available to Junior Wildcats as long as they observed the rules that applied to all members. The boys' behavior in the neighborhood, however, required additional attention, and it was agreed that area youth work service be provided the group through the project.

During the weeks that followed the attack on Pete, increasing ref-

[1] The Youth Services Association was responsible for coordinating the area youth work programs of various agencies on a city-wide basis.

erence to the Junior Wildcats was made in Falcon meetings. A retaliatory move had been made on the Wildcats, not by the Falcons, but by the Little C's through a prearranged agreement as the Falcons were under close police observation. Shots were fired, but no one was injured. Actually many of the Falcons were in the police station when the retaliatory act occurred because of reported gang movement in the neighborhood. None of these decisions had been shared with workers. The crisis situation and the discussions that followed demonstrated a willingness on the part of some members to place increasing trust in the worker regarding gang activities. The recent events had made a deep impression on Gus, as the following report indicates.

[4/23] Individual conference with Gus B. Following the meeting with the Falcons, I accompanied Gus B. through the housing project. I asked him if the situation between themselves and the Junior Wildcats had improved. He responded, "I was talking to their runner in school today, and he said that some of the boys want to cut the corner loose." I explained that the agency, through the area youth work program was interested in helping all corner groups with something constructive. Gus replied, "I think that Warren Green would be interested." He agreed to talk to Warren tomorrow. I said that I was pleased that he was willing to share such information with me. He turned his head toward me and remarked, "If I didn't trust you, I wouldn't even be walking with you."

The phrase "to cut the corner loose" refers to a decision of a member or a group to leave the gang and gang activities. Gus was able to follow through on his self-imposed responsibility, which showed considerable maturity on his part.

When service can be provided to the principal groups in conflict, a system of more direct communication through agencies, workers, and group members can be established. One of the means of improving communication between various groups with similar purposes is the intergroup council. Such programs offer opportunity for broad experiences of democratic participation and representation. Some recreation agencies that have a number of teen-age groups in their membership use councils so that programs of each group can be coordinated and related to one another. The principal of face-to-face communication through group representatives is also applicable to antisocial groups.

During the period of service to the Falcons, workers were also assigned to the Little C's and the Junior Wildcats. A council was established for the purpose of bringing together the leaders of each group to 1) discuss specific conflicts between members of their groups, and 2) decide alternative means of settling differences, other than gang fighting. The

long-range goal of these meetings was aimed at increasing positive relationships between the groups.

Each group had selected a permanent representative who was fully
informed about the group's activities and attitudes. In each case this was
the leader. The second representative provided for rotation so that each
member of the group had an opportunity to attend a council meeting. The
place of a meeting was known only to workers. Meetings were held in a
variety of places, and attempts were made not to have two successive
meetings in the same location. All groups agreed to meeting places not being announced, as this prevented any group from congregating outside of
the particular location.

The following is an account of an early council meeting. A Junior
Wildcat member had related a story to his worker that five boys had attempted to beat up Warren. One of the five boys was a member of a group
represented on the council, and this served as the basis for calling a council
meeting. As there had been some agreement that the groups represented
on the council would attempt to improve relationships with one another,
the Junior Wildcats were interested in knowing why a member of Little
C's named Thomas was present when four other boys attempted to attack
Warren. The following record points out how a problem is created when
communication breaks down within a gang. Thomas had not been an active member of the Little C's social club. His affiliation with the gang had
been affirmed by the group members to the workers prior to the meeting.

[6/3] Dominic and Thomas, Little C's; Warren and Clyde, Junior Wildcats; Robert and Paul, Falcons; three workers. Worker B of the Falcons
opened the meeting as the misunderstanding was between the Little C's
and the Junior Wildcats. He stated that something has occurred at Fourth
and Lincoln between members of the Little C's and the Wildcats. He added
that there had been an agreement of the council that as certain developments occurred they would be brought to the attention of the council.
(Pause.)

Worker C: "Perhaps it would help if Dominic gave an account of the
incident." (Pause.)

Dominic: "Understand that I wasn't there, so I can only tell you how it
was run down to me, understand. Well, it seems that some boys from
another corner met Warren. One of these boys—well, things ain't too cool
between him and Warren."

Warren: "No, Man. It's not that way at all. I mean things ain't too cool
between me and the boy, you know, but there was five of them and I'm with
my girl, Man."

Thomas: "And you—you sent her back to get your boys, Man."

Warren: "I don't know what she did, Man. But I told her to make it,
Man, because she might get smashed, too. You know."

Thomas: "Why didn't you give that boy a fair one, Man?"

Warren: "I would have, Man, but you started to throw one, Man."

Thomas: "Aw-w-w, Man!"

Worker: "It appears to me that we have talked about each group member's responsibility to other groups in other council meetings. I believe this point has been discussed in each group, hasn't it? Have you been attending group meetings, Thomas?"

Thomas: "No, not lately."

Worker A: "I think that the groups represented here tonight had agreed to work toward a better understanding with each other. Did you know about such an agreement, Thomas?"

Thomas: "Well, I knew that some talk was going on, but I didn't understand. You know, I heard something, but not like you just said."

Worker C: "It seems to me that a member of a group carries the group's name wherever he goes, and it is important that each member follows through on decisions reached by the group."

Worker B: "In this situation, it appears that Thomas did not have a clear understanding of what had been decided in earlier council meetings."

Dominic: "It seems to me that we have reached a point of understanding. Thomas says that he did not know what had taken place at these meetings. If Warren is any kind of a man, he should be willing to forget the whole thing. But that is up to him."

Warren: "It's all right with me, Man. But you know, I just wanted to find out what's to it, Man."

Worker B: "I believe Warren is right. Thomas is a member of the Little C's, and we had agreed that as an incident occurred between members of the three groups, we would bring it to the attention of the council. I regard this as a proper move on the part of the Wildcats."

Council meetings became scheduled on a regular basis, and relationships between the groups continued to improve. By midsummer the Falcons challenged the Junior Wildcats to a game of softball. While there was an interest and willingness on the part of each group for the game, the following accounts illustrate some of the uncertainties of members immediately prior to the proposed activity.

[7/25] Junior Wildcats. It was an hour before game time. Ham and Frank were the only two members on the corner. Frank commented that Warren had not returned from work and was doubtful that he would be present. Ham complained that there were not enough gloves. The worker asked Ham if gloves might be available at the playground. He seemed very doubtful. Frank was worried that their coach had forgotten about the game. The worker asked if something had happened recently that made the game with the Falcons unadvisable. Ham smiled and said he knew of nothing. He added, "You know all the guys haven't got together for something good in two years." The worker asked them if they thought the Falcons might also be wondering how the get-together would work out. The worker then suggested we ride to the Falcon corner and find out. The worker mentioned that their worker was already with them. They agreed.

[7/25] Falcons. Gus continued to complain about the lack of equipment and the fact that the group had never practiced. I asked if he was suggesting that the game be postponed or called off. This was too much for him. He replied "If it's left up to me, we play. But I don't know about these other cats." Pete asked why the game wasn't scheduled at the Preston playground. Someone called him stupid and remarked that the Wildcats would never leave that playground alive. I said that Pete had made a good point and asked if they were concerned about playing at Goddard's Field. Robert laughed and said, "No, not if we get enough baseball bats." Allen added, "If any of those punks make one move toward me, I'll smash them." Paul explained that the boys at Goddard's Field were allies to the Wildcats. I said that I could not be party to arranging a riot, only a softball game. Robert responded immediately with the opinion that he did not think anything would happen. I said that I would notify the playground supervisor to phone to the police if it appeared that fighting was to take place. This was acceptable to them and considered a wise move.

When Ham, Frank, and their worker arrived at the Falcon corner, the members of each group became more concerned about their status and their commitment to playing the game than about their apprehensions. They began joking with each other, and this eased the tension considerably. Frank, hedging, told the Falcons that the Wildcats were ready, and they had wanted to know if the Falcons were still interested in playing. Robert remarked that if Frank had arrived three minutes later, the Falcons would have already been at the field.

The Falcons were somewhat tense at the field, but the Junior Wildcats talked in a very friendly manner, which helped to put the small number of spectators at ease about the Falcons' presence. The Falcons made a number of errors, and by the fifth inning some of their members walked off the field disgusted with themselves. This was the first time that the Falcons had shown hostility among themselves in the presence of another group. In spite of the defeat, the important result of the game was that members of both groups gathered together outside the playing field after the game. Their discussion became so friendly that they were inviting each other to dances that they were contemplating. This never actually occurred as each group was fearful that other neighborhood boys might do harm to members of the invited groups.

While providing service to a group, the worker is concerned with individuals and the ways in which experiences within the group contribute to their growth and development. "New" members very often are boys returning from institutions, and they rebuild their associations in the group with mixed feelings. The person on parole regards the worker with great caution as his affiliation with the agency represents the law-abiding community. Also his affiliation with gang members can be considered a parole violation. The following account points out the beginning of a relationship with Fred. The conversation occurred prior to the third group meeting that Fred attended. Fred's participation in the two meetings had been limited to a few comments that expressed a commitment on his part to help the group plan an activity. The worker therefore carried a very positive impression of him. Observe how the group helped to support the individual by granting Fred time to speak to the worker alone.

[7/28]   Fred Johnson. I had been waiting outside fifteen minutes when Fred arrived, alone. I greeted him and asked if he had seen the others. He said that they were at Gus's house and would be along soon. I thought that it was odd that he did not wait for the group, but I made no mention of it. He asked if the door was open. I answered that it was, and then he asked if I was going inside. I replied that it seemed like a good idea and suggested that we arrange the table and chairs for the meeting. I asked him about his job. He replied with comments that had no particular importance. He appeared nervous. After further general conversation, I excused myself to go to the bathroom. He asked if it was alright for him to accompany me. I smiled and shrugged my shoulders.

As the bathroom door closed, he pushed a white slip in front of me. He said, "Could you sign this?" I asked what it was. He remarked, "It's just a piece of paper that I have to get signed." I noticed that the name of the state was printed in large letters on the form. I asked, "Can anyone sign this?" He said, "Anyone that is a sponsor." I remarked that I wasn't a sponsor. He appeared like he wanted to shout but replied in a low voice, "That's what I mean. Will you be my sponsor?" He was quite tense, and I replied, "I'm very pleased that you asked me."

I explained that while I was very interested in being his sponsor, the parole board might not approve as I was not in a position to report him to his parole officer. He replied, "That means you won't sign it." In answer to my question, he commented that his report was overdue by a week. I said that I understood the pressure he was under and complimented him for his willingness to ask me to do this as we did not know each other very well. I told him that I would make every effort to see his parole officer tomorrow, and I would give him my decision tomorrow evening. He folded the form slowly and placed it in his pocket. He felt disappointed and skeptical about this postponement. I said, "I know that this is very important to you. I would like to be your sponsor, but if I am not approved by the parole officer—and I were to sign the slip—it might only create further problems for you."

The immediate pressure on Fred to submit his overdue report made it difficult for him to accept the necessity of the worker to become more fully informed about the requirements of sponsorship. The worker, of course, had no alternative. He indicated his pleasure in Fred's willingness to consider the worker as a sponsor and tried to avoid Fred's misinterpreting the postponement of the slip signing with a rejection of Fred as a person.

The worker met with the parole officer, and an understanding was reached between the two persons. Later, Fred was able to express his appreciation to the worker for delaying the signing of the report form. Much later, Fred was able to discuss the incident that had led to his commitment to a correctional institution in another state.

A worker's relationship with a corner group requires him to maintain a general positive interpretation of the functions of public institutions. Many youngsters have negative experiences with agencies, police, schools, and courts, and there is, understandably, a tendency for a youngster on the basis of a single situation to condemn the entire system. There are instances, also, when a youngster is justified in a complaint toward the action of a public employee. The worker helps the youth to focus on his own responsibilities in his relationship with others. He also takes advantage of opportunities that help create better understanding between the youngster and staff persons of other agencies. The worker is most effective in this regard when it is clear that he does not have the authority of a public official. That is, he does not arrest nor provide information leading to the arrest of individuals. For example, the worker's relationship with a probation officer does not include providing information that might lead to court action.

[8/15] Mr. Crowley, probation officer. Mr. Crowley commented that he was investigating the arrest of Charles Green on a disorderly conduct charge. He said that he had visited the house of the address listed and found it to be a vacant lot. I explained that I knew Charles as he was a member of a group to which I was assigned. Mr. Crowley seemed somewhat resigned to the situation. He said, "It will take a while, but I'll find him." I suggested that I could notify Charles that the court was investigating a recent arrest and Mr. Crowley, who was assigned to the case, was looking for him. If Charles could voluntarily come forward, it would indicate that he was able to approach such a situation in a responsible manner. Mr. Crowley agreed that the approach had some merit and added that regardless of what happened, his investigation would focus on the basic facts of the incident. I replied that beyond getting the two of them together, I had no further responsibility.

[8/15] Pete, Allen, and Paul. I introduced the fact that Mr. Crowley had been to the office and was planning to get in touch with Charles concerning last week's arrest. I indicated that it was my suggestion that Charles be given the opportunity to decide whether or not he wanted to take the initiative on this matter. Paul commented that Charles was in the movies but he would see him tonight and let him know.

[8/18]   Mr. Crowley, phone call. Mr. Crowley said that he had not heard from Charles; therefore, he planned to write the place of employment of Charles' mother. He indicated that he would prefer to avoid this approach, but he had no alternative. I said that I had not seen Charles, but some of the boys reported that he had been given the message. I asked if it were advisable for me to tell Charles that he, Mr. Crowley, was planning to write his mother's employer. He said that he was very much in favor of the idea.

[8/19]   Charles, phone call. I had relayed the information provided me by Mr. Crowley on August 18 to Robert, Paul, and Fred. They had made a visit to Charles' house and given the information to his sister as Charles was not home at the time.

Charles spoke in a very low voice when he phoned. He said, "I understand that you are looking for me." I replied that I was not looking for him. He said, "That's not what I mean. That man wants to see me, huh?" I agreed that a man wanted to see him. He continued, angrily, "What the hell does Mr. Crowley want me for?" I asked if his friends had given him any information. He said they had told him about the disorderly conduct charge. He explained, "You know, the police lied in that report. That's not the way it happened." I explained that while I was interested, it was more important for him to confer with Mr. Crowley as he was the person who would make recommendations to the court. He asked how he would go about reaching Mr. Crowley. I explained that Mr. Crowley's schedule was office in the morning, the area in the afternoon. He asked if he could see me after he spoke to Mr. Crowley. I said that I would be willing to talk to him before or after his interview with the probation officer. Charles answered, "Well, you know, I'll just feel better after this is out of the way."

In the above situation, as in other similar instances, the worker is careful not to dismiss the healthy anxiety affecting the individual. He might have told Charles "not to worry" or remarked that, "Everything will be all right," but this approach would be very unrealistic as the worker's help was limited. He also wanted to avoid a role that would have made him appear as a probation officer. When Charles suggested that the worker might help him in reviewing the whole situation, the worker made himself available. In doing so, the worker demonstrated his real interest in Charles, saying in effect, "This I can help you with; this is my function."

Most of all, the worker is not interested in protecting the individual or the group from the consequences of their own behavior. When they assume responsibility for planning and executing their program interests, they are able to fully appreciate and grow from their successes and failures. The worker helps them to realize the extent of their responsibilities and supports the members in their implementation of program. When a program becomes completely dependent upon the efforts of the worker, then it becomes the worker's program rather than that of the group.

The Falcons had become increasingly confident of their ability to put on dances. They usually had refreshments. They always had some form of simple decorations. The members were neatly dressed. The major criterion for a successful dance in their neighborhood, however, was that it did not end up in a "free for all." Mr. Morris and Mr. Jones were satisfied. The Falcons felt good about the fact that their affairs were convincing others that teen-agers could be responsible persons—this was becoming recognized by adults and other teen-agers.

In August they had another dance. Robert had phoned the local police district and requested that the patrol car stop from time to time during the dance. They had failed to get chaperones, and the worker reminded them of the housing policy and stated that the dance would not begin until a chaperone was present. Pete convinced his mother to leave the house of a friend that she was visiting, and the dance began.

> Later, the project guard reported to me that he was planning to call the police because some boys were drinking wine near a building close by. It was reported later that Allen and the project guard had exchanged words in anger and profanity flowed freely from each of them. Paul, Robert, and I spoke to the boys who had the wine, which resolved the problem for the evening. However, the incidents had created enough tension that the group members felt relieved when the dance was closed early because of an insufficient number of chaperones. I was relieved, also, as I had spent some time pacifying the damaged pride of the project guard. Apparently, Allen, in addition to being rude, had made some truthful comments that the project guard preferred not to have publicly stated.

The agency was notified the next day by telephone that the facility was no longer available to the Falcons for dances or meetings. A letter confirming the action arrived the day after. When the letter was shared with the members on the corner, their main objection was that the action was based on one person's opinion, the project guard. A conference was arranged with Mr. Morris. Three members and the worker discussed the activity and the letter with him. The members admitted that the dance had fallen short of their standards. Mr. Morris explained that his action was the result of increasing complaints of gang activity in and near the project. While the Falcons had not been mentioned in the earlier reports, he felt that their gatherings constituted a risk that he could not presently afford. He agreed to meet with them at a later date and reconsider their request for a meeting place.

During the months that followed, the Falcons held their meetings in one another's houses. At first, attendance at these meetings averaged between seven to ten members. Interest in program lessened, and between meetings the members tended to develop stronger subgroups. Robert, Fred, and Paul spent much of their spare time together. This was usually in the evening and on week ends as Fred was employed full-time and Robert continued his part-time job. Gus B. had left school and was employed full-time in a grocery store. He was giving serious consideration to becoming a meat-cutter. Morton had married. Phil B., James, Leon, Pete, and Charles spent much time together and were interested in neighborhood activity. Some of the boys came to the attention of the police for truancy and corner lounging. Their interest in girls was generalized and uncertain as compared to Paul and Robert who dated and went steady.

Hank and Roland were inseparable and often spent their time in athletic pursuits at the recreation center, which was no longer dominated by the Junior Wildcats. Allen was committed to a correctional institution for participating in gang fight with a group that was younger than the average Falcon members. Edward, Arnold, George, and Roger, of whom little attention was given in the reports, never seriously engaged in the organizational aspects of the social club. With the exception of Arnold, who participated erratically with zest and energy, the other persons never committed themselves to group program. They were regarded by the members as drifters and avoided forming close relationships with their peers or adults.

Gang members are affected by the dynamics of human behavior, essentially the same in all groups. In addition, members of a gang or corner group have to resolve in some way to conflicting sets of values: the gang subcultural values and the value system of the larger society. Some can never adopt the value system of the larger society, and their only form of adjustment is within the antisocial subculture. For members who have severe limitations in their basic personalities, the appeal of the gang as a social means to individual status fulfills a need that is not found elsewhere. For instance to Edward, George, and Roger who had difficulty even in gang relationships due to their real insecurity, the larger society is seen as frightening and threatening, and probably always will be. For the majority of Falcon members, however, as their positive experiences in the larger society increase, their need for and identification with the value structure of the subculture decreases. Most of them will very likely make a suitable adjustment in terms of being responsible citizens, fathers, and employees.

As it was indicated earlier, the Falcons were considered as a marginal delinquent group. They formed a gang more for reasons of protection than for aggressively establishing a reputation through gang activity. They regarded gang conflict as inevitable for survival in the neighborhood subculture. The gang system was dependent on loyalty to one another and independence of the adult world; yet they wanted and needed the guidance that adults could provide because they felt that gang fighting did not prepare them for the future. How they were able to regard the agency's service to their dilemma was best expressed by a member one year after their social club formation. In the company of two other members, Gus remarked to the worker, "Until you came along, nobody cared what we did, even if we killed each other, except the police and they only wanted us in jail."

15

COMMUNITY ORGANIZATION FOR SOCIAL WELFARE

Common background of casework, group work, and community organization

Casework and group work grew out of the social conditions forged by the industrial revolution, especially the uncertain transition from a rural to an urban orientation of life that transformed our whole social system. Community organization is more nearly a product of the maturation process than of the beginnings. The increasingly complex and interdependent nature of modern society makes community organization almost a prerequisite for existence, let alone for reasonably smooth functioning. It is because of this all-pervasive aspect that community organization for social welfare, and particularly that aspect that is social work, is so difficult to isolate and define. Community organization in some form or other is an inherent part of the over-all operation of a variety of agencies, organizations, and other social institutions.

Being so new in the social work family, it is still quite flexible. Being so essential, it must mature more rapidly than either casework or group work had to do. Community organization had not yet developed a professional association when it combined with several professional associations in 1954 to form the National Association of Social Workers. It was the Association for the Study of Community Organization that merged with the others. In comparison, group work, the second youngest social work specialization, had changed from a study group to a professional association in 1946. Because of this stage of professional development, community organization did not enter the National Association of Social Workers on the same administrative level as casework and group work.

With this pressure to mature in too short a period of time, there has not been the consolidation of theory, philosophy, and methods that one might hope. It is still somewhat of a "collection" rather than an integrated whole. On the other hand, like some youths thrown into adult responsibility at an early age, maturation can take place at a much accelerated pace. In spite of obvious gaps in knowledge and skills, community organization is performing adult responsibilities.

Definitions

What is this process so essential to our modern culture? One widely used definition is:

Community organization for social welfare has been defined as the process of bringing about and maintaining a progressively more effective adjustment between social welfare resources and social welfare needs within a geographic area or functional field. Its goals are consistent with all social work goals in that its primary focus is upon needs of people and provision of means of meeting these needs in a manner consistent with the precepts of democratic living.[1]

A second definition describes it as

. . . a process by which a community identifies its needs and objectives, orders (or ranks) these needs or objectives, develops the confidence and will to work at these needs or objectives, finds the resources (internal and/or external) to deal with these needs or objectives, takes action in respect to them, and in doing so extends and develops cooperation and collaborative attitudes and practices in the community.[2]

By definition, it is disarmingly simple and logical, essentially identifying social needs and doing something about them. But like many seemingly simple processes, this is one of almost unbelievable complexity. It involves, on the one hand, all of the variations of individual personalities and motivations, and on the other, all of the variations of environmental factors.

---

[1] C. F. McNeil, "Community Organization for Social Welfare," *Social Work Year Book, 1951* (New York: American Association of Social Workers, 1951), p. 123.

[2] Murray G. Ross, *Community Organization—Theory and Principles* (New York, Harper & Row, Publishers, 1955), p. 39.

Historical development

One of the first attempts at organization on a community-wide basis was that carried out by the Charity Organization Societies in the latter part of the nineteenth century. They had been organized to bring about order in the confusion of variety and quality of services and relationships between agencies, as well as to provide direct service. It was out of this experience that one of the basic principles of community organization was formulated. It soon became apparent, through sad experience, that it was impossible for the same agency to give direct service and at the same time attempt to coordinate and pass judgment on the quality of service of the same kind (primarily casework performed by other agencies). From this and similar experiences came separate organizations for fund raising, program coordination, and standard setting on the one hand, and direct service on the other. The objectivity, the position of noncompetition, the broad community outlook, as opposed to the one agency focus, all made it necessary for the two types of service to be separate and distinct.

Fund raising

Our present-day fund-raising groups, commonly known as community chest, community fund, or united fund drives, had their origin in the interests and concerns of the people who contributed a large share of the funds to support voluntary social agencies. As the complexity and number of social agencies grew, it became less possible for the large contributors to know personally both the staff and operation of the social agencies. It soon reached a stage where there was much honest searching for some kind of service that would help contributors know whether an agency soliciting funds was not only really offering a needed type of work but also was operating with a quality of service that would warrant financial support in comparison to others also seeking funds. The search for this type of help resulted in the community fund movement.

The biggest development came during and immediately after World War I although there had been some preliminary work on this problem before that time. As early as 1889 Denver had grouped together some fifteen or sixteen agencies in a cooperative joint fund-raising venture, although at that time this group did not raise all of the funds for these agencies nor did it promise the community only one drive. About 1900 the Cleveland Chamber of Commerce, in attempting to meet this need for some type of accreditation, set up a Committee on Benevolent Institutions to investigate and approve or disapprove the validity of an agency's claim to community support.

The impetus for these developments came primarily from the lay group rather than from the professional social workers of that time. There were at least four reasons behind this development. Big contributors (1) felt that they were being asked to give more than their share, (2) believed that an educational program was necessary to encourage the wider public to assume a share of these community enterprises, (3) deplored the inefficiency and high cost of so many agencies conducting individual, separate fund-raising drives, and (4) thought that there was more and more duplication of services, but that they were not always competent to identify the most effective and indispensable.

The war chests of World War I furnished the real proving grounds for the chest movement. Soon after the Armistice these war chests were converted into the peacetime community chests. From these early partial explorations evolved the present community-wide drives based on the philosophy that it is more efficient and administratively sound to have one strong drive, which reduces the heavy overhead necessary for ten, eighty, or a hundred separate drives; which releases the time of the agency professional staff for the service job; which provides machinery for investigation and approval of community programs, thus protecting the public from fraud and incompetency; where the contributor is approached once rather than dozens of times. One of the problems created is that in a campaign covering so many programs and agencies it is difficult to "pinpoint" the appeal. The personal interest growing out of the intimate knowledge that a person had when he contributed directly to a specific agency is usually not carried over when many agencies are united in one drive.

Coordinating and standard-setting programs

While the fund-raising drives were inaugurated largely through the interest and initiative of the layman, the standard-setting and coordinating programs, known today as councils of social agencies, community planning councils, welfare federations, and similar names, originated for the most part through the interest and initiative of the social workers who carried the responsibility for service to clients and members. This program also reached its developmental stride in the years during and following World War I although it too had its beginnings prior to the war in Pittsburgh, Rochester, Milwaukee, and Cleveland. These early experiences were attempts to coordinate the services of existing programs and to improve the quality of the services. Concentrated interest in the quality of the programs, however, was a later development. There was an exchange of ideas, plans, and programs leading to better coordination, cooperation, joint planning, and common agreement on the setting of standards. The central idea always was to improve the quality of service.

In the early days, the names "council of social agencies" or "federation of social agencies" were commonly used. More recent changes in titles are indicative of a steady pattern of growth that has vastly broadened the scope and outlook and as a result, the effectiveness of such programs. From councils of social agencies the names have been changing to community councils, community planning councils, and health and welfare councils. The vital progress reflected in these name changes has been the result of the inclusion of an increasing number of public agencies (whereas the earlier councils had been composed primarily of private organizations) and a much wider representation of lay membership, including not only representatives of the boards of the member organizations but also representatives of various related fields, such as medicine, nursing, public health, education, religion, labor, and business.

There is one basic difference in the relationship between the council and its membership and the chest and its member agencies. Since the chest allocates funds, it has potentially a much greater degree of control over member agencies. All agreements between council members are arrived at after joint discussion, but the council neither has nor wants any power other than voluntary agreement to enforce such decisions. Only as the members are convinced of the soundness of the decisions and operate in a spirit of cooperation are the desired results likely to be achieved. Chests, on the other hand, having the responsibility of allocation or withholding of funds, have a powerful source of sanction or control.

There can never be, nor should there be, a complete separation of the social-planning responsibilities from the fund-raising and allocation responsibility. There is the utmost necessity for planning, fund raising, and allocation to be carefully integrated and coordinated. Funds can be effectively allocated only on the basis of a carefully devised procedure that takes into consideration total community needs, total community resources, both public and private, and the quality and quantity of services rendered. There are seldom sufficient funds to meet total requests, even after the most careful scrutiny and study by allocating groups. Budget committees are constantly faced with the question: Given a limited amount of money acknowledged to be insufficient, how can it be used in the best interest of the total community? The question of new services usually brings up this point. If there are not enough funds available to meet acknowledged needs of existing programs, why should new services be sanctioned? This points up the fact that social-planning and fund allocation is a process of continual evaluation, both of over-all needs and of existing resources.

The social work component of community organization

Over the years the National Conference of Social Work has played an important role in the efforts to develop a comprehensive definition of community organization and its social work component. In 1939 one of the conference committees reported on a year's work focused on the study of the concept of community organization and its implications for the conference. The report was based on the results of discussion groups in six different cities.[3] It was found that, even as today, the definition was used to mean both a process and a field of work and frequently was used with these meanings confused; that some community organization was carried on within the field of social work and some outside; that in social work, community organization was conducted in some agencies as a primary process and in others as a secondary or incidental phase of the program; and that community organization was carried on at a variety of levels from the local neighborhood to the national scene [4] (and today on an international level). Throughout succeeding years various meetings and papers attempted further refinement in the definitions, techniques, concepts, and philosophy.

A more recent series of meetings and papers, a milestone in this process of definition and study, occurred in 1947 when the National Conference of Social Work met in San Francisco. Papers by Kenneth Pray of the Pennsylvania School of Social Work, Wilbur I. Newstetter of the Pittsburgh School of Social Work, and Lester Granger of the National Urban League, among others, made significant contributions toward the definition of that portion of community organization which is an integral part of social work and that which is outside the area of social work but nonetheless is important to total community development.

Mr. Pray's paper discussed "When Is Community Organization Social Work Practice?" Before delving too far into that topic, Mr. Pray had to first answer the question, not when, but whether community organization was social work. He concluded that it:

> . . . is social work practice, that is practitioners can share in the development of a single profession of social work, on three conditions: (1) if and when their focal concerns and their primary objectives relate always to the development and guidance of the process by which people find satisfying and fruitful social relationships, and not to the attainment of specific, pre-

---

[3] Boston, Buffalo, Detroit, New York, Pittsburgh, and Chicago.
[4] Wayne McMillen, *Community Organization for Social Welfare* (Chicago: University of Chicago Press, 1945), pp. 36–39.

conceived products or forms of relationship; (2) if and when these objectives are sought consistently through the realization of a democratic philosophy and faith which respects the right and the responsibility of communities, as of individuals, to create their own satisfying relationships, and to use those relationships to their own chosen ends; and (3) if and when the basic processes, methods, and skills that are demanded and employed in actual practice are those that inhere in the worker's capacity to initiate and sustain a helping, not a controlling, relationship with individuals and groups.[5]

Social intergroup work process

Mr. Newstetter's paper was entitled "The Social Intergroup Work Process." The term "social intergroup work" introduced a new concept into the attempt to clarify the social work component of community organization. It in turn is based on a specific viewpoint of the community itself. There are many different ways of looking at or defining a community. In some instances it is considered as a geographical area with man-made boundaries or with natural topographical boundaries; some define it in terms of psychological identification and so on. The idea of intergroup work is based on a definition of the community that is a paraphrase of Eubank's definition of a group, namely: "A group is two or more persons in a relationship of psychic interaction, whose relationship with one another may be abstracted and distinguished from their relationship with all others, so that they may be thought of as an entity." [6] Mr. Newstetter's definition of community substitutes the word "community" for group and "groups" for persons.

This definition is based on the concept that there must be genuine relationships, psychic interaction, between the groups before there is any feeling of community. Just being present with no relationship interactions is not sufficient. It is also based on the belief that the individual who has status and influence, who truly is in a position to exercise leadership within the community, is in that position because of his association with certain groups and his ability to enlist the support or influence of those groups. It may be a family group, a religious group, a business association, a labor union, a professional organization, or any of a wide variety that could be identified. The individual, as such, has little influence in contemporary community life separate from his group ties.

---

[5] Kenneth L. M. Pray, "When Is Community Organization Social Work Practice?" *Proceedings of the National Conference of Social Work, 1947*, pp. 203–204.

[6] Earle E. Eubank, *The Concepts of Sociology* (Boston: D.C. Heath and Company, 1932), p. 163.

Effective community organization in this sense is thought of in terms of relationships between community groups that are involved in or are in a position to influence a particular program. Since it would obviously be impossible, as well as impractical, for numerous large or even small groups to sit down en masse, these relationships are fostered and facilitated through representatives. If a community organization project was aimed at better recreation facilities for the community, representatives from the city recreation department, from the school, from parent-teacher groups, citizen groups, from the YMCA and the YWCA, settlements, boys' clubs, and many other leisure-time programs might get together and have a very congenial meeting and even agree on a plan for meeting the needs of their community. But this would avail nothing unless the groups they represent (the city government, the school board, the leisure-time organizations, and the churches) actually get together and provide services and facilities.

The educational and promotional process

At the same time he was defining intergroup work as the social work component of community organization, Mr. Newstetter identified two other processes in community organization that he felt were of importance, but were not considered to be social work processes. One of these was the educational and promotional or selling process. In this instance, the decision to carry out a particular program may be made by some central group with all major policies and program procedures determined by that group. The plan is then "sold" to a number of communities or groups, who carry out essentially the program worked out on the central level, whether it be local, state, regional, or national. The polio, cancer, or heart drives are examples of this educational and promotional procedure.

The administrative process in community organization

The administrative process identified in community organization programs was the third. Again, this is not a social work process in itself, but it is an essential part of all community organization.

It should be clearly understood, however, that the three processes identified: intergroup, educational and promotional, and administrative, never occur in a "pure" state, so to speak, to the complete exclusion of the other two. The three overlap in almost every instance. It is more accurate to say that the name applied to any one or the other is appropriate when that particular process is the major focus. The administrative process is involved to some degree in each of the others.

Roles of the social worker in community organization

As with casework and group work, the professional social worker in community organization is called upon to carry a variety of responsibilities, not all social work, but all within the framework of social work values, goals, and methods. These include direct practice, administration, supervision, consultation, and research.

Direct Practice

The "client" in casework is the individual, in group work, the group, and in community organization, the community. In each instance, however, the welfare of the individual is the ultimate goal. The direct practice of community organization, then, involves helping community groups such as councils, block groups, committees, work shops, conferences, and many others.

There is a major difference in the relation of the social worker in community organization to his client and the relationship of the case-worker and the group worker. The casework client comes because of a problem, one he feels incapable of handling satisfactorily himself and so he asks for help. In group work, the motivation is more often an interest than a problem as such. Members want to enjoy activities with others, such as a club program, dramatics, or learning a skill. There may be problems with which the individual does need help, but the large majority do not come consciously asking for that kind of help. In community organization, the participants come primarily to *help others* through working on community problems, not to get personal help. It is true that many community problems are dealt with by such groups so that the total community or neighborhood benefits, frequently including the participants too, but the focus is largely on others.

In the course of helping community groups identify and deal with their community concerns a variety of methods and techniques are employed. These include committees, discussion groups, study groups, research, individual conferences, consultation, and many others.

The community organization worker is not only using a variety of methods and techniques, he is also dealing with a variety of groups and organizations.[7] Numerous health and welfare agencies, both public and voluntary, may be involved. Citizen organizations concerned with business, civic, professional, educational, religious, or similar interests on a community, city-wide, regional, or national basis may be involved, and in some instances the scope may be international. Community work may involve planning groups such as a health and welfare council, board of education, city or county planning commission, urban redevelopment authority, or a housing authority. Responsibility may include working with individuals as well as groups, in their various roles and capacities within the community organization program. These individuals may be top leaders in the community—the power structure—or the unknown citizens in the block organization. This relationship may be with the skilled, experienced, sophisticated leadership or with the fumbling but earnest first attempts of newly developing leadership ability. The work may require merely that the facts and implications be made known to the "right people" who have the "know how" and desire to deal with the situation, or it might mean a slow process of interpretation and laborious effort in enabling local leadership to mobilize sufficient strength and vision to act. Results may be produced by calling a committee together for two or three sessions, or it may mean a long process of individual conferences, preparation, encouragement, helping to plan agendas, assistance in how to conduct a meeting and how to state the problem in terms that encourage interest and participation.

Even this brief and limited review makes it clear that the community organization worker in social welfare needs to be deeply rooted in social work philosophy, principles, and ethics; must understand individual and group behavior; must have some knowledge of the intricacies of urban, suburban, and rural organization and growth patterns and of community resources, health, welfare, education, religious, business, civic, and all others pertinent to successful community living.

It becomes clear from the above discussion that all knowledge concerning individuals, relationship skills and group process is of major importance to the social worker in community organization. The interviews, the conferences, and sometimes the consultation require the skill of the one-to-one relationship. The committees, group conferences and discussions require skill in using group process. As a matter of fact, the committees and similar groups require two types of group process skill simultaneously. One relates to the functioning of the group itself, how to help it operate effectively, how to have the participants work together toward a common goal. The other relates to the community action objective of achieving community goals. It is possible for a group to function

---

[7] See record, pp. 528–550.

effectively and to the satisfaction and benefit of participants individually but still stop short of community achievement.

Administration

As with group workers, administrative responsibilities come early in the community organization practice. The lines of demarcation between direct practice and administrative responsibility are not always clear.

Fact finding and research on the part of the social worker in community organization are essentially administrative responsibilities. The worker assembles material, analyzes it, and interprets to the appropriate community groups. On the basis of these facts and interpretation, priority decisions are made; which are the most urgent needs for the allocation of staff time and funds? Some time ago, an article in *The New York Times Magazine* [8] discussing teen-agers made a distinction between choices and decisions. The point was that anyone can make a choice. A decision, however, can be made *only* when the *facts* are known, when the advantages and disadvantages of the alternatives are known. Then a decision can be made. This same principle holds for adults as well as teen-agers. Too many times community or neighborhood groups and even budget committees are forced to make choices rather than decisions because they do not have the data to make a decision possible. Part of this reflects gaps in our understanding of community, institutional, and individual behavior and their influence on one another. What would be the ultimate effect on the community if the limited funds available were put into a "crash" delinquency program on one hand, or used to strengthen the regular preventive services, on the other? Would raising fees for a particular service make it inaccessible to some who need it most or would it attract more people? Actual examples of each result can be documented. How are we to anticipate in any specific instance?

Public relations is also a part of administrative responsibility. This involves interpretation of health, welfare, and recreation programs including the goals and objectives, the need for such services, the need for planning and coordination, problems in obtaining such community-wide programs and results that are obtained. One of the important public relations goals of the community worker is to have everyone involved in community projects assume some responsibility for interpretation.

These and other administrative skills such as recording, budgeting, or financing are essential tools of the community organization worker.

---

[8] Dorothy Barclay, "Deciding Who Should Make Decisions," *The New York Times Magazine*, March 8, 1959, p. 57.

Without these, program skills may be wasted on fruitless efforts, for planning alone is not enough—something must happen!

Supervision

Community organization practice, similar to casework and group work, carries in many instances supervisory responsibility. This may involve full-time professional staff, part-time staff, or volunteers and students.

More positions are now available for younger, less experienced staff. This is largely due to the fact that there are now more experienced workers in the field qualified to offer supervision. For a number of years, staff shortages were so great that only individuals with considerable maturity and prior experience in at least a related type of responsibility were encouraged to enter community organization. Many entered the field after experience in casework or group work. The availability of additional supervisors has opened up more adequate field instruction placements for graduate students and a steadily increasing number of initial positions with responsibilities conmensurate with the abilities of the beginner.

The community organization worker's skills in supervision are the same as those discussed in relation to casework and group work even though the content dealt with and the responsibilities carried vary somewhat.

Consultation

Consultation is a skill of major importance for many community organization positions. This type of responsibility assumes a wide background of experience and knowledge of the content of the services involved.

The work may require skill and understanding in such matters as how to chair meetings, how to conduct productive group discussions, how to elicit the ideas of all committee members, and other procedural knowledge needed by presidents, chairmen, discussion leaders, and others carrying responsibilities at various levels.

It may involve an understanding of standards and criteria for evaluation of the quality of service such as institutional care, family welfare, delinquency programs, leisure-time services, and others. Consultation of this nature may be with boards of directors, executives, or staff. It may be with old, established organizations attempting to continually improve their service or it may be a new agency about to organize and offer a service for the first time.

It may involve standards of physical facilities and equipment for institutions, boarding homes, foster homes, camps, and similar services.

It may be the interpretation of national agency policies and procedures to state and local units or cooperating organizations.

Thus, consultation is carried on at a variety of levels on many subjects and areas of concern. For some community organization staff, consultation is a major responsibility, for others a small but important segment.

Teaching

With the acceptance of community organization educational programs, both by schools of social work and the organizations that employ their graduates, teaching opportunities have increased. The most recent development in this recognition of community organization education is the initiation, in at least one graduate school of social work, of a full two-year curriculum in community organization. Prior to this program, community organization was a second year specialization, the first year being in casework or group work with a larger number coming from group work.

Differences of opinion arising out of this step highlight the major questions around the place of community organization in the social work family; namely, Is it necessary for a student to have casework or group work experience before specializing in community organization? Many persons in the field still think of casework and group work as the basic "direct service" practice and fear that community organization deals so heavily in administration, research, education, promotion, and consultation that community organization field experience would provide insufficient social work experience in relationship. Others believe community organization can furnish as rich a social work experience in relationships as casework or group work. They base their belief on the fact that the portion of community organization identified as social work [9] offers through representative committees and similar groups a process of identifying problems, or needs, analyzing them, and working out an approach for dealing with solutions that is the same basic social work process as that carried on with an individual or a group. It does require careful selection of field instruction experiences with a progressively more complex level of social work relationships involved, but there is a rapidly increasing and widespread acceptance that it can and is being done.

Local programs

Developments in the last few years have widened very materially the scope of local community organization programs in the field of social

---

[9] Kenneth L. M. Pray, "When Is Community Organization Social Work Practice?" *Proceedings of the National Conference of Social Work, 1947,* pp. 194–204.

welfare. For purposes of this discussion, "local" will be limited to neighborhood, community, city, or county-wide and regional in the restricted sense of two or three counties or similar geographic areas.

The types of agency programs operating at this level include community chest, united funds, health and welfare councils or community welfare councils, human relations councils, community or coordinating councils, and block organizations.

Community chests, united funds, and health and welfare councils function at least on a city-wide basis and many in the county or regional area. These programs have been discussed above in the historical background.

Another type of community organization program on the local level operates in the small neighborhood. These programs go by various names. In many places they are called coordinating councils, in others, community councils, and in still others, neighborhood councils. By and large, however, organization and structure, as well as operating practices, are quite similar. The major focus is on the improvement of life in the neighborhood, and the range of activities is limited only by the scope of the members' interests and imagination. Many of the early councils were mainly interested in juvenile delinquency with the emphasis on prevention and reduction of juvenile offenses. The councils soon found that any group interested in delinquency had to be concerned with a wide range of social factors, for they were all related to delinquency. This included school programs, health programs, police protection, the caliber of movies and radio programs (and now television), the kind of literature available to youth, and many others. In the last analysis, almost any influence affecting the life of the community comes within the scope of the councils. Some of the councils fell under the control of one particular individual or group trying to use it for selfish purposes. This situation led to almost inevitable downfall, for the strength of such a program rests in the fact that all groups—business, labor, professional, religious, racial, and all of the rest— are acting in the best interest of the total community and not for any one segment. Such councils might be described as the modern town hall, an attempt to return to the neighborhood or small community the opportunity for democratic, grass roots participation that is fast disappearing in urban communities. More use is being made of this type of organization on the block level, that is, all the homes facing one particular street on one block. These smaller organizations, with the same objectives as community councils, are frequently joined together for mutual assistance and over-all effectiveness through a council formed of representatives from all of the organized blocks in a particular community. Block organizations were first developed during World War I and have been in existence in various cities since then. More social welfare organizations, particularly settlements, now make formation of and staff service to such groups an integral part of their program.

Human relations councils are playing an increasingly important role in many communities. Some of these councils are voluntary organizations and some are public, being initiated by legislation. Some operate on a national level, but this discussion will be limited to local activities. In general, these programs are geared to the easing of tensions arising out of strained relationships between religious, ethnic, racial, or cultural groups or the reaction of a majority section of a community to some minority group. The problem of concern for such programs range from prejudice and discrimination in their various ramifications to segregation and acts of violence. Such organizations are striving for the difficult goal of actually bringing to fruition in our communities the things that we say in our religious creeds, the Declaration of Independence, and in our democratic ideals should happen, such as the recognition of the dignity of all individuals, the right of all persons to the opportunity to develop their potentials, and the others we know so well. This is a long term and difficult task. It is also an educational and a community organization task. It means organizing for community action, trying to create the kind of a community we would like our children to inherit. Many persons with community organization education and experience in social work have entered this type of work.

State programs

One example of state-wide operation is the state conference of social work. These conferences are associations of both lay and professional membership. One of their major methods is to provide an open forum as a means of exchanging information and stimulating discussion toward the development of sound public and private welfare services through the particular state. Usually an annual state-wide conference of two or three days duration and sometimes smaller regional conferences throughout the state are held. Various committees are active throughout the year, both for the preparation of the state-wide or regional conferences and for on-going year-round programs of study, research, and interpretation. Membership is usually both individual and agency. When an organization belongs, one or more members, depending on membership arrangements and the amount of dues paid, represent the agency when they attend.

Another type of state-wide association is interested in bringing about within the state the best welfare program possible through both public and private sources, but turns particular attention to the legislative programs as they affect facilities and services. These organizations are usually independent, nonprofit, voluntary, citizens associations. They function through programs of research and information to create an informed public opinion and understanding leading to community action on problems of health, welfare, and recreation needing state-wide attention. An example of such an association is the Pennsylvania Citizens Association with offices at both Philadelphia and Pittsburgh. The type of organizational pattern such associations use has real meaning in terms of their effectiveness. Some concentrate their efforts on securing individual members. Such members are almost always key people in their community and as such are in a position to enlist the cooperation and interest of many groups. However, with the membership largely individual rather than delegate, there is not the direct tie into the activities of the groups whose support is needed. Whichever plan of organization is followed, one of the objectives is to get public support for or against proposed welfare or health legislation.

Other examples of community organization responsibilities are YMCA programs sponsored through a state-wide organization or consultation by various state departments or bureaus such as public welfare, aging, or recreation. The 1960 White House Conference on Children and Youth used state-wide as well as county committees to promote citizen interest and participation in programs and services for youth. A few states have experimented with united funds on a state-wide basis to finance those voluntary services offered on a state-wide basis.

National programs

To give some indication of the tremendous scope and varied roles of public and voluntary national organizations in the health and welfare field, the 1960 *Social Work Year Book* [10] lists some 335 voluntary and sixty-three federal agencies. They range in the voluntary field all the way from Alcoholics Anonymous to the National Travelers Aid Association; from Save the Children Federation to the Young Women's Christian Association of U. S. A., National Board, the National Urban League, or the Boys' Clubs of America.

---

[10] Russell Kurtz, ed., *Social Work Year Book, 1960* (New York: National Association of Social Workers, 1960), pp. 631–730.

International programs

Many of the organizations having strong national programs also affiliate their national units through an international organization. Examples of this type of organization are the YMCA, the YWCA, the International Conference of Social Work, or the International Association of Schools of Social Work. Others operate on the problem focus. This approach includes such organizations as the International Prisoners Aid Association, International Social Service, or the United Nations Childrens' Emergency Fund. Over thirty such international organizations are listed in the 1960 *Social Work Year Book*.[11]

Some of these operate with individual memberships while others have delegates and official representatives. The international type of program is expanding rapidly. These developments are encouraged and facilitated as more students from other countries study in our schools of social work; as there is more exchange of students between various countries; as interest and participation increase in the International Conference of Social Work, which meets every other year in cities around the world; as teams of social workers from the United States spend several months in different countries; as there is a wider circulation of social work literature available in different languages; and as there is an increase in the exchange of social work faculty members.

Trends

Tendency toward Wider Planning Areas

Historically, most social welfare planning and fund-raising groups such as councils, chests, and funds, developed in cities and were mostly limited in scope to the urban areas. As the trend to suburbia continues and the problems facing the city and the surrounding suburban areas become increasingly intertwined, the scope of planning organizations is becoming regional rather than city based. This means a county-wide or even a two or three county area. If the related communities are so situated, such organizations may even cross state boundaries.

United funds or similar fund-raising agencies are covering metropolitan areas and in some instances, as mentioned previously, are state-wide, using the big cities and heavily populated sections to help balance the lack of resources in some rural and sparsely settled areas.

---

[11] *Ibid.*, pp. 621–630.

Since many of the direct service agencies serve counties or states, the overhead cost of several fund-raising drives can be reduced to one. There are still instances where one agency may get funds from as many as nine or more different community chests. This kind of wasted effort is being eliminated by area and regional organization.

One of the crucial requirements facing an organization that cuts across many governmental administrative units is the necessity of developing and maintaining an over-all look at planning and dealing with needs that cut across boundaries while simultaneously providing for sufficient autonomy to meet problems principally local in nature. This is not an easy matter since most smaller communities have a deep fear of being swallowed up by the "big city." However, the very complexity and interrelatedness of these matters are making possible advances in cooperative planning and working together that were neither considered necessary or advisable a few years ago.

Wider Scope of Community Organization Efforts

As planning and cooperative enterprises play an increasingly essential role in modern communities, the scope of effective activities seems to be widening in both directions, that is, at the top and at the "grass roots" level.

At the top level there is willingness and ability for planners and administrators from a variety of settings but with interrelated and overlapping interests to sit down together and consider mutual problems and concerns. These discussions may include the health and welfare council, united fund, housing authority, urban redevelopment authority, city or county planning commission, board of education, various citizen groups with special interest in housing, city planning, and similar concerns, a top administrative officer such as the city manager or coordinator, and other similar interests. Such activities make possible a blending of social and physical planning and coordination that has been sadly lacking by and large. There are always exceptions, but the pattern has been far from common.

At the same time, there has been a growing recognition that no matter how excellent the plans that may be developed by top planners for a community, if the citizens affected by their plans do not understand or approve of them, they can be rendered largely ineffective. Planning is being seen as a two-way process with channels of communication running *up* as well as down.

This opportunity for citizen participation at the local level has developed in several ways. Health and welfare councils have offered this opportunity through two common types of structure. One is by sponsoring or encouraging community or neighborhood councils throughout the city in designated planning sections or in selected neighborhood areas. While they are autonomous groups representing a cross section of the community, the council provides professional staff service to them. A second method is for the council to operate, in part at least, on a decentralized basis with staff assigned to districts. Here they either work with neighborhood groups already existing or help them form when they are lacking. Both methods place a high priority on citizen understanding and participation and the development of indigenous leadership.

Streamlining Planning Structure

Over the country numerous planning councils have been conducting serious review of their administrative structure and some have already made extensive revisions.

The traditional council structure in cities large enough to support a staff of several persons has been through divisions and departments or bureaus. The council usually has a delegate body composed of two representatives of each member agency plus interested persons in the community commonly designated as delegates-at-large. This delegate group ordinarily determines the constitution and bylaws of the organization and elects the board of directors.

Divisions vary in number according to the size of the organization but include such designations as family and children, group work and recreation, health or aging. Divisions also usually have a delegate body from the division member agencies including interested delegates-at-large.

Bureaus or departments frequently have less administrative structure, namely, no delegate body, but frequently do have an advisory group. These departments might include research, volunteer bureau, community councils, information and referral service, and similar concerns.

One of the major forces behind the tendency to streamline the structure has been the fact that many social problems such as delinquency, aging, and others cut across most division lines. The difficulty of crossing so much administrative structure frequently involves delay and impairs efficient action especially if it is imperative to do so rapidly.

One of the issues faced in structure revision is that individual agencies have usually been most closely related to the divisions. A "problem-centered" approach usually means that separate divisions are eliminated or are all combined into one. Specialized staff and volunteer time can be directed, in any appropriate combination, to the question at hand. Keeping the close agency relationship while at the same time providing additional flexibility and unity of approach is still a major administrative concern.

The direction is clear, however. The interrelatedness of most social problems makes a unified approach essential in spite of the danger of some specialized interests receiving less attention. Each community will work out variations in light of their peculiarities and resources.

Relation of United Funds to Other Major Fund Drives

When community chests and united funds were discussed, it was pointed out that a major selling point and one of the most important contributions of this method of financing was one drive, which replaced numerous individual ones. In recent years this has again become a matter of concern. There are a growing number of organizations, local and national, that raise their funds outside of united fund drives. Since affiliation with community chests and united funds is voluntary, no agency can or should be made to participate, but major contributors are again asking why so many solicitations? If one of the big advantages is elimination of numerous expensive drives and provision of a channel through which money can be given with the assurance that the program has been reviewed and approved as a valid health, welfare, or recreation service, why are so many outside? Even though such organizations as the American Red Cross, the March of Dimes, heart or cancer drives, to mention a few, have never been questioned as necessary and essential programs, the multitude of campaigns did and does raise serious questions. The development of united funds made considerable progress as a solution, and some of the national organizations, such as the American Red Cross joined such united efforts. However, this move has been only partially successful.

Among some of the major objectors are the national health drives, such as tuberculosis, polio, cancer, and others, which feel that any combined drive kills or seriously weakens the special appeal of any one agency; they feel they not only can raise more money on their own, and thus provide more extensive and improved services, but they can do a better job of interpretation and public education through their own, single, one-emphasis drive. The over-all type of campaign, on the other hand, has the advantage of getting the whole community active at one time, and with this truly united effort it is possible to operate a more efficient campaign. One reason it is hard to make a decision on this question is the absolute sincerity on both sides and the fact that they both have only one goal in mind, the best possible service that will meet the needs of the community. The variance is over methods more than goals, but methods also involve philosophy and goals.

A few communities are experimenting with a new approach. A health research organization is established to receive funds from the united fund for medical research. These funds are allocated for research purposes

to appropriate institutions and individuals conducting outstanding research in the field of interest. This program is one answer to the numerous
health drives and the "splintering" effect on the total approach to health
and welfare needs. Human beings are not a myriad of parts functioning
independently. Many groups see the need for some unity and joint planning in health research, not for independent groups with one interest
competing with each other for funds. The final answer is far from solution,
but the need for a new approach is clear.

Conceptualization and Identification of Basic Community Organization Principles

One of the indications that community organization is fast becoming of age is the accelerated attempt to provide a sound conceptual base
for identifying and defining principles and guides. At the same time,
there has been an attempt to draw into this process the applicable concepts from the social and behavioral sciences. This trend is reflected in
recent literature and in the academic requirements of graduate schools of
social work. There is still much to be done, but the results have been
encouraging.

Community Organization as a Two-Year Program

As was mentioned earlier, a start toward making community organization a two-year program on a par with casework and group work
has already taken place. There is every indication that this will progress
further as other schools study this experience.

In an age of specialization, coordination, planning and integration
are not luxuries but basic necessities of life. Community organization in
the field of health, welfare, and recreation is an important step toward
making these services available to the total community.

Bibliography

Andrews, Emerson F., "New Trends in Corporate Giving," *Social Work Journal,*
        XXXIII (October 1952), pp. 172–176.
Bachman, Richard S., "Public Agency Participation in Community Planning,"
        Community Organization, 1961. New York: Columbia University Press,
        1961, pp. 146–152.

Barry, Mildred M., "Current Concepts in Community Organization," *Group Work and Community Organization, 1956*. New York: Columbia University Press, 1956, pp. 3–20.
Benjamin, Paul, "State-Wide Community Organization," *Proceedings of the National Conference of Social Work, 1946*, pp. 139–148.
Biddle, William W., *The Cultivation of Community Leaders*. New York: Harper & Row, Publishers, 1953.
Buell, Bradley, and Associates, *Community Planning for Human Services*. New York: Columbia University Press, 1952.
Clark, William E., "A Project for Pilgrims—The United Fund as an Experiment in Democracy," *Community*, XXIX (September 1953), pp. 4–5.
"Code of the Chest and Council Movement," *Community*, XXVIII (April 1953), pp. 160–161.
Cohen, Nathan E., "Planned Community Change, A Multiple Responsibility," *Community Organization, 1960*. New York: Columbia University Press, 1960, pp. 3–21.
Colcord, Joanna C., *Your Community: Its Provisions for Health, Education, Safety and Welfare*, rev. ed. New York: Russell Sage Foundation, 1947.
Community Chests and Councils of America, Inc., *Neighbors Unite for Better Communities: A Handbook on District Community Councils*. New York, 1956.
———, *Policy Statement on Community Planning for Social Welfare*. New York, 1950.
Culberson, George W., "Intergroup Relations and Community Welfare Planning," *Community Organization, 1961*. New York: Columbia University Press, 1961, pp. 132–145.
Dillick, Sidney, *Community Organization for Neighborhood Development: Past and Present*. New York: Whiteside, Inc., 1953.
Dunham, Arthur, *Community Welfare Organization: Principles and Practice*. New York: Thomas Y. Crowell Company, 1958.
Farra, Kathryn, "Neighborhood Councils," *Proceedings of the National Conference of Social Work, 1940*, pp. 445–455.
Granger, Lester B., "Educational and Promotional Process in Community Organization," *Proceedings of the National Conference of Social Work, 1947*, pp. 218–226.
Harper, Ernest B., and Arthur Dunham, *Community Organization in Action*. New York: Association Press, 1959.
Hillman, Arthur, *Community Organization and Planning*. New York: The Macmillan Company, 1950.
Howard, Donald S., ed., *Community Organization—Its Nature and Setting*. New York: American Association of Social Workers, 1948.
Hunter, Floyd, *Community Power Structure*. Chapel Hill: University of North Carolina Press, 1953.
Johns, Ray, *The Cooperative Process among National Social Agencies*. New York: Association Press, 1946.
———, and David F. DeMarche, *Community Organization and Agency Responsibility*. New York: Association Press, 1951.
Lynde, Edward D., "The Role of the Community Organization Practitioner," *Selected Papers in Group Work and Community Organization*. Raleigh: Health Publications Institute, 1952, pp. 118–128.
———, "Two-Pronged Approach to Community Planning," *Selected Papers in*

Group Work and Community Organization. Raleigh: Health Publications Institute, 1951, pp. 104–107.

Manning, Seaton W., "Community Organization in the Intergroup Relations Setting," *Community Organization, 1959*. New York: Columbia University Press, 1959, pp. 61–70.

Markey, Sydney B., "Social Work in Planned Community Change," *Community Organization, 1960*. New York: Columbia University Press, 1960, pp. 42–55.

McMillen, Wayne, *Community Organization for Social Welfare*. Chicago: University of Chicago Press, 1945.

Murphy, Campbell G., *Community Organization Practice*. Boston: Houghton Mifflin Company, 1954.

———, "Community Organization for Social Welfare," *Social Work Year Book, 1960*. New York: National Association of Social Workers, 1960, pp. 186–191.

National Conference on Social Welfare, "Community Organization in Public Housing and Urban Renewal," I, Downing, Willard E., "Special Problems of the Urban Newcomer"; II, Hollenbeck, Howard B., "The Province of the Social Services," *Community Organization, 1959*. New York: Columbia University Press, 1959, pp. 71–88.

Newstetter, Wilbur I., "The Social Intergroup Work Process," *Proceedings of the National Conference of Social Work, 1947*, pp. 205–217.

Nicholson, James T., "Effective Development in International Social Welfare Programs to Improve Conditions of Living," *Selected Papers in Group Work and Community Organization*. Raleigh: Health Publications Institute, 1952, pp. 73–79.

Nisbet, R. A., *The Quest for Community*. New York: Oxford University Press, 1953.

Norton, William J., *The Cooperative Movement in Social Work*. New York: The Macmillan Company, 1927.

Ogden, Jean C., and Jess Ogden, *Small Communities in Action*. New York: Harper & Row, Publishers, 1946.

Ogg, Elizabeth, *Good Neighbors—The Rise of Community Welfare Councils*. New York: Public Affairs Committee, Inc., 1959.

Pray, Kenneth L. M., "When Is Community Organization Social Work Practice?" *Proceedings of the National Conference of Social Work, 1947*, pp. 194–204.

Ross, Murray G., *Community Organization: Theory and Principles*. New York: Harper & Row Publishers, 1955.

Schorr, Alvin L., "Governmental and Voluntary Agencies," *Community Organization, 1961*, New York: Columbia University Press, 1961, pp. 153–160.

Sieder, Violet M., "Community Organization Developments in our Cities and Metropolitan Areas," *Group Work and Community Organization, 1955*. New York: Columbia University Press, 1955, pp. 3–11.

———, "The Tasks of the Community Organization Worker," *The Community Organization Method in Social Work Education*. New York: Council on Social Work Education, 1959, pp. 246–259.

———, Mildred C. Barry, and Ernest F. Witte, *Practice in Old and New Settings*, Papers presented at the 83rd Annual Forum of the National Conference of Social Work, 1956.

Stroup, Herbert H., *Community Welfare Organization*. New York: Harper & Row, Publishers, 1952.

United States Woman's Bureau, *The Outlook for Women in Community Organization in Social Work*. Washington, D.C.: Government Printing Office, 1951.

Van Valen, Donald, "Community Organization: Manipulation or Group Process?" *Proceedings of the National Conference of Social Work, 1949*, pp. 325–342.

"What Make a Good Council?" *Community*, XXVIII (March 1953), pp. 126–127.

Pittsfield Health Services Committee: A Process Record[1]

JAMES O. F. HACKSHAW
Assistant Professor of Social Work
New York School of Social Work

Background Information

The Pittsfield neighborhood is one of several neighborhoods in the northern area of a large metropolitan community. Health and welfare planning is carried out through a Planning Area Committee, which has representation from civic groups, business and labor organizations, social and health services, as well as key community leaders. There are active committees on health, housing, and recreation. The Health Committee has been concerned with the Pittsfield neighborhood because of the high health hazards that are prevalent.

Description of Area

The Pittsfield area is one of the most densely populated in the city. It is mainly residential but with some industry and commercial establishments. During the last twenty-five years, it has changed from one of upper middle-class white, single-family homes to one primarily of lower-class, nonwhite, multiple-family homes. The neighborhood has a predominance of row housing and one public housing project.

Physical Characteristics

According to the 1950 United States Census, the area covers 128 acres with a population of 19,000 living in 5505 dwelling units. The two census tracts within the area have net density population per residential area rates of 327 and 221 as compared to a city average of 100.5. One tract has one of the highest density rates in the city. The average number of persons per household is 3.32. Houses are in most cases old and in need of repairs. 62 per cent are dilapidated or have no private bath.

Thirty-two per cent of the land area is used for streets, and one of the common neighborhood complaints is about the volume and speed of

---

[1] This record has been disguised to preserve the confidential nature of the staff record.

traffic and limited street-playing facilities for children because of automobile parking.

Social Characteristics

Most of the residents are Negroes. The majority of residents employed outside the home are unskilled, semiskilled, or service workers. The median educational level is about eight years, which is one year less than the median for the total city. The median income is well below the city average.

The appearance of the neighborhood varies from block to block. Some blocks have newly painted houses, flower boxes, and clean sidewalks, while other blocks have dilapidated houses, vacant lots with debris, and sidewalks covered with litter.

The neighborhood is characterized by multiple social, economic, and health problems. Juvenile arrests are more than double the city average. Public Assistance rates are five times the city average. There are an exceptionally large number of health problems, including high premature births and a very high infant mortality rate.

Because of the many health hazards in the neighborhood, the area field secretary of the Welfare Council arranged with the Tuberculosis and Health Association to assign a worker trained in community work to develop a program of neighborhood improvement, which, it was hoped, would lead to improved health standards. The community worker would work with existing organizations in the neighborhood and with city-wide agencies offering services to the community to stimulate the development of block organizations. Through this program, many excellent lay leaders were identified and involved in neighborhood improvement programs.

The problem

In the Department of Public Health District serving the neighborhood, the neonatal death rate (infants under 28 days old) was 31.9 per 1000 live births as compared to a rate of 23.3 per 1000 live births for the city as a whole. According to the Committee on Maternal and Child Care of the local county medical society, prenatal care tends to diminish maternal and neonatal mortality. Such care is considered adequate when it begins no later than the fifth month of pregnancy.

Statistics on the number of mothers from the neighborhood who delivered babies at the city's general hospital showed serious inadequacies of prenatal care. In a sample study of 192 mothers delivered, 62 received prenatal care by the fifth month; 65 mothers received prenatal care after the fifth month; and 65 had not registered for any care before delivery.

Resources available for tackling the problem

Planning

The Welfare Council provides a structure through which health and welfare planning can take place. The Area Planning Committee, covering eight neighborhoods such as Pittsfield, facilitates health planning through its Health Services Committee. The Welfare Council also has throughout the metropolitan area centralized divisions in various specialized fields, one being the Health Division.

Direct Health Services

These are provided mainly through the city's Department of Public Health. Services include child health conferences, health education, public health nursing services, dental clinics, and control of communicable diseases.

Public schools provide certain medical services to school-age children, including home visiting on health problems.

The Visiting Nurse Society provides public health nursing to the neighborhood. Four hospitals serve residents of the neighborhood but are not located within the neighborhood.

Potential for Citizen Participation

The following resources are available for developing citizen interest and participation in programs of health improvement:

BLOCK CLUBS. Composed of residents of a city block interested in block cleanliness and neighborhood improvement. A listing of such clubs is available from the staff worker of the Tuberculosis and Health Association.

COMMUNITY COUNCILS. Some clubs have recently joined into a representative-type of community council—the East Devon Community Council. There is also one loosely organized community council north of East Devon composed of individuals and some block clubs. Both of these councils are tied in with the Health Committee.

CHURCHES. A complete listing of all churches and pastors is

available in office files. Where churches are composed mostly of local members, rather than city-wide, these will probably be concerned.

PARENT-TEACHER ASSOCIATIONS. These will reach a wide cross section of the population.

SOCIAL AND RECREATIONAL CENTERS. There are three such centers in, or adjacent to, the Pittsfield neighborhood. These centers provide a core of community interest through their programs.

BUSINESSMEN'S GROUPS. There is one functioning Businessmen's Association in the neighborhood that has participated in the past in community-action programs.

Data on the health services committee

The Health Services Committee has been functioning for ten years as an integral part of the Area Planning Committee, which is one of the six planning units of the Welfare Council. Many health action programs have been undertaken, all being successfully completed. Included among these were: Tuberculosis X-ray Survey; V.D. Survey; and "Meals on Wheels," a project to serve hot meals to the home-bound aged. For the past year, the committee has been "chafing at the bit" for some major problem to tackle. For the past few months committee meetings have been informal in nature, which, as the chairman said, gave them a respite from their last successful project of stimulating the building of a community health center.

The committee is a community planning committee concerned with developing programs to meet the health needs of the Pittsfield and adjacent neighborhoods.

Staff Consultant Service

Staff service included work with the Health Services Committee's Program Planning Committee and subcommittees appointed for specific tasks. The staff worker also served as director of the Planning Committee of the Welfare Council, as well as staff consultant to the Area Recreation and Housing Committees.

The following example from the worker's files deals with the work of the Health Services Committee in showing how organized community effort at the agency-consumer level was successful in providing prenatal care services for the alleviation of the high infant death rate in a neighborhood of a metropolitan community.

Obviously, a great deal of material has been omitted—material that would clearly show in greater detail the worker's role in working with the many interrelationships involved in such a project. The primary emphasis has been to show the gradual involvement of agencies and citizen groups in a total process directed toward a specific goal.

It will be seen that the Community Organization Worker takes on a multiplicity of roles. He is developing and strengthening relationships in his immediate community and, at the same time, is relating to his sponsoring organization, the Welfare Council, to ensure that local plans are an integral part of metropolitan planning.

The record shows the worker in the role of secretary to the Committee, enabler to the chairmen and group members, resource on community services and facilities, liaison between city-wide planning organizations and the neighborhood, consultant to agencies serving a section, and administrator to make sure that all the wheels are moving at the same time. The role of the worker is identified in the margin.

AUGUST 1

Mr. Brian Turner, consultant of the Health Division of the Welfare Council, called worker to express his concern over the high neonatal death rate in the district staffed by the worker.

Maintains liaison between city-wide Health Division and the neighborhood

He reviewed the latest statistical report from the City Health Department showing high neonatal rate as compared with other sections of the city. Mr. Turner asked whether this was a concern that could be discussed in the District Health Committee. He said he would be glad to meet with the committee and share all information he had on this problem.

AUGUST 3

Enables chairman to focus on the problem

Worker called Mrs. Keel, chairman of the Health Services Committee, to discuss the problem identified by Mr. Turner. Worker found Mrs. Keel extremely interested. She asked what the Health Services Committee should do. Worker suggested an early meeting of the Program Planning Committee to determine the advisability of the Health Services Committee undertaking this problem as a priority assignment. This would give some opportunity for exploratory thinking on the problem before it was taken to the Health Services Committee. A meeting was set up for the following week in Mrs. Keel's office.

AUGUST 8

**Attempts to assess
degree of interest
in the problem**

Worker called District Health Director to indicate the possibility of the Health Services Committee undertaking further considerations of this problem. Dr. Jamison said he "would be delighted if the Committee could do something about this problem because it was also a concern of his Department." Since he was a member of the Program Planning Committee, he would bring in additional information on the problem to the next meeting.

Worker contacted Miss Janice Littlefield, directing supervisor of the Visiting Nurse Society, to see if her staff had expressed concern over the infant mortality problem. Miss Littlefield indicated a similar concerned had been expressed by Dr. Jamison and said she would ask her staff to share their experiences on this problem before the next program-planning meeting.

Program Planning Committee Meeting
AUGUST 14

**Helps committee
focus on the
problem**

Mrs. Keel opened the meeting by stating that the Program Planning Committee needed to establish some program priorities for the coming year. These in turn would then be reviewed by the Health Services Committee in September when a specific health problem would be selected for action. Mrs. Keel gave a résumé of the successful achievements of the past year noting that, since all current projects had been completed, the committee should concern itself with a different health problem this year. Worker suggested that Mr. Turner might discuss with the committee the Health Division's concern about the infant mortality problem. Mr. Turner presented statistical data on the problem, stating that it appeared on the surface as if the high rates of neonatal deaths were due to inadequate prenatal care. Miss Littlefield pointed out that she had checked with her staff nurses on this problem and that many had noted the lack of prenatal care on the part of many mothers in the neighborhood. Mrs. Keel said

her hospital provided prenatal care on a fee basis
and was not yet aware of any particular problem although she did feel that cost was a factor in mothers
not getting early prenatal care.

The committee agreed that the problem was
serious enough to merit consideration by the total
Helps committee   Health Services Committee at its next meeting. Dr.
formulate a plan   Jamison suggested that the committee's focus might
be on (a) factoring out the causes of high mortality
rates in children under one month of age; and (b)
finding ways of alleviating this grave health problem.

Pittsfield Health Committee Meeting
SEPTEMBER 15

The Health Services Committee went on record in support of giving highest priority to finding
a solution to the serious neonatal problem in the
Pittsfield neighborhood. Mrs. Keel asked Dr. Jamison to prepare a statement, outlining the background of the problem and some proposals for
committee action that could be considered at the
next meeting.

SEPTEMBER 16

Since the neighborhood of highest rate was
predominantly Negro, worker contacted Mrs. Myola
Seeks to get   Davis, community services secretary of the Urban
broader agency   League, to alert her on the committee's action. Mrs.
involvement in the   Davis felt she needed to know more about the prob-
project   lem and what might be an appropriate role for her
agency should any action program be undertaken.
Worker called Mrs. Keel to suggest that Mrs. Davis
be asked to serve on the committee in light of her
agency's ultimate concern with this problem, which
affected the Negro community so severely. Mrs.
Keel agreed to call Mrs. Davis and ask her to serve
on the Health Services Committee.

SEPTEMBER 17

Worker called Dr. Jamison to give him information pertinent to the population, characteristics,

Serves as resource to committee member on neighborhood data

agencies, etc., of the Pittsfield neighborhood, which were in the files of the Area Welfare Council and would be made available to him should he need it for the statement he was preparing on the problem. Dr. Jamison expressed the belief that this would be of tremendous help and that he would visit the area office to go over the materials so that he and worker could determine what might be incorporated in his statement.

Health Services Committee Meeting

OCTOBER 12

Dr. Jamison was asked to present his statement and proposals on the neonatal problem. He stated that he had reviewed the problem with Department chiefs at the Central Health Department headquarters to determine the city-wide scope of the problem before narrowing it down to the district level. A summary of the statement was that neonatal death rate is related to lack of use of prenatal care facilities by expectant mothers. A preliminary assessment indicates this is due to (a) lack of adequate health education, and (b) inability of patients to afford clinic fees. Therefore, the committee should (a) encourage a health education program, and (b) put forth a concentrated effort to encourage community residents to use existing prenatal care facilities.

Miss Beatrice Horter from St. Barnabas Hospital questioned whether voluntary hospitals could absorb the increased costs to meet this need if this approach stimulated tremendous use of existing facilities. She suggested that the Department of Health provide subsidies to local hospitals to allow services to be offered at a fee in keeping with the patient's ability to pay. Miss Littlefield wondered how such a program should be started and to whom referrals should be made. Miss Talbot asked if there was sufficient motivation for expectant mothers to go to clinics outside the geographic area. Because of the questions raised, the committee agreed that a subcommittee should be appointed to formulate a plan which would (a) study all factors causing inadequate prenatal care; and (b) formulate a proposal for action based on these findings.

The chairman was asked to appoint the subcommittee.

OCTOBER 14

Serves as resource to chairman on selection of committee members

Mrs. Keel, the committee chairman, called worker to discuss appointments for the subcommittee. Worker outlined some of the types of representation that she should consider in making appointments: the Department of Public Assistance, because of its high caseload of expectant mothers; hospitals, because of possible increase in clinic caseloads; the Department of Health, because of its ultimate responsibility with the problem; and possibly the Urban League, because of its interest in problems affecting the Negro community. Mrs. Keel agreed to give this some further thought and said she would appoint the subcommittee within the next few days.

OCTOBER 16

Helps to arrange committee meetings

Mrs. Keel called to indicate that she had appointed Miss Littlefield of the Visiting Nurse Society; Miss Talbot of the Department of Public Assistance; Dr. Jamison of the Department of Health; and Miss Lutz, the District's school nurse supervisor, who had a wealth of knowledge about the neighborhood. She asked if the worker would call Miss Talbot, who had been named subcommittee chairman, to set up a meeting time for the subcommittee.

OCTOBER 17

Miss Talbot, subcommittee chairman, convened a meeting of the group. Present were: Miss Littlefield, Dr. Jamison, Miss Lutz, and worker. Miss Talbot circulated the Statement of the Charge. The subcommittee agreed to a plan that suggested a Case-finding Survey to determine the number of women in the Pittsfield neighborhood in need of prenatal care and who were not utilizing existing facilities.

Miss Talbot indicated that her D.P.A. staff workers might undertake this assignment in line with their regular visits to clients in the neighborhood. The committee felt that, while this would not give a complete picture of the need, at least it would provide some factual basis for a plan since the D.P.A. caseload was so high in this community.

Dr. Jamison suggested a survey of existing prenatal care services to determine their appropriateness for meeting the particular need in the Pittsfield neighborhood and to point out where a new prenatal clinic, designed to meet this need, might be located. Miss Lutz agreed to undertake this assignment and asked Mrs. Florence Barnes, the district health educator, and a representative from the Bayview Civic League to serve with her. The committee felt that there should be consultations with local hospitals serving the neighborhood to determine how prenatal clinic facilities might be coordinated with necessary hospital services. Since Mrs. Keel, the Health Services Committee chairman, was also a hospital administrator, the committee agreed that she be asked to make the necessary explorations with the other hospitals. Miss Talbot then asked the subcommittee chairmen to report back their findings within three weeks.

Meeting of Miss Talbot's Subcommittee
NOVEMBER 15

Serves as staff secretary to delineate the problem and the plan

Miss Talbot asked subcommittee chairmen to report on developments. She began by stating that one of her staff members who was intrigued by the project had arranged with casework staff for them to inquire of their pregnant clients whether or not they were receiving prenatal care and, if not, what were their reasons for not seeking such care. A preliminary report indicated that of those clients so interviewed, between 40 and 50 percent were not receiving any prenatal care, the most frequently noted reasons being (1) a lack of financial resources and (2) the inability to provide for the supervisory care of their children while the expectant mothers

attended the prenatal clinic. The subcommittee
agreed that this preliminary survey documented the
need for some type of prenatal clinic facility.

Miss Lutz reported that her subcommittee
had made a fairly extensive survey of the hospitals serving the neighborhood and had found that
they were not easily accessible to the neighborhood;
in every case two transportation lines were necessary
to reach the hospitals. One hospital was within
walking distance but did not have clinic facilities
available or even space in which to locate such a
facility. Miss Lutz said she believed the factors of
a highly mobile community and a predominance of
residents with limited educational background
meant it would be necessary to have an approach
to developing a prenatal care program that would
"maximize the identification of the service with the
local community, both geographically and socially."
Miss Talbot summarized the meeting by stating
that the subcommittee had documented the need for
a prenatal program; that existing facilities were not
adequate to meet the need; and that the committee
seemed to feel that "an experimental neighborhood
approach, with maximum involvement of the local
community, was necessary for providing the type of
prenatal care needed." There was total agreement
with this summary. At this point, Miss Talbot asked
worker if he would draft a report that would include
a summary of the population and socioeconomic
characteristics of the neighborhood, the D.P.A.
statistical material, and the findings of Miss Lutz'
subcommittee on Resources. The report would be
duplicated for the next meeting of the Health Services Committee. Worker agreed to prepare a summary, but indicated that it would be a first draft,
subject to Miss Talbot's review for additions and/or
deletions. Miss Talbot thought this would be fine,
and worker agreed to forward the draft within a
week.

NOVEMBER 18

Worker prepared draft of statement, "Proposal—A Pilot Project Aimed at Reducing the High

Neonatal Death Rate in Health District No. 7." The statement of proposal included:

A. Background on problem
B. Barriers to prenatal care
C. Proposed plan for establishment of clinic
    (1) Suggested geographic area for service
    (2) Case finding—proposed source of referrals
    (3) Plan for community involvement
    (4) Source of staff service for
        (a) clinic operation
        (b) neighborhood groups
    (5) Relationship with health and medical services and facilities
D. Procedure for evaluation

This draft was forwarded to Miss Talbot for revisions.

NOVEMBER 21

Miss Talbot called worker to indicate approval of statement prepared by him on the proposal, but suggested further elaboration on arrangement of statistical data and a rearrangement of headings on final page. Worker made changes on his copy as per suggestions and said report would be ready for Miss Talbot's distribution at the next meeting of the Health Services Committee.

NOVEMBER 25

Helps chairman to identify the need to relate the project to city-wide resources

Worker called Mrs. Keel to discuss agenda for the December meeting of the Health Services Committee. Mrs. Keel said that Miss Talbot had informed her that her Committee Report would be ready for discussion at the meeting. Worker suggested that perhaps it might be helpful if Dr. Jamison would invite his superior, Dr. John Hamilton, the director of Public Health Services, to the December meeting to determine what assistance the Central Health Department might be able to offer in this prenatal project. Mrs. Keel agreed to make contact with Dr. Jamison before extending an invitation to Dr. Hamilton to attend the meeting. It was also decided that she would call worker within the week to suggest what should be included in the written notice to be sent out for the December meeting of the committee.

DECEMBER 1

Endeavors to keep channels open to community agencies

Worker called Mrs. Davis, community services secretary of the Urban League, to bring her up to date on developments. Mrs. Davis said she had reported back to her Departmental Advisory Committee on the Pittsfield Health Services Committee's concern over prenatal care. Her committee, in turn, was most enthusiastic about giving maximum support to any program that could be developed. Worker said the December meeting would probably provide more specific information on immediate next steps, which could then be shared with Mrs. Davis' Advisory Committee.

DECEMBER 15

Attempts to keep involvement of the Health Department in the project

At the meeting of the Pittsfield Health Services Committee, twenty-two persons were present, including Dr. John Hamilton. Mrs. Keel called on Miss Talbot for her subcommittee report. Copies of the "Proposal—A Pilot Project Aimed at Reducing the High Neonatal Death Rate in Health District No. 7" were distributed.

Miss Rose Innes of St. Andrews Hospital was the first to react to the proposal. She expressed great concern over the high rate of mothers not receiving adequate prenatal care in the Pittsfield neighborhood. "Something just has to be done by our committee," she said. Miss Littlefield stressed the need for some sort of "outpost clinic" that would be within walking distance for expectant mothers and that would offer waiting-room facilities where the mothers might leave their small children under supervision care while they received their prenatal examinations. This, she felt, would cover two points in Miss Talbot's report. Dr. Hamilton expressed the great concern of the Central Health Department about the prenatal problem. However, he stated that at that moment the Department of Health had neither the staff nor sufficient funds available to assist the project. Worker wondered if Health Education staff time could not be given to the project to develop community understanding of the prenatal problem. This action would not necessitate any additional outlay of departmental funds and would at least show the interest of the City's Health Department in the problem. Dr. Hamilton agreed that this would be quite appropriate.

Seeks to maintain close liaison between the committee and the Health Division to ensure wider community acceptance of the plan

There was full agreement that the Health Services Committee would go on record in support of the establishment of a demonstration prenatal clinic, located in the Pittsfield neighborhood, and providing free services with maximum community participation from within the neighborhood, this pilot project to last approximately one year. The purpose of the demonstration would be to show how previously unserved segments of the population might be reached with needed services.

Helps committee to focus on the need of professional service to the project

Worker suggested that the Health Division of the Welfare Council be asked to review the proposal and to advise the Health Services Committee accordingly. Worker was asked to contact Mr. Brian Turner, Health Division Consultant, and arrange for a review of the proposal as soon as possible. Also, to ensure maximum neighborhood support, the Urban League was asked to assign professional staff service to the project. Worker noted that the Urban League worker, who was trained in community organization, would bring knowledge and skills essential in accomplishing the development of neighborhood understanding and support.

DECEMBER 17

Worker, in conference with Mr. Turner, arranged for Mrs. Keel to make presentation of the Health Services Committee's proposal at the January meeting of the Health Division. Worker then met with Mrs. Keel to go over the proposal prior to the January meeting to make sure all points would be covered.

JANUARY 12

The Health Division of the Welfare Council endorsed the proposal. A Neonatal Technical Ad-

visory Committee was appointed to give advice on
the project throughout its duration. The Health
Division suggested that endorsement of the project
be sought from the County Medical Society to avoid
the possible misinterpretation of the prenatal project as an invasion of private medical practice.

JANUARY 14

After further consultation with Mrs. Keel,
worker wrote to the County Medical Society, out-

**Aims to facilitate
interaction of
groups concerned
with the problem
to ensure
maximum use of
community
resources**

lining the problem and enclosing a copy of the
Health Services Committee's proposal. Worker suggested a meeting with the appropriate County Medical Society Committee and the Pitsfield Health
Services Committee to arrive at a working agreement. Three days later, Dr. Joseph Kenman, chairman of the County Medical Society's Committee on
Neonatal Deaths, called worker to say he would
meet with the committee. On the basis of the proposal he felt that his committee would be in total
accord with the project.

JANUARY 29

**Acts as clearing
center to
organizations
involved in
the project**

Worker received call from Dr. Kenman giving official endorsement of his Committee on Neonatal Deaths and indicating he would seek the
endorsement of the Committee on Maternal and
Child Health of the County Medical Society.

FEBRUARY 2

Worker wrote to Urban League indicating
Pittsfield Health Services Committee's request that

**Attempts to clarify
role of the
participating
agency in the
project**

the League undertake responsibility for developing
community support for the prenatal program in
terms of (1) interpreting the program to professional, church, and medical leaders in the Negro
community; and (2) working with citizen groups to
develop an education program for waiting mothers
and a recreation program for children accompanying
their mothers.

FEBRUARY 15

Reply from Mrs. Davis to worker's February
2 communication informed him that her Advisory
Committee had agreed that, since the request dealt

with a serious problem affecting a predominantly Negro community and, since the focus of the request was on developing Negro community leadership, the Urban League accepted the request as an appropriate function of its program. Further, that Mrs. Davis could devote staff time to the project in keeping with her other agency commitments.

MARCH 1

Helps chairman to focus on the need to develop suitable structure to implement the project

Mrs. Keel, in telephone conversation, told worker that the board of her hospital was very much interested in the prenatal project and, if necessary, would lend medical staff to the clinic for a one-year demonstration period. She also reported that Dr. Nathan Paley, chairman of the County Medical Society's Committee on Maternal and Child Health, had called her to express the interest of his committee in the project. He voiced also his own personal interest as chief of obstetrics at Hanson Hospital. He indicated he would be happy to have his medical students participate in any way feasible on the medical staffing of the prenatal clinic.

Worker suggested a meeting of the total Health Services Committee to draw together elements of the plan and decide on immediate next steps.

MARCH 10

Serves as resource on neighborhood facilities

Worker followed up with Miss Lutz, chairman of the Resources Committee, on possible locations for the prenatal clinic. Although a number of agencies offered their facilities, none had adequate space for play supervision for children who might accompany their mothers. Worker conferred with The Reverend Silas Spain, minister of the Elvira Community Church, located centrally in the Pittsfield neighborhood. Previously, Reverend Spain had expressed interest in having his church render service to the community. He agreed to seek the approval of his board for use of the church as a clinic site.

MARCH 15

The Reverend Spain called worker to say that not only had his church given permission to use the

Attempts to develop greater church involvement in the project

building but had offered to make extensive appropriate renovations to the basement in keeping with what the committee would suggest as meeting basic medical standards. Worker suggested that the congregation would provide an important channel for developing community support and acceptance of the new facility, which would ultimately lead to full utilization of the prenatal services.

Meeting of the Total Health Services Committee

MARCH 20

Attempts to relate interests of civic league to the work to be developed by the Urban League

Mrs. Keel reviewed the status of clinic developments, pointing out that the essentials of the plan had been reviewed and endorsed by many elements in the Pittsfield community. Mrs. Ruth Dennison, chairman of the Bayview Civic League, emphasized the need for developing maximum support for the clinic. Worker suggested that she would be of great assistance in helping Mrs. Davis, community services secretary of the Urban League, who had assumed responsibility for developing neighborhood understanding and support of the project. Mrs. Keel asked Mrs. Dennison to work with Mrs. Davis on this phase of the program.

The committee agreed to set the target date of June 6 for opening of the clinic for a one-year demonstration.

The committee authorized a Steering Committee to move ahead on clinic plans. Members to serve would represent key groups concerned with operation of the clinic.

MARCH 22

Consultant to participating agency on neighborhood resources

Worker had a conference with Mrs. Davis who reported that her Health Services Advisory Committee was anxious to move ahead on the assignment. She saw as a first step identifying sources of local neighborhood leadership and would need a listing of neighborhood groups—churches, home and school associations, etc.—in the Pittsfield neighborhood. Worker offered to compile and mail to her such a list in the next few days. He also suggested she might contact local social agencies with community programs who might suggest additional names. Mrs. Davis indicated that Mrs. Dennison, chairman of the Bayview Civic League, was working closely with her.

APRIL 10

A meeting of neighborhood leaders was convened by Mrs. Edith Walters, chairman of the Urban League Health Committee, to plan ways of developing community support in the neighborhood to be served by the clinic. Eighteen neighborhood leaders attended. Mrs. Walters discussed the infant death rate in the neighborhood and explained plans for a demonstration prenatal clinic. All present expressed great enthusiasm for the proposed project. The group agreed on two approaches:

(1) Each person would interpret to the membership of his organization the need to know more about the infant death problem. To aid in this program an interpretation team would be formed, this team to be composed of the district health educator and the Tuberculosis and Health Association staff person, to provide the necessary technical data on the problem;

(2) Money would be raised for purchase of necessary items of medical equipment for the prenatal clinic.

APRIL 22

**Keeps abreast
of developments
in the project**

Worker met with Mrs. Davis to ascertain progress of the "informational program." Mrs. Davis was most enthusiastic in reporting that twelve meetings on the problem had been set up. Already, a local fraternal group had contributed $100. Movies were being used in some groups, and local newspapers were carrying several stories on the prenatal project.

APRIL 23

Worker met with Mrs. Keel to secure a list of items that the medical staff thought would be basic equipment for the clinic. Mrs. Keel agreed to compile such a list in consultation with Dr. Paley. She also mentioned that Dr. Daniel Bergstein, a staff obstetrician at Kingston Hospital, had volunteered his services as medical director of the prenatal project.

MAY 4

Mrs. Davis called worker to say that enough money had been contributed to purchase at least some of the needed equipment for the clinic and that a neighborhood committee was planning to go, on May 6, to the Penn Surgical Supply Company to buy equipment in line with Mrs. Keel's memorandum outlining the necessary items.

MAY 8

Administrative role to tie together various parts of the project

Worker convened a meeting of the Steering Committee with the Health Division Committee to work out details of clinic operations. Target date of June 6 was agreed on. Kingston Hospital would supply a registered nurse, a social worker, and a laboratory technician, as well as some delivery service. Dr. Paley of Hanson Hospital agreed to supply medical consultation, resident physicians in obstetrics, and delivery service. The Reverend Spain stated that alterations had been completed in accordance with specifications of Dr. Paley, the Medical Consultant of the clinic. Mrs. Davis mentioned the enthusiasm of neighborhood residents and reported that they were currently initiating a door-to-door campaign in a concerted effort to contact as many expectant mothers as possible informing them of the clinic and stressing the need and importance of prenatal care. Mrs. Dennison and members of her Bayview Civic League had provided a supply of examining gowns for both patients and physicians, as well as curtains for the examining rooms and dressing rooms. The neighborhood clinic had enrolled thirty-five volunteers for actual work in the clinic—such as supervision of children while mothers were being examined; clerks; typists; receptionists; mopping and cleaning squads. Dr. Paley pointed out the fact that while the basic equipment had been purchased, some larger, more expensive items were still needed.

Members of the Technical Committee agreed to make contact with hospitals to secure two obstetrical examining tables and scales. This committee would also work on an evaluation schedule to test the effectiveness of the operation.

MAY 26

Members of all the neighborhood participating organizations were asked to meet at the clinic to help with a number of jobs that had to be done—cleaning and mopping, unpacking equipment, arranging furniture, etc.

MAY 27

Invitations were sent out to attend the opening of the clinic on June 6. All group representatives who had participated in setting up the clinic were invited.

JUNE 6

The clinic officially opened with twenty-nine representatives of community groups present. Refreshments were served by the Women's Guild of the church. Six patients came in for service. Worker noticed they were pleased and awed by the attention they received. After the clinic session, most of the representatives present stayed on to discuss how they could iron out "kinks" in the operation—taking care of certain jobs such as laundering gowns and sheets; opening and closing clinic; securing additional pieces of equipment, etc. There was general agreement that a steering committee of local citizens be set up to perform the necessary functions to insure smooth operation of the clinic in consultation with the medical staff. Mrs. Lorington was unanimously chosen to head up the Steering Committee. The name "York Prenatal Center," was agreed upon. Mrs. Lula Jones was appointed to serve as secretary to the Steering Committee.

JUNE 10

Mrs. Davis of the Urban League called worker to describe how she saw her role in working

Consultant to Urban League on spelling out staff functions

with Mrs. Lorington, the newly elected chairman of the clinic's Steering Committee. We decided that the role would include

(1) helping the lay chairman, Mrs. Lorington, to formulate issues to be handled by the Steering Committee, for example, purchase of equipment; scheduling of jobs, etc.;

(2) helping chairman plan ways of orienting new volunteers to clinic services and ways in which the chairman could carry out her responsibilities as coordinator of volunteer services;

(3) helping the lay secretary, Mrs. Jones, to evaluate the content of meetings in terms of what should be recorded so that minutes would be useful and meaningful to committee members as a record of accomplishments and as a reminder of things to be done, as well as a way to give recognition to the contributions of individual members;

(4) helping individual members to develop leadership rather than taking over the role.

Administrative follow-up

These were incorporated in a memorandum and sent to Mrs. Keel, Mrs. Lorington, and Dr. Bergstein.

Worker's Summary

The record and summary will serve as basis for a report to be sent to participating agencies and community groups

The demonstration project was carried on for one year as per plan. Four hundred and forty expectant mothers were examined; 257 babies were delivered at Kingston and Hanson Hospitals; the others were referred to other hospitals that could absorb the heavy caseload.

Evaluation of the project was completed by the Health Division's Neonatal Technical Committee of the Welfare Council. The Technical Committee reported that a substantially higher proportion of pregnant women had used the clinic's services as compared with the records of prenatal clinics operated in comparable areas of the city. It recommended that the City Department of Health undertake the staffing of the clinic and the continued utilization of volunteers in appropriate capacities.

The department has accepted the report and is currently implementing the findings.

Worker's Assessment of the Project

An assessment of the project is incorporated into the office files to be used later with the Area Planning Committee when all the year's projects will be evaluated and priorities determined for the next program year

1. Local community pride and a feeling of status and worth has been gained by residents in the Pittsfield neighborhood. The volunteers, as well as the patients, have become extremely active in many other community-improvement projects.

2. The Central Department of Health has expressed great interest in utilizing similar procedures of citizen involvement in its other clinics in the future.

3. Many local leaders, who have already been involved in agency advisory committee work, community projects, etc., have been identified.

4. A pattern of cooperative working relationships between various agencies serving the local area in developing and carrying out joint planning has been firmly built into the neighborhood. This has been enhanced by the continued interaction with policy makers at the city-wide level through the Health Division of the Welfare Council.

5. Strong endorsement has been given by the local planning groups and the Welfare Council to the need for professional staff services to community groups. The demonstration of the effectiveness of Urban League staff service with the York Prenatal Center Steering Committee has served to document this need.

Worker's role in the project

The record showed the staff worker performing a number of different functions. He met with the committee, subcommittees, and their chairmen. He prepared minutes and a draft proposal. He developed and maintained relationships with all segments of the neighborhood and attempted to involve committee members and representatives from the community in planning and participating in the project.

The worker helped the chairman to set up appropriate committee structure to carry out the project. At the same time, he maintained close liaison with the city-wide Health Division of the Welfare Council so that planning at the neighborhood level was geared into city-wide planning.

In essence, the primary role of the worker in this instance was to help the committee to focus on the problem, formulate a plan of approach, gain broad community acceptance of the plan, and finally, to implement the plan so that the goal was achieved—in this instance the establishment of a prenatal care clinic.

INDEX

INDEX